McGraw-Hill Reading

Wonders

Education

Bothell, WA • Chicago, IL • Columbus, OH • New York, NY

 **TextEvaluator**™

ETS and the ETS logo are registered trademarks of Educational Testing Service (ETS). TextEvaluator is a trademark of Educational Testing Service.

**Cover and Title Pages:** Nathan Love

**www.mheonline.com/readingwonders**

c

**Mc Graw Hill** **Education**

Send all inquiries to:
McGraw-Hill Education
Two Penn Plaza
New York, New York 10121

Printed in China

7 8 9 DSS 17 16 15 14

# McGraw-Hill Reading Wonders

## CCSS Reading/Language Arts Program

## Program Authors

**Dr. Diane August**
Managing Director,
American Institutes for Research
Washington, D.C.

**Dr. Donald Bear**
Iowa State University
Ames, Iowa

**Dr. Janice A. Dole**
University of Utah
Salt Lake City, Utah

**Dr. Jana Echevarria**
California State University, Long Beach
Long Beach, California

**Dr. Douglas Fisher**
San Diego State University
San Diego, California

**Dr. David J. Francis**
University of Houston
Houston, Texas

**Dr. Vicki Gibson**
Educational Consultant
Gibson Hasbrouck and Associates
Wellesley, Massachusetts

**Dr. Jan Hasbrouck**
Educational Consultant
and Researcher
J.H. Consulting
Vancouver, Washington
Gibson Hasbrouck and Associates
Wellesley, Massachusetts

**Margaret Kilgo**
Educational Consultant
Kilgo Consulting, Inc.
Austin, Texas

**Dr. Jay McTighe**
Educational Consultant
Jay McTighe and Associates
Columbia, Maryland

**Dr. Scott G. Paris**
Vice President, Research
Educational Testing Service
Princeton, New Jersey

**Dr. Timothy Shanahan**
University of Illinois at Chicago
Chicago, Illinois

**Dr. Josefina V. Tinajero**
University of Texas at El Paso
El Paso, Texas

McGraw Hill Education

Bothell, WA • Chicago, IL • Columbus, OH • New York, NY

# PROGRAM AUTHORS

**Dr. Diane August**

American Institutes for Research, Washington, D.C.

Managing Director focused on literacy and science for ELLs for the Education, Human Development and the Workforce Division

**Dr. Donald R. Bear**

Iowa State University

Professor, Iowa State University

Author of *Words Their Way, Words Their Way with English Learners, Vocabulary Their Way,* and *Words Their Way with Struggling Readers, 4–12*

**Dr. Janice A. Dole**

University of Utah

Professor, University of Utah

Director, Utah Center for Reading and Literacy

Content Facilitator, National Assessment of Educational Progress (NAEP)

CCSS Consultant to Literacy Coaches, Salt Lake City School District, Utah

**Dr. Jana Echevarria**

California State University, Long Beach

Professor Emerita of Education, California State University

Author of *Making Content Comprehensible for English Learners: The SIOP Model*

**Dr. Douglas Fisher**

San Diego State University

Co-Director, Center for the Advancement of Reading, California State University

Author of *Language Arts Workshop: Purposeful Reading and Writing Instruction* and *Reading for Information in Elementary School*

**Dr. David J. Francis**

University of Houston

Director of the Center for Research on Educational Achievement and Teaching of English Language Learners (CREATE)

**Dr. Vicki Gibson**

Educational Consultant Gibson Hasbrouck and Associates

Author of *Differentiated Instruction: Grouping for Success, Differentiated Instruction: Guidelines for Implementation,* and *Managing Behaviors to Support Differentiated Instruction*

**Dr. Jan Hasbrouck**

J.H. Consulting Gibson Hasbrouck and Associates

Developed Oral Reading Fluency Norms for Grades 1–8

Author of *The Reading Coach: A How-to Manual for Success* and *Educators as Physicians: Using RTI Assessments for Effective Decision-Making*

**Margaret Kilgo**

Educational Consultant Kilgo Consulting, Inc., Austin, TX

Developed Data-Driven Decisions process for evaluating student performance by standard

Member of Common Core State Standards Anchor Standards Committee for Reading and Writing

**Dr. Scott G. Paris**

Educational Testing Service,
Vice President, Research

Professor, Nanyang Technological
University, Singapore, 2008–2011

Professor of Education and Psychology,
University of Michigan, 1978–2008

**Dr. Timothy Shanahan**

University of Illinois at Chicago

Distinguished Professor, Urban Education

Director, UIC Center for Literacy

Chair, Department of Curriculum &
Instruction

Member, English Language Arts Work
Team and Writer of the Common Core
State Standards

President, International Reading
Association, 2006

**Dr. Josefina V. Tinajero**

University of Texas at El Paso

Dean of College of Education

President of TABE

Board of Directors for the American
Association of Colleges for Teacher
Education (AACTE)

Governing Board of the National Network
for Educational Renewal (NNER)

# Consulting Authors

**Kathy R. Bumgardner**

National Literacy Consultant

Strategies Unlimited, Inc.
Gastonia, NC

**Jay McTighe**

Jay McTighe and Associates

Author of *The Understanding by Design
Guide to Creating High Quality Units* with
G. Wiggins; *Schooling by Design: Mission,
Action, Achievement* with G. Wiggins;
and *Differentiated Instruction and
Understanding By Design* with C. Tomlinson

**Dr. Doris Walker-Dalhouse**

Marquette University

Associate Professor, Department
of Educational Policy & Leadership

Author of articles on multicultural
literature, struggling readers, and
reading instruction in urban schools

**Dinah Zike**

Educational Consultant

Dinah-Might Activities, Inc.
San Antonio, TX

# Program Reviewers

**Kelly Aeppli-Campbell**
Escambia County School District
Pensacola, FL

**Marjorie J. Archer**
Broward County Public Schools
Davie, FL

**Whitney Augustine**
Brevard Public Schools
Melbourne, FL

**Antonio C. Campbell**
Washington County School District
Saint George, UT

**Helen Dunne**
Gilbert Public School District
Gilbert, AZ

**David P. Frydman**
Clark County School District
Las Vegas, NV

**Fran Gregory**
Metropolitan Nashville Public Schools
Nashville, TN

**Veronica Allen Hunt**
Clark County School District
Las Vegas, NV

**Michele Jacobs**
Dee-Mack CUSD #701
Mackinaw, IL

**LaVita Johnson Spears**
Broward County Public Schools
Pembroke Pines, FL

**Randall B. Kincaid**
Sevier County Schools
Sevierville, TN

**Matt Melamed**
Community Consolidated School
District 46
Grayslake, IL

**Angela L. Reese,**
Bay District Schools
Panama City, FL

**Eddie Thompson**
Fairfield City School District
Fairfield Township, OH

**Patricia Vasseur Sosa**
Miami-Dade County Public Schools
Miami, FL

**Dr. Elizabeth Watson**
Hazelwood School District
Hazelwood, MO

# TEACHING WITH

## INTRODUCE

### Weekly Concept
Grade Appropriate
Topics, including Science
and Social Studies

**Reading/Writing Workshop**

- Videos
- Photographs
- Interactive Graphic
  Organizers

## TEACH

### Close Reading
Short Complex Texts

### Minilessons
Comprehension
Strategies and Skills
Genre
Vocabulary Strategies
Writing Traits

### Grammar Handbook

**Reading/Writing Workshop**

- Visual Glossary
- Interactive Minilessons
- Interactive Graphic
  Organizers

## APPLY

### Close Reading
Anchor Texts
Extended Complex Texts
Application of
Strategies and Skills

**Literature Anthology**

- e Books
- Interactive Texts
- Listening Library
- English/Spanish
  Summaries

# CCSS Master the Common Core State Standards!

## DIFFERENTIATE

- e Books
- Interactive Texts
- Leveled Reader Search
- Listening Library
- Interactive Activities

**Leveled Readers**

**Leveled Readers**
Small Group Instruction
with Differentiated Texts

## INTEGRATE

- Online Research
- Writer's Workspace
- Interactive Group Projects

**Collection of Texts**

**Research and Inquiry**
Short and Sustained Research Projects

**Text Connections**
Reading Across Texts

**Write About Reading**
Analytical Writing

## ASSESS

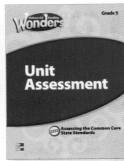

- Online Assessment
- Test Generator
- Reports

**Weekly Assessment**

**Unit Assessment**

**Benchmark Assessment**

**Weekly Assessment**

**Unit Assessment**

**Benchmark Assessment**

# PROGRAM COMPONENTS

**Reading/Writing Workshop**

**Literature Anthology**

**Teacher Editions**

**Leveled Readers**

**Classroom Library Tradebooks**

**Your Turn Practice Book**

**Visual Vocabulary Cards**

**Leveled Workstation Activity Cards**

**CCSS Assessing the Common Core State Standards**

**Sound-Spelling Cards**

**High-Frequency Word Cards**

**Response Board**

**Weekly Assessment**

**Unit Assessment**

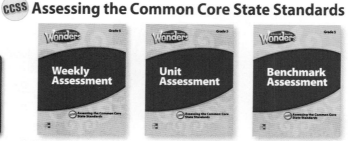
**Benchmark Assessment**

**Go Digital**

**For the Teacher**

**For the Students**

**Plan**
Customizable Lesson Plans

**Assess**
Online Assessments
Reports and Scoring

**Professional Development**
Lesson and CCSS Videos

**Teach**
Classroom Presentation Tools
Instructional Lessons

**Collaborate**
Online Class Conversations
Interactive Group Projects

**Additional Online Resources**
Leveled Practice
Grammar Practice
Phonics/Spelling
ELL Activities
Genre Study
Reader's Theater
Tier 2 Intervention

**Manage and Assign**
Student Grouping and Assignments

**School to Home**
Digital Open House
Activities and Messages

**My To Do List**
Assignments
Assessment

**Words to Know**
Build Vocabulary

**Read**
e Books
Interactive Texts

**Play**
Interactive Games

**Write**
Interactive Writing

**School to Home**
Activities for Home
Messages from the Teacher
Class Wall of Student Work

www.connected.mcgraw-hill.com

# UNIT 6 CONTENTS

## Unit Planning

## Weekly Lessons

## Writing Process · Genre Writing: Opinion

## Model Lesson · Extended Complex Text

### Program Information

(t to b) George Marks/Retrofile/Getty Images; Yva Momatiuk & John Eastcott/Minden Pictures; Isao Enomoto/Nature Production/Minden Pictures; Penny Tweedie/Corbis; Brad Walker/SuperStock/Getty Images

# UNIT OVERVIEW

**Text Complexity Range for Grades 4–5**

Lexile

740       *TextEvaluator™*       1010

23                      51

|  | **Week 1** | **Week 2** | **Week 3** |
|---|---|---|---|
|  | **JOINING FORCES** | **GETTING ALONG** | **ADAPTATIONS** |

## READING

### Week 1 — JOINING FORCES

**ESSENTIAL QUESTION**
*How do different groups contribute to a cause?*

**Build Background**

**Vocabulary** (CCSS L.5.6)
*bulletin, contributions, diversity, enlisted, intercept, operations, recruits, survival*
Homophones

**Comprehension** (CCSS RL.5.2)
Strategy: Summarize
Skill: Theme
Genre: Historical Fiction
*Analytical Writing* Write About Reading

**Word Study** (CCSS RF.5.3a)
Words with Greek Roots

**Fluency** (CCSS RF.5.4b)
Expression and Phrasing

### Week 2 — GETTING ALONG

**ESSENTIAL QUESTION**
*What actions can we take to get along with others?*

**Build Background**

**Vocabulary** (CCSS L.5.6)
*abruptly, ally, collided, confident, conflict, intervene, protective, taunting*
Connotation and Denotation

**Comprehension** (CCSS RL.5.2)
Strategy: Summarize
Skill: Theme
Genre: Realistic Fiction
*Analytical Writing* Write About Reading

**Word Study** (CCSS RF.5.3a)
Words with Latin Roots

**Fluency** (CCSS RF.5.4b)
Intonation

### Week 3 — ADAPTATIONS

**ESSENTIAL QUESTION**
*How are living things adapted to their environment?*

**Build Background**

**Vocabulary** (CCSS L.5.6)
*adaptation, agile, cache, dormant, forage, frigid, hibernate, insulates*
Context Clues

**Comprehension** (CCSS RI.5.3)
Strategy: Ask and Answer Questions
Skill: Text Structure: Cause and Effect
Genre: Expository Text
*Analytical Writing* Write About Reading

**Word Study** (CCSS RF.5.3a)
Words from Mythology

**Fluency** (CCSS RF.5.4c)
Rate and Accuracy

## LANGUAGE ARTS

### Week 1

**Writing** (CCSS W.5.10)
Trait: Organization

**Grammar** (CCSS L.3.1a)
Adverbs

**Spelling** (CCSS L.5.2e)
Words with Greek Roots

**Vocabulary** (CCSS L.5.4b)
Build Vocabulary

### Week 2

**Writing** (CCSS W.5.3c)
Trait: Word Choice

**Grammar** (CCSS L.3.1g)
Adverbs That Compare

**Spelling** (CCSS L.5.2e)
Words with Latin Roots

**Vocabulary** (CCSS L.5.4)
Build Vocabulary

### Week 3

**Writing** (CCSS W.5.10)
Trait: Sentence Fluency

**Grammar** (CCSS L.5.1)
Negatives

**Spelling** (CCSS L.5.2e)
Words from Mythology

**Vocabulary** (CCSS L.5.4a)
Build Vocabulary

 **Writing Process**   **Genre Writing: Opinion**   Review T344–T349

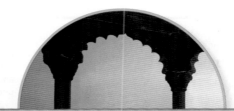

## Review and Assess

| Week 4 | Week 5 | Week 6 |
|---|---|---|

### MAKING A DIFFERENCE

**ESSENTIAL QUESTION**
*What impact do our actions have on our world?*

**Build Background**

**CCSS Vocabulary**
L.5.6
export, glistening, influence, landscape, native, plantations, restore, urged
Synonyms and Antonyms

**CCSS Comprehension**
RI.5.5
Strategy: Ask and Answer Questions
Skill: Text Structure: Problem and Solution
Genre: Biography
*Analytical Writing* Write About Reading

**CCSS Word Study**
RF.5.3a
Number prefixes *uni-, bi-, tri-, cent-*

**CCSS Fluency**
RF.5.4b
Expression and Phrasing

**CCSS Writing**
W.5.1
Trait: Ideas

**CCSS Grammar**
L.5.1e
Sentence Combining

**CCSS Spelling**
L.5.2e
Number Prefixes *uni-, bi-, tri-, cent-*

**CCSS Vocabulary**
L.5.5c
Build Vocabulary

### OUT IN THE WORLD

**ESSENTIAL QUESTION**
*What can our connections to the world teach us?*

**Build Background**

**CCSS Vocabulary**
L.5.6
assonance, blares, connection, consonance, errand, exchange, imagery, personification
Personification

**CCSS Comprehension**
RL.5.6
Literary Elements: Assonance and Consonance
Skill: Point of View
Genre: Lyric and Narrative
*Analytical Writing* Write About Reading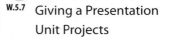

**CCSS Word Study**
RF.5.3a
Suffixes *-ible* and *-able*

**CCSS Fluency**
RF.5.4b
Expression and Phrasing

**CCSS Writing**
W.5.3d
Trait: Word Choice

**CCSS Grammar**
L.5.1a
Prepositional Phrases

**CCSS Spelling**
L.5.2e
Suffixes *-ible* and *-able*

**CCSS Vocabulary**
L.5.5c
Build Vocabulary

**CCSS Reader's Theater**
RF.5.4a
Focus on Vocabulary
Fluency: Accuracy, Rate, and Prosody

**CCSS Reading Digitally**
RI.5.7
Notetaking
Navigating Links

**CCSS Research and Inquiry**
W.5.7
Giving a Presentation
Unit Projects
Presentation of Ideas

### Unit 6 Assessment

**Unit Assessment Book**
pages 137–163

**Fluency Assessment**
pages 292–301

**CCSS Writing**
SL.5.5
Share Your Writing
Portfolio Choice

 **Writing Process Genre Writing: Opinion** Opinion Letter T350–T355

# UNIT OPENER

**Reading/Writing Workshop**

**READING/WRITING WORKSHOP, pp. 376–377**

Contents of image panel:

Unit 6

**Linked In**

**The BIG Idea**
How are we all connected?

376

Peace can be made and kept only by the united determination of free and peace-loving peoples who are willing to work together — willing to help one another — willing to respect and tolerate and try to understand one another's opinions and feelings.

— **FRANKLIN D. ROOSEVELT,** President of the United States, 1933-1945, from *State of the Union Address, January 6, 1945*

377

## The Big Idea *How are we all connected?*

### Talk About It

Have students read the Big Idea aloud. Ask them to identify a time they connected with others in order to accomplish something. Students may mention cleaning up a school playground or completing a difficult science project.

Ask: *What benefits come from interacting and making connections with others?* Have students discuss in partners or in groups, then share their ideas with the class.

**Music Links** Introduce a song at the start of the unit. Go to www.connected.mcgraw-hill.com, Resources Media: Music to find audio recordings, song lyrics, and activities.

### Read the Quote

Read aloud the quote by Franklin D. Roosevelt. Ask students questions to explore the theme.

→ What does Roosevelt mean when he refers to "united determination"?

→ What does Roosevelt think people must do to make and keep the peace?

→ Why is it important to try and understand one another's opinions and feelings?

**Repetition** Have students skim the quote and identify repeated words or phrases (*peace, willing to*) and words that have similar meanings (*united, work together*). Ask why speakers use repetition (to clarify their points, to be memorable, to help the speech flow). Have students identify the theme of the quote and tell how repetition made it clear.

# RESEARCH AND INQUIRY

**Weekly Projects** Each week students will produce a project related to the Essential Question. They will then develop one of these projects more fully for the Week 6 Unit Project. Through their research, students will focus their attention on:

→ communicating clearly.

→ organizing and enhancing presentations.

**Shared Research Board** You may wish to develop a Shared Research Board. Students can post ideas and information about the unit theme as well as summaries, examples, illustrations, lists, or notes they gather as they do their research. They can also post notes with questions they have as they conduct their research.

### WEEKLY PROJECTS

Students work in pairs or small groups.

**Week 1** Class Web Site, T28

**Week 2** Oral Presentation, T92

**Week 3** Oral Presentation, T156

**Week 4** Research Display, T220

**Week 5** Interview Summary, T284

### WEEK 6 UNIT PROJECT

Students work in small groups to complete and present one of the following projects.

→ Oral Presentation

→ List of Guidelines

→ Slide Show

→ Rap or Jingle

→ Mock Interview

# WRITING

**Write About Reading** As students read and reread each week for close reading of text, students will take notes, cite evidence to support their ideas and opinions, write summaries of text, or develop character sketches.

## Writing Every Day: Focus on Writing Traits

Each week, students will focus on a writing trait. After analyzing an expert and student model, students will draft and revise shorter writing entries in their writer's notebook, applying the trait to their writing.

## Writing Process: Focus on Opinion Writing

Over the course of the unit, students will develop one to two longer opinion texts. They will work through the various stages of the writing process, allowing them time to continue revising their writing and conferencing with peers and teacher.

### WEEKLY WRITING TRAITS

**Week 1** Organization, T30

**Week 2** Word Choice, T94

**Week 3** Sentence Fluency, T158

**Week 4** Ideas, T222

**Week 5** Word Choice, T286

### GENRE WRITING: OPINION TEXT

Choose one or complete both 2–3 week writing process lessons over the course of the unit.

Book Review, T344–T349

Opinion Letter, T350–T355

  **Go Digital**

**COLLABORATE**
Post student questions and monitor student online discussions. Create a Shared Research Board.

  **Go Digital**

**WRITER'S WORKSPACE**
Ask students to work through their genre writing using the online tools.

**Text Complexity Range for Grades 4–5**

| Lexile | |
|---|---|
| 740 | 1010 |
| *TextEvaluator*™ | |
| 23 | 51 |

**McGraw-Hill Reading**
# Wonders

**Reading/Writing Workshop**

Mc Graw Hill

# TEACH AND MODEL

CCSS **Shared Read** Genre • Historical Fiction

# SHIPPED OUT

**Essential Question**
**How do different groups contribute to a cause?**
Read about how a young girl learns how to contribute to the war effort during World War II.

382

My name is Libby Kendall, and I am a prisoner of war. Well, not really, but some days it feels that way. Just like my dad, I've packed up my things and shipped out. Unlike my dad, however, nothing I do will ever help the Allies win World War II.

My father is a mechanic on a battleship in the Pacific Ocean. I'm trapped in a little apartment above my Aunt Lucia's bakery downtown. Mom says it's just for a few months while she works double shifts at the clothing factory. She makes uniforms, mostly sewing pockets on jackets. I asked her once if she snuck things into the pockets for soldiers to find, like little poems written in calligraphy. She said soldiers wore jackets with pockets to hold tools they might need for war **survival**, not silly things like poetry.

It seems no one appreciates my creative **contributions** to the war effort, but Aunt Lucia says my help to her is important, since both her workers joined the army.

On my first day with Aunt Lucia, she explained the daily **operations** of the bakery. First, we get up before dawn to knead the dough. Next, we bake breads and muffins. Then,

while I help customers, Lucia makes cakes and cookies for sale in the afternoon. Whenever the phone rings, she races from the back room to **intercept** the call. She's always worried that it might be bad news, so she wants to be the first to hear it.

After dinner, Aunt Lucia invites neighbors over to listen to the radio. Some are immigrants from a wide **diversity** of backgrounds. Lucia and others help translate the news into several languages for everyone to understand. I always listen closely for any **bulletin** about fighting in the Pacific.

383

## ✔ Vocabulary

bulletin
contributions
diversity
enlisted
intercept
operations
recruits
survival

## 🔍 Close Reading of Complex Text

**Shared Read** "Shipped Out," 382–389

**Genre** Historical Fiction

**Lexile** 810L
 *TextEvaluator*™ 50

## Minilessons

## ✔ Tested Skills CCSS

**Comprehension Strategy** .............. Summarize, T18–T19

✔ **Comprehension Skill** ................... Theme, T20–T21

✔ **Genre** ................................................. Historical Fiction, T22–T23

✔ **Vocabulary Strategy** ................... Homophones, T24–T25

✔ **Writing Traits** ................................ Organization, T30–T31

**Grammar Handbook** ...................... Adverbs, T34–T35

 ☞ **Go Digital**

www.connected.mcgraw-hill.com

# JOINING FORCES

**Essential Question**
How do different groups contribute to a cause?

# APPLY WITH CLOSE READING

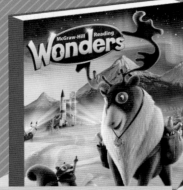

**Literature Anthology**

## Complex Text

**PAIRED READ**

*The Unbreakable Code,* 430–443
**Genre** Historical Fiction
**Lexile** 640L
**ETS** TextEvaluator™ 40

"Allies in Action," 446–449
**Genre** Expository Text
**Lexile** 870L
**ETS** TextEvaluator™ 52

## Differentiated Text

**Leveled Readers** *Include Paired Reads*

APPROACHING
**Lexile** 730L
**ETS** TextEvaluator™ 36

ON LEVEL
**Lexile** 770L
**ETS** TextEvaluator™ 46

BEYOND
**Lexile** 900L
**ETS** TextEvaluator™ 51

ELL
**Lexile** 640L
**ETS** TextEvaluator™ 28

## Extended Complex Text

*No Talking*
**Genre** Realistic Fiction
**Lexile** 820L
**ETS** TextEvaluator™ 45

*The Midnight Fox*
**Genre** Realistic Fiction
**Lexile** 990L
**ETS** TextEvaluator™ 45

**Classroom Library**

Classroom Library lessons available online.

No Talking: Illustration © Mark Elliott

# TEACH AND MANAGE

## How You Teach

### INTRODUCE

**Weekly Concept**
Joining Forces

**Reading/Writing Workshop**
378–379

### TEACH

**Close Reading**
"Shipped Out"

**Minilessons**
Summarize, Theme, Historical Fiction, Homophones, Writing Traits

**Reading/Writing Workshop**
382–391

### APPLY

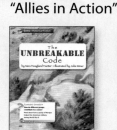

**Close Reading**
*The Unbreakable Code*

"Allies in Action"

**Literature Anthology**
430–449

 **Go Digital**

 Interactive Whiteboard

 Interactive Whiteboard

Mobile

## How Students Practice

### WEEKLY CONTRACT

**PDF Online**

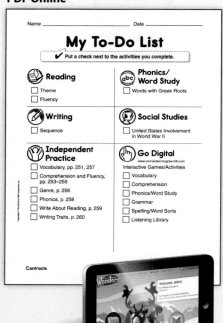

Name _____ Date _____

#### My To-Do List
✔ Put a check next to the activities you complete.

📖 **Reading**
☐ Theme
☐ Fluency

🔤 **Phonics/Word Study**
☐ Words with Greek Roots

✏️ **Writing**
☐ Sequence

📚 **Social Studies**
☐ United States Involvement in World War II

🏆 **Independent Practice**
☐ Vocabulary, pp. 251, 257
☐ Comprehension and Fluency, pp. 253–255
☐ Genre, p. 256
☐ Phonics, p. 258
☐ Write About Reading, p. 259
☐ Writing Traits, p. 260

👆 **Go Digital**
www.connected.mcgraw-hill.com
Interactive Games/Activities
☐ Vocabulary
☐ Comprehension
☐ Phonics/Word Study
☐ Grammar
☐ Spelling/Word Sorts
☐ Listening Library

Contracts

### LEVELED PRACTICE and ONLINE ACTIVITIES

**Your Turn Practice Book**
251–260

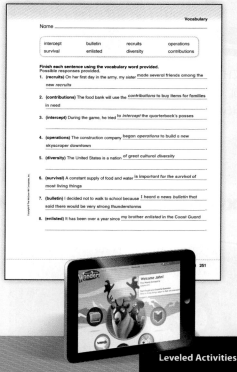

Name _____

Vocabulary

| intercept | bulletin | recruits | operations |
| survival | enlisted | diversity | contributions |

Finish each sentence using the vocabulary word provided.
Possible responses provided.

1. (recruits) On her first day in the army, my sister made several friends among the new recruits

2. (contributions) The food bank will use the contributions to buy items for families in need

3. (intercept) During the game, he tried to intercept the quarterback's passes

4. (operations) The construction company began operations to build a new skyscraper downtown

5. (diversity) The United States is a nation of great cultural diversity

6. (survival) A constant supply of food and water is important for the survival of most living things

7. (bulletin) I decided not to walk to school because I heard a news bulletin that said there would be very strong thunderstorms

8. (enlisted) It has been over a year since my brother enlisted in the Coast Guard

251

**Leveled Readers**

👆 **Go Digital**

Online To-Do List

Leveled Activities

Writer's Workspace

## DIFFERENTIATE

**SMALL GROUP INSTRUCTION**

**Leveled Readers**

**Mobile**

## INTEGRATE

**Research and Inquiry**
Research Presentation, T28

**Text Connections**
Compare How Groups
Contribute to a Cause, T29

**Write About Reading**
*Analytical Writing* Write an Analysis, T29

**Online Research
and Writing**

## ASSESS

**Weekly Assessment
301–312**

**Online
Assessment**

# LEVELED WORKSTATION CARDS

More
Activities
on back

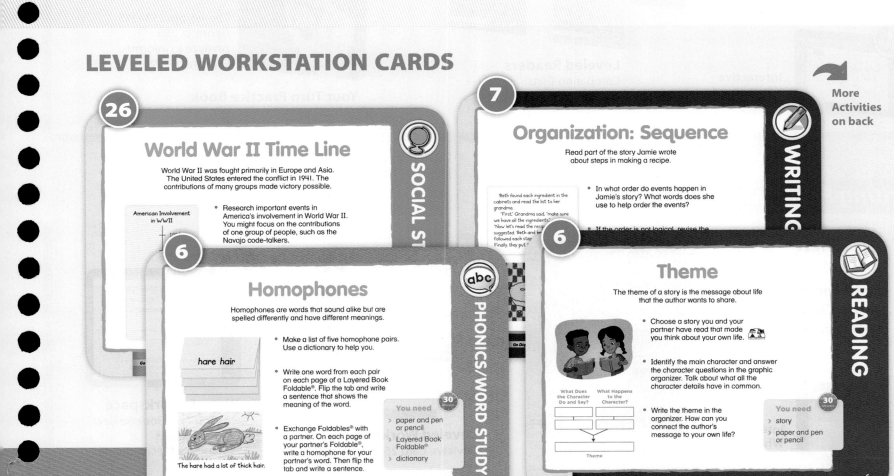

**26**

### World War II Time Line

SOCIAL STUDIES

World War II was fought primarily in Europe and Asia.
The United States entered the conflict in 1941. The
contributions of many groups made victory possible.

American Involvement
in WWII

- Research important events in
America's involvement in World War II.
You might focus on the contributions
of one group of people, such as the
Navajo code-talkers.

**6**

### Homophones

PHONICS/WORD STUDY

Homophones are words that sound alike but are
spelled differently and have different meanings.

hare  hair

- Make a list of five homophone pairs.
Use a dictionary to help you.

- Write one word from each pair
on each page of a Layered Book
Foldable®. Flip the tab and write
a sentence that shows the
meaning of the word.

The hare had a lot of thick hair.

- Exchange Foldables® with
a partner. On each page of
your partner's Foldable®,
write a homophone for your
partner's word. Then flip the
tab and write a sentence.

**You need**
> paper and pen
or pencil
> Layered Book
Foldable®
> dictionary

30 minutes

Go Digital! • www.connected.mcgraw-hill.com • Interactive Games and Activities • Grade 5    6

**7**

### Organization: Sequence

WRITING

Read part of the story Jamie wrote
about steps in making a recipe.

"Beth found each ingredient in the
cabinets and read the list to her
grandma.
'First,' Grandma said, 'make sure
we have all the ingredients'...
'Now let's read the recipe'...
suggested. Beth and her...
followed each step...
Finally, they put..."

- In what order do events happen in
Jamie's story? What words does she
use to help order the events?

- If the order is not logical, revise the...

**6**

### Theme

READING

The theme of a story is the message about life
that the author wants to share.

- Choose a story you and your
partner have read that made
you think about your own life.

- Identify the main character and answer
the character questions in the graphic
organizer. Talk about what all the
character details have in common.

| What Does
the Character
Do and Say? | What Happens
to the
Character? |
|---|---|

Theme

- Write the theme in the
organizer. How can you
connect the author's
message to your own life?

**You need**
> story
> paper and pen
or pencil

30 minutes

Go Digital! • www.connected.mcgraw-hill.com • Interactive Games and Activities • Grade 5    6

# DEVELOPING READERS AND WRITERS

## Write to Sources and Research

Theme, T20–T21

Note Taking, T25B, T25R

Summarize, T25P

Theme, T25P

Make Connections: Essential Question, T25P, T25T, T29

Key Details, T25R, T25S

Research and Inquiry, T28

Analyze to Inform/Explain, T29

Comparing Texts, T41, T49, T53, T59

Predictive Writing, T25B

**Teacher's Edition**

**Literature Anthology**

Summarize, p. 445
Theme, p. 445

**Interactive Whiteboard**

**Leveled Readers**
Comparing Texts
Theme

**Your Turn Practice Book**

Theme, pp. 253–255
Genre, p. 256
Analyze to Inform/
Explain, p. 259

---

**Opinion Text**
Book Review, T344–T349

**Conferencing Routines**
Teacher Conferences, T346
Peer Conferences, T347

**Interactive Whiteboard**

**Teacher's Edition**

**Leveled Workstation Card**
Reviews, Card 26

**Writer's Workspace**
Opinion Text: Book Review
Writing Process
Multimedia Presentations

## *Writing Traits • Write Every Day*

**Writing Trait: Organization**
Sequence, T30–T31

**Conferencing Routines**
Teacher Conferences, T32
Peer Conferences, T33

**Teacher's Edition**

Organization:
Sequence,
pp. 390–391

**Reading/Writing Workshop**

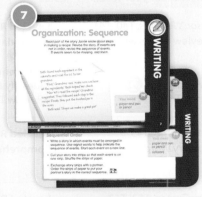

Organization:
Sequence, 7

**Leveled Workstation Card**

Organization:
Sequence, p. 260

**Your Turn Practice Book**

**Interactive
Whiteboard**

## *Grammar and Spelling*

**Grammar**
Adverbs, T34–T35

**Spelling**
Words with Greek Roots,
T36–T37

**Interactive
Whiteboard**

**Teacher's Edition**

**GRAMMonster!**
Answer each question and try
to drive the GRAMMonster
out of his castle!

Adverbs

**Spelling: Long a**

Words with
Greek Roots
Word Sorts

**Online Spelling and Grammar Games**

# SUGGESTED LESSON PLAN

✔ TESTED SKILLS  CCSS

| | | DAY 1 | DAY 2 |
|---|---|---|---|
| **READING** | | | |

## Whole Group

**Teach, Model and Apply**

Reading/Writing Workshop

### DAY 1
**Build Background** Joining Forces, T10–T11
**Listening Comprehension** Interactive Read Aloud: "Hope for the Troops," T12–T13
**Comprehension**
• Preview Genre: Historical Fiction, T22–T23
• Preview Strategy: Summarize, T18–T19
✔ **Vocabulary** Words in Context, T14–T15
**Practice** *Your Turn* 251

**Close Reading of Complex Text** "Shipped Out," 382–385

### DAY 2
✔ **Comprehension**
• Strategy: Summarize, T18–T19
• Skill: Theme, T20–T21
• Write About Reading ● Analytical Writing
• Genre: Historical Fiction, T22–T23
✔ **Vocabulary** Strategy: Homophones, T24–T25
**Practice** *Your Turn* 252–257

---

## DIFFERENTIATED INSTRUCTION  Choose across the week to meet your students' needs.

## Small Group

### Approaching Level

**DAY 1**
**Leveled Reader** *Mrs. Gleeson's Records*, T40–T41
**Word Study/Decoding** Review Words with Greek Roots, T42 (TIER 2)
**Vocabulary**
• Review High-Frequency Words, T44 (TIER 2)
• Understand Word Meanings, T45

**DAY 2**
**Leveled Reader** *Mrs. Gleeson's Records*, T40–T41
**Vocabulary** Review Vocabulary Words, T44 (TIER 2)
**Comprehension**
• Identify Details, T46 (TIER 2)
• Review Theme, T47

### On Level

**DAY 1**
**Leveled Reader** *Norberto's Hat*, T48–T49
**Vocabulary** Review Vocabulary Words, T50

**DAY 2**
**Leveled Reader** *Norberto's Hat*, T48–T49
**Comprehension** Review Theme, T51

### Beyond Level

**DAY 1**
**Leveled Reader** *The Victory Garden*, T52–T53
**Vocabulary** Review Domain-Specific Words, T54

**DAY 2**
**Leveled Reader** *The Victory Garden*, T52–T53
**Comprehension** Review Theme, T55

### English Language Learners

**DAY 1**
**Shared Read** "Shipped Out," T56–T57
**Word Study/Decoding** Review Words with Greek Roots, T42
**Vocabulary**
• Preteach Vocabulary, T60
• Review High-Frequency Words, T44

**DAY 2**
**Leveled Reader** *Norberto's Hat*, T58–T59
**Vocabulary** Review Vocabulary, T60
**Writing** Writing Trait: Organization, T62
**Grammar** Adverbs, T63

---

## LANGUAGE ARTS  Writing Process: Book Review T344–T349                                    Use with Weeks 1–3

## Whole Group

### Writing
### Grammar
### Spelling
### Build Vocabulary

**DAY 1**
✔ **Readers to Writers**
• Writing Trait: Organization/Sequence, T30–T31
• Writing Entry: Prewrite and Draft, T32
**Grammar** Adverbs, T34
**Spelling** Words with Greek Roots, T36
**Build Vocabulary**
• Connect to Words, T38
• Academic Vocabulary, T38

**DAY 2**
**Readers to Writers**
• Writing Trait: Organization/Sequence, T30–T31
• Writing Entry: Revise, T32
**Grammar** Adverbs, T34
**Spelling** Words with Greek Roots, T36
**Build Vocabulary**
• Expand Vocabulary, T38
• Review Root Words, T38

☞ **Go**
**Digital**

CUSTOMIZE YOUR OWN
LESSON PLANS
www.connected.mcgraw-hill.com

WEEK 1 →

| **DAY 3** | **DAY 4** | **DAY 5** Review and Assess |
|---|---|---|

**READING**

**Word Study/Decoding** Words with Greek Roots, T26–T27
**Practice** *Your Turn* 258

**Close Reading** *The Unbreakable Code*, 430–445

**Fluency** Expression and Phrasing, T27
**Integrate Ideas** *Analytical Writing*
• Research and Inquiry, T28
**Practice** *Your Turn* 253–255

**Close Reading** "Allies in Action," 446–449 *Analytical Writing*

**Integrate Ideas** *Analytical Writing*
• Research and Inquiry, T28
• Text Connections, T29
• Write About Reading, T29
**Practice** *Your Turn* 259

**DIFFERENTIATED INSTRUCTION**

**Leveled Reader** *Mrs. Gleeson's Records*, T40–T41
**Word Study/Decoding** Build Words with Greek Roots, T42 **TIER 2**
**Fluency** Expression and Phrasing, T46 **TIER 2**
**Vocabulary** Homophones, T45

**Leveled Reader** Paired Read: "Scrap Drives and Ration Books," T41 *Analytical Writing*
**Word Study/Decoding** Practice Words with Greek Roots, T43

**Leveled Reader** Literature Circle, T41
**Comprehension** Self-Selected Reading, T47

**Leveled Reader** *Norberto's Hat*, T48–T49
**Vocabulary** Homophones, T50

**Leveled Reader** Paired Read: "The *Bracero* Program," T49 *Analytical Writing*

**Leveled Reader** Literature Circle, T49
**Comprehension** Self-Selected Reading, T51

**Leveled Reader** *The Victory Garden*, T52–T53
**Vocabulary**
• Homophones, T54 *Gifted and Talented*
• Analyze, T54

**Leveled Reader** Paired Read: "Gardening for Uncle Sam," T53 *Analytical Writing*

**Leveled Reader** Literature Circle, T53
**Comprehension**
• Self-Selected Reading, T55
• Independent Study: Joining Forces, T55 *Gifted and Talented*

**Leveled Reader** *Norberto's Hat*, T58–T59
**Word Study/Decoding** Build Words with Greek Roots, T42
**Vocabulary** Homophones, T61
**Spelling** Words with Greek Roots, T62

**Leveled Reader** Paired Read: "The *Bracero* Program," T59 *Analytical Writing*
**Vocabulary** Additional Vocabulary, T61
**Word Study/Decoding** Practice Words with Greek Roots, T43

**Leveled Reader** Literature Circle, T59

**LANGUAGE ARTS**

**Readers to Writers**
• Writing Entry: Prewrite and Draft, T33
**Grammar** Mechanics and Usage, T35
**Spelling** Words with Greek Roots, T37
**Build Vocabulary**
• Reinforce the Words, T39
• Homophones, T39

**Readers to Writers**
• Writing Entry: Revise, T33
**Grammar** Adverbs, T35
**Spelling** Words with Greek Roots, T37
**Build Vocabulary**
• Connect to Writing, T39
• Shades of Meaning, T39

**Readers to Writers**
• Writing Entry: Share and Reflect, T33
**Grammar** Adverbs, T35
**Spelling** Words with Greek Roots, T37
**Build Vocabulary**
• Word Squares, T39
• Morphology, T39

# DIFFERENTIATE TO ACCELERATE

  Scaffold to **A**ccess **C**omplex **T**ext

**IF** the text complexity of a particular selection is too difficult for students

**THEN** see the references noted in the chart below for scaffolded instruction to help students Access Complex Text.

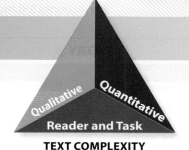

Qualitative | Quantitative

**Reader and Task**

**TEXT COMPLEXITY**

| | Reading/Writing Workshop | Literature Anthology | Leveled Readers | | Classroom Library |
|---|---|---|---|---|---|
| **Quantitative** | **"Shipped Out"**<br>Lexile 810<br>*TextEvaluator™* 50<br><br>**"Allies in Action"**<br>Lexile 870<br>*TextEvaluator™* 52 | *The Unbreakable Code*<br>Lexile 640<br>*TextEvaluator™* 40 | **Approaching Level**<br>Lexile 730<br>*TextEvaluator™* 36<br><br>**Beyond Level**<br>Lexile 900<br>*TextEvaluator™* 51 | **On Level**<br>Lexile 770<br>*TextEvaluator™* 46<br><br>**ELL**<br>Lexile 640<br>*TextEvaluator™* 28 | *No Talking*<br>Lexile 820<br>*TextEvaluator™* 45<br><br>*The Midnight Fox*<br>Lexile 990<br>*TextEvaluator™* 45 |
| **Qualitative** | **What Makes the Text Complex?**<br>• **Prior Knowledge** World War II T17<br>• **Organization** Flashbacks T23<br><br> *See Scaffolded Instruction in Teacher's Edition T17 and T23.* | **What Makes the Text Complex?**<br>• **Sentence Structure** T25A, T25H, T25K<br>• **Specific Vocabulary** Word Parts T25C; Military T25E, T25S<br>• **Prior Knowledge** Navajo T25D; Iwo Jima T25K<br>• **Connection of Ideas** Navajo Code T25G; War Training T25I; Earlier Information T25M<br>• **Organization** Multiple Structures T25Q<br><br> *See Scaffolded Instruction in Teacher's Edition T25A–T25T.* | **What Makes the Text Complex?**<br>• **Specific Vocabulary**<br>• **Sentence Structure**<br>• **Connection of Ideas**<br>• **Genre**<br><br><br><br><br> *See Level Up lessons online for Leveled Readers.* | | **What Makes the Text Complex?**<br>• **Genre**<br>• **Specific Vocabulary**<br>• **Prior Knowledge**<br>• **Sentence Structure**<br>• **Organization**<br>• **Purpose**<br>• **Connection of Ideas**<br><br> *See Scaffolded Instruction in Teacher's Edition T360-T361.* |
| **Reader and Task** | The Introduce the Concept lesson on pages T10-T11 will help determine the reader's knowledge and engagement in the weekly concept. See pages T16-T25 and T28-T29 for questions and tasks for this text. | The Introduce the Concept lesson on pages T10-T11 will help determine the reader's knowledge and engagement in the weekly concept. See pages T25A-T25T and T28-T29 for questions and tasks for this text. | The Introduce the Concept lesson on pages T10-T11 will help determine the reader's knowledge and engagement in the weekly concept. See pages T40-T41, T48-T49, T52-T53, T58-T59, and T28-T29 for questions and tasks for this text. | | The Introduce the Concept lesson on pages T10-T11 will help determine the reader's knowledge and engagement in the weekly concept. See pages T360-T361 for questions and tasks for this text. |

No Talking: Illustration © Mark Elliott

## Monitor and *Differentiate*

**IF** → you need to differentiate instruction

**THEN** → use the Quick Checks to assess students' needs and select the appropriate small group instruction focus.

### ✓ Quick Check

**Comprehension Strategy** Summarize T19
**Comprehension Skill** Theme T21
**Genre** Historical Fiction T23
**Vocabulary Strategy** Homophones T25
**Word Study/Fluency** Words with Greek Roots, Expression and Phrasing T27

**If No** →
| Approaching Level | **Reteach** T40–T47 |
| ELL | **Develop** T56–T63 |

**If Yes** →
| On Level | **Review** T48–T51 |
| Beyond Level | **Extend** T52–T55 |

## Level Up with Leveled Readers

**IF** → students can read their leveled text fluently and answer comprehension questions

**THEN** → work with the next level up to accelerate students' reading with more complex text.

## ENGLISH LANGUAGE LEARNERS
### SCAFFOLD

**IF** → ELL students need additional support **THEN** → scaffold instruction using the small group suggestions.

| Reading/Writing Workshop "Shipped Out" T56–T57 | Leveled Reader *Norberto's Hat* T58–T59 "The *Bracero* Program" T59 | Additional Vocabulary T61 harvest    military fascinated    navy immigrants    wallet | Homophones T61 | Writing Trait: Organization T62 | Spelling Words with Greek Roots T62 | Grammar Adverbs T63 |
|---|---|---|---|---|---|---|

**Note: Include ELL Students in all small groups based on their needs.**

# → Introduce the Concept

**Reading/Writing Workshop**

**MINILESSON**
**10 Mins**

## Build Background

### ESSENTIAL QUESTION

*How do different groups contribute to a cause?*

Have students read the Essential Question on page 378 of the **Reading/Writing Workshop**. Tell them that it takes a **diversity**, or variety, of talents, skills, and people to contribute to a cause.

Discuss the photograph of the women working in the factory. Focus on their **contributions**, or what they gave or did, to support the war effort.

→ During World War II, everyone had to pool their talents and resources to contribute to the war effort.

→ Instead of their usual **diversity** of products, some factories helped by making weapons and war equipment.

→ With the men away at war, many women went to work in these factories. Together everyone made contributions to help.

## Talk About It

**COLLABORATE**

**Ask:** *What **contributions** have you made to a cause? When working together for a cause, why is there strength in **diversity**?* Have students discuss in pairs or groups.

→ Model adding words about causes and contributions to the graphic organizer. Then generate words and phrases with students and add their ideas.

→ Have partners discuss what they have learned about contributing to a cause. Have them add related ideas to the organizer.

### Collaborative Conversations

**Add New Ideas** As students engage in partner, small-group, and whole-class discussions, encourage them to add new ideas to their conversations. Remind students to

→ stay on topic.

→ connect their own ideas to things their peers have said.

→ look for ways to connect their personal experiences or prior knowledge to the conversation.

---

### OBJECTIVES

**CCSS**

Engage effectively in a range of collaborative discussions (one-on-one, in groups, and teacher-led) with diverse partners on *grade 5 topics and texts*, building on others' ideas and expressing their own clearly. Come to discussions prepared, having read or studied required material; explicitly draw on that preparation and other information known about the topic to explore ideas under discussion. **SL.5.1a**

Build background knowledge on contributing to a cause.

---

### ACADEMIC LANGUAGE

• *diversity, contributions*

• Cognates: *diversidad, contribuciones*

---

**Go Digital**

**Discuss the Concept**

**Watch Video**

**Use Graphic Organizer**

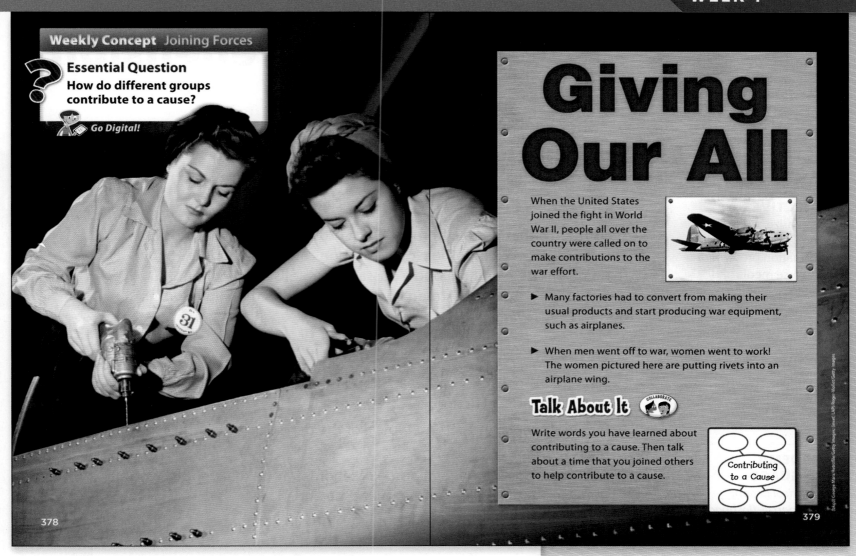

**Weekly Concept** Joining Forces

**Essential Question**
How do different groups contribute to a cause?

Go Digital!

# Giving Our All

When the United States joined the fight in World War II, people all over the country were called on to make contributions to the war effort.

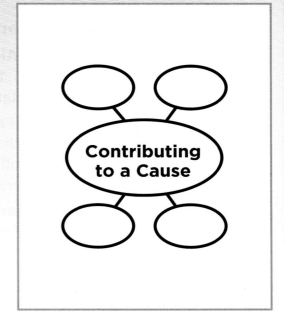

▶ Many factories had to convert from making their usual products and start producing war equipment, such as airplanes.

▶ When men went off to war, women went to work! The women pictured here are putting rivets into an airplane wing.

**Talk About It**

Write words you have learned about contributing to a cause. Then talk about a time that you joined others to help contribute to a cause.

Contributing to a Cause

378    379

**READING/WRITING WORKSHOP, pp. 378–379**

## ELL ENGLISH LANGUAGE LEARNERS SCAFFOLD

| **Beginning** | **Intermediate** | **Advanced/High** |
|---|---|---|
| **Use Visuals** Point to the women in the photograph. Say: *These women wanted to help during the war, so they worked in factories. This was their contribution.* Elicit that a contribution is something given to help. Ask: *Did these women help their country during the war?* Elaborate. Say: *When people join forces, they work together.* | **Describe** Have students describe what is happening in the photograph. Ask: *What contributions did these women make during the war? What are some other ways to make contributions to a cause?* Correct for grammar and pronunciation as needed. | **Discuss** Ask students to discuss the women in the photograph. Ask: *What contributions did the women make when they joined forces to help the war effort? How were they helping the cause? Why are contributions important?* Clarify or restate students' responses as needed. |

**GRAPHIC ORGANIZER 62**

Contributing to a Cause

# → Listening Comprehension

MINILESSON
**10**
Mins

## Interactive Read Aloud

**View Illustrations**

### OBJECTIVES

CCSS Summarize a written text read aloud or information presented in diverse media and formats, including visually, quantitatively, and orally. **SL.5.2**

- Listen for a purpose.
- Identify characteristics of historical fiction

### ACADEMIC LANGUAGE

- *historical fiction, summarize, flashback*
- Cognates: *ficción histórica, resumir*

### Connect to Concept: Joining Forces

Tell students that people from different groups and backgrounds often join forces, or work together, for a common cause. Let students know that you will be reading aloud a passage that tells about when USO entertainers visited U.S. Armed Forces personnel in the South Pacific during World War II.

### Preview Genre: Historical Fiction

Explain that the text you will read aloud is historical fiction. Discuss the features of historical fiction:

→ features events and setting typical of the period in which the action takes place

→ features lifelike characters, some of whom may be real people, who think and act like people from that time and place

→ usually unfolds in time order but may contain flashbacks

### Preview Comprehension Strategy: Summarize

Point out that skillful readers often summarize information as they read to help remember main ideas and key details. A helpful summary leaves out the reader's opinions and focuses on important information.

Use the Think Alouds on page T13 to model the strategy.

### Respond to Reading

**Think Aloud Clouds** Display Think Aloud Master 5: *This was mostly about…* to reinforce how you used the summarize strategy to understand content.

**Genre Features** With students, discuss the elements of the Read Aloud that let them know that it is historical fiction. Ask them to think about other texts that you have read or they have read independently that were historical fiction.

**Summarize** Have students restate the main ideas of "Hope for the Troops" in their own words.

**Model Think Alouds**

**Genre Chart**

# Hope for the Troops

Stuart stared down at the potatoes and meatball stew on his plate. Back home in North Dakota, he enjoyed hot meals with lots of gravy. Here on a South Pacific island during World War II, however, his appetite sank with his spirits. After days of surviving a summer heat wave with high humidity, he would rather bite into a homemade snowball than another U.S. Army meatball. **1**

"Look at this," said Stuart's friend Jerry, a radio operations assistant. He placed a handwritten note on the table that read, "Hope, USO, Summer, 1944."

"What does this mean?" Stuart asked.

"It means Bob Hope is coming to our island outpost next month!" Jerry said. "He's doing a USO show here—you know, the United Service Organizations. We just got a radio transmission about the schedule, and they're coming here to this base!"

At last, Stuart thought, after weeks of building an air strip, here was something fun to look forward to.

Officers and enlisted personnel watched the plane touch down on the airstrip they themselves had built. Within minutes, the comedian Bob Hope stepped out of the aircraft, grinned, and waved to the crowd.

All day long the base buzzed with activity. Everyone pitched in to help the USO set up. Smiles and back slaps replaced the grim and tired faces from the week before. **2**

That afternoon, Bob Hope cracked jokes on a makeshift stage in front of hundreds of enlisted men. People laughed so hard that tears streamed down their faces. Soon after, more performers took the stage. Stuart and the other soldiers tapped their feet and clapped their hands as singers and dancers put on a star-studded show.

Jerry elbowed Stuart in the ribs. "I haven't seen you so happy in days," he said.

"I can't wait to write my folks," Stuart replied. "They would've loved this show!" **3**

**1 Think Aloud** As I read, I will **summarize** what I have read: The main character, Stuart, is on an Army base in World War II. He is tired of the heat and feeling homesick.

**2 Think Aloud** Things on the island have changed. I will **summarize** the plot so far to help explain this: Performers from the USO have come to put on a show, and they are lifting everyone's spirits.

**3 Think Aloud** Now that I'm finished, I will **summarize** the story: A visit from the USO performers helps to cheer up Stuart and other soldiers on a U.S. Army base in WWII.

moodboard/Corbis

# → Vocabulary

**Reading/Writing Workshop**

### OBJECTIVES

Acquire and use accurately grade-appropriate general academic and domain-specific words and phrases, including those that signal contrast, addition, and other logical relationships (e.g., *however, although, nevertheless, similarly, moreover, in addition*). **L.5.6**

### ACADEMIC LANGUAGE

• *contributions, diversity*

• Cognates: *contribuciones, diversidad*

MINILESSON **10** Mins

## Words in Context

### Model the Routine

Introduce each vocabulary word using the Vocabulary Routine found on the **Visual Vocabulary Cards**.

**Visual Vocabulary Cards**

Vocabu...

Define:

Example:

Ask:

---

### Vocabulary Routine

**Define:** A **bulletin** is a short announcement of the latest news.

**Example:** Kip posted a bulletin in the neighborhood about his missing dog.

**Ask:** Why else might you post a bulletin?

---

### Definitions

→ **contributions**   **Contributions** are gifts of money, time, or effort given to a cause. **Cognate:** *contribuciones*

→ **diversity**   **Diversity** is a great difference or variety. **Cognate:** *diversidad*

→ **enlisted**   If people **enlisted**, they joined the armed forces of their own free will.

→ **intercept**   If you **intercept** something, you stop it from moving from one place to another. **Cognate:** *interceptar*

→ **operations**   **Operations** are plans or processes for doing something. **Cognate:** *operaciones*

→ **recruits**   **Recruits** are new members of the armed forces. **Cognate:** *reclutas*

→ **survival**   **Survival** is the act of continuing to live.

### Talk About It

COLLABORATE

Have partners read the sentence and discuss the definition for each word. Have them talk about how the photograph relates to the definition. Then ask students to choose three words and write questions for their partner to answer.

**Go Digital**

**bulletin**

**Use Visual Glossary**

## CCSS Words to Know

# Vocabulary

Use the picture and the sentences to talk with a partner about each word.

**bulletin**

Kip posted a **bulletin** in the neighborhood about his missing dog.

*Why else might you post a bulletin?*

**contributions**

The school art exhibit will feature **contributions** from many student artists.

*What other events rely on contributions from others?*

**diversity**

There was a great **diversity** of breeds at the dog show.

*Where else might you see a wide diversity of animals?*

**enlisted**

Citizens who have **enlisted** in the military are sworn in before training begins.

*Why have people enlisted for military duty?*

**intercept**

I jumped up to **intercept** the pass and prevent a touchdown by the other team.

*In what other sports might you intercept a ball?*

**operations**

The crew of workers began **operations** to clean up after the disaster.

*What other operations might help in a disaster?*

**recruits**

The officer addressed the **recruits** as they prepared for training.

*What kinds of services look for new recruits?*

**survival**

A first aid kit, a blanket, and water are important for **survival** in an emergency.

*What other items are important for survival in an emergency?*

### Your Turn    COLLABORATE

Pick three words. Write three questions for your partner to answer.

*Go Digital!* *Use the online visual glossary*

380

381

**READING/WRITING WORKSHOP, pp. 380–381**

---

## ELL ENGLISH LANGUAGE LEARNERS SCAFFOLD

### Beginning

**Use Visuals** Say: *Let's look at the photograph for the word* bulletin. Point to the bulletin. Say: *A bulletin has printed words that give important news and information.* Have students repeat. Ask: *Where would you be more likely to find a bulletin, on a chair or on the wall?* Elaborate on students' answers.

### Intermediate

**Describe** Have partners describe the photograph for *bulletin* and review the definition. Ask: *Where might you find a bulletin posted at school?* (in the hall or cafeteria) *What kind of information might you find in a bulletin?* (events, dates, rules) Allow time for discussion with a partner. Circulate and elicit details.

### Advanced/High

**Discuss** Ask partners to discuss the photograph for *bulletin*. Tell them to discuss places they've seen bulletins posted and what was on them. Then have them write a sentence giving an example of information they might find in a bulletin. Ask volunteers to share their sentences. Clarify as needed.

---

### ON-LEVEL PRACTICE BOOK p. 251

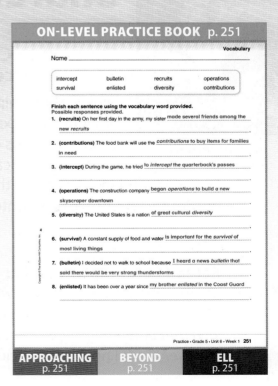

**APPROACHING** p. 251    **BEYOND** p. 251    **ELL** p. 251

CCSS **Shared Read** ❯ Genre • Historical Fiction

# SHIPPED OUT

**Essential Question**

**How do different groups contribute to a cause?**

Read about how a young girl learns how to contribute to the war effort during World War II.

382

My name is Libby Kendall, and I am a prisoner of war. Well, not really, but some days it feels that way. Just like my dad, I've packed up my things and shipped out. Unlike my dad, however, nothing I do will ever help the Allies win World War II.

My father is a mechanic on a battleship in the Pacific Ocean. I'm trapped in a little apartment above my Aunt Lucia's bakery downtown. Mom says it's just for a few months while she works double shifts at the clothing factory. She makes uniforms, mostly sewing pockets on jackets. I asked her once if she snuck things into the pockets for soldiers to find, like little poems written in calligraphy. She said soldiers wore jackets with pockets to hold tools they might need for war **survival**, not silly things like poetry.

It seems no one appreciates my creative **contributions** to the war effort, but Aunt Lucia says my help to her is important, since both her workers joined the army.

On my first day with Aunt Lucia, she explained the daily **operations** of the bakery. First, we get up before dawn to knead the dough. Next, we bake breads and muffins. Then,

while I help customers, Lucia makes cakes and cookies for sale in the afternoon. Whenever the phone rings, she races from the back room to **intercept** the call. She's always worried that it might be bad news, so she wants to be the first to hear it.

After dinner, Aunt Lucia invites neighbors over to listen to the radio. Some are immigrants from a wide **diversity** of backgrounds. Lucia and others help translate the news into several languages for everyone to understand. I always listen closely for any **bulletin** about fighting in the Pacific.

383

---

![Reading/Writing Workshop — McGraw-Hill Reading Wonders]

**Reading/Writing Workshop**

**READING/WRITING WORKSHOP, pp. 382–383**

# Shared Read

**Lexile** 810    *TextEvaluator*™ 50

### Connect to Concept: Joining Forces

Explain that "Shipped Out" will provide more examples of how different groups of people can contribute to a cause. Read "Shipped Out" with students. Note that the vocabulary words previously taught are highlighted in the text.

### Close Reading

**Reread Paragraphs 1 and 2:** Reread the first two paragraphs of "Shipped Out" with students. Ask: *What information in these paragraphs supports the idea that different groups of people can contribute to a cause?* Model how to cite evidence in answers.

In paragraph one, I learn that the story takes place during World War II. In paragraph two, the narrator, Libby, explains that her father is a mechanic on a battleship in the Pacific Ocean. I also learn that her mother makes uniforms in a clothing factory. Libby's parents are contributing to a cause.

**Reread Paragraph 3:** Model how to summarize important details in the story and use them to identify the main character's problem.

In paragraph one, Libby says nothing she does "will ever help the Allies win World War II." In paragraph three, she complains that no one appreciates her creative contributions. So Libby's problem seems to be that she feels unable to contribute meaningfully to the war effort.

I remember how intently my parents read reports about the war, which I rarely understood. They often whispered to one another, and I'd shout out something like, "Speak up! I can't hear you!" They'd frown and leave me alone to talk in private.

One night, they came into the living room and turned off the radio. At first I was angry, but they had serious expressions on their faces. "Our country's at war," Dad said. "The military will be looking for new **recruits**. I know something about boats and ship engines, so I intend to join the navy."

My face grew hot, but my hands felt cold. "You can't just leave," I said. I stomped on the floor for emphasis and stormed off to my bedroom. Looking back on that now, I feel ashamed of how selfishly I had acted.

This morning, Aunt Lucia can tell I'm feeling down. She asks me to help her decorate cupcakes for a fundraiser tonight. At first I'm not interested. I just slather on frosting and plop a berry on top. Then I realize that I can make red stripes out of strawberries and a patch of blue from blueberries. Soon I have a whole tray of cupcakes decorated like flags to show Aunt Lucia.

Sean Qualls

384

"These are wonderful!" Lucia says. "I'm sure they'll sell better than anything else!"

For the first time in weeks, I feel like I've done something right. I think of all the money we might make at the sale, and how it may buy supplies for my father.

"I **enlisted** in the navy to help restore democracy in the world," my dad said on the day he left. "Now you be a good navy daughter and

sail straight, young lady." I promised I would. As he went out the door, I slipped a little poem into his coat pocket. "Here's a little rhyme to pass the day," it said. "I love you back in the U.S.A.!"

I look at the cupcakes and wish I could send one to my dad. Instead, I'll draw a platter on which they're piled high and send the picture off to the Pacific with a letter. That way, my dad will have plenty to share with everyone there.

**Make Connections**

? What kinds of contributions to the war effort do characters make in this story? **ESSENTIAL QUESTION**

Think about an event in your own life that required contributions from others. How did they all work together? **TEXT TO SELF**

385

**READING/WRITING WORKSHOP, pp. 384–385**

## Make Connections

### ESSENTIAL QUESTION

Encourage students to reread the text for details and evidence as they discuss the characters' contributions to the war effort. Ask students to explain, using the text, how different groups of people can contribute to a cause.

## Continue Close Reading

Use the following lessons for focused rereadings.

→ Summarize, pp. T18–T19

→ Theme, pp. T20–T21

→ Historical Fiction, pp. T22–T23

→ Homophones, pp. T24–T25

**A C T  A**ccess **C**omplex **T**ext

▶ **Prior Knowledge**

Provide World War II background information to help students understand key references.

→ World War II lasted from 1939 to 1945. The United States entered the war in 1941.

→ The two sides were known as the Allies and the Axis powers. The Allies included the United States, Great Britain, and France. The Axis powers included Germany, Japan, and Italy.

→ Critical events of World War II took place in the Pacific Ocean and East Asia, where the Allies fought the Empire of Japan. These events are sometimes called the Pacific War.

# → **Comprehension Strategy**

**Reading/Writing Workshop**

**MINILESSON 10 Mins**

## Summarize

**Go Digital**

**Present the Lesson**

### OBJECTIVES

**CCSS** Quote accurately from a text when explaining what the text says explicitly and when drawing inferences from the text. **RL.5.1**

**CCSS** Summarize a written text read aloud or information presented in diverse media and formats, including visually, quantitatively, and orally. **SL.5.2**

### ACADEMIC LANGUAGE

• *summarize, historical fiction*

• Cognates: *resumir, ficción histórica*

### 1 Explain

Remind students that when they **summarize**, they restate a story's important events, ideas, and details in their own words.

→ Students should pause while reading to summarize what they have just read.

→ Using their own words, they should restate important events; important things the characters do, say, and feel; and other significant details in the story.

→ Point out that summarizing the beginning, middle, and end of a story can help students remember important events, ideas, and details.

→ Remind students that summaries should not include personal opinions about the characters or events. The goal of a summary is to capture important events, ideas, and details the author includes in the story.

### 2 Model Close Reading: Text Evidence

Model how summarizing the first three paragraphs of "Shipped Out" can help you clearly understand the setting (a city during World War II), the main characters (Libby, her father, her mother, and Aunt Lucia), and the plot (Libby is unhappy with the changes in her life caused by her father going off to war and her mother working long hours in a clothing mill).

### 3 Guided Practice of Close Reading

Have pairs read aloud the fourth and fifth paragraphs on page 383, the fourth paragraph on page 384, and the first and second paragraphs on page 385 and summarize Libby's experiences at Aunt Lucia's bakery. Encourage students to summarize Libby's tasks at the bakery, her relationship with her aunt, and what Libby does that impresses her aunt and helps Libby feel more useful. Have partners identify other parts of the story they might want to summarize.

**CCSS** Comprehension Strategy

# Summarize

Summarizing can help readers remember details as they read. You may want to summarize the important details at the beginning of a story that help you understand the setting and plot events. Remember that a summary should not include your opinions.

 **Find Text Evidence**

Summarizing the opening paragraphs of "Shipped Out" on page 383 may help you understand the setting and plot of the story.

page 383

My name is Libby Kendall, and I am a prisoner of war. Well, not really, but some days it feels that way. Just like my dad, I've packed up my things and shipped out. Unlike my dad, however, nothing I do will ever help win World War II.

My father is a mechanic on a battleship in the Pacific Ocean. I'm trapped in a little apartment above my Aunt Lucia's bakery downtown. Mom says it's just for a few months while she works double shifts at the clothing factory. She makes uniforms, mostly sewing pockets on jackets. I asked her once if she stuck things into the pockets for soldiers to find, like little poems written in calligraphy. She said soldiers wore jackets with pockets to hold tools they might need for war survival, not silly things like poetry.

while I help customers, Lucia makes cakes and cookies for sale in the afternoon. Whenever the phone rings, she races from the back room to intercept the call. She's always worried that it might be bad news.

*The first paragraphs introduce Libby Kendall, a girl living during World War II. Because her father has gone off to war and her mother must work long hours, Libby has been sent to live with her Aunt Lucia. I can infer that the war has caused many changes.*

 COLLABORATE

### Your Turn

Summarize Libby's experiences at her aunt's bakery. Include details showing the war's effect on events.

386

**READING/WRITING WORKSHOP, p. 386**

---

 **Monitor and Differentiate**

✔ **Quick Check**

Do students' summaries include important ideas and details in the passage? Do students take care not to include their personal opinions in their summaries?

⬇

## Small Group Instruction

If No → | Approaching Level | Reteach p. T40
| ELL | Develop p. T57

If Yes → | On Level | Review p. T48
| Beyond Level | Extend p. T52

---

## ENGLISH LANGUAGE LEARNERS SCAFFOLD

**ELL**

| Beginning | Intermediate | Advanced/High |
|---|---|---|
| **Understand** Reread the first three paragraphs on page 383. Point out difficult words and phrases, such as *mechanic, double shifts, clothing factory, calligraphy,* and *war effort.* Define them for students. Help students replace these words with words and phrases they know. | **Derive Meaning** Help students reread the first three paragraphs. The text may be confusing because of figurative language. Ask: *To what does Libby compare herself in the first sentence?* (a prisoner of war) *Why does she make this comparison?* (Her father is away at war, her mother is working long hours, and Libby must live with her aunt.) | **Demonstrate Comprehension** Have students reread the first three paragraphs on page 383. Elicit from students why this text might be confusing. Ask: *When does this story take place? What has changed for Libby recently? How are Libby and her family contributing to a cause?* Have students turn to a partner and summarize. Elaborate. |

---

**ON-LEVEL PRACTICE BOOK** pp. 253–254

Comprehension and Fluency

Name _____

Read the passage. Use the summarizing strategy to help you understand what you are reading.

**Books for Victory**

    As Carlos shivered on the snowy porch, he noticed a drooping banner
12  in the front window. "Happy New Year 1943!" it said. "Huh, they
24  could've taken that down by now," he thought as he pressed the doorbell
37  once more. "Hurry up," he muttered. "I'm turning blue out here." As he
50  waited for his neighbor to answer the door, Carlos blew on his hands to
64  warm them. Glancing at his wagon piled with books, he thought back to
77  last year and the reason he was out here again collecting for the Victory
91  Book Campaign.
93      His brother Tomás had been in the army and stationed at a military
106 camp across the country. Carlos had missed Tomás and looked forward
117 to his letters. Carlos knew one of those letters by heart. "There's nothing
130 new to tell you," Tomás had written. "We still train and drill every day.
144 When we're not training and drilling there's not much to do. I wish I had
159 something good to read."
163     Carlos had felt bad for Tomás. He wondered how he could help him.
176 The next day, in morning assembly, Principal Ramírez told the students
187 about the Victory Book Campaign. All over Oregon and the rest of the
200 country, people were collecting books to send to soldiers, sailors, and
211 others fighting in the war.
216     Principal Ramírez added that the campaign needed volunteers. As soon
226 as he said that, hands shot up all over the auditorium.
237     Carlos had promised himself he would collect as many books as
248 he possibly could and during the following month he took his wagon
260 throughout the neighborhood. At each house he explained the campaign
270 and asked people to donate books. In its first year, the campaign had lasted
284 from January to November. It had been an outstanding success. By the
296 time it was over, people across the country had donated more than eleven
309 million books.

Practice • Grade 5 • Unit 6 • Week 1  **253**

| **APPROACHING** pp. 253–254 | **BEYOND** pp. 253–254 | **ELL** pp. 253–254 |

#  Comprehension Skill

 MINILESSON **10** Mins

## Theme

**Reading/Writing Workshop**

**CCSS** Determine a theme of a story, drama, or poem from details in the text, including how characters in a story or drama respond to challenges or how the speaker in a poem reflects upon a topic; summarize the text. **RL.5.2**

---

### ACADEMIC LANGUAGE
- *theme, details*
- Cognates: *tema, detalles*

---

### SKILLS TRACE

**THEME**

**Introduce** U2W4

**Review** U2W5, U2W6, U3W1, U3W2, U4W5, U4W6, U6W1, U6W2, U6W6

**Assess** U2, U3, U4, U6

### 1 Explain

Explain to students that the **theme** of a story is the important message about life that the author wants to share with readers. Point out that a story's theme is usually not stated directly.

→ Students can determine the theme by thinking about what the characters say and do and how their behavior affects other characters and the way the events in the story unfold.

→ Students should also consider what happens to the characters and how they change as a result of their experiences. Sometimes a lesson that a character learns is closely related to the theme.

Point out that thinking about the characters and events in a story and how they relate to the story's theme can help students remain engaged in their reading. As the story progresses, they may revise their ideas about the theme.

### 2 Model Close Reading: Text Evidence

Model how to identify important details about what Libby does and says and what happens to her in the first three paragraphs of the story. Then model using the details written on the graphic organizer to determine a possible theme, such as that people can contribute to a cause in different ways.

 **Analytical Writing** **Write About Reading: Summary** Model how to use notes from the organizer to summarize how Libby feels at the beginning of the story and why.

### 3 Guided Practice of Close Reading

 COLLABORATE Have students work in pairs to complete the graphic organizer with details about what Libby does and says and what happens to her during the story. Have them discuss what Libby learns from Aunt Lucia about contributing to the war effort. Then have them use the organizer to determine the story's theme.

 **Analytical Writing** **Write About Reading: Summary** Ask partners to work together to summarize how Libby changes as a result of living and working with Aunt Lucia. Select pairs of students to share their summaries.

**Go Digital**

**Present the Lesson**

## Comprehension Skill  CCSS

# Theme

To identify a story's **theme**, or overall message, consider what the characters say and do, and how their behavior affects the events and other characters. Finally, think about how characters change as a result of what happens to them.

### Find Text Evidence

*On page 383 of "Shipped Out," Libby says that she feels like a prisoner of war at her aunt's apartment. This is because her father has gone to war and her mother has had to go to work. Libby feels her war efforts are not appreciated, but Aunt Lucia needs her help. These events will help me identify the theme.*

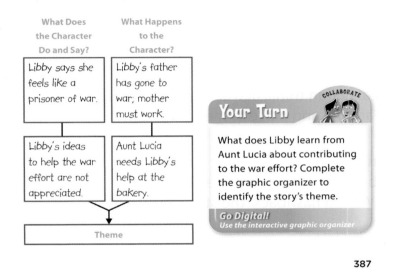

| What Does the Character Do and Say? | What Happens to the Character? |
|---|---|
| Libby says she feels like a prisoner of war. | Libby's father has gone to war; mother must work. |
| Libby's ideas to help the war effort are not appreciated. | Aunt Lucia needs Libby's help at the bakery. |

Theme

**Your Turn** COLLABORATE

What does Libby learn from Aunt Lucia about contributing to the war effort? Complete the graphic organizer to identify the story's theme.

*Go Digital!*
*Use the interactive graphic organizer*

387

**READING/WRITING WORKSHOP,** p. 387

---

## Monitor and *Differentiate*

 **Quick Check**

Can students identify important details about characters and events? Can they use these details to determine the theme of the story?

### Small Group Instruction

| | | |
|---|---|---|
| If No → | **Approaching Level** | Reteach p. T47 |
| | **ELL** | Develop p. T57 |
| If Yes → | **On Level** | Review p. T51 |
| | **Beyond Level** | Extend p. T55 |

---

## ENGLISH LANGUAGE LEARNERS

**ELL SCAFFOLD**

---

**ON-LEVEL PRACTICE BOOK** pp. 253–255

Comprehension: Theme and Fluency

Name _____

A. Reread the passage and answer the questions. Possible responses provided.

1. How does Carlos feel when he hears about the Victory Book Campaign?
He is excited and ready to volunteer.

2. Why does he feel that way?
The campaign is a way he can help people who are fighting in the war.

3. What does Carlos learn from his experience? What might be the theme, or message, of this story?
Everyone can make a contribution.

B. Work with a partner. Read the passage aloud. Pay attention to expression and phrasing. Stop after one minute. Fill out the chart.

| | Words Read | – | Number of Errors | = | Words Correct Score |
|---|---|---|---|---|---|
| First Read | | – | | = | |
| Second Read | | – | | = | |

Practice · Grade 5 · Unit 6 · Week 1 **255**

| APPROACHING pp. 253–255 | BEYOND pp. 253–255 | ELL pp. 253–255 |
|---|---|---|

→ # Genre: Literature

**Reading/Writing Workshop**

**OBJECTIVES**

 **CCSS** Quote accurately from a text when explaining what the text says explicitly and when drawing inferences from the text. **RL.5.1**

**CCSS** By the end of the year, read and comprehend literature, including stories, dramas, and poetry, at the high end of the grades 4–5 text complexity band independently and proficiently. **RL.5.10**

Identify characteristics of historical fiction.

**ACADEMIC LANGUAGE**

• *historical fiction, events, setting, characters, details, flashback*

• Cognates: *ficción histórica, detalles*

**MINILESSON 10 Mins**

## Historical Fiction

**Go Digital**

**Present the Lesson**

### 1 Explain

Share with students the following key characteristics of **historical fiction:**

→ Historical fiction features events that really happened or could have happened and places that really existed or could have existed at a particular time in history.

→ The characters in historical fiction think, act, and speak like real people from the particular time and place in the past in which the story is set.

→ Like other kinds of fiction, historical fiction may include flashbacks, which describe events that happened before the main action of the story. After a flashback, the story returns to the main action.

### 2 Model Close Reading: Text Evidence

Model identifying text evidence that helps you determine that "Shipped Out" is historical fiction.

**Details** Point out realistic details typical of the 1940s: World War II, battleship in the Pacific Ocean, clothing mill.

**Flashback** Explain that the main action of the story takes place during Libby's stay with her Aunt Lucia. The events described in the first three paragraphs on page 384, however, occurred before the main action of the story. They help explain why Libby had to go and live with her aunt. This is an example of a flashback.

### 3 Guided Practice of Close Reading

**COLLABORATE**

Have students work with partners to find another example of a flashback in the story and explain why an author might use flashbacks in a work of historical fiction. Have partners share their work with the class.

**Genre** Literature

# Historical Fiction

The selection "Shipped Out" is historical fiction.

**Historical fiction:**
- Features events and settings typical of the period in which the story is set
- Features realistic characters who speak and act like people from a particular time and place in the past
- May include flashback

 **Find Text Evidence**

*I can tell that "Shipped Out" is historical fiction. The first paragraph mentions a real event, World War II. In flashback, we learn why Libby, the main character, has to live with her aunt.*

page 384

**Flashback** Flashbacks describe events and actions that occurred before the main action of the story. Key words, such as *once* or *I remember*, may show a character remembering past events.

**Your Turn**

Find another example of a flashback in "Shipped Out." Why might an author use flashbacks in a work of historical fiction?

384

388

**READING/WRITING WORKSHOP, p. 388**

## A C T Access Complex Text

▶ **Organization**

Explain that this story contains several flashbacks. Help students see how signal words can help them identify flashbacks.

→ Point out *One night* in the second paragraph on page 384. Ask: *What key story details are given in this flashback?* (reasons Libby's father joined the navy)

→ *Which words tell you that the action has returned to the main story?* (*This morning*) *Which words on page 385 indicate that the dialogue between Libby and her dad takes place at an earlier time?* (*on the day he left*)

## Monitor and *Differentiate*

 **Quick Check**

Can students find another example of a flashback in the story? Are they able to explain why an author might use flashbacks in historical fiction?

⬇

### Small Group Instruction

| | | |
|---|---|---|
| **If No** → | **Approaching Level** | **Reteach p. T41** |
| | **ELL** | **Develop p. T59** |
| **If Yes** → | **On Level** | **Review p. T49** |
| | **Beyond Level** | **Extend p. T53** |

**ON-LEVEL PRACTICE BOOK** p. 256

*Genre/Literary Element*

Name _____

**The Scrap Drive**

   Alice watched the young girl drop the bottle into the recycle bin. She remembered how she had started recycling when she was the girl's age. During World War II, everything was rationed, and people needed to recycle. She recalled how schools in her city had a Scrap Drive contest every month and collected paper, metal, rubber, and fabric. One day she had asked her father, "Dad, how can I help my school win the contest?"
   "That old, bald tire in the garage might help," Dad had said. "A rubber tire can be reused to make 20 pairs of boots."
   Alice and her dad had found the tire and started to roll it to the collection center at the bottom of the hill. The tire slipped from Dad's grasp and rolled downhill. "Stop that tire!" Dad had shouted. They raced after the tire, but it had crashed into the collection center building. Alice smiled to herself and remembered how proud she had felt when her school had won the contest that month.

**Answer the questions about the text.**  Possible responses provided.

1. **How do you know this text is historical fiction?**
   The story is set in a place that could have existed during World War II. The characters act and talk the way real people from the time would have acted and talked.

2. **A flashback is a scene from the past that interrupts a story. What sentence tells that a flashback is coming?**
   One day she had asked her father, "Dad, how can I help my school win the contest?"

3. **What two time clues signal that this takes place in the past?**
   The writer says, "During World War II," and "One day."

256 Practice • Grade 5 • Unit 6 • Week 1

| APPROACHING | BEYOND | ELL |
|---|---|---|
| p. 256 | p. 256 | p. 256 |

# → Vocabulary Strategy

**MINILESSON 10 Mins**

## Homophones

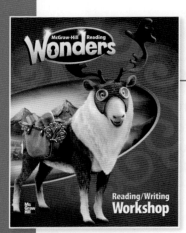

**Reading/Writing Workshop**

**OBJECTIVES**

**CCSS** Use context (e.g., cause/effect relationships and comparisons in text) as a clue to the meaning of a word or phrase. **L.5.4a**

**ACADEMIC LANGUAGE**
*homophones, context clues*

### 1 Explain

Remind students that homophones are words that sound the same but are spelled differently and have different meanings. For example, the words *not* and *knot* are homophones.

→ Students can use context clues to figure out the meaning of a homophone.

→ Context clues may appear in the same sentence or in surrounding sentences.

→ Suggest that students keep a list of homophones and their meanings. Reviewing the list now and then can help them remember the definitions of homophones.

### 2 Model Close Reading: Text Evidence

Model using context clues in the last sentence of the second paragraph on page 383 to figure out the meanings of *wore* and *war*. For example, point out that the word *jackets* helps show the meaning of *wore* and the words *tools they might need* and *survival* help show the meaning of *war*.

### 3 Guided Practice of Close Reading

Have students work in pairs to distinguish the meanings of *need* and *knead*, *read* and *red*, and *sale* and *sail* in "Shipped Out." Encourage partners to reread the text and use context clues in the same sentence and in the surrounding sentences to help them figure out the meaning of each word.

**SKILLS TRACE**

**HOMOPHONES**

**Introduce** U6W1

**Review** U6W1, U6W4

**Assess** U6

## Go Digital

**Present the Lesson**

## Vocabulary Strategy CCSS

# Homophones

Sometimes when you read, you come across **homophones**, or words that sound the same but are spelled differently and have different meanings. Surrounding words and sentences can help you figure out the meaning of a homophone.

 **Find Text Evidence**

In "Shipped Out" on page 383, I see the words war and wore, which are pronounced the same. From the surrounding words, I can tell that war means a large conflict, and that wore is the past tense of the verb wear, which means to have clothing on.

> She said soldiers ⟦wore jackets⟧ with pockets to hold tools they might need for ⟦war survival,⟧ not silly things like poetry.

### Your Turn COLLABORATE

Use context clues to distinguish between the meanings of the following homophones from "Shipped Out."

**need** and **knead**, page 383
**read** and **red**, page 384
**sale** and **sail**, page 385

389

**READING/WRITING WORKSHOP, p. 389**

---

## ELL ENGLISH LANGUAGE LEARNERS SCAFFOLD

### Beginning

**Distinguish** Point out the homophones *need/knead, read/red,* and *sale/sail* and define them. Use pantomime, gestures, and images to reinforce their meanings. Write the homophone pairs on the board and circle the spellings that make the words different. Provide sentence frames:
*I _____ a new jacket. I _____ the dough.*

### Intermediate

**Demonstrate Comprehension** Help students reread the sentences that contain the homophones *need/knead, read/red,* and *sale/sail.* Define each word for students. Then help them find and read aloud the context clues that help them understand the meaning of each homophone.

### Advanced/High

**Know and Use** Point out the homophones *need/knead, read/red,* and *sale/sail.* Ask students to determine the meaning of each word in the pair by using context clues in the story. Then have partners write a sentence for each pair that uses both words correctly, such as *The book I read had a bright red cover.*

---

## Monitor and Differentiate

### ✓ Quick Check

Can students use context clues to determine the meanings of homophones?

⬇

### Small Group Instruction

If No → **Approaching Level** Reteach p. T45
**ELL** Develop p. T61
If Yes → **On Level** Review p. T50
**Beyond Level** Extend p. T54

---

**ON-LEVEL PRACTICE BOOK** p. 257

Vocabulary Strategy: **Homophones**

Name _____

Read the sentences below and circle the correct word to complete each one. Underline the context clues that help you figure out which word to use. Then use that word in a new sentence.

1. This morning the wind _____ so hard that I nearly fell over.   (blew)   blue
I blew on my soup to cool it down.

2. I thought I _____ all the answers to her questions.   (knew)   new
I knew where her house was because I had been there before.

3. I didn't recognize you when we _____ on the street.   (passed)   past
I've passed that store a dozen times but have never been inside.

4. Call your dog to come _____ now.   hear   (here)
I like it here in the winter.

5. He seems like a nice person and a good friend. _____   to   (too)
Do you want to go to the mall too?

Practice • Grade 5 • Unit 6 • Week 1   **257**

APPROACHING p. 257    BEYOND p. 257    ELL p. 257

# Develop Comprehension

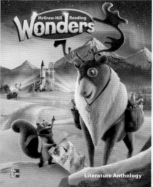

**Literature Anthology**
*Although the selection score falls below the Lexile range, this selection requires some prior knowledge of American history.*

## The Unbreakable Code

### Text Complexity Range

**Lexile**

▲740    1010
*640

**TextEvaluator™**

23        ▲        51
          40

## Options for Close Reading

→ Whole Class
→ Small Group
→ Independent

---

**CCSS Genre · Historical Fiction**

# The UNBREAKABLE Code

by Sara Hoagland Hunter • illustrated by Julia Miner

**Essential Question**
**How do different groups contribute to a cause?**
Read about how a group of Navajos helped the American military during World War II.

*Go Digital!*

430

---

## A C T Access Complex Text

### What makes this text complex?

▶ **Sentence Structure**
▶ **Specific Vocabulary**
▶ **Prior Knowledge**
▶ **Connection of Ideas**

### ▶ Sentence Structure

Point out that in the first paragraph the narrator says, "They would be looking for him now," without identifying who "they" are. This creates suspense.

→ *Reread the second paragraph. Who are "they"?* (John's mother and the man from Minnesota, his stepfather)

John raced up the trail, sending pebbles skidding behind him. When he reached his favorite hiding place, he fell to the ground out of breath. Here between the old piñon tree and the towering walls of the canyon, he felt safe. The river full of late-summer rain looked like a silver thread winding through his grandfather's farm land. They would be looking for him now, but he was never coming down.

His mother had married the man from Minnesota. There was nothing he could do about that. But he was not going with them. He closed his eyes and rested in the stillness. The faint bleat of a mountain goat echoed off the canyon walls.

431

**LITERATURE ANTHOLOGY,** pp. 430–431

## Predictive Writing

Have students read the title, preview the illustrations, and write their predictions about what this story will be about.

### ESSENTIAL QUESTION

Ask a student to read aloud the Essential Question. Have students discuss how the story might help them answer the question.

### Note Taking: Use the Graphic Organizer

*Analytical Writing*

As students read the selection, ask them to take notes by filling in the graphic organizer on **Your Turn Practice Book page 252** to help them determine the theme.

### ❶ Author's Craft: Figurative Language

A simile compares two things using *like* or *as*. To what is the river compared? (a thin silver thread winding through the farm land) What is the effect of the comparison on the reader? (It helps the reader picture the beauty of the river from John's viewpoint.)

**ELL** Review the pronouns *he, they,* and *them* with ELLs. Explain that *he* replaces *John* and *they* and *them* replace *his mother and the man from Minnesota.*

→ Say: *His mom and the man from Minnesota are looking for John.* They *are looking for* him.

→ *Why is John hiding? Use pronouns to answer the question.* (He does not want to go with them.)

# Develop Comprehension

2 **Strategy: Summarize**

**Teacher Think Aloud** As I read, I pause from time to time to **summarize** what I've read. John is hiding in the canyon because he doesn't want to move to Minnesota. When his grandfather finds him, John tells him that he wants to stay with him. His grandfather tries to comfort him by telling him that he will be all right since he has an unbreakable code. To explain what that is, he begins speaking in Navajo.

Suddenly a voice boomed above him: "Shouldn't you be packing?"

John's eyes flew open. It was his grandfather on horseback.

"Your stepfather's coming with the pickup in an hour."

"I'm not going," John said.

"You have to go. School's starting soon," said Grandfather, stepping down from his horse. "You'll be back next summer."

John dug his toe deeper into the dirt. "I want to stay with you," he said.

Grandfather's soft, brown eyes disappeared in the wrinkles of a smile. John thought they were the kindest eyes he had ever seen.

"You're going to be all right," Grandfather said. "You have an unbreakable code."

"What's that?" asked John.

Grandfather sat down and began to speak gently in Navajo. The sounds wove up and down, in and out, as warm and familiar as the patterns of one of Grandmother's Navajo blankets. John leaned against his  grandfather's knee.

432

## A C T  Access Complex Text

### ▶ Specific Vocabulary

Review with students strategies, such as using word parts, for finding the meanings of unfamiliar words. Point to the word *unbreakable* in paragraph eight on page 432.

→ *What word parts do you see in* unbreakable? (*un-, break, -able*)

→ Help students determine the meaning of each part and combine them to find the meaning of *unbreakable.* If necessary, review that *un-* means "not" and *-able* means "able to be."

"The unbreakable code is what saved my life in World War II," he said. "It's the Navajo language."

John's shoulders sagged. Navajo couldn't help him. Nobody in his new school spoke Navajo.

"I'll probably forget how to speak Navajo," he whispered.

"Navajo is your language," said his grandfather sternly. "Navajo you must never forget."

The lump in John's throat was close to a sob. "You don't know what it's like there!" he said.

His grandfather continued quietly in Navajo. "I had to go to a government boarding school when I was five. It was the law.

"They gave me an English name and cut my hair off. I wasn't allowed to speak my language. Anyone who spoke Navajo had to chew on squares of soap. Believe me, I chewed a lot of soap during those years. 'Speak English,' they said. But Navajo was my language and Navajo I would never forget.

"Every summer I went home to herd the sheep and help with the crops. I cried when the cottonwoods turned gold and it was time to go back.

**3**

**4**

433

**LITERATURE ANTHOLOGY, pp. 432–433**

**❸ Genre: Historical Fiction**

**What elements of historical fiction do you notice on page 433?** (In the first sentence, Grandfather talks about World War II. Even though Grandfather and John are fictional characters, World War II is a real historical event.)

**❹ Skill: Theme**

Grandfather knows how John feels about leaving home. **What does Grandfather do when he is forbidden to speak Navajo at the government boarding school?** (He keeps speaking Navajo because it was his language.) **What happens as a result?** (He often gets punished by having to chew soap, but he does not forget the language.)

| What Does the Character Do and Say? | What Happens to the Character? |
|---|---|
| Grandfather keeps speaking Navajo at the school. | He is often punished, but he does not forget the language. |

▶ **Prior Knowledge**

Share the following information about the Navajo Nation.

→ The Navajo are the second-largest Native American tribe. They live mostly in New Mexico, Arizona, and Utah.

→ The Navajo language is an unwritten language with a complex pronunciation.

**ELL** To help students understand why John is so upset, use a map to show the distance from Minnesota to the southwestern states of Utah, New Mexico, and Arizona, where many Navajo live.

→ *Is Minnesota near or far from John?* (far)

→ *Who speaks Navajo at the school in Minnesota?* (nobody)

# Develop Comprehension

**⑤ Literary Device: Flashback**

A flashback describes events and actions that occurred before the main action of the story. Turn to a partner and discuss the main action of the story. (John has run away because he does not want to move to Minnesota. His grandfather is telling him about his past to make him feel better.) When does Grandfather's story take place? (The events take place many years before the main story, when John's grandfather is in the tenth grade.)

---

**STOP AND CHECK**

**Summarize** Why does Grandfather leave the boarding school? (Grandfather hears a bulletin recruiting Navajo who can speak both their native language and English, and he decides to enlist in the Marines.)

---

⑤ "Finally, one night in the tenth grade, I was working in the kitchen when I heard a bulletin on the school radio: 'Navajo needed for special duty to the Marines. Must be between the ages of seventeen and thirty-two, fluent in English and Navajo, and in excellent physical condition.'

"Just before lights out, I snuck past the bunks and out the door towards the open plain. I felt like a wild horse with the lasso finally off its neck. Out in the open, the stars danced above me and the tumbleweeds blew by my feet as I ran. The next day, I enlisted."

⑥ "But you weren't seventeen," said John.

"The reservation had no birth records," Grandfather said with a grin. "Two weeks later I was on a bus headed for boot camp with twenty-eight other Navajos. I stared out the window into the darkness. I was going outside of the Four Sacred Mountains for the first time in my life."

434

**STOP AND CHECK**

Summarize Why does Grandfather leave the boarding school? Summarizing the events may help you.

---

# A C T Access Complex Text

## Specific Vocabulary

Point out that authors of historical fiction sometimes use special vocabulary related to their subject—in this case, the military. Guide students to use context to determine the meaning of *platoon, boot camp,* and *drills* in paragraph four on page 435.

→ *What is a* platoon? *Use text clues and the illustration to help you.* (a group of soldiers)

→ *What is* boot camp? *Use the text clues to help you.* (a training camp for soldiers)

→ *What are* drills? *Use the examples to help you.* (Drills are exercises such as marching and hiking.)

"Were you scared?" asked John.

"Of course," said his grandfather. "I didn't know where I was going or what our mission was. Most of all, I didn't know how I would measure up to the people out there I had heard so much about."

"How did you?" asked John, chewing his fingernail.

His grandfather began to laugh. "We were known as the toughest platoon at boot camp. We had done so much marching at boarding school that the drills were no problem. Hiking in the desert of California with a heavy pack was no worse than hauling water in the canyon in midsummer. And I'd done that since I was four years old.

"As for the **survival** exercises, we had all gone without food for a few days. A Navajo learns to survive.

435

## 6 Author's Craft: Figurative Language

To what does Grandfather compare himself? (a wild horse with the lasso finally off its neck) What does the comparison tell you about Grandfather's feelings? (It tells you that Grandfather felt freed when he snuck out of the school.)

## 7 Ask and Answer Questions

Generate a question of your own and share it with a partner. To find the answer, try rereading and paraphrasing the text. For example, you might ask, "How was Grandfather able to measure up to others?" To find the answer, you can reread the last two paragraphs on page 435 and paraphrase the relevant information. (Grandfather was able to measure up because he had marched a lot in boarding school, hauled water in the desert, and gone a few days without food.)

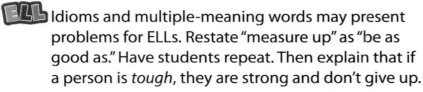

**ELL** Idioms and multiple-meaning words may present problems for ELLs. Restate "measure up" as "be as good as." Have students repeat. Then explain that if a person is *tough*, they are strong and don't give up.

→ *Was it hard or easy for the Navajo platoon to hike with a heavy pack?* (easy)

→ *Did they measure up to the others, or were they even tougher?* (They were even tougher.)

# Develop Comprehension

**8** **Skill: Theme**

On page 434, we read that John's grandfather enlists in the Marines. The text on this page tells how he is brought to San Diego with other Navajo recruits. What happens to him there? (He is given a top secret mission to code words using the Navajo language. He realizes the government now values the language it tried to destroy.) **Add these details to your organizer.**

| What Does the Character Do and Say? | What Happens to the Character? |
|---|---|
| Grandfather enlists and uses the Navajo language to create a code. | He is locked in a classroom and was told their mission was top secret. |

"One weekend they bused us to a new camp in San Diego. On Monday we were marched to a building with bars on every window. They locked us in a classroom at the end of a long, narrow corridor. An officer told us our mission was top secret. We would not even be allowed to tell our families. We were desperately needed for a successful invasion of the Pacific Islands. So far the Japanese had been able to **intercept** and decode all American messages in only minutes. This meant that no information could be passed between American ships, planes, and land forces.

"The government thought the Navajo language might be the secret weapon. Only a few outsiders had ever learned it. Most importantly, the language had never been written down, so there was no alphabet for the Japanese to discover and decode.

 "He gave us a list of more than two hundred military terms to code. Everything had to be memorized. No trace of the code could ever be found in writing. It would live or die with us in battle.

"When the officer walked out of the room, I looked at the Navajo next to me and began to laugh. 'All those years they told us to forget Navajo, and now the government needs it to save the country!'

436

## A C T  **A**ccess **C**omplex **T**ext

▶ **Connection of Ideas**

Help students understand why the Navajo code was different from other codes.

→ *Why did the American military need a code?* (The military needed a code to keep enemies who intercept their communication from knowing what they were planning.)

→ *What have the Japanese been able to do to this point in the war?* (They have decoded all American messages in minutes.)

→ *How is the Navajo code different?* (Since it has never been written down, and few outsiders know it, it will be very hard for the Japanese to decode.)

"We were marched every day to that classroom. We were never allowed to leave the building. We couldn't even use the bathroom by ourselves. Each night, an officer locked our notes in a safe. **10**

"The code had to be simple and fast. We would have only one chance to send each message. After that, the Japanese would be tracing our location to bomb us or trying to record the code.

"We chose words from nature that would be easy to remember under fire. Since Navajo has no alphabet, we made up our own.

"'A' became *wollachee*."

"Ant?" asked John in English.

Grandfather nodded.

"'B' was *shush*."

"Bear," said John.

"'C' was *moasi*. 'D', *be*. 'E', *dzeh*." His grandfather continued through the alphabet. Each time he named the Navajo word, John answered with the English.

"We named the aircraft after birds. The dive-bomber was a chicken hawk. The observation plane was an owl. A patrol plane was a crow. Bomber was buzzard.

"At night we would lie in our bunks and test each other. Pretty soon I was dreaming in code.

> **STOP AND CHECK**
>
> **Summarize** How do the Navajo soldiers create a code? Summarizing what they did may help you.

437

**LITERATURE ANTHOLOGY, pp. 436–437**

**9 Vocabulary: Homophones**

The words *allowed*, A-L-L-O-W-E-D, and *aloud*, A-L-O-U-D, are homophones. They sound the same but have different meanings and spellings. Use the context to choose the correct meaning for the word on the page, *allowed*. (I used the clue "top secret" to figure out that *allowed* means "permitted.")

**10 Skill: Make Inferences**

What can you infer about the mission, based on the way the Navajo coders are treated? Paraphrase the evidence from the text that supports your inference. (I can infer that the mission is very important and no one is trusted because the coders are not allowed to leave the building. The notes are locked in a safe. Nothing can be written down.)

**STOP AND CHECK**

**Summarize** How do the Navajo soldiers create a code? (The Navajo soldiers make up their own alphabet using words from nature that will be easy to remember under fire. They name aircraft after birds.)

---

▶ **Sentence Structure**

Remind students that words from other languages are often italicized.

→ *What are the words in italics?* (Navajo words)

→ *In the code, what is the word for the English letter* A? (wollachee)

→ *What does* wollachee *mean in Navajo?* (ant)

**ELL** Before reading, clarify the meanings of vocabulary words related to the military code:

→ Decode *means "figure out, or understand." Would you decode messages or ships?* (messages)

→ Memorize *means "learn it by memory." Why might you memorize something?* (so you don't have to write it down or read it off a piece of paper)

# Develop Comprehension

**11** **Strategy: Summarize**

**Teacher Think Aloud** The paragraph gives information about how the Navajo coders are tested. How can we remember the most important information?

Prompt students to apply the strategy in a Think Aloud by paraphrasing how the Navajos are tested and then summarizing it in a sentence or two. Have them turn to a partner to summarize.

**Student Think Aloud** An officer gives John's grandfather a message. John's grandfather speaks the message in code. A Navajo on the other end translates the message into English.

"Since we would be radiomen, we had to learn all kinds of radio **operations**. We were taught how to take a radio apart and put it together blindfolded. The Japanese fought at night, so we would have to do most of our work in complete darkness. Even the tiniest match flame could be a target.

"When the day came for the code to be tested in front of the top Marine officers, I was terrified. I knelt at one end of a field with our radio ground set. The officers marched towards me. Behind a building at the other end of the field, another code talker sat under military guard waiting for my transmission. One officer handed me a written message:

"'Receiving steady machine gun fire. Request reinforcements.'

"It took only seconds for me to speak into the microphone in Navajo code. The officer sent a runner to the end of the field to check the speed and accuracy of the message. The Navajo at the other end handed him the exact message written in English before he even came around the corner of the building! They tested us over and over. Each time, we were successful. The government requested two hundred Navajo **recruits** immediately. Two of our group stayed behind to train them. The rest of us were on our way."

**11**

438

## A C T Access Complex Text

### ▶ Connection of Ideas

Help students connect the events of Grandfather's war training, told through dialogue.

→ *As radiomen, what was their first task?* (They had to learn to take a radio apart and put it back together, so they could work in darkness.)

→ *How were the men tested?* (They had to receive and speak messages in Navajo code over and over again.)

→ *Why does Grandfather explain his training and testing in such detail?* (Because it was a war and people could get killed, recruits had to be well trained.)

"Tell me about the fighting!" said John.

Suddenly Grandfather's face looked as creased and battered as the canyon walls behind him. After a long pause he said, "What I saw is better left back there. I would not want to touch my home or my family with those pictures.

"Before we invaded, I looked out at that island. It had been flattened and burned. 'Let this never happen to a beautiful island again,' I thought. I just stayed on the deck of the ship thinking about the ceremonies they were doing for me at home. We invaded at dawn.

"I almost drowned in a bomb crater before I even got to shore. I was trying to run through the water and the bullets when I felt myself sinking into a bottomless hole. My eighty-pound radio pack pulled me straight down. I lost my rifle paddling to the surface.

"On the beach, it was all I could do just to survive. I remember lying there with gunfire flying past my ears. A creek that ran to the beach was clear when I first lay there. By noon it was blood red.

439

**LITERATURE ANTHOLOGY,** pp. 438–439

**⑫ Skill: Theme**

What does John's grandfather think about before they invade? (He hopes a beautiful island is never destroyed again and about his own people performing ceremonies for him.) What happens to John's grandfather during the invasion? (He almost drowns and he hears gunfire fly past him.) Add these details to your organizer.

| What Does the Character Do and Say? | What Happens to the Character? |
|---|---|
| He thinks about the destruction and the people performing ceremonies for him at home. | He almost drowns, and gunfire flies past his ears. |

**ELL** Encourage students to notice cognates on pages 438 and 439: radio/*radio,* transmission/*transmisión,* ceremonies/*ceremonias.*

→ *What is a* transmission? *Point to the text that gives you a clue.* (a message)

→ Read aloud with students the transmission that Grandfather has to make: *Receiving steady machine gun fire. Request reinforcements.*

# Develop Comprehension

**13** **Strategy: Summarize**

Reread page 440. Turn to your partner and summarize what happens when Grandfather meets another American soldier.

**Student Think Aloud** The American soldier thinks that John's grandfather is a spy because he had just heard him speaking a foreign language. The soldier was going to shoot him, and a friend has to save him.

"The worst were the fallen soldiers I had to run over to go forward. I couldn't even stop to say I was sorry. I just had to run over them and keep going.

"I had to move through the jungle at night, broadcasting in code from different locations. One unit needed medical supplies. Another needed machine-gun support. I had just begun broadcasting to another code talker. 'Arizona! New Mexico!' I called. The next thing I knew, an American soldier behind me was yelling, 'Do you know what we do to spies?'

"'Don't shoot!' I said. 'I'm American. Look at my uniform.' He didn't believe me. He had just heard the foreign language. He had seen my hair and my eyes. Japanese spies had been known to steal uniforms from fallen soldiers.

**13** "One of my buddies jumped out of the bushes right at that moment and saved my life."

440

## A C T  Access Complex Text

### ▶ Sentence Structure

Explain the use of double and single quotation marks in paragraph three on page 441.

→ *Double quotation marks show that a character is speaking. When a speaking character quotes another person, those words are in single quotation marks. Who is speaking here?* (Grandfather)

→ *Whom does Grandfather quote?* (the medicine man)

### ▶ Prior Knowledge

Share this information about the Battle of Iwo Jima.

→ Iwo Jima was the bloodiest battle the Marine Corps had ever fought. The flag was raised on February 23, but fighting continued into April.

→ Capturing the island of Iwo Jima was vital. It allowed the United States to use Iwo Jima's airstrips to protect U.S. fighter planes over Japan.

"How did you stay alive the rest of the time?" asked John.

"My belief was my shield," Grandfather answered.

He drew a ragged wallet from deep inside of his shirt pocket. "Inside of this, I carried corn pollen from the medicine man. 'Never be afraid,' he said. 'Nothing's going to touch you.' And nothing ever did. More than four hundred code talkers fought in some of the bloodiest battles of World War II. All but a few of us survived.

"The Japanese never did crack the code. When they finally discovered what language it was, they captured and tortured one poor Navajo. He wasn't a code talker and couldn't understand the message they had intercepted. He told them we were talking about what we ate for breakfast. Our code word for bombs was 'eggs.'

"Six months before the war ended, Navajo code talkers passed more than eight hundred messages in two days during the invasion of Iwo Jima.

"When the American flag was raised on top of Iwo Jima's mountain, the victory was announced in code to the American fleet. 'Sheep-Uncle-Ram-Ice-Bear-Ant-Cat-Horse-Itch' came the code."

John tried to spell out the letters.

"Suribachi?" asked John.

"Yes," said Grandfather. "Mount Suribachi.

441

**LITERATURE ANTHOLOGY, pp. 440–441**

## 14 Skill: Theme

According to Grandfather, what kept him alive as he continued to fight in the war? (Grandfather says that his belief kept him alive. He carried corn pollen from a medicine man who told him that nothing would touch him.) **What might Grandfather's belief tell you about the theme?** (Your culture can give you strength and help you hold onto the things that you value.) **Add the details and theme to your organizer.**

| What Does the Character Do and Say? | What Happens to the Character? |
|---|---|
| He carries pollen seeds from a medicine man who said that nothing would harm him. | He stays alive during battle and believes that the pollen protects him. |

Your culture can give you strength and help you hold on to what you value.

Theme

---

**ELL** Use the illustration on page 441 to help students understand the text.

→ Point to the mountain and say *Mount Suribachi.* Have students repeat.

→ *What are the soldiers putting on Mount Suribachi?* Students can point to the flag or answer orally.

Point out the cognate: victory/*victoria.*

→ *Did the Americans win or lose at Iwo Jima?* (They won.)

→ Read aloud the text with students that gives the clue: "When the American flag was raised on top of Iwo Jima's mountain, the victory was announced in code to the American fleet."

# Develop Comprehension

**15** **Skill: Make Inferences**

Why do you think Grandfather says he will never leave again? What evidence from the text supports your inference? (When he was at war, he thought about the ceremonies people performed for him, and he believed that the corn pollen from the Navajo medicine man protected him, so I can infer that being Navajo was very important to him.)

"When I came home, I walked the twelve miles from the bus station to this spot. There weren't any parades or parties.

"I knew I wasn't allowed to tell anyone about the code. I looked down at that beautiful canyon floor and thought, 'I'm never leaving again.'"

**15**

442

# A C T Access Complex Text

## ▶ Connection of Ideas

To understand characters' actions, students may need to make connections with information that was presented earlier in the selection.

→ *What is special about Grandfather's wallet?* (It once held corn pollen from a medicine man. Grandfather believed it would keep him safe.)

→ *How did the unbreakable code, the Navajo language, help save the country?* (It made it possible for the Americans to transmit messages that the Japanese could not decode. The coded messages the Navajo sent helped America and its allies to win the war.)

"But why did you leave in the first place?" asked John.

His grandfather lifted him gently onto the horse. "The answer to that is in the code," he said. "The code name for America was 'Our Mother.' You fight for what you love. You fight for what is yours."

He swung his leg behind John and reached around him to hold the reins.

"Keep my wallet," he said. "It will remind you of the unbreakable code that once saved your country."

John clutched the wallet with one hand and held the horse's mane with the other. He wasn't as scared of going to a new place any more. His grandfather had taught him who he was and what he would always have with him. He was the grandson of a Navajo code talker and he had a language that had once helped save his country.

**STOP AND CHECK**

**Ask and Answer Questions** How does Grandfather's story affect John? Go back to the text to find the answer.

443

**LITERATURE ANTHOLOGY,** pp. 442–443

---

**STOP AND CHECK**

**Ask and Answer Questions** How does Grandfather's story affect John? (John is no longer scared of going to a new place. He knows that he will always have his Navajo culture, and that his Navajo language played an important role in the history of the United States.)

**Return to Predictions**

Review students' predictions and purposes for reading. Ask them to answer the Essential Question. (The Navajos contributed to the U.S. victory in World War II by using their language to create an unbreakable code.)

# About the Author

## Meet the Author and the Illustrator

### Sara Hoagland Hunter and Julia Miner

Have students read the biographies of the author and illustrator. Ask:

→ Why did Sara Hoagland Hunter spend so much time interviewing the Navajo?

→ How did the Navajo feel about Julia Miner's illustrations for this story?

## Author's Purpose

### To Inform

Remind students that when authors write to inform, they try to represent people accurately. Students may say that Sara Hoagland Hunter describes Grandfather as gentle and kind. Grandfather comforts John when he expresses concern about moving. When asked to fight for his country, Grandfather proudly offers his services as a code talker, even though he is often saddened by the war. In the end, he tells John that "you fight for what you love."

## Author's Craft

### Figurative Language

Explain that authors use figurative language to help us think about familiar ideas in new ways. Discuss what this adds to the writing.

→ Authors use similes when they say that one thing is like something else. Example: *I felt like a wild horse with a lasso finally off its neck.* (page 434)

→ Have students find other examples of figurative language, such as "… [his] face looked as creased and battered as the canyon walls…." (page 439)

---

## ABOUT THE AUTHOR AND ILLUSTRATOR

(t) Durant Hunter; (b) Courtesy Rowman & Littlefield Publishing Group

**Sara Hoagland Hunter** traveled to the Southwest to write this story. There, she interviewed some of the Navajo people who had served in World War II. After much discussion, the tribal elders finally agreed that Sara should tell their story. The Navajo men were eager to pass along their experiences to their own children and grandchildren, and a children's book would be a fine way to achieve that.

Sara wanted to represent Navajo culture accurately. She respected the generosity and peaceful wisdom of the people she interviewed. During the writing process, she even shared drafts with the people she had met. *The Unbreakable Code* turned into one of Sara's favorite works.

**Julia Miner** is an artist and architect who enjoys illustrating stories with a regional or historical focus. For that reason, she was eager to accompany Sara Hoagland Hunter on her research trip to the Southwest. Julia fell in love with the landscape and was excited to draw and paint the scenery. When she shared her artwork with the Navajos, they were delighted by her realistic drawings.

### Author's Purpose

Sara Hoagland Hunter found the Navajo people she interviewed to be generous, peaceful, and wise. How does she show these characteristics in *The Unbreakable Code*?

444

**LITERATURE ANTHOLOGY, pp. 444–445**

# RESPOND TO READING

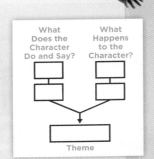

## Summarize

Summarize how Grandfather helped the military in *The Unbreakable Code*. Details from your Theme Chart may help you.

## Text Evidence

| What Does the Character Do and Say? | What Happens to the Character? |
|---|---|

Theme

1. What major historical event happens in *The Unbreakable Code*? How can you tell the story is fictional? **GENRE**

2. What does Grandfather do when he faces challenges as a boy at school and as a soldier at war? What does this tell about the importance of culture? **THEME**

3. Find the word *plain* on page 434. What word on page 437 is a homophone for *plain*? What is the meaning of each word? Use context clues to help you. **HOMOPHONES**

4. Write the message the author is trying to communicate by having Grandfather give John his wallet. Explain how John's response supports the author's message. **WRITE ABOUT READING**

### Make Connections

Talk about how the Navajo code talkers and other people in the military contributed to a cause. **ESSENTIAL QUESTION**

Give another example when people of different backgrounds worked together for a cause. How does a group benefit from the contributions of different people? **TEXT TO WORLD**

445

# Make Connections · *Analytical Writing*

**Essential Question** Have partners work together to cite evidence from the text that shows how the Navajos and others worked together to contribute to a cause.

**Text to World** After students discuss ways that groups of people can contribute to a cause and work together to achieve success, have students suggest other causes to which groups of people might contribute.

# Respond to Reading

## Summarize

Review with students the notes in their organizer. Model how to use the information to summarize *The Unbreakable Code*.

*Analytical Writing* **Write About Reading: Summarize** Ask students to write a summary using the notes in their organizer to guide them. Remind them to state the theme at the end of their summary. Have partners share summaries.

## Text Evidence

1. **Genre** <u>Answer</u> World War II. The story must be fiction because the dialogue is a private conversation that wasn't recorded by the author. <u>Evidence</u> John and Grandfather are alone, talking in John's hiding place.

2. **Theme** <u>Answer</u> He remembers his Navajo culture. Culture can get people through hard times. <u>Evidence</u> Grandfather says, "Navajo was my language and Navajo I would never forget." At war, he recalled the ceremonies the Navajo were doing for him at home; he kept the Navajo medicine man's corn pollen with him so as not to be afraid.

3. **Homophones** <u>Answer</u> *Plane*. A *plain* is an open area of land; a *plane* is something that flies through the air. <u>Evidence</u> Grandfather describes the plain as "open," and he is outdoors. The word part *air* in *aircraft* in the preceding sentence tells me *plane* means "something that flies through the air."

*Analytical Writing* 4. **Write About Reading: Theme** The author is trying to show that the strength of the Navajo culture will pass on to future generations. Grandfather says the wallet will remind John of the unbreakable code, the Navajo language. John isn't scared anymore, which shows that the strength of

# Develop Comprehension

**Literature Anthology**
*Complex vocabulary places this selection above TextEvaluator range. Content is grade-level appropriate.*

## "Allies in Action"

### Text Complexity Range

**Lexile**

740 ▲ 1010
870

**TextEvaluator™**

23 51 ▲
*52

## Options for Close Reading

→ Whole Class
→ Small Group
→ Independent

---

**CCSS Genre · Expository Text**

**Compare Texts**
Read about how groups of people contributed to one effort during World War II.

# Allies in Action

During the 1930s, many countries faced hard economic times. Leaders of two nations, Germany and Japan, saw an opportunity and invaded neighboring countries to expand their power. Other countries, such as Italy, joined them. These forces were called the Axis powers. In response, a number of countries including Great Britain, France, and later the Soviet Union, joined together. This group came to be known as the Allied forces. The conflict worsened and expanded, eventually involving over fifty nations. It became known as World War II.

Keystone/Hulton Archive/Getty Images

446

---

## A C T Access Complex Text

### What makes this text complex?
▷ **Organization**
▷ **Specific Vocabulary**

### ▷ Organization

Point out that authors of complex texts may use more than one organizational structure. "Allies in Action" includes both a sequential structure and a cause-and-effect structure.

→ *What caused the worker shortage in the United States during World War II?* (Many men and women left to serve.)

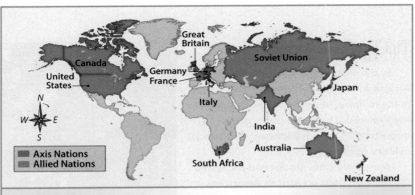

By 1941, Germany and Japan had invaded a number of countries. In response, the United States, the Soviet Union, France, and Great Britain (and countries that were part of its commonwealth) joined together to oppose them.

## Joining the Allies

At first the United States tried to remain neutral. However, after Japan attacked Pearl Harbor in December of 1941, the U.S. had to act. The country joined the Allies and sent troops to fight in the Pacific and in Europe.

Many men left the United States to fight in the war. Women also **enlisted**, often serving in the Army Nurse Corps. The large number of **recruits** that went overseas caused a worker shortage back home. In response, many women took jobs previously held by men. They held positions in government and worked in factories. They also raised funds and collected materials that would be recycled into supplies for the troops.

The shortage of workers in agriculture led the United States to institute the Bracero Program with Mexico. *Bracero* is the Spanish word for laborer. This program encouraged Mexican workers to offer assistance to farm owners in the United States. These skilled workers helped maintain crops, keeping the country's economy productive during the war.

**WOMAN'S PLACE IN WAR**
The Army of the United States has 239 kinds of jobs for women
**THE WOMEN'S ARMY CORPS**

Though women could enlist in the army reserve, most were not sent directly into battle.

(r) Hulton Archive/Getty Images

447

**LITERATURE ANTHOLOGY, pp. 446–447**

## Compare Texts ✎ *Analytical Writing*

Students will read an informational text describing the wartime contributions of diverse groups in the United States, including the Navajo. Ask students to do a close reading to understand the content. Then have students reread, **summarizing** or using other strategies they know to help them. They will also take notes and then use the text evidence they gathered to compare this text with *The Unbreakable Code.*

### ❶ Ask and Answer Questions

What caused the United States to join forces with the Allies? What did they do to help?

*Analytical Writing* **Write About Reading** Write a short summary explaining why the United States joined forces with the Allies and what our country did to help. (After Japan attacked Pearl Harbor, the United States joined the Allied forces. They sent troops to Europe and the Pacific.)

→ Point out the words *In response* and explain that they signal to readers that the effect will follow.

→ *What were some effects of this shortage?* (Many women joined the workforce, taking the jobs of the men who were fighting. The United States started the Bracero Program wth Mexico.)

**ELL** Help ELLs understand the cause-and-effect relationship by explaining key words and phrases: *shortage back home, held positions, raised funds.*

→ *Why did Mexican workers and many women get U.S. jobs during the war?* (There was a worker shortage.)

# Develop Comprehension

## ② Ask and Answer Questions

What role did the Tuskegee airmen play in World War II? Turn to a partner and paraphrase what they did. (The Tuskegee airmen flew many missions during World War II and became well known for their flying skills.)

## ③ Ask and Answer Questions

Why did Philip Johnston think the Navajo could help during World War II?

**Analytical Writing** **Write About Reading** Write a sentence or two explaining why Philip Johnston thought the Navajo could be helpful. (Johnston remembered that the Choctaw tribe had put messages in code during World War I. He thought the Navajo could do the same.)

## The Tuskegee Airmen

By the start of the war, a number of African American men were already active in the military. However, their positions were limited. They were rarely given opportunities for advancement and special military **operations**.

Many civil rights groups had protested these restrictions on African Americans. In response, the U.S. Army Air Corps began a new training program in 1941. They taught African Americans how to become pilots and navigators. This program was based in Tuskegee, Alabama. Those who completed aeronautic, or pilot, training there became known as "The Tuskegee Airmen."

The Tuskegee Airmen flew many missions during World War II. Over time, they gained a strong reputation for their skills. Their success would lead the U.S. military to recognize African American service and ② offer them more training opportunities in different fields.

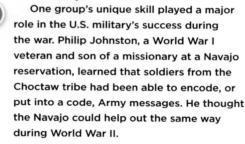

Nearly 1,000 African Americans completed the pilot training program in Tuskegee, Alabama.

## The Navajo Code Talkers

③ One group's unique skill played a major role in the U.S. military's success during the war. Philip Johnston, a World War I veteran and son of a missionary at a Navajo reservation, learned that soldiers from the Choctaw tribe had been able to encode, or put into a code, Army messages. He thought the Navajo could help out the same way during World War II.

(t) U.S. Air Force photo; (b) Corbis

448

---

## A C T Access Complex Text

### ▶ Specific Vocabulary

Review with students that authors sometimes provide definitions or restatements to help readers determine the meaning of unfamiliar domain-specific words.

→ *What clue in the last sentence of paragraph two on page 448 helps you figure out what* aeronautic *means?* (the word *pilot*, which is set off in commas)

→ *What does the word* encode *mean in paragraph four on page 448?* (put into code)

→ Explain that antonyms can also help students find meaning. Point to the second sentence on page 449. Ask: *What is an antonym for the word* decipher? (encode) *What does* decipher *mean?* (to decode, or figure out)

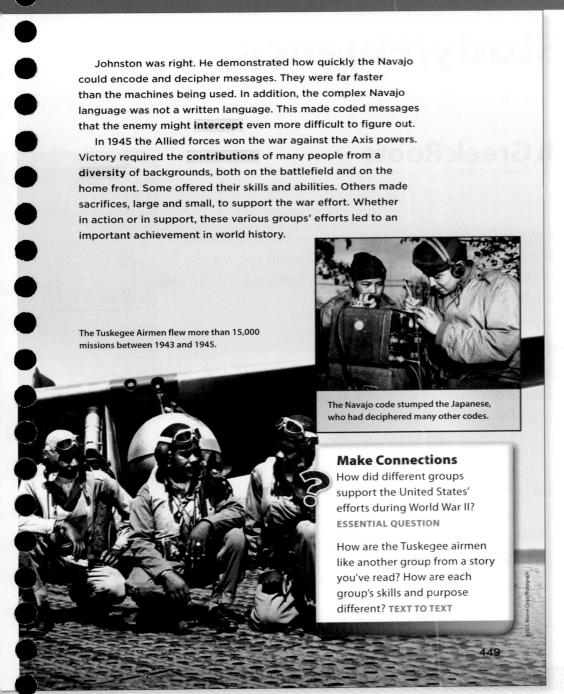

Johnston was right. He demonstrated how quickly the Navajo could encode and decipher messages. They were far faster than the machines being used. In addition, the complex Navajo language was not a written language. This made coded messages that the enemy might **intercept** even more difficult to figure out.

In 1945 the Allied forces won the war against the Axis powers. Victory required the **contributions** of many people from a **diversity** of backgrounds, both on the battlefield and on the home front. Some offered their skills and abilities. Others made sacrifices, large and small, to support the war effort. Whether in action or in support, these various groups' efforts led to an important achievement in world history.

The Tuskegee Airmen flew more than 15,000 missions between 1943 and 1945.

The Navajo code stumped the Japanese, who had deciphered many other codes.

**Make Connections**
How did different groups support the United States' efforts during World War II?
**ESSENTIAL QUESTION**

How are the Tuskegee airmen like another group from a story you've read? How are each group's skills and purpose different? **TEXT TO TEXT**

449

**LITERATURE ANTHOLOGY, pp. 448–449**

## Make Connections · Analytical Writing

**Essential Question** Have students paraphrase and share information about how different groups supported the U.S. war effort in World War II. Suggest that they look back at the headings and skim each section to identify the contributions of each group.

**Text to Text** Have groups of students compare and contrast their responses to the Ask and Answer Questions prompts with what they learned in *The Unbreakable Code*. Have groups discuss how the Tuskegee Airmen were similar to the Navajo. (Both groups trained to help the military, and both groups were important to the military's success. Both groups risked their lives during the war, and both groups were not always treated fairly in the United States.) Then have groups share differences. (The Navajos used their language and their ability to encode and decode quickly. The Tuskegee Airmen flew missions during the war, and they became known for their great skill and success.)

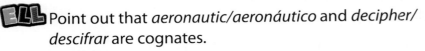

**ELL** Point out that *aeronautic/aeronáutico* and *decipher/descifrar* are cognates.

To help students understand the terminology related to the civil rights movement referred to on page 448, point out that *protested/protestar*, *civil/civil*, and *restrictions/restricciones* are also cognates.

→ *Were African Americans restricted in what they could do in the military before the war?* (yes)

→ *Who protested restrictions on their roles?* (civil rights groups)

→ *Did the protests make a difference?* (yes)

# Word Study/Fluency

**MINILESSON 20 Mins**

## Words with Greek Roots

### OBJECTIVES

**CCSS** Know and apply grade-level phonics and word analysis skills in decoding words. Use combined knowledge of all letter-sound correspondences, syllabication patterns, and morphology (e.g. roots and affixes) to read accurately unfamiliar multisyllabic words in context and out of context. **RF.5.3a**

**CCSS** Read on-level prose and poetry orally with accuracy, appropriate rate, and expression on successive readings. **RF.5.4b**

Rate: 129–149 WCPM

### ACADEMIC LANGUAGE
• expression, phrasing
• Cognates: expresión, fraseo

Refer to the sound transfers chart to identify sounds that do not transfer in Spanish, Cantonese, Vietnamese, Hmong, and Korean.

### 1 Explain

Tell students that in the English language, many words are of Greek origin, or come from the Greek language. They will often see words with Greek roots in their science and social studies textbooks. Write the following example on the board:

**Greek root:** *psych*, meaning "mind" or "soul"

**English words:** *psychology, psychic, psychiatrist*

Discuss the meaning of each English word. Tell students that learning the meanings of common Greek roots can help them access the meaning of unfamiliar words.

### 2 Model

Write the following common Greek roots and their meanings on the board.

| | | | |
|---|---|---|---|
| **astro**, star | **auto**, self | **graph**, write | **geo**, earth |
| **hydro**, water | **phon**, sound | **tele**, far off | **bio**, life |
| **photo**, light | **myth**, beliefs | **naut**, ship | **therm**, heat |

Read aloud each Greek root and its meaning. Then model using the roots to read and define the following words: *astrology, autograph, geography, hydropower, telephone, biology, photosynthesis, mythology, nautical, thermometer.*

### 3 Guided Practice

Write the following words with Greek roots on the board. Have students underline the root or roots in each word. Then have them read the words chorally. Help students use the meanings of the Greek roots to define the words. Then have them verify their definitions by consulting a dictionary.

| | | | |
|---|---|---|---|
| geology | telegraph | graphite | dehydrate |
| autobiography | mythical | photograph | phonics |

## Go Digital

**Words with Greek Roots**

Present the Lesson

View "Shipped Out"

## Read Multisyllabic Words

**Transition to Longer Words** Help students transition to multisyllabic words with Greek roots. Write the following Greek roots and example words on the board. Have students read a word or word root in the first column. Then model how to read the longer word in the second column. Help students use the meaning of the Greek roots, as well as the meaning of common prefixes and suffixes, to determine each word's meaning.

| | | | |
|---|---|---|---|
| hydrate | rehydration | mobile | mobility |
| phone | phonographic | geo | geology |
| graph | autobiographic | mech | mechanical |
| myth | mythological | promote | promotion |

After students complete the activity, ask them to use four multisyllabic words from the list in sentences. Then have them share their sentences with partners.

## Monitor and *Differentiate*

 **Quick Check**

Can students identify Greek roots in unfamiliar English words? Can they use the meanings of those roots to define the words?

### Small Group Instruction

| | | |
|---|---|---|
| **If No** → | **Approaching Level** | Reteach pp. T42, T46 |
| | **ELL** | Develop pp. T59, T62 |
| **If Yes** → | **On Level** | Apply pp. T48–T49 |
| | **Beyond Level** | Apply pp. T52–T53 |

## FLUENCY ←

### Expression and Phrasing

**Explain/Model** Remind students that using proper expression helps make the writer's ideas clear and enlivens the text. Review that pauses, marked by punctuation, can create drama or clarify information contained in phrases. Model reading the first page of "Shipped Out," **Reading/Writing Workshop** pages 382–385. Emphasize the use of expression and phrasing as you read.

Remind students that you will be listening for their use of expression and phrasing as you monitor their reading during the week.

**Practice/Apply** Have partners alternate reading paragraphs in the passage, modeling the expression you used.

### Daily Fluency Practice

Students can practice fluency using **Your Turn Practice Book** passages.

**ON-LEVEL PRACTICE BOOK** p. 258

Name _____

Word Study: Words with Greek Roots

A. Add the word parts to create a word with a Greek root. Write the word on the line. Then circle the word below that has the same Greek root.

1. tele + vision = television
   automated    (telegram)    asteroid

2. auto + mobile = automobile
   disaster    (automatic)    microwave

3. photo + genic = photogenic
   philosophy    (telephoto)    program

4. homo + phone = homophone
   (phonics)    mechanic    psychic

5. para + graph = paragraph
   videophone    invite    (graphic)

B. Read each sentence. Replace the underlined words with one of the words from the word box below and rewrite the sentence.

| mechanical | phonics | autograph | astronomer | photograph |

6. The scientist who studies stars and planets was able to see Mars.
   The astronomer was able to see Mars.

7. My uncle is studying how to take a picture with his new camera.
   My uncle is studying how to take a photograph with his new camera.

8. They were able to get the handwritten name of the famous actress.
   They were able to get the autograph of the famous actress.

9. I understand the science of sounds, so I can read almost any word.
   I understand phonics, so I can read almost any word.

10. People who are able to fix machines will always be able to find a job.
    People who are mechanical will always be able to find a job.

258 Practice · Grade 5 · Unit 6 · Week 1

| **APPROACHING** p. 258 | **BEYOND** p. 258 | **ELL** p. 258 |

 **Go** Digital

www.connected.mcgraw-hill.com
**RESOURCES**
**Research and Inquiry**

→ **Wrap Up the Week**

# Integrate Ideas

## RESEARCH AND INQUIRY

**Joining Forces**

### OBJECTIVES

**CCSS** Write routinely over extended time frames (time for research, reflection, and revision) and shorter time frames (a single sitting or a day or two) for a range of discipline-specific tasks, purposes, and audiences. **W.5.10**

**CCSS** Include multimedia components (e.g., graphics, sound) and visual displays in presentations when appropriate to enhance the development of main ideas or themes. **SL.5.5**

- Use media to publish information.
- Work in teams.
- Use technology to present information.

### ACADEMIC LANGUAGE
- *media, publish, technology*
- Cognates: *publicar, tecnología*

### Publish Research Findings

Explain that students will work in small groups to research how people came together in response to a natural disaster that occurred in the United States during the past ten years. Tell them that their research should answer the questions *Who? What? When?* and *Where?* Then they will share their findings on a class Web site. Discuss the following steps:

**1** **Choose a Topic**  Have groups brainstorm natural disasters that occurred in the United States during the past ten years. Have them think about events such as hurricanes, tornadoes, earthquakes, and wildfires. Ask them to select one of the natural disasters as their topic.

**2** **Find Resources**  Have students do an Internet search of reliable Web sites to find news articles, photographs, and first-person accounts of how people responded to the natural disaster they select. Remind them to seek answers to the questions *Who? What? When?* and *Where?*

**3** **Guided Practice**  Tell students that multimedia components make presentations more enjoyable for the audience. Help them understand how to use clip art, create a chart, or add audio or video files to illustrate points in their presentation.

**4** **Create the Project: Class Web Site**  Have students use their research and various multimedia components to create a presentation they can post to a class Web site.

### Present the Web Site

Have groups share their findings on a class Web site. Evaluate the presentation using Presenting Checklist 1.

# TEXT CONNECTIONS  *Analytical Writing*

## OBJECTIVES

**CCSS** Integrate information from several texts on the same topic in order to write or speak about the subject knowledgeably. **RI.5.9**

**CCSS** Engage effectively in a range of collaborative discussions (one-on-one, in groups, and teacher-led) with diverse partners on *grade 5 topics and texts*, building on others' ideas and expressing their own clearly. Review the key ideas expressed and draw conclusions in light of information and knowledge gained from the discussions. **SL.5.1d**

## Text to Text

**Cite Evidence** Tell students they will work in small groups to compare the information they have read this week about how groups can contribute to a cause. Model how to make comparisons using examples from this week's **Leveled Readers** and "Shipped Out," **Reading/Writing Workshop** pages 382–385. Have students review the week's selections and their completed graphic organizers. Help them set up an Accordion Foldable® to organize their findings. Students should record information about who contributed to the cause, what they did, and how it helped. They can then draw conclusions about the Essential Question.

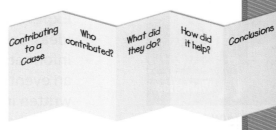

Dinah Zike's **FOLDABLES**

**Present Information** Have groups meet to present their notes and conclusions. Encourage discussion by asking students to comment on information each group found that is similar to and different from other groups' findings.

# WRITE ABOUT READING  *Analytical Writing*

**CCSS** Draw evidence from literary or informational texts to support analysis, reflection, and research. **W.5.9**

**CCSS** Determine a theme of a story, drama, or poem from details in the text, including how characters in a story or drama respond to challenges or how the speaker in a poem reflects upon a topic; summarize the text. **RL.5.2**

## Write an Analysis

**Cite Evidence** Explain that students will write about one of the stories they read this week. Using text evidence, students will analyze the way the author's descriptions of a character's feelings help to convey the theme.

Discuss how to analyze a text by asking *how* and *why* questions.

→ How does the author show what a character's feelings are?

→ Why are the character's feelings important to the theme of the story?

Use **Your Turn Practice Book** page 259 to read and discuss the student model. Then have students select a story and review its theme. Have them write to show how the author's descriptions of the characters' feelings help to convey the theme. Remind students that good explanatory writers end with a strong concluding sentence and use transitions to link ideas, such as *therefore* and *also*.

**Present Your Ideas** Ask partners to share their paragraphs and discuss how the evidence they cited from the text supports their ideas.

# → Readers to Writers

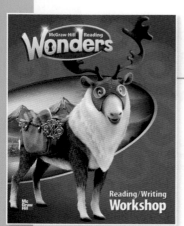

**Reading/Writing Workshop**

**ACADEMIC LANGUAGE**
- *organization, sequence*
- Cognates: *organización, secuencia*

## Writing Traits: Organization

### Sequence

**Expert Model** Explain that writers may use sequence to organize ideas. Sequence is a logical way to tell what happens first, next, and last. Informational writing that explains steps in a process or that recounts an event usually uses sequence. Narrative writing is also usually written in sequence. The beginning usually introduces the problem the main character faces. The middle shows the sequence of events that develops the story's action and characters. The end shows how the problem is solved.

**Read aloud** the expert model from "Shipped Out." Ask students to listen for the sequence of events in the story. Have students work with partners to discuss how putting events in order helps readers understand the story.

**Student Model** Remind students that writers usually tell about events in the order they happened. Read aloud the student model "Fleas Flee at the Pet Shelter." As students follow along, have them focus on how each event leads logically to the next.

**Invite** partners to talk about the model and the changes the writer made to improve the sequence. Ask them to suggest other changes Jay could make to create an organized story with a clear sequence of events.

**Go Digital**

**Expert Model**

**Student Model**

**Genre Writing**

**Opinion Writing**

For full writing process lessons and rubrics see:
→ Book Review, pp. T344–T349
→ Opinion Letter, pp. T350–T355

**CCSS Writing Traits** Organization

 # Readers to...

Writers often tell the events of a story in order, or **sequence**. Writers organize the sequence of events in a logical way. The middle of the story often includes a description of events, in order, that develop the story's action and characters. Reread this paragraph from "Shipped Out."

**Expert Model**

**Sequence**

Why is the **sequence** of events important in this paragraph?

On my first day with Aunt Lucia, she explained the daily operations of the bakery. First, we get up before dawn to knead the dough. Next, we bake breads and muffins. Then, while I help customers, Lucia makes cakes and cookies for sale in the afternoon. Whenever the phone rings, she races from the back room to intercept the call. She's always worried that it might be bad news, so she wants to be the first to hear it.

Sean Qualls

390

# Writers

Jay wrote an article about the Service Club at his school. Read Jay's revision of this section.

**Student Model**

## Fleas Flee
### at the Pet Shelter!

Our school's Service Club sponsored a "Flea Bath" for the Shady Brook Animal Shelter. Volunteers showed up ^early Saturday morning. ^First, Luke and Heidi filled tubs with warm water. ^When The first dogs arrived. They lathered them up with flea soap. Keith and Astrid dried them gently with towels. Danielle rinsed off (there) fur. ^By the end of the day, We raised $200 to help animals at the shelter.

**Editing Marks**

∧ Add
⌃ Add a comma.
⟍ Take out.
(SP) Check spelling.
≡ Make a capital letter.

**Grammar Handbook**

**Adverbs**
See page 469.

**Your Turn**  COLLABORATE

✔ How does Jay indicate the sequence of events in his article?
✔ Find adverbs that Jay included.
✔ Tell how Jay's revisions improved his article.

*Go Digital!*
*Write online in Writer's Workspace*

391

**READING/WRITING WORKSHOP, pp. 390–391**

## ELL ENGLISH LANGUAGE LEARNERS SCAFFOLD

Provide support to help English Language Learners understand the writing trait.

| Beginning | Intermediate | Advanced/High |
|---|---|---|
| **Respond Orally** Help students complete the sentence frames about the student model. *First, Luke and Heidi filled tubs with ____. Then they washed the ____. In the end, they had ____ dollars.* | **Practice** Ask students to complete the sentence frames. *First, Heidi and Luke ____. When the dogs arrived, Heidi and Luke ____. Next, Danielle ____. Then Keith and Astrid ____. By the end of the day, the club raised ____.* | **Understand** Check for understanding. Ask: *What happens first in the story? Then what happens? What events happen after that? What happens at the end of the story?* |

# Writing Every Day: Organization

**DAY**

**1**

**DAY**

**2**

### Writing Entry: Sequence

**Prewrite** Provide students with the prompt below.

*Explain what an organization in your school or community has done to complete a project. Use sequence to explain in order the actions the organization took.*

Have partners list different projects. Ask them to jot down what the people did to complete each project.

**Draft** Have each student select a project to write about. Remind students to write the events in the order they happened.

### Focus on Sequence

Use **Your Turn Practice Book** page 260 to model writing events in sequence.

*Last week, we held a paper drive. We took the paper to the recycling center. But first we set out bins for magazines and newspapers. We had also advertised.*

Rewrite the second sentence to make the sequence clearer.

*We set out bins for magazines and newspapers. Later, we took the paper to the recycling center.*

Have students continue revising to improve sequence.

### Writing Entry: Sequence

**Revise** Have students revise their writing from Day 1 by arranging events in the order they happened.

Use the **Conferencing Routines**. Circulate among students and stop briefly to talk with individuals. Provide time for peer review.

**Edit** Have students use Grammar Handbook page 469 in the **Reading/Writing Workshop** to edit for errors in adverbs.

# Conferencing Routines

## Teacher Conferences

**STEP 1**

Talk about the strengths of the writing.

*You have included details that really bring the event to life!*

**STEP 2**

Focus on how the writer uses the target trait for the week.

*Some of the events in the middle are out of order. Rearrange the events so they flow more logically.*

**STEP 3**

Make concrete suggestions for revisions. Have students work on a specific assignment, such as those to the right, and then meet with you to review progress.

## DAY  3

### Writing Entry: Sequence

**Prewrite** Ask students to search their Writer's Notebooks for topics for a new draft. Or, provide a prompt such as the following:

*Tell about a problem that required many people to come together to solve and the steps they took to solve it.*

**Draft** Once students have chosen their topics, ask them to create a sequence chart to organize their writing. Students can use their charts to begin their drafts.

## DAY  4

### Writing Entry: Sequence

**Revise** Have students revise their writing from Day 3 by making sure events are in order. As students revise, hold teacher conferences with individual students. You may also wish to have students work with partners to peer conference.

**Edit** Invite students to review the rules for adverbs on Grammar Handbook page 469 in the **Reading/Writing Workshop** and then edit their drafts for errors.

## DAY 5

### Share and Reflect

Discuss with students what they learned about sequence. Invite volunteers to read and compare draft text with text that has been revised. Have students discuss the writing by focusing on the importance of putting events in order. Allow time for individuals to reflect on their own writing progress and record observations in their Writer's Notebooks.

McGraw-Hill Companies Inc./Ken Karp, photographer

### Suggested Revisions

Provide specific direction to help focus young writers.

**Focus on a Sentence**
Read the draft and target one sentence for revision. *Rewrite this sentence to make it clear when the event happened.*

**Focus on a Section**
Underline a section that needs to be revised. Provide specific suggestions. *Is something missing? Add a sentence explaining how this event leads to this later event.*

**Focus on a Revision Strategy**
Underline a section. Have students use a specific revision strategy, such as rearranging. *Reorder the events so that they are told in the order they happened.*

## Peer Conferences

Focus peer response groups on arranging events in the order they happened.

- ☑ Are the events written in the order they happened?
- ☑ Are any important events left out?
- ☑ Do events flow logically from one to the next?

# Grammar: Adverbs

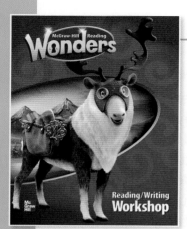

**Reading/Writing Workshop**

## OBJECTIVES

**CCSS** Demonstrate command of the conventions of standard English grammar and usage when writing or speaking. Explain the function of nouns, pronouns, verbs, adjectives, and adverbs in general and their functions in particular sentences. **L.3.1a**

**CCSS** Use relative pronouns *(who, whose, whom, which, that)* and relative adverbs *(where, when, why).* **L.4.1a**

## Go Digital

Adverbs

**Grammar Activities**

---

### DAY 1

### Introduce Adverbs

→ An **adverb** can tell how, when, where, or how often an action happens. *I run _quickly_.* (tells *how*)

→ Some adverbs tell how much or how intensely. *I am _completely_ exhausted.* (tells *how intensely*)

→ Transitional words, such as the **conjunctive adverb** *therefore*, connect two clauses. *I want to win; _therefore_, I train hard.*

→ The **relative adverbs** *where, when,* and *why* can also introduce clauses. *My sister writes ads _where_ she works.*

Have partners discuss adverbs using page 469 of the Grammar Handbook in **Reading/Writing Workshop**.

---

### DAY 2

### Review Adverbs

Review adverbs of manner, time, and place. Point out that adverbs serve as modifiers of adjectives, verbs, or other adverbs.

### Introduce Adverbs Before Adjectives and Other Adverbs

→ An adverb is a word that can describe an adjective. *Mark is _extremely_ kind.*

→ An adverb can describe another adverb. *My sister woke up _quite early_.*

Have partners discuss adverbs using page 469 of the Grammar Handbook.

---

 **COLLABORATE** ## TALK ABOUT IT

### USE ADVERBS

Ask partners to write a paragraph about two groups in their school that have worked together to accomplish something. Have them use each kind of adverb discussed in the lesson.

### MATCH THEM

Provide students with a list of adverbs and adjectives. Have pairs create as many adverb-modifying-adverb and adverb-modifying-adjective combinations as possible. Have pairs share with the class.

---

## DAY  3

**DAILY LANGUAGE ACTIVITY**

"You're cookies are the most tastiest I've ever had!" said Mark. "Their yummy!" (1: Your; 2: the tastiest; 3: They're)

### Mechanics and Usage: Capitalization and Abbreviations in Letters and Formal E-mails

→ Capitalize the first word and all proper nouns in a greeting: *Dear Aunt Millicent.*

→ Capitalize the first word in the closing: *Sincerely.*

→ Capitalize these abbreviations commonly used in letters and formal e-mails: *Mrs., Mr., Inc.*

As students write, refer them to Grammar Handbook pages 473, and 475–476.

## DAY  4

**DAILY LANGUAGE ACTIVITY**

Mrs Wu eager waited for the mail too be delivered. (1: Mrs. ; 2: eagerly; 3: to)

### Proofread

Have students correct errors in this letter:

> dear Mr Blackwell,
>
> I was verily pleased to receive your note. i grinned wide when I read it. Thanks you very much!
>
> You're neighbor,
>
> Carlos

(1: Dear; 2: Mr.; 3: very; 4: I; 5: widely; 6: Thank; 7: Your)

Have students check their work using Grammar Handbook pages 469, 473, and 475–476.

## DAY 5

**DAILY LANGUAGE ACTIVITY**

"When is the choir concert." asked Pablo. "Its november 12," said Ava. (1: concert?"; 2: It's; 3: November)

### Assess

Use the Daily Language Activity and Grammar Practice Reproducibles page 130 for assessment.

### Reteach

Use Grammar Practice Reproducibles pages 126–129 and selected pages from the Grammar Handbook for additional reteaching. Remind students that it is important to use adverbs correctly as they speak and write.

Check students' writing for use of the skill and listen for it in their speaking. Assign Grammar Revision Assignments in their Writer's Notebooks as needed.

**See Grammar Practice Reproducibles pp. 126–130.**

---

### ADD AN ADVERB

Have each student write a paragraph about a cause that is important to him or her and then exchange the paragraph with a partner. Students then add adverbs to their partner's paragraph. Have volunteers share their paragraphs.

### ADVERB MANIA

Group students into two teams. Read aloud sentences with adverbs, including some examples from the lesson. Have team members identify the adverb and whether the adverb modifies a verb, an adjective, or an adverb.

### FIND THOSE ADVERBS

Have partners choose a story they have read in class and identify adverbs used in the text. Have partners record the adverbs they find. Ask pairs to share and create a cumulative list to display in class.

# Spelling: Words with Greek Roots

**DAY 1**

**DAY 2**

## OBJECTIVES

**CCSS** Spell grade-appropriate words correctly, consulting references as needed.
**L.5.2e**

## Spelling Words

| | | |
|---|---|---|
| astronaut | phonics | telegram |
| telephone | astronomer | telephoto |
| automobile | photograph | autograph |
| telescope | photography | automatic |
| mechanical | mythical | disaster |
| myth | homophone | telegraph |
| television | mechanic | |

**Review** correction, discussion, decoration
**Challenge** videophone, photogenic

## Differentiated Spelling

**Approaching Level**

| | | |
|---|---|---|
| astronaut | automatic | autograph |
| telephone | photograph | disaster |
| telescope | photography | mythical |
| mechanical | videophone | auto |
| myth | mechanic | graph |
| television | telegram | homophone |
| phonics | telephoto | |

**Beyond Level**

| | | |
|---|---|---|
| astronaut | phonics | telegram |
| telephone | automatic | telephoto |
| automobile | mechanic | autograph |
| astronomer | photography | telescope |
| mechanical | mechanized | mythical |
| myth | homophone | telegraph |
| television | photosynthesis | |

## Assess Prior Knowledge

Read the spelling words aloud, emphasizing the Greek roots.

Display the word *astronaut*. Point out that two Greek roots placed together form the word. Tell students that recognizing Greek roots can help them remember how to spell words.

Use the roots *astr/aster, photo, tele, auto, phon, mech, myth,* and *graph* to demonstrate sorting spelling words that share the same Greek roots. Sort a few words, pointing out the Greek roots. Ask students to name other everyday words with these roots.

Use the Dictation Sentences from Day 5 to give the pretest. Say the underlined word, read the sentence, and repeat the word. Have students write the words. Then have students check their papers.

## Spiral Review

Review the suffixes in *correction, discussion,* and *decoration*. Read each sentence below, repeat the review word, and have students write the word.

1. Jon made a <u>correction</u> on his test before turning it in.
2. We had a <u>discussion</u> about dinosaurs.
3. The room had no <u>decoration</u>.

Have students trade papers and check their spellings.

**Challenge Words** Review this week's spellings of Greek roots. Read each sentence below, repeat the challenge word, and have students write the words.

1. They held the meeting by <u>videophone</u>.
2. Fashion models are <u>photogenic</u>.

Have students check and correct their spellings and write the words in their word study notebooks.

 **WORD SORTS**

**COLLABORATE**

### OPEN SORT

Have students cut apart the **Spelling Word Cards** in the Online Resource Book and initial the back of each card. Have them read the words aloud with partners. Then have partners do an **open sort**. Have them record their sorts in their word study notebooks.

### PATTERN SORT

Complete the **pattern sort** from Day 1 by using the Spelling Word Cards. Point out the different Greek roots. Partners should compare and check their sorts. Have them record their sorts in their word study notebooks.

## DAY 3

### Word Meanings

Have students copy the three words below into their word study notebooks. Say the words aloud. Then ask students to write words with the same root for each spelling word.

1. automatic (Possible responses: automatically, automate)
2. photograph (Possible responses: photography, photographic, photographer)
3. myth (Possible responses: mythical, mythic, mythology)

Challenge students to write related words for their other spelling, review, or challenge words. Encourage them to include words that are different parts of speech. Have students discuss their word lists with a partner.

## DAY 4

### Proofread and Write

Write these sentences on the board. Have students circle and correct each misspelled word. Have students use a print or a digital dictionary to check and correct their spellings.

1. No one has ever taken a phottograph of the mithical beast. (photograph, mythical)
2. The astronommer showed us how to use the tellescope. (astronomer, telescope)
3. Our local machanic can fix any automobil. (mechanic, automobile)
4. We watched the news of the dissaster on the televission. (disaster, television)

**Error Correction** Tell students that the spellings of Greek roots can change slightly from word to word.

## DAY 5

### Assess

Use the Dictation Sentences for the posttest. Have students list the misspelled words in their word study notebooks. Look for students' use of these words in their writings.

**Dictation Sentences**
1. The <u>astronaut</u> floated in space.
2. The <u>telephone</u> rang loudly.
3. We drove in our <u>automobile</u>.
4. I looked through the <u>telescope</u>.
5. It's a <u>mechanical</u> can opener.
6. A goddess appeared in the <u>myth</u>.
7. I watched the game on <u>television</u>.
8. We're learning <u>phonics</u> in school.
9. The <u>astronomer</u> studied the stars.
10. She smiled for the <u>photograph</u>.
11. Sam's hobby is <u>photography</u>.
12. <u>Mythical</u> stories are fascinating.
13. A <u>homophone</u> is a word that sounds the same as another word.
14. A <u>mechanic</u> will fix your car.
15. A <u>telegram</u> announced the news.
16. Sharon used a <u>telephoto</u> lens.
17. I asked for the star's <u>autograph</u>.
18. The <u>automatic</u> door slid open.
19. We prevented the <u>disaster</u>.
20. The <u>telegraph</u> was an important invention.

Have students self-correct their tests.

**See Phonics/Spelling Reproducibles pp. 151–156.**

### SPEED SORT

Have partners do a **speed sort** to see who is fastest and then compare and discuss their sorts. Then have them do a word hunt in this week's readings to find words with Greek roots. Have them record the words in their word study notebooks.

### BLIND SORT

Have partners do a **blind sort:** one reads a Spelling Word Card; the other tells under which Greek root it belongs. Have partners compare and discuss their sorts. Then have students write a reflection of how they sorted the words.

# → Build Vocabulary

**DAY**
**1**

**DAY**
**2**

## OBJECTIVES

Determine or clarify the meaning of unknown and multiple-meaning words and phrases based on grade 5 reading and content, choosing flexibly from a range of strategies. Use common, grade-appropriate Greek and Latin affixes and roots as clues to the meaning of a word (e.g., *photograph, photosynthesis)*.
**L.5.4b**

Expand vocabulary by adding inflectional endings and suffixes.

## Vocabulary Words

| | |
|---|---|
| bulletin | intercept |
| contributions | operations |
| diversity | recruits |
| enlisted | survival |

## Go Digital

**Vocabulary**

**Vocabulary Activities**

### Connect to Words

Practice this week's vocabulary words.

1. What might you learn from a school **bulletin**?
2. What **contributions** do people make to charities?
3. Give an example of **diversity** in musical interests.
4. Is **enlisting** a choice or a law?
5. When might you **intercept** a note to someone?
6. What **operations** can you do using a calculator?
7. What kinds of things do **recruits** learn to do?
8. What is necessary for **survival**?

### Expand Vocabulary

Help students generate different forms of this week's words by adding, changing, or removing inflectional endings.

→ Draw a four-column chart on the board. Write *intercept* in the first column. Then write *intercepts, intercepted,* and *intercepting* in the next three columns. Read aloud the words with students.

→ Have students share sentences using each form of *intercept*.

→ Students should add *enlisted* to the chart, and then share sentences using the different forms of the word.

→ Have students copy the chart in their word study notebooks.

## BUILD MORE VOCABULARY

**COLLABORATE**

### ACADEMIC VOCABULARY

→ Display *creative, immigrants,* and *government*.

→ Define the words and discuss their meanings with students.

→ Write *create* under *creativity*. Have partners write other words with the same root and define them. Then have partners ask and answer questions using the words.

→ Repeat with *immigrants* and *government*.

### ROOT WORDS  Review

Remind students to look for root words to help figure out the meanings of unfamiliar words.

→ Write: *manuscript.* Explain that the Latin root *man(u)* means "hand" and *script* means "write."

→ Have partners discuss the meaning of *manuscript.* Then have them search for other words with these roots and discuss.

→ Have students write the words and their meanings in their word study notebooks.

**DAY**

### Reinforce the Words

Review this week's and last week's vocabulary words. Have students orally complete each sentence stem.

1. Jodi ran to <u>intercept</u> the mail carrier _____.
2. The <u>bulletin</u> says _____.
3. The <u>recruits</u> began their training with _____.
4. The <u>operations</u> of a _____ are difficult to learn.
5. Plants need _____ for <u>survival</u>.
6. He <u>enlisted</u> in the _____.

Display the previous week's vocabulary: *declined, disorder, identify, probable, unexpected, widespread*. Have partners ask and answer questions for each word.

**DAY**

### Connect to Writing

→ Have students write sentences in their word study notebooks using this week's vocabulary.

→ Tell them to write sentences that provide word information they learned from this week's readings.

→ **ELL** Provide the Day 3 sentence stems 1–6 for students needing extra support.

**Write About Vocabulary**  Have students write something they learned from this week's words in their word study notebooks. For example, they might write about the kinds of things announced in a *bulletin* or how *survival* is hard for some plants and animals.

**DAY**

### Word Squares

Ask students to create Word Squares for each vocabulary word.

→ In the first square, students write the word. (e.g., *diversity*)

→ In the second square, students write their own definition of the word and any related words, such as synonyms. (e.g., *variety, mixture*)

→ In the third square, students draw a simple illustration that will help them remember the word. (e.g., drawing of many diverse plants)

→ In the fourth square, students write nonexamples, including antonyms for the word. (e.g., *uniformity*)

Have partners discuss their squares.

---

### HOMOPHONES

Remind students to look for context clues to help figure out the meanings of homophones.

→ Display **Your Turn Practice Book pages 253–254.** Read paragraph one. Model using context clues to distinguish between *blew* and *blue*.

→ Have students complete page 257.

→ Partners can confirm meanings in a print or online dictionary.

### SHADES OF MEANING

Help students generate words related to *intercept*. Draw a T-chart. Head one column *Synonyms* and the other *Antonyms*.

→ Have partners generate words to add to the T-chart. Ask students to use a thesaurus.

→ Add words and phrases not included such as (synonyms) *capture, seize*; (antonyms) *let pass, miss*.

→ Ask students to copy the words in their word study notebooks.

### MORPHOLOGY

Use *recruits* as a springboard for students to learn more words. Draw a T-chart. Write *recruits* in the left column.

→ In the right column of the T-chart, write *-ment*, and *-er*. Discuss how the suffixes change the meaning.

→ Have students add the suffixes to *recruits*, dropping the *-s*. Review the meanings of the new words.

→ Ask partners to do a search for other words with these suffixes.

# Approaching Level

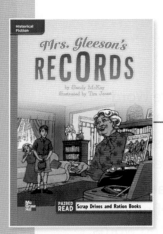

**Lexile** 730
*TextEvaluator*™ 46

---

## OBJECTIVES

**CCSS** Determine a theme of a story, drama, or poem from details in the text, including how characters in a story or drama respond to challenges or how the speaker in a poem reflects upon a topic; summarize the text. **RL.5.2**

**CCSS** Read on-level prose and poetry orally with accuracy, appropriate rate, and expression on successive readings. **RF.5.4b**

---

## ACADEMIC LANGUAGE

• *historical fiction, summarize, theme, homophones*
• Cognates: *ficción histórica, resumir, tema, homófonos*

## Leveled Reader:
## *Mrs. Gleeson's Records*

**Leveled Readers**

### Before Reading

#### Preview and Predict

→ Read the Essential Question with students.

→ Have students preview the title, table of contents, and first page of *Mrs. Gleeson's Records* and predict what they think the selection will be about. Tell them to try to confirm or revise their predictions as they continue reading.

#### Review Genre: Historical Fiction

Tell students that this selection is historical fiction. Explain that historical fiction features settings that could have existed and events that could have happened during a particular period in history. Characters in historical fiction act and speak like real people from that time and place. Historical fiction often includes flashbacks, which describe events that happened before the main action of the story. Have students identify features of historical fiction in the story.

### During Reading

#### Close Reading

**Note Taking:** Ask students to use their graphic organizer as they read.

**Use Graphic Organizer**

**Pages 2–5** *A story's setting can help you understand the story's theme. What is the setting in this story?* (an American town in 1943 during World War II) *Turn to a partner and summarize important events during Andrew's Boy Scouts meeting.* (The scoutmaster shows the scouts an ad for a scrap collection and says they will hold their own scrap collection.)

**Pages 6–8** *Why do Andrew and Emily visit Mrs. Gleeson?* (They bring her tomatoes.) *Describe Mrs. Gleeson's feelings about records.* (They make people want to dance. Years ahead, people will hear the records and know that people kept their spirits up during the war.) *On page 7, the word* led *sounds the same as the word* lead, *but the two words have different meanings. What is the meaning of* led? *Use context clues to help you answer.* ("to direct or conduct someone in a certain direction")

**Pages 9–11** *What are some items Andrew's group collects?* (tin cans, grease, galoshes, soda bottles, newspapers)

*What does Mrs Gleeson want to contribute?* (her records) *What does Andrew tell her? Why?* (He says they are not collecting records. He doesn't want Mrs. Gleeson to give up the things she loves so much.)

**Pages 12–15** *Paraphrase how Mr. Dalwinkle finds out about Andrew's fib and what happens as a result.* (He runs into Mrs. Gleeson. She donates her records.) *Summarize what happens at Mrs. Gleeson's after the war.* (Everyone dances to records.) *What theme do the characters' actions help you identify?* (Everyone can contribute to an effort; the most important contributions are the ones that are hardest to make.)

## After Reading

**Respond to Reading** Revisit the Essential Question and ask students to complete the Text Evidence questions on page 16.

**Analytical Writing** **Write About Reading** Check that students have written about why people contributed and how this connects to the theme.

### Fluency: Expression and Phrasing

**Model** Model reading aloud page 8 with appropriate expression and phrasing. Next reread the page aloud and have students read along.

**Apply** Have students practice reading the passage with partners.

## PAIRED READ

## "Scrap Drives and Ration Books"

**Leveled Reader**

### Make Connections: Write About It **Analytical Writing**

Before reading, ask students to note that the genre of this text is expository text. Then discuss the Essential Question. After reading, ask students to write connections between what they learned about how different groups contribute to a cause in *Mrs. Gleeson's Records* and "Scrap Drives and Ration Books."

### FOCUS ON LITERARY ELEMENTS

Students can extend their knowledge of how authors use flashbacks in fiction by completing the literary elements activity on page 20.

---

## Literature Circles

Ask students to conduct a literature circle using the Thinkmark questions to guide the discussion. You may wish to have a whole-class discussion, using both selections in the Leveled Reader, about how different groups of people can contribute to a cause.

## Level Up

Level-up lessons available online.

**IF** students read the **Approaching Level** fluently and answered the questions

**THEN** pair them with students who have proficiently read the **On Level** and have students

• echo-read the **On Level** main selection.

• identify two traits that help them know that the story is historical fiction.

### A C T Access Complex Text

The **On Level** challenges students by including more **complex sentence structures** and **vocabulary**.

# Approaching Level

## Word Study/Decoding

### REVIEW WORDS WITH GREEK ROOTS

 **TIER 2**

 **OBJECTIVES**

**CCSS** Know and apply grade-level phonics and word analysis skills in decoding words. Use combined knowledge of all letter-sound correspondences, syllabication patterns, and morphology (e.g., roots and affixes) to read accurately unfamiliar multisyllabic words in context and out of context. **RF.5.3a**

Decode words with Greek roots.

 **I Do**  Write the Greek root *psych* on the board and read it aloud. Explain that it means "mind" or "soul." Then write the Greek suffix *-logy* on the board. Explain that it means "study of." Write the word *psychology*, read it aloud, and model using the meaning of the root and suffix to define the word.

 **We Do**  Write the words *geology* and *telegraph* on the board and read them aloud. Explain that *geology* is made up of *geo* ("earth") and *-logy* ("study of") and that *telegraph* is made up of *tele* ("far off") and *graph* ("write"). Guide students to use the meanings of the Greek roots to determine the meanings of the words.

**You Do**  Write these words on the board: *mythology, psychiatrist,* and *graphite.* Have partners identify and use the meanings of the Greek roots and a dictionary to determine the meanings of the words.

### BUILD WORDS WITH GREEK ROOTS

 **TIER 2**

 **OBJECTIVES**

**CCSS** Know and apply grade-level phonics and word analysis skills in decoding words. Use combined knowledge of all letter-sound correspondences, syllabication patterns, and morphology (e.g., roots and affixes) to read accurately unfamiliar multisyllabic words in context and out of context. **RF.5.3a**

Build words with Greek roots.

 **I Do**  Write the roots *auto, bio,* and *graph* on the board and display the **Word-Building Card** *ic.* Read them aloud. Review the meaning of the Greek roots: *auto* ("self"), *bio* ("life"), *graph* ("write").

 **We Do**  Guide students to combine the Word-Building Card and all three Greek roots to create a new word: *autobiographic.* Guide students to use the meanings of the roots to determine the meaning of the word *autobiographic:* "about one's own life as written by oneself."

 **You Do**  Write on the board the Greek roots *auto* and *bio* and the words *mobile, pilot, hazard, sphere.* Have students combine the words and the roots to create new words. Then have students use the meaning of the root and a dictionary to determine the meaning of each word. Ask them to share their work with the class.

# PRACTICE WORDS WITH GREEK ROOTS

## OBJECTIVES

 Know and apply grade-level phonics and word analysis skills in decoding words. Use combined knowledge of all letter-sound correspondences, syllabication patterns, and morphology (e.g., roots and affixes) to read accurately unfamiliar multisyllabic words in context and out of context. **RF.5.3a**

 Determine or clarify the meaning of unknown and multiple-meaning words and phrases based on *grade 5 reading and content,* choosing flexibly from a range of strategies. Use common, grade-appropriate Greek and Latin affixes and roots as clues to the meaning of a word (e.g., *photograph, photosynthesis*). **L.5.4b**

Practice words with Greek roots.

 Write the words *photograph* and *autograph* on the board. Review the meaning of the Greek prefix *photo-* ("light") and the roots *graph* ("write") and *auto* ("self) and underline these in the words. Read the words aloud. Model using the meaning of the prefix and the roots to determine each word's meaning.

 Write the words *biology* and *telephone* on the board. Model how to use the Greek root *bio* ("life") and the suffix *-logy* ("study of") to figure out the meaning of *biology*. Then have students use the Greek roots *tele* ("far off") and *phon* ("sound") to determine the meaning of *telephone*.

 To provide additional practice, write the words below on the board. Read aloud the first word, identify the Greek roots, and give the word's meaning.

| | | |
|---|---|---|
| geography | astrology | phonetics |
| hydrology | nautical | phonograph |
| psychological | astral | psychic |

Then have students read aloud the remaining words. Ask them to identify each Greek root or affix and give the meaning of each word. As necessary, allow students to use a dictionary to determine the words' meanings.

Afterward, point to the words in the list in random order for students to read chorally, clarifying pronunciation as needed.

## ELL ENGLISH LANGUAGE LEARNERS

For the **ELLs** who need **phonics, decoding,** and **fluency** practice, use scaffolding methods as necessary to ensure students understand the meaning of the words. Refer to the **Language Transfers Handbook** for phonics elements that may not transfer in students' native languages.

# → Approaching Level

## Vocabulary

### REVIEW HIGH-FREQUENCY WORDS

**TIER 2**

**OBJECTIVES**

CCSS Acquire and use accurately grade-appropriate general academic and domain-specific words and phrases, including those that signal contrast, addition, and other logical relationships (e.g., *however, although, nevertheless, similarly, moreover, in addition*). **L.5.6**

 Use **High-Frequency Word Cards** 201–210. Display one word at a time, following the routine:

Display the word. Read the word. Then spell the word.

 Ask students to state the word and spell the word with you. Model using the word in a sentence and have students repeat after you.

 Display the word. Ask students to say the word and then spell it. When completed, quickly flip through the word card set as students chorally read the words. Provide opportunities for students to use the words in speaking and writing. For example, provide sentence starters such as *It is time to ____.* Ask students to write each word in their Writer's Notebook.

### REVIEW VOCABULARY WORDS

**TIER 2**

**OBJECTIVES**

CCSS Acquire and use accurately grade-appropriate general academic and domain-specific words and phrases, including those that signal contrast, addition, and other logical relationships (e.g., *however, although, nevertheless, similarly, moreover, in addition*). **L.5.6**

 Display each **Visual Vocabulary Card** and state the word. Explain how the photograph illustrates the word. State the example sentence and repeat the word.

 Point to the word on the card and read the word with students. Ask them to repeat the word. Engage students in structured partner talk about the image as prompted on the back of the vocabulary card.

 Display each visual in random order, hiding the word. Have students match the definitions and context sentences of the words to the visuals displayed.

## UNDERSTAND VOCABULARY WORDS

**OBJECTIVES**

(ccss) Acquire and use accurately grade-appropriate general academic and domain-specific words and phrases, including those that signal contrast, addition, and other logical relationships (e.g., *however, although, nevertheless, similarly, moreover, in addition*).
**L.5.6**

**I Do** Display the *bulletin* **Visual Vocabulary Card** and ask: *Is a* bulletin *a long letter or a short announcement?* Explain that it is a short announcement.

**We Do** Ask these questions. Help students explain their answers.

→ If people *enlisted* in the United States Navy, did they join because they wanted to or because they had to?

→ To *intercept* the ball, do you stop it or let it keep going?

→ Do people need clean-up *operations* after a storm or after a piano recital?

**You Do** Ask these questions. Help students explain their answers.

→ Are *recruits* members of the armed forces or an orchestra?

→ Is living or dying the opposite of *survival*?

→ Are *contributions* of money more like gifts or paychecks?

→ If there is *diversity* at a zoo, are the animals the same or different?

## HOMOPHONES

**OBJECTIVES**

(ccss) Determine or clarify the meaning of unknown and multiple-meaning words and phrases based on *grade 5 reading and content*, choosing flexibly from a range of strategies. Use context (e.g., cause/effect relationships and comparisons in text) as a clue to the meaning of a word or phrase. **L.5.4a**

**I Do** Remind students that homophones are words that sound the same but are spelled differently and have different meanings. They can use context clues within the sentence or the paragraph to find the meaning of an unknown homophone. Display the Comprehension and Fluency passage on **Approaching Reproducibles** pages 253–254. Choral-read the first paragraph. Point to the words *blue* and *blew*.

**Think Aloud** I know that the words *blue* and *blew* are homophones. Carlos says he is turning blue, so *b-l-u-e* must be the color blue. Since he blew on his hands, *b-l-e-w* must refer to the action of breathing out air.

**We Do** Ask students to point to the homophones *knew* and *new* in the second paragraph. Choral-read both sentences. Help students identify context clues for each meaning. Ask them to give the definitions of *knew* and *new*.

**You Do** Have students use context clues to identify the meaning of the homophones *here, hear* (page 254, paragraphs 2 and 3) and *too, to* (page 254, last paragraph), and then use them to determine the meanings of the words.

→ **Approaching Level**

# Comprehension

## FLUENCY

**TIER 2**

**OBJECTIVES**

CCSS Read on-level prose and poetry orally with accuracy, appropriate rate, and expression on successive readings. **RF.5.4b**

Read fluently with good expression and phrasing.

 **I Do** Explain that good readers change the sound of their voices to show the text's meaning. They also group words into phrases, using punctuation cues. Read the first paragraph of the Comprehension and Fluency passage on **Approaching Reproducibles** pages 253–254. Have students listen for the way you change the sound of your voice and how you group words into phrases. Point out that you read the text in quotation marks as if the person were speaking.

 **We Do** Read the next three paragraphs aloud. Have students repeat each sentence after you, imitating your phrasing and expression. Explain that you changed the sound of your voice to reveal the character's emotions.

 **You Do** Have partners take turns reading sentences from the Comprehension and Fluency passage. Remind them to read dialogue as if the speakers were talking to each other. Listen in and provide corrective feedback as needed by modeling proper fluency.

## IDENTIFY IMPORTANT DETAILS

**TIER 2**

**OBJECTIVES**

CCSS Quote accurately from a text when explaining what the text says explicitly and when drawing inferences from the text. **RL.5.1**

 **I Do** Remind students that in historical fiction, the author includes many details about what the characters say, do, and feel. These details help readers understand how characters respond to each other and events in the story. Details may also show how characters change by the end of the story.

 **We Do** Read the first paragraph of the Comprehension and Fluency passage on **Approaching Reproducibles** pages 253–254. Point out the name of the character, the line of dialogue, and the character's actions. Discuss when the story takes place and how the character feels.

 **You Do** Have students read the rest of the passage. After each paragraph, have them identify important details about what the characters say, do, and feel. Remind students to pay attention to how the characters respond to each other and to events in the story. Review students' lists with them and help them explain why the details they chose are important.

## REVIEW THEME

### OBJECTIVES

**CCSS** Determine a theme of a story, drama, or poem from details in the text, including how characters in a story or drama respond to challenges or how the speaker in a poem reflects upon a topic; summarize the text. **RL.5.2**

 **I Do** Remind students that the theme of a story is the overall message that the author wants to share with readers. The theme usually is not stated directly in the text. Readers can determine the theme by considering what the characters say, do, and feel and how they respond to events in the story.

**We Do** Choral-read the first three paragraphs of the Comprehension and Fluency passage on **Approaching Reproducibles** pages 253–254. Refer to the list of details the students have already compiled about the characters. Model using these details to determine a possible theme, such as: even though it can be a lot of work to contribute to a cause, it is worth it to be able to help others.

 **You Do** Have partners read the rest of the passage and add details to their lists. Then have students use the details about the characters to determine the story's theme.

## SELF-SELECTED READING

### OBJECTIVES

**CCSS** Determine a theme of a story, drama, or poem from details in the text, including how characters in a story or drama respond to challenges or how the speaker in a poem reflects upon a topic; summarize the text. **RL.5.2**

Summarize text to increase understanding.

### Read Independently

Have students choose a historical fiction text for sustained silent reading. Remind students that:

→ they can determine the theme of the story by considering what the characters say and do and how they respond to events.

→ as they read, they should identify the most important details and use them to summarize the text in their own words.

### Read Purposefully

Using Graphic Organizer 102, have students record details about what the characters say, do, and experience and then determine a possible theme based on this information. After they finish, they can conduct a Book Talk about their reading.

→ Students should share their organizers and answer this question: *What did you like most about this story?*

→ They should also tell the group when they summarized portions of text to increase their understanding.

# On Level

**Lexile** 770
*TextEvaluator*™ 46

## OBJECTIVES

**CCSS** Determine a theme of a story, drama, or poem from details in the text, including how characters in a story or drama respond to challenges or how the speaker in a poem reflects upon a topic; summarize the text. **RL.5.2**

**CCSS** Read on-level prose and poetry orally with accuracy, appropriate rate, and expression on successive readings. **RF.5.4b**

## ACADEMIC LANGUAGE

• *historical fiction, summarize, theme, homophones*

• Cognates: *ficción histórica, resumir, tema, homófonos*

## Leveled Reader:
### *Norberto's Hat*

**Leveled Readers**

### Before Reading

#### Preview and Predict

→ Read the Essential Question with students.

→ Have students preview the title, table of contents, and first page of *Norberto's Hat* and predict what they think the selection will be about. Tell them to try to confirm or revise their predictions as they continue reading.

#### Review Genre: Historical Fiction

Tell students that this selection is historical fiction. Explain that historical fiction features settings that could have existed and events that could have happened during a particular period in history. Characters in historical fiction act and speak like real people from that time and place. Historical fiction often includes flashbacks, which describe events that happened before the main action of the story. Have students identify features of historical fiction in *Norberto's Hat*.

### During Reading

#### Close Reading

**Note Taking:** Ask students to use their graphic organizer as they read.

**Pages 2–4** *What is the setting at the beginning of the story?* (a California house in 1962) *Turn to a partner and summarize the events at the beginning of the story.* (David finds a sombrero. His discovery inspires his father to tell him about events during World War II, 20 years earlier.)

**Pages 5–6** *How does the setting of the story change in Chapter 2?* (It changes to Henry Johnson's house in 1943.) *Who is Henry?* (David's father, at 14) *Where is he going?* (a sugar beet farm) *Who are* braceros? (Mexican workers who helped American farmers harvest crops in WWII)

**Pages 7–9** *What happens to Henry's wallet?* (He loses it.) *What does the farm manager think happened?* (A *bracero* stole it.) *What happens at the end of the chapter?* (Norberto, a *bracero,* finds Henry's wallet and returns it. The boys share photographs of their families. Henry asks Norberto to help him learn Spanish, and Norberto agrees.)

**Use Graphic Organizer**

*Using context clues, determine whether the homophone* wore *on page 8 means "had on" or "passed."* (The word *hat* indicates it means "had on.")

**Pages 10–12** *How does Henry thank Norberto for his kindness?* (He invites Norberto to visit his home.) *What problem does Norberto share?* (He worries that the money he sends home isn't being delivered by the courier.) *What does Mrs. Johnson tell him to do?* (use certified mail)

**Pages 13–15** *What exchange takes place?* (Norberto gives Ralf his sombrero. Ralf gives Norberto his cap.) *What does the story tell you about how different people can work together?* (People from different cultures can help each other and contribute to a cause together.)

## After Reading

**Respond to Reading** Revisit the Essential Question and ask students to complete the Text Evidence questions on page 16.

**Write About Reading** Check that students have correctly identified Henry and Mrs. Johnson's attitude toward the *braceros* and how their attitude conveys the author's message.

### Fluency: Expression and Phrasing

**Model** Model reading aloud page 3 with appropriate expression and phrasing. Next reread the page aloud and have students read along.

**Apply** Have students practice reading the passage with partners.

## PAIRED READ

### "The Bracero Program"

**Leveled Reader**

#### Make Connections:
#### Write About It 📝 *Analytical Writing*

Before reading, ask students to note that the genre of this text is expository text. Then discuss the Essential Question. After reading, ask students to make connections between what they learned about how different groups contribute to a cause in *Norberto's Hat* and "The Bracero Program."

### FOCUS ON LITERARY ELEMENTS

Students can extend their knowledge of how authors use flashbacks in fiction by completing the literary elements activity on page 20.

## Literature Circles

Ask students to conduct a literature circle using the Thinkmark questions to guide the discussion. You may wish to have a whole-class discussion, using both selections in the Leveled Reader, about how different groups of people can contribute to a cause.

## Level Up

Level-up lessons available online.

**IF** students read the On Level fluently and answered the questions

**THEN** pair them with students who have proficiently read the Beyond Level and have students

• partner-read the Beyond Level main selection.

• identify two details that help them understand the theme of the story.

### A C T Access Complex Text

The Beyond Level challenges students by requiring more synthesis of information to **connect ideas** and including more **complex sentence structures**.

→ ## On Level

# Vocabulary

## REVIEW VOCABULARY WORDS

**OBJECTIVES**

Acquire and use accurately grade-appropriate general academic and domain-specific words and phrases, including those that signal contrast, addition, and other logical relationships (e.g., *however, although, nevertheless, similarly, moreover, in addition*). **L.5.6**

 **I Do**
Use the **Visual Vocabulary Cards** to review the key selection words *bulletin, enlisted, intercept, operations, recruits,* and *survival*. Point to each word, read it aloud, and have students chorally repeat it.

**We Do**
Ask these questions and help students respond.
→ What might be written on a school *bulletin*?
→ Why might people have *enlisted* in the Army?
→ How can you *intercept* a ball that is thrown to someone near you?

**You Do**
Have students work in pairs to respond to these questions.
→ What *operations* are necessary at your school?
→ What might Navy *recruits* need to learn?
→ How do some animals manage their *survival* in the desert?

## HOMOPHONES

**OBJECTIVES**

Determine or clarify the meaning of unknown and multiple-meaning words and phrases based on *grade 5 reading and content,* choosing flexibly from a range of strategies. Use context (e.g., cause/effect relationships and comparisons in text) as a clue to the meaning of a word or phrase. **L.5.4a**

 **I Do**
Remind students that homophones are words that sound the same but are spelled differently and have different meanings. They can use context clues within the sentence or the paragraph to find the meaning of a homophone. Display the Comprehension and Fluency passage on **Your Turn Practice Book** pages 253–254. Read aloud the first paragraph.

**Think Aloud** I see the homophones *blue* and *blew*. Carlos turned *blue*, so b-l-u-e refers to a color. He *blew* on his hands, so b-l-e-w must refer to breathing out air.

 **We Do**
Have students read aloud the first paragraph on page 254, where they encounter the homophones *past* and *passed*. Point out the context clues they can use to figure out the meaning of each homophone. Ask students to state the meanings of *past* and *passed* in their own words.

 **You Do**
Have partners identify the meanings of: *knew, new* (page 253, paragraph 2); *here, hear* (page 254, paragraphs 2 and 3); *too, to* (page 254, last paragraph).

# Comprehension

## REVIEW THEME

**OBJECTIVES**

Determine a theme of a story, drama, or poem from details in the text, including how characters in a story or drama respond to challenges or how the speaker in a poem reflects upon a topic; summarize the text. **RL.5.2**

 **I Do**

Remind students that the theme of a story is the overall message that the author wants to share with readers. The theme usually is not stated directly in the text. Readers can determine the theme by considering what the characters do and say and how they respond to events in the story.

 **We Do**

Have volunteers read the first three paragraphs of the Comprehension and Fluency passage on **Your Turn Practice Book** pages 253–254. Have students record important details about what the characters do and say and how they respond to events. Guide students to use these details to consider a possible theme.

 **You Do**

Have partners read the rest of the passage. Tell them to pause to identify key details about the characters. Remind them to pay attention to how the characters respond to events. Then have them determine a theme for the passage.

## SELF-SELECTED READING

**OBJECTIVES**

Determine a theme of a story, drama, or poem from details in the text, including how characters in a story or drama respond to challenges or how the speaker in a poem reflects upon a topic; summarize the text. **RL.5.2**

Summarize text to increase understanding.

### Read Independently

Have students choose a historical fiction text for sustained silent reading.

→ Remind them to pay attention to what characters say and do, how they respond to events, and how they change during the course of the story.

→ Tell students to summarize the text by restating the story's important ideas and details in their own words.

### Read Purposefully

Encourage students to read different books to learn about a variety of time periods.

→ Using Graphic Organizer 102, have them record details about what the characters say and do and then use these to determine the theme.

→ They can use this organizer to help write a summary of the book.

→ Ask students to share their reactions to the book with classmates.

# → Beyond Level

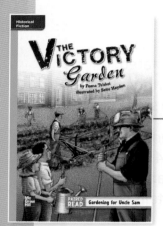

**Lexile** 900
*TextEvaluator™* 51

**OBJECTIVES**

**CCSS** Determine a theme of a story, drama, or poem from details in the text, including how characters in a story or drama respond to challenges or how the speaker in a poem reflects upon a topic; summarize the text. **RL.5.2**

**CCSS** Read on-level prose and poetry orally with accuracy, appropriate rate, and expression on successive readings. **RF.5.4b**

**ACADEMIC LANGUAGE**

• historical fiction, summarize, theme, homophones

• Cognates: *ficción histórica, resumir, tema, homófonos*

## Leveled Reader:
## *The Victory Garden*

### Before Reading

**Preview and Predict**

→ Have students read the Essential Question.

→ Have students preview the title, table of contents, and first page of *The Victory Garden* to make predictions about what might happen in the story. Tell students to find details as they read that help them confirm or revise their predictions.

**Review Genre: Historical Fiction**

Tell students that this selection is historical fiction. Explain that historical fiction features settings that could have existed and events that could have happened during a particular period in history. Characters in historical fiction act and speak like real people from that time and place. Historical fiction often includes flashbacks, which describe events that happened before the main action of the story. Have students identify features of historical fiction in the story.

### During Reading

**Close Reading**

**Note Taking:** Ask students to use their graphic organizer as they read.

**Pages 2–4** *What problem does Betty have?* (Because of rationing shortages during World War II, she cannot buy spinach.) *What is Betty's solution?* (grow her own garden) *Identify the characters and setting in the flashback. What does it show?* (Betty's mom, Lillian, is a young girl in the flashback to World War I. She is speaking with her father about her own garden. It shows that Betty's mom knows that gardens take work.)

**Pages 5–7** *What problem do Betty and her friends discuss?* (where to plant a garden) *Summarize her teacher's feedback.* (He agrees to use the schoolyard for the garden, but says it must be removed if the principal doesn't approve when she returns from the hospital.)

**Pages 8–10** *Allowed* and *aloud* are homophones. What is the meaning of *allowed* at the top of page 8? ("permitted") *Why does Betty address the school assembly?* (to convince other students to participate)

**Go Digital**

**Leveled Readers**

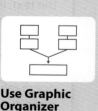

**Use Graphic Organizer**

*How do community members help them prepare?* (Some lend equipment and give seeds. Others volunteer their time and labor.)

**Pages 11–13** *Reread page 11. Summarize how different people help make the garden.* (Dorothy and Eli mark off a rectangle. George and Betty hammer stakes. They all tie twine around the stakes. Mr. Montgomery and others loosen the soil. Robert plows rows of dirt.)

**Pages 14–15** *What happens just after the garden is finished?* (A reporter interviews them.) *What theme does the ending help you identify?* (Different groups can work together to support a helpful cause.)

### After Reading

**Respond to Reading** Revisit the Essential Question and ask students to complete the Text Evidence questions on page 16.

**Analytical Writing** **Write About Reading** Check that students have correctly identified reasons for the garden and how they connect to the theme.

### Fluency: Expression and Phrasing

**Model** Model reading aloud page 2 with appropriate expression and phrasing. Next reread the page aloud and have students read along.

**Apply** Have students practice reading the passage with partners.

### PAIRED READ

## "Gardening for Uncle Sam"

### Make Connections:
**Write About It** **Analytical Writing**

**Leveled Reader**

Before reading, ask students to note that the genre of this selection is expository text. Then discuss the Essential Question. After reading, ask students to write connections between what they learned about how different groups can contribute to a cause in *The Victory Garden* and "Gardening for Uncle Sam."

---

### FOCUS ON LITERARY ELEMENTS

Students can extend their knowledge of how authors use flashbacks in fiction by completing the literary elements activity on page 20.

---

## Literature Circles

Ask students to conduct a literature circle using the Thinkmark questions to guide the discussion. You may wish to have a whole-class discussion, using both selections in the Leveled Reader, about how different groups of people can contribute to a cause.

## Gifted and Talented

**Synthesize** Challenge students to think of what might happen in a sequel to *The Victory Garden*. Students should consider the success that Betty and her friends have with getting the garden started and the different people who become involved. Students could write a brief description of what they think will happen to the characters and their garden, or they could write a historical fiction story about another plan Betty and her friends make to help the war effort.

**Beyond Level**

# Vocabulary

## REVIEW DOMAIN-SPECIFIC WORDS

 **OBJECTIVES**
Acquire and use accurately grade-appropriate general academic and domain-specific words and phrases, including those that signal contrast, addition, and other logical relationships (e.g., *however, although, nevertheless, similarly, moreover, in addition*). **L.5.6**

 **Model** Use the **Visual Vocabulary Cards** to review the meaning of the words *contributions* and *diversity*. Write genre-related sentences on the board using the words.

Write the words *rationing* and *victory* on the board and discuss the meanings with students. Then help students write sentences using these words.

 **Apply** Have students work in pairs to review the meanings of the words *campaign* and *soldiers*. Then have partners write sentences using these words.

## HOMOPHONES

 **OBJECTIVES**
Determine or clarify the meaning of unknown and multiple-meaning words and phrases based on *grade 5 reading and content*, choosing flexibly from a range of strategies. Use context (e.g., cause/effect relationships and comparisons in text) as a clue to the meaning of a word or phrase. **L.5.4a**

 **Model** Read aloud the second paragraph of the Comprehension and Fluency passage on **Beyond Reproducibles** pages 253–254.

**Think Aloud** I see the homophones *knew* and *new*. Carlos says he knew the letter by heart, so *k-n-e-w* relates to understanding or remembering. The letter from Tomás says nothing is new, and he describes things he does every day. So *n-e-w* must mean "different from the old."

With students, read aloud the first paragraph. Point out the homophones *blue* and *blew* and the context clues that explain their meanings.

 **[Apply]** Have pairs of students read the rest of the passage and use context clues to determine the meanings of *past, passed* (page 254, paragraph 1); *here, hear* (page 254, paragraphs 2 and 3); and *too, to* (page 254, paragraph 9).

 *Gifted and Talented* **Analyze** Challenge students to find other words in the passage that have homophones (*be, by, do, for, him, in, missed, not, one, read, war, you*). Have them list the words and their homophones. Have them use three homophone pairs in sentences that include context clues. Tell them to trade papers and have partners check the accuracy of the context clues.

# Comprehension

## REVIEW THEME

**OBJECTIVES**
**CCSS** Determine a theme of a story, drama, or poem from details in the text, including how characters in a story or drama respond to challenges or how the speaker in a poem reflects upon a topic; summarize the text. **RL.5.2**

**Model** Review that the theme of a story is the overall message that the author wants to share with readers. The theme usually is not stated directly in the text. Readers can determine the theme by considering what the characters do and say and how they respond to events in the story.

Have students read the first three paragraphs of the Comprehension and Fluency passage on **Beyond Reproducibles** pages 253–254. Help students identify key details about the characters and their responses to events.

**Apply** As students fill out Graphic Organizer 102 independently, have them identify details about what the characters do, say, and experience. Have them use these details to determine the theme. Then have them share their completed organizers with the class.

## SELF-SELECTED READING

**OBJECTIVES**
**CCSS** Determine a theme of a story, drama, or poem from details in the text, including how characters in a story or drama respond to challenges or how the speaker in a poem reflects upon a topic; summarize the text. **RL.5.2**

Summarize text to increase understanding.

### Read Independently

Have students choose a historical fiction text for sustained silent reading.

→ Have students use Graphic Organizer 102 to record details about what the characters say, do, and experience and use these to determine the theme.

→ Remind students to summarize as they read.

### Read Purposefully

Encourage students to keep a reading journal. Ask them to read a variety of historical fiction texts to increase their understanding of the genre.

→ Students can write summaries of the books in their journals.

→ Ask students to share their reactions to the books with classmates.

**Independent Study** Challenge students to discuss how their books relate to the weekly theme of joining forces. Have them use all of their reading materials to identify how different groups can contribute to a cause.

# English Language Learners

**Reading/Writing Workshop**

## OBJECTIVES

CCSS Quote accurately from a text when explaining what the text says explicitly and when drawing inferences from the text. **RL.5.1**

CCSS Determine a theme of a story, drama, or poem from details in the text, including how characters in a story or drama respond to challenges or how the speaker in a poem reflects upon a topic; summarize the text. **RL.5.2**

## LANGUAGE OBJECTIVE

Identify details that help determine the theme of a story.

## ACADEMIC LANGUAGE

• *summarize, homophones, theme*

• Cognates: *resumir, homófonos, tema*

## Shared Read
### *Shipped Out*

**Go Digital**

View "Shipped Out"

### Before Reading

#### Build Background

Read the Essential Question: *How do different groups contribute to a cause?*

→ Explain the meaning of the Essential Question, including the vocabulary in the question: Contribute *means "to add to or give to something," and a cause is an event or idea that people believe in and support.*

→ **Model an answer:** *During World War II, many different groups of people contributed to the war effort. For example, women went to work in factories. They made airplanes and other equipment for the military. Kids collected scrap metal to be used for artillery.*

→ Ask students a question that ties the Essential Question to their own background knowledge: *Turn to a partner and think of a cause that you or people you know believe in. How do you or the people contribute to the cause?* Call on several pairs.

### During Reading

#### Interactive Question-Response

→ Ask questions that help students understand the meaning of the text after each paragraph.

→ Reinforce the meanings of key vocabulary.

→ Ask students questions that require them to use key vocabulary.

→ Reinforce strategies and skills of the week by modeling.

## Page 382

**Paragraphs 1–2**
Point to "shipped out." Explain that it is a term that means "packed up and left." *Where is Libby living now?* (in a little apartment above a bakery)

**Explain and Model the Strategy** Reread to help students identify the cause to which people are contributing. *The cause in this story is World War II, a war the United States fought from 1941 to 1945.*

Guide students to summarize how Libby's father and mother are contributing to the cause. (Libby's father is a mechanic on a battleship. Her mother works in a factory making jackets for soldiers.)

**Explain and Model Homophones** Choral-read the last sentence in the second paragraph. Point out the homophones *wore* and *war*. Explain how the word *jackets* after *wore* and the phrase *tools they might need* before *war* show the meanings of the words.

**Paragraph 3**
**Explain and Model Theme** *Understanding the challenge that Libby faces can help us understand the theme, or message, of the story.* Choral-read the paragraph. *What problem is Libby having?* Guide students to the answer. (She doesn't think anyone appreciates her creative contributions.)

**Paragraph 4**
Turn to a partner and tell what Libby does at the bakery. (She and her aunt knead the dough and bake bread and muffins. Libby also helps the customers.)

*The word* knead *sounds like another word,* need. *Let's show what the word* knead *means.* Have students imitate your actions as you demonstrate the act of kneading dough.

**Paragraph 5**
*Why does Aunt Lucia invite the neighbors over after dinner?* (to listen to news on the radio) *Do you think Aunt Lucia is contributing to the war effort?* (yes)

## Page 384

**Paragraphs 1–3**
Point out that the action of the first two paragraphs takes place before Libby went to live with her aunt. Explain that this is called a flashback. Have partners summarize what happens in the flashback. (Libby's father tells her that he is joining the navy to help with the war cause.)

**Paragraph 4**
*Why is Aunt Lucia decorating cupcakes?* (She is decorating cupcakes for a fundraiser.) **Explain** that a fundraiser is a way to raise money. They are raising money to buy supplies for the soldiers. Have students complete the sentence: *Libby decorates the cupcakes to look like _____.* (flags)

## Page 385

**Paragraphs 1–2**
*What makes Libby begin to feel better about her contribution to the war cause?* (Her aunt tells her that her cupcakes will sell well at the fundraiser.)

**Paragraph 4**
*Can Libby send a cupcake to her dad?* (no) *What will she do instead?* (She will send him a picture of the cupcakes and a letter.)

Turn to a partner and tell at least two ways people in this story contributed to the war effort. What does this tell you about the theme of the story? (There are many different ways to contribute to important causes.)

### After Reading

**Make Connections**

→ Review the Essential Question.

→ Make text connections and have students complete **ELL Reproducibles** pages 253–255.

# English Language Learners

## Leveled Reader:
### *Norberto's Hat*

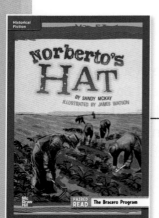

**Lexile** 640
*TextEvaluator* 28

---

**OBJECTIVES**

**CCSS** Determine a theme of a story, drama, or poem from details in the text, including how characters in a story or drama respond to challenges or how the speaker in a poem reflects upon a topic; summarize the text. **RL.5.2**

**CCSS** Read on-level prose and poetry orally with accuracy, appropriate rate, and expression on successive readings. **RF.5.4b**

---

**ACADEMIC LANGUAGE**
- summarize, theme, historical fiction
- Cognates: *resumir, tema, ficción histórica*

### Before Reading

**Preview and Predict**

→ Read the Essential Question: *How do different groups contribute to a cause?*

→ Refer to Giving Our All: *How did different groups contribute to the war effort during World War II?*

→ Preview *Norberto's Hat* and "The Bracero Program": *Our purpose for reading is to learn about how to work together for a common cause.*

**Vocabulary**

Use the **Visual Vocabulary Cards** to pre-teach the ELL vocabulary: *sympathized, repay, engrossed, legacy.* Use the routine found on the cards.

### During Reading

**Interactive Question-Response**

**Note Taking:** Ask students to use the graphic organizer on **ELL Reproducibles** page 252. Use the questions below after each page is read with students. As you read, define vocabulary in context and use visuals to help students understand key vocabulary.

**Pages 2–3** Choral read the chapter title and heading. *Titles and headings tell important details about a story. What is going to happen in Chapter 1?* (David is going to find a hat.) *Does the beginning of the story take place in California?* (yes) *Whose hat was it?* (Uncle Ralf's)

**Pages 4–6** *Whom did the sombrero originally belong to?* (Norberto) *Where is Norberto from?* (Mexico) On a map, show California and Mexico. Choral read the last paragraph on page 4. *What is David's dad doing?* (He is remembering the past.) *Does Henry like his work?* (yes) *Who are braceros?* (Mexican workers who help farmers)

**Pages 7–9** *What happens to Henry's wallet?* (He loses it.) *How does Henry find his wallet?* (Norberto finds it and gives it back.) *What do Henry and Norberto talk about?* (photographs of their families)

Go Digital

**Leveled Readers**

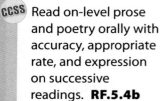
**Use Graphic Organizer**

**Pages 10–12** Point to the illustration and labels on page 11. *What does this picture show?* (Norberto and Henry's family sitting and talking in a room) *How does Mrs. Johnson help Norberto?* (She tells him how to send money to his family.)

**Pages 13–15** Choral read the first four paragraphs on page 14, and have pairs of students pantomime the scene. *Did David's father ever see Norberto again?* (no) *Whom does he meet?* (Norberto's brother, Fidel)

### After Reading

**Respond to Reading** Revisit the Essential Question and ask students to complete the Text Evidence questions on page 16.

**Analytical Writing** **Write About Reading** Check that students have correctly identified Henry and Mrs. Johnson's attitude toward the *braceros* and how their attitude conveys the author's message.

### Fluency: Expression and Phrasing

**Model** Model reading page 2 with proper expression and phrasing. Next, reread the page aloud and have students read along with you.

**Apply** Have students practice reading with partners.

### PAIRED READ

## "The Bracero Program"

### Make Connections: Write About It **Analytical Writing**

**Leveled Reader**

Before reading, ask students to note that the genre of this selection is expository text. Then discuss the Essential Question. After reading, ask students to list connections between what they learned from *Norberto's Hat* and "The Bracero Program."

### FOCUS ON LITERARY ELEMENTS

Students can extend their knowledge of how flashbacks are used in stories by completing the literary elements activity on page 20.

## Literature Circles

Ask students to conduct a literature circle using the Thinkmark questions to guide the discussion. You may wish to have a whole-class discussion about how different groups of people can contribute to a cause using information from both selections in the Leveled Reader.

## Level Up

Level-up lessons available online.

**IF** students read the **ELL Level** fluently and answered the questions

**THEN** pair them with students who have proficiently read **On Level** and have ELL students

• echo-read the **On Level** main selection.

• list words with which they have difficulty and discuss them with a partner.

### A C T Access Complex Text

The **On Level** challenges students by including a more complex **organization** and **complex sentence structures**.

→ # English Language Learners
## Vocabulary

## PRETEACH VOCABULARY

**OBJECTIVES**
CCSS Acquire and use accurately grade-appropriate general academic and domain-specific words and phrases, including those that signal contrast, addition, and other logical relationships. **L.5.6**

**LANGUAGE OBJECTIVE**
Use vocabulary words.

 **I Do** Preteach vocabulary from "Shipped Out" following the Vocabulary Routine found on the **Visual Vocabulary Cards** for the words *bulletin, contributions, diversity, enlisted, intercept, operations, recruits,* and *survival.*

 **We Do** After completing the Vocabulary Routine for each word, point to the word on the card and read the word with students. Ask them to repeat the word.

**You Do** Have students work with a partner to use two or more words in sentences or questions. Then have each pair read the sentences aloud.

| Beginning | Intermediate | Advanced/High |
|---|---|---|
| Help students write the sentences correctly and read them aloud. | Ask students to write one sentence and one question. | Challenge students to write one sentence and one question for each word. |

## REVIEW VOCABULARY

**OBJECTIVES**
CCSS Acquire and use accurately grade-appropriate general academic and domain-specific words and phrases, including those that signal contrast, addition, and other logical relationships. **L.5.6**

**LANGUAGE OBJECTIVE**
Use vocabulary words.

 **I Do** Review the previous week's vocabulary words. The words can be reviewed over a few days. Read each word aloud, pointing to the word on the **Visual Vocabulary Card**. Have students repeat after you. Then follow the Vocabulary Routine on the back of each card.

 **We Do** Review the words quickly again. Then model saying a sentence and omit the vocabulary word for students to guess.

 **You Do** Have partners write sentences for all of the words, omitting the vocabulary word in each sentence. Ask them to read the sentences aloud for the class to guess the missing word.

| Beginning | Intermediate | Advanced/High |
|---|---|---|
| Help students read aloud the sentences and determine the missing words. | Ask students to include a context clue in each sentence. | Have students use two or more vocabulary words in each sentence. |

# HOMOPHONES

**OBJECTIVES**

 Determine or clarify the meaning of unknown and multiple-meaning words and phrases based on grade 5 reading and content, choosing flexibly from a range of strategies. Use context (e.g., cause/effect relationships and comparisons in text) as a clue to the meaning of a word or phrase. **L.5.4a**

**LANGUAGE OBJECTIVE**
Identify and use homophones.

 **I Do** Read aloud the first paragraph of the Comprehension and Fluency passage on **ELL Reproducibles** pages 253–254 while students follow along. Point to the homophones *blue* and *blew*. Explain that identifying context clues will help them figure out the meaning of each homophone.

**Think Aloud** Carlos was turning blue from the cold, so I think that *blue* refers to the color. He blew on his hands to make them warm, so *blew* must mean he breathed air on them.

 **We Do** Have students point to the homophones *knew* and *new* in the second paragraph on page 253. Explain that the context clue *by heart* tells that *knew* has to do with understanding. The context clues *nothing* and *every day* tell that *new* refers to things that happen recently. Ask students to give the meanings of *knew* and *new* in their own words.

 **You Do** Have partners use context clues to determine the meaning of *past, passed* (page 254, paragraph 1); *here, hear* (page 254, paragraphs 2 and 3); and *too, to* (page 254, paragraph 9).

| **Beginning** | **Intermediate** | **Advanced/High** |
|---|---|---|
| Help students locate the homophones on the page and read them aloud. | Have students find the homophones on the page and locate context clues. | Have students explain how they used context to find meaning of homophones. |

# ADDITIONAL VOCABULARY

**OBJECTIVES**

 Acquire and use accurately grade-appropriate general academic and domain-specific words and phrases, including those that signal contrast, addition, and other logical relationships. **L.5.6**

**LANGUAGE OBJECTIVE**
Use academic vocabulary and high-frequency words.

 **I Do** List some academic vocabulary and high-frequency words from "Shipped Out": *immigrants, military, navy*; and *Norberto's Hat*: *harvest, fascinated, wallet*. Define each word for students: *Immigrants are people who have come to live in a new land.*

 **We Do** Model using the words for students in a sentence: *Immigrants may need to learn a new language. Many of Aunt Lucia's neighbors are immigrants.* Then provide sentence frames and complete them with students: *Immigrants may come to the United States from _____.*

 **You Do** Have pairs make up their own sentences and share them with the class to complete them.

| **Beginning** | **Intermediate** | **Advanced/High** |
|---|---|---|
| Provide sentence frames and help students correctly complete them. | Provide sentence starters for students, if necessary. | Have students define the words they used and give related words when possible. |

English Language Learners

# Writing/Spelling

## WRITING TRAIT: ORGANIZATION

 **OBJECTIVES**
Produce clear and coherent writing in which the development and organization are appropriate to task, purpose, and audience. **W.5.4**

**LANGUAGE OBJECTIVE**
Use sequence of events in writing.

 **I Do** Explain that good writers organize their writing in a logical way. Writers use time-order words to show the sequence of events, or what happens first, next, and last. Read the Expert Model passage aloud as students follow along. Point out time-order words that show sequence.

 **We Do** Read aloud the fourth paragraph on page 384 of "Shipped Out". Identify the sequence of events in the passage. Use a sequence chart to record the time-order words and the events they signal. Model writing sentences that include time-order words and a sequence of events.

**You Do** Have partners write their own short paragraph, using the same chart. They should use time-order words to write the sequence of events.

| Beginning | Intermediate | Advanced/High |
|---|---|---|
| Help students copy the edited sentences. | Have students revise, checking for correct use of time-order words, and edit for errors. | Have students revise, adding time-order words and events, and edit for errors. |

## SPELL WORDS WITH GREEK ROOTS

 **OBJECTIVES**
Spell grade-appropriate words correctly, consulting references as needed. **L.5.2e**

**LANGUAGE OBJECTIVE**
Spell words with Greek roots.

**I Do** Read aloud the Spelling Words on page T36, segmenting them into syllables and stressing the Greek root. Point out that some of the roots have one syllable, while others have two syllables.

 **We Do** Read the Dictation Sentences on page T37 aloud for students. With each sentence, read the underlined word slowly, stressing the Greek root. Have students repeat after you and write the words.

 **You Do** Display the words. Have students exchange their list with a partner to check the spelling and write the words correctly.

| Beginning | Intermediate | Advanced/High |
|---|---|---|
| Have students copy the words with correct spelling and say them aloud. | After students make corrections, have pairs quiz each other. | Have students make corrections, then tell why some words were difficult. |

# Grammar

## ADVERBS

**OBJECTIVES**

Demonstrate command of the conventions of standard English grammar and usage when writing or speaking. Explain the function of nouns, pronouns, verbs, adjectives, and adverbs in general and their functions in particular sentences. **L.3.1a**

**LANGUAGE OBJECTIVE**

Identify and use adverbs.

**Language Transfers Handbook**

Speakers of Cantonese and Korean may put the adverb before the verb as they do in their native languages. In Haitian Creole and Hmong, adjectives and adverb forms are interchangeable. Work with students to identify adverbs and point out their position in the sentence.

 **I Do**

Tell students that an adverb describes a verb, an adjective, or another adverb. Compare adverbs with adjectives and tell how they are different. Explain that adverbs tell more about how an action happens; when, where, or how often it happens; how much; and the intensity of the action. Write the following sentences on the board, underline the adverb, and explain its function: *Josh turned <u>slowly</u>.* (how an action happens); *Grandma arrived <u>yesterday</u>.* (when); *Put the bag <u>here</u>.* (where); *<u>Sometimes</u> we play games.* (how often); *We wrote <u>many</u> letters.* (how much); *She was <u>totally</u> surprised.* (intensity)

**We Do**

Write the sentence frames below on the board. Identify the function of the adverb in each sentence and have students name appropriate adverbs to fill in the blank. Then read the completed sentences aloud for students to repeat.

> *Lynn spoke _____ to the baby.* (how)
>
> *Please call me _____.* (when)
>
> *The dish belongs _____.* (where)
>
> *You should _____ forget your manners.* (how frequently)
>
> *Did you spend _____ time on your homework?* (how much)
>
> *The blizzard turned the yard _____ white.* (intensity)

 **You Do**

Write the words *how, when, where, how frequently, how much,* and *intensity* in columns on the board. Have partners name an adverb that belongs in each column. Have them choose one adverb from each column and write it in a sentence.

| Beginning | Intermediate | Advanced/High |
|---|---|---|
| Help students copy their sentences and help them underline the adverb. Read the sentence aloud for students to repeat. | Ask students to underline the adverb and indicate the word it modifies. | Have students underline the adverb and tell the word it modifies. Ask them to explain how they identified the adverb and the word it modifies. |

For extra support, have students complete the activities in the **Grammar Practice Reproducibles** during the week, using the routine below.

→ Explain the grammar skill.

→ Model the first activity in the Grammar Practice Reproducibles.

→ Have the whole group complete the next couple of activities, then do the rest with a partner.

→ Review the activities with correct answers.

# PROGRESS MONITORING

## Weekly Assessment

**TESTED SKILLS**

| ✓COMPREHENSION: | ✓VOCABULARY: | ✓WRITING: |
|---|---|---|
| Theme **RL.5.2** | Homophones **L.5.4a** | Writing About Text **RL.5.2, W.5.9a** |

### Assessment Includes

→ Performance Tasks

→ Approaching-Level Assessment online PDFs

**Fluency Goal** 129 to 149 words correct per minute (WCPM)

**Accuracy Rate Goal** 95% or higher

Administer oral reading fluency assessments using the following schedule:

→ **Weeks 1, 3, 5** Provide Approaching-Level students at least three oral reading fluency assessments during the unit.

→ **Weeks 2 and 4** Provide On-Level students at least two oral reading fluency assessments during the unit.

→ **Week 6** If necessary, provide Beyond-Level students an oral reading fluency assessment at this time.

**Also Available: Selection Tests online PDFs**

*Go Digital!* www.connected.mcgraw-hill.com

# Using Assessment Results

| TESTED SKILLS | If ... | Then ... |
|---|---|---|
| **COMPREHENSION** | Students answer 0–6 multiple-choice items correctly ... | ... assign Lessons 34–36 on Theme from the *Tier 2 Comprehension Intervention online PDFs.* |
| **VOCABULARY** | Students answer 0–6 multiple-choice items correctly ... | ... assign Lesson 170 on Homographs and Homophones from the *Tier 2 Vocabulary Intervention online PDFs.* |
| **WRITING** | Students score less than "3" on the constructed responses ... | ... assign Lessons 34–36 on Theme and/or Write About Reading Lesson 194 from the *Tier 2 Comprehension Intervention online PDFs.* |
| **FLUENCY** | Students have a WCPM score of 120–128 ... | ... assign a lesson from Section 1, 7, 8, 9, or 10 of the *Tier 2 Fluency Intervention online PDFs.* |
| | Students have a WCPM score of 0–119 ... | ... assign a lesson from Section 2, 3, 4, 5, or 6 of the *Tier 2 Fluency Intervention online PDFs.* |

# Response to Intervention

Use the appropriate sections of the *Placement and Dignostic Assessment* as well as students' assessment results to designate students requiring:

 **Intervention Online PDFs**

 **WonderWorks Intervention Program**

McGraw-Hill Reading
**Wonders**

**Reading/Writing Workshop**

Mc Graw Hill

## TEACH AND MODEL

CCSS **Shared Read** Genre · Realistic Fiction

**The Bully**

**Essential Question**
What actions can we take to get along with others?

Read about how one student tries to deal with a bully.

396

Michael saw the trouble coming from all the way at the end of the school hallway. There standing by the stairs was J.T., the school bully who enjoyed **taunting** anyone he felt like at any given moment. J.T. was tall and strong, so few of his victims were willing to stand up to him and defend themselves. Michael hated the idea that he let J.T. get away with these offenses. Yet like most of the other kids who were picked on, he just took it quietly and waited for the unpleasant moment to pass.

J.T. walked directly toward Michael, his eyes locked on the books that Michael carried under his arms. When they met in the middle of the hallway, J.T. stopped **abruptly** and snapped at Michael, "Hey, let me see those books!" A group of students watched as Michael held out the books he was carrying, trying not to tremble to reveal how nervous he was.

J.T. grabbed a math book, looked inside for a second, and then shoved the book at Michael, who dropped all the books he held. "Hey, those books are school property," J.T. barked, "so don't let them fall to the floor!" Then he walked away, laughing loudly.

Michael, his cheeks turning red, half kicked the fallen books. Suddenly a hand appeared beside Michael and picked up an adventure novel as it slid away. "You look like you could use an **ally**," a friendly voice said with a laugh.

397

## ✔ Vocabulary

abruptly

ally

collided

confident

conflict

intervene

protective

taunting

## 🔍 Close Reading of Complex Text

**Shared Read** "The Bully," 396–403

**Genre** Realistic Fiction

**Lexile** 850L

ⒺⓉⓈ *TextEvaluator™* 32

## Minilessons

 **Tested Skills** CCSS

| | |
|---|---|
| ✔ **Comprehension Strategy** | Summarize, T82–T83 |
| ✔ **Comprehension Skill** | Theme, T84–T85 |
| ✔ **Genre** | Realistic Fiction, T86–T87 |
| ✔ **Vocabulary Strategy** | Connotation and Denotation, T88–T89 |
| ✔ **Writing Traits** | Word Choice, T94–T95 |
| **Grammar Handbook** | Adverbs That Compare, T98–T99 |

☞ **Go** Digital

www.connected.mcgraw-hill.com

# APPLY WITH CLOSE READING

## Complex Text

**Literature Anthology**

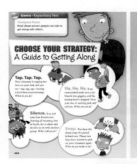

**PAIRED READ**

*The Friend Who Changed My Life,* 450–461
**Genre** Realistic Fiction
**Lexile** 860L
ETS *TextEvaluator* 56

"Choose Your Strategy: A Guide to Getting Along," 464–467
**Genre** Expository Text
**Lexile** 850L
ETS *TextEvaluator* 42

## Differentiated Text

**Leveled Readers**   *Include Paired Reads*

APPROACHING
**Lexile** 680L
ETS *TextEvaluator* 43

ON LEVEL
**Lexile** 840L
ETS *TextEvaluator* 56

BEYOND
**Lexile** 900L
ETS *TextEvaluator* 50

ELL
**Lexile** 700L
ETS *TextEvaluator* 27

## Extended Complex Text

*No Talking*
**Genre** Realistic Fiction
**Lexile** 820L
ETS *TextEvaluator* 45

*The Midnight Fox*
**Genre** Realistic Fiction
**Lexile** 990L
ETS *TextEvaluator* 45

**Classroom Library**

Classroom Library lessons available online.

No Talking: Illustration © Mark Elliott

# TEACH AND MANAGE

## How You Teach

### INTRODUCE

**Weekly Concept**
Getting Along

**Reading/Writing Workshop**
392–393

### TEACH

**Close Reading**
"The Bully"

**Minilessons**
Summarize, Theme, Realistic Fiction, Connotation and Denotation, Writing Traits

**Reading/Writing Workshop**
396–405

### APPLY

**Close Reading**
*The Friend Who Changed My Life*

"Choose Your Strategy: A Guide to Getting Along"

**Literature Anthology**
450–467

**Go Digital**

Interactive Whiteboard | Interactive Whiteboard | Mobile

## How Students Practice

### WEEKLY CONTRACT

**PDF Online**

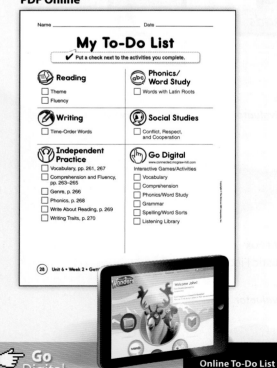

### LEVELED PRACTICE AND ONLINE ACTIVITIES

**Your Turn Practice Book**
261–270

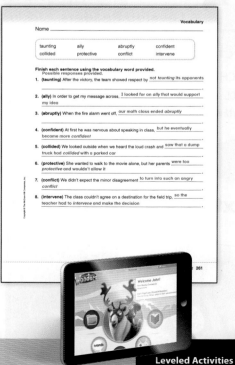

**Leveled Readers**

**Go Digital**

Online To-Do List | Leveled Activities | Writer's Workspace

## DIFFERENTIATE

**SMALL GROUP INSTRUCTION**

**Leveled Readers**

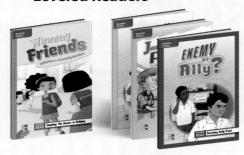

## INTEGRATE

**Research and Inquiry**
Oral Presentation, T92

**Text Connections**
Compare Stories and Texts, T93

**Write About Reading**
 Write an Analysis, T93

## ASSESS

**Weekly Assessment**
313–324

Mobile

Online Research
and Writing

Online
Assessment

## LEVELED WORKSTATION CARDS

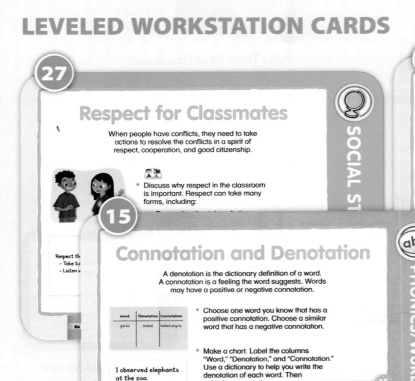

**27**

### Respect for Classmates

When people have conflicts, they need to take actions to resolve the conflicts in a spirit of respect, cooperation, and good citizenship.

• Discuss why respect in the classroom is important. Respect can take many forms, including:

Respect the
- Take tu
- Listen w

SOCIAL ST

**15**

### Connotation and Denotation

A denotation is the dictionary definition of a word. A connotation is a feeling the word suggests. Words may have a positive or negative connotation.

| Word | Denotation | Connotation |
|------|-----------|-------------|
| glared | looked | looked angrily |

I observed elephants at the zoo.

The woman glared at me, and I knew she was angry.

• Choose one word you know that has a positive connotation. Choose a similar word that has a negative connotation.

• Make a chart. Label the columns "Word," "Denotation," and "Connotation." Use a dictionary to help you write the denotation of each word. Then write the connotation.

• Use one of the words in a sentence. Give it to a partner. Can your partner say what the connotation of the word is?

**You need**
› dictionary
› paper and pen or pencil

PHONICS/WORD STUDY

**19**

### Word Choice: Time-Order Words

Saturday
Today, I went to the dinosaur museum with Uncle Jim. At the end of the day, we took the bus home. After lunch, I watched a skit about dinosaur fossils. First, I looked at the huge dinosaur model rex. I learned about d flew. I ate lunch.

• What time-order words does Mark use?

• Revise and rewrite Mark's journal entry to put the events

WRITING

**6**

### Theme

The theme of a story is the message about life that the author wants to share.

• Choose a story you and your partner have read that made you think about your own life.

• Identify the main character and answer the character questions in the graphic organizer. Talk about what all the character details have in common.

| What Does the Character Do and Say? | What Happens to the Character? |
|---|---|

• Write the theme in the organizer. How can you connect the author's message to your own life?

**You need**
› story
› paper and pen or pencil

READING

More
Activities
on back

# DEVELOPING READERS AND WRITERS

## Write to Sources and Research

Theme, T84–T85

Note Taking, T89B, T89P

Summarize, T89N

Theme, T89N

Make Connections: Essential Question, T89N, 789R, T93

Key Details, T89Q

Research and Inquiry, T92

Analyze to Share an Opinion, T93

Comparing Texts, T105, T113, T117, T123

Predictive Writing, T89B

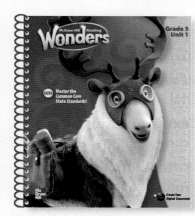

**Teacher's Edition**

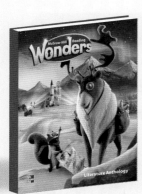

Summarize, p. 463
Theme, p. 463

**Literature Anthology**

**Interactive Whiteboard**

**Leveled Readers**
Comparing Texts
Theme

Theme, pp. 263–265
Genre, p. 266
Analyze to Share an Opinion, p. 269

**Your Turn Practice Book**

---

**Opinion Text**
Book Review, T344–T349

**Conferencing Routines**
Teacher Conferences, T346
Peer Conferences, T347

**Interactive Whiteboard**

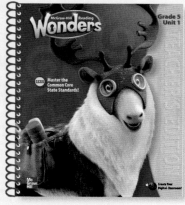

**Teacher's Edition**

**Leveled Workstation Card**
Reviews, Card 26

**Writer's Workspace**
Opinion Text: Book Review
Writing Process
Multimedia Presentations

## Writing Traits • Write Every Day

**Writing Trait: Word Choice**
Time-Order Words, T94–T95

**Conferencing Routines**
Teacher Conferences, T96
Peer Conferences, T97

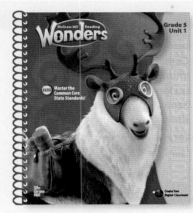
**Teacher's Edition**

Word Choice:
Time-Order Words,
pp. 404–405
**Reading/Writing Workshop**

**Interactive
Whiteboard**

Word Choice:
Time-Order
Words, 19
**Leveled Workstation Card**

Word Choice: Time-
Order Words, p. 270
**Your Turn Practice Book**

## Grammar and Spelling

**Grammar**
Adverbs That Compare,
T98–T99

**Spelling**
Words with Latin Roots,
T100–T101

**Interactive
Whiteboard**

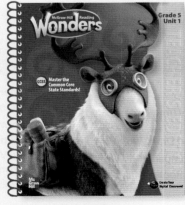
**Teacher's Edition**

Adverbs that Compare

Words with
Latin Roots
Word Sorts

**Online Spelling and Grammar Games**

# SUGGESTED LESSON PLAN

| | | **DAY 1** | **DAY 2** |
|---|---|---|---|

## ✓ TESTED SKILLS CCSS

### READING

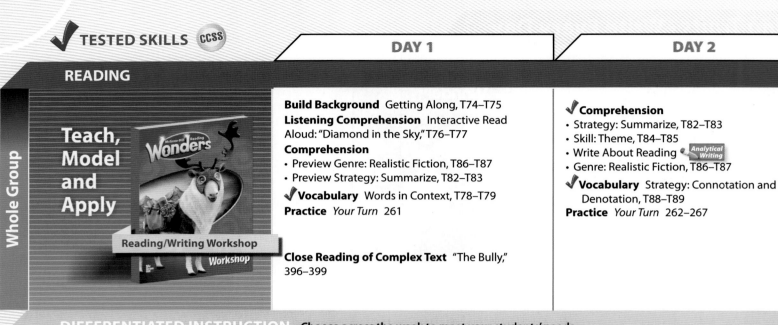

**Teach, Model and Apply**
Reading/Writing Workshop

**DAY 1**

**Build Background** Getting Along, T74–T75
**Listening Comprehension** Interactive Read Aloud: "Diamond in the Sky," T76–T77
**Comprehension**
• Preview Genre: Realistic Fiction, T86–T87
• Preview Strategy: Summarize, T82–T83
✓ **Vocabulary** Words in Context, T78–T79
**Practice** *Your Turn* 261

**Close Reading of Complex Text** "The Bully," 396–399

**DAY 2**

✓ **Comprehension**
• Strategy: Summarize, T82–T83
• Skill: Theme, T84–T85
• Write About Reading *Analytical Writing*
• Genre: Realistic Fiction, T86–T87
✓ **Vocabulary** Strategy: Connotation and Denotation, T88–T89
**Practice** *Your Turn* 262–267

---

### DIFFERENTIATED INSTRUCTION — Choose across the week to meet your students' needs.

#### Approaching Level

**DAY 1**
**Leveled Reader** *Winning Friends*, T104–T105
**Word Study/Decoding** Review Words with Latin Roots, T106
**Vocabulary**
• Review High-Frequency Words, T108 (TIER 2)
• Identify Related Words, T109

**DAY 2**
**Leveled Reader** *Winning Friends*, T104–T105
**Vocabulary** Review Vocabulary Words, T108 (TIER 2)
**Comprehension**
• Identify Important Details, T110 (TIER 2)
• Review Theme, T111

#### On Level

**DAY 1**
**Leveled Reader** *Enemy or Ally?*, T112–T113
**Vocabulary** Review Vocabulary Words, T114

**DAY 2**
**Leveled Reader** *Enemy or Ally?*, T112–T113
**Comprehension** Review Theme, T115

#### Beyond Level

**DAY 1**
**Leveled Reader** *Jamayla to the Rescue*, T116–T117
**Vocabulary** Review Domain-Specific Words, T118

**DAY 2**
**Leveled Reader** *Jamayla to the Rescue*, T116–T117
**Comprehension** Review Theme, T119

#### English Language Learners

**DAY 1**
**Shared Read** "The Bully," T120–T121
**Word Study/Decoding** Review Words with Latin Roots, T106
**Vocabulary**
• Preteach Vocabulary, T124
• Review High-Frequency Words, T108

**DAY 2**
**Leveled Reader** *Enemy or Ally?*, T122–T123
**Vocabulary** Review Vocabulary, T124
**Writing** Writing Trait: Word Choice, T126
**Grammar** Adverbs That Compare, T127

---

### LANGUAGE ARTS — Writing Process: Book Review T344–T349 — Use with Weeks 1–3

#### Writing, Grammar, Spelling, Build Vocabulary

**DAY 1**
✓ **Readers to Writers**
• Writing Trait: Word Choice/Time-Order Words, T94–T95
• Writing Entry: Prewrite and Draft, T96
**Grammar** Adverbs That Compare, T98
**Spelling** Words with Latin Roots, T100
**Build Vocabulary**
• Connect to Words, T102
• Academic Vocabulary, T102

**DAY 2**
**Readers to Writers**
• Writing Entry: Revise, T96
**Grammar** Adverbs That Compare, T98
**Spelling** Words with Latin Roots, T100
**Build Vocabulary**
• Expand Vocabulary, T102
• Review Adages and Proverbs, T102

| DAY 3 | DAY 4 | DAY 5  Review and Assess |
|---|---|---|

## READING

**Word Study/Decoding** Words with Latin Roots, T90–T91
**Practice** *Your Turn* 268

**Close Reading** *The Friend Who Changed My Life*, 450–463
*Analytical Writing*

Literature Anthology

**Fluency** Intonation, T91
**Integrate Ideas** *Analytical Writing*
• Research and Inquiry, T92

**Practice** *Your Turn* 263–265

**Close Reading** "Choose Your Strategy: A Guide to Getting Along," 464–467 *Analytical Writing*

**Integrate Ideas** *Analytical Writing*
• Research and Inquiry, T92
• Text Connections, T93
• Write About Reading, T93

**Practice** *Your Turn* 269

## DIFFERENTIATED INSTRUCTION

**Leveled Reader** *Winning Friends*, T104–T105
**Word Study/Decoding** Build Words with Latin Roots, T106 🔵TIER 2
**Fluency** Intonation, T110 🔵TIER 2
**Vocabulary** Connotation and Denotation, T109

**Leveled Reader** Paired Read: "Empathy: The Answer to Bullying," T105 *Analytical Writing*
**Word Study/Decoding** Practice Words with Latin Roots, T107

**Leveled Reader** Literature Circle, T105
**Comprehension** Self-Selected Reading, T111

---

**Leveled Reader** *Enemy or Ally?*, T112–T113
**Vocabulary** Connotation and Denotation, T114

**Leveled Reader** Paired Read: "Becoming Bully Proof," T113 *Analytical Writing*

**Leveled Reader** Literature Circle, T113
**Comprehension** Self-Selected Reading, T115

---

**Leveled Reader** *Jamayla to the Rescue*, T116–T117
**Vocabulary**
• Connotation and Denotation, T118
• Analyze, T118
*Gifted and Talented*

**Leveled Reader** Paired Read: "Bullying," T117
*Analytical Writing*

**Leveled Reader** Literature Circle, T117
**Comprehension**
• Self-Selected Reading, T119
• Independent Study: Get Along, T119
*Gifted and Talented*

---

**Leveled Reader** *Enemy or Ally?*, T122–T123
**Word Study/Decoding** Build Words with Latin Roots, T106
**Vocabulary** Connotation and Denotation, T125
**Spelling** Words with Latin Roots, T126

**Leveled Reader** Paired Read: "Becoming Bully Proof," T123 *Analytical Writing*
**Vocabulary** Additional Vocabulary, T125
**Word Study/Decoding** Practice Words with Latin Roots, T107

**Leveled Reader** Literature Circle, T123

## LANGUAGE ARTS

**Readers to Writers**
• Writing Entry: Prewrite and Draft, T97

**Grammar** Mechanics and Usage, T99
**Spelling** Words with Latin Roots, T101
**Build Vocabulary**
• Reinforce the Words, T103
• Connotation and Denotation, T103

**Readers to Writers**
• Writing Entry: Revise, T97

**Grammar** Adverbs That Compare, T99
**Spelling** Words with Latin Roots, T101
**Build Vocabulary**
• Connect to Writing, T103
• Shades of Meaning, T103

**Readers to Writers**
• Writing Entry: Share and Reflect, T97

**Grammar** Adverbs That Compare, T99
**Spelling** Words with Latin Roots, T101
**Build Vocabulary**
• Word Squares, T103
• Morphology, T103

# DIFFERENTIATE TO ACCELERATE

 **Scaffold to Access Complex Text**

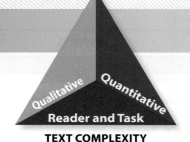

**IF** ▶ the text complexity of a particular selection is too difficult for students

**THEN** ▶ see the references noted in the chart below for scaffolded instruction to help students Access Complex Text.

Qualitative / Quantitative
**Reader and Task**
**TEXT COMPLEXITY**

| | **Reading/Writing Workshop** | **Literature Anthology** | **Leveled Readers** | | **Classroom Library** |
|---|---|---|---|---|---|

## Quantitative

**Reading/Writing Workshop**

"The Bully"
Lexile 850
TextEvaluator™ 32

**Literature Anthology**

*The Friend Who Changed My Life*
Lexile 860
TextEvaluator™ 56

"Choose Your Strategy: A Guide to Getting Along"
Lexile 850
TextEvaluator™ 42

**Leveled Readers**

**Approaching Level**
Lexile 680
TextEvaluator™ 43

**Beyond Level**
Lexile 900
TextEvaluator™ 50

**On Level**
Lexile 840
TextEvaluator™ 56

**ELL**
Lexile 700
TextEvaluator™ 27

**Classroom Library**

*No Talking*
Lexile 820
TextEvaluator™ 45

*The Midnight Fox*
Lexile 990
TextEvaluator™ 45

## Qualitative

**What Makes the Text Complex?**

• **Connection of Ideas** Inferences T81
• **Specific Vocabulary** Proverbs T85

**What Makes the Text Complex?**

• **Specific Vocabulary** Figurative Language T89A; Sarcasm T89C; Context Clues T89G, T89K, T89Q
• **Organization** Pacing T89F; Plot and Setting T89I
• **Connection of Ideas** Read On T89D; Past Events T89E
• **Purpose** Explain T89O

**What Makes the Text Complex?**

• **Specific Vocabulary**
• **Sentence Structure**
• **Connection of Ideas**
• **Genre**

**What Makes the Text Complex?**

• Genre
• Specific Vocabulary
• Prior Knowledge
• Sentence Structure
• Organization
• Purpose
• Connection of Ideas

**ACT** *See Scaffolded Instruction in Teacher's Edition T81 and T85.*

**ACT** *See Scaffolded Instruction in Teacher's Edition T89A–T89R.*

**ACT** *See Level Up lessons online for Leveled Readers.*

**ACT** *See Scaffolded Instruction in Teacher's Edition T360-T361.*

## Reader and Task

The Introduce the Concept lesson on pages T74–T75 will help determine the reader's knowledge and engagement in the weekly concept. See pages T80–T89 and T92–T93 for questions and tasks for this text.

The Introduce the Concept lesson on pages T74–T75 will help determine the reader's knowledge and engagement in the weekly concept. See pages T89A–T89R and T92–T93 for questions and tasks for this text.

The Introduce the Concept lesson on pages T74–T75 will help determine the reader's knowledge and engagement in the weekly concept. See pages T104–T105, T112–T113, T116–T117, T122–T123, and T92–T93 for questions and tasks for this text.

The Introduce the Concept lesson on pages T74–T75 will help determine the reader's knowledge and engagement in the weekly concept. See pages T360-T361 for questions and tasks for this text.

## Monitor and *Differentiate*

**IF** → you need to differentiate instruction

**THEN** → use the Quick Checks to assess students' needs and select the appropriate small group instruction focus.

### ✓ Quick Check

**Comprehension Strategy** Summarize T83
**Comprehension Skill** Theme T85
**Genre** Realistic Fiction T87
**Vocabulary Strategy** Connotation and Denotation T89
**Word Study/Fluency** Words with Latin Roots, Intonation T91

**If No →**

| Approaching Level | Reteach T104–T111 |
| ELL | Develop T120–T127 |

**If Yes →**

| On Level | Review T112–T115 |
| Beyond Level | Extend T116–T119 |

## Level Up with Leveled Readers

**IF** → students can read their leveled text fluently and answer comprehension questions

**THEN** → work with the next level up to accelerate students' reading with more complex text.

T113

On Level

T105    T123

## ENGLISH LANGUAGE LEARNERS
### SCAFFOLD

**IF** → ELL students need additional support    **THEN** → scaffold instruction using the small group suggestions.

| Reading/Writing Workshop "The Bully" T120–T121 | Leveled Reader *Enemy or Ally?* T122–T123 "Becoming Bully Proof" T123 | Additional Vocabulary T125 apologize  enemies offenses  intervene electricity  trouble | Connotation and Denotation T125 | Writing Trait: Word Choice T126 | Spelling Words with Latin Roots T126 | Grammar Adverbs That Compare T127 |
| --- | --- | --- | --- | --- | --- | --- |

**Note: Include ELL Students in all small groups based on their needs.**

# → Introduce the Concept

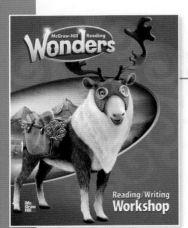

**Reading/Writing Workshop**

## OBJECTIVES

**CCSS** Engage effectively in a range of collaborative discussions (one-on-one, in groups, and teacher-led) with diverse partners on *grade 5 topics and texts,* building on others' ideas and expressing their own clearly. Follow agreed-upon rules for discussions and carry out assigned roles. **SL.5.1b**

Build background knowledge on solving conflicts.

## ACADEMIC LANGUAGE
• *conflict, intervene*
• Cognates: *conflicto, intervenir*

**MINILESSON 10 Mins**

## Build Background

### ESSENTIAL QUESTION
***What actions can we take to get along with others?***

Have students read the Essential Question on page 392 of the **Reading/Writing Workshop**. Tell them that when we don't get along with others, a **conflict,** or a disagreement, can occur. Sometimes a third party may need to **intervene**, or get involved, to help solve the disagreement.

Discuss the photograph of the animals on the crowded beach. Focus on how the animals are living together without **conflict.**

→ These penguins and seals are different in many ways, but they are able to live together and share the same space peacefully.

→ Animals communicate with each other in their own way. A King Penguin knows its chick's voice among the masses. Sometimes it may need to **intervene** to help a chick in trouble.

## Talk About It

COLLABORATE

**Ask:** *How did you resolve a* ***conflict*** *with another person? Did someone have to* ***intervene****, or were you able to resolve the problem on your own?* Explain. Have students discuss in pairs or groups.

→ Generate words and phrases related to getting along with others. Model adding them to the graphic organizer.

→ Have partners discuss what they have learned about getting along with others. Have them add related ideas to the organizer.

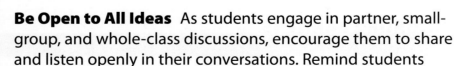

### Collaborative Conversations

**Be Open to All Ideas** As students engage in partner, small-group, and whole-class discussions, encourage them to share and listen openly in their conversations. Remind students

→ that all ideas, questions, or comments should be heard.

→ to ask a question if something is unclear.

→ to respect the opinions of others.

→ to offer opinions, even if they are different from others' viewpoints.

## Go Digital

**Discuss the Concept**

**Watch Video**

**Use Graphic Organizer**

**Weekly Concept** Getting Along

**Essential Question**
What actions can we take to get along with others?

Go Digital!

# Trying to Fit In

It's a big crowded world out there, and we must work to figure out ways to live together. What can we do to get along well with others?

▶ This beach crowd consists of a colony of King Penguins and their chicks, and Southern Elephant Seals. Somehow they make it work!

▶ Part of getting along is learning to resolve a conflict when it arises. If we cannot resolve it, someone else may need to intervene.

## Talk About It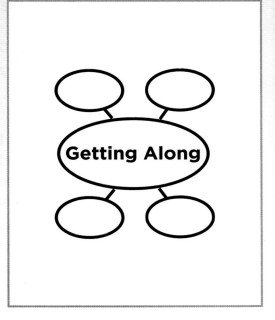

Write words you have learned about how to get along with others. Then talk about a time you did not get along with someone and how you handled it.

Getting Along

392        393

**READING/WRITING WORKSHOP, pp. 392–393**

## ELL ENGLISH LANGUAGE LEARNERS SCAFFOLD

| Beginning | Intermediate | Advanced/High |
|---|---|---|
| **Use Visuals** Help students understand the phrase *get along*. Smile and make an inclusive gesture. Say: *We work and play together. We do not fight. We get along well.* Point to the photograph and ask: *Are these animals fighting?* [pause] *No, because they all get along.* Ask: *How do you know the animals are getting along?* Elicit details. | **Describe** Have students describe the scene on the beach in the photograph. Ask: *What do you think happens when the animals have conflicts and don't get along well?* Provide sentence frames, such as *When the animals have conflicts, they might ____.* Restate students' responses for clarity as needed. | **Discuss** Ask students to discuss the photograph. Ask questions to help them elaborate. *Do you think these animals ever have conflicts? What might they have to do to get along? Why is it important that they all get along?* Correct grammar and pronunciation as needed. |

**GRAPHIC ORGANIZER 62**

Getting Along

# → Listening Comprehension

## Interactive Read Aloud

**OBJECTIVES**

CCSS Summarize a written text read aloud or information presented in diverse media and formats, including visually, quantitatively, and orally. **SL.5.2**

• Listen for a purpose.
• Identify characteristics of realistic fiction.

**ACADEMIC LANGUAGE**
• *realistic fiction, summarize*
• Cognates: *ficción realista, resumir*

### Connect to Concept: Getting Along

Invite students to recall times in their lives when they have not been able to get along with someone because of a conflict. Ask them what caused the conflict and what they did or might have done to resolve it. Tell them that in the story you are going to read aloud, a boy and his next-door neighbor resolve their differences when they discover a common interest.

### Preview Genre: Realistic Fiction

Explain that the text you will read aloud is realistic fiction. Discuss features of realistic fiction:

→ is set in places and times that could exist

→ has characters and events similar to those in real life

→ has descriptive details and pacing that make the story realistic

### Preview Comprehension Strategy: Summarize

Explain that when readers summarize a story, they focus on the most important details and events. As students listen to you read aloud "Diamond in the Sky," tell them to decide which details and events are most important. Point out that if they can't understand the story without a particular detail, then that detail is important.

Use the Think Alouds on page T77 to model the strategy.

### Respond to Reading

**Think Aloud Clouds** Display Think Aloud Master 5: *This was mostly about…* to reinforce how you used the summarize strategy to understand content.

**Genre Features** With students, discuss the elements of the Read Aloud that let them know it is realistic fiction. Ask them to think about other texts that you have read or they have read independently that were realistic fiction.

**Summarize** Invite students to try retelling the story of "Diamond in the Sky" in their own words. Encourage them to focus on main events and most important details that make up the plot.

**Go Digital**

**View Illustrations**

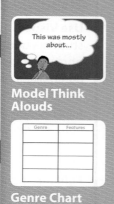

**Model Think Alouds**

**Genre Chart**

# Diamond in the Sky

Jon Davis stood in his yard, watching excitedly as his new kite climbed higher and higher. Suddenly, the wind shifted and the kite took a nosedive into an old oak tree on his neighbors' front lawn. Jon tugged on the string, but the kite wouldn't budge. "Oh, no!" he thought. "The Stowes are going to be so mad!" Jon didn't know his neighbors very well, but he knew they didn't appreciate rowdy kids. **1**

Grabbing a broom, Jon sneaked across the lawn. "I bet this will get my kite down," Jon thought, boldly taking a swipe at the branches. On his third try, a branch cracked loudly.

"What was that noise?" wondered Mr. Stowe, who was gardening in the backyard. Jogging around front, he caught Jon sticking the broken branch back into the tree. "How many times have I told you to keep out of my yard!" he huffed.

Marching Jon next door, Mr. Stowe related the story of the broken branch to Jon's mother. "What if Jon helps you in your garden to make things right?" Jon's mother asked. "Okay," said Mr. Stowe. "We'll start now."

At first, Jon sulked as he raked reluctantly. Then Mr. Stowe began telling tales of his own kite-flying days. "Maybe he's not so grouchy after all," Jon thought. **2**

Later, Mr. Stowe used a ladder to get Jon's kite, which had a classic diamond shape. "This is pretty broken up," he noted. "Why don't you come over tomorrow? I'll show you how to make your own kite."

"Thanks," Jon said. "I'll ask my parents."

Mr. Stowe was waiting by his workbench when Jon arrived. Trading tools back and forth, they built the kite together. Would it fly? Jon was eager to find out. Rain poured down outside, so Mrs. Stowe suggested they all test the kite at the park on Saturday and have a picnic. **3**

On Saturday, breezes chased flocks of clouds across the sky. Jon released the kite and it took off rapidly, fluttering like a diamond sparkling in the sunlight.

Everyone cheered. "Say, Jon," called Mr. Stowe, "How about you, your dad, and I build a dragon kite next week?"

**1** **Think Aloud** To better understand a story, I can **summarize** important events and key details. An important event is Jon's kite getting stuck in his neighbor's tree. A key detail is that Jon knows the neighbors don't appreciate rowdy kids.

**2** **Think Aloud** I can **summarize** to help me remember what has happened so far. Jon's kite got stuck in Mr. Stowe's tree. To apologize, he is helping Mr. Stowe in the garden. Now Mr. Stowe is telling Jon about his kite-flying days.

**3** **Think Aloud** When I **summarize** the story, I want to remember important events. I know a key event is when Jon and Mr. Stowe work together to build a kite. This shows the actions that two people took to get along with each other.

Ariel Skelley/Blend Images/ Getty Images

→ # Vocabulary

**Reading/Writing Workshop**

 **Go** Digital

### OBJECTIVES

**CCSS** Acquire and use accurately grade-appropriate general academic and domain-specific words and phrases, including those that signal contrast, addition, and other logical relationships (e.g., *however, although, nevertheless, similarly, moreover, in addition*). **L.5.6**

### ACADEMIC LANGUAGE

• *conflict, intervene*
• Cognates: *conflicto, intervenir*

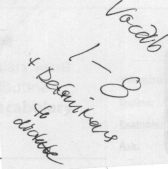

## MINILESSON 10 Mins  Words in Context

### Model the Routine

Introduce each vocabulary word using the Vocabulary Routine found on the **Visual Vocabulary Cards**.

Visual Vocabulary Cards

**abruptly**
**Use Visual Glossary**

---

#### Vocabulary Routine

**Define:** If something ends **abruptly**, it stops suddenly without warning.

**Example:** Playing in the park ended abruptly because of a sudden rainstorm.

**Ask:** What else might cause an activity to end abruptly?

---

### Definitions

→ **ally**         An **ally** is a person or nation on the same side during a conflict. **Cognate:** *aliado(a)*

→ **collided**     If the bikes **collided**, they hit or crashed against each other.

→ **confident**    When you are **confident**, you have a strong belief in your abilities.

→ **conflict**     A **conflict** is a strong disagreement. **Cognate:** *conflicto*

→ **intervene**    When you **intervene**, you get involved in a disagreement to help solve it. **Cognate:** *intervenir*

→ **protective**   Something that is **protective** helps keep you safe. **Cognate:** *protector*

→ **taunting**     **Taunting** is teasing, or making fun of someone.

### Talk About It

COLLABORATE

Have students work with a partner and talk about the photograph and definition for each word. Ask them to discuss how the sentence relates to the definition. Then ask students to choose three words and write questions for their partner to answer.

## CCSS Words to Know

# Vocabulary

Use the picture and the sentences to talk with a partner about each word.

**abruptly**
Playing in the park ended **abruptly** because of a sudden rainstorm.

*What else might cause an activity to end abruptly?*

**ally**
My little brother says that a dog is the best **ally**, even for a superhero.

*When might an ally be important?*

**collided**
The players **collided** on the field, and both fell down.

*What could happen if two cars collided?*

**confident**
The more you practice a song before a concert, the more **confident** you will feel.

*How might practicing a lot make you feel more confident?*

**conflict**
To resolve their **conflict** over who would use the remote control, the sisters finally agreed to take turns.

*What else can cause a conflict?*

**intervene**
When the referee saw the players arguing, he had to **intervene** to stop them.

*When else might a person need to intervene?*

**protective**
Every bicycle rider should always wear a **protective** helmet.

*How is an umbrella protective?*

**taunting**
Outside the window, a squirrel seemed to be **taunting** my cat.

*When have you seen people taunting other people?*

**Your Turn** COLLABORATE

Pick three words. Write three questions for your partner to answer.

**Go Digital!** *Use the online visual glossary*

394

395

**READING/WRITING WORKSHOP, pp. 394–395**

## ELL ENGLISH LANGUAGE LEARNERS SCAFFOLD

### Beginning

**Recognize** Elicit that another word for *abruptly* is *quickly*. Then sing a melody two ways: first stopping suddenly and then gradually fading out. Ask: *Which time did I stop abruptly?* Point out that *abruptly* is *abruptamente* in Spanish.

### Intermediate

**Describe** Have students describe the photograph for *abruptly*. Help them with the pronunciation. Ask: *What is another word for* abruptly? (quickly, suddenly) *What word means the opposite of* abruptly? (slowly) Repeat correct responses.

### Advanced/High

**Discuss** Ask pairs to discuss the photograph for *abruptly*. *Have them complete the following sentence frame: The ____ ended abruptly when ____.* Then have them share their work with the class. Correct responses as needed.

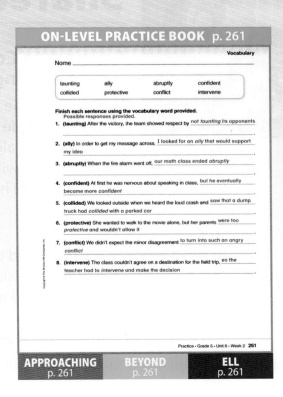

**ON-LEVEL PRACTICE BOOK** p. 261

Name _____

| taunting | ally | abruptly | confident |
| collided | protective | conflict | intervene |

**Finish each sentence using the vocabulary word provided.**
Possible responses provided.

1. **(taunting)** After the victory, the team showed respect by not *taunting* its opponents

2. **(ally)** In order to get my message across, I looked for an *ally* that would support my idea

3. **(abruptly)** When the fire alarm went off, our math class ended *abruptly*

4. **(confident)** At first he was nervous about speaking in class, but he eventually became more *confident*

5. **(collided)** We looked outside when we heard the loud crash and saw that a dump truck had *collided* with a parked car

6. **(protective)** She wanted to walk to the movie alone, but her parents were too *protective* and wouldn't allow it

7. **(conflict)** We didn't expect the minor disagreement to turn into such an angry *conflict*

8. **(intervene)** The class couldn't agree on a destination for the field trip, so the teacher had to *intervene* and make the decision

Practice • Grade 5 • Unit 6 • Week 2 **261**

| APPROACHING p. 261 | BEYOND p. 261 | ELL p. 261 |

**CCSS** **Shared Read** ⟩ Genre • Realistic Fiction

# The Bully

**?** **Essential Question**

**What actions can we take to get along with others?**

Read about how one student tries to deal with a bully.

396

Michael saw the trouble coming from all the way at the end of the school hallway. There standing by the stairs was J.T., the school bully who enjoyed **taunting** anyone he felt like at any given moment. J.T. was tall and strong, so few of his victims were willing to stand up to him and defend themselves. Michael hated the idea that he let J.T. get away with these offenses. Yet like most of the other kids who were picked on, he just took it quietly and waited for the unpleasant moment to pass.

J.T. walked directly toward Michael, his eyes locked on the books that Michael carried under his arms. When they met in the middle of the hallway, J.T. stopped **abruptly** and snapped at Michael, "Hey, let me see those books!" A group of students watched as Michael held out the books he was carrying, trying not to tremble to reveal how nervous he was.

J.T. grabbed a math book, looked inside for a second, and then shoved the book at Michael, who dropped all the books he held. "Hey, those books are school property," J.T. barked, "so don't let them fall to the floor!" Then he walked away, laughing loudly.

Michael, his cheeks turning red, half kicked the fallen books. Suddenly a hand appeared beside Michael and picked up an adventure novel as it slid away. "You look like you could use an **ally**," a friendly voice said with a laugh.

397

**READING/WRITING WORKSHOP, pp. 396–397**

# Shared Read

**Lexile** 850    *TextEvaluator.* 32

**Reading/Writing Workshop**

## Connect to Concept: Getting Along

Explain that "The Bully" will provide another example of actions people can take to get along with others. Read the story with students. Note that the vocabulary words are highlighted.

## Close Reading

**Reread Paragraph 1:** Reread the first paragraph of "The Bully" with students. Ask: *Based on details in this paragraph, what predictions might we make about the characters and events?* Model how to use text evidence to answer the question.

In the first sentence, I learn that a character named Michael is expecting some trouble. Then I read about J. T., a tall, strong boy who is the school bully. I predict that Michael will be bullied again by J.T. However, because the text says that Michael doesn't like allowing J.T. to get away with bullying, I predict that later something will change.

**Reread Paragraphs 2 and 3:** Model how to summarize what happens in the second and third paragraphs. Remind students that summarizing can help them understand what they have read.

J. T. stops Michael in the crowded hallway, grabs a book out of his hands, and then shoves it back at Michael, causing Michael to drop all his books. J. T. walks away laughing. This summary confirms my prediction: Michael is bullied by J.T. again.

Michael turned around and saw that it was Ramon. He was the school's star baseball player, basketball player, and everything-else-player you could name. Michael couldn't believe that Ramon was stopping to help him. The two had barely spoken to each other since the school year began.

"Thanks," Michael sighed with relief. "It's so confusing. I don't know what his problem is."

"I've been watching you in the halls," Ramon said, "and as I see it, you need to find a way to end this **conflict** with J.T." Michael nodded, stuck for what to say. "Well," Ramon continued, "I can tell you what my grandmother used to tell me whenever I had a problem with someone. She'd say, 'You can catch more flies with honey than with vinegar.'"

Looking puzzled, Michael asked, "What does that mean?"

"It means that being kind to your enemies may be more effective than being angry at them," Ramon explained.

"What if you just **intervene** and tell J.T. to stop picking on me?" Michael suggested. "I think he'd leave me alone if you threatened him."

"That's vinegar," Ramon laughed as he walked away. "Try honey instead."

That night, Michael thought about the advice that Ramon had given him. It sounded like a good plan, but deep down Michael wasn't very **confident** that it would actually work with J.T.

The next day in school brought Michael's usual misery. There stood J.T., and Michael knew it would be just a matter of seconds before the two of them **collided** in the middle of the hall.

398

As J.T. came nearer, Michael wished he had Ramon's **protective** arm to stop the bully from attacking. Then, suddenly, the unexpected happened. J.T. accidentally tripped. He fell down, and his own armful of books went flying across the floor.

For a moment, all was silent. The crowd of students in the hallway froze, waiting to see what J.T. would do next. As J.T. slowly stood up, Michael had an idea. He bent down, quickly picked up J.T.'s books from the floor, and offered them to him.

Michael said, "You look like you could use an ally."

J.T. was speechless, completely thrown by Michael's act of kindness. He took the books and muttered quickly, "Uh, thanks."

As J.T. walked away, Michael caught Ramon in the corner of his eye. Ramon gave him a big smile and a "thumbs-up." "My grandmother would be proud of you," Ramon said.

"It's just honey," Michael grinned. "I hope it sticks."

**Make Connections**

? Talk about how Ramon's advice affected Michael's problem with J.T. **ESSENTIAL QUESTION**

What advice would you give to someone being bullied? Give reasons to support your opinion. **TEXT TO SELF**

399

**READING/WRITING WORKSHOP, pp. 398–399**

## Make Connections

### ESSENTIAL QUESTION

Encourage students to reread the text for evidence as they discuss how Ramon's advice affected Michael's problem with J.T. Ask students to explain, using details in the text, what actions people can take to get along with others.

## Continue Close Reading

Use the following lessons for focused rereadings.

→ Summarize, pp. T82–T83

→ Theme, pp. T84–T85

→ Realistic Fiction, pp. T86–T87

→ Connotation and Denotation, pp. T88–T89

**A C T Access Complex Text**

### ▶ Connection of Ideas

Help students identify details they can use to make inferences about the characters.

→ *On page 397, Michael kicks his own books. What details on the page help you infer why he does so?* (On page 397, we learn that "Michael hated the idea that he let J.T. get away with these offenses." So he's probably angry that he just let it happen again.)

→ *Ramon helps Michael. Why do you think he does this?* (Ramon's grandmother gave him good advice about how to solve problems with others. Ramon probably knows how Michael feels and wants to help.)

→ # Comprehension Strategy

**Reading/Writing Workshop**

---

**OBJECTIVES**

 Quote accurately from a text when explaining what the text says explicitly and when drawing inferences from the text. **RL.5.1**

Summarize a written text read aloud or information presented in diverse media and formats, including visually, quantitatively, and orally. **SL.5.2**

---

**ACADEMIC LANGUAGE**

• summarize, realistic fiction

• Cognates: resumir, ficción realista

**MINILESSON 10 Mins**

## Summarize

### 1 Explain

Remind students that when they **summarize** a story, they restate the most important events, ideas, and details in their own words.

→ Tell students to pause now and then to summarize what they have just read.

→ Remind students that a summary includes only the most important events, ideas, and details. To determine if a piece of information is important, students should ask themselves if they would understand the story without it. If they answer *no*, then it is important.

Point out that it is a good idea to summarize the beginning, middle, and end of a story. Doing so can help students better remember the characters and events.

### 2 Model Close Reading: Text Evidence

Reread aloud the first paragraph of "The Bully" on page 397. Then model how determining important details about the characters and events in this first paragraph helps you summarize the beginning of the story.

### 3 Guided Practice of Close Reading

Have partners take turns rereading the rest of "The Bully" aloud. Ask them to retell the most important events, ideas, and details in their own words in order to summarize the story. To help students summarize the middle and end of the story, direct them to pages 398 and 399 for details about how Ramon helps Michael and how Michael finally solves his problem.

Remind students that they can ask themselves, "Would I understand the story without knowing this event, idea, or detail?" Doing so will help them decide which information is important enough to include in their summaries.

**Go Digital**

**Present the Lesson**

**CCSS Comprehension Strategy**

# Summarize

When you summarize a story, you include the most important details. As you read, you can decide which details are most important by asking yourself, *Would I understand the story without this detail?* If the answer is no, the detail is important.

## 🔍 Find Text Evidence

To help your understanding of the first part of "The Bully" on page 397, you can identify the important details and summarize that section.

**page 397**

Michael saw the trouble coming from all the way at the end of the school hallway. There standing by the stairs was J.T., the school bully who enjoyed taunting anyone he felt like at any given moment. J.T. was tall and strong, so few of his victims were willing to stand up to him and defend themselves. Michael hated the idea that he let J.T. get away with these offenses. Yet like most of the other kids who were picked on, he just took it quietly and waited for the unpleasant moment to pass.

J.T. walked directly toward Michael, his eyes locked on the books that Michael carried under his arms. When they met in the middle of the hallway, J.T. stopped abruptly and snapped at Michael, "Hey, let me see those books?" A group of students watched as Michael held out the books he was carrying, trying not to tremble to reveal how nervous he was.

J.T. grabbed a math book, looked inside for a second, and then shoved the book at Michael, who dropped all the books he held. "Hey, those books are school property," J.T. barked, "so don't let them fall to the floor!" Then he walked away, laughing loudly.

*I read that J.T. picks on kids in school, including Michael. The text then says that Michael* just took it quietly and waited for the unpleasant moment to pass. *These seem like important details, so I will use them as I summarize.*

### Your Turn  COLLABORATE

Use the most important details to summarize the rest of "The Bully." As you read, use the strategy Summarize.

400

**READING/WRITING WORKSHOP,** p. 400

---

## ENGLISH LANGUAGE LEARNERS SCAFFOLD

### Beginning

**Understand** Reread the first paragraph on page 397. Point out difficult words such as *bully, victims, defend, offenses,* and *unpleasant* and define them. Help students replace these words with words or phrases they know. Point out the two Spanish cognates: *victims/víctimas, defend/defender.*

### Intermediate

**Identify** Help students reread the first paragraph. Point out that the second sentence may be confusing because of its unusual word order. Ask: *Who is the school bully?* (J.T.) *Where is he?* (standing by the stairs) *What does the phrase* at any given moment *mean?* (at any time, whenever he feels like it) Have partners restate the sentence.

### Advanced/High

**Explain** Have students reread the first paragraph on page 397. Elicit from students why this paragraph may be confusing. Ask: *Why is it important to understand what Michael and J.T. are like? Turn to a partner and explain.* Have partners summarize the beginning of the story. Clarify student responses.

---

## Monitor and *Differentiate*

### ✓ Quick Check

Do students identify important events, ideas, and details in the story? Do they retell this information in their own words to summarize the story?

⬇

## Small Group Instruction

| | | |
|---|---|---|
| **If No →** | **Approaching Level** | **Reteach p. T104** |
| | **ELL** | **Develop p. T121** |
| **If Yes →** | **On Level** | **Review p. T112** |
| | **Beyond Level** | **Extend p. T116** |

---

**ON-LEVEL PRACTICE BOOK** pp. 263–264

Comprehension and Fluency

Name

Read the passage. Use the summarizing strategy to help you understand what you are reading.

**The Battle of the Bedroom**

13 My older sister, Marta, glares at me from across the room. Her dark
26 brown eyes blaze with anger; she's ready to burst. I almost say something
43 to set her off, but Dad said if he heard any more noise from our room that
48 we would both be grounded.
62 Sure, we fight like all sisters do, but the battle lines were redrawn when
77 we moved into our new house a week ago. In our old house, we each
93 had our own bedroom. Now we have to share, and it has led to an all-out
107 war. We still haven't unpacked a thing because we can't agree on how to
117 decorate the room. Right now, we're stuck with cardboard boxes.
129 Marta wants dark walls, gray curtains, and posters of her favorite bands.
142 I want a mural of ocean creatures against bright blue walls. Our family
159 took a trip to the Gulf of Mexico last year, and I fell in love with the
174 sparkling blue water. I think it would be fun to have a reminder of that.
189 Marta despises my idea, and I sure don't like hers, so now we're stuck in
191 a stalemate.
206 Dad pops his head into the room. "Lucia, Marta, can we see you in the
220 living room, please?" He and Mom are sitting on the couch. Marta and I
226 sit in chairs across from them.
237 Dad starts by telling us how disappointed he is, especially about
250 the disrespect we've shown them and each other. I squirm in my seat,
257 embarrassed that we've been acting so childish.
272 Mom cuts to the chase and says, "It's a mystery to us how two bright
285 and reasonable girls can be so inflexible." She hands us each a spiral
298 notebook and a ballpoint pen. "You both have good ideas. So we're giving
313 you one hour to come up with a plan..." she looks back and forth between
327 us, "for the other person's idea. Lucia, you'll tell us why Marta's idea is
the best, and vice versa."

Practice · Grade 5 · Unit 6 · Week 2   **263**

| APPROACHING pp. 263–264 | BEYOND pp. 263–264 | ELL pp. 263–264 |
|---|---|---|

# Comprehension Skill

**Reading/Writing Workshop**

**ACADEMIC LANGUAGE**
- *theme, details*
- Cognates: *tema, detalles*

 **MINILESSON 10 Mins**

## Theme

### 1 Explain

Explain to students that the **theme** of a story is the important message about life that the author wants to share with readers. Point out that a story's theme is usually not stated directly. Provide students with these tips for identifying the theme.

→ Students should pay attention to what the main characters do and say, what happens to them, and how they respond to events. These details may be clues to the theme.

→ Students should think about how characters change from the beginning to the end. A lesson that a character learns is often closely related to the theme.

### 2 Model Close Reading: Text Evidence

Using the first page of the story, model how to identify details about what the characters in "The Bully" do and say and what happens to them. Then model using the details written on the graphic organizer to begin thinking about a possible theme in the story—for example, that people must find ways to get along, even with bullies.

 **Write About Reading: Summary** Model for students how to use the notes from the organizer to write a summary of the events at the beginning of the story.

### 3 Guided Practice of Close Reading

 Have partners reread the rest of the story and complete the graphic organizer with additional details from "The Bully." Discuss the details as students identify them. Then discuss the theme that students identify after considering all of the details they have compiled.

 **Write About Reading: Summary** Ask partners to write a summary of the middle and end of the story, including Ramon's advice and the actions Michael takes to get along with J. T. Have volunteers share their summaries with the class.

**Go Digital**

**Present the Lesson**

---

**SKILLS TRACE**

**THEME**

**Introduce** U2W4

**Review** U2W5, U2W6, U3W1, U3W2, U4W5, U4W6, U6W1, U6W2, U6W6

**Assess** U2, U3, U4, U6

---

 **Comprehension Skill** CCSS

# Theme

The **theme** of a story is the message or truth about life that the author wants readers to understand. To identify the theme, think about what the characters do and say and what happens to them. Then decide what lessons or truths about life can be learned from the events.

 **Find Text Evidence**

When I read the first page of "The Bully," I learned that Michael is regularly bullied by J.T. Because J.T. is taller and stronger, Michael is afraid to do anything to stop J.T. from bullying him.

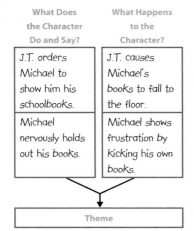

| What Does the Character Do and Say? | What Happens to the Character? |
|---|---|
| J.T. orders Michael to show him his schoolbooks. | J.T. causes Michael's books to fall to the floor. |
| Michael nervously holds out his books. | Michael shows frustration by kicking his own books. |

Theme

**Your Turn** COLLABORATE

Reread the rest of "The Bully." Find the most important things that the characters say and do and what happens to them. Record the details in the graphic organizer and use them to identify the theme.

*Go Digital!*
*Use the interactive graphic organizer*

401

**READING/WRITING WORKSHOP, p. 401**

## A C T Access Complex Text

▶ **Specific Vocabulary**

Ramon tells Michael "you can catch more flies with honey than with vinegar." Tell students that this statement is a *proverb*, or saying that is often repeated. Help students connect the proverb to the story's theme.

→ *What action does Ramon say would be like trying to catch a fly with something the fly does not like?* (threatening J.T.)

→ *What solution does Michael try that is like catching a fly with something the fly might respond to?* (helping J.T. when he trips)

 **Monitor and** *Differentiate*

 **Quick Check**

Can students identify what characters do, say, and experience? Can they use these details to determine the theme of the story?

⬇

**Small Group Instruction**

If No → **Approaching Level** Reteach p. T111
**ELL** Develop p. T121
If Yes → **On Level** Review p. T115
**Beyond Level** Extend p. T119

**ON-LEVEL PRACTICE BOOK** pp. 263–265

Comprehension: Theme and Fluency

Name _____

**A. Reread the passage and answer the questions.**
Possible responses provided.
1. **What problem does sharing a bedroom create for Marta and Lucia?**
They cannot agree on how to decorate the room.

2. **Why do the girls' parents give them each a notebook and a pen?**
The idea is that they can each write down why the other's decorating ideas are the best.

3. **What happens when the sisters discuss their ideas with each other?**
They start coming up with ideas that both of them like.

4. **What is the theme of the passage?**
People can often work out differences by talking about them and coming to a compromise.

**B. Work with a partner. Read the passage aloud. Pay attention to intonation. Stop after one minute. Fill out the chart.**

| | Words Read | – | Number of Errors | = | Words Correct Score |
|---|---|---|---|---|---|
| First Read | | – | | = | |
| Second Read | | – | | = | |

Practice · Grade 5 · Unit 6 · Week 2 **265**

| **APPROACHING** pp. 263–265 | **BEYOND** pp. 263–265 | **ELL** pp. 263–265 |
|---|---|---|

# → Genre: Literature

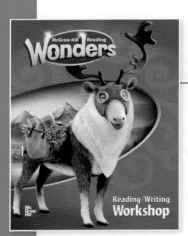

**Reading/Writing Workshop**

## ACADEMIC LANGUAGE

• *realistic fiction, details, pacing*

• Cognates: *ficción realista, detalles*

 **MINILESSON 10 Mins**

## Realistic Fiction

**Go Digital**

**Present the Lesson**

### 1 Explain

Share with students the following key characteristics of **realistic fiction**:

→ Realistic fiction takes place in settings that could actually exist, such as shopping malls, apartments, parks, and schools.

→ Characters and events in realistic fiction are like those found in real life.

→ Like other kinds of fiction, realistic fiction contains descriptive details that help readers visualize the setting, characters, and events in the story.

→ Authors of realistic fiction use sentence length and descriptive details to control the pacing, or the speed at which actions occur.

### 2 Model Close Reading: Text Evidence

Model identifying and using text evidence from page 397 of "The Bully" to help you understand that the story is realistic fiction.

**Descriptive Details** Point out details, such as "school hallway" and "standing by the stairs," that the author uses to create a realistic setting. Other details, such as those that describe J. T.'s appearance and behavior and explain Michael's feelings, help readers connect the story to the real-life problem of school bullying.

**Pacing** Point out that in the first paragraph, very little action actually happens, but in the second paragraph, several actions happen quickly. The author's use of brisk action and vivid language, such as *abruptly* and *snapped*, set the quick pace of the paragraph and create a feeling of suspense about what will happen next.

### 3 Guided Practice of Close Reading

 **COLLABORATE**

Have partners list three other details in the story that indicate how the characters, problems, and events are like those found in real life. Ask students to share their work and their reactions to the way in which Michael solves his problem.

## CCSS Genre Literature

# Realistic Fiction

The selection "The Bully" is realistic fiction.

**Realistic fiction:**
- Is set in places and times that could actually exist
- Has characters and events like those found in real life
- Includes descriptive details and appropriate pacing

### Find Text Evidence

*I can tell that "The Bully" is realistic fiction. For example, Michael attends a school like those found in the real world. Being bullied is a real problem that some students face in school. Descriptive details and pacing help to make events of the story seem realistic.*

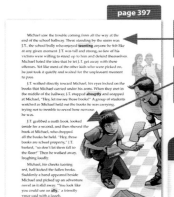

**Descriptive Details** Descriptive details tell you more about the setting, characters, and events.

**Pacing** Authors deliver details at a pace, or rate, that creates effects such as suspense or excitement.

### Your Turn

List three other details in "The Bully" that indicate how the characters, problems, and story events are similar to those found in real life.

402

**READING/WRITING WORKSHOP, p. 402**

## ELL ENGLISH LANGUAGE LEARNERS SCAFFOLD

### Beginning

**Use Visuals** Read aloud the first two paragraphs on page 397. Have students look at the illustration on page 396 as you repeat these descriptive details from the text: *school hallway, books, group of students.* Have students point to appropriate details in the illustration and repeat the words from the text.

### Intermediate

**Recognize** Help students reread the first two paragraphs. Guide them to notice that several things happen quickly in the second paragraph. Ask: *What descriptive details in the second paragraph help you visualize the scene?* (eyes locked on the books, a group of students watched, trying not to tremble)

### Advanced/High

**Demonstrate Comprehension** Have students reread the first two paragraphs on page 397. Elicit details that describe the story's realistic setting. Ask: *What descriptive details create suspense and help readers visualize the scene? Is the pace faster in the first paragraph or the second? Why? Turn to a partner and discuss.*

---

# Monitor and *Differentiate*

## ✓ Quick Check

Can students identify details in the story that indicate how the characters, problems, and events are similar to those found in real life?

⬇

## Small Group Instruction

| | | |
|---|---|---|
| If No → | **Approaching Level** | Reteach p. T105 |
| | **ELL** | Develop p. T123 |
| If Yes → | **On Level** | Review p. T113 |
| | **Beyond Level** | Extend p. T117 |

---

**ON-LEVEL PRACTICE BOOK** p. 266

Genre/Literary Element

Name _____

**Paying it Forward**

Andy frowned at his cast-enclosed leg. He'd broken his tibia and fibula, and cracked his patella—three important leg bones—the doctor had said.

Suddenly, his mom walked in. His classmate Peter followed her, grasping something secretively in his hand.

*Oh, great!* Andy thought. *Peter's come to be mean to me, like always.*

"Just go home!" he snapped.

"Chill out," Peter replied. "I broke an arm last summer, and a friend made it better for me. I've come to do the same for you." He held out a video game.

"I just picked up a copy of a great new video game," Peter said. "Want to play?"

**Answer the questions about the text.**

1. **Name a detail that lets you know this text is realistic fiction. How does it do that?**
   Possible response: Andy has broken his leg. Things like that happen
   in real life.

2. **Write an example of a descriptive detail from the text. How does the detail add to the text's setting, characters, or events?**
   Answers will vary but should include an example of a descriptive detail and
   explain how it contributes to the text's setting, characters, or events.

3. **How does the author use pacing in this text? How does the pacing help make the text seem realistic?**
   Possible response: The dialogue between Andy and Peter is fast. This makes
   the dialogue realistic, like the way real people talk.

266 Practice · Grade 5 · Unit 6 · Week 2

| APPROACHING p. 266 | BEYOND p. 266 | ELL p. 266 |
|---|---|---|

# → Vocabulary Strategy

**Reading/Writing Workshop**

MINILESSON
**10** Mins

## Connotation and Denotation

### Go Digital

**Present the Lesson**

### 1 Explain

Explain that a word may have different kinds of meaning.

→ A word's **denotation** is its dictionary definition.

→ A word's **connotation** is the feeling it suggests.

→ Explain that words may have positive or negative connotations. Words such as *bounce* and *shine* usually have positive connotations. Words such as *cold* and *shiver* usually have negative connotations.

### 2 Model Close Reading: Text Evidence

Point to the word *froze* in the second paragraph on page 399. Provide the dictionary definition and explain that this is its denotation. Then discuss the context in which the word is used and the feeling it suggests. Explain that *froze* sometimes has a negative connotation. In this paragraph, it describes students who have stopped out of fear and are anxious to see what will happen next.

### 3 Guided Practice of Close Reading

COLLABORATE

Have students work in pairs to determine whether the words *tremble, barked,* and *muttered* have positive or negative connotations and then identify each word's meaning in context.

---

**Use Reference Sources**

**Print Dictionary and Online Glossary** Have students check a dictionary to find the pronunciations and compare the definitions of *tremble, barked,* and *muttered* with the connotations the words have in the story. If the dictionary gives more than one definition, have students choose the one that is closest to the meaning in the selection.

Extend the activity to review the vocabulary word *protective*. Have students look up the word and choose the dictionary definition that matches the usage in the selection. Then have them look up the word in the online glossary. Ask: *Is the online glossary definition the same as the definition you chose? Explain.*

---

**OBJECTIVES**

**CCSS** Consult reference materials (e.g., dictionaries, glossaries, thesauruses), both print and digital, to find the pronunciation and determine or clarify the precise meaning of key words and phrases. **L.5.4c**

---

**ACADEMIC LANGUAGE**

• *connotation, denotation*

• Cognates: *connotación, denotación*

---

**SKILLS TRACE**

**CONNOTATION AND DENOTATION**

**Introduce** U6W2

**Review** U6W2, U6W3

**Assess** U6

## Vocabulary Strategy CCSS

# Connotation and Denotation

Every word has a dictionary meaning, or **denotation**. The same word may also have a **connotation**—a feeling the word suggests. Connotations are often negative or positive. Paying attention to word connotations as well as denotations will increase your understanding of a text.

### Find Text Evidence

*I read* The crowd of students in the hallway froze *and realized that the word* froze *was another way of saying that the crowd stopped moving. The connotation of* froze, *however, suggests that they stopped out of fear and could not move at all.*

> For a moment, all was silent. The crowd of students in the hallway froze, waiting to see what J.T. would do next. As J.T. slowly stood up, Michael had an idea.

### Your Turn COLLABORATE

Decide whether each of the following words from "The Bully" has a positive or negative connotation. Then tell what each word means in the story.

**tremble,** *page 397*
**barked,** *page 397*
**muttered,** *page 399*

403

Marcelo Baez

**READING/WRITING WORKSHOP,** p. 403

## ENGLISH LANGUAGE LEARNERS
## SCAFFOLD

### Beginning

**Listen** Say aloud the words *tremble, barked,* and *muttered* and define them for students. Pantomime or act out the words to reinforce their meanings. Help students replace each word with a word or phrase they know. Point out that *tremble* has a Spanish cognate: *temblar.*

### Intermediate

**Identify** Point out *tremble, barked,* and *muttered* and define each. Help students tell whether each has a positive or negative connotation. Ask: *What kind of character is J.T.? How does this help you determine the connotations of* barked *and* muttered*? How does Michael feel about J.T.? How does this help you determine the connotation of* tremble*?*

### Advanced/High

**Actively Engage** Point out the words *tremble, barked,* and *muttered.* Ask students to determine the denotation and connotation of each. Have students replace the words with words that have similar denotations and connotations. Then have students find a cognate and tell it to their partner.

---

## Monitor and *Differentiate*

### ✓ Quick Check

Can students decide if each word has a positive or negative connotation? Can they tell what each word means in the story?

⬇

### Small Group Instruction

| If No → | Approaching Level | Reteach p. T109 |
| | ELL | Develop p. T125 |
| If Yes → | On Level | Review p. T114 |
| | Beyond Level | Extend p. T118 |

---

**ON-LEVEL PRACTICE BOOK** p. 267

Vocabulary Strategy: **Connotation and Denotation**

Name _____

Read each passage. Then, on the lines below the passage, give the denotation, or definition, and connotation of the words in bold. Identify the connotation as positive, negative, or neutral. **Possible responses provided.**

1. My older sister, Marta, glares at me from across the room. Her dark brown eyes **blaze** with anger; she's ready to burst.

   look intense; negative

2. Sure, we fight like all sisters do, but the **battle lines** were redrawn when we moved into our new house a week ago.

   place where a battle occurs; negative

3. Marta **despises** my idea, and I sure don't like hers, so now we're stuck in a stalemate.

   hates; negative

4. "That isn't fair," Marta **screeches,** her shrill voice rising another octave. "Lucia's idea is childish and awful!"

   screams; negative

5. I leap to defend myself but quickly **choke** back my words. Our parents' faces are bleak.

   smother; negative

Practice • Grade 5 • Unit 6 • Week 2 **267**

| APPROACHING p. 267 | BEYOND p. 267 | ELL p. 267 |

# Develop Comprehension

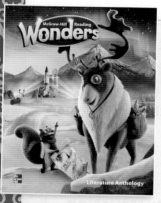

### The Friend Who Changed My Life

**Literature Anthology**
*Complex vocabulary and organization place this selection above TextEvaluator range. Content is grade-level appropriate.*

**Text Complexity Range**

Lexile

740 ▲ 1010
890

TextEvaluator™

23 51 ▲
*56

## Options for Close Reading

→ Whole Class

→ Small Group

→ Independent

This selection is suggested for use as an Extended Complex Text. See pages T356–T361.

**CCSS Genre · Realistic Fiction**

# The Friend Who Changed My Life

by Pam Muñoz Ryan
illustrated by Carl Pearce

**? Essential Question**
**What actions can we take to get along with others?**
Read about how one girl's confrontation with a bully changes her life.

**Go Digital!**

450

Copyright © by Pam Muñoz Ryan.

---

# A C T Access Complex Text

## What makes this text complex?

▶ **Specific Vocabulary**

▶ **Connection of Ideas**

▶ **Organization**

## ▶ Specific Vocabulary

Help students find the meaning of difficult words and figurative language on page 451.

→ Help students use context to determine the meaning of *atrocity* in the third sentence.

→ Discuss the personification of the word *vulnerability*. Ask: *Can you wear vulnerability? Why or why not?* (No, it's a feeling.)

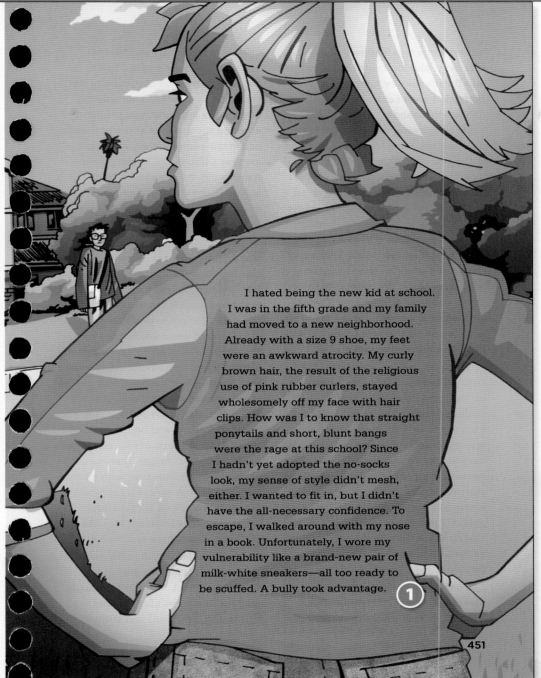

I hated being the new kid at school. I was in the fifth grade and my family had moved to a new neighborhood. Already with a size 9 shoe, my feet were an awkward atrocity. My curly brown hair, the result of the religious use of pink rubber curlers, stayed wholesomely off my face with hair clips. How was I to know that straight ponytails and short, blunt bangs were the rage at this school? Since I hadn't yet adopted the no-socks look, my sense of style didn't mesh, either. I wanted to fit in, but I didn't have the all-necessary confidence. To escape, I walked around with my nose in a book. Unfortunately, I wore my vulnerability like a brand-new pair of milk-white sneakers—all too ready to be scuffed. A bully took advantage. **①**

451

**LITERATURE ANTHOLOGY, pp. 450–451**

## Predictive Writing

Have students read the title, preview the illustrations, and skim the text to look for characters and dialogue. Ask them to write their predictions about what this story is about.

### ESSENTIAL QUESTION

Ask a student to read aloud the Essential Question. Have students discuss how the story might help them answer the question.

### Note Taking: Use the Graphic Organizer

As students read the selection, ask them to take notes by filling in the graphic organizer on **Your Turn Practice Book page 262** to record details related to the theme.

### ① Genre: Realistic Fiction

What qualities of the narrator show that this story is realistic fiction? Turn to a partner and paraphrase your answer. (The narrator seems like a real fifth-grader. She doesn't like being the new kid and feels embarrassed by her feet and hairstyle. These are feelings that many fifth-graders have.)

→ *Why does the author use the phrase "I wore my vulnerability"?* (She wants to show that the narrator's vulnerability is obvious.)

→ *To what does the narrator compare her vulnerability?* (new, milk-white sneakers) *Which words show how her vulnerability and new white sneakers are similar?* ("all too ready to be scuffed")

**ELL** ELLs may be unfamiliar with some expressions.

→ Point out the idiom "were the rage" on page 451. Help students use context clues to unlock the meaning of this idiom. Ask: *What is the meaning of "were the rage"?* (The narrator says that she "wanted to fit in," so "were the rage" must mean "popular" or "in style.")

# Develop Comprehension

## 2 Skill: Theme

On page 452, what does the narrator do when Theresa bullies her? What happens as a result? (The narrator does nothing. She just stands there and takes it, so Theresa keeps bullying her.) Add these details to your organizer.

| What Does the Character Do and Say? | What Happens to the Character? |
|---|---|
| The narrator does not stand up for herself with Theresa. | The narrator continues to be bullied by Theresa. |

Her name was Theresa. She was tiny, wiry, and loud, with blond bangs and the mandatory tightly-pulled-back ponytail. I swore she walked with a deliberate swagger just to get her ponytail to swing back and forth. For a reason unknown to me, she decided that I was worthy of her undivided attention, and every day she waltzed up to me and kicked me in the shins or the back of the legs. I could expect a wallop any time I was off guard, while I was standing in line to go to class after a recess, on my way out of the girls' bathroom, or as I pushed my lunch tray along the counter in front of the cafeteria ladies. *Bam!* Theresa was smart and quick. No teacher ever saw her, and my legs were black, blue, purple, and green within a week.

My mom noticed the marks, but I pacified her by saying that I played on the jungle gym at recess and had bruised them on the bars. I could tell from my mom's expression that she was suspicious of my story. She made me promise I'd play somewhere else. I knew that if I kept coming home with mottled legs one of my parents would eventually go to my teacher. I could only imagine the price I'd have to pay among the other kids if I was seen as both the new kid *and* a crybaby tattletale.

I used to lie in bed every night dreading school and trying to figure out complicated routes to walk from one place to another so Theresa couldn't get to me easily. I had a convoluted method of getting to my classroom, which involved walking outside the fenced school yard and entering the grounds at the opposite end of the campus, then working my way through the kindergarten playground. At recess and lunch I stayed in the open spaces on the grassy field because if I saw Theresa coming, I could at least run.

One day, Theresa chased me on the playground, about to close in with yet another successful attack. Frantically, I ran away from her, glancing back every few seconds to see where she was. I looked to one side and was relieved when I didn't see her. Thinking she had given up, I stopped **abruptly** and turned around, unaware that Theresa had been running full-speed toward me from the other side. She didn't expect my sudden stop and **collided** into me and bounced toward the ground. A group of kids standing nearby laughed. Angry, Theresa got up and began kicking me with a fury, over and over. A scrape on my knee reopened and blood trickled down my leg. As much as I wanted to, I didn't cry. I just stood there and took it.

Mary Lou, also in the fifth grade, was the tallest and biggest girl in the entire school, including the sixth graders. She wasn't fat but was sturdy and big-boned and strong.

**452**

# A C T  Access Complex Text

## ▶ Specific Vocabulary

Point out this line on page 452: "…she decided that I was worthy of her undivided attention." Help students understand that the narrator is using sarcasm—saying the opposite of what she means.

→ *Does this line show that Theresa thinks well of the narrator?* (No, the narrator means the opposite: Theresa is trying to make her life miserable.)

Point out the word *convoluted* on page 452.

→ *What context clues help you figure out what* convoluted *means?* ("complicated routes"; The narrator describes the long, complicated route that she takes to get to class.)

→ *What is the meaning of* convoluted? (complicated)

Her red hair, thousands of freckles, and fair skin gave her a gentle giant appearance. Still, no one ever messed with her. When Mary Lou shoved her way through the crowd of kids and took my elbow, everyone backed away, including Theresa.

Mary Lou ushered me to the girls' bathroom. As I stood there, shaking, she took a wad of paper towels, wet them, handed them to me, and pointed to my bloodied leg.

"So, Theresa's been bothering you."

I nodded, hoping that the next words out of Mary Lou's mouth would

be, *Well, I'm going to take care of her for you.* I had visions of having a personal hero to protect me—fantasies of Mary Lou escorting me around the school with a **protective** arm over my shoulder, clobbering anyone who came near me.

Instead Mary Lou said, "You can't let her keep doing this to you. She's never going to stop unless you make her stop. Get it?"

I didn't really get it, but I nodded.

"Listen, she's a pain. But if you don't stick up for yourself, things will get worse. You know that, don't you?"

453

**LITERATURE ANTHOLOGY, pp. 452–453**

**③ Vocabulary: Connotation and Denotation**

The narrator uses the word *sturdy* on page 452 to describe Mary Lou. What is the denotation of *sturdy*? (solid and strong) Does *sturdy* have a positive or negative connotation? What clues help you figure out the connotation? (It has a positive connotation. The narrator says Mary Lou "wasn't fat," which has a negative connotation, "but was sturdy." This contrast shows that *sturdy* is positive.)

**④ Strategy: Summarize**

**Teacher Think Aloud** While reading a story, I pause from time to time to **summarize** the most important details and events on pages 452–453. I read that "no one ever messed with" Mary Lou. The text then says that "Mary Lou shoved her way through the crowd" and "ushered" the narrator away. These seem like important details, so I will use them to summarize this scene: *Mary Lou fearlessly shoves the kids aside and takes the narrator away from the bully.*

▶ **Connection of Ideas**

Remind students that the strategy to read on can often clear up confusing parts of the text.

→ Have students reread paragraph two on page 452. *Why does the narrator tell her mom she was bruised on the jungle gym?* (to hide the fact that she was bullied) *Where do we find out her reasons for lying?* (in the last sentence of the paragraph)

**ELL** Understanding idioms can be challenging to ELLs. Point out the following idioms on pages 452–453 and explain their meanings: "waltzed up," "off guard," "price I'd have to pay," "took it," "messed with her," "get it," and "stick up for yourself." Invite students to say what words they might use instead. Have students role play to demonstrate these idioms.

# Develop Comprehension

## 5 Author's Craft: Character Development

Authors develop characters through what they say and do. Characters may surprise readers. Paraphrase why it is surprising when Mary Lou says that she might hit the narrator. (Mary Lou rescued the narrator.) Do you think Mary Lou will follow through on her threat? Why or why not? (Possible response: No, Mary Lou just wants the narrator to stick up for herself.)

### STOP AND CHECK

**Summarize** Why does the narrator confront Theresa?

**Teacher Think Aloud** Mary Lou tells the narrator that she has to stand up for herself.

Prompt students to build on the beginning of your summary to answer the question.

**Student Think Aloud** Mary Lou nudges the narrator toward Theresa. When Theresa goes to kick her, the narrator defends herself and then punches Theresa.

---

How could it get worse? I was already paralyzed with fear and had turned into a whipping post for some girl who was half my size. Besides, what did Mary Lou mean about sticking up for myself? Did she want me to *fight* Theresa? That idea terrified me more than being kicked every day.

**5** "I'm not kidding," said Mary Lou. "And if you don't *do* something, I'm going to start hitting you, too. Understand?" She made a fist and held it in front of my face.

I thought about Mary Lou's size and weight and gulped. Things could *definitely* get worse. "Yes," I whispered.

"Okay then, get back out there."

Now? Did she mean stand up for myself right now?

I walked back to the playground with Mary Lou smugly following behind. I couldn't see a way out of the situation. In front of me was Theresa and in back of me was Mary Lou. The first bell rang and kids began to assemble in their assigned lines on the blacktop in front of the classrooms. In a few minutes, the second bell would ring and teachers would walk out and get their students for class. The yard duty teacher was out on the grassy field blowing her whistle and rounding up the stragglers. As usual, no teachers would be around to witness my destruction.

**454**

Theresa stood in a huddle of girls. Mary Lou nudged me toward her. I had never started a fight before in my life. I had never hit anyone and didn't have an inkling of what to do. My insides shook worse than my outsides. When Theresa saw me approaching, she set her mouth in a grim line, marched toward me, and swung her leg back to haul off and kick me. I jumped back to avoid the kick. I made a fist and flailed my arm wildly, in some sort of ridiculous motion. *Pop!* In a miraculous blow, I caught Theresa in the nose and blood sprayed across her clothes. I don't know which of us was more surprised.

### STOP AND CHECK

**Summarize** Why does the narrator confront Theresa? Summarizing the events may help you.

---

# A C T Access Complex Text

## ▶ Connection of Ideas

Tell students that it's important to keep past events in mind to understand what's happening in the present.

→ Point to this text on page 454: "In front of me was Theresa and in back of me was Mary Lou." Have students locate earlier text that explains why the narrator is especially afraid of Theresa right now.

(On page 452, Theresa kicked her "with a fury, over and over.")

→ *Why is she afraid of Mary Lou? Point to the text that shows the reason.* (In the second paragraph on page 454, Mary Lou said she would hit the narrator if she didn't stand up to Theresa.)

**6** I don't remember what happened next. I know we brawled on the blacktop. Gritty sand scraped the bare skin on my arms. (I would notice the burns later.) As we rolled over and over, tiny pebbles embedded in my face. One of them made a substantial puncture that didn't heal for weeks. (The pock remained for years.) I'm not sure who separated us and broke it up. In a matter of minutes, someone retrieved the yard duty teacher, and she corralled and ceremoniously walked us to the principal's office. I, the nice girl, the good girl, was going to the principal's office for fighting. Devastated, I hung my head.

Sitting on the bench outside the principal's office and waiting to be called in, I worried about several things. Would the school tell my parents? What would my punishment be? What would Theresa do to get back at me? What would the other kids think? Branded, I was now a bad girl.

The yard duty teacher deposited us in two chairs, side by side, in the principal's office and placed the referral slip on his desk. Our principal was a balding man, with glasses and a kind, grandfatherly face. He seemed happy to see us.

Smiling, he said, "Well, girls, I want you to put your heads together and decide what your punishment should be while I make a phone call."

455

**LITERATURE ANTHOLOGY,** pp. 454–455

## 6 Skill: Theme

What does the narrator do after Mary Lou tells her to stick up for herself? (The narrator gets into a fight with Theresa and gives her a bloody nose.) Continue reading to find out what happens as a result.

| What Does the Character Do and Say? | What Happens to the Character? |
|---|---|
| The narrator does not stand up for herself with Theresa. | The narrator continues to be bullied by Theresa. |
| The narrator fights Theresa after Mary Lou tells her to stick up for herself. | |

## ▶ Organization

Reread the first paragraph on page 455 to help students understand the pacing of the story.

→ Have students point to the two parenthetical sentences. *Why does the author set these references in parentheses?* (It shows that these references are out of sequence with the story: they happen in the future.)

**ELL** Point out sequential clues to students on page 455, such as "what happened next," "later," "for weeks," "for years," and "in a matter of minutes." Work with students to identify whether these words and phrases reference the past, the present, or the future.

# Develop Comprehension

## 7 Author's Craft: Word Choice

Theresa whispers "remorsefully." Why is *remorsefully* a better word choice than *sadly*? What new understanding does it give the reader about Theresa? (*Remorsefully* shows that Theresa is both sad and sorry about what she did. Up to this point, Theresa only acted mean and tough. Being remorseful shows that she has a more thoughtful side.)

## 8 Literary Element: Pacing

Page 456 includes a paragraph that is noticeably longer than the others. How does this organizational pacing differ from the rest of the page? (The rest of the page includes brief periods of dialogue.) Why might this part of the story be paced this way? Discuss your answer with a partner. (Possible response: The author wanted to add several important, descriptive details to this part of the story.)

He picked up the phone, and as he made his call, I stared at his desk. I realized I could read the referral slip upside down. The yard duty teacher had written: *Benched for one week.*

**7** Theresa leaned toward me and whispered, remorsefully, "I guess we should be benched for two weeks." She felt worse than I had suspected.

I glared at her and shook my head no.

The principal put down the phone. "Well, young ladies?"

"We should be benched for a week," I blurted.

"I agree…and I don't want to see you back here anytime soon." He signed the referral and sent us back to class.

"How did you know to say one week?" Theresa asked on our way back to class.

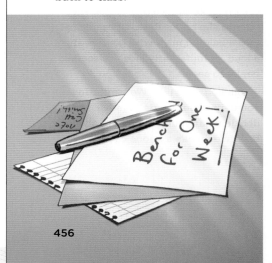

456

"I could read what the yard duty teacher put on the slip. Upside down," I told her.

"Wow, you can read upside down?" Theresa said, her ponytail swinging like a pendulum.

I didn't answer her.

That night I told my mother that I fell, trying to jump rope double Dutch.

Theresa and I were confined at every recess and lunchtime to the same green bench next to the stucco wall of the cafeteria building. It was indisputably the Bad Kids' Bench. Kindergartners and first graders had to file by to get to their classrooms and they always gave us a wide berth, their orderly line snaking away from us, then back in formation, as if our badness might be contagious. The bench faced the playground so the entire recess population could see who was *not privileged* enough to play. The yard duty teacher could keep an eye on us, too, in case we decided to jump up and sneak in a hopscotch game. Indignant and humiliated, I refused to talk to Theresa, who didn't seem to have any inhibitions about being chatty.

She bragged to me about all sorts of things, but I was aloof until she said, "My mom takes me to the *big* downtown library every Tuesday after school."

## A C T  Access Complex Text

### ▶ Specific Vocabulary

Help students access difficult vocabulary and phrases in the long paragraph on page 456.

→ The word *dispute* means "to argue" and the prefix *in-* means "not." What does the sentence "It was indisputably the Bad Kids' Bench" mean? (Without any doubt, the bench was obviously for bad kids.)

→ What does the phrase "gave us a wide berth" mean?

*How do you k_____ ts gave them a lot o_____ king away.")

→ What conte_____ what *contagious* m_____ far away to avoid becoming bad themselves. *Contagious* must mean something that others can "catch.")

Point out that the author is using humor.

I rode my bike to the small branch library near my house every weekend, but my parents both worked full-time and couldn't always manage after-school activities or driving to the main branch. The *big* library had a hundred times the selection of the branch library and a huge children's room with comfy pillows. They sometimes had puppet shows, story times, free bookmarks, and writing contests.

"Yep, every single Tuesday I go to the *big* downtown library to check out as many books as I like."

Before I could pretend I didn't care, I said, "You're lucky." I was suddenly jealous of Theresa, but I didn't want her to know how much. So I returned to my determined martyrdom. Instead of listening to her, I stared at the dirt and ignored her prattle.

The week was over soon enough. The principal never called my parents. The other kids didn't seem to care that I had been disciplined on the Bad Kids' Bench. In fact, I actually detected a subtle reverence from some of my classmates. From then on, Theresa left me alone and Mary Lou was my widely acknowledged **ally**. I didn't know how I'd ever repay her.

**STOP AND CHECK**

**Summarize** How do the narrator and Theresa behave while they are benched? Summarize to help you.

457

**LITERATURE ANTHOLOGY, pp. 456–457**

**9 Literary Element: Descriptive Details**

What descriptive details does the author give about the main library that show why it would attract the narrator? (It has a much larger selection than her local branch library; there are comfy pillows in the children's room; they have puppet shows, story times, free bookmarks, and writing contests.)

**STOP AND CHECK**

**Summarize** How do Theresa and the narrator behave while they are benched? (The narrator won't talk to Theresa, but Theresa becomes much friendlier and chats with her anyway. Theresa brags about going to the *big* library, which makes the narrator jealous.)

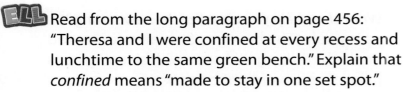 Read from the long paragraph on page 456: "Theresa and I were confined at every recess and lunchtime to the same green bench." Explain that *confined* means "made to stay in one set spot."

→ Why do the girls have to stay on the bench? (They are being punished for fighting.)

→ *From the picture, what clues can you get about how the girls feel on the bench?* (They are sitting far apart and frowning.)

Read the last sentence in the paragraph. Point out the cognates: indignant/*indignado(a),* humiliated/*humillado(a),* inhibitions/*inhibiciones.* Help students define *indignant, humiliated,* and *inhibitions.*

# Develop Comprehension

### 10 Ask and Answer Questions

Generate a question of your own about the text and share it with a partner. To find the answer, try rereading the text. For example, you might ask, "Why doesn't the narrator like ghost stories?" To find the answer, you can reread the second paragraph on page 458 and paraphrase what the narrator says about ghost stories. (The narrator doesn't like ghost stories because she has an active imagination and can't turn off the dark, scary world after she hears a story.)

### 11 Strategy: Summarize

Reread page 458. Turn to your partner and summarize what happens at the slumber party.

**Student Think Aloud** At the slumber party, the narrator and Mary Lou get scared when the girls begin telling ghost stories. Mary Lou starts crying and decides to call her parents to pick her up, even though the other girls tease her.

---

A few weeks passed and one of the girls in our class had a slumber party. All the fifth-grade girls were invited. The barrage of females descended on the birthday girl's house with sleeping bags, pillows, and overnight cases. Mary Lou and I set up our sleeping bags right next to each other. The night progressed happily... until someone suggested we tell ghost stories.

10 I hated ghost stories. I had far too active an imagination, which always took me much farther than the storytelling. I couldn't seem to turn off the dark, scary world. If I saw even a slightly scary movie on television, my stomach would churn for days and I'd have to sleep with my bedside lamp on all night. Mary Lou must have felt the same, because she moved closer to me. We huddled together behind the avid listeners with our pillows almost covering our faces. There was no way *not* to listen. One girl told a particularly gruesome tale about a tree whose giant branches turned into fingers and could grab and capture children. Most of the girls squealed and clutched one another in mock terror before they ended up giggling. Already fraught with anxiety, I couldn't imagine how I would get through the night. I suddenly wanted to be in my own house, in my own bed, with my parents down the hall and my trusty bedside lamp. There

didn't seem to be any way out of the situation that wasn't humiliating. At least Mary Lou was by my side.

Suddenly, Mary Lou started crying. "I'm scared," she said. "I want to go home."

Mary Lou had read my mind but had voiced it with her own tears.

One of the girls said, "Don't be such a baby!"

Others chimed in, "Mary Lou's a scaredy-cat!"

"I'm calling my parents," said Mary Lou through her giant sniffles.

"The baby's calling her mommy and daddy," the girls chanted.

458

---

## ACT Access Complex Text

### Organization

Ask students to pay attention to how the plot and setting shift on page 458.

→ *Where did most of the earlier scenes take place?* (at school) *What has been the narrator's main problem up to this point?* (She was bullied by Theresa.)

→ *What sequential clue tells you that the story has shifted to a different time?* ("a few weeks passed")

→ *What clues help you visualize the new setting?* (first paragraph: "The barrage of females descended on the birthday girl's house with sleeping bags, pillows, and overnight cases.")

→ *What is the narrator's main problem in this new scene?* (The other girls want to tell ghost stories, but ghost stories scare her.)

I shivered in my sleeping bag, my stomach sick with fear. Sick that Mary Lou was leaving. Sick that I was next to a window, with a tree looming on the other side.

Mary Lou headed toward the phone and didn't seem to care about the **taunting**. She called her parents with her chin up, set down the phone, and methodically began packing up her things.

My sleeping area looked bare without Mary Lou's sleeping bag and blanket. A tree branch brushed against the window from the wind. I was convinced it was the same tree from the story and that I would be its next victim.

I stood up and began rolling up my sleeping bag. "I'm going home, too. Mary Lou, can your dad give me a ride?"

I heard more giggles.

Then, from across the room, a small voice said, "Me, too?"

Mary Lou nodded.

I secretly celebrated. I knew that we'd suffer the consequences of the gossip and finger-pointing at school on Monday, but now I didn't care. There was safety in numbers. As I dragged my things into the hallway, I saw the third person.

It was Theresa.

459

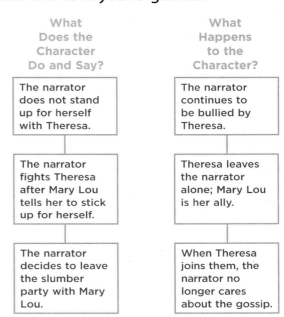

**12 Skill: Theme**

On page 457, what happens to the narrator as a result of her fight with Theresa? (Theresa finally leaves the narrator alone and Mary Lou is seen as the narrator's ally.) On page 459, what does the narrator do? What happens then? (The narrator decides to leave the slumber party with Mary Lou, even though it's embarrassing. Then Theresa joins them, creating safety in numbers.) **Add these events to your organizer.**

| What Does the Character Do and Say? | What Happens to the Character? |
|---|---|
| The narrator does not stand up for herself with Theresa. | The narrator continues to be bullied by Theresa. |
| The narrator fights Theresa after Mary Lou tells her to stick up for herself. | Theresa leaves the narrator alone; Mary Lou is her ally. |
| The narrator decides to leave the slumber party with Mary Lou. | When Theresa joins them, the narrator no longer cares about the gossip. |

Invite students to share what they know about slumber parties using clues in the text as well as their prior knowledge. Repeat students' responses, modeling correct pronunciation and grammar. Take opportunities to elaborate by using details in their responses to ask more questions.

CLOSE READING

# Develop Comprehension

**13 Skill: Make Inferences**

In the first paragraph on page 460, the narrator says that she "was never so grateful to see station wagon headlights." Why does she feel this way? Use text evidence to support your answer. (The narrator was happy to see headlights because Mary Lou's dad was there to take her, Mary Lou, and Theresa home. Pages 458–459 state that the girls are scared of ghost stories. The other girls made fun of them and belittled them. For these reasons the narrator, Mary Lou, and Theresa decided it was best to leave.)

**14 Skill: Theme**

Reread the last two paragraphs on page 461. What lesson does the main character learn in this story? (The narrator learns that it takes courage to reveal our weaknesses and that we're stronger with support.) Use the information in your organizer to find the theme of the story. What is the theme? (Don't be afraid to be yourself.) Add the theme to your organizer.

The three of us huddled on the front porch waiting for Mary Lou's dad. In a final gesture of belittlement, one of the girls turned off the porch light so we had to wait on the front steps in the dark, directly under the tree with the sprawling branches. On the other side of the door, the party howled with laughter. I was never so grateful to see **13** station wagon headlights.

Mary Lou's dad headed toward Theresa's house first. On the way, we were mostly quiet, but I felt happy. Happy I was going home to my own room. Happy that Mary Lou's tearful exit scene had been watered down by our group departure. I was puzzled, though, that Theresa had been frightened, too. She always seemed so **confident**, so tough.

In front of Theresa's house, she climbed out of the car and said, "So do you guys want to go to the *big* library with me after school on Tuesdays? My mom drives me and she could drive you, too."

*I would* love *to go to the* big *downtown library on Tuesdays after school,* I thought. *But with Theresa?* My mind battled with my emotions.

Theresa eagerly continued. "My mom can call your moms to… you know…make sure it's okay and everything."

I hesitated. "Are *you* going?" I asked Mary Lou.

"I can't," she said. "But you should go if you want to."

Theresa sounded sincere enough.

Mary Lou nudged me in the backseat as if to say, *Go!*

I finally nodded.

460

## A C T  Access Complex Text

**▶ Specific Vocabulary**

Help students access difficult vocabulary and phrases in the second paragraph on page 461.

→ *What context clue helps you identify the meaning of the expression "domino effect"?* ("the premise that one action triggers another")

→ *How can you figure out the meaning of* antithesis *in the second-to-last paragraph?* (The narrator uses opposite words to describe herself and Mary Lou, so *antithesis* must mean "opposite.")

→ *What else could help you figure out the meaning of* antithesis? (The prefix *anti-* means "opposite.")

It was a strange camaraderie, given our history. Theresa and I shared many trips to the library together on Tuesdays. I've often wondered if, in some convoluted way, Theresa's abuse had been an attempt to get my attention. She liked the library and I always had my nose in a book, so she targeted me. Too bad for my legs that she didn't have better social skills!

Mary Lou is still my hero. If a person believes in the domino effect, the premise that one action triggers another, then I am deeply indebted to her. If she had never made me stand up to Theresa, I would have existed on the outskirts of fifth-grade society, always defenseless. I would have never gained Mary Lou's respect or become her friend. I wouldn't have gone home with her that night at the slumber party. Instead, I would have suffered through my worst imaginings. And if it weren't for Mary Lou, I might not have had the opportunity or courage to accept Theresa's invitation to the *big* library on Tuesdays, which fueled my affection for books in a dramatic way. After all, I was entering the enemy's camp.

It's sometimes easier to be brave if you have someone with whom you can stand beside or who you know is always standing behind you. Being Mary Lou's friend was always comforting, even when she

revealed her own vulnerability. Big, strong people have fears (as do tiny, wiry people), and it often takes more courage to reveal a weakness than to cover it up. She was confident, determined, fair-minded, and unafraid of her emotions. I was her antithesis: naive, insecure, and desperately wanting to be a part of something. Mary Lou fit in because she didn't try to be anything but herself. **(14)**

I wanted to be just like her.

> **STOP AND CHECK**
>
> **Reread** Why is Mary Lou the narrator's hero? Reread to check your understanding.

461

**LITERATURE ANTHOLOGY,** pp. 460–461

---

**STOP AND CHECK**

**Reread** Why is Mary Lou the narrator's hero? (Mary Lou is the narrator's hero because she made the narrator stand up for herself, which gave the narrator self-respect and courage. Mary Lou is also her hero because she has admirable personality traits, such as confidence, determination, and the ability to show her feelings. Finally, the narrator admired Mary Lou for not being anything but herself.)

## Return to Predictions

Review students' predictions and purposes for reading. Ask them to answer the Essential Question. (We can try understanding other people's points of views, talking things over, and looking for common interests to get along with others.)

---

**ELL** Point out the cognate at the top of page 461: camaraderie/*camaradería*. Help ELLs use context clues to determine the meaning of this word.

→ *Why does the narrator say her camaraderie with Theresa was strange?* (because of their history)

→ *What is the narrator's history with Theresa?* (The narrator did not like Theresa at the beginning of the story. After the slumber party she wasn't sure how she felt about her. At the end of the story, they became friends.)

# About the Author

## Meet the Author and the Illustrator

### Pam Muñoz Ryan and Carl Pearce

Have students read the biographies of the author and illustrator. Ask:

→ How did Pam Muñoz Ryan's own experiences help her create the narrator of this story?

→ How do Carl Pearce's drawings help you understand the story better?

## Author's Purpose

### To Entertain

Remind students that authors write fiction stories to entertain readers. Students may say that Pam Muñoz Ryan chose to write the story in first person because she, too, had been a new kid in a new school and knew what it was like not to fit in. The first-person point of view helps the reader see how the narrator feels about herself and others.

## Author's Craft

### Figurative Language

Explain that authors use figurative language, such as exaggeration, to create a strong feeling. Discuss what this adds to the writing.

→ Authors use exaggeration when they say that something is more or greater than it really is. For example, on page 451 the author writes, "Already with a size 9 shoe, my feet were an awkward atrocity."

→ Have students find other examples of exaggeration, such as, "The *big* library had a hundred times the selection of the branch library" on page 457.

## About the Author and Illustrator

**Pam Muñoz Ryan** knows what it feels like to be the new kid in school. When she was in fifth grade, her parents moved to a new neighborhood. Pam faced the challenge of making new friends and fitting in. What helped her adjust? Reading books! Like reading, Pam says that writing is also a journey—but one she can create. She says writing can help her "sort out the issues of life." Pam has written over 30 books and won many awards, and her journey as a writer continues.

**Carl Pearce** lives in Wales in the United Kingdom. He sometimes uses scenes from local places to help him illustrate settings in books. His work is also influenced by his love of movies. Carl brings characters and events described in books to life through his colorful drawings.

### Author's Purpose

Why do you think the author chose to write the story in first-person? How does this point of view help you understand the events?

462

**LITERATURE ANTHOLOGY, pp. 462–463**

# Respond to Reading

## Summarize

Summarize what happened to the characters in *The Friend Who Changed My Life* that led them to get along. Details from your Theme Chart may help you.

| What Does the Character Do and Say? | What Happens to the Character? |
|---|---|
| ☐ | ☐ |
| ☐ | ☐ |

Theme

## Text Evidence

1. How is the narrator like a real person? Give examples of what she says and does that make her realistic. **GENRE**

2. How are Theresa, Mary Lou, and the narrator alike and different? What does the narrator learn from her relationship with them? **THEME**

3. Does the word *sincere* on page 460 suggest a positive or a negative feeling? What clues help you figure out the connotation? **CONNOTATION AND DENOTATION**

4. Write the message the author is trying to communicate by including the scene at the slumber party. Use details to support your answer. **WRITE ABOUT READING**

### Make Connections

Talk about what leads the characters in this story to get along. **ESSENTIAL QUESTION**

Give an example of one action that a character from the story takes to get along with others. In what other ways can people get along? **TEXT TO WORLD**

463

## Make Connections · *Analytical Writing*

**Essential Question** Have partners work together to cite evidence from the text that explains how Mary Lou's actions toward the narrator affect the narrator's life.

**Text to World** After students discuss a way that a character in the story takes action to get along with others, have students suggest some positive ways classmates can get along.

# Respond to Reading

## Summarize

Review with students the information from their organizers. Model how to use the information to summarize *The Friend Who Changed My Life*.

**·** *Analytical Writing* **Write About Reading:**

**Summarize** Remind students that a summary retells only the most important story events. Ask students to write a summary of the story, using the information in their organizers to help them. Have students share their summaries with a partner.

## Text Evidence

1. **Genre** <u>Answer</u> The narrator feels awkward at her new school and she wants to fit in, just as any fifth-grader might in the same situation. <u>Evidence</u> On page 451, she says she "hated being the new kid at school."

2. **Theme** <u>Answer</u> The narrator feels awkward; Theresa and Mary Lou seem confident. All of them have similar likes and fears, which helps them get along. <u>Evidence</u> The narrator walked around with her "nose in a book," Theresa walks with a "deliberate swagger," Mary Lou is "sturdy." They are all afraid of ghost stories.

   *finished here*

3. **Connotation and Denotation** <u>Answer</u> The word *sincere* has a positive connotation. <u>Evidence</u> The word *sincere* describes the way Theresa invites the narrator to the party and she accepts. This tells me *sincere* must have a positive connotation.

4. **·** *Analytical Writing* **Write About Reading: Theme** The author's message is to be yourself. At the slumber party, the narrator is frightened but afraid to say so. Mary Lou is scared too, and she is comfortable saying so. With Mary Lou's help, the narrator and Theresa can

# Develop Comprehension

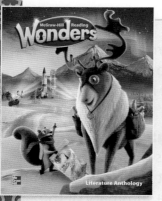

**Literature Anthology**

## "Choose Your Strategy: A Guide to Getting Along"

### Text Complexity Range

**Lexile**

740 ▲ 850 1010

**TextEvaluator™**

23 ▲ 42 51

## Options for Close Reading

→ Whole Class
→ Small Group
→ Independent

---

**CCSS Genre · Expository Text**

**Compare Texts**
Read about actions people can take to get along with others.

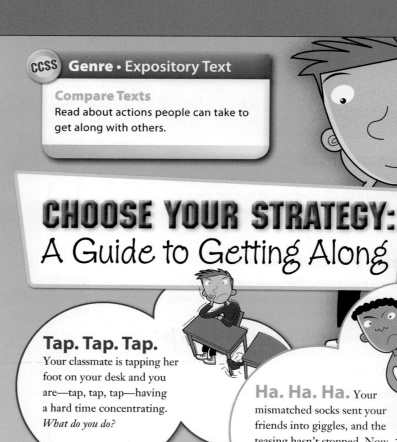

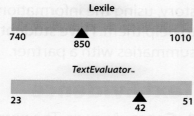

# CHOOSE YOUR STRATEGY:
## A Guide to Getting Along

**Tap. Tap. Tap.** Your classmate is tapping her foot on your desk and you are—tap, tap, tap—having a hard time concentrating. *What do you do?*

**Ha. Ha. Ha.** Your mismatched socks sent your friends into giggles, and the teasing hasn't stopped. Now your face is turning pink and red too. *What can you do?*

**Silence.** You and your best friend were chatting all morning, but at lunch, she is silent and decides to sit with another group. *What will you do?*

**Snap.** You hear the sharp snap of a pencil behind you. Those two boys have started to pick on your classmate again. *What do you decide to do?*

464

---

# A C T  Access Complex Text

## What makes this text complex?
▶ **Purpose**
▶ **Specific Vocabulary**

---

▶ **Purpose**

Remind students that knowing an author's purpose can help them to get the most from an article.

→ *Reread the title. What is the purpose of this text?* (to suggest ways that help people get along)

→ *What problem does the first bubble describe?* (A noisy classmate makes it hard to concentrate.)

Sound like problems? You can probably imagine what it's like to be in each circumstance, because, unfortunately, problems do happen. What you decide to do and how you respond in these kinds of situations is important: Your reaction can affect how you feel about yourself and others, and how others feel about you.

Because each person and problem is different, the strategies you use to resolve problems will be different, too. These are just some of the ways people can get along with others.

## Consider Other Perspectives

A good way to approach any problem is to think about the other person's perspective of a situation. Have you ever heard the expression, "Put yourself in someone else's shoes"? No, you will not be slipping on another person's pair of shoes. It means to imagine what it might be like to be in someone else's position. After all, maybe your classmate was concentrating and didn't realize her tapping was affecting you. Considering the other possibilities and points of view can help you decide how best to respond. Also, before you react impulsively, stop and ask yourself: Is this a *big* problem? Then you can decide whether it's worth saying or doing something.

**1**

465

Illustration: John Haslam

**LITERATURE ANTHOLOGY, pp. 464–465**

## Compare Texts

Students will read an informational text about getting along with others. Ask students to do a close reading of the text to understand the content. As they reread, encourage them to **summarize** or use other strategies they know to help them. They will also take notes. Then students will use the text evidence they gathered to compare this text with *The Friend Who Changed My Life.*

### 1 Ask and Answer Questions

How is it helpful to think about someone else's point of view? With a partner, paraphrase ways that this strategy is helpful. (Thinking about someone else's point of view helps you imagine how they feel. It helps you decide how to respond.)

→ *Where do the situations take place?* (at school)

→ *Why do you think the author addresses the reader directly?* (The author wants readers to imagine how they would feel in these situations.)

→ *What might be the author's purpose in addressing these problems?* (to explain how to solve certain problems that students might face)

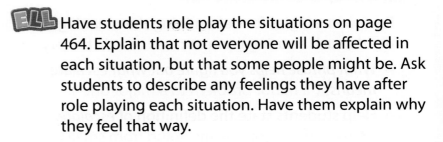 Have students role play the situations on page 464. Explain that not everyone will be affected in each situation, but that some people might be. Ask students to describe any feelings they have after role playing each situation. Have them explain why they feel that way.

# Develop Comprehension

## ❷ Ask and Answer Questions

How can "talking it out" help you solve a problem?

**Analytical Writing** **Write About Reading** Write a short summary of how a conversation can help. (A short conversation can help you understand another person's point of view and fix misunderstandings.)

## ❸ Ask and Answer Questions

What things can a person do to show a positive attitude?

**Analytical Writing** **Write About Reading** Make a list of actions that indicate a positive attitude. (1. Use a friendly tone of voice. 2. Act politely. 3. Look for humor in a situation.)

---

### Talk it Out

❷ Problems often arise when people misunderstand each other. Sometimes it's difficult to know how another person is feeling, and you may not be able to guess what's wrong. Talking things through is one way to solve the problem. But where do you begin? A simple "What's up?" can open up discussion. For example, if a friend is suddenly avoiding you, asking her what's wrong might clue you in. Maybe you didn't realize you made a remark that hurt her feelings. Having a simple conversation can help you to see each other's point of view and clear up misunderstandings.

### Adjust Your Attitude

One of the best ways to get along with others is to have a positive attitude. Remember, your attitude and your tone of voice affect those around you. If you respond to your classmate by yelling, it is likely that your classmate will react negatively, too, and this can escalate a minor problem to a major one. If you ask politely, you may get a better result.

❸ Finding a little humor in a situation can also make it less tense. So you are mortified by your mismatched socks, but stop and consider whether it is really worth getting angry. On second thought, it *is* funny. Sometimes laughter can be the best medicine, and a change of attitude can change your day.

466

---

# A C T Access Complex Text

## ▶ Specific Vocabulary

Review strategies for determining the meaning of words, such as using context clues or a dictionary.

→ *What phrase helps you figure out what* escalate *means?* ("a minor problem to a major one")

→ Help students state the definition of *escalate*. ("Minor" to "major" means going from small to big. So *escalate* must mean "to increase or grow.")

Point to the word *mortified*. Guide students to use context to determine a meaning.

→ *How might you feel if you found you had mismatched socks or shoes?* (embarrassed)

→ Confirm the meaning of *mortified* by using a dictionary.

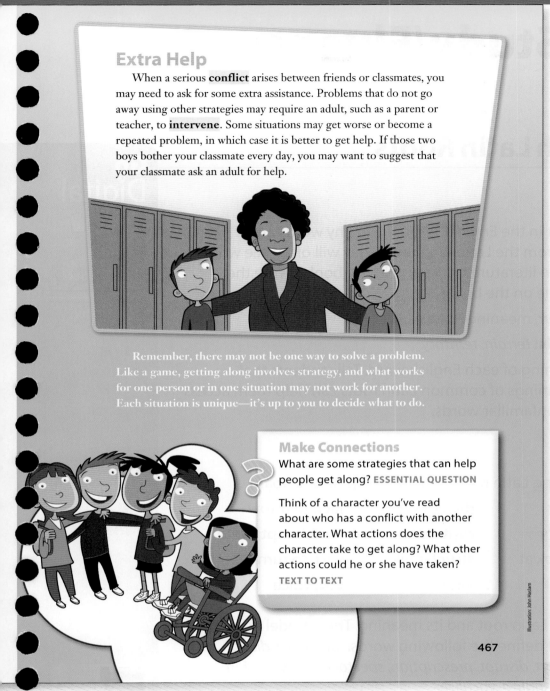

### Extra Help

When a serious **conflict** arises between friends or classmates, you may need to ask for some extra assistance. Problems that do not go away using other strategies may require an adult, such as a parent or teacher, to **intervene**. Some situations may get worse or become a repeated problem, in which case it is better to get help. If those two boys bother your classmate every day, you may want to suggest that your classmate ask an adult for help.

Remember, there may not be one way to solve a problem. Like a game, getting along involves strategy, and what works for one person or in one situation may not work for another. Each situation is unique—it's up to you to decide what to do.

**Make Connections**

What are some strategies that can help people get along? **ESSENTIAL QUESTION**

Think of a character you've read about who has a conflict with another character. What actions does the character take to get along? What other actions could he or she have taken? **TEXT TO TEXT**

Illustration: John Haslam

467

**LITERATURE ANTHOLOGY,** pp. 466–467

## Make Connections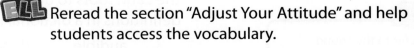

**Essential Question** Have students paraphrase and share information about actions people can take to get along with each other. Suggest that they review the headings to recall some basic strategies people can use.

**Text to Text** Have groups of students use the responses to their Ask and Answer Questions prompts to help them determine other actions the narrator in *The Friend Who Changed My Life* could have taken. Each group can report back to the class by naming the actions that the character takes in the story and suggesting another action she could have taken. Have the class vote on which strategy they think would work best. (The narrator could have talked to Theresa directly about the bullying or she could have gone to her mother, teacher, or another adult for help or advice.)

→ Explain that the idiom "laughter can be the best medicine" means it is not always necessary to take things too seriously.

**ELL** Reread the section "Adjust Your Attitude" and help students access the vocabulary.

→ Point out difficult words such as *attitude, negatively, escalate,* and *mortified.* Define them for students, using facial expressions and gestures to demonstrate their meanings. Help them replace the difficult words with words they know.

# Word Study/Fluency

 MINILESSON **20** Mins

## Words with Latin Roots

 **ELL**

Refer to the sound transfers chart to identify sounds that do not transfer in Spanish, Cantonese, Vietnamese, Hmong, and Korean.

### 1 Explain

Tell students that in the English language, many words are of Latin origin, or come from the Latin language. They will often see words with Latin roots in literature books and in textbooks. Write the following example on the board:

> **Latin root:** *terr*, meaning "land"
>
> **English words:** *terrain, territory*

Discuss the meaning of each English word. Tell students that learning the meanings of common Latin roots can help them access the meaning of unfamiliar words.

### 2 Model

Write the following Latin roots and meanings on the board.

| | | |
|---|---|---|
| **aud**, to hear | **dict**, to say | **ject**, to throw |
| **port**, to carry | **rupt**, break | **scrib/script**, write |
| **spect**, to look at | **struct**, build | **vert**, to turn |
| **tract**, to pull | **vis**, to see | **voc**, voice |

Read aloud each Latin root and its meaning. Then model using the roots to read and define the following words: *audience, diction, projectile, transport, disrupt, prescription, spectacle, construction, revert, traction, visualize, vocalize.*

### 3 Guided Practice

Write the following words with Latin roots on the board. Have students underline the root or roots in each word. Then have them read the words chorally. Help students use the meanings of the Latin roots to define the words. Then have them check their definitions in a dictionary.

| | | | |
|---|---|---|---|
| audible | dictate | project | portable |
| rupture | scribble | inspect | structure |
| visible | tractor | vocal | invert |

 **Go Digital**

**Words with Latin Roots**

**Present the Lesson**

 View "The Bully"

## Read Multisyllabic Words

**Transition to Longer Words** Help students transition to multisyllabic words with Latin roots. Write the following Latin roots and example words on the board. Have students read a root in the first column. Then model how to read the longer word in the second column. Help students use the meaning of the Latin roots, as well as the meaning of common prefixes and suffixes, to determine each word's meaning.

| aud | inaudible | dic | predictable |
| rupt | interruption | ject | projection |
| voc | vocalizing | struct | destruction |
| tract | extraction | spec | spectator |

After students complete the activity, ask them to use four multisyllabic words from the list in sentences. Then have them share their sentences with partners.

## Monitor and *Differentiate*

 **Quick Check**

Can students identify Latin roots in unfamiliar English words? Can they use the meanings of those roots to define the words?

### Small Group Instruction

**If No →** **Approaching Level** Reteach pp. T106, T110

**ELL** Develop pp. T123, T126

**If Yes →** **On Level** Apply pp. T112–T113

**Beyond Level** Apply pp. T116–T117

## FLUENCY

### Intonation

**Explain/Model** Remind students that intonation involves changes in the voice's tone or pitch during reading. Model reading the first two paragraphs of "The Bully," **Reading/Writing Workshop** pages 396–399. Emphasize the use of intonation by varying the pitch of your voice as you read.

Remind students that you will be listening for their use of intonation as you monitor their reading during the week.

**Practice/Apply** Have partners alternate reading paragraphs in the passage, modeling the intonation you used.

### Daily Fluency Practice

Students can practice fluency using **Your Turn Practice Book** passages.

**ON-LEVEL PRACTICE BOOK** p. 268

Word Study: Words with Latin Roots

Name

**Latin Roots and Their Meanings**

| tract: to pull | miss/mitt: to send |
| port: to carry | aud: to hear |
| spect: to look at | vis: to see |

Complete each sentence with a word from the word box below. A definition of each missing word is given in parentheses ( ).

| audible | tractor | portable | import | spectator |
| distract | vision | inaudible | dismiss | visible |

1. The tall mountains were _visible_ from our balcony. (able to be seen)
2. The farmer used his _tractor_ to tow the wagon. (vehicle that is used to pull farm equipment)
3. The new line of luggage was designed to be _portable_ (easy to carry)
4. It was so loud outside that the music was nearly _inaudible_ (unable to be heard)
5. The principal decided to _dismiss_ the students earlier than usual. (send away)
6. Every _spectator_ in the stadium cheered when the winning touchdown was scored. (person who goes to look at an event)

268 Practice · Grade 5 · Unit 6 · Week 2

**APPROACHING** p. 268  **BEYOND** p. 268  **ELL** p. 268

☞ **Go** Digital

**www.connected.mcgraw-hill.com**
**RESOURCES**
**Research and Inquiry**

→ **Wrap Up the Week**
# Integrate Ideas

# RESEARCH AND INQUIRY

**Getting Along**

**OBJECTIVES**

CCSS Recall relevant information from experiences or gather relevant information from print and digital sources; summarize or paraphrase information in notes and finished work, and provide a list of sources. **W.5.8**

CCSS Report on a topic or text or present an opinion, sequencing ideas logically and using appropriate facts and relevant, descriptive details to support main ideas or themes; speak clearly at an understandable pace. **SL.5.4**

• Evaluate media.
• Draw conclusions.
• Organize a speech.

**ACADEMIC LANGUAGE**

• *social media, conclusion*
• Cognates: *medios sociales, conclusión*

## Give an Oral Presentation

Explain that students will work with partners to list as many forms of social media as possible. They will also list ways in which social media can help us to get along. Finally, they will organize their conclusions and include them in an oral presentation. Discuss the following steps:

❶ **List Social Media**  Have partners brainstorm and list different forms of social media and the types of information people share through social media. Post the list of social media forms on the Shared Research Board.

❷ **Analyze Social Media**  Have partners analyze each form of social media they identify. Ask them to list features of each form, focusing on how they help people socialize with one another.

❸ **Guided Practice**  Lead students in a discussion of the ways they use social media in their lives. Have them take notes during the discussion. Students may use the Listening Checklist to evaluate their listening skills.

❹ **Create the Project: Oral Presentation**  Have partners use the lists they made about social media and the notes they took during the class discussion to draw conclusions about how social media can help people get along. Have them organize their conclusions to present in a speech to another pair.

## Present the Oral Presentation

Have partners present their organized conclusions to another pair. Encourage pairs to discuss similarities and differences between each presentation.

# TEXT CONNECTIONS

 *Analytical Writing*

## OBJECTIVES

**CCSS** Integrate information from several texts on the same topic in order to write or speak about the subject knowledgeably. **RI.5.9**

**CCSS** Engage effectively in a range of collaborative discussions (one-on-one, in groups, and teacher-led) with diverse partners on *grade 5 topics and texts*, building on others' ideas and expressing their own clearly. Review the key ideas expressed and draw conclusions in light of information and knowledge gained from the discussions. **SL.5.1d**

## Text to Text

**Cite Evidence** Tell students they will work in groups to compare the stories and texts they have read this week about getting along with others and then draw some conclusions about the Essential Question: *What actions can we take to get along with others?* Model how to make comparisons using examples from the week's **Leveled Readers** and "The Bully," **Reading/Writing Workshop** pages 396–399. Have students review the week's selections and their notes and graphic organizers. Help them set up an Accordion Foldable® to organize their findings. Students should take notes on who took action, what they did, and what the results were. They can then draw some conclusions related to the week's Essential Question.

Dinah Zike's
**FOLDABLES**

**Present Information** Have groups meet to present their summaries and conclusions. Prompt discussion of differences in students' interpretations of how characters took action to get along with others and in their overall conclusions.

# WRITE ABOUT READING

 *Analytical Writing*

**Analyze to Share an Opinion**

## OBJECTIVES

**CCSS** Draw evidence from literary or informational texts to support analysis, reflection, and research. **W.5.9**

## Write an Analysis

**Cite Evidence** Explain that students will write about a story they read this week. Using text evidence, students will analyze how well an author developed realistic characters and events.

Discuss how to analyze characters by asking *how* and *why* questions.

→ How does the author use descriptive details to make the characters realistic?

→ Why does the author do a good job of making the events seem realistic?

Use **Your Turn Practice Book** page 269 to read and discuss the student model. Have students choose a story they have read and review their notes on the characters. Have them write to give their opinion as to how well the author developed realistic characters and events. Remind students that good opinion writing clearly introduces the topic and states an opinion. Remind students to use adverbs that compare correctly.

**Present Your Ideas** Ask partners to share their paragraphs and discuss how the evidence they cited from the text supports their opinions.

# → Readers to Writers

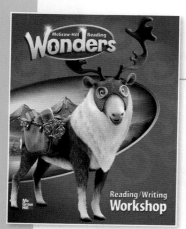

**Reading/Writing Workshop**

**OBJECTIVES**

**CCSS** Use a variety of transitional words, phrases, and clauses to manage the sequence of events. **W.5.3c**

**CCSS** Write routinely over extended time frames (time for research, reflection, and revision) and shorter time frames (a single sitting or a day or two) for a range of discipline-specific tasks, purposes, and audiences. **W.5.10**

• Analyze models to understand word choice.

• Write about coming to an agreement.

**ACADEMIC LANGUAGE**

• *sequence, time order, phrases, clauses*

• Cognates: *secuencia, cláusulas*

MINILESSON 10 Mins

## Writing Traits: Word Choice

### Time-Order Words

**Expert Model** Explain that writers make the sequence of events clear for readers by using time-order words (*next, as, then, while, finally*), phrases (*in the meantime, after a while, before long*), and clauses (*As the ball soared, before I awoke*). Time-order words show how events are connected.

COLLABORATE **Read aloud** the expert model from "The Bully." Ask students to listen for the sequence of events in the story. Have students talk with a partner to identify the time-order words, phrases, and clauses used in the passage.

**Student Model** Remind students that writers use time-order words to show the order in which events happen. Read aloud the student model "Making Peace." As students follow along, have them focus on the time-order words Karen used.

COLLABORATE **Invite** partners to talk about the model and the changes the writer made to clarify the sequence of events. Ask them to suggest other words, phrases, or clauses Karen could add to help readers understand the sequence of events.

**Expert Model**

**Student Model**

Go Digital

 **Genre Writing**

**Opinion Writing**

For full writing process lessons and rubrics see:

→ Book Review, pp. T344–T349

→ Opinion Letter, pp. T350–T355

## CCSS Writing Traits › Word Choice

# Readers to ...

To help readers understand the sequence of events in a story, writers may use **time-order words**, such as *first*, *next*, *then*, *later*, *as*, *before*, *after*, *last*, and *finally*. The words may introduce longer phrases. Reread the passage below from "The Bully."

### Time-Order Words

What time-order words are used in the passage?

Explain how the use of the time-order words helps make the sequence of events clear.

**Expert Model**

The next day in school brought Michael's usual misery. There stood J.T., and Michael knew it would be just a matter of seconds before the two of them collided in the middle of the hall.

As J.T. came nearer, Michael wished he had Ramon's protective arm to stop the bully from attacking. Then, suddenly, the unexpected happened. J.T. accidentally tripped. He fell down, and his own armful of books went flying across the floor.

Marcelo Baez

404

# Writers

Karen wrote a narrative about friends who come to an agreement. Read Karen's revision of this section.

**Student Model**

## Making Peace

At first,
^ Amy and I were best friends. It

had been that way since Kindergarten.
Later,
^ We both entered fifth grade, and

         I felt bad because
trouble began. ^ Amy made new friends

    more easily        Soon
in class easier^ than I did. ^ She spent

                Eventually
little time with me. ^ She ignored me

completely. I felt worse than ever and

tried to think of a way to bring us

            Finally
back together. ^ I got an idea.

### Editing Marks

∧ Add
∧ Add a comma.
⌐ Take out.
(sp) Check spelling.
≡ Make a capital letter.

### Grammar Handbook

**Adverbs that Compare**
See page 470.

### Your Turn

☑ Identify the time-order words that Karen included in her narrative.

☑ Explain how Karen used adverbs that compare.

☑ Tell how Karen's revisions improved her writing.

*Go Digital!*
**Write online in Writer's Workspace**

405

**READING/WRITING WORKSHOP, pp. 404–405**

## ELL ENGLISH LANGUAGE LEARNERS SCAFFOLD

Provide support to help English Language Learners understand the writing trait.

| Beginning | Intermediate | Advanced/High |
|---|---|---|
| **Respond Orally** Help students complete the sentence frames about the student model. ____, *Amy and Karen were best friends.* ____ *trouble began when they were in the fifth grade. Amy made new friends.* ____ *she ignored Karen.* | **Practice** Ask students to complete the sentence frames. *At first, ____. Later, ____. Amy made new friends, and eventually, ____.* | **Understand** Check for understanding. Ask: *Which time-order words does Karen use? What happens first? Next? Last? How do the time-order words help you understand the narrative?* |

# Writing Every Day: Word Choice

 **DAY 1**

 **DAY 2**

### Writing Entry: Time-Order Words

**Prewrite** Provide students with the prompt below.

*Write about a time when you and a friend came to an agreement.*

Have partners list times they came to an agreement with a friend. Ask them to jot down what the disagreement was and how they came to an agreement.

**Draft** Have students select a topic from the list to write about. Remind students to use time-order words, phrases, and clauses to show the sequence of events.

### Focus on Time-Order Words

Use **Your Turn Practice Book** page 270 to model using time-order words, phrases, and clauses.

*Maria and I could not agree on a science project. I wanted to grow crystals. Maria wanted to make a volcano. We chose a project we both liked—making a robot.*

Model adding time-order words to the first sentence.

*At first, Maria and I could not agree on a science project.*

Discuss how using time-order words helps clarify the sequence of events. Guide students to add more time-order words to the model.

### Writing Entry: Time-Order Words

**Revise** Have students revise their writing from Day 1 by adding time-order words, phrases, and clauses.

Use the **Conferencing Routines**. Circulate among students and stop briefly to talk with individuals. Provide time for peer review.

**Edit** Have students use Grammar Handbook page 470 in the **Reading/Writing Workshop** to edit for errors in adverbs that compare.

# Conferencing Routines

## Teacher Conferences

**STEP 1**

Talk about the strengths of the writing.

*You have a clear beginning in which you introduce the problem. It makes we want to keep reading.*

**STEP 2**

Focus on how the writer uses the target trait for the week.

*Your story events seem to be in order, but it would help me understand the sequence if you added some time-order words.*

**STEP 3**

Make concrete suggestions for revisions. Have students work on a specific assignment, such as those to the right, and then meet with you to review progress.

## DAY 3

### Writing Entry: Time-Order Words

**Prewrite** Ask students to search their Writer's Notebooks for topics for a new draft. Or, provide a prompt such as the following:

*Tell about a time you disagreed with a family member. How did you come to an agreement?*

**Draft** Once students have chosen their topics, ask them to create a sequence chart to plan their writing. Then have them think about time-order words they might include in their writing. Students can use their charts to begin their drafts.

## DAY 4

### Writing Entry: Time-Order Words

**Revise** Have students revise their writing from Day 3 by making sure they use time-order words, phrases, and clauses. As students revise, hold teacher conferences with individual students. You may also wish to have students work with partners to peer conference.

**Edit** Invite students to review the rules for adverbs that compare on Grammar Handbook page 470 in the **Reading/Writing Workshop** and then edit their drafts for errors.

## DAY 5

### Share and Reflect

Discuss with the class what they learned about using time-order words. Invite volunteers to read and compare draft text with text that has been revised. Have students discuss the writing by focusing on the importance of using time-order words to help readers understand the sequence of events. Allow time for individuals to reflect on their own writing progress and record observations in their Writer's Notebooks.

---

### Suggested Revisions

Provide specific direction to help focus young writers.

**Focus on a Sentence**
Read the draft and target one sentence for revision. *Rewrite this sentence by adding a time-order word to make the sequence clear.*

**Focus on a Section**
Underline a section that needs to be revised. Provide specific suggestions. *Add time-order words to help the reader understand how the events are related.*

**Focus on a Revision Strategy**
Underline a section. Have students use a specific revision strategy such as substituting. *Replace overused time-order words, such as* then *and* next, *with more descriptive phrases and clauses.*

## Peer Conferences

Focus peer response groups on adding time-order words to make the sequence of events clear.

- ☑ Are the events written in a logical sequence?
- ☑ Do time-order words, phrases, and clauses make the sequence clear?
- ☑ Does the writer need to add additional time-order words?

# → Grammar: Adverbs That Compare

**Reading/Writing Workshop**

## OBJECTIVES

**CCSS** Demonstrate command of the conventions of standard English grammar and usage when writing or speaking. Form and use comparative and superlative adjectives and adverbs, and choose between them depending on what is to be modified. **L.3.1g**

- Distinguish how to use *good* and *well*.
- Proofread sentences.

**Go Digital**

**Adverbs That Compare**

**Grammar Activities**

---

### DAY 1

**DAILY LANGUAGE ACTIVITY**

**When I eat chinese food I use chopsticks. I use them best than Lyn does.** (1: Chinese; 2: food,; 3: chopsticks; 4: better)

## Introduce Adverbs that Compare

→ An **adverb** can compare two or more actions.

→ Adverbs that compare two actions use -*er* or *more*. *Lars runs <u>faster</u> than Lee. Vance talks <u>more rapidly</u> than his sister.*

→ Actions that compare three or more actions use -*est* or *most*. *Kathy runs the <u>fastest</u> out of all the girls in our class. Kaylee talks the <u>most rapidly</u> of anyone in our class.*

Have partners discuss adverbs that compare using page 470 of the Grammar Handbook in **Reading/Writing Workshop**.

---

### DAY 2

**DAILY LANGUAGE ACTIVITY**

**Cara walked quick to her brothers room. "Where is my bat," she asked.** (1: quickly; 2: brother's; 3: bat?")

## Review Using Adverbs that Compare

Discuss examples of adverbs that compare two actions and adverbs that compare three or more actions.

## Introduce Comparative Adverbs -*er*, -*est*, *more*, *most*

→ Add -*er* or -*est* to most short adverbs to compare actions: *ran faster, ran the fastest.*

→ Add *more* or *most* to adverbs that have two or more syllables or to adverbs that end in -*ly*: *more carefully, most carefully.*

Have partners discuss adverbs that compare using page 470 of the Grammar Handbook.

---

 **TALK ABOUT IT**

**COLLABORATE**

### ADVERBS THAT COMPARE

Set a timer and ask pairs to list ten actions. Then have pairs use adverbs to make comparisons using the actions in their list. One partner records the comparisons; the other reads them to the class.

### MODIFY IT

Call out a verb. Ask students to write -*ly* adverbs that could modify the verb. Then have students write sentences using the -*ly* adverbs to compare two or more actions. Ask volunteers to share their sentences.

---

## DAY  3

### DAILY LANGUAGE ACTIVITY

**I usual run three miles every morning but I woke up extreme late today.** (1: usually; 2: morning,; 3: extremely)

### Mechanics and Usage: Using *good, well; more, most; -er, -est*

→ *Good* is often an adjective, and *well* is often an adverb that tells *how*. *Good* and *well* cannot be used interchangeably. *Well* is an adjective when it means healthy. *I do not feel* <u>well</u> *today*.

→ Use *more* or *most* to form comparisons with adverbs that have two or more syllables. *More* or *most* almost always appears in front of the adverb.

→ Never add *-er* and *more* or *-est* and *most* to the same adverb.

Have students check their writing using Grammar Handbook pages 469–470.

## DAY  4

### DAILY LANGUAGE ACTIVITY

**Sean recovered from the flu quickly more than I did. He felt good enough to go to the play.** (1: more quickly; 2: well)

### Proofread

Have students correct errors in these sentences:

1. Tony packed more hurriedlier than his sister. (hurriedly)

2. Tara sang most beautifullier of all the singers. (beautifully)

3. Randell did good on his spelling test, though he is not always a well speller. (1: well; 2: good)

4. At last week's race, Shana ran more faster than Lisa. (ran faster)

Have students check their work using Grammar Handbook pages 469–470 on adverbs.

## DAY 5

### DAILY LANGUAGE ACTIVITY

**"Lara, please turn down the t.v," said mrs Lincoln. "Thats the annoyingest show."** (1: TV; 2: Mrs.; 3: That's; 4: most annoying)

### Assess

Use the Daily Language Activity and Grammar Practice Reproducibles page 135 for assessment.

### Reteach

Use Grammar Practice Reproducibles pages 131–134 and selected pages from the Grammar Handbook for additional reteaching. Remind students that it is important to use adverbs to compare correctly as they speak and write.

Check students' writing for use of the skill and listen for it in their speaking. Assign Grammar Revision Assignments in their Writer's Notebooks as needed.

**See Grammar Practice Reproducibles pp. 131–135.**

### ADJECTIVES TO ADVERBS

List the following adjectives: *slow, constant, quiet, soft*. Have partners add *-ly* to form the adverbs. Then have them compare two or more actions using the *-ly* adverbs. Have pairs write sentences with the comparisons.

### TWO THEN TWO OR MORE

Display the following adverbs: *fast, tiredly, gracefully*. Have one partner use each adverb to compare two actions and the other partner use the adverb to compare more than two actions.

### ACTIONS AND YOU

Have students use adverbs that compare to write a paragraph about actions they can take to get along with others. Brainstorm a list of possible adverbs with the class.

# Spelling: Words with Latin Roots

**DAY 1**

**DAY 2**

## OBJECTIVES

CCSS Spell grade-appropriate words correctly, consulting references as needed.
**L.5.2e**

### Spelling Words

| | | |
|---|---|---|
| subtraction | transport | spectacle |
| transportation | tractor | inspect |
| missile | spectator | mission |
| portable | attraction | import |
| intermission | export | dismiss |
| committee | inspector | suspect |
| respect | distract | |

**Review** telescope, astronaut, photograph
**Challenge** spectacular, protractor

### Differentiated Spelling

**Approaching Level**

| | | |
|---|---|---|
| subtract | transport | spectacle |
| port | tractor | inspect |
| missile | spectator | mission |
| portable | traction | import |
| intermission | export | dismiss |
| commit | inspector | suspect |
| respect | distract | |

**Beyond Level**

| | | |
|---|---|---|
| subtraction | transport | spectacle |
| transportation | intractable | inspect |
| circumspect | spectator | mission |
| portable | attraction | import |
| intermission | export | dismissal |
| committee | inspector | missile |
| prospector | distract | |

## Assess Prior Knowledge

Read the spelling words aloud, emphasizing the Latin roots.

Display the word *export*. Point out the Latin root *port*, drawing a line under the root as you say it. Explain that many English words are based on Latin roots such as *port*, from the Latin word meaning "to carry."

Demonstrate sorting spelling words by Latin roots: *port, tract, spect,* and *miss/mit*. Sort a few spelling words that have a similar root, such as *export, distract, suspect,* and *mission*. Point out the root in each word as it is sorted. Ask students to name other words that have these roots.

Use the Dictation Sentences from Day 5 to give the pretest. Say the underlined word, read the sentence, and repeat the word. Have students write the words. Then have students check their papers.

## Spiral Review

Review the Greek roots in *telescope astronaut,* and *photograph.* Read each sentence below, repeat the review word, and have students write the words.

1. I saw Mars through a <u>telescope</u>.
2. The <u>astronaut</u> walked on the moon.
3. The <u>photograph</u> of the African savannah is stunning.

Have students trade papers and check their spellings.

**Challenge Words** Review this week's spelling words with Latin roots. Read each sentence below, repeat the challenge word, and have students write the words.

1. The vista was a <u>spectacular</u> sight!
2. Use a <u>protractor</u> to measure angles.

Have students check and correct their spellings and write the words in their word study notebooks.

 **WORD SORTS**

**COLLABORATE**

### OPEN SORT

Have students cut apart the **Spelling Word Cards** in the Online Resource Book and initial the back of each card. Have them read the words aloud with partners. Then have partners do an **open sort**. Have them record their sorts in their word study notebooks.

### PATTERN SORT

Complete the **pattern sort** from Day 1 by using the Spelling Word Cards. Point out the different Latin roots. Partners should compare and check their sorts. Have them record their sorts in their word study notebooks.

**DAY**  **3**

## Word Meanings

Have students copy the cloze sentences below into their word study notebooks. Say the sentences aloud. Then ask students to fill in the blanks with a spelling word.

1. Mr. Riley needs a _____ computer so he can work from anywhere. (portable)

2. I always _____ items for any flaws before I buy them. (inspect)

3. Public _____ in our town includes buses and the subway. (transportation)

Challenge students to create cloze sentences using their other spelling, review, or challenge words. Have students post their sentences on the board.

**See Phonics/Spelling Reproducibles pp. 157–162.**

### SPEED SORT

Have partners do a **speed sort** to see who is fastest and then compare and discuss their sorts. Then have them do a word hunt in this week's readings to find words with Latin roots. Have them record the words in their word study notebooks.

**DAY**  **4**

## Proofread and Write

Write these sentences on the board. Have students circle and correct each misspelled word. Have students use a print or a digital dictionary to check and correct their spellings.

1. One spectater left the concert before intermishion. (spectator, intermission)

2. The transportashion comittee hired buses for the trip. (transportation, committee)

3. The tracter pull was quite a spectackle. (tractor, spectacle)

4. The firm's mishion is to exxport high-quality goods. (mission, export)

**Error Correction** Once students write a word, prompt them to recheck it for the spelling of the Latin root by segmenting the syllables.

### BLIND SORT

Have partners do a **blind sort:** one reads a Spelling Word Card; the other tells under which Latin root it belongs. Have partners compare and discuss their sorts. Then have partners play Go Fish with the cards, using Latin roots as the "fish."

**DAY** **5**

## Write

Use the Dictation Sentences for the posttest. Have students list the misspelled words in their word study notebooks. Look for students' use of these words in their writings.

### Dictation Sentences

1. We learned <u>subtraction</u> in class.
2. A bike is my <u>transportation</u>.
3. He worked on the secret <u>missile</u>.
4. I carried the <u>portable</u> radio.
5. He left the theater at <u>intermission</u>.
6. A <u>committee</u> chose the book.
7. We will <u>respect</u> the camp rules.
8. Big items are hard to <u>transport</u>.
9. The farmer rode the <u>tractor</u>.
10. The <u>spectator</u> watched the game.
11. Lions are the main <u>attraction</u> at the zoo.
12. Corn is our country's <u>export</u>.
13. The <u>inspector</u> examined the restaurant.
14. Loud music will <u>distract</u> me.
15. What a <u>spectacle</u> the circus was!
16. Please <u>inspect</u> the sleeping bags.
17. Her <u>mission</u> is to finish the job.
18. It's expensive to <u>import</u> goods.
19. The teacher will <u>dismiss</u> the class.
20. I <u>suspect</u> she is upset with me.

Have students self-correct their tests.

# Build Vocabulary

**DAY**  **1**

**DAY**  **2**

## OBJECTIVES

 **CCSS** Determine or clarify the meaning of unknown and multiple-meaning words and phrases based on *grade 5 reading and content,* choosing flexibly from a range of strategies. **L.5.4**

**CCSS** Demonstrate understanding of figurative language, word relationships, and nuances in word meanings. Recognize and explain the meaning of common idioms, adages, and proverbs. **L.5.5b**

Expand vocabulary by adding inflectional endings and suffixes.

### Vocabulary Words

| | |
|---|---|
| abruptly | conflict |
| ally | intervene |
| collided | protective |
| confident | taunting |

## Go Digital

**Vocabulary**

**Vocabulary Activities**

### Connect to Words

Practice this week's vocabulary words.

1. Demonstrate stopping a conversation **abruptly**.
2. How is an **ally** different from a friend?
3. Tell about a time when you **collided** with someone.
4. Describe something that you feel **confident** doing.
5. How might you resolve a **conflict** between friends?
6. Why might you **intervene** in an argument?
7. What people or things are you **protective** of?
8. Why is **taunting** other people wrong?

### Expand Vocabulary

Help students generate different forms of this week's words by adding, changing, or removing inflectional endings.

→ Draw a T-chart on the board. Write *ally* in the first column. Then write *allies* in the next column. Read aloud the words with students.

→ Have students share sentences using each form of *ally*.

→ Students can fill in the chart for *conflict*, and then share sentences using the different forms of the words.

→ Have students copy the chart in their word study notebooks.

## BUILD MORE VOCABULARY

**COLLABORATE**

### ACADEMIC VOCABULARY

→ Display *concentrating, strategies,* and *respond*.

→ Define the words and discuss their meanings with students.

→ Write *concentrate* under *concentrating*. Have partners write other words with the same root and define them. Then have partners ask and answer questions using the words.

→ Repeat with *strategies* and *respond*.

### ADAGES AND PROVERBS

Remind students that adages and proverbs are common sayings.

→ Write the sentence *A friend in need is a friend indeed.* Elicit what students think the adage means.

→ Have partners research other adages and proverbs and share their ideas with the class.

→ Have students write the adages and proverbs and their meanings in their word study notebooks.

**DAY**

**3**

## Reinforce the Words

Review this week's and last week's vocabulary words. Have students orally complete each sentence stem.

1. When the bully was <u>taunting</u> Sean and Ted, _____.
2. Lena's <u>ally</u> helped _____.
3. Mr. Gable <u>abruptly</u> dropped the plate when _____.
4. Lexi is <u>confident</u> that she will _____ the test.
5. After Carla <u>collided</u> with Ray, she _____.
6. Kim wears <u>protective</u> clothing when he _____.

Display the previous week's vocabulary: *bulletin, enlisted, intercept, operations, recruits, survival.* Have partners ask and answer questions for each word.

**DAY**

**4**

## Connect to Writing

→ Have students write sentences in their word study notebooks using this week's vocabulary.

→ Tell them to write sentences that provide word information they learned from this week's readings.

→ **ELL** Provide the Day 3 sentence stems 1–6 for students needing extra support.

**Write About Vocabulary** Have students write something they learned from this week's words in their word study notebooks. For example, they might write about how an *ally* can be helpful or about ways to be *protective* of a younger sibling.

**DAY**

**5**

## Word Squares

Ask students to create Word Squares for each vocabulary word.

→ In the first square, students write the word. (e.g., *collided*)

→ In the second square, students write their own definition of the word and any related words, such as synonyms. (e.g., *bumped, ran into*)

→ In the third square, students draw a simple illustration that will help them remember the word. (e.g., drawing of two ball players who collided)

→ In the fourth square, students write nonexamples, including antonyms for the word. (e.g., *avoided, missed*)

Have partners discuss their squares.

## CONNOTATION AND DENOTATION

Remind students to consider the connotation and denotation of words to understand what they read.

→ Display **Your Turn Practice Book pages 263–264.** Discuss the denotation and connotation of *glares* in the first paragraph.

→ Have students complete page 267.

→ Partners can confirm meanings in a print or an online dictionary.

## SHADES OF MEANING

Help students generate words related to *conflict.* Draw a T-chart. Head one column *Conflict* and the other *Conflict Resolution.*

→ Have partners generate words to add to the T-chart. Ask students to use a thesaurus.

→ Add words not included such as (conflict) *argument, fight, struggle, disagreement*; (conflict resolution) *peace, agreement, mediation, compromise.*

## MORPHOLOGY

Use *intervene* as a springboard for students to learn more words.

→ Have students research the origin of *intervene* using a dictionary.

→ Elicit from students that the word is from the Latin *venire* meaning "to come."

→ Ask partners to use their knowledge of the root to discuss the meaning of *convene* and write the word in their word study notebooks.

# (→) Approaching Level

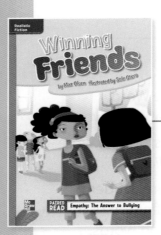

**Lexile** 680
*TextEvaluator™* 43

**ACADEMIC LANGUAGE**

• *realistic fiction, theme, summarize, details, connotation, denotation*

• Cognates: *ficción realista, tema, resumir, detalles, connotación, denotación*

## Leveled Reader: *Winning Friends*

**Go Digital**

**Leveled Readers**

### Before Reading

**Preview and Predict**

→ Read the Essential Question with students.

→ Have students preview the title, table of contents, and first page of *Winning Friends*. Students should predict what they think the selection will be about. Encourage students to confirm or revise their predictions as they read.

### Review Genre: Realistic Fiction

Tell students that this text is realistic fiction. Explain that realistic fiction contains settings that could exist and includes characters and events like those found in real life. Authors use descriptive details to help readers visualize the people and places in the story. Have students identify features of realistic fiction in *Winning Friends* as they read.

### During Reading

**Close Reading**

**Note Taking:** Ask students to use their graphic organizer as they read.

**Use Graphic Organizer**

**Pages 2–5** *What is Jalissa and Ella's relationship?* (They are best friends.) *How does Ella feel about Jalissa getting into the school musical?* (Ella realizes that it's the first thing they haven't done together.) *Turn to a partner and summarize what happens at school the next day.* (Ella listens as Jalissa talks to two other girls about the play. Jalissa does not want to play basketball with Ella. Ella thinks that Jalissa doesn't want to hang out with her anymore.) *What does Ella agree to do at the end of the chapter?* (watch the next rehearsal, so she won't feel so left out)

**Pages 6–7** *Does attending the rehearsal make Ella feel better or worse?* (worse) *Summarize what happens between Jalissa and Ella afterwards.* (Jalissa walks off with her new friends, ignoring Ella. Jalissa tells Ella she can't go to Alana's house.) *How does Ella react?* (She is very hurt.)

**Pages 8–9** *Summarize what happens when Ella and her mother visit the public library.* (Ella's mother shows her a leaflet about a talent contest. Ella gets an idea about how she and Jalissa can spend time together.)

*Does Jalissa agree to enter the contest?* (not at first; she'll call back)

**Pages 10–12** *How does Jalissa act during the rehearsal for the contest?* (bored and impatient) *On page 11, does* shrugged *have a positive or negative connotation?* (negative; It shows that Jalissa isn't enthusiastic.) *What important event happens at the end of Chapter 3?* (Ella and Jalissa argue, and Jalissa quits the contest.)

**Pages 13–15** *What does Jalissa do at the beginning of Chapter 4?* (apologize; suggest that they practice over the phone) *How do they feel about not winning? What might this say about the story's theme?* (They feel they won back their friendship; getting along is more important.)

## After Reading

**Respond to Reading** Revisit the Essential Question and ask students to complete the Text Evidence questions on page 16.

**Write About Reading** Check that students have identified the message the author communicates by using details from the story.

### Fluency: Intonation

**Model** Model reading page 3 with proper intonation. Next reread the page aloud and have students read along with you.

**Apply** Have students practice reading the passage with partners.

## PAIRED READ

**Leveled Reader**

# "Empathy: The Answer to Bullying"

## Make Connections:
## Write About It

Before reading, ask students to note that the genre of this selection is expository text. Then discuss the Essential Question. After reading, ask students to write connections between *Winning Friends* and "Empathy: The Answer to Bullying."

> ### FOCUS ON LITERARY ELEMENTS
>
> Students can extend their knowledge of how authors create a mood, or feeling, in a story by completing the literary elements activity on page 20.

## Literature Circles

Ask students to conduct a literature circle using the Thinkmark questions to guide the discussion. You may wish to have a whole-class discussion, using information in both selections in the Leveled Reader, about actions we can take to get along with others.

# Level Up

Level-up lessons available online.

**IF** students read the **Approaching Level** fluently and answered the questions,

**THEN** pair them with students who have proficiently read the **On Level** and have students

• echo-read the **On Level** main selection.

• identify two traits that help them know that the story is realistic fiction.

## A C T Access Complex Text

The **On Level** challenges students by including more **complex sentence structures** and a more complicated **story structure**.

**Approaching Level**

# Word Study/Decoding

## REVIEW WORDS WITH LATIN ROOTS

 **TIER 2**

**OBJECTIVES**

**CCSS** Know and apply grade-level phonics and word analysis skills in decoding words. Use combined knowledge of all letter-sound correspondences, syllabication patterns, and morphology (e.g., roots and affixes) to read accurately unfamiliar multisyllabic words in context and out of context. **RF.5.3a**

Decode words with Latin roots.

 **I Do** Write the Latin root *vis* on the board and read it aloud. Explain that the Latin root *vis* means "to see." Then write the word *revise* on the board and read it aloud. Model using the meaning of the Latin root *vis* and the prefix *re-* ("again") to define the word as "to see again."

**We Do** Write the word *vision* on the board and read it aloud. Guide students to use the meaning of the root and the suffix *-ion* ("act or process") to determine the meaning of the word: "the act of seeing."

**You Do** Add the Latin root *aud* to the board. Read it aloud, and give its meaning ("to hear"). Ask students to use the meaning of the Latin root *aud* and the meaning of the suffix *-ible* ("capable of") to define the word *audible*: "able to be heard."

## BUILD WORDS WITH LATIN ROOTS

 **TIER 2**

**OBJECTIVES**

**CCSS** Know and apply grade-level phonics and word analysis skills in decoding words. Use combined knowledge of all letter-sound correspondences, syllabication patterns, and morphology (e.g., roots and affixes) to read accurately unfamiliar multisyllabic words in context and out of context. **RF.5.3a**

Build words with Latin roots.

 **I Do** Display the **Word-Building Cards** *ex, sup,* and *or* and write the Latin roots *port* ("to carry") and *tract* ("to pull") on the board. Model reading the Word-Building Cards and the Latin roots, and discuss each root's meaning.

 **We Do** Work with students to combine the Word-Building Cards and Latin roots to form the words *export, support, extract,* and *tractor*. Guide them to use the meanings of the Latin roots and a dictionary to define the words.

 **You Do** Write on the board and review the meanings of the prefix *pre-* ("before") and the Latin roots *dict* ("to say") and *scrib/script* ("write"). Ask pairs of students to combine the prefix with the Latin roots to build words. Have them determine the meaning of each word by using the meaning of its prefix and root. Have them share their work with the class.

# PRACTICE WORDS WITH LATIN ROOTS

## OBJECTIVES

 Know and apply grade-level phonics and word analysis skills in decoding words. Use combined knowledge of all letter-sound correspondences, syllabication patterns, and morphology (e.g., roots and affixes) to read accurately unfamiliar multisyllabic words in context and out of context. **RF.5.3a**

Practice words with Latin roots.

 Write these words with Latin roots on the board: *portable, scripted, terrain.* Review the meaning of the Latin roots *port* ("to carry"), *scrib/script* ("write"), and *terr* ("land") and underline them in the words. Read each word aloud. Model using the meaning of the root to determine the meaning of each word.

 Write the words *structure, spectator,* and *interject* on the board. As necessary, help students identify and define the Latin root in each word (*struct*: "build"; *spect*: "to look at"; *ject*: "to throw"). Model how to decode and figure out the meaning of the first word. Then have students decode and give the meaning of the remaining words.

**You Do** To provide additional practice, write these words on the board. Read aloud the first word, identify the Latin root, and give the word's meaning.

| | | |
|---|---|---|
| spectacle | territory | scribble |
| terrestrial | subtraction | visualize |
| rejection | dictation | transport |

Then have students read aloud the remaining words. Ask them to identify each Latin root and give the meaning of each word. As necessary, have students use a dictionary to determine the meaning of the words.

Afterward, point to the words in the list in random order for students to read chorally.

## ELL ENGLISH LANGUAGE LEARNERS

For the **ELLs** who need **phonics, decoding,** and **fluency** practice, use scaffolding methods as necessary to ensure students understand the meaning of the words. Refer to the **Language Transfers Handbook** for phonics elements that may not transfer in students' native languages.

# → Approaching Level

## Vocabulary

### REVIEW HIGH-FREQUENCY WORDS

**TIER 2**

**OBJECTIVES**
Acquire and use accurately grade-appropriate general academic and domain-specific words and phrases, including those that signal contrast, addition, and other logical relationships (e.g., *however, although, nevertheless, similarly, moreover, in addition*).
**L.5.6**

Review high-frequency words.

 Use **High-Frequency Word Cards** 211–220. Display one word at a time, following the routine:

Display the word. Read the word. Then spell the word.

 Ask students to state the word and spell the word with you. Model using the word in a sentence and have students repeat after you.

 Display the word. Ask students to say the word then spell it. When completed, quickly flip through the word card set as students chorally read the words. Provide opportunities for students to use the words in speaking and writing. For example, provide sentence starters such as *I want to ____*. Ask students to write each word in their Writer's Notebook.

### REVIEW VOCABULARY WORDS

**TIER 2**

**OBJECTIVES**
Acquire and use accurately grade-appropriate general academic and domain-specific words and phrases, including those that signal contrast, addition, and other logical relationships (e.g., *however, although, nevertheless, similarly, moreover, in addition*).
**L.5.6**

 Display each **Visual Vocabulary Card** and state the word. Explain how the photograph illustrates the word. State the example sentence and repeat the word.

 Point to the word on the card and read the word with students. Ask them to repeat the word. Engage students in structured partner talk about the image as prompted on the back of the vocabulary card.

 Display each visual in random order, hiding the word. Have students match the definitions and context sentences of the words to the visuals displayed.

# IDENTIFY RELATED WORDS

**OBJECTIVES**

**CCSS** Demonstrate understanding of figurative language, word relationships, and nuances in word meanings. Use the relationship between particular words (e.g., synonyms, antonyms, homographs) to better understand each of the words. **L.5.5.c**

 **I Do** Display the *abruptly* **Visual Vocabulary Card** and say aloud the word set *abruptly, quickly, suddenly, slowly*. Point out that *slowly* does not belong.

 **We Do** Display the vocabulary card for the word *ally*. Say aloud the word set *ally, friend, enemy, supporter*. With students, identify the word that does not belong (*enemy*) and discuss why.

 **You Do** Using the word sets below, display the remaining cards one at a time, saying aloud the word set. Ask students to identify the word that does not belong.

*collided, missed, crashed, bumped*

*confident, uncertain, secure, sure*

*protective, shielding, dangerous, defensive*

*taunting, teasing, complimenting, mocking*

*conflict, fight, argument, agreement*

*intervene, withdraw, intrude, block*

# CONNOTATION AND DENOTATION

**OBJECTIVES**

**CCSS** Determine or clarify the meaning of unknown and multiple-meaning words and phrases based on *grade 5 reading and content*, choosing flexibly from a range of strategies. **L.5.4**

**CCSS** Demonstrate understanding of figurative language, word relationships, and nuances in word meanings. **L.5.5**

Identify the connotation and denotation of words to understand their meanings.

 **I Do** Remind students that a word's *denotation* is its dictionary definition. A word's *connotation* is the specific feeling it suggests or creates in readers. A word can have a positive or a negative connotation. Using connotations and denotations can increase understanding of a text. Display the Comprehension and Fluency passage on **Approaching Reproducibles** pages 263–264. Read the first five paragraphs. Point to *squirm* in paragraph 5.

**Think Aloud** I know the denotation of *squirm* is "to twist about like a worm." In the context of the story, *squirm* has a negative connotation. The narrator squirms in her seat because she is embarrassed by her childish behavior.

 **We Do** Have students point to the word *inflexible* in paragraph 6. Have them use a dictionary to find the denotation ("rigidly firm in will or purpose"). Guide students to see how the word *inflexible* has a negative connotation in this context, since being inflexible prevents the sisters from coming to an agreement.

 **You Do** Have partners use a dictionary to find the denotation of the word *slumps* in the third paragraph on page 264 and use context clues to determine if it has a positive or negative connotation.

# Approaching Level

## Comprehension

### FLUENCY

**TIER 2**

**OBJECTIVES**

**CCSS** Read on-level prose and poetry orally with accuracy, appropriate rate, and expression on successive readings. **RF.5.4b**

Read fluently with good intonation.

 **I Do** Explain that reading a selection out loud is not just about reading accurately. Readers should change the tone of their voices to show the meaning of what they read. Read the first three paragraphs of the Comprehension and Fluency passage on **Approaching Reproducibles** pages 263–264. Have students listen for when you change the volume or tone of your voice.

 **We Do** Read the rest of the page aloud. Have students repeat each sentence after you, using the same intonation. Explain that you raised your voice and emphasized certain words and phrases to show they are important.

 **You Do** Have partners take turns reading sentences from the Comprehension and Fluency passage. Remind them to focus on intonation. Listen in and provide corrective feedback as needed by modeling proper fluency.

### IDENTIFY IMPORTANT DETAILS

**TIER 2**

**OBJECTIVES**

**CCSS** Quote accurately from a text when explaining what the text says explicitly and when drawing inferences from the text. **RL.5.1**

Identify key details to increase understanding.

 **I Do** Remind students to pay attention to details about what the characters do and say and how they respond to events. Identifying these details helps readers understand how characters change throughout the story—which is a good way to start identifying the story's theme.

 **We Do** Echo-read the first four paragraphs of the Comprehension and Fluency passage on **Approaching Reproducibles** pages 263–264. Model how to identify the things that Lucia and her family members say and do and how they respond to events.

 **You Do** Have partners read the rest of the passage aloud to each other. After each paragraph, have students list details about what the characters say and do and how they respond to events. Review their lists with them and help them explain why the details they chose are important.

## REVIEW THEME

**OBJECTIVES**
CCSS Determine a theme
of a story, drama, or
poem from details in
the text, including how
characters in a story
or drama respond
to challenges or
how the speaker in a
poem reflects upon a
topic; summarize the
text. **RL.5.2**

 **I Do**   Remind students that the theme of a story is the important message about life that the author wants to share with readers. The theme usually is not stated directly in the text. Readers can determine the theme by paying attention to what characters say and do and how they respond to events. For example, a lesson the characters learn is often related to the theme.

 **We Do**   Choral-read the first four paragraphs of the Comprehension and Fluency passage on **Approaching Reproducibles** pages 263–264. Refer to the list of details students have already compiled to identify details about the characters. Model using the details to brainstorm ideas about what the theme might be, such as that being inflexible leads to conflict.

 **You Do**   Have partners read the rest of the passage and reread their lists. Tell them to add details about how the characters change from the beginning to the end and about the lesson they learn. Then have students use the details to determine the overall theme of the passage.

## SELF-SELECTED READING

**OBJECTIVES**
CCSS Determine a theme
of a story, drama, or
poem from details in
the text, including how
characters in a story
or drama respond
to challenges or
how the speaker in a
poem reflects upon a
topic; summarize the
text. **RL.5.2**

Summarize
text to increase
understanding.

### Read Independently

Have students choose a realistic fiction text for sustained silent reading. Remind students that:

→ they can determine the story's theme by noting how the characters change and the lesson the characters learn.

→ as they read, they should summarize the beginning, middle, and end of a story in their own words.

### Read Purposefully

Have students use Graphic Organizer 102 to record details about what the characters say and do and then use these details to determine the story's theme. After they finish, students can conduct a Book Talk about what they read.

→ Students should share their organizers and answer this question: *What did you like most about this story?*

→ They should also share times when they summarized in order to better understand ideas in the text.

# On Level

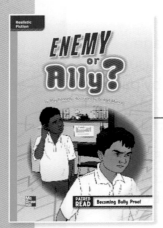

**Lexile** 840
*TextEvaluator* 56

---

## OBJECTIVES

**CCSS** Determine a theme of a story, drama, or poem from details in the text, including how characters in a story or drama respond to challenges or how the speaker in a poem reflects upon a topic; summarize the text. **RL.5.2**

**CCSS** Read on-level prose and poetry orally with accuracy, appropriate rate, and expression on successive readings. **RF.5.4b**

---

## ACADEMIC LANGUAGE

• *realistic fiction, theme, summarize, details, connotation, denotation*

• Cognates: *ficción realista, tema, resumir, detalles, connotación, denotación*

---

## Leveled Reader:
## *Enemy or Ally?*

### Before Reading

#### Preview and Predict

→ Read the Essential Question with students.

→ Have students preview the title, table of contents, and first page of *Enemy or Ally?* Students should predict what they think the selection will be about. Encourage students to confirm or revise their predictions as they read.

#### Review Genre: Realistic Fiction

Tell students that this text is realistic fiction. Explain that realistic fiction contains settings that could actually exist and includes characters and events like those found in real life. Authors use descriptive details to help readers visualize the people and places in the story. As they read, have students identify features of realistic fiction in *Enemy or Ally?*

### During Reading

#### Close Reading

**Note Taking:** Ask students to use their graphic organizer as they read.

**Pages 2–5** *Are Adam and Toby friends?* (no) *What do Adam and Toby think about one another?* (Adam thinks that Toby should have outgrown art. Toby thinks that Adam could be more active instead of reading about electricity.) *On page 2, the text indicates that Adam slumped in his seat. Does* slumped *have a positive or negative connotation? Why?* (negative; The word makes it sound like Adam is not excited that Toby is his partner.) *Turn to a partner and summarize what happens on page 5 as they work on their project.* (They disagree about whether to use electricity or art in their project and do not make any progress.)

**Pages 6–7** *How does the meeting at Adam's house go?* (It goes badly. Adam and Toby argue, and Toby leaves.)

**Pages 8–10** *What does Toby realize later that night?* (He overreacted. He must apologize to Adam.) *Summarize what happens the next morning.* (Toby apologizes. Adam accepts his apology. They suggest that there might be a way to use both electricity and art in their project.)

**Go Digital**

**Leveled Readers**

**Use Graphic Organizer**

*What does Adam realize about Toby when he visits Toby's house?* (He realizes that he and Toby are actually very similar; they just have different obsessions.) *By the end of Chapter 2, the boys have an idea for their project. What two qualities will it have?* (creative and electronic)

**Pages 11–15** *Why do you think Mrs. Tyler is worried as she watches Adam and Toby working?* (Adam is working with electricity, and Toby is working on art. They do not seem to be working together.) *Reread the last paragraph on page 13. How would you state the theme of this story?* (Although people are different, they can learn to appreciate one another's differences and get along.)

## After Reading

**Respond to Reading** Revisit the Essential Question and ask students to complete the Text Evidence questions on page 16.

*Analytical Writing* **Write About Reading** Check that students have correctly identified the author's message by showing how Adam and Toby learned to respect each other despite their differences.

### Fluency: Intonation

**Model** Model reading page 4 with proper intonation. Next, reread the page aloud and have students read along with you.

**Apply** Have students practice reading the passage with partners.

## PAIRED READ

### "Becoming Bully Proof"

### Make Connections:
### Write About It *Analytical Writing*

Before reading, ask students to note that the genre of this selection is expository text. Then discuss the Essential Question. After reading, ask students to write connections between *Enemy or Ally?* and "Becoming Bully Proof."

**Leveled Reader**

### FOCUS ON LITERARY ELEMENTS

Students can extend their knowledge of how authors create a mood, or feeling, in a story by completing the literary elements activity on page 20.

## Literature Circles

Ask students to conduct a literature circle using the Thinkmark questions to guide the discussion. You may wish to have a whole-class discussion, using both selections in the Leveled Reader, about actions we can take to get along with others.

## Level Up

Level-up lessons available online.

**IF** students read the On Level fluently and answered the questions

**THEN** pair them with students who have proficiently read the Beyond Level and have students

• partner-read the Beyond Level main selection.

• identify two details that help them understand the theme of the story.

### A C T Access Complex Text

The Beyond Level challenges students by having a more complicated **purpose** and including more **complex sentence structures**.

**On Level**

# Vocabulary

## REVIEW VOCABULARY WORDS

**OBJECTIVES**

 Acquire and use accurately grade-appropriate general academic and domain-specific words and phrases, including those that signal contrast, addition, and other logical relationships (e.g., *however, although, nevertheless, similarly, moreover, in addition*). **L.5.6**

**I Do** Use the **Visual Vocabulary Cards** to review the key selection words *abruptly, ally, collided, confident, protective,* and *taunting*. Point to each word, read it aloud, and have students chorally repeat it.

**We Do** Ask these questions and help students respond.
- → Why might an outdoor event end *abruptly*?
- → How can you be an *ally* to someone?
- → What could happen if two water balloons *collided*?

**You Do** Have students respond individually to these questions.
- → How can you show that you are *confident* in your abilities?
- → Why should you wear *protective* sports gear?
- → How can you help stop people from *taunting* others?

## CONNOTATION AND DENOTATION

**OBJECTIVES**

 Determine or clarify the meaning of unknown and multiple-meaning words and phrases based on *grade 5 reading and content,* choosing flexibly from a range of strategies. **L.5.4**

 Demonstrate understanding of figurative language, word relationships, and nuances in word meanings. **L.5.5**

**I Do** Review denotation and connotation with students. The connotation of a word can be positive or negative. Display the Comprehension and Fluency passage on **Your Turn Practice Book** pages 263–264. Read aloud the first five paragraphs. Point to *squirm* in the fifth paragraph.

**Think Aloud** The denotation of *squirm* is "to twist about like a worm." In the story, Lucia squirms because she feels embarrassed, so *squirm* has a negative connotation in this context.

**We Do** Have students find the word *inflexible* in the sixth paragraph on page 263. Model using a dictionary to find the word's denotation. Help students identify that the word has a negative connotation in the context of the story because being inflexible has prevented the girls from compromising.

**You Do** Have partners use a dictionary to find the denotation of *slumps* (page 264, paragraph 3) and use context clues to determine its connotation.

# Comprehension

## REVIEW THEME

**OBJECTIVES**

**CCSS** Determine a theme of a story, drama, or poem from details in the text, including how characters in a story or drama respond to challenges or how the speaker in a poem reflects upon a topic; summarize the text. **RL.5.2**

 **I Do** Remind students that the theme of a story is the important message about life that the author wants to share with readers. The theme usually is not stated directly in the text. Readers can determine the theme by paying attention to what characters say and do and how they respond to events. How characters change and the lessons they learn are often related to the theme.

 **We Do** Have volunteers read the first four paragraphs of the Comprehension and Fluency passage on **Your Turn Practice Book** pages 263–264. Have students identify details about what the characters say and do and how they respond to events. Guide students to use these details to propose ideas about what the theme might be, such as that being inflexible can lead to conflict.

 **You Do** Have partners read the rest of the passage. Tell them to stop after each paragraph and identify key details about what the characters do and say and how they respond to events. Remind them to add details about how the characters change and about the lesson each learns. Then have students determine the theme of the passage.

## SELF-SELECTED READING

**OBJECTIVES**

**CCSS** Determine a theme of a story, drama, or poem from details in the text, including how characters in a story or drama respond to challenges or how the speaker in a poem reflects upon a topic; summarize the text. **RL.5.2**

Summarize text to increase understanding.

### Read Independently

Have students choose a realistic fiction text for sustained silent reading.

→ Tell them to use details about how characters change and what lessons they learn to determine the theme.

→ Remind students to summarize the beginning, middle, and end of the story in their own words to increase their understanding of important events.

### Read Purposefully

Encourage students to read different realistic fiction texts to learn about a variety of topics.

→ Have them use Graphic Organizer 102 to record details about the characters and then use these to determine the theme.

→ They can use this organizer to help them write a summary of the book.

→ Ask students to share their reactions to the book with classmates.

# → Beyond Level

## Leveled Reader:
### *Jamayla to the Rescue*

**Lexile** 900
*TextEvaluator* 50

### OBJECTIVES

**CCSS** Determine a theme of a story, drama, or poem from details in the text, including how characters in a story or drama respond to challenges or how the speaker in a poem reflects upon a topic; summarize the text. **RL.5.2**

**CCSS** Read on-level prose and poetry orally with accuracy, appropriate rate, and expression on successive readings. **RF.5.4b**

### ACADEMIC LANGUAGE

• realistic fiction, theme, summarize, details, connotation, denotation

• Cognates: *ficción realista, tema, resumir, detalles, connotación, denotación*

## Before Reading

### Preview and Predict

→ Have students read the Essential Question.

→ Have students preview the title, table of contents, and first page of *Jamayla to the Rescue*. They should make a prediction about what might happen in the story. Encourage students to confirm or revise their predictions as they read.

### Review Genre: Realistic Fiction

Tell students that this text is realistic fiction. Explain that realistic fiction contains settings that could actually exist and includes characters and events like those found in real life. Authors use descriptive details to help readers visualize the people and places in the story. Have students identify features of realistic fiction in *Jamayla to the Rescue* as they read.

## During Reading

### Close Reading

**Note Taking:** Ask students to use their graphic organizer as they read.

**Pages 2–4** *Reread the first paragraph on page 2. What does it tell you about the setting of the story?* (The story takes place in a seaside town that has existed for over 200 years.) *How do Shawn and Han respond to the news of the contest?* (They are sure that they can win the contest.) *What do they argue about?* (Shawn wants to take the prize boat to the lake where his family vacations; Han wants to keep it at his house.) *Reread this line on page 3: "'No way!' Han shot back." Does* shot *have a positive or negative connotation. Why?* (negative; It suggests that Han is angry.) *What consequences to their argument does Jamayla point out?* (She points out that if they don't cooperate, neither will win.)

**Pages 5–7** *Summarize how Shawn and Han plan to sabotage one another.* (Shawn hides Han's boat. Han notices that his boat is missing and looks for it with Jamayla. Han grabs a pair of scissors and leaves the room. Just as he is about to cut a hole in Shawn's boat, Jamayla finds him and prevents him from doing so.)

**Go Digital**

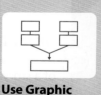

**Leveled Readers**

**Use Graphic Organizer**

**Pages 8–10** *Summarize Jamayla's solution for solving the argument.* (The boys should apologize, agree to share the prize if they win, and realize that their friendship is more important than winning.) *How do Shawn and Han respond to Jamayla's suggestion?* (They agree.)

**Pages 11–15** *What discovery does Han make?* (He discovers the speed of the catamaran, made of two boat hulls joined by one set of sails.) *How do the friends finish their boat for the contest?* (They join their individual boats.) *The author does not tell how the contest ends. Why?* (to convey the theme that getting along is more important than winning)

## After Reading

**Respond to Reading** Revisit the Essential Question and ask students to complete the Text Evidence questions on page 16.

**Analytical Writing** **Write About Reading** Check that students have correctly written about the message the author conveys by using details from the story to tell what Jamayla did to help Han and Shawn.

### Fluency: Intonation

**Model** Model reading page 4 with proper intonation. Next, reread the page aloud and have students read along with you.

**Apply** Have students practice reading the passage with partners.

## PAIRED READ

**Leveled Reader**

## "Bullying"

**Make Connections:**
**Write About It** **Analytical Writing**

Before reading, ask students to note that the genre of this selection is expository text. Then discuss the Essential Question. After reading, ask students to write connections between *Jamayla to the Rescue* and "Bullying" in terms of what actions people can take to get along with others.

> ### FOCUS ON LITERARY ELEMENTS
>
> Students can extend their knowledge of how authors create a mood in realistic fiction by completing the literary elements activity on page 20.

### Literature Circles

Ask students to conduct a literature circle using the Thinkmark questions to guide the discussion. You may wish to have a whole-class discussion, using information in both selections in the Leveled Reader, about what actions we can take to get along with others.

## Gifted and Talented

**Synthesize** Challenge students to think of what might have happened if Jamayla had not intervened between the two friends. Students should identify a likely plot scenario and then write an alternative middle and ending for the story without Jamayla as a mediator. Encourage students to use descriptive details to convey the characters' words, actions, and feelings and to create a mood, or feeling, in their writing.

# → Beyond Level

# Vocabulary

## REVIEW DOMAIN-SPECIFIC WORDS

**OBJECTIVES**

Acquire and use accurately grade-appropriate general academic and domain-specific words and phrases, including those that signal contrast, addition, and other logical relationships (e.g., *however, although, nevertheless, similarly, moreover, in addition*). **L.5.6**

 **Model** Use the **Visual Vocabulary Cards** to review the meaning of the words *conflict* and *intervene*. Write genre-related sentences on the board using the words.

Write the words *petitioning* and *obstinate* on the board and discuss the meanings with students. Then help students write sentences using these words.

 **Apply** Have students work in pairs to review the meanings of the words *cooperate* and *salvage* and write sentences using the words.

## CONNOTATION AND DENOTATION

**OBJECTIVES**
Determine or clarify the meaning of unknown and multiple-meaning words and phrases based on *grade 5 reading and content,* choosing flexibly from a range of strategies. **L.5.4**

Demonstrate understanding of figurative language, word relationships, and nuances in word meanings. **L.5.5**

 **Model** Choral-read the first paragraph of the Comprehension and Fluency passage on **Beyond Reproducibles** pages 263–264.

**Think Aloud** The denotation of the word *puckered* is "gathered into wrinkles." The girls are fighting, and Marta scowls, so I think *puckered* has a negative connotation. To Lucia, Marta's expression is angry and unpleasant.

Have students find the word *squirm* in the fifth paragraph. Guide students to use context clues about Lucia squirming because she is embarrassed to determine that *squirm* has a negative connotation in the story.

 **Apply** Have partners read the rest of the passage. Have them use a dictionary to find the denotation of the word *stiffly* (page 264, paragraph 3). Then have them discuss whether the word has a positive or a negative connotation and explain what context clues lead them to think so.

 **Analyze** Challenge students to use each of the exemplar words from the passage in a sentence that conveys a positive connotation and in a sentence that conveys a negative connotation. Have partners read their sentences aloud and identify the connotation from the context.

# Comprehension

## REVIEW THEME

### OBJECTIVES

Determine a theme of a story, drama, or poem from details in the text, including how characters in a story or drama respond to challenges or how the speaker in a poem reflects upon a topic; summarize the text. **RL.5.2**

 **Model** Review that the theme of a story is the important message about life that the author wants to share with readers. The theme usually is not stated directly in the text. Readers can determine the theme by paying attention to what characters say and do and how they respond to events. How characters change and the lessons they learn are often related to the theme.

Have students read the first four paragraphs of the Comprehension and Fluency passage on **Beyond Reproducibles** pages 263–264. Work with them to identify what the characters do or say and what happens to them. As they continue reading, help students identify how the characters change.

 **Apply** Have students fill out Graphic Organizer 102 independently. Tell them to use the information on the chart to determine the overall theme and then share their ideas with the class.

## SELF-SELECTED READING

### OBJECTIVES

Determine a theme of a story, drama, or poem from details in the text, including how characters in a story or drama respond to challenges or how the speaker in a poem reflects upon a topic; summarize the text. **RL.5.2**

Summarize text to increase understanding.

### Read Independently

Have students choose a realistic fiction text for sustained silent reading.

→ As students read, have them fill in Graphic Organizer 102 with details about what the characters do, say, and experience and then use these to determine the theme.

→ Remind them to summarize the most important details as they read.

### Read Purposefully

Encourage students to keep a reading journal. Suggest that they read realistic fiction texts with characters and plots that interest them.

→ Students can write summaries of the books in their journals.

→ Ask students to share their reactions to the books with classmates.

 **Independent Study** Challenge students to discuss how their books relate to the weekly theme of getting along. Have them use all of their reading materials to identify actions people can take to get along with others.

# English Language Learners

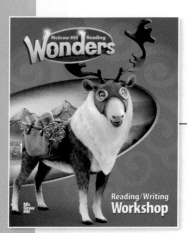

**Reading/Writing Workshop**

**OBJECTIVES**

CCSS Quote accurately from a text when explaining what the text says explicitly and when drawing inferences from the text. **RL.5.1**

CCSS Determine a theme of a story, drama, or poem from details in the text, including how characters in a story or drama respond to challenges or how the speaker in a poem reflects upon a topic; summarize the text. **RL.5.2**

**LANGUAGE OBJECTIVES**

Identify details that help determine the theme of a story.

**ACADEMIC LANGUAGE**

• *theme, connotation, denotation, summarize*

• Cognates: *tema, connotación, denotación, resumir*

## Shared Read
### *The Bully*

**View "The Bully"**

### Before Reading

#### Build Background

Read the Essential Question: *What actions can we take to get along with others?*

→ Explain the meaning of the Essential Question, including the vocabulary in the question: *Actions are the things we do or say, and when we get along with people, we are friendly with them.*

→ **Model an answer:** *When people have trouble getting along, they can take action by looking for common ground and compromising. Sometimes people might have to apologize to get along.*

→ Ask students a question that ties the Essential Question to their own background knowledge: *Turn to a partner and think of a time when you or someone you know had to overcome a problem with a friend or family member. What did you have to do to get along?* Call on several pairs.

### During Reading

#### Interactive Question-Response

→ Ask questions that help students understand the meaning of the text after each paragraph.

→ Reinforce the meanings of key vocabulary.

→ Ask students questions that require them to use key vocabulary.

→ Reinforce strategies and skills of the week by modeling.

## Page 397

### Paragraph 1

*Let's look at the illustration together. Where does this story take place? What can you tell about the characters?* (It takes place in school. It looks like there will be a problem between the characters.)

Read the first two sentences aloud. Point out the word *taunting* and have students repeat. Explain that *taunting* means "teasing in a mean way." This shows that J.T. enjoys threatening, or scaring, people.

*Michael and J.T. are not getting along. What is the problem?* (Michael is being bullied by J.T., who is larger and stronger than Michael. Michael doesn't know how to deal with J.T.)

### Paragraphs 2–3

*I know that Michael is having a problem with J.T. What happens in these paragraphs that supports that idea?* (J.T. knocks Michael's books out of his hands, makes fun of Michael, and walks away laughing.) *Do you think this made Michael feel good or bad?* (bad)

**Explain and Model Theme** *Think about the details you have read so far and how they help you understand the challenge Michael faces. How do you think Michael will respond?* (Michael is probably scared. He may run away, or he may fight back.)

### Paragraph 4

**Model Connotation and Denotation** Choral-read the paragraph. Point to the word *ally*. *This word has a positive connotation, or feeling.* Help students identify clues in the sentence that show this. (The phrase "a friendly voice said with a laugh" shows that *ally* has positive connotations.)

## Page 398

### Paragraphs 1–2

*Why is Michael surprised when he sees that it's Ramon who spoke to him?* (Ramon is very popular and a star athlete. He and Michael are not really friends.) *Is Michael glad to have Ramon's help?* (yes)

### Paragraphs 3–5

*Ramon gives Michael some advice. Does Michael understand it at first?* (no) *How do you know this?* (Michael says "What does that mean?" at the end of paragraph 4.)

*Ramon explains his grandmother's saying. What is the advice that Ramon gives Michael?* (He tells Michael to be kind to J.T. rather than acting angry or scared.) *Do you think this is good advice?* Call on pairs to share their ideas.

### Paragraphs 6–8

*Does Michael agree with Ramon about being nice to J.T.?* (no) *Does Ramon agree to step in and help Michael?* (no) *When does Michael decide that Ramon's advice might be helpful?* (that night at home)

## Page 399

### Paragraph 1

**Model the Strategy** Summarize the scene for students. *How is this situation like the beginning of the story? How is it different?* (J.T. meets Michael in the hall and starts toward him. This time, J.T. trips and drops his books instead of knocking books out of Michael's hands.)

### Paragraphs 2–6

*What does Michael do that shows he agrees with Ramon's advice?* (He helps J.T. pick up his books.) *Does being kind to J.T. seem to have solved the problem between J.T. and Michael?* (yes) *Do you think they will get along better now?* (yes)

### After Reading

**Make Connections**

→ Review the Essential Question: *What actions can we take to get along with others?*

→ Make text connections.

→ Have students complete **ELL Reproducibles** pages 263–265.

# → English Language Learners

**Lexile** 700
*TextEvaluator* 27

## Leveled Reader:
### *Enemy or Ally?*

**Go Digital**

**Leveled Readers**

### Before Reading

#### Preview

→ Read the Essential Question: *What actions can we take to get along with others?*

→ Refer to Trying to Fit In: *What are some different ways people cooperate and get along with one another?*

→ Preview *Enemy or Ally?* and "Becoming Bully Proof": *Our purpose for reading is to learn about how we all can get along.*

#### Vocabulary

Use the **Visual Vocabulary Cards** to pre-teach the ELL vocabulary: *cooperate, compromise, corresponding, impressed*. Use the routine found on the cards. Point out the cognate: *cooperar.*

### During Reading

#### Interactive Question-Response

**Note Taking:** Ask students to use the graphic organizer on **ELL Reproducibles** page 262. Use the questions below after each page is read with students. As you read, define vocabulary in context and use visuals to help students understand key vocabulary.

**Pages 2–3** Choral read the last paragraph on page 2 and the first paragraph on page 3. *Understanding the main characters in a story can help us understand the author's message. How are Adam and Toby different?* (Adam likes science. Toby likes art.) *Illustrations can tell us a lot about a story. Look at the illustration on page 3. Do Adam and Toby look happy or unhappy?* (unhappy)

**Pages 4–5** *Do Adam and Toby get along in class?* (no) *How do you think their teacher feels?* (frustrated)

**Pages 6–7** Choral read the first two paragraphs on page 6. *What must the boys do?* (get along) Reread the first paragraph on page 7. Pantomime shuffling your feet. *When I shuffle my feet, am I excited or bored?* (bored)

**Use Graphic Organizer**

## OBJECTIVES

**CCSS** Quote accurately from a text when explaining what the text says explicitly and when drawing inferences from the text. **RL.5.1**

**CCSS** Determine a theme of a story, drama, or poem from details in the text, including how characters in a story or drama respond to challenges or how the speaker in a poem reflects upon a topic; summarize the text. **RL.5.2**

**CCSS** Read on-level prose and poetry orally with accuracy, appropriate rate, and expression on successive readings. **RF.5.4b**

## ACADEMIC LANGUAGE

• *summarize, realistic fiction, theme*

• Cognates: *resumir, ficción realista, tema*

**Pages 8–10** *This part of the story is important. What does Toby do?* (He apologizes.) Choral-read the last two paragraphs on page 9. *Does Adam think Toby is a good artist?* (yes)

**Pages 11–15** Point out the illustration and labels on page 15. *Describe the project that Adam and Toby did for class.* (They created sculptures of a cat and a plant. They used lights.) Write the following sentence frame on the board and complete it with students: *Even people who are different can ____.* (work together to get along)

## After Reading

**Respond to Reading** Revisit the Essential Question and ask students to complete the Text Evidence questions on page 16.

*Analytical Writing* **Write About Reading** Check that students have correctly identified the author's message by showing how Adam and Toby learned to respect each other despite their differences.

### Fluency: Intonation

**Model** Model reading page 2 with proper intonation. Next, reread the page aloud and have students read along with you.

**Apply** Have students practice reading with partners.

## PAIRED READ

# "Becoming Bully Proof"

### Make Connections:
### Write About It *Analytical Writing*

Before reading, point out that the genre
of this selection is expository text and discuss the Essential Question. After reading, ask students to list connections between what they learned from *Enemy or Ally?* and "Becoming Bully Proof."

**Leveled Reader**

## FOCUS ON LITERARY ELEMENTS

Students can extend their knowledge of how writers use words to create a mood, or feeling, in a story by completing the literary elements activity on page 20.

### Literature Circles

Ask students to conduct a literature circle using the Thinkmark questions to guide the discussion. You may wish to use both Leveled Reader selections to conduct a whole-class discussion about the topic of getting along.

# Level Up

Level-up lessons available online.

**IF** students read the **ELL Level** fluently and answered the questions,

**THEN** pair them with students who have proficiently read **On Level** and have ELL students

• echo-read the **On Level** main selection.

• list words with which they have difficulty and discuss them with a partner.

### A C T Access Complex Text

The **On Level** challenges students by including a more complex **organization** and **complex sentence structures**.

 # English Language Learners
## Vocabulary

## PRETEACH VOCABULARY

**OBJECTIVES**

 Acquire and use accurately grade-appropriate general academic and domain-specific words and phrases, including those that signal contrast, addition, and other logical relationships. **L.5.6**

**LANGUAGE OBJECTIVE**
Use vocabulary words.

 **I Do** Preteach vocabulary from "The Bully" following the Vocabulary Routine found on the **Visual Vocabulary Cards** for the words *abruptly, ally, collided, confident, conflict, intervene, protective,* and *taunting*.

 **We Do** After completing the Vocabulary Routine for each word, point to the word on the card and read the word with students. Ask them to repeat the word.

 **You Do** Have students work with a partner to use two or more words in sentences or questions. Then have each pair read the sentences aloud.

| Beginning | Intermediate | Advanced/High |
|---|---|---|
| Help students write the sentences correctly and read them aloud. | Ask students to write one sentence and one question. | Challenge students to write one sentence and one question for each word. |

## REVIEW VOCABULARY

**OBJECTIVES**

Acquire and use accurately grade-appropriate general academic and domain-specific words and phrases, including those that signal contrast, addition, and other logical relationships. **L.5.6**

**LANGUAGE OBJECTIVE**
Use vocabulary words.

 **I Do** Review the previous week's vocabulary words. The words can be reviewed over a few days. Read each word aloud pointing to the word on the **Visual Vocabulary Card**. Have students repeat after you. Then follow the Vocabulary Routine on the back of each card.

 **We Do** Model saying a sentence and omitting the vocabulary word for students to guess.

 **You Do** In pairs, have students write sentences for all of the words, omitting the vocabulary word in each sentence. Ask them to read the sentences aloud for the class to guess the missing word.

| Beginning | Intermediate | Advanced/High |
|---|---|---|
| Help students read aloud the sentences and determine the missing words. | Ask students to include a context clue in each sentence. | Have students use two or more vocabulary words in each sentence. |

# CONNOTATION AND DENOTATION

## OBJECTIVES
 Demonstrate understanding of figurative language, word relationships, and nuances in word meanings. **L.5.5**

## LANGUAGE OBJECTIVE
Identify the connotation and denotation of given words.

 **I Do** Have students echo-read the fourth paragraph of the Comprehension and Fluency passage on **ELL Reproducibles** pages 263–264. Point to the word *squirm* in the last sentence. Explain that the word has both a denotation, or dictionary meaning, and a connotation, or specific feeling.

**Think Aloud** The denotation of the word *squirm* is "twist from side to side." From the rest of the paragraph I know Lucia is embarrassed, which helps me understand that *squirm* has a negative connotation.

 **We Do** Have students point to the word *stubborn* in the last paragraph on page 263. Explain that the denotation is "determined not to change." Help students see that the connotation is negative: Lucia's mom contrasts *stubborn* with *bright* and *reasonable,* two words with positive meanings.

 **You Do** Have partners use print and digital dictionaries to find the denotations of *shrieks* (page 264, paragraph 1) and *silly* (page 264, paragraph 5). Then have them explain if the connotations are positive or negative and why.

| Beginning | Intermediate | Advanced/High |
|---|---|---|
| Help students locate the denotations in a dictionary and use context to find connotations. | Have students explain the denotations and the clues that helped them find the connotations. | Have students explain how they used the context clues to determine the connotation of each word. |

# ADDITIONAL VOCABULARY

## OBJECTIVES
 Acquire and use accurately grade-appropriate general academic and domain-specific words and phrases, including those that signal contrast, addition, and other logical relationships. **L.5.6**

## LANGUAGE OBJECTIVE
Use academic vocabulary and high-frequency words.

 **I Do** List some academic vocabulary and high-frequency words from "The Bully": *offenses, enemies, trouble;* and *Enemy or Ally?*: *electricity, intervene, apologize.* Define each word for students: Trouble *is a situation that is hard or dangerous.*

 **We Do** Model using the words for students in a sentence: *Our dog got into trouble when she dug up Mom's plants. Michael saw trouble coming at the end of the school hallway.* Then provide sentence frames and complete them with students: *I knew trouble was coming when _____.*

 **You Do** Have pairs make up their own sentence frames to complete with the class.

| Beginning | Intermediate | Advanced/High |
|---|---|---|
| Provide the sentence frames and have students complete them. | Help students complete the sentence frames and read them aloud. | Challenge students to write sentences with two missing words. |

# → English Language Learners
## Writing/Spelling

### WRITING TRAIT: WORD CHOICE

**OBJECTIVES**

 Write narratives to develop real or imagined experiences or events using effective technique, descriptive details, and clear event sequences. Use a variety of transitional words, phrases, and clauses to manage the sequence of events. **W.5.3c**

**LANGUAGE OBJECTIVE**
Use time-order words in writing.

 **I Do** Explain that writers use time-order words to show the sequence of events. Some time-order words are *first, next, last, later,* and *finally.* Read the Expert Model passage aloud as students follow along. Point out that the time-order words *next, before, as,* and *then* tell the reader when each event happens.

**We Do** Read aloud the second paragraph on page 399 of "The Bully" as students follow along. Point out the time-order words *for a moment, next,* and *as.* Then use a sequence chart to record the time-order words and events, showing how the words signal the events. Model writing sentences that include time-order words and a sequence of events.

**You Do** Have pairs write their own short paragraph, using words from the chart. They should use time-order words to write the sequence of events.

| Beginning | Intermediate | Advanced/High |
|---|---|---|
| Help students write sentences using time-order words. | Have students check use of time-order words and edit for errors. | Have students add events using time-order words and edit for errors. |

### SPELL WORDS WITH LATIN ROOTS

**OBJECTIVES**

 Spell grade-appropriate words correctly, consulting references as needed. **L.5.2e**

**LANGUAGE OBJECTIVE**
Spell words with Latin roots.

 **I Do** Read aloud the Spelling Words on page T100, segmenting them into syllables and stressing the Latin roots *port, tract, spect,* and *miss/mit.* Point out that each of the roots has one syllable.

 **We Do** Read the Dictation Sentences on page T101 aloud for students. With each sentence, read the underlined word slowly, stressing the Latin root. Have students repeat after you and create a list labeled *port, trac, spec,* and *miss/mit.* Place the correct words under each label.

 **You Do** Display the words. Have students exchange their list with a partner to check the spelling and write the words correctly.

| Beginning | Intermediate | Advanced/High |
|---|---|---|
| Have students copy the words with correct spelling and say the word aloud. | After students have corrected their words, have pairs quiz each other. | Have students correct their words and explain why some words were difficult. |

# Grammar

## ADVERVS THAT COMPARE

### OBJECTIVES

 **CCSS** Demonstrate command of the conventions of standard English grammar and usage when writing or speaking. Form and use comparative and superlative adjectives and adverbs, and choose between them depending on what is to be modified. **L.3.1g**

### LANGUAGE OBJECTIVE

Identify and use adverbs that compare.

**Language Transfers Handbook**

In Haitian Creole and Hmong, adjectives and adverb forms are interchangeable. Speakers of these languages may use an adjective where an adverb is needed. Work with students to differentiate between adverbs and adjectives in a sentence.

 **I Do** Remind students that an adverb can compare two or more actions. Compare adverbs with verbs and point out how they are different. Explain that adverbs that compare two actions use *–er* or *more*. Adverbs that compare three or more actions use *–est* or *most*. Write the following sentences on the board, underline the adverb, and explain the comparison: *My dog barks <u>louder</u> than your dog.* (compares two actions); *Your dog learns tricks <u>more easily</u> than my dog.* (compares two actions); *My dog barks the <u>loudest</u> of all the dogs on the block.* (compares three or more actions); *Your dog learns tricks the <u>most easily</u> of all the dogs on our block.* (compares three or more actions)

 **We Do** Write the sentence frames below on the board. Have students fill in the correct form of the adverb. Then read the completed sentences aloud for students to repeat.

> *Susan dances _____ than Tim dances. (gracefully)*
>
> *Harry dances the _____ of anyone in the class. (gracefully)*
>
> *Emma worked _____ than Ming worked. (late)*
>
> *Jim worked the _____ of all the volunteers. (late)*

**You Do** Write the endings *–er* and *–est* and the words *more* and *most* in columns on the board. Have students work in pairs to name an adverb that belongs in each column. Have them choose one adverb from each column and write it in a sentence.

| Beginning | Intermediate | Advanced/High |
|---|---|---|
| Help students to copy their sentence and underline the adverb. Read the sentence aloud for students to repeat after you. | Ask students to underline the adverb and the actions it compares. | Have students underline the adverb and the actions it compares. Ask them to explain how they identified the adverb and made the comparison. |

For extra support, have students complete the activities in the **Grammar Practice Reproducibles** during the week, using the routine below.

→ Explain the grammar skill.

→ Model the first activity in the Grammar Practice Reproducibles.

→ Have the whole group complete the next couple of activities, then do the rest with a partner.

→ Review the activities with correct answers.

# PROGRESS MONITORING

## Weekly Assessment

### CCSS TESTED SKILLS

| ✓ **COMPREHENSION:** | ✓ **VOCABULARY:** | ✓ **WRITING:** |
|---|---|---|
| Theme **RL.5.2** | Connotation and Denotation **L.5.4c** | Writing About Text **RL.5.2, W.5.9a** |

### Assessment Includes
→ Performance Tasks
→ Approaching-Level Assessment online PDFs

**Fluency Goal** 129 to 149 words correct per minute (WCPM)

**Accuracy Rate Goal** 95% or higher

Administer oral reading fluency assessments using the following schedule:

→ **Weeks 1, 3, 5** Provide Approaching-Level students at least three oral reading fluency assessments during the unit.

→ **Weeks 2 and 4** Provide On-Level students at least two oral reading fluency assessments during the unit.

→ **Week 6** If necessary, provide Beyond-Level students an oral reading fluency assessment at this time.

**Also Available: Selection Tests online PDFs**

*Go Digital!* www.connected.mcgraw-hill.com

# Using Assessment Results

| TESTED SKILLS | If ... | Then ... |
|---|---|---|
| **COMPREHENSION** | Students answer 0–6 multiple-choice items correctly ... | ... assign Lessons 34–36 on Theme from the ***Tier 2 Comprehension Intervention online PDFs.*** |
| **VOCABULARY** | Students answer 0–6 multiple-choice items correctly ... | ... assign Lesson 172 on Connotation and Denotation from the ***Tier 2 Vocabulary Intervention online PDFs.*** |
| **WRITING** | Students score less than "3" on the constructed responses ... | ... assign Lessons 34–36 on Theme and/or Write About Reading Lesson 194 from the ***Tier 2 Comprehension Intervention online PDFs.*** |
| 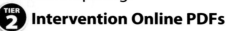 | Students have a WCPM score of 120–128 ... | ... assign a lesson from Section 1, 7, 8, 9, or 10 of the ***Tier 2 Fluency Intervention online PDFs.*** |
| | Students have a WCPM score of 0–119 ... | ... assign a lesson from Section 2, 3, 4, 5, or 6 of the ***Tier 2 Fluency Intervention online PDFs.*** |

# Response to Intervention

Use the appropriate sections of the ***Placement and Dignostic Assessment*** as well as students' assessment results to designate students requiring:

**TIER 2** **Intervention Online PDFs**

**TIER 3** **WonderWorks Intervention Program**

**Text Complexity Range for Grades 4–5**

| Lexile | |
|---|---|
| 740 | 1010 |
| *TextEvaluator*™ | |
| 23 | 51 |

Reading/Writing Workshop

# TEACH AND MODEL

**Deep Diving**

It has no mouth, eyes, or stomach. Its soft body is encased in a white cylinder and topped with a red plume. It can grow to be eight feet tall. It is a sea creature known as a giant tube worm, and it lives without any sunlight on the deep, dark ocean floor.

What we sometimes call the deep ocean, in contrast to shallow waters, covers almost two-thirds of Earth's surface. On average, oceans are about two miles deep. However, the deepest point known on Earth, Challenger Deep, descends nearly seven miles.

◄ Some deep ocean fish are swimming among tube worms. New ocean species are being discovered all the time.

The ocean's floor is varied, consisting of vast plains, steep canyons, and towering mountains. It includes active, **dormant**, and extinct volcanoes. This undersea world is a harsh environment because of its **frigid** temperatures and lack of sunshine.

The deep ocean is also a mysterious environment that remains largely unexplored. Little is known about it or its creatures. Do any of them **cache** food the way land animals do? Do any ocean species **hibernate**? As one example among countless mysteries, not a single, live giant squid had ever been spotted until a few years ago. We knew they existed only because their corpses had been found.

The Challenger Deep is located in an undersea canyon called the Mariana Trench.

**The Deepest Known Point on Earth**

**Essential Question**

How are living things adapted to their environment?

Read about the adaptation of sea creatures to the deep ocean.

## ✔ Vocabulary

adaptation
agile
cache
dormant
forage
frigid
hibernate
insulates

☞ **Go Digital**

www.connected.mcgraw-hill.com

## 🔍 Close Reading of Complex Text

**Shared Read** "Mysterious Oceans," 410–417

**Genre** Expository Text

**Lexile** 980L

ETS *TextEvaluator*™ 45

## Minilessons

✔ **Comprehension Strategy**
✔ **Comprehension Skill**

✔ **Genre**
✔ **Vocabulary Strategy**
✔ **Writing Traits**
**Grammar Handbook**

## ✔ Tested Skills CCSS

Ask and Answer Questions, T146–T147
Text Structure: Cause and Effect, T148–T149
Expository Text, T150–T151
Context Clues, T152–T153
Sentence Fluency, T158–T159
Negatives, T162–T163

## ADAPTATIONS
**Essential Question**
How are living things adapted to their environment?

# WEEK 3

# APPLY WITH CLOSE READING

## Complex Text

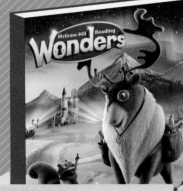

**Literature Anthology**

**PAIRED READ**

*Survival at 40 Below,* 468–483
**Genre** Expository Text
**Lexile** 990L
(ETS) *TextEvaluator™* 36

"Why the Evergreen Trees Never Lose Their Leaves," 486–489
**Genre** Pourquoi Story
**Lexile** 850L
(ETS) *TextEvaluator™* 34

## Differentiated Text

**Leveled Readers** *Include Paired Reads*

APPROACHING
**Lexile** 760L
(ETS) *TextEvaluator™* 28

ON LEVEL
**Lexile** 900L
(ETS) *TextEvaluator™* 35

BEYOND
**Lexile** 1010L
(ETS) *TextEvaluator™* 43

ELL
**Lexile** 750L
(ETS) *TextEvaluator™* 25

## Extended Complex Text

*Spiders: Biggest! Littlest!*
**Genre** Expository Text
**Lexile** 820L
(ETS) *TextEvaluator™* 13

*Earth Heroes: Champions of the Wilderness*
**Genre** Collection of Biographies
**Lexile** 920L
(ETS) *TextEvaluator™* 53

Classroom Library lessons available online.

**Classroom Library**

# TEACH AND MANAGE

## How You Teach

### INTRODUCE

**Weekly Concept**
Adaptations

**Reading/Writing Workshop**
406–407

### TEACH

**Close Reading**
"Mysterious Oceans"

**Minilessons**
Ask and Answer Questions, Cause and Effect, Expository Text, Context Clues: Paragraph Clues, Writing Traits

**Reading/Writing Workshop**
410–419

### APPLY

**Close Reading**
*Survival at 40 Below*

"Why the Evergreen Trees Never Lose Their Leaves"

**Literature Anthology**
468–489

☞ **Go** Digital

Interactive Whiteboard

Interactive Whiteboard

Mobile

## How Students Practice

### WEEKLY CONTRACT

**PDF Online**

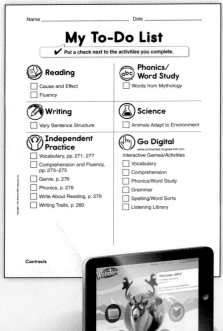

My To-Do List
✔ Put a check next to the activities you complete.

📖 **Reading**
☐ Cause and Effect
☐ Fluency

🔤 **Phonics/Word Study**
☐ Words from Mythology

✏️ **Writing**
☐ Vary Sentence Structure

🔬 **Science**
☐ Animals Adapt to Environment

✋ **Independent Practice**
☐ Vocabulary, pp. 271, 277
☐ Comprehension and Fluency, pp. 273–275
☐ Genre, p. 276
☐ Phonics, p. 278
☐ Write About Reading, p. 279
☐ Writing Traits, p. 280

☞ **Go Digital**
www.connected.mcgraw-hill.com
Interactive Games/Activities
☐ Vocabulary
☐ Comprehension
☐ Phonics/Word Study
☐ Grammar
☐ Spelling/Word Sorts
☐ Listening Library

Contracts

### LEVELED PRACTICE AND ONLINE ACTIVITIES

**Your Turn Practice Book**
271–280

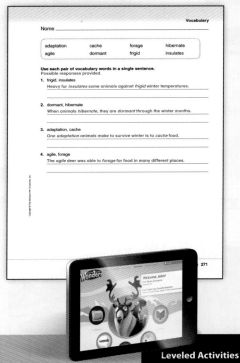

Vocabulary

Name _____

| adaptation | cache | forage | hibernate |
| agile | dormant | frigid | insulates |

**Use each pair of vocabulary words in a single sentence.**
Possible responses provided.

1. frigid, insulates
   *Heavy fur* insulates *some animals against* frigid *winter temperatures.*

2. dormant, hibernate
   *When animals* hibernate, *they are* dormant *through the winter months.*

3. adaptation, cache
   *One* adaptation *animals make to survive winter is to* cache *food.*

4. agile, forage
   *The* agile *deer was able to* forage *for food in many different places.*

271

**Leveled Readers**

☞ **Go** Digital

Online To-Do List

Leveled Activities

Writer's Workspace

## DIFFERENTIATE

**SMALL GROUP INSTRUCTION**

**Leveled Readers**

## INTEGRATE

**Research and Inquiry**
Oral Presentation, T156

**Text Connections**
Compare Animal Adaptations, T157

**Write About Reading**
*Analytical Writing* Write an Analysis, T157

## ASSESS

**Weekly Assessment**
**325–336**

Mobile

Online Research and Writing

Online Assessment

## LEVELED WORKSTATION CARDS

**More Activities on back**

**28**

### Antarctic Animals

Many animals have adaptations that help them survive in a particular environment. The animals of Antarctica have adapted to living under extremely cold conditions.

* Research to identify adaptations that allow animals, such as penguins and seals, to survive Antarctica's harsh climate.

*SCIENCE*

**12**

### Sentence Fluency: Sentence Structure

Read this part of Ernesto's campaign speech.

Vote for me for class president. I will listen to everyone's ideas. I will work hard. Also, I will talk to the principal about important issues. I will try to get a class pet. Vote for...

* Discuss Ernesto's sentence structure and sentence lengths. Where does Ernesto vary his sentence structure well? Where do sentences sound too much the same?

*WRITING*

**1**

### Context Clues

Clues to word meanings may appear in **sentences** and **paragraphs**, or as **definitions** or **restatements**.

Kaylie used <u>calligraphy</u>, or beautiful writing, when she wrote the letter.

* Find a selection you read this week that contains a word did not know. Write the word.

* Look for context clues to help you figure out the meaning. Use a dictionary to check the definition.

* Write a sentence for the word and provide a context clue for its meaning. Underline the word.

* Exchange sentences with a partner. Identify context clues to figure out the word's meaning.

**You need**
› reading selection
› paper and pen or pencil
› dictionary

**20**

*PHONICS/WORD STUDY*

**11**

### Text Structure: Cause and Effect

A cause is an action or event that makes something happen. An effect happens as a result of the cause.

* Choose an informational text you have read this week.

* Identify causes and effects the author discusses. Use the graphic organizer to help you.

* Look for effects that in turn cause other events or problems to happen.

| Cause | | Effect |
|---|---|---|
| | → | |
| | → | |
| | → | |

* Write a paragraph about the cause and effect process. How does this text structure help you understand information?

**You need**
› informational text
› paper and pen or pencil

**30**

*READING*

Go Digital! www.connected.mcgraw-hill.com • Interactive Games and Activities • Grade 5

## *Write About Reading* • Analytical Writing

### Write to Sources and Research

Text Structure: Cause and Effect, T148–T149

Note Taking, T153B, T153T

Summarize, T153R

Cause and Effect, T153R

Make Connections: Essential Question, T153R, T153V, T157

Key Details: T153T, T153U

Research and Inquiry, T156

Analyze to Share an Opinion, T157

Comparing Texts, T169, T177, T181, T187

Predictive Writing, T153B

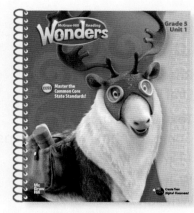
**Teacher's Edition**

**Literature Anthology**

Summarize, p. 485
Cause and Effect, p. 485

**Interactive Whiteboard**

**Leveled Readers**
Comparing Texts
Cause and Effect

**Your Turn Practice Book**

Cause and Effect, pp. 273–275
Genre, p. 276
Analyze to Share an Opinion, p. 279

## *Writing Process* • Genre Writing

**Opinion Text**
Book Review, T344–T349

**Conferencing Routines**
Teacher Conferences, T346
Peer Conferences, T347

**Interactive Whiteboard**

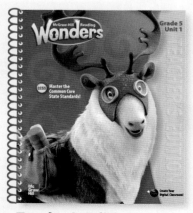
**Teacher's Edition**

**Leveled Workstation Card**
Reviews, Card 26

**Writer's Workspace**
Opinion Text: Book Review
Writing Process
Multimedia Presentations

## *Writing Traits* • **Write Every Day**

**Writing Trait: Sentence Fluency**
Vary Sentence Structure, T158–T159

**Conferencing Routines**
Teacher Conferences, T160
Peer Conferences, T161

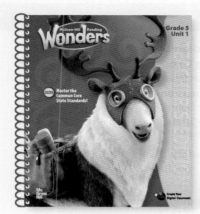
**Teacher's Edition**

Sentence Fluency:
Sentence Structure,
pp. 418–419
**Reading/Writing Workshop**

**Go Digital**

**Interactive
Whiteboard**

Sentence
Fluency:
Sentence
Structure, 12
**Leveled Workstation Card**

Sentence Fluency:
Sentence Structure,
p. 280
**Your Turn Practice Book**

## *Grammar and Spelling*

**Grammar**
Negatives, T162–T163

**Spelling**
Words from Mythology,
T164–T165

**Go Digital**

**Interactive
Whiteboard**

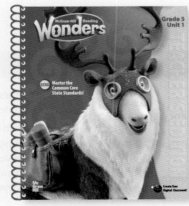
**Teacher's Edition**

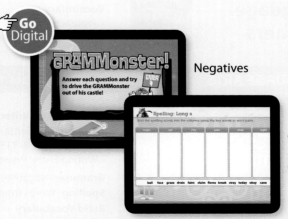
**Go Digital**

Negatives

Words from
Mythology
Word Sorts

**Online Spelling and Grammar Games**

✔ **TESTED SKILLS** CCSS

| | DAY 1 | DAY 2 |
|---|---|---|

## READING

### Whole Group

**Teach, Model and Apply**

Reading/Writing Workshop

**DAY 1**

**Build Background** Adaptations, T138–T139
**Listening Comprehension** Interactive Read Aloud: "Bacteria: They're Everywhere," T140–T141
**Comprehension**
• Preview Genre: Expository Text, T150–T151
• Preview Strategy: Ask and Answer Questions, T146–T147
✔ **Vocabulary** Words in Context, T142–T143
**Practice** *Your Turn* 271

**Close Reading of Complex Text** "Mysterious Oceans," 410–413

**DAY 2**

✔ **Comprehension**
• Strategy: Ask and Answer Questions, T146–T147
• Skill: Text Structure: Cause and Effect, T148–T149
• Write About Reading 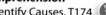 *Analytical Writing*
• Genre: Expository Text, T150–T151
✔ **Vocabulary** Strategy: Context Clues, T152–T153
**Practice** *Your Turn* 272–277

## DIFFERENTIATED INSTRUCTION  Choose across the week to meet your students' needs.

### Small Group

**Approaching Level**

**DAY 1**
**Leveled Reader** *Cave Creatures,* T168–T169
**Word Study/Decoding** Review Words from Mythology, T170 TIER 2
**Vocabulary**
• Review High-Frequency Words, T172 TIER 2
• Understand Vocabulary Words, T173

**DAY 2**
**Leveled Reader** *Cave Creatures,* T168–T169
**Vocabulary** Review Vocabulary Words, T172 TIER 2
**Comprehension**
• Identify Causes, T174 TIER 2
• Review Text Structure: Cause and Effect, T175

**On Level**

**DAY 1**
**Leveled Reader** *Cave Creatures,* T176–T177
**Vocabulary** Review Vocabulary Words, T178

**DAY 2**
**Leveled Reader** *Cave Creatures,* T176–T177
**Comprehension** Review Text Structure: Cause and Effect, T179

**Beyond Level**

**DAY 1**
**Leveled Reader** *Cave Creatures,* T180–T181
**Vocabulary** Review Domain-Specific Words, T182

**DAY 2**
**Leveled Reader** *Cave Creatures,* T180–T181
**Comprehension** Review Text Structure: Cause and Effect, T183

**English Language Learners**

**DAY 1**
**Shared Read** "Mysterious Oceans," T184–T185
**Word Study/Decoding** Review Words from Mythology, T170
**Vocabulary**
• Preteach Vocabulary, T188
• Review High-Frequency Words, T172

**DAY 2**
**Leveled Reader** *Cave Creatures,* T186–T187
**Vocabulary** Review Vocabulary, T188
**Writing** Writing Trait: Sentence Fluency, T190
**Grammar** Negatives, T191

## LANGUAGE ARTS  Writing Process: Book Review T344–T349
Use with Weeks 1–3

### Whole Group

**Writing**
**Grammar**
**Spelling**
**Build Vocabulary**

**DAY 1**
✔ **Readers to Writers**
• Writing Trait: Sentence Fluency/Vary Sentence Structure, T158–T159
• Writing Entry: Prewrite and Draft, T160
**Grammar** Negatives, T162
**Spelling** Words from Mythology, T164
**Build Vocabulary**
• Connect to Words, T166
• Academic Vocabulary, T166

**DAY 2**
**Readers to Writers**
• Writing Entry: Revise, T160
**Grammar** Negatives, T162
**Spelling** Words from Mythology, T164
**Build Vocabulary**
• Expand Vocabulary, T166
• Review Connotation and Denotation, T166

☞ **Go**
Digital

CUSTOMIZE YOUR OWN
LESSON PLANS
www.connected.mcgraw-hill.com

WEEK 3 →

| DAY 3 | DAY 4 | DAY 5  Review and Assess |
|---|---|---|

## READING

**Word Study/Decoding** Words from Mythology, T154–T155
**Practice** *Your Turn* 278

**Close Reading** *Survival at 40 Below*, 468–485 ● *Analytical Writing*

Literature Anthology

**Fluency** Rate and Accuracy, T155
**Integrate Ideas** ● *Analytical Writing*
• Research and Inquiry, T156
**Practice** *Your Turn* 273–275

**Close Reading** "Why the Evergreen Trees Never Lose Their Leaves," 486–489 ● *Analytical Writing*

**Integrate Ideas** ● *Analytical Writing*
• Research and Inquiry, T156
• Text Connections, T157
• Write About Reading, T157
**Practice** *Your Turn* 279

## DIFFERENTIATED INSTRUCTION

**Leveled Reader** *Cave Creatures*, T168–T169
**Word Study/Decoding** Build Words from Mythology, T170 ⓶
**Fluency** Rate and Accuracy, T174 ⓶
**Vocabulary** Context Clues, T173

**Leveled Reader** Paired Read: "Why Bat Flies at Night," T169 ● *Analytical Writing*
**Word Study/Decoding** Practice Words from Mythology, T171

**Leveled Reader** Literature Circle, T169
**Comprehension** Self-Selected Reading, T175

---

**Leveled Reader** *Cave Creatures*, T176–T177
**Vocabulary** Context Clues, T178

**Leveled Reader** Paired Read: "Why Bat Flies at Night," T177 ● *Analytical Writing*

**Leveled Reader** Literature Circle, T177
**Comprehension** Self-Selected Reading, T179

---

**Leveled Reader** *Cave Creatures*, T180–T181
**Vocabulary**
• Context Clues, T182
• Analyze, T182

*Gifted and Talented*

**Leveled Reader** Paired Read: "Why Bat Flies at Night," T181 ● *Analytical Writing*

**Leveled Reader** Literature Circle, T181
**Comprehension**
• Self-Selected Reading, T183
• Independent Study: Adapting, T183

*Gifted and Talented*

---

**Leveled Reader** *Cave Creatures*, T186–T187
**Word Study/Decoding** Build Words from Mythology, T170
**Vocabulary** Context Clues, T189
**Spelling** Words from Mythology, T190

**Leveled Reader** Paired Read: "Why Bat Flies at Night," T187 ● *Analytical Writing*
**Vocabulary** Additional Vocabulary, T189
**Word Study/Decoding** Practice Words from Mythology, T171

**Leveled Reader** Literature Circle, T187

## LANGUAGE ARTS

**Readers to Writers**
• Writing Entry: Prewrite and Draft, T161
**Grammar** Mechanics and Usage, T163
**Spelling** Words from Mythology, T165
**Build Vocabulary**
• Reinforce the Words, T167
• Context Clues, T167

**Readers to Writers**
• Writing Entry: Revise, T161
**Grammar** Negatives, T163
**Spelling** Words from Mythology, T165
**Build Vocabulary**
• Connect to Writing, T167
• Shades of Meaning, T167

**Readers to Writers**
• Writing Entry: Share and Reflect, T161
**Grammar** Negatives, T163
**Spelling** Words from Mythology, T165
**Build Vocabulary**
• Word Squares, T167
• Morphology, T167

# DIFFERENTIATE TO ACCELERATE

## Scaffold to **A**ccess **C**omplex **T**ext

**IF** ▶ the text complexity of a particular selection is too difficult for students

**THEN** ▶ see the references noted in the chart below for scaffolded instruction to help students Access Complex Text.

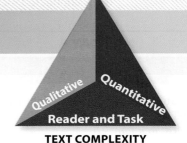

Qualitative — Quantitative
**Reader and Task**
**TEXT COMPLEXITY**

|  | **Reading/Writing Workshop** | **Literature Anthology** | **Leveled Readers** | | **Classroom Library** |
|---|---|---|---|---|---|
| |  |  |  | |  |

<table>
<tr><th>Quantitative</th><td>

**"Mysterious Oceans"**
- **Lexile** 980
- *TextEvaluator* 45

</td><td>

*Survival at 40 Below*
- **Lexile** 990
- *TextEvaluator* 36

"Why the Evergreen Trees Never Lose Their Leaves"
- **Lexile** 850
- *TextEvaluator* 34

</td><td colspan="2">

**Approaching Level**
**Lexile** 760
*TextEvaluator* 28

**Beyond Level**
**Lexile** 1010
*TextEvaluator* 43

**On Level**
**Lexile** 900
*TextEvaluator* 35

**ELL**
**Lexile** 750
*TextEvaluator* 25

</td><td>

*Spiders: Biggest! Littlest!*
- **Lexile** 820
- *TextEvaluator* 13

*Earth Heroes: Champions of the Wilderness*
- **Lexile** 920
- *TextEvaluator* 53

</td></tr>

<tr><th>Qualitative</th><td>

**What Makes the Text Complex?**
- **Specific Vocabulary** Context Clues T145
- **Connection of Ideas** Ask Questions T147

**ACT** *See Scaffolded Instruction in Teacher's Edition T145 and T147.*

</td><td>

**What Makes the Text Complex?**
- **Specific Vocabulary** Context Clues T153A, T153C, T153G, T153K
- **Genre** Pourquoi Story T153U; Illustrations T153E; Folktale T153U
- **Prior Knowledge** Insulation T153I; Arctic T153O
- **Organization** Structures T153M, T153S
- **Connection of Ideas** Prior Reading T153O

**ACT** *See Scaffolded Instruction in Teacher's Edition T153A–T153V.*

</td><td colspan="2">

**What Makes the Text Complex?**
- **Specific Vocabulary**
- **Prior Knowledge**
- **Sentence Structure**
- **Connection of Ideas**
- **Genre**

**ACT** *See Level Up lessons online for Leveled Readers.*

</td><td>

**What Makes the Text Complex?**
- **Genre**
- **Specific Vocabulary**
- **Prior Knowledge**
- **Sentence Structure**
- **Organization**
- **Purpose**
- **Connection of Ideas**

**ACT** *See Scaffolded Instruction in Teacher's Edition T360-T361.*

</td></tr>

<tr><th>Reader and Task</th><td>

The Introduce the Concept lesson on pages T138–T139 will help determine the reader's knowledge and engagement in the weekly concept. See pages T144–T153 and T156–T157 for questions and tasks for this text.

</td><td>

The Introduce the Concept lesson on pages T138–T139 will help determine the reader's knowledge and engagement in the weekly concept. See pages T153A–T153V and T156–T157 for questions and tasks for this text.

</td><td colspan="2">

The Introduce the Concept lesson on pages T138–T139 will help determine the reader's knowledge and engagement in the weekly concept. See pages T168–T169, T176–T177, T180–T181, T186–T187, and T156–T157 for questions and tasks for this text.

</td><td>

The Introduce the Concept lesson on pages T138–T139 will help determine the reader's knowledge and engagement in the weekly concept. See pages T360-T361 for questions and tasks for this text.

</td></tr>
</table>

## Monitor and *Differentiate*

**IF** → you need to differentiate instruction

**THEN** → use the Quick Checks to assess students' needs and select the appropriate small group instruction focus.

### ✔ Quick Check

**Comprehension Strategy** Ask and Answer Questions T147

**Comprehension Skill** Text Structure: Cause and Effect T149

**Genre** Expository Text T151

**Vocabulary Strategy** Context Clues: Paragraph Clues T153

**Word Study/Fluency** Words from Mythology, Rate and Accuracy T155

**If No** →
| Approaching Level | Reteach T168–T169 |
| ELL | Develop T184–T191 |

**If Yes** →
| On Level | Review T176–T179 |
| Beyond Level | Extend T180–T183 |

## Level Up with Leveled Readers

**IF** → students can read their leveled text fluently and answer comprehension questions

**THEN** → work with the next level up to accelerate students' reading with more complex text.

Beyond — T49

On Level

Approaching — T169

ELL — T187

## ENGLISH LANGUAGE LEARNERS
### ELL SCAFFOLD

**IF** ELL students need additional support **THEN** scaffold instruction using the small group suggestions.

| Reading/Writing Workshop | Leveled Reader | Additional Vocabulary T189 | | Context Clues: Synonyms T189 | Writing Trait: Sentence Fluency T190 | Spelling | Grammar Negatives T191 |
|---|---|---|---|---|---|---|---|
| "Mysterious Oceans" T184–T185 | *Cave Creatures* T186–T187 | classify | prey | | | Words from Mythology T190 | |
| | "Why Bat Flies at Night" T187 | discovered | species | | | | |
| | | explore | survive | | | | |

**Note: Include ELL Students in all small groups based on their needs.**

# → Introduce the Concept

**MINILESSON**
**10** Mins

## Build Background

**Reading/Writing Workshop**

**OBJECTIVES**

**CCSS** Follow agreed-upon rules for discussions and carry out assigned roles. **SL.5.1b**

Build background knowledge on adaptations.

**ACADEMIC LANGUAGE**
- *adaptation, hibernate*
- Cognates: *adaptación, hibernar*

**ESSENTIAL QUESTION**

*How are living things adapted to their environment?*

Have students read the Essential Question on page 406 of the **Reading/Writing Workshop**. Tell them an **adaptation** is a change in a plant or animal that allows it to survive. For example, some animals **hibernate**, or sleep through the winter, to survive the extreme cold.

Discuss the photograph of the thorny devil. Focus on the traits it has developed to live in its environment.

→ Thorny devils have sharp thorns to protect them from predators.

→ They can duck their heads beneath their necks. This **adaptation** also helps keep them safe.

→ They have grooves on their bodies that move water to their mouths. This **adaptation** helps them get water.

## Talk About It

COLLABORATE

**Ask:** *What **adaptations** protect the thorny devils from predators? How do these **adaptations** help them survive?* Have partners discuss.

→ Model using the graphic organizer to generate words and phrases related to **adaptations**. Add students' responses.

→ Have partners continue the discussion by sharing what they know about an animal, how or if it might **hibernate**, and how it adapts. Ask them to compare and contrast the adaptions of the animals they discuss. They can then complete the organizer, generating additional related words and phrases.

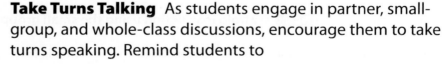

**Collaborative Conversations**

**Take Turns Talking** As students engage in partner, small-group, and whole-class discussions, encourage them to take turns speaking. Remind students to

→ wait for a person to finish before they speak.

→ raise their hand to let others know they would like to speak.

→ allow others to share their own opinions.

**Go Digital**

**Discuss the Concept**

**Watch Video**

**View Photos**

**Use Graphic Organizer**

**Essential Question**
How are living things adapted to their environment?

Go Digital!

# Creature Comforts

Every living thing, including human beings, has developed ways to live in its environment.

▶ Take me, for example. I'm an Australian lizard called a Thorny Devil. My thorns protect me from predators. Also, I can duck my head, and up pops a "false head" at the back of my neck!

▶ I have another adaptation so I can get water from wherever it touches my body: Grooves on my body move water up into my mouth!

## Talk About It

Write words you have learned about adapting to an environment. Then talk about an animal you know about and how it has adapted.

Adaptations

406

407

**READING/WRITING WORKSHOP, pp. 406–407**

## ENGLISH LANGUAGE LEARNERS SCAFFOLD

| Beginning | Intermediate | Advanced/High |
|---|---|---|
| **Use Visuals** Point to the photograph. Say: *The thorny devil has sharp thorns.* Clarify meaning by touching a sharp pencil point. Say: *Its thorns are an adaptation.* Have students repeat *adaptation*, then clarify the word's meaning. Say: *The thorns help the thorny devil stay safe.* Clarify or restate as needed. | **Describe** Help students describe the thorny devil. Elicit that an adaptation helps an animal to survive. Ask: *How does the thorny devil protect itself?* Provide the sentence frame: *Thorny devils have _____, and this adaptation helps them survive.* Repeat student responses slowly and clearly for the class. | **Discuss** Have students look at the photograph and discuss adaptations that help the thorny devil survive. Ask questions to help them elaborate. *What protects the thorny devil? How does it get water? Which adaptation is the most unusual?* Elicit details to support students' responses. |

**GRAPHIC ORGANIZER 140**

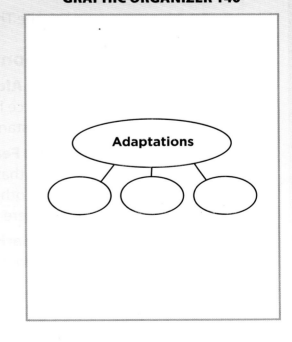

Adaptations

# Listening Comprehension

MINILESSON
**10** Mins

## Interactive Read Aloud

**OBJECTIVES**

CCSS Summarize a written text read aloud or information presented in diverse media and formats, including visually, quantitatively, and orally. **SL.5.2**

• Listen for a purpose.
• Identify characteristics of expository text

**ACADEMIC LANGUAGE**

• *expository text, ask and answer questions, summarize, cause, effect*
• Cognates: *texto expositivo, resumir, causa, efecto*

### Connect to Concept: Adaptations

Tell students that people can learn about connections by exploring how living things adapt to their environments. Let students know that you will be reading aloud an essay that describes bacteria, a type of living thing that adapts many ways and can be found nearly everywhere in the world—even inside people!

### Preview Genre: Expository Text

Explain that the text you will read aloud is expository text. Discuss the features of expository text:

→ presents information about a topic with main ideas and key details

→ may be organized to show cause-and-effect relationships

→ may include text features such as maps, charts, and graphs

### Preview Comprehension Strategy: Ask and Answer Questions

Point out that experienced readers ask themselves questions before, during, and after reading. Finding the answers and asking new questions can assist in comprehension. When reading expository text, readers should also keep in mind how the key details support a main idea.

Use the Think Alouds on page T141 to model the strategy.

### Respond to Reading

**Think Aloud Clouds** Display Think Aloud Master 1: *I wonder…* to reinforce how you used the ask and answer questions strategy to understand content.

Model Think Alouds

**Genre Features** With students, discuss the elements of the Read Aloud that let them know that it is expository text. Ask them to think about other texts that you have read or they have read independently that were expository text.

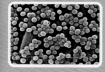
Genre Chart

**Summarize** Have students restate the main ideas of "Bacteria: They're Everywhere" in their own words.

# Bacteria: They're Everywhere

They hide in plain sight. Some are moving around on your hands right now, and others are living in your mouth. Some can make you sick, but others help you stay healthy. What are they? Bacteria. **1**

Among Earth's oldest living things, bacteria are so small you need a microscope to see them. They live almost everywhere: on mountaintops and ocean floors, on plant roots and in animal guts. They are so common that your body contains more bacteria cells than human cells!

How many types of bacteria are there? Scientists don't know for sure, but they estimate that there are millions of different bacteria on the planet.

## A Bad Reputation

People may think bacteria are bad. After all, bacteria cause some frightening diseases, such as a flesh-eating rash. Disease-causing bacteria, however, make up only a small segment of the bacterial world.

Most bacteria benefit humans. Bacteria in the intestines help us digest our food, while others help our immune system fight off illnesses. We use bacteria to make bread and to turn milk into yogurt. Antibiotic medicines, which kill bacterial diseases, are made with bacteria.

Many ecological cycles depend on bacteria. Bacteria convert nitrogen gas from the air into a form that plants can absorb. They also break down dead organisms, releasing needed nutrients. **2**

## A Talent for Adaptability

What allows bacteria to live in so many places and serve so many different functions? Adaptability. Bacteria can adapt to almost any environment.

Some bacteria, such as the bacteria that live in the human digestive tract, are anaerobic. Anaerobic bacteria do not need oxygen to live. Other bacteria are aerobic and require oxygen. Some bacteria are so flexible they can live with or without oxygen.

Bacteria continue adapting to change. Some disease-causing bacteria, for example, have developed a resistance to antibiotics.

The next time you think you are alone, remember: there are millions of bacteria keeping you company. **3**

Jamie Grill/Iconica/Getty Images

**1** **Think Aloud** I have a **question** about this section: "If bacteria are everywhere, why can't I see them?" I will read on to find the answer.

**2** **Think Aloud** I can **ask and answer a question** about this section: "How can bacteria be helpful?" The text says bacteria help digestion. They are used to make food and medicine. Ecological cycles depend on bacteria.

**3** **Think Aloud** Now that I'm finished, I'm going to **ask and answer a question**: "How is bacteria able to live in so many different environments?" I read that bacteria can adapt to change. That is how they survive in different environments.

# → **Vocabulary**

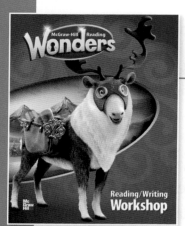

MINILESSON **10** Mins

## Words in Context

### Model the Routine

Introduce each vocabulary word using the Vocabulary Routine found on the **Visual Vocabulary Cards**.

**Visual Vocabulary Cards**

Vocabu...
Define:
Example:
Ask:

**Vocabulary Routine**

<u>Define:</u>  If something is **dormant**, it is sleeping or not active.

<u>Example:</u>  The guide explained that the volcano was dormant, so we felt safe standing near it.

<u>Ask:</u>  Why is it safe to visit a dormant volcano?

**Go Digital**

dormant

**Use Visual Glossary**

**CCSS**

**OBJECTIVES**
Acquire and use accurately grade-appropriate general academic and domain-specific words and phrases, including those that signal contrast, addition, and other logical relationships (e.g., *however, although, nevertheless, similarly, moreover, in addition*).
**L.5.6**

**ACADEMIC LANGUAGE**
• *adaptation, hibernate*
• Cognates: *adaptación, hibernar*

### Definitions

→ **adaptation**   An **adaptation** is a change in a plant or animal that helps it survive.
   **Cognate:** *adaptación*

→ **agile**   If you are **agile**, you are able to move and react quickly and easily.  **Cognate:** *ágil*

→ **cache**   If you **cache** something, you hide or store it in a hiding place.

→ **forage**   When animals **forage**, they hunt or search for food.
   **Cognate:** *forrajear*

→ **frigid**   If the temperature is **frigid**, it is very cold.

→ **hibernate**   When animals **hibernate**, they spend the winter sleeping.
   **Cognate:** *hibernar*

→ **insulates**   An animal's fur **insulates**, or keeps the animal warm.

### Talk About It

COLLABORATE

Have students work with a partner and look at each photograph and discuss the definition of each word. Then ask students to choose three words and write questions for their partner to answer.

## CCSS Words to Know

# Vocabulary

Use the picture and the sentences to talk with a partner about each word.

**adaptation** Changing color is an **adaptation** some lizards have made to their environment.

How is fur an example of an adaptation?

**agile** Kim was such an **agile** gymnast, she could do a back bend on a balance beam.

Why should athletes be agile?

**cache** My parents **cache** jewelry and other treasures in an old wooden chest.

Where else might people cache special things?

**dormant** The guide explained that the volcano was **dormant**, so we felt safe standing near it.

Why is it safe to visit a dormant volcano?

**forage** When winter comes, elk, deer, and other animals often have to **forage** for food.

Why is it hard to forage for food during winter?

**frigid** We drank a hot beverage to warm up after being outside on that **frigid** day.

Do you usually wear shorts in frigid weather?

**hibernate** Some animals, such as the dormouse, **hibernate** in some way during the winter.

Why do some animals hibernate in winter?

**insulates** My coat **insulates** my body against the cold.

What kind of coat insulates a cat?

### Your Turn COLLABORATE

Pick three words. Write three questions for your partner to answer.

**Go Digital!** *Use the online visual glossary*

408

409

**READING/WRITING WORKSHOP, pp. 408–409**

## ELL ENGLISH LANGUAGE LEARNERS SCAFFOLD

### Beginning

**Use Visuals** Say: *This volcano is not hot. People can go near this volcano because it is dormant.* Elicit that another word for *dormant* is *sleeping.* Have students repeat. Ask: *Is it safe to visit this dormant volcano?* Elaborate on answers.

### Intermediate

**Describe** Guide students to describe the photograph for *dormant.* Review the meaning of *dormant.* Ask: *What do we know about this volcano?* Have partners discuss other things that can be dormant. Clarify responses as needed.

### Advanced/High

**Discuss** Have partners discuss the photograph for *dormant.* Tell them to write a sentence about it using the word *dormant.* Then have pairs share the sentence with the class. Correct for grammar and pronunciation.

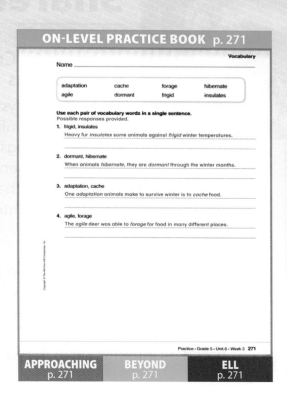
| APPROACHING p. 271 | BEYOND p. 271 | ELL p. 271 |

CCSS **Shared Read** | Genre • Expository Text

# Mysterious Oceans

**? Essential Question**

**How are living things adapted to their environment?**

Read about the adaptation of sea creatures to the deep ocean.

410

## Deep Diving

It has no mouth, eyes, or stomach. Its soft body is encased in a white cylinder and topped with a red plume. It can grow to be eight feet tall. It is a sea creature known as a giant tube worm, and it lives without any sunlight on the deep, dark ocean floor.

What we sometimes call the deep ocean, in contrast to shallow waters, covers almost two-thirds of Earth's surface. On average, oceans are about two miles deep. However, the deepest point known on Earth, Challenger Deep, descends nearly seven miles.

◀ Some deep ocean fish are swimming among tube worms. New ocean species are being discovered all the time.

The ocean's floor is varied, consisting of vast plains, steep canyons, and towering mountains. It includes active, **dormant**, and extinct volcanoes. This undersea world is a harsh environment because of its **frigid** temperatures and lack of sunshine.

The deep ocean is also a mysterious environment that remains largely unexplored. Little is known about it or its creatures. Do any of them **cache** food the way land animals do? Do any ocean species **hibernate**? As one example among countless mysteries, not a single, live giant squid had ever been spotted until a few years ago. We knew they existed only because their corpses had been found.

The Challenger Deep is located in an undersea canyon called the Mariana Trench.

### The Deepest Known Point on Earth

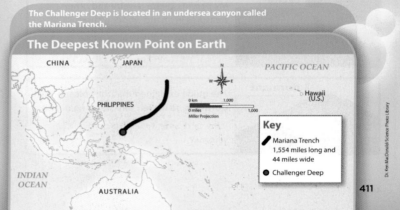

**Key**

▬ Mariana Trench
1,554 miles long and
44 miles wide

● Challenger Deep

411

**READING/WRITING WORKSHOP, pp. 410–411**

**Reading/Writing Workshop**

# Shared Read

**Lexile** 980   *TextEvaluator*™ 45

## Connect to Concept: Adaptations

Explain that "Mysterious Oceans" will give more information about how living things are adapted to their environment. Read "Mysterious Oceans" with students. Note that previously taught vocabulary words are highlighted in the text.

## Close Reading

**Reread Paragraph 1:** Reread the first paragraph of the selection with students. Ask: *Why does the author begin the selection with a description of the giant tube worm?* Model how to make inferences based on information in the paragraph.

I know that this selection will explore how living things adapt to their environment. In the last sentence of this paragraph, I read that the giant tube worm lives without sunlight in the deep ocean. I think this is a good example of a creature that has adapted to its environment. That is why the author begins the selection by describing it.

**Reread Paragraphs 2 and 3:** Model how to use information in these paragraphs to identify how and why the author organizes ideas in the text.

Paragraph two indicates that much of Earth is covered by deep ocean. Paragraph three provides specific details about this harsh environment (volcanoes, cold, lack of sunlight). I think the author includes this information in the introduction to show why living things must adapt to survive.

This fish, the striated frogfish, lures prey. The nose is an adaptation to life in the deep ocean.

A basket starfish rests in a deep-sea coral reef.

## Amazing Adaptations

When a submersible, or submarine, was invented that could descend farther than any other craft, scientists were then able to make the odyssey to the deep ocean floor. However, exploration remains difficult, and they have since seen merely five percent of the underwater world.

As scientists anticipated, life generally seems sparse at the bottom of the deep ocean. Few creatures can survive there. Food sources that sea creatures depend on, such as dead plants and animals, rarely drift down from the ocean's surface. As a result, animals have to adapt to an environment that is not only frigid and dark but also has little food.

One example of an **adaptation** to this environment is seen in the starfish. Deep sea starfish grow larger and more aggressive than their shallow water relatives. They can't afford to wait for an occasional snail to pass by. Instead, deep sea starfish are predators that actively **forage** for food. They reach up their five arms, which have pincers at the ends, to catch meals of **agile**, fast-moving shrimp.

Anglerfish also are adapted to the herculean task of finding scarce food. Each has a bioluminous, or naturally glowing, lure on the top of its head. This shining pole is sensitive to vibrations and allows them to attract other fish. With their huge jaws, they quickly seize their prey.

412

## Heated Habitats

What has truly surprised scientists, however, is the discovery of another, very different type of environment on the deep ocean floor. They found that cracks, or vents, in Earth's surface exist underwater, just as they do on dry land. Sea water rushes into these vents, where it mingles with chemicals. The water is also heated by magma, or hot melted rock. When the water from the vent bursts back into the ocean, it creates geysers and hot springs.

To scientists' amazement, the habitats around these vents teem with life. In addition to tube worms, there are huge clams, eyeless shrimp, crabs, and mussels, along with many kinds of bacteria. One odd creature is the Pompeii worm. It has a fleece of bacteria on its back that, as far as scientists can determine, **insulates** it from heat.

Mussels, worms, and spider crabs live near heated vents.

How can so much life exist where there is so little food or sunlight? Scientists have discovered that many creatures transform the chemicals from the vents into food. The process is called chemosynthesis. Because of this process, animals are able to flourish in these remarkable habitats. Creatures that don't use chemosynthesis for food, such as crabs, eat the ones that do.

There are many mysteries to be found and solved at the bottom of the deep sea. In the last few decades alone, scientists have discovered more than 1,500 ocean species! If scientists continue sea exploration, they are bound to discover many more.

### Make Connections

Talk about the ways some sea creatures adapt to the deep ocean. **ESSENTIAL QUESTION**

Compare one sea creature adaptation to that of another animal you have seen. **TEXT TO SELF**

413

**READING/WRITING WORKSHOP, pp. 412–413**

## Make Connections

### ESSENTIAL QUESTION

Encourage students to reread the text for evidence as they discuss how sea creatures adapt to the deep ocean. Ask students to identify and explain, using the text, the adaptations of living things that help them survive in a particular environment.

## Continue Close Reading

Use the following lessons for focused rereadings.

→ Ask and Answer Questions, pp. T146–T147
→ Text Structure: Cause and Effect, pp. T148–T149
→ Expository Text, pp. T150–T151
→ Context Clues, pp. T152–T153

## A C T Access Complex Text

### ▶ Specific Vocabulary

A dictionary or context clues help readers find the meaning of scientific terms in text.

→ *What context clue helps you determine the meaning of* vents *in the second sentence on page 413?* (the restatement "cracks")

→ *What context clue helps you determine the meaning of* magma *in the fourth sentence on page 413?* (the definition "hot melted rock")

→ Have students determine the meanings of *submersible* (page 412), *bioluminous* (page 412), *chemosynthesis* (page 413).

# → Comprehension Strategy

**Reading/Writing Workshop**

 MINILESSON **10** Mins

## Ask and Answer Questions

**Go Digital**

**Present the Lesson**

### 1 Explain

Explain to students that they can improve their understanding of a text by asking and answering questions as they read. This strategy is especially helpful when reading scientific texts that may cover unfamiliar or complex topics. Scientific texts sometimes pose questions or raise issues that are not addressed until later in the text.

→ Good readers pause while reading scientific texts to ask themselves questions about what they have read. They may question themselves to see if they can recall the most important facts and details or identify the main idea.

→ Students should also stop and ask questions whenever they do not understand a section of text or they become confused.

→ Once students have asked questions about a section of text, they should reread to find answers.

### 2 Model Close Reading: Text Evidence

Model how asking questions can help you better understand text that may be confusing. Reread the last paragraph in the section "Deep Diving" on page 411. Point out that the text poses several questions about oceans but does not answer them right away, leading you to ask, "Why is the deep ocean so mysterious?" Tell students that your purpose for rereading will be to try to find answers to this question.

### 3 Guided Practice of Close Reading

COLLABORATE

Have students work in pairs to identify details and evidence in the first three paragraphs of "Deep Diving" that will help them begin to answer the question "Why is the deep ocean so mysterious?" Partners should ask questions about other sections of "Mysterious Oceans" and then reread for answers.

---

**OBJECTIVES**

**CCSS** Quote accurately from a text when explaining what the text says explicitly and when drawing inferences from the text. **RI.5.1**

Ask and answer questions to increase understanding of text.

---

**ACADEMIC LANGUAGE**

• *ask and answer questions, expository text*

• Cognate: *texto expositivo*

---

## Comprehension Strategy

# Ask and Answer Questions

Asking and answering questions can help you check your understanding of complex scientific text. You can ask yourself what the main ideas are, or whether you need to reread a section of text.

 **Find Text Evidence**

The last paragraph in the section "Deep Diving" on page 411 of "Mysterious Oceans" asks several questions about oceans. You may wonder how to find the answers.

**page 411**

The deep ocean is also a mysterious environment that remains largely unexplored. Little is known about it or its creatures. Do any of them **cache** food the way land animals do? Do any ocean species **hibernate**? As one example among countless mysteries, not a single, live giant squid had ever been spotted until a few years ago. We knew they existed only because their corpses had been found.

*There must be reasons why we know so little about ocean life. I'm going to ask myself, "Why is the deep ocean so mysterious?" I will reread the section to try to answer this question.*

**Your Turn** COLLABORATE

Use the information in the first two paragraphs of "Deep Diving" on page 411 to begin to answer the question "Why is the deep ocean so mysterious?"

414

**READING/WRITING WORKSHOP, p. 414**

 **Access Complex Text**

▶ **Connection of Ideas**

Asking and answering questions can help students link ideas in a text.

→ *What features of the deep ocean are similar to those on land?* (canyons, mountains, volcanoes) *What makes the deep ocean environment different from most places on land?* (It gets no sunlight.)

→ *Photosynthesis is a process in which plants use sunlight to change carbon dioxide and water into food. How is chemosynthesis similar?* (Deep ocean animals change the chemicals from the ocean vents into food.)

## Monitor and *Differentiate*

 **Quick Check**

Do students ask questions about the text as they read? Do they reread in order to find answers to their questions?

**Small Group Instruction**

| | | |
|---|---|---|
| If No → | **Approaching Level** | Reteach p. T168 |
| | **ELL** | Develop p. T185 |
| If Yes → | **On Level** | Review p. T176 |
| | **Beyond Level** | Extend p. T180 |

**ON-LEVEL PRACTICE BOOK** pp. 273–274

Comprehension and Fluency

Name _____

Read the passage. Use the ask and answer questions strategy to help you understand what you read.

**Life in the Desert**

What do you think of when you hear the word *desert*? You probably
13   picture a place that is hot and dry. Although there are some desert areas
27   that are cold, most deserts are as you imagine them. They are dry and hot.
42       A desert is an area that gets less than ten inches of rain each year. Many
58   types of animals live in these harsh climates. Survival for desert animals
70   depends on their ability to adapt, or change.

78   **Structural Adaptation**
80       One kind of adaptation is structural. This means the animal's body has
92   changed so that it can survive in the climate. The gundi is an example of
107  this adaptation. A gundi is a small animal that looks a lot like a guinea
122  pig. Gundis live in the deserts of Africa. The desert has very little drinking
136  water, but gundis get all the moisture they need from their diet of plants.
150  Gundis' fur helps them stay cool during the day and warm at night.

163  **Behavioral Adaptation**
165      Another type of adaptation is behavioral. Desert animals act in ways
176  that help them survive. Since it is so hot during the day, many animals are
191  nocturnal. They rest under rocks or in other cool places during the day and
205  come out at night to hunt for food.

213  **Thriving in the Desert**
217      Most desert animals adapt in a combination of ways. Dromedary
240  camels live in the deserts of Africa and the Arabian Peninsula. They raise
240  their body temperature to reduce loss of water, and they can live for days
254  without eating or drinking. Dromedaries have a hump on their backs that
266  is made up of fat. They use the fat for energy when food is scarce. These
282  animals sweat very little, which saves water. When they do drink, they can
295  take in as many as thirty gallons of water in a little over ten minutes!

Practice · Grade 5 · Unit 6 · Week 3 **273**

| **APPROACHING** pp. 273–274 | **BEYOND** pp. 273–274 | **ELL** pp. 273–274 |
|---|---|---|

# → Comprehension Skill

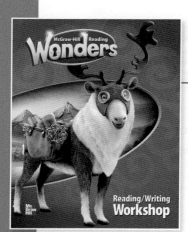

**Reading/Writing Workshop**

---

**OBJECTIVES**

**CCSS** Explain the relationships or interactions between two or more individuals, events, ideas, or concepts in a historical, scientific, or technical text based on specific information in the text. **RI.5.3**

Identify the overall structure of a text.

---

**ACADEMIC LANGUAGE**

• *text structure, cause, effect*

• Cognates: *causa, efecto*

---

**SKILLS TRACE**

**TEXT STRUCTURE**

**Introduce** U1W3

**Review** U1W4, U1W6, U2W1, U2W3, U4W6, U5W3, U5W4, U5W6, U6W3, U6W4

**Assess** U1, U2, U3, U5, U6

---

**MINILESSON 10 Mins**

## Text Structure: Cause and Effect

### 1 Explain

Remind students that text structure refers to the way ideas in a text are organized. A text organized by **cause and effect** explains how or why something happens.

→ Explain that a **cause** is an event or action that makes something happen. An **effect** is what happens as a result of a cause.

→ Certain words and phrases can signal cause-and-effect relationships. These include *because of, as a result, if/then,* and *when*.

→ Point out that some causes and effects are implied instead of being stated directly. To identify these causes and effects, students must ask themselves whether one event is the cause or result of another event.

### 2 Model Close Reading: Text Evidence

Point out that the word *when* in the first paragraph of the section "Amazing Adaptations" signals a cause-and-effect relationship. Explain that the invention of the submersible, or submarine, was the cause and ocean floor exploration was the effect.

**Analytical Writing** **Write About Reading: Text Structure** Model how to use the cause-and-effect relationship in the organizer to restate the main idea of the paragraph: *The invention of the submersible enabled scientists to go deep down into the ocean and explore its floor.*

### 3 Guided Practice of Close Reading

Have partners identify cause-and-effect relationships in the rest of the section "Amazing Adaptations" on page 412 and record them on the graphic organizer. Ask them to explain each cause-and-effect relationship they identify.

**Analytical Writing** **Write About Reading: Text Structure** Ask pairs to use the cause-and-effect relationships they listed on the organizer to summarize the text as a whole. Have them share their summaries with the class.

**Go Digital**

**Present the Lesson**

## Comprehension Skill CCSS

# Cause and Effect

To figure out cause and effect relationships in a text, first look for an event or action that makes something happen. This is the **cause**. Then look for what happens as a result of that cause. This is the **effect**. Words and phrases such as *because of*, *as a result*, *if/then*, or *when* can signal cause and effect.

### Find Text Evidence

*In the first paragraph of the section "Amazing Adaptations" on page 412 of "Mysterious Oceans," the author explains that a new type of submersible was invented. The word* when *signals a cause and effect relationship. This invention caused something else to happen.*

| Cause | → | Effect |
|---|---|---|
| Invention of submersible | → | Exploration of ocean floor |

### Your Turn COLLABORATE

Reread the rest of the section "Amazing Adaptations" on page 412. Identify the cause and effect relationships explained in these paragraphs.

*Go Digital!* *Use the interactive graphic organizer*

415

**READING/WRITING WORKSHOP, p. 415**

## Monitor and *Differentiate*

### ✓ Quick Check

Are students able to identify cause-and-effect relationships in the section "Amazing Adaptations" and record them on the graphic organizer?

### Small Group Instruction

| If No → | Approaching Level | Reteach p. T175 |
|---|---|---|
| | ELL | Develop p. T185 |
| If Yes → | On Level | Review p. T179 |
| | Beyond Level | Extend p. T183 |

## ELL ENGLISH LANGUAGE LEARNERS SCAFFOLD

### Beginning

**Comprehend** Reread the first paragraph of "Amazing Adaptations." Ask: *Did the invention of the submarine make something happen?* (yes) *So the invention of the submarine is the* cause. Then ask: *Did ocean exploration happen as a result of this invention?* (yes) *So ocean exploration is the* effect. Point out cognates *causa* and *efecto*.

### Intermediate

**Identify** Help students reread the first paragraph of "Amazing Adaptations." Ask: *What cause-and-effect signal word do you see?* (when) *Why were scientists able to explore the ocean floor?* (The submarine was invented.) Have partners describe the cause-and-effect relationship. *The cause was _____. The effect was _____.*

### Advanced/High

**Explain** Have students reread the first paragraph of "Amazing Adaptations" and explain the cause-and-effect relationship. Students should explain to partners how they identified both the cause and the effect. Encourage students to use the words *cause, effect,* and *signal word* in their explanations.

### ON-LEVEL PRACTICE BOOK pp. 273–275

Comprehension: Cause and Effect and Fluency

Name _____

A. Reread the passage and answer the questions.
Possible responses provided.

1. What causes many desert animals to adapt their behavior so that they sleep during the day instead of at night?
The desert climate is very hot during the day, so animals seek shelter in cool places.

2. What evidence in the fifth paragraph shows the structural effects of a desert climate on an animal's body?
Dromedary camels store fat in a hump on their backs. When food is scarce, they use the fat for energy. They also sweat very little and can drink thirty gallons of water at one time.

3. What are three ways the fennec fox has adapted to its harsh desert climate?
Their light color keeps them cool; fur on the bottoms of their feet protects them from the hot sand; their bodies lose water very slowly, so they can go for days without drinking.

B. Work with a partner. Read the passage aloud. Pay attention to rate and accuracy. Stop after one minute. Fill out the chart.

| | Words Read | – | Number of Errors | = | Words Correct Score |
|---|---|---|---|---|---|
| First Read | | – | | = | |
| Second Read | | – | | = | |

Practice • Grade 5 • Unit 6 • Week 3 **275**

| APPROACHING pp. 273–275 | BEYOND pp. 273–275 | ELL pp. 273–275 |
|---|---|---|

COMPREHENSION SKILL **T149**

# → Genre: Informational Text

**Reading/Writing Workshop**

**OBJECTIVES**

CCSS By the end of the year, read and comprehend informational texts, including history/ social studies, science, and technical texts, at the high end of the grades 4–5 text complexity band independently and proficiently. **RI.5.10**

CCSS Interpret information presented visually, orally, or quantitatively (e.g., in charts, graphs, diagrams, time lines, animations, or interactive elements on Web pages) and explain how the information contributes to an understanding of the text in which it appears. **RI.4.7**

**ACADEMIC LANGUAGE**
• *expository text, map*
• Cognates: *texto expositivo, mapa*

MINILESSON
**10** Mins

## Expository Text

### 1 Explain

Share with students these key characteristics of **expository text**:

→ An expository text, such as a scientific article, gives readers information about a topic. The text presents main ideas as well as evidence and key details that support those ideas.

→ The information in an expository text may be organized to show cause-and-effect relationships. Signal words and phrases help readers recognize and understand these relationships.

→ Helpful features in an expository text may include headings, charts, graphs, maps, and photographs with captions.

### 2 Model Close Reading: Text Evidence

Model identifying features of "Mysterious Oceans" that help you understand that the selection is an expository text. Point out factual information about oceans on page 411 and about the deep sea starfish and anglerfish on page 412.

**Map** Point to the map on page 411. Remind students that a map is a flat picture of an area. Explain that most maps have certain features, including a title, a scale to show how many miles are represented by an inch, a compass rose to show directions, and a key that explains colors or symbols.

Identify each of these features on the map with students. Then ask: *How does this map help you better understand the Challenger Deep, which is described in the text under the heading "Deep Diving"?*

### 3 Guided Practice of Close Reading

COLLABORATE

Have students work in pairs to use the map on page 411 to find the approximate length and width of the Mariana Trench. Partners should discuss how they found this information and how the map helps them visualize the Mariana Trench. Have students share and compare their findings with the class.

## Go Digital

**Present the Lesson**

## CCSS Genre | Informational Text

# Expository Text

The selection "Mysterious Oceans" is expository text.

**Expository text:**
- Presents information about a topic, with main ideas and key details
- May be organized to show cause and effect relationships
- May include text features such as photos and maps

###  Find Text Evidence

*I can tell "Mysterious Oceans" is expository text. The text gives information about oceans and includes main ideas and cause and effect relationships. A map gives visual information.*

**page 411**

**Map** A map is a flat picture of an area. Most maps have a title, a scale to show how many miles are represented by an inch, a compass rose to show directions, and a key that explains colors or symbols.

### Your Turn

Study the map on page 411. What is the approximate length and width of the Mariana Trench? How does the map help you visualize it?

416

**READING/WRITING WORKSHOP, p. 416**

## Monitor and *Differentiate*

### ✓ Quick Check

Are students able to use the map on page 411 to find the approximate length and width of the Mariana Trench? Can they describe how the map helps them visualize?

⬇

### Small Group Instruction

| | | |
|---|---|---|
| If No → | **Approaching Level** | Reteach p. T169 |
| | **ELL** | Develop p. T187 |
| If Yes → | **On Level** | Review p. T177 |
| | **Beyond Level** | Extend p. T181 |

---

## ELL ENGLISH LANGUAGE LEARNERS SCAFFOLD

### Beginning

**Recognize** Have students point to the map on page 411. Read aloud the title. Ask: *Does this map show the deepest known point on Earth?* (yes) *Is this point on land or in the ocean?* (in the ocean) Point to each map feature as you say it aloud: *scale, compass rose, key.* Have students repeat. Point out Spanish cognate: *escala.*

### Intermediate

**Identify** Have students read the title of the map on page 411. Ask: *What does the map show?* (the deepest known point on Earth) Help students point to and name different features of the map, including the scale, compass rose, and key. Then have partners discuss what the map shows about the Mariana Trench.

### Advanced/High

**Distinguish** Have students locate text features characteristic of expository texts (photos, maps, section headings). Ask: *What information does each text feature provide? Why is the map on page 411 particularly helpful?* Have partners discuss their answers and share with the class. Elicit details to support responses.

---

**ON-LEVEL PRACTICE BOOK** p. 276

Name _____

Genre/Text Feature

**Desert Plant Adaptations**

Plants adapt to living in the Mojave Desert in many ways. One way plants survive is by conserving water. They have spines or thorns that direct air flow and reflect hot sunlight. Waxy leaves hold moisture in to reduce water loss. Shallow roots help plants use every bit of rainfall. Other plants have long roots that allow them to get water from deep in the ground. Desert flowers bloom only when it rains. These adaptations enable a wide variety of plants to survive in the desert.

**Answer the questions about the text.**

1. How do you know this is expository text?
   It gives information about how plants survive in the Mojave Desert.

2. What is the heading? Is it a strong heading for this text? Why or why not?
   Desert Plant Adaptations; Possible response: It would be stronger if it were more specific, such as "Mojave Desert Plant Adaptations."

3. What other text feature does this text include? What information does it give you?
   It includes a map that shows where the Mojave Desert is located.

275 Practice • Grade 5 • Unit 6 • Week 3

| APPROACHING p. 276 | BEYOND p. 276 | ELL p. 276 |
|---|---|---|

# → Vocabulary Strategy

**Reading/Writing Workshop**

**OBJECTIVES**

**CCSS** Determine or clarify the meaning of unknown and multiple-meaning words and phrases based on grade 5 reading and content, choosing flexibly from a range of strategies. Use context (e.g., cause/effect relationships and comparisons in text) as a clue to the meaning of a word or phrase. **L.5.4a**

**ACADEMIC LANGUAGE**
- context clues, paragraph
- *párrofo*

**MINILESSON · 10 Mins**

## Context Clues

### 1 Explain

Explain to students that when they come across an unfamiliar or multiple-meaning word, they can use context clues in the paragraph that contains it to help them figure out its meaning.

→ Clues to a word's meaning can be found at the beginning, middle, or end of the paragraph.

→ When students encounter a word they don't know, they can read ahead to find clues to its meaning. If they still are not sure what the word means, they can reread from the beginning of the paragraph.

→ One kind of context clue may be a description or restatement of the unknown word. Other context clues include examples of the word.

### 2 Model Close Reading: Text Evidence

Model using context clues to determine the meaning of *cylinder* in the first paragraph of "Mysterious Oceans" on page 411. Point out that the last sentence of the paragraph refers to the creature whose body is encased in a cylinder as a "tube worm." This helps you recognize that the words *cylinder* and *tube* are closely related.

### 3 Guided Practice of Close Reading

COLLABORATE

Have students work in pairs to figure out the meanings of *sparse*, *aggressive*, and *predators* on page 412 of "Mysterious Oceans." Remind students to reread the paragraphs that contain these words to find context clues that will help them determine each word's meaning.

**Go Digital**

**Present the Lesson**

**SKILLS TRACE**

**PARAGRAPH CLUES**

**Introduce** U5W3

**Review** U5W3, U6W3

**Assess** U5, U6

## Context Clues

If you read an unfamiliar or multiple meaning word that puzzles you, you can look for clues to its meaning as you read the paragraph in which it appears. Clues to a word's meaning can be found in the beginning, middle, or end of a paragraph.

### Find Text Evidence

*In first paragraph of "Mysterious Oceans" on page 411, I see the word* cylinder. *I'm not sure what* cylinder *means. Since the creature being discussed is called a tube worm, I think that a cylinder may refer to the tube around the worm.*

> It has no mouth, eyes, or stomach. Its soft body is encased in a white cylinder and topped with a red plume. It can grow to be eight feet tall. It is a sea creature known as a giant tube worm, and it lives without any sunlight on the deep, dark ocean floor.

### Your Turn

With a partner, use context clues to figure out the meaning of the following words in "Mysterious Oceans." Remember, you may find context clues in the beginning, middle, or end of a paragraph.

**sparse,** *page 412*
**aggressive,** *page 412*
**predators,** *page 412*

417

**READING/WRITING WORKSHOP, p. 417**

## ENGLISH LANGUAGE LEARNERS SCAFFOLD

### Beginning

**Understand** Point out the words *sparse, aggressive,* and *predators* and define them. Give students examples of things that are sparse (open land in a city) and aggressive (a hungry lion). Name predators, such as tigers, hawks, wolves. Help students replace the words with words they know. Point out cognates *agresivo* and *depredador.*

### Intermediate

**Identify** Point out the words *sparse, aggressive,* and *predators* and define them. Assist students in finding context clues within the paragraphs that help them identify each word's meaning. Elicit from students how cognates helped them understand the words (*agresivo, depredador*).

### Advanced/High

**Actively Engage** Point out the words *sparse, aggressive,* and *predators.* Have students identify paragraph clues that help them figure out the meaning of each word. Ask students to find cognates, both among the words and in the paragraph clues, and tell them to their partners. Finally, have students list examples of each word.

---

## Monitor and *Differentiate*

### ✓ Quick Check

Can students identify and use paragraph clues to determine the meanings of *sparse, aggressive,* and *predators*?

### Small Group Instruction

If No → **Approaching Level** Reteach p. T173
**ELL** Develop p. T189
If Yes → **On Level** Review p. T178
**Beyond Level** Extend p. T182

---

**ON-LEVEL PRACTICE BOOK** p. 277

Vocabulary Strategy: **Context Clues**

Name _____

Read each passage. Underline the context clues that help you figure out the meaning of each word in bold. Then, in your own words, write the definition of the word. Possible responses provided.

1. One kind of adaptation is **structural**. This means the animal's body has changed so that it can survive in the climate.
   relating to the way the parts work together

2. Another type of adaptation is **behavioral**. Desert animals act in ways that help them survive.
   having to do with the way an animal acts

3. Since it is so hot during the day, many animals are **nocturnal**. They rest under rocks or in other cool places during the day and come out at night to hunt for food.
   active at night

4. Gila monsters come out only at night during the summer. In winter the lizards **hibernate**. During this period of inactivity, they use very little food and energy.
   sleep during winter

5. Many different types of snakes live in the desert. Because they are **cold-blooded**, snakes' body temperatures change with that of their surroundings.
   having a body temperature that changes depending on the temperature of the air

6. Meerkats are members of the mongoose family that live in Africa. They hunt early in the day to avoid the heat. They live in **mobs**, or groups, of as many as thirty members. The mob helps keep its members safe.
   large groups or crowds

Practice • Grade 5 • Unit 6 • Week 3 **277**

| APPROACHING p. 277 | BEYOND p. 277 | ELL p. 277 |

# Develop Comprehension

**Literature Anthology**

## Survival at 40 Below

### Text Complexity Range

**Lexile**

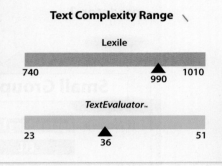

740     990     1010

**TextEvaluator™**

23     36     51

## Options for Close Reading

→ Whole Class

→ Small Group

→ Independent

**CCSS** Genre • Expository Text

# SURVIVAL AT 40 BELOW

by Debbie S. Miller,
illustrated by Jon Van Zyle

**Essential Question**

**How are living things adapted to their environment?**

Read about how some animals are adapted to the Arctic environment.

*Go Digital!*

468

---

# A C T Access Complex Text

## What makes this text complex?

⊳ **Specific Vocabulary**

⊳ **Genre**

⊳ **Prior Knowledge**

⊳ **Organization**

⊳ **Connection of Ideas**

## ▶ Specific Vocabulary

Tell students that vocabulary in this text is specific to Arctic animals and regions. Review strategies for finding the meanings of unfamiliar words, such as using context clues, word parts, or a dictionary.

→ Have students read paragraphs two and three on page 469. Have them use illustrations and text clues to find the meaning of *caribou* and *tundra*.

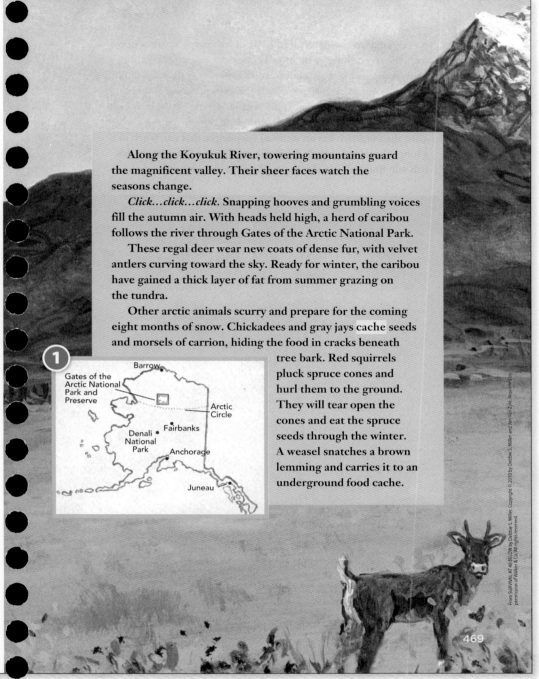

Along the Koyukuk River, towering mountains guard the magnificent valley. Their sheer faces watch the seasons change.

*Click…click…click.* Snapping hooves and grumbling voices fill the autumn air. With heads held high, a herd of caribou follows the river through Gates of the Arctic National Park.

These regal deer wear new coats of dense fur, with velvet antlers curving toward the sky. Ready for winter, the caribou have gained a thick layer of fat from summer grazing on the tundra.

Other arctic animals scurry and prepare for the coming eight months of snow. Chickadees and gray jays cache seeds and morsels of carrion, hiding the food in cracks beneath tree bark. Red squirrels pluck spruce cones and hurl them to the ground. They will tear open the cones and eat the spruce seeds through the winter. A weasel snatches a brown lemming and carries it to an underground food cache.

Barrow

Gates of the Arctic National Park and Preserve

Arctic Circle

Fairbanks

Denali National Park

Anchorage

Juneau

469

From SURVIVAL AT 40 BELOW by Debbie S. Miller. Copyright © 2010 by Debbie S. Miller and Jon Van Zyle. Reprinted by permission of Walker & Co. All rights reserved.

**LITERATURE ANTHOLOGY, pp. 468–469**

## Predictive Writing

Have students read the title, preview the map and illustrations, and write their predictions about what this selection will be about.

### ESSENTIAL QUESTION

Ask a student to read aloud the Essential Question. Have students discuss what information they expect to learn.

### Note Taking:
### Use the Graphic Organizer *Analytical Writing*

As students read the selection, ask them to take notes by filling in the graphic organizer on **Your Turn Practice Book page 272** to record the cause-and-effect relationships in the text.

### ❶ Text Features: Map

Look at the map on page 469. It is a map of Alaska. What cities do you see on the map? What parks do you see on the map? (Barrow, Fairbanks, Anchorage, and Juneau; Denali and Gates of the Arctic National Parks)

→ Choral read the first two sentences in paragraph four. Point to *carrion*. *What context clues help you find the meaning of* carrion? (morsels, food)

→ Recall the vocabulary word *cache*, a verb meaning "to hide or store something." Point out that *cache* is used as a noun in the last sentence. Elicit that it refers to a place for hiding or storing the food.

**ELL** Explain that the author uses different verbs that all relate to how animals gather food in the Arctic: *grazing, pluck, snatches.* Then ask:

→ *Chickadees and gray jays are birds. They eat _____.*

→ *Red squirrels eat _____.*

→ *A weasel is a small animal. Weasels eat _____.*

# Develop Comprehension

## ② Skill: Text Structure: Cause and Effect

We can understand how animals survive Arctic winters by looking at cause-and-effect relationships. On page 470, what causes ice to form on the pond? (Nights are growing colder.) How does the lack of oxygen in the frozen ponds affect the Alaska blackfish? (The fish's esophagus works like a lung. The fish finds holes in the ice and breathes through its mouth.) Add the causes and effects to your organizer.

| Cause | → | Effect |
|---|---|---|
| Nights grow colder. | → | Ice forms on the ponds. |
| Frozen ponds have little oxygen. | → | The Alaska blackfish gets oxygen by finding holes in the ice and breathing through its mouth. |

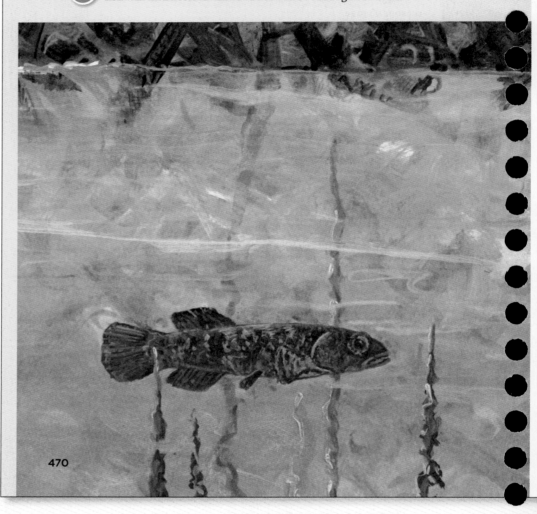

Nights grow colder. A thin layer of ice creeps across a pond near the river. Snug in their lodge, beavers rest after cutting many saplings for their underwater cache. Near their food pile, an Alaska blackfish paddles slowly through pond vegetation, searching for insect larvae. This bottom dweller can survive the winter in shallow frozen ponds with little oxygen. Along with gills, the blackfish has an unusual esophagus that can work like a lung, absorbing oxygen from the air. During the winter, this fish will find holes in the ice and breathe through its mouth.

470

## A C T Access Complex Text

### ▶ Specific Vocabulary

Help students use strategies to access content vocabulary on page 470.

→ Point out *vegetation. What word part do you recognize that gives a clue to the word's meaning?* (veg) *What other word has this word part?* (vegetable) *What does vegetation mean?* (plants)

→ Read aloud the word *larvae* in the fourth sentence. Explain that *larvae* is the plural form of *larva.* Have students use context and a dictionary to determine that *larvae* means "young insects."

→ Have students use a dictionary to find the meaning of *esophagus* in the sixth sentence.

Leaves rustle softly as a wood frog burrows into the duff of the forest floor. Suddenly, the frog feels its skin freezing. Its heart begins to beat rapidly. The frog's liver quickly produces lots of glucose. This sugary fluid, which the frog pumps through its body for several hours, will protect the insides of the cells from ice crystals. When more than three-quarters of its body freezes, the frog stops breathing and its heart stops beating.

**3**

But, like magic, the frog is still alive. Beneath the insulating layers of duff and snow, this frozen amphibian will hibernate until spring. It's a live frogsicle!

**4**

471

**LITERATURE ANTHOLOGY,** pp. 470–471

**3 Vocabulary: Context Clues**

What clues in the paragraph help you figure out the meaning of *glucose*? Turn to a partner and share your response. (The phrases "this sugary fluid" and "pumps through its body" are in the next sentence of the paragraph. These phrases tell me that *glucose* is a sugary fluid inside the frog's body.)

**4 Strategy: Ask and Answer Questions**

**Teacher Think Aloud** I can **ask and answer questions** about what I am reading to help me understand the text. I read that when the frog hibernates, it does not breathe, and its heart does not beat. I wonder how it stays alive if it can't breathe and its heart is not beating. I will reread and paraphrase the answer. The frog's liver produces glucose. The frog pumps it through its body to protect the cells from ice crystals. Protecting the cells keeps the frog alive.

**ELL** Provide additional vocabulary support on page 470.

→ Read aloud the third sentence on page 470. Explain that *snug* means "comfortable" and *lodge* means home. *What does it look like to be snug?*

→ Explain that a *bottom dweller* is a fish that stays near the bottom of the pond. *Point to the place in the illustration where the bottom dweller stays.*

→ Help students simplify the second to the last sentence and read it aloud: *The blackfish has an unusual esophagus that can work like a lung.*

→ Point out the location of your esophagus. Draw a tube on the board and use it to explain how the esophagus is a pathway for food that is being used to take in oxygen.

# Develop Comprehension

**5 Skill: Text Structure: Cause and Effect**

The text explains the effect of the Arctic on many different animals. On page 472, why is the arctic ground squirrel plump? (He ate tundra plants and seeds during the summer.) The shorter days are a sign that winter is coming. What effect do the shorter days have on the ground squirrel? (It tunnels into the earth to prepare its burrow.) Add the causes and effects to your organizer.

| Cause | → | Effect |
|---|---|---|
| The squirrel eats plants and seeds in summer. | → | He gets plump in time for winter. |
| The days grow shorter. | → | The squirrel prepares its burrow. |

**5** Farther up the valley, a small golden mammal is plump after a summer diet of tundra plants and seeds. As days grow shorter, the male arctic ground squirrel tunnels into the earth to prepare its burrow. He digs an underground chamber, about the size of a basketball, and stuffs it with grasses and tufts of caribou fur. Then he collects and stores seeds and berries.

472

## A C T  Access Complex Text

▶ **Genre**

Remind students that informational text often includes descriptions and illustrations to help readers visualize scenes and events.

→ *What do the text and the illustration on page 472 tell you about the ground squirrel?* (It is a small golden mammal; it is plump; it stands on its back legs to look around.)

→ *Reread page 473 and look at the illustration. How do descriptions of the squirrel's sounds and the bear's activity help you understand the scene?* (The squirrel's warning sounds and the description of the bear's claws, as well as the illustration, help me picture the squirrel's hurry to hide from the bear.)

*Sik...sik...sik.* The squirrel chatters a warning signal. Across the river, a grizzly bear browses on berries and digs up thick potato-like roots with her sharp claws. Alarmed by this huge predator, the squirrel dashes beneath the tundra. Like the squirrel, this grizzly will soon dig her winter den on a mountain slope.  **6** **7**

**STOP AND CHECK**

**Ask and Answer Questions** How does the change in season affect the arctic ground squirrel? Go back to the text to find the answer.

473

**LITERATURE ANTHOLOGY, pp. 472–473**

**6 Author's Craft: Text Structure**

The word *like* is often used as a signal word for comparison and contrast. What is the author comparing? (The author compares how the squirrel and the grizzly bear prepare for winter.)

**7 Genre: Expository Text**

Expository texts may use cause-and-effect relationships to tell about a topic. What relationship is explained on these pages? (The purpose of these pages is to show how two animals, the squirrel and the grizzly bear, prepare for winter.)

**STOP AND CHECK**

**Ask and Answer Questions** How does the change in season affect the arctic ground squirrel? (The squirrel prepares its burrow and collects and stores seeds and berries to get ready for winter.)

**ELL** Help students use the illustration to understand what happens before and after this scene. Read aloud pages 472–473, explaining words such as *burrow, warning, predator, dashes,* and *den.*

→ *What happens before this scene? Does the squirrel prepare its winter burrow or run away?* (It prepares its burrow.)

→ *What does the text "sik … sik … sik" on page 473 mean?* (It is the squirrel's warning sound.)

→ *What does the squirrel do after it sees the predator?* (It dashes away.)

→ *What will the bear do next?* (She will dig her winter den.)

# Develop Comprehension

**8 Skill: Text Structure: Cause and Effect**

What is the effect of the squirrel warming his body by burning brown fat? (It protects his vital organs and acts like a heating pad.) **Why does the squirrel warm himself, sleep, and supercool about a dozen times during the winter?** (He does this in order to conserve enough energy to survive.) **Add this information to your organizer.**

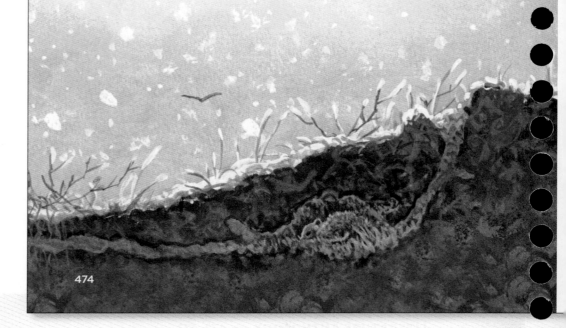

As snowflakes swirl, the squirrel is ready to hibernate. He curls into a ball in his burrow, then slowly supercools his body, lowering his temperature to just below the freezing point of water. His heart rate gradually drops to three beats per minute, and his brain activity ceases. This ice-cold furry squirrel looks dead, but, amazingly, he is only in the inactive state of torpor.

**8** After three weeks, something triggers the squirrel to wake up. His heart rate increases. He warms his body by burning brown fat. This insulating fat protects his vital organs and acts like a heating pad. Within several hours, his heartbeat and temperature are normal.

After rearranging his nest, the squirrel curls back into a ball and falls asleep. He dreams and sleeps soundly for about twelve hours. Then his body supercools again. Like a yo-yo, the squirrel warms himself, sleeps, and supercools about a dozen times during the winter to conserve enough energy to survive.

474

## A C T Access Complex Text

### ▶ Specific Vocabulary

Remind students that clues to an unfamiliar word can often be found in sentences surrounding the word. These are context clues.

→ Reread the first paragraph on page 474. Point out the word *torpor* in the last line. *What two words in the last sentence help you understand what* torpor *means?* (inactive state)

→ *Describe the squirrel when it is in the state of torpor.* (Its body is just below the freezing point of water, and its heart rate is slow. Its brain activity stops. It looks dead.)

→ Have students give a definition of *torpor.* (a time of decreased activity when all body functions slow down or stop)

Above the squirrel's burrow, an arctic fox searches for prey. The fox picks up the scent of voles beneath the snow. These mouselike animals are huddling in their nest to keep warm. Like an acrobat, the fox springs high in the air and pounces on the voles. Breaking through the snow, he traps one by surprise.

The arctic fox keeps warm in frigid temperatures because he wears two winter coats. His dense underfur insulates him like the down in a fluffy sleeping bag. His thick outer coat has tiny air pockets inside the hair shafts, instead of color pigment. The snow-white coat perfectly camouflages the fox for hunting prey and escaping predators. Fur also covers the soles of his paws, and his big, bushy tail provides extra warmth.

475

**9** **Strategy: Ask and Answer Questions**

**Teacher Think Aloud** As I read the second paragraph, I wonder how the fox's fur camouflages him. I'll reread the paragraph to see if I can find the answer. I learn that his outer coat of fur has air pockets instead of color pigment. This means his fur is white. I know that snow is white. Now I understand that the snow camouflages the fox because his fur is white.

Prompt students to apply the strategy in a Think Aloud by generating their own question and rereading to find the answer. Have them share their questions with a partner and paraphrase the answer they found.

**Student Think Aloud** After reading, I didn't understand what the fox was hunting. I reread the first paragraph to find the answer. The text explains that the fox was hunting a vole. I kept reading, and the text says the voles are mouse-like. The fox was hunting voles, which look like mice.

**ELL** ELLs may not be familiar with the content vocabulary on page 474. Encourage students to notice cognates: inactive/*inactivo*, temperature/*temperatura*, conserve/*conservar*.

→ Point out context clues that help define the meaning of *supercools*: "lowering his temperature to just below the freezing point of water."

Help students understand the squirrel's cycle between torpor and wakefulness.

→ *When the squirrel's body is supercooled, is he active or inactive?* (inactive) *Does he use energy or conserve energy?* (conserves energy)

→ *When the squirrel wakes up, does his temperature get warmer or colder?* (warmer)

# Develop Comprehension

**10 Skill: Text Structure: Cause and Effect**

The Arctic's deep snow makes walking difficult. **Why do snowshoe hares and ptarmigan have insulated feet that spread out their weight?** (So they can travel lightly across the snow.) **Why does the ptarmigan dive into snow drifts at night?** (The snow provides warmth so it can survive the lethal temperatures during the night.) **Add the causes and effects to your organizer.**

| Cause | → | Effect |
|---|---|---|
| Animals have insulated feet that spread out their weight. | → | The animals can travel lightly over the deep snow. |
| Arctic winter nights have lethal temperatures. | → | The ptarmigan dives into the snow at night for warmth. |

Inch by inch, the layer of snow deepens with each winter storm. On a frigid January day, the temperature plummets to 40 below zero. Thick pond ice cracks and makes eerie sounds. The fluffy quilt of snow insulates and protects the many animals, plants, and insects beneath it. It is much warmer under the snow layer than in the open air.

Other animals are well adapted to survive the colder air temperatures above the ice and snow. Snowshoe hares and ptarmigan zigzag between the willow bushes. Both animals can travel lightly across the snow with insulated feet that help spread out their weight. But the ptarmigan can't survive the **10** lethal night temperatures and fly off at dusk to seek shelter.

476

## A C T  Access Complex Text

▶ **Prior Knowledge**

Students may not understand how cold snow can keep plants and animals warm. Introduce them to the concept of insulation.

→ *Why do people wear layers of clothes when it gets cold?* (The layers help keep the cold out. They also help keep body heat in.)

→ Explain to students that the snow acts a bit like clothing or a blanket. The air spaces between the flakes trap animals' body heat and protect them from wind and the colder air temperatures above.

*Puff!* They dive into a drift of powdery snow. Invisible to the world, the ptarmigan roost inside their snow burrows, protected from predators and the extreme cold. **⑪**

Another bird combats the deep freeze. A black-capped chickadee flits from tree to tree, eating his cached food. He must gain enough fat each day to survive the night.

But this small bird needs more than food to survive. He fluffs up his dense feathers for better insulation. Tiny muscles control the angle of each feather, while other muscles shiver to produce heat. The chickadee can also lower his temperature and metabolism to save energy. He roosts in a thick forest or in tree cavities that give him the best shelter.

477

**LITERATURE ANTHOLOGY, pp. 476–477**

## ⑪ Author's Craft: Word Choice

The author chooses descriptive words that appeal to the reader's senses in order to explain the topic. These words help readers picture and understand the text. What sense or senses does the word *Puff* appeal to? (It appeals to the senses of hearing and sight.) What do you picture when you read this word? (I picture the bird diving and soft snow flying up in the air.) What other words on this page appeal to your senses? (*Snow burrows, black-capped chickadee, flits,* and *shiver* all appeal to the senses.)

## CONNECT TO CONTENT
### ADAPTATION AND INTERDEPENDENCY

Adaptations such as life cycle variations, animal behaviors, and physical characteristics enable plants and animals to survive the climate of the Arctic tundra. On pages 476–477, students learn how two different birds survive the Arctic winter. The ptarmigan burrows under the insulating snow to roost at night, while the chickadee is able to roost in tree cavities, staying warm by fluffing its feathers for insulation, shivering to produce heat, and saving energy by lowering its temperature and metabolism.

**STEM**

**ELL** Use a jacket or blanket to demonstrate that snow, though it feels cold to touch, can provide warmth.

→ Choral read the sentence "It is much warmer under the snow layer than in the open air."

→ *Am I warmer or colder under the jacket?* (warmer) *Are animals warmer or colder under the snow?* (warmer)

# Develop Comprehension

## 12 Skill: Make Inferences

The caribou are looking for food. Why do they avoid the burned area of an old forest fire? Use evidence from the second paragraph to make an inference. (They are looking for lichens. A burned area likely would not have any vegetation to eat.)

### STOP AND CHECK

**Ask and Answer Questions** How are the caribou adapted to a cold environment? (A special liquid fat protects their joints. Blood traveling to their hooves helps warm the blood returning to the heart. The flow protects the legs and reduces heat loss.)

While birds roost beneath a full moon, all is not quiet. A wolf howls on a distant ridge as caribou crunch through the snow with their broad hooves. These deer are well insulated for the Arctic by dense fur and hollow guard hairs. They sniff the snow and detect the smell of ashes from an old forest fire. Turning away, the caribou avoid this burned area.

Muzzles to the ground, the caribou later detect the mushroomlike scent of lichens. They dig craters and forage on clumps of these rootless plants. Their hooves and thin legs are well adapted for digging. A special liquid fat protects their joints. Blood traveling directly to the hooves helps warm the returning blood to the heart. This circular flow protects the legs and reduces heat loss.

### STOP AND CHECK

**Ask and Answer Questions** How are the caribou adapted to a cold environment? Go back to the text to find the answer.

478

# A C T Access Complex Text

## ► Specific Vocabulary

Remind students that authors of informational text use specific words that may be unfamiliar. Have students use strategies they have learned, or a dictionary, to determine word meanings.

→ *What clues tell you the meaning of* muzzles*?* (The text says, "With muzzles to the ground, the caribou later detect the mushroomlike scent of lichens." We find scents with the nose. The muzzle must be the area of the nose and mouth.)

Help students determine the meanings of other words, including *insulated, guard hairs* (p. 478), *storehouse, sedges* and *lee* (p. 479). Knowing these words will help them better understand adaptations.

While caribou wander, the grizzly bear is snug in her den with two newborn cubs. The drowsy bear nurses them and rests to save energy. The three survive off her large storehouse of fat. As she sleepily feeds her fast-growing cubs, she doesn't notice the faint sound of steps across the snow.

Sure-footed and agile, Dall sheep pick their way across the mountain slope. Fierce winds have blown snow off the alpine tundra, exposing frozen grasses and sedges. The sheep graze on these withered plants, then seek shelter from the wind by bedding down in the lee of some rocky crags.

479

**LITERATURE ANTHOLOGY, pp. 478–479**

**⑬ Skill: Text Structure: Cause and Effect**

The text has explained that food is hard to come by in the Arctic. Why does the grizzly bear rest? (The bear rests to save energy.) Why does it need to save energy? (The bears must survive off the energy stored in the mother's fat.)

What effect do the fierce winds have on the Dall sheep? (The wind blows snow off the tundra and exposes grasses and plants that Dall sheep eat; the sheep take shelter from the wind.) Add the causes and effects to your organizer.

| Cause | → | Effect |
|---|---|---|
| The grizzly bear rests. | → | It saves energy so the bears can survive off the mother's stored fat. |
| Fierce winds blow. | → | Grasses and plants that Dall sheep eat become exposed. |
| | | The sheep take shelter from the wind. |

**ELL** ELLs may have difficulty understanding how the caribou find lichens.

→ Point out the cognate: lichen/*liquen. Reread the first two sentences in the last paragraph on p. 478. What are lichens?* (plants with no roots) *How do you know? Point to the text that tells you that.*

→ Use gestures to explain *muzzles, detect, dig craters, forage.*

→ *How do caribou detect lichens?* (They use their muzzles and look for the smell.)

→ *What do the caribou do when they detect lichens?* (They dig craters and forage.)

# Develop Comprehension

**14** **Skill: Text Structure: Cause and Effect**

What danger does the musk ox sense? (A wolf approaches.) What effect does this danger have on the oxen? (They gather together and form a circular wall of fur and horns. One ox charges the wolf as it approaches, driving it away.) Add the causes and effects to your organizer.

| Cause | → | Effect |
|-------|---|--------|
| Wolves approach the musk oxen. | → | Oxen form a circular wall and work as a team to drive off hungry wolves. |

Month by month, winter passes slowly. Backs to the wind, a group of musk oxen stands on the snow-covered tundra, conserving energy. Short legs, small ears, and fluffy underwool, known as *qiviut*, insulate musk oxen from even the deepest cold. One musk ox sees wolves approaching and senses danger. Immediately, the musk oxen gather together. Shoulder to shoulder they form a circular wall of thick fur and horns. As one wolf draws near, a large bull lowers his deadly sharp horns. With a sudden burst, he charges the wolf.

**14** Wheeling away, the wolf quickly retreats. The musk oxen continue to work as a team, charging and driving off the hungry wolves.

480

## A C T Access Complex Text

▶ **Organization**

Explain that the author describes the movement of winter into spring chronologically. Each change is shown by the effects on different plants and animals, as well as on the environment. Point out the passage about musk oxen on page 480.

→ *How do musk oxen survive the winter?* (They have a fluffy underwool called *qiviut* to keep them warm in the deepest cold. To ward off predators such as the wolf, they come together, shoulder to shoulder in a circle, and use their horns to drive the wolves back.)

*Trickle...tinkle...drip.* The snow and ice begin to melt.  As temperatures rise, bumblebees, butterflies, and other dormant insects begin to stir. A woolly bear caterpillar basks in the sun after being snow-covered for eight months. His dark, furry body traps the sun's heat. Inching his way to a budding willow, he chews on a tiny leaf.

These fuzzy creatures, and other northern insects, have antifreeze substances that prevent ice crystals from forming in their bodies. The woolly bear will spend up to fourteen winters in the Arctic as a caterpillar. Then this amazing survivor will transform into a moth, but for only one short summer!

481

**LITERATURE ANTHOLOGY, pp. 480–481**

**15 Author's Craft: Word Choice**

Why does the author use the words *trickle, tinkle,* and *drip*? (It appeals to the reader's sense of hearing. These words help the reader picture what it sounds like when the snow and ice start to melt. )

**16 Strategy: Ask and Answer Questions**

Reread page 481. Generate a question of your own about the text and share it with a partner. Look for the answer in the text. Turn back to your partner and paraphrase the text where you found the answer to your question.

**Student Think Aloud** As I read the second paragraph on page 481, I see it begins "These fuzzy creatures." I'm not sure what these "fuzzy creatures" are. I will reread the first paragraph to find the answer. I see that the author is referring to woolly bear caterpillars, and as I keep reading I learn that they are furry insects that spend fourteen winters as caterpillars before they turn into moths for just one summer.

→ *Summarize the effect of rising temperatures on the woolly bear caterpillar on page 481.* (As snow and ice begin to melt, the woolly bear caterpillar comes out of its dormant state. An antifreeze substance helps it live up to fourteen winters in the Arctic. It lives as a moth only one summer.)

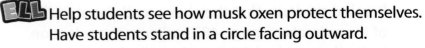Help students see how musk oxen protect themselves. Have students stand in a circle facing outward.

→ *Can someone sneak up on us like this?* (no) *Why not?* (We can see in all directions.) Have one student show what one musk ox does when a wolf approaches by lowering his or her head and running a few steps away from the circle.

# Develop Comprehension

**17 Skill: Text Structure: Cause and Effect**

What are the animals doing on page 482?
(The wood frog thaws and calls for a mate,
the beavers dive, the blackfish dart after
prey, the ground squirrel eats his stored
food and looks for a mate.) What has caused
this behavior? If you need help, look back at
page 480 or read on to page 483. (Winter is
coming to an end.) Add the information to
your organizer.

| Cause → | Effect |
|---|---|
| Winter is coming to an end. → | The wood frog thaws and calls for a mate, the beavers dive, the blackfish dart after prey, the ground squirrel eats his stored food and looks for a mate. |

One by one, moist leaves rustle near the pond. The
wood frog slowly thaws out, and its heart beats once again.
*rrrrRuk… rrrrRuk.* The frog begins calling for a mate, making
a ducklike sound near the pond's edge. Slapping their tails in
the open water, the beavers dive while the blackfish dart after
prey on the pond's bottom. Farther up the valley, the male
ground squirrel eats his stored cache of food, then leaves his
**17** burrow in search of a mate.

482

## A C T  Access Complex Text

### ▶ Connection of Ideas

Remind students that they have read about each
of the animals on page 482 earlier in the selection.
Invite them to look back and recall what each
animal has done to survive the winter.

### ▶ Prior Knowledge

Students may not be familiar with the term "Land of
the Midnight Sun" on page 483. Have students refer
back to the map on page 469.

→ *Where do the animals described in the text live?*
(They live above the Arctic Circle in Alaska.)

Hour by hour, day by day, the pulse of life increases with warmer June days and greening plants. Caribou feast upon a summer buffet, while playful grizzly bear cubs tussle and explore the tundra as their mother searches for prey. Birds that migrated south for the winter return to their birthplace, building nests on the tundra and filling the air with music. For more than two months the days will be endless, as the top of the world tilts toward the sun and the magical Land of the Midnight Sun explodes with life.

**STOP AND CHECK**

Visualize  How does the warmer weather affect life in the Arctic? Visualizing the animals and their actions may help you.

483

**LITERATURE ANTHOLOGY, pp. 482–483**

**STOP AND CHECK**

**Visualize**  How does the warmer weather affect life in the Arctic? (Animals leave their winter homes and begin to move around and make noise. For example, the grizzly bear cubs play and explore, and birds that migrated south return.)

## Return to Predictions

Review students' predictions and purposes for reading. Ask them to answer the **Essential Question.** (Animals that live in the Arctic have adapted to survive the cold. Some animals hibernate, some have fur that keeps them warm, and some migrate to warmer places.)

→ Tell students that Earth has a tilted axis. In the summer, the tilt causes the land north of the Arctic Circle to face the sun constantly during the day and night, resulting in 24 hours of sunlight.

→ Use a globe and a flashlight to demonstrate.

→ *Why do you think the area above the Arctic Circle is referred to as the Land of the Midnight Sun?* (The sun can still be seen at midnight.)

# About the Author

## Meet the Author and the Illustrator

### Debbie S. Miller and Jon Van Zyle

Have students read the biographies of the author and illustrator. Ask:

→ How might Debbie S. Miller use her experiences living in Alaska to gather facts and details for books?

→ Why is Jon Van Zyle a good choice as the illustrator of *Survival at 40 Below*?

## Author's Purpose

### To Inform

Remind students that authors who write to inform present facts about a topic. Explain that authors also think about the best way to organize the facts. Students may say that organizing the text throughout the course of the seasons helps readers understand how survival depends on preparation and activities during other seasons.

## Author's Craft

### Sensory Images

Remind students that authors use sensory images to help readers visualize the text.

→ The author uses specific words to help readers visualize the cold. Example: "thin layer of ice creeps across a pond" (p. 470).

→ Have students find other examples of sensory images, such as "Leaves rustle softly…" (p. 471).

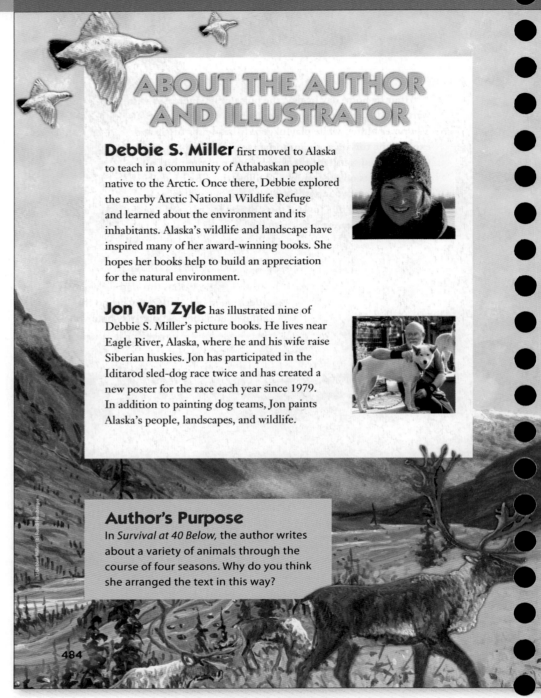

## ABOUT THE AUTHOR AND ILLUSTRATOR

**Debbie S. Miller** first moved to Alaska to teach in a community of Athabaskan people native to the Arctic. Once there, Debbie explored the nearby Arctic National Wildlife Refuge and learned about the environment and its inhabitants. Alaska's wildlife and landscape have inspired many of her award-winning books. She hopes her books help to build an appreciation for the natural environment.

**Jon Van Zyle** has illustrated nine of Debbie S. Miller's picture books. He lives near Eagle River, Alaska, where he and his wife raise Siberian huskies. Jon has participated in the Iditarod sled-dog race twice and has created a new poster for the race each year since 1979. In addition to painting dog teams, Jon paints Alaska's people, landscapes, and wildlife.

### Author's Purpose

In *Survival at 40 Below*, the author writes about a variety of animals through the course of four seasons. Why do you think she arranged the text in this way?

484

**LITERATURE ANTHOLOGY, pp. 484–485**

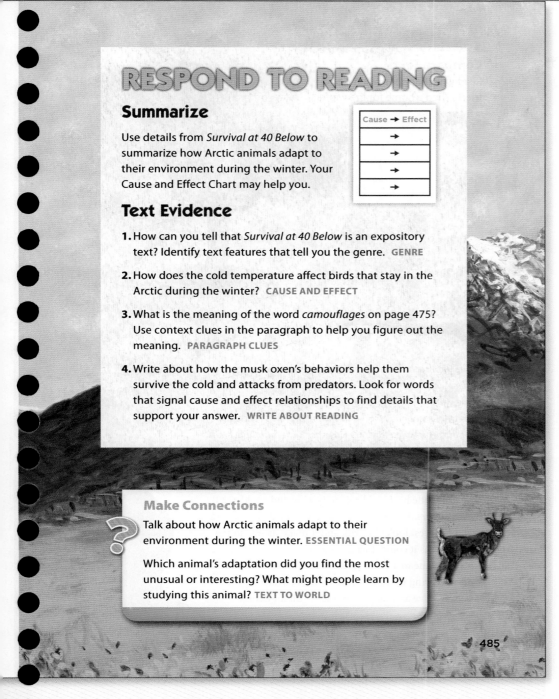

# RESPOND TO READING

## Summarize

Use details from *Survival at 40 Below* to summarize how Arctic animals adapt to their environment during the winter. Your Cause and Effect Chart may help you.

| Cause → Effect |
|---|
| → |
| → |
| → |
| → |

## Text Evidence

1. How can you tell that *Survival at 40 Below* is an expository text? Identify text features that tell you the genre. **GENRE**

2. How does the cold temperature affect birds that stay in the Arctic during the winter? **CAUSE AND EFFECT**

3. What is the meaning of the word *camouflages* on page 475? Use context clues in the paragraph to help you figure out the meaning. **PARAGRAPH CLUES**

4. Write about how the musk oxen's behaviors help them survive the cold and attacks from predators. Look for words that signal cause and effect relationships to find details that support your answer. **WRITE ABOUT READING**

### Make Connections

Talk about how Arctic animals adapt to their environment during the winter. **ESSENTIAL QUESTION**

Which animal's adaptation did you find the most unusual or interesting? What might people learn by studying this animal? **TEXT TO WORLD**

485

# Make Connections ⏺ *Analytical Writing*

**Essential Question** Have partners work together to cite evidence from the text of how animals have adapted to the environment in the winter. Ask partners to discuss their findings with the class.

**Text to World** After students name the adaptation about an animal they found most unusual, discuss what people can learn by studying this animal.

# Respond to Reading

## Summarize

Review with students the information from their graphic organizers. Model how to use the information to summarize *Survival at 40 Below*.

⏺ *Analytical Writing* **Write About Reading: Paraphrase** Remind students that to paraphrase is to restate the text in your own words. You can paraphrase a section of a text or an entire text.

Ask students to write a paragraph that paraphrases how one of the animals in the text survives the winter, using the causes and effects they recorded in their organizers. Have students share their writing with a partner.

## Text Evidence

1. **Genre** <u>Answer</u> The selection is set in a real location and tells about real animals. <u>Evidence</u> The location is identified on a map. Animals, such as the gray jay and the red squirrel, are identified and described.

2. **Cause and Effect** <u>Answer</u> Birds store food caches, find shelter, and change behavior and body temperatures to produce heat. <u>Evidence</u> Chickadees store seeds and fluff up their feathers; ptarmigans burrow into the snow.

3. **Context Clues** <u>Answer</u> It means "disguises, or changes in appearance to hide." <u>Evidence</u> I used the paragraph clues "His thick outer coat has tiny air pockets inside the hair shafts, instead of color pigment" and "The snow-white coat."

⏺ *Analytical Writing* 4. **Write About Reading: Cause and Effect** The body shape and fur of the oxen insulate them. They have short legs, small ears, and fluffy underwool that protects them from the deepest cold. Oxen stand in a circle and take turns charging to fend off predators.

# Develop Comprehension

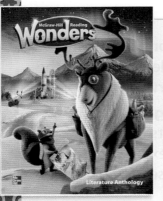

**Literature Anthology**

## "Why the Evergreen Trees Never Lose Their Leaves"

**Text Complexity Range**

Lexile

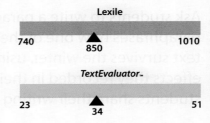

740    850    1010

*TextEvaluator*

23    34    51

## Options for Close Reading

→ Whole Class

→ Small Group

→ Independent

---

**CCSS** Genre • Pourquoi Story

**Compare Texts**
Read what happens when a bird tries to find a home for the winter.

## Why the Evergreen Trees Never Lose Their Leaves

*The approach of winter brings changes to many northern environments that can send animals on the move, seeking warmer regions. Other animals stay, but they must* **hibernate** *or seek out food and shelter that will keep them warm through the cold winter months. Each animal has an* **adaptation** *that helps it survive.*

Winter was coming, and the birds had flown far to the south, where the air was warm and they could find berries to eat. One little bird had broken its wing and could not fly with the others. It was alone in the cold world of frost and snow. The forest looked warm, and it made its way to the trees as well as it could, to ask for help.

First it came to a birch-tree. "Beautiful birch-tree," it said, "my wing is broken, and my friends have flown away. May I live among your branches till they come back to me?"

486

---

# A C T   Access Complex Text

## What makes this text complex?

▷ **Genre**

▷ **Organization**

## ▶ Genre

Explain that some folktales explain natural phenomena in an entertaining way. Tell students that a pourquoi story tells why something happens. The French word *pourquoi* means *why*.

→ *Reread the title. What is this folktale going to explain?* (why, in fall, some trees turn color and lose their leaves, but evergreens do not)

"No, indeed," answered the birch-tree, drawing her fair leaves away. "We of the great forest have our own birds to help. I can do nothing for you."

"The birch is not very strong," said the little bird to itself, "and it might be that she could not hold me easily. I will ask the oak." So the bird said, "Great oak-tree, you are so strong, will you not let me live on your boughs till my friends come back in the springtime?"

"In the springtime!" cried the oak. "That is a long way off. How do I know what you might do in all that time? Birds are always looking for something to eat, and you might even eat up some of my acorns."

"It may be that the willow will be kind to me," thought the bird, and it said, "Gentle willow, my wing is broken, and I could not fly to the south with the other birds. May I live on your branches till the springtime?"

The willow did not look gentle then, for she drew herself up proudly and said, "Indeed, I do not know you, and we willows never talk to people whom we do not know. Very likely there are trees somewhere that will take in strange birds. Leave me at once."

**1**

487

**LITERATURE ANTHOLOGY, pp. 486–487**

## Compare Texts

Students will read a folktale about how a bird learns to adapt when it can't fly south for the winter. Ask students to do a close reading of the story. Encourage them to **ask and answer questions** or use other strategies they know. Then have students reread, taking notes. Students will use the text evidence they gather to compare this story with *Survival at 40 Below*.

### 1 Ask and Answer Questions

What reasons do the first three trees give for not letting the bird live on their branches?

**Write About Reading** Make a list of reasons that the trees would not let the bird stay. Share your list with a partner. (The birch only helps its own birds. The bird might eat all of the oak tree's acorns. Willows never talk to strange birds.)

→ *What problem does the bird need to solve?* (The little bird has a broken wing. Since he cannot fly to a warmer place for the winter, he needs to live in the woods.)

→ *What kinds of trees does the little bird ask the help of on pages 486 and 487?* (the birch, oak, and willow trees, which lose their leaves in the winter)

**ELL** Help students understand problem-solution organization. Point out the cognates: problem/*problema*, solution/*solución*.

→ *The bird has a problem. Its wing is _____.* (broken)

→ Explain the phrases *made its way* and *as well as it could* in the second paragraph. Ask students to use one of these phrases in a sentence.

# Develop Comprehension

**2 Ask and Answer Questions**

How does the spruce-tree offer to help the bird? Turn to a partner and paraphrase the text to answer the question. (The spruce-tree tells the bird it can live on one of its thickest, softest branches to stay warm.)

**3 Ask and Answer Questions**

How do the pine-tree and the juniper-tree offer to help the little bird?

*Analytical Writing* **Write About Reading** Take notes on what these two trees offer the bird. (The pine-tree tells the bird it will help it stay warm by keeping the north wind from blowing on it. The juniper-tree tells the bird it will give it berries to eat all winter long.)

The poor little bird did not know what to do. Its wing was not yet strong, but it began to fly away as well as it could. Before it had gone far, a voice was heard. "Little bird," it said, "where are you going?"

"Indeed, I do not know," answered the bird sadly. "I am very cold."

"Come right here, then," said the friendly spruce-tree, for it was her voice that had called. "You shall live on my warmest branch all winter if you choose."

"Will you really let me?" asked the little bird eagerly.

"Indeed, I will," answered the kind-hearted spruce-tree. "If your friends have flown away, it is time for the trees to help you. Here is the branch where my leaves are thickest and softest."

"My branches are not very thick," said the friendly pine-tree, "but I am big and strong, and I can keep the north wind from you and the spruce."

"I can help too," said a little juniper-tree. "I can give you berries all winter long, and every bird knows that juniper berries are good."

So the spruce gave the lonely little bird a home, the pine kept the cold north wind away from it, and the juniper gave it berries to eat.

Illustration: Richard Downs

488

# A C T  Access Complex Text

## ▶ Organization

Remind students that this story began with the little bird looking for help to solve a problem. Prompt students to see that the author summarizes the solution in the last paragraph on page 488.

→ *What is the solution to the little bird's problem?* (The spruce lets it live on its branches. The pine blocks the cold wind. The juniper provides berries.)

## ▶ Genre

Remind students that when they read a folktale, they must distinguish between fact and fiction.

→ *What is the purpose of this folktale?* (to explain why some trees lose their leaves and others don't)

→ *What do you read about trees in this folktale that is factual?* (Spruces, pines, and junipers don't lose their leaves in winter.)

The other trees looked on and talked together wisely.

"I would not have strange birds on my boughs," said the birch.

"I shall not give my acorns away for any one," said the oak.

"I never have anything to do with strangers," said the willow, and the three trees drew their leaves closely about them.

In the morning all those shining leaves lay on the ground, for a cold north wind had come in the night, and every leaf that it touched fell from the tree.

"May I touch every leaf in the forest?" asked the wind in its frolic.

"No," said the frost king. "The trees that have been kind to the little bird with the broken wing may keep their leaves."

This is why the leaves of the spruce, the pine, and the juniper are always green.

**Make Connections**

How does the bird adapt to changes in its environment? What happens as a result? ESSENTIAL QUESTION

How is the bird's adaptation in this story different from other animal adaptations you've read about? TEXT TO TEXT

489

**LITERATURE ANTHOLOGY, pp. 488–489**

## Make Connections

**Essential Question** Have students paraphrase and share information about how the bird adapted to changes in the environment. Suggest that they look back at the story's introduction and the solution.

**Text to Text** Have groups of students compare their responses to the Ask and Answer Questions prompts with what they learned in *Survival at 40 Below*. Each group can report back to the whole class. Ask one group to compare the way the ptarmigan stays warm in the winter and how the little bird stayed warm. (The ptarmigan burrows under the snow for warmth. The little bird used the tree's branches to keep out the wind and cold.) **Ask other groups to compare the chickadee and the ground squirrel with the little bird.** (The chickadee can fluff up and move its feathers to keep warm. The squirrel digs a burrow and hibernates to keep warm. The little bird must use the spruce and pine trees to keep warm.)

---

**ELL** ELLs may be unfamiliar with the names of trees in English.

→ Pronounce the name of each tree. Have students repeat after you.

→ Use illustrations or photographs of a spruce, pine, and juniper tree. Point to each kind of tree and say its name.

→ Use pictures of birch, oak, and willow trees and say each tree's name as you point to it.

→ *Which trees lose their leaves?* (The birch, oak, and willow trees lose their leaves.)

→ *Which trees get to keep their leaves?* (The spruce, pine, and juniper trees get to keep their leaves.)

# → Word Study/Fluency

MINILESSON
**20** Mins

## Words from Mythology

### OBJECTIVES

**CCSS** Know and apply grade-level phonics and word analysis skills in decoding words. Use combined knowledge of all letter-sound correspondences, syllabication patterns, and morphology (e.g. roots and affixes) to read accurately unfamiliar multisyllabic words in context and out of context. **RF.5.3a**

**CCSS** Use context to confirm or self-correct word recognition and understanding, rereading as necessary. **RF.5.4c**

Rate: 129–149 WCPM

### ACADEMIC LANGUAGE

• *rate, accuracy*

• Cognate: *ritmo*

Refer to the sound transfers chart to identify sounds that do not transfer in Spanish, Cantonese, Vietnamese, Hmong, and Korean.

## 1 Explain

Tell students that many words in English have origins in mythology, especially from the Greeks and Romans. Explain that Vulcan was the Roman god of fire. The English word *volcano* has its origin in *Vulcan*. Discuss the relationship between the name from mythology and the English word. Tell students that recognizing and understanding these relationships can help them access the meaning of many unfamiliar words.

## 2 Model

On the board, write each of the following words from mythology and the related English words. Model how to recognize and understand the relationship between each name from mythology and its English counterpart.

→ **Ceres/cereal:** In Roman mythology, Ceres was the goddess of grain and the harvest. The word *cereal* has its origin in her name.

→ **Pan/panic:** Pan was the Greek god of goatherds and shepherds. The word *panic* comes from his name. One explanation of how this came to be is that Pan created noise in the woods at night to scare travelers.

→ **Titan/titanic:** In Greek mythology, the Titans were the gigantic sons of Gaia and Uranus. They were huge and powerful. The adjective *titanic* has its origin in this name.

## 3 Guided Practice

Write the following words on the board. Help students identify the mythological origin of each word and explain the relationship between the word and its origin. Encourage students to use a dictionary or reliable sources on the Internet to verify their explanations and extend their understanding.

| | | | |
|---|---|---|---|
| atlas | jovial | marathon | nectar |
| martial | echo | herculean | tantalize |

### Go Digital

**Words from Mythology**

**Present the Lesson**

**View "Mysterious Oceans"**

## Read Multisyllabic Words

**Transition to Longer Words** Help students transition to multisyllabic words with roots in mythology. Write the following words on the board. Have students read the words aloud. Then ask them to use a dictionary to identify each word's origin and its meaning.

| | |
|---|---|
| colossally | narcissistic |
| ambrosial | Amazonian |
| nocturnal | labyrinthine |
| January | iridescent |

## Monitor and *Differentiate*

 **Quick Check**

Can students decode words from Greek and Roman mythology? Can students read with appropriate rate and accuracy?

### Small Group Instruction

| | | |
|---|---|---|
| If No → | **Approaching Level** | **Reteach** pp. T170, T174 |
| | **ELL** | **Develop** pp. T187, T190 |
| If Yes → | **On Level** | **Apply** pp. T176–T177 |
| | **Beyond Level** | **Apply** pp. T180–T181 |

 ←

## Rate and Accuracy

**Explain/Model** Tell students that using a slower rate may help them read selections with scientific terms or unfamiliar words more accurately. Model reading the first page of "Mysterious Oceans," **Reading/Writing Workshop** pages 410–413. Use a slow and measured rate as you read.

Remind students that you will be listening for appropriate rate and accuracy as you monitor their reading during the week.

**Practice/Apply** Have partners alternate reading paragraphs in the passage, modeling the rate you used.

## Daily Fluency Practice

Students can practice fluency using **Your Turn Practice Book** passages.

### ON-LEVEL PRACTICE BOOK p. 278

Word Study: **Words from Mythology**

Name _____

Read each sentence below. Circle the word that has origins in mythology.
Then write the meaning of the word on the line. You may use a dictionary.

**Janus:** Roman god of beginnings
**Atlas:** Greek giant who supported the world on his shoulders
**Luna:** Roman goddess of the moon
**Clotho:** Greek goddess who spins the thread of human life
**Oceanus:** Greek god of the stream of water encircling the world
**Olympus:** mountain in Greece known as home of the gods
**Furies:** Greek goddesses of law and punishment
**Fortuna:** Roman goddess of luck

1. The ocean is home to a wide variety of plants and animals.
   the salt water that covers much of the earth

2. They used an atlas to plan their trip around the world.
   a book of maps

3. Some people start a new hobby or exercise routine in January.
   the first month of the calendar year

4. Many people watched the first lunar landing on television.
   having to do with the moon

5. The other team was furious when the referee made an incorrect call.
   very angry

6. In the winter, people wear several layers of clothes to keep warm.
   garments that people wear

7. The summer Olympics in 2008 were held in China.
   international sports competition

8. In many fairy tales the main characters set out to seek their fortune.
   good luck or riches

278 Practice • Grade 5 • Unit 6 • Week 3

| APPROACHING | BEYOND | ELL |
|---|---|---|
| p. 278 | p. 278 | p. 278 |

**Go** Digital

www.connected.mcgraw-hill.com
RESOURCES
Research and Inquiry

→ **Wrap Up the Week**

# Integrate Ideas

# RESEARCH AND INQUIRY 🔬 SCIENCE

**Adaptations**

### OBJECTIVES

**CCSS** Conduct short research projects that use several sources to build knowledge through investigation of different aspects of a topic. **W.5.7**

**CCSS** Include multimedia components (e.g., graphics, sound) and visual displays in presentations when appropriate to enhance the development of main ideas or themes. **SL.5.5**

• Avoid plagiarism.
• Work in teams.

### ACADEMIC LANGUAGE
• *plagiarism*
• Cognate: *plagio*

## Prepare an Oral Presentation

Explain that students will work in small groups to research animals that are found on the African island nation of Madagascar and nowhere else on Earth. They will then share their findings in short presentations to other groups. Discuss the following steps:

**1** **Find Resources** Have groups use reliable print and online resources to identify five different animal species that are unique to Madagascar. Have them make a list of these animals and post it to the Shared Research Board.

**2** **Research Animals** Ask students to identify and record interesting facts about Madagascar's animals. Caution students to restate information from the resources in their own words to avoid plagiarism. Use online Research Process Checklist 3 to evaluate their research.

**3** **Guided Practice** Help groups organize their information logically for oral presentations. For example, they might first talk about animals that live in trees and then discuss animals that live on the ground. Encourage groups to assign specific roles to each group member so everyone has a chance to participate in some way.

**4** **Create the Project: Oral Presentation** Have groups use the notes they took to organize and prepare information to present to another group. Encourage them to use video, pictures, music, or other multimedia elements to enliven their presentations.

## Give an Oral Presentation

Have each group present its findings to another group. Ask groups to provide feedback on each presentation.

**STEM**

Isao Enomoto/Nature Production/Minden Pictures

# TEXT CONNECTIONS  *Analytical Writing*

## OBJECTIVES

**CCSS** Integrate information from several texts on the same topic in order to write or speak about the subject knowledgeably. **RI.5.9**

**CCSS** Review the key ideas expressed and draw conclusions in light of information and knowledge gained from the discussions. **SL.5.1d**

### Text-to-Text

COLLABORATE

**Cite Evidence** Explain to students that they will work in groups to compare information they have learned about animal adaptations from all the texts they have read this week. Model how to compare this information by using examples from the week's **Leveled Readers** and "Mysterious Oceans," **Reading/Writing Workshop** pages 410–413. Have students review the week's selections and their completed graphic organizers. Help them set up a Two-Tab Foldable® to record their comparisons from each text. Instruct them to write notes about how animals on land adapt on the first tab and notes about how sea creatures adapt on the other tab.

Land Animals

Sea Creatures

Dinah Zike's
**FOLDABLES**

**Present Information** Ask groups to present their findings to the class. Encourage discussion by asking students to comment on information each group found that is similar to and different from other groups' findings.

# WRITE ABOUT READING  *Analytical Writing*

## OBJECTIVES

**CCSS** Draw evidence from literary or informational texts to support analysis, reflection, and research. **W.5.9**

### Write an Analysis

**Cite Evidence** Explain that students will write about one of the texts they read this week. Using text evidence, students will analyze how well the author uses cause-and-effect relationships to explain a topic.

Discuss how to analyze a text by asking *how* and *why* questions.

→ How does describing causes and effects help explain the topic?

→ Why does the author do a good job of explaining the topic?

Use **Your Turn Practice Book** page 279 to read and discuss the student model. Then have students choose a text and review causes and effects they recorded. Have them write their opinion as to how well the author used cause-and-effect relationships to explain a topic. Remind students that good opinion writers clearly state an opinion. Remind students to use negatives or negative contractions correctly.

COLLABORATE

**Present Your Ideas** Ask partners to share their paragraphs and discuss how the evidence they cited from the text supports their opinions.

# → Readers to Writers

MINILESSON
**10 Mins**

## Writing Traits: Sentence Fluency

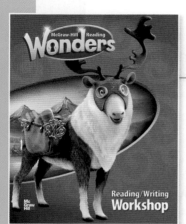

**Reading/Writing Workshop**

### OBJECTIVES

**CCSS** With guidance and support from peers and adults, develop and strengthen writing as needed by planning, revising, editing, rewriting, or trying a new approach. **W.5.5**

**CCSS** Write routinely over extended time frames (time for research, reflection, and revision) and shorter time frames (a single sitting or a day or two) for a range of discipline-specific tasks, purposes, and audiences. **W.5.10**

Analyze models to understand sentence variety.

### ACADEMIC LANGUAGE

• fluency, sentence structure, simple, compound, complex

• Cognate: *estructura*

### Vary Sentence Structure

**Expert Model** Writers vary sentence structure to give their writing rhythm, style, and interest. To add variety, writers may expand, combine, or shorten sentences as they write and revise.

To vary sentence structure, writers may use simple, compound, and complex sentences. They may also begin sentences in different ways. A sentence might begin with a participial phrase—a short phrase that relates to the subject. It might begin with an appositive, which gives another name for a nearby noun. It might begin with a phrase that starts with a preposition.

**Read aloud** the expert model from "Mysterious Oceans." Ask students to listen for different sentence structures. Have students talk with a partner to discuss the ways the writer varied sentences in the passage and how that makes the writing lively.

**Student Model** Remind students that good writers vary sentences to add interest. Read aloud the student model "My Cat and the Cold." As students follow along, have them focus on how Juan combined some sentences and divided others to vary the structure.

**Invite** partners to talk about the model and the changes the writer made. Ask them to suggest other changes Juan could make to improve sentence variety.

Go Digital

**Expert Model**

**Student Model**

**Genre Writing**

**Opinion Writing**

For full writing process lessons and rubrics see:

→ Book Review, pp. T344–T349

→ Opinion Letter, pp. T350–T355

## CCSS Writing Traits • Sentence Fluency

# Readers to ...

Writers vary their sentences by expanding, combining, and reducing them. A combination of long and short sentences makes the text livelier. A variety of **sentence structures** also makes the writing clearer and more interesting to read. Reread this passage from "Mysterious Oceans."

**Expert Model**

### Sentence Structure

Identify some of the ways the writer varies her sentences to make the writing lively.

The ocean's floor is varied, consisting of vast plains, steep canyons, and towering mountains. It includes active, dormant, and extinct volcanoes. This undersea world is a harsh environment because of its frigid temperatures and lack of sunshine.

The deep ocean is also a mysterious environment that remains largely unexplored. Little is known about it or its creatures. Do any of them cache food the way land animals do? Do any ocean species hibernate? As one example among countless mysteries, not a single, live giant squid had ever been spotted until a few years ago. We knew they existed only because their corpses had been found.

418

# Writers

Juan wrote an expository text about living in a cold environment. Read his revision of this section.

**Student Model**

## My Cat and the Cold

Another reason that I would rather live in a cold climate is my cat, Blue. When We got my cat from the shelter. Our vet said it would be a good idea to keep her inside, and we think she though must have lived outside before. happily For one thing, she trots out in cold weather and she also likes to hunt for a pool food. To get warm, Blue curls up in of sunlight. When it's very hot, though, and she lies around. She looks really sad.

### Grammar Handbook

**Adverbs**
See page 469.

### Your Turn

☑ What kinds of sentences does Juan use?

☑ Identify adverbs that come before adjectives and other adverbs.

☑ Tell how other revisions improved Juan's writing.

**Go Digital!**
*Write online in Writer's Workspace*

419

**READING/WRITING WORKSHOP, pp. 418–419**

## ELL ENGLISH LANGUAGE LEARNERS SCAFFOLD

Provide support to help English Language Learners understand the writing trait.

| Beginning | Intermediate | Advanced/High |
|---|---|---|
| **Respond Orally** Help students complete the sentence frames about the student model: *Juan combines some sentences to make them _____. He divides some sentences to make them _____. He _____ the last two sentences into a compound sentence.* | **Practice** Ask students to complete the sentence frames. *The writer includes simple and _____ sentences. He starts sentences in _____ ways. At the end of the text, he _____.* | **Understand** Check for understanding. Ask: *What kinds of sentence structures does the writer use? How does varying sentences make the writing more interesting?* |

# Writing Every Day: Sentence Fluency

**DAY 1**

**DAY 2**

### Writing Entry: Vary Sentence Structure

**Prewrite** Provide students with the prompt below.

*Would you rather live in an extremely hot or an extremely cold environment? Give reasons for your opinion.*

Have partners list examples of hot and cold environments. Ask them to jot down reasons to live in each environment.

**Draft** Have each student select an environment to write about. Remind students to vary sentence structure in their drafts.

### Focus on Varying Sentence Structure

Use **Your Turn Practice Book** page 280 to model varying sentence structures.

*I would rather live in an extremely cold environment. I like cold weather. I can put on a sweater. I can also put on a coat.*

Model combining sentences to add interest.

*I would rather live in an extremely cold environment because I like cold weather.*

Discuss how varying sentences adds interest. Guide students to continue revising the model.

### Writing Entry: Vary Sentence Structure

**Revise** Have students revise their writing from Day 1 by varying sentence structure.

Use the **Conferencing Routines**. Circulate among students and stop briefly to talk with individuals. Provide time for peer review.

**Edit** Have students use Grammar Handbook page 469 in the **Reading/Writing Workshop** to edit for errors in adverbs.

# Conferencing Routines

## Teacher Conferences

**STEP 1**

Talk about the strengths of the writing.

*You support your opinion with solid, logical reasons. It is very convincing!*

**STEP 2**

Focus on how the writer uses the target trait for the week.

*You used some great simple and compound sentences. You could add more interest if you used complex sentences as well.*

**STEP 3**

Make concrete suggestions for revisions. Have students work on a specific assignment, such as those to the right, and then meet with you to review progress.

DAY

## Writing Entry: Vary Sentence Structure

**Prewrite** Ask students to search their Writer's Notebooks for topics for a new draft. Or provide a prompt such as the following.

*Tell about an extreme environment, such as a tundra or a desert, that you would <u>not</u> like to visit.*

**Draft** Once students have chosen their topics, ask them to create a word web to plan their writing. Have them name the environment in the center and add reasons in the surrounding circles. Students can use their webs to begin their drafts.

DAY

## Writing Entry: Vary Sentence Structure

**Revise** Have students revise the draft writing from Day 3 by varying sentence structure. As students revise, hold teacher conferences with individual students. You may also wish to have students work with partners to peer conference.

**Edit** Invite students to review the rules for adverbs on Grammar Handbook page 469 in the **Reading/Writing Workshop** and then check their drafts for errors.

DAY 5

## Share and Reflect

Discuss with the class what they learned about variety in sentence structure. Invite volunteers to read and compare draft text with text that has been revised. Have students discuss the writing by focusing on the importance of varying sentence structure to add interest and make writing flow. Allow time for individuals to reflect on their own writing progress and record observations in their Writer's Notebooks.

McGraw-Hill Companies Inc./Ken Karp, photographer

### Suggested Revisions

Provide specific direction to help focus young writers.

**Focus on a Sentence**
Read the draft and target one sentence for revision. *Try rearranging this sentence to begin with an introductory phrase.*

**Focus on a Section**
Underline a section that needs to be revised. Provide specific suggestions. *These sentences have related ideas. How can you combine them?*

**Focus on a Revision Strategy**
Underline a section. Have students use a specific revision strategy, such as rearranging. *Rearrange the parts of sentences so sentences begin in different ways.*

## Peer Conferences

Focus peer response groups on varying sentence structures to add interest.

☑ Does the writer use a mix of simple, compound, and complex sentences?

☑ Does the writing have a good rhythm when read aloud?

☑ Do sentences begin in different ways?

# → Grammar: Negatives

**Reading/Writing Workshop**

## OBJECTIVES

 **CCSS** Demonstrate command of the conventions of standard English grammar and usage when writing or speaking. **L.5.1**

**CCSS** Demonstrate command of the conventions of standard English capitalization, punctuation and spelling when writing. **L.5.2**

- Identify negatives, negative contractions, and double negatives.
- Proofread sentences.

## Go Digital

**Negatives**

**Grammar Activities**

---

### DAY 1

**DAILY LANGUAGE ACTIVITY**

**Although Juan is faster Julia still swims good. The pool is the crowdedest at 4:00.** (1: faster,; 2: well; 3: most crowded)

### Introduce Negatives

→ A **negative** is a word or phrase that means "no."

→ Do not use more than one negative in a spoken or written sentence.

→ Negatives include *no* and *not*, as well as *nobody, nothing, never, no one,* and *nowhere*.

→ Positives include words such as *any, ever, anything, anybody, anyone,* and *anywhere*.

Have partners discuss negatives using page 470 of the Grammar Handbook in **Reading/Writing Workshop**.

---

### DAY 2

**DAILY LANGUAGE ACTIVITY**

**Mr. Simms a marathon runner is training for a race. Its in october.** (1: Simms,; 2: runner,; 3: It's; 4: October)

### Review Negatives

Discuss examples of negatives and positives and how negatives should be used in a sentence.

### Introduce Negative Contractions

→ A **negative contraction** is made up of a verb and the word *not*. An apostrophe is used in place of the letter *o*: *is not/isn't; are not/aren't*.

→ Do not use another negative in a sentence that has a negative contraction.

---

 ## TALK ABOUT IT

**COLLABORATE**

### USE NEGATIVES

Have pairs use the following negatives in sentences that tell about animal adaptations: *nobody, nothing, never, no one, nowhere, no, not*.

### USE NEGATIVE CONTRACTIONS

Have students work individually to create sentences using the following negative contractions: *aren't, haven't, shouldn't, won't*. Ask volunteers to share their sentences.

**DAY**  3

**Jill is the most kind person I know. When I was sick she brought me soup crackers and juice.** (1: kindest; 2: sick,; 3: soup,; 4: crackers,)

## Mechanics and Usage: Correct Double Negatives

→ Do not use two negatives in the same sentence. This is known as a double negative. *She <u>didn't</u> know <u>nobody</u>. She <u>won't never</u> walk the dog.*

→ Correct a sentence with two negatives by changing one negative to a positive word. *She didn't know <u>anybody</u>. She won't <u>ever</u> walk the dog.*

Have students check their writing using Grammar Handbook page 470 for negatives.

**DAY** 4

**The train couldn't fit nobody else on it. We had to walk their.** (1: anybody; 2: there)

## Proofread

Have students correct errors in these sentences:

1. We don't know nothing about fishing. (don't know anything / know nothing)

2. My brother won't never play with me. (won't ever / will never)

3. I've never eaten no sushi. (never eaten sushi / I've eaten no sushi)

4. The children didn't want no broccoli. (didn't want any / wanted no)

Have students check their work using Grammar Handbook page 470 for negatives.

**DAY** 5

**I should have left earliest so I wouldnt be late. My sister is most prompt than I am.** (1: earlier; 2: wouldn't; 3: more)

## Assess

Use the Daily Language Activity and Grammar Practice Reproducibles page 140 for assessment.

## Reteach

Use Grammar Practice Reproducibles pages 136–139 and selected pages from the Grammar Handbook for additional reteaching. Remind students that it is important to correct negatives.

Check students' writing for use of the skill and listen for it in their speaking. Assign Grammar Revision Assignments in their Writer's Notebooks as needed.

**See Grammar Practice Reproducibles pp. 136–140.**

## IT AIN'T RIGHT

Have pairs write five sentences using double negatives. Have partners trade sentences and correct the double negatives.

## NEGATIVE CHARADES

Have volunteers perform an action such as jumping, walking, skipping, or laughing. Ask other students to use negatives to describe the action. For example: *She won't jump. / She never jumps.*

## NEGATIVE SEARCH

Have pairs use a story from this week's readings. Ask students to identify negatives in the readings. Have students make a list. Have pairs share their list with the class.

# Spelling: Words from Mythology

**DAY**

## OBJECTIVES

 Spell grade-appropriate words correctly, consulting references as needed.
**L.5.2e**

## Spelling Words

| | | |
|---|---|---|
| clothes | salute | territory |
| January | fury | terrace |
| cereal | echo | parasol |
| strength | cycle | fortune |
| lunar | cyclone | furious |
| atlas | gigantic | gracious |
| ocean | Olympics | |

**Review** suspect, inspect, mission
**Challenge** jovial, venerable

## Differentiated Spelling

### Approaching Level

| | | |
|---|---|---|
| clothes | salute | Titanic |
| January | fury | terrace |
| cereal | echo | siren |
| strength | cycle | fortune |
| lunar | python | furious |
| atlas | gigantic | music |
| ocean | Olympics | |

### Beyond Level

| | | |
|---|---|---|
| arachnid | salute | territory |
| lethargic | fury | terrace |
| muse | nemesis | parasol |
| hygiene | sphinx | nocturnal |
| ogre | cyclone | furious |
| hypnosis | gigantic | gracious |
| martial | Olympics | |

## DAY 1

### Assess Prior Knowledge

Read the spelling words aloud, enunciating each syllable.

Tell students that many words in the English language are connected to mythology. Point out the word *January*. Explain that *Janus* was the Roman god of beginnings.

Have groups use a dictionary or the Internet to research the origins of four other spelling words. Have students share their research.

Then use the words *echo* and *January* to demonstrate sorting a few spelling words according to their connection to Greek or Roman mythology or some other aspect of those cultures.

Use the Dictation Sentences from Day 5 to give the pretest. Say the underlined word, read the sentence, and repeat the word. Have students write the words. Then have students check their papers.

## DAY 2

### Spiral Review

Review the Latin roots in *suspect*, *inspect*, and *mission*. Read each sentence below, repeat the review word, and have students write the word.

1. I began to <u>suspect</u> Julio.
2. The police had to <u>inspect</u> the room.
3. The <u>mission</u> of the group is to help people learn to read.

Have students trade papers and check their spellings.

**Challenge Words** Review this week's words from mythology. Read each sentence below, repeat the challenge word, and have students write the word.

1. The <u>jovial</u> old man laughed heartily.
2. Members of the <u>venerable</u> family have been politicians for generations.

Have students check and correct their spellings and write the words in their word study notebooks.

 **WORD SORTS**

**COLLABORATE**

### OPEN SORT

Have students cut apart the **Spelling Word Cards** in the Online Resource Book and initial the back of each card. Have them read the words aloud with partners. Then have partners do an **open sort**. Have them record their sorts in their word study notebooks.

### PATTERN SORT

Complete the **pattern sort** from Day 1 by using the Spelling Word Cards. Point out the different Greek and Roman associations. Partners should compare and check their sorts. Have them record their sorts in their word study notebooks.

## DAY 3

### Word Meanings

Have students copy the three analogies below into their word study notebooks. Say the sentences aloud. Then ask students to fill in the blanks with a spelling word.

1. *Air* is to *atmosphere* as *sea* is to _____. (ocean)
2. *Furious* is to *fury* as _____ is to *grace*. (gracious)
3. *Shirt* is to *clothes* as _____ is to *book*. (atlas)

Challenge students to create analogies with their other spelling, review, or challenge words. Encourage them to use synonyms and antonyms. Have students discuss their analogies with a partner.

**See Phonics/Spelling Reproducibles pp. 163–168.**

### SPEED SORT

Have partners do a **speed sort** to see who is fastest and then compare and discuss their sorts. Then have them research other words from mythology. Have them record the words in their word study notebooks.

## DAY 4

### Proofread and Write

Write these sentences on the board. Have students circle and correct each misspelled word. Have them use a print or a digital dictionary to check and correct their spellings.

1. The country's teritory is shown clearly in the attlas. (territory, atlas)
2. Marta was grashious enough to loan me some cloathes. (gracious, clothes)
3. The scylone started over the Indian Oshun. (cyclone, Ocean)
4. The Winter Olympicks usually begin in Januery or February. (Olympics, January)

**Error Correction** Students may struggle with spelling patterns in words such as *gracious* (/sh/ sound) and *gigantic* (two sounds for the letter *g*). Have students write sentences with these words. They can use print or electronic resources to help check or correct their spellings.

### BLIND SORT

Have partners do a **blind sort:** one reads a Spelling Word Card; the other names its connection to Greek or Roman mythology. Then have partners play Concentration. Have them match words with a Greek or a Roman association.

## DAY 5

### Assess

Use the Dictation Sentences for the posttest. Have students list the misspelled words in their word study notebooks. Look for students' use of these words in their writings.

#### Dictation Sentences

1. They wore colorful <u>clothes</u>.
2. <u>January</u> is a cold month.
3. She had <u>cereal</u> for breakfast.
4. Exercise can increase your <u>strength</u>.
5. The <u>lunar</u> eclipse is rare.
6. An <u>atlas</u> contains maps.
7. <u>Ocean</u> water tastes salty.
8. Soldiers <u>salute</u> each other.
9. We tried to calm her <u>fury</u>.
10. Voices <u>echo</u> in the hall.
11. The seasons follow a <u>cycle</u>.
12. The <u>cyclone</u> missed our path.
13. The statue is <u>gigantic</u>.
14. Athletes compete in the <u>Olympics</u>.
15. Flags marked their <u>territory</u>.
16. We ate lunch on the <u>terrace</u>.
17. Her <u>parasol</u> blocked the sun.
18. Nancy inherited a <u>fortune</u>.
19. I was <u>furious</u> after the fight.
20. Paul is <u>gracious</u> to his guests.

Have students self-correct their tests.

# Build Vocabulary

**DAY 1**

**DAY 2**

## OBJECTIVES

**CCSS** Determine or clarify the meaning of unknown and multiple-meaning words and phrases based on *grade 5 reading and content,* choosing flexibly from a range of strategies. Use context (e.g., cause/effect relationships and comparisons in text) as a clue to the meaning of a word or phrase. **L.5.4a**

**CCSS** Use the relationship between particular words (e.g., synonyms, antonyms, homographs) to better understand each of the words. **L.5.5c**

### Vocabulary Words

| | |
|---|---|
| adaptation | forage |
| agile | frigid |
| cache | hibernate |
| dormant | insulates |

## Go Digital

**Vocabulary**

**Vocabulary Activities**

### Connect to Words

Practice this week's vocabulary words.

1. Describe a useful **adaptation** for hot weather.
2. Name an animal that is **agile**.
3. If you **cache** food, do you hide it or share it?
4. Show me what it looks like to be **dormant**.
5. What might a bird **forage** for?
6. What would you wear if it were **frigid** outside?
7. When animals **hibernate**, are they active or inactive?
8. What **insulates** a cat?

### Expand Vocabulary

Help students generate different forms of this week's words by adding, changing, or removing inflectional endings.

→ Draw a four-column chart on the board. Write *forage* in the first column. Then write *forages, foraged,* and *foraging* in the next three columns. Read aloud the words with students.

→ Have students share sentences using each form of *forage.*

→ Students can fill in the chart for *insulates, cache,* and *hibernate,* and then share sentences using the different forms of the words.

→ Have students copy the chart in their word study notebooks.

## BUILD MORE VOCABULARY

**COLLABORATE**

### ACADEMIC VOCABULARY

→ Display *cylinder, consisting,* and *submarine.*

→ Define the words and discuss their meanings with students.

→ Write *consistency* under *consisting.* Have partners write other words with the same root and define them. Then have partners ask and answer questions using the words.

→ Repeat with *cylinder* and *submarine.*

### CONNOTATION AND DENOTATION

→ Ask: *What is the denotation, or dictionary meaning, of* forage?

→ Have partners use a thesaurus to find similar words, such as *scavenge* or *search.*

→ Have partners distinguish between the connotations of each word. Ask: *How is* scavenge *different from* search?

→ Have students write each word's denotation and connotation in their word study notebooks.

DAY

DAY

DAY **5**

## Reinforce the Words

Review this week's and last week's vocabulary words. Have students orally complete each sentence stem.

1. Animals <u>cache</u> _____ to eat during <u>frigid</u> weather.
2. A warm coat <u>insulates</u> _____.
3. <u>Dormant</u> flowers _____.
4. The <u>agile</u> dancer _____.
5. Animals <u>forage</u> for _____.
6. The crowd began <u>taunting</u> the team when _____.
7. An <u>ally</u> should be <u>protective</u> when _____.
8. I stopped <u>abruptly</u> after _____.
9. Sonya felt <u>confident</u> doing _____ until she <u>collided</u> _____.

## Connect to Writing

→ Have students write sentences in their word study notebooks using this week's vocabulary.

→ Tell them to write sentences that provide word information they learned from this week's readings.

→ **ELL** Provide the Day 3 sentence stems 1–5 for students needing extra support.

**Write About Vocabulary** Have students write something they learned from this week's words in their word study notebooks. For example, they might write about things in nature that are *dormant* or about characteristics of *frigid* environments.

## Word Squares

Ask students to create Word Squares for each vocabulary word.

→ In the first square, students write the word. (e.g., *dormant*)

→ In the second square, students write their own definition of the word and any related words, such as synonyms. (e.g., *resting, inactive, sleeping*)

→ In the third square, students draw a simple illustration that will help them remember the word. (e.g., drawing of a seed under dirt with snow on ground above)

→ In the fourth square, students write nonexamples, including antonyms. (e.g., *active, awake, dynamic, functioning*)

Have partners discuss their squares.

### CONTEXT CLUES

Remind students to look for clues in a paragraph to help figure out the meanings of unfamiliar words.

→ Display **Your Turn Practice Book pages 273–274.** Model figuring out the meaning of the word *structural* in the third paragraph.

→ Have students complete page 277.

→ Partners can confirm meanings in a print or online dictionary.

### SHADES OF MEANING

Help students generate words related to *agile*. Draw a synonym/antonym scale.

→ Have small groups use a thesaurus to find at least two synonyms and two antonyms for the word.

→ Ask groups to write the words on the scale in order from most to least and share with the class.

→ Ask groups to add all words to their scale and copy it in their word study notebooks.

### MORPHOLOGY

Use *insulates* as a springboard for students to learn more words.

→ Have students research the origin of *insulates*, using a dictionary.

→ Elicit from students that *insulates* comes from the Latin word *insula*, meaning "island."

→ Have partners search for other words with the same origin and write them in their word study notebooks (e.g., *insular, insulin*).

# → Approaching Level

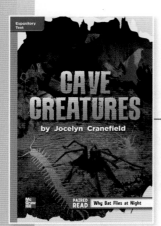

**Lexile** 760
*TextEvaluator* 28

---

## OBJECTIVES

CCSS Explain the relationships or interactions between two or more individuals, events, ideas, or concepts in a historical, scientific, or technical text based on specific information in the text. **RI.5.3**

CCSS Use context to confirm or self-correct word recognition and understanding, rereading as necessary. **RF.5.4c**

---

## ACADEMIC LANGUAGE
• cause, effect, expository text
• Cognates: *causa, efecto, texto expositivo*

## Leveled Reader:
### *Cave Creatures*

**Go**
Digital

**Leveled Readers**

### Before Reading

#### Preview and Predict

→ Read the Essential Question with students.

→ Have students preview the title, table of contents, and first page of *Cave Creatures* and predict what they think the selection will be about. Encourage students to confirm or revise their predictions as they read.

#### Review Genre: Expository Text

Tell students that this selection is an expository text. Expository text provides factual information about a topic. Main ideas within the text are supported by evidence and key details. The text may include features such as headings, captions, labels, maps, charts, or graphs. Have students identify features of expository text in *Cave Creatures*.

### During Reading

#### Close Reading

**Note Taking:** Ask students to use their graphic organizer as they read.

**Use Graphic Organizer**

**Pages 2–3** *Dark, rocky caves provide homes to animals. How has cave living affected many animals?* (They have developed adaptations that help them survive in caves.)

**Pages 4–5** *What adaptation do bats have that allows them to navigate in dark caves?* (Bats have developed echolocation. They can navigate by making high-pitched squeaking sounds and listening for an echo.)

**Pages 6–7** *What are some adaptations of creatures that live in the twilight zone?* (strong senses of hearing and touch, the ability to glow, long antennae) *Which cave characteristics caused these adaptations?* (coolness, dampness, and lack of food and light)

**Pages 8–9** *Study the cave food web. Bats are an important part of this web. What do they eat?* (mosquitoes, gnats, glowworms, crickets) *How does this diagram help you understand the food cycle in a cave?* (It shows that the creatures who live in caves depend on each other for food.)

**Pages 10–12** *Creatures that live in the dark zone have adapted due to the lack of light and plant life. What adaptations have they made?* (They have small bodies, long limbs, long antennae, and the ability to detect small vibrations and smells, which help them move in the pitch black.)

**Pages 13–15** *Some caves have extreme conditions that cause creatures to adapt. Using paragraph clues, turn to a partner and explain the meaning of the word* frigid. (*Frigid* means "extremely cold," based on the clues *ice, most animals could not survive,* and *sub-zero temperatures.*)

**Pages 16–17** *Ask a partner a question about the strategies scientists use to study cave creature adaptations. Answer it together using text details.*

## After Reading

**Respond to Reading** Revisit the Essential Question and ask students to complete the Respond to Reading section on page 18.

**Write About Reading** Check that students have correctly identified and described some cave creatures and their adaptations.

### Fluency: Rate and Accuracy

**Model** Model reading page 5 with proper rate and accuracy. Next reread the page aloud and have students read along with you.

**Apply** Have students practice reading the passage with partners.

## PAIRED READ

**Leveled Reader**

### "Why Bat Flies at Night"

**Make Connections:**
**Write About It** *Analytical Writing*

Before reading, ask students to note that the genre of this text is a *pourquoi* story. Then discuss the Essential Question. After reading, ask students to write connections between what they learned about how living things adapt to their environments in *Cave Creatures* and "Why Bat Flies at Night."

 **FOCUS ON SCIENCE**

Students can extend their knowledge of adaptations by completing the science activity on page 24. **STEM**

### Literature Circles

Ask students to conduct a literature circle using the Thinkmark questions to guide the discussion. You may wish to have a whole-class discussion, using both selections in the Leveled Reader, about how livings things are adapted to their environment.

## Level Up

Level-up lessons available online.

**IF** students read the **Approaching Level** fluently and answered the questions

**THEN** pair them with students who have proficiently read the **On Level** and have students

- echo-read the **On Level** main selection.
- list two causes and effects in the text.

### A C T **Access Complex Text**

The **On Level** challenges students by including more **domain-specific words** and **complex sentence structures**.

# Approaching Level
## Word Study/Decoding

### REVIEW WORDS FROM MYTHOLOGY

**TIER 2**

 **OBJECTIVES**
**CCSS** Know and apply grade-level phonics and word analysis skills in decoding words. Use combined knowledge of all letter-sound correspondences, syllabication patterns, and morphology (e.g., roots and affixes) to read accurately unfamiliar multisyllabic words in context and out of context. **RF.5.3a**

Decode words from mythology.

**I Do** Review with students that many words in the English language come from mythology, especially from the Greeks and Romans. Explain that these words are often used to describe characteristics exhibited by mythological gods, people, or creatures.

 **We Do** Write the word *herculean* on the board. Explain that Hercules was a hero in Greek mythology who accomplished difficult tasks. Model how to use this information to determine that *herculean* means "requiring great strength or effort."

 **You Do** Add the word *volcano* to the board. Explain that Vulcan was the Roman god of fire. Ask students to use this information to determine the meaning of *volcano*. Discuss students' definitions.

### BUILD WORDS FROM MYTHOLOGY

**TIER 2**

 **OBJECTIVES**
**CCSS** Know and apply grade-level phonics and word analysis skills in decoding words. Use combined knowledge of all letter-sound correspondences, syllabication patterns, and morphology (e.g., roots and affixes) to read accurately unfamiliar multisyllabic words in context and out of context. **RF.5.3a**

Build words from mythology.

 **I Do** Write the name *Pan* on the board and display the **Word-Building Card** *ic*. Model reading the name and the Word-Building Card. Explain that Pan was a Greek god of shepherds and goatherds. He created frightening noises in the woods at night to scare travelers.

 **We Do** Work with students to combine the mythological name and the Word-Building Card to build the word *panic*. Ask students to use what they know about Pan to determine the meaning of the word *panic*.

 **You Do** Write the word *Titan* on the board and display the Word-Building Card *ic*. Review that Titans were gigantic. Ask students to combine *Titan* and *ic* to form the word *titanic*. Then have them determine the meaning of the word based on what they know about Titans.

# PRACTICE WORDS FROM MYTHOLOGY

## OBJECTIVES

(CCSS) Know and apply grade-level phonics and word analysis skills in decoding words. Use combined knowledge of all letter-sound correspondences, syllabication patterns, and morphology (e.g., roots and affixes) to read accurately unfamiliar multisyllabic words in context and out of context. **RF.5.3a**

Decode words from mythology.

**I Do** Write the word *cereal* and the name *Ceres* from Roman mythology on the board. Read the words aloud. Model using information about the Roman goddess Ceres, who was the goddess of grain and the harvest, to determine the meaning of *cereal*.

**We Do** Write the word *martial* and the name *Mars* on the board. Read the words aloud. Explain that Mars was the Roman god of war. Then have students use what they know about Mars to determine the meaning of *martial*.

**You Do** To provide additional practice, write the words below on the board. Read aloud the first word, identify the mythological origin of the word, and give the word's meaning.

| | | |
|---|---|---|
| tantalize | echo | jovial |
| ambrosial | colossal | atlas |

Have students read aloud the remaining words. Tell partners to use a dictionary to find the mythological origin of each word and the word's meaning. Encourage partners to discuss the connection between the word's origin and its definition.

Afterward, point to the words in the list in random order for students to read chorally.

## ELL ENGLISH LANGUAGE LEARNERS

For the **ELLs** who need **phonics, decoding,** and **fluency** practice, use scaffolding methods as necessary to ensure students understand the meaning of the words. Refer to the **Language Transfers Handbook** for phonics elements that may not transfer in students' native languages.

# → Approaching Level

## Vocabulary

### REVIEW HIGH-FREQUENCY WORDS

 **TIER 2**

 **OBJECTIVES**
Acquire and use accurately grade-appropriate general academic and domain-specific words and phrases, including those that signal contrast, addition, and other logical relationships (e.g., *however, although, nevertheless, similarly, moreover, in addition*).
**L.5.6**

 **I Do** Use **High-Frequency Word Cards** 221–230. Display one word at a time, following the routine:

Display the word. Read the word. Then spell the word.

 **We Do** Ask students to state the word and spell the word with you. Model using the word in a sentence and have students repeat after you.

 **You Do** Display the word. Ask students to say the word and then spell it. When completed, quickly flip through the word card set as students chorally read the words. Provide opportunities for students to use the words in speaking and writing. For example, provide sentence starters such as *We use water to _____.* Ask students to write each word in their Writer's Notebook.

### REVIEW VOCABULARY WORDS

**TIER 2**

 **OBJECTIVES**
Acquire and use accurately grade-appropriate general academic and domain-specific words and phrases, including those that signal contrast, addition, and other logical relationships (e.g., *however, although, nevertheless, similarly, moreover, in addition*).
**L.5.6**

 **I Do** Display each **Visual Vocabulary Card** and state the word. Explain how the photograph illustrates the word. State the example sentence and repeat the word.

 **We Do** Point to the word on the card and read the word with students. Ask them to repeat the word. Engage students in structured partner talk about the image as prompted on the back of the vocabulary card.

 **You Do** Display each visual in random order, hiding the word. Have students match the definitions and context sentences of the words to the visuals displayed.

# UNDERSTAND VOCABULARY WORDS

**OBJECTIVES**

**CCSS** Acquire and use accurately grade-appropriate general academic and domain-specific words and phrases, including those that signal contrast, addition, and other logical relationships (e.g., *however, although, nevertheless, similarly, moreover, in addition*). **L.5.6**

**I Do**

Use the **Visual Vocabulary Cards** to review the key selection words *adaptation, agile, cache, dormant, forage, frigid, hibernate,* and *insulates.* Point to each word, read it aloud, and have students chorally repeat it.

**We Do**

Ask these questions and help students respond.

→ If a plant makes an *adaptation,* does it change or stay the same?

→ If an animal is *agile*, is it clumsy or graceful?

→ If you *cache* your favorite DVDs, do you hide them or give them away?

**You Do**

Have students work in pairs to respond to these questions.

→ When an animal is *dormant,* is it awake or asleep?

→ Is it easier for animals to *forage* for food in the winter or in the summer?

→ If it is *frigid* outside, would you be more likely to shiver or sweat?

→ Which one *insulates* you better, a warm coat or a thin jacket?

→ Are animals active or sleeping when they *hibernate?*

# CONTEXT CLUES

**OBJECTIVES**

**CCSS** Determine or clarify the meaning of unknown and multiple-meaning words and phrases based on *grade 5 reading and content,* choosing flexibly from a range of strategies. Use context (e.g., cause/effect relationships and comparisons in text) as a clue to the meaning of a word or phrase. **L.5.4a**

**I Do**

Remind students that they can use context clues in the surrounding paragraph to help them figure out the meaning of a word. Display the Comprehension and Fluency passage on **Approaching Reproducibles** pages 273–274. Echo-read paragraph 3. Then point out the word *structural.*

**Think Aloud** The second sentence explains what *structural* change means. The rest of the paragraph gives an example of an animal whose body helps it adapt. I think *structural* refers to the way a body is organized.

**We Do**

Ask students to point to the word *behavioral* in the fourth paragraph. Point out the comparison word *act* in the next sentence. Choral-read the paragraph, noting examples of different actions or behaviors. Then have students explain the meaning of *behavioral* in their own words.

**You Do**

Have students use paragraph clues to identify the meaning of *nocturnal* (page 273, paragraph 4), *hibernate* (page 274, paragraph 2), and *mobs* (page 274, paragraph 4).

# Approaching Level

# Comprehension

## FLUENCY

**TIER 2**

### OBJECTIVES

**CCSS** Read with sufficient accuracy and fluency to support comprehension. Read on-level prose and poetry orally with accuracy, appropriate rate, and expression on successive readings. **RF.5.4b**

**CCSS** Use context to confirm or self-correct word recognition and understanding, rereading as necessary. **RF.5.4c**

Read fluently with appropriate rate and accuracy.

**I Do** Explain that when reading a selection out loud, students should read at an appropriate rate for the type and difficulty of the material in order to ensure accuracy. Read the first two paragraphs of the Comprehension and Fluency passage on **Approaching Reproducibles** pages 273–274. Tell students to listen for the way you read at the appropriate rate for an informational science article, as well as for the accuracy of your words and phrasing.

**We Do** Read the rest of the page aloud and have students repeat each sentence after you, reading at the same rate. Explain that since this selection is informational text with a lot of scientific facts, you read slowly, taking care to read words correctly and observing punctuation cues.

**You Do** Have partners take turns reading sentences from the Comprehension and Fluency passage. Have them reread as needed to ensure understanding, focusing on appropriate rate and accuracy. Listen in and provide corrective feedback as needed by modeling proper fluency.

## IDENTIFY CAUSES

**TIER 2**

### OBJECTIVES

**CCSS** Explain the relationships or interactions between two or more individuals, events, ideas, or concepts in a historical, scientific, or technical text based on specific information in the text. **RI.5.3**

Identify important events.

**I Do** Remind students that in an informational text, the author may describe many events. One event may cause another to happen. Explain that a *cause* is what makes something happen and an *effect* is what happens.

**We Do** Read the first three paragraphs of the Comprehension and Fluency passage on **Approaching Reproducibles** pages 273–274. Point out that the need to survive in the hot desert environment caused the gundis' bodies to adapt.

**You Do** Have students read the rest of the passage. After each paragraph, have them write down important causes or events that make other events happen. Review students' lists of causes with them and help them explain what effects they had.

## REVIEW TEXT STRUCTURE: CAUSE AND EFFECT

**OBJECTIVES**

 Explain the relationships or interactions between two or more individuals, events, ideas, or concepts in a historical, scientific, or technical text based on specific information in the text. **RI.5.3**

 **I Do** Remind students that in an informational text, an author may use a cause-and-effect text structure to explain how or why something happens. Some causes and effects are directly stated, while others are implied. Signal words such as *because of, as a result, if/then, so,* and *when* alert readers to a cause and effect described in the text.

**We Do** Choral-read the fourth paragraph of the Comprehension and Fluency passage on **Approaching Reproducibles** pages 273–274. Guide students to use the signal word *so* as well as details in the text to identify a cause and effect related to life in the desert: *desert days are very hot, so many animals are nocturnal.*

**You Do** Have partners read the rest of the passage and identify different causes and effects described in the text. Ask them to use their lists to identify the text's overall message about desert animals.

## SELF-SELECTED READING

**OBJECTIVES**

 Explain the relationships or interactions between two or more individuals, events, ideas, or concepts in a historical, scientific, or technical text based on specific information in the text. **RI.5.3**

Ask and answer questions to increase understanding.

### Read Independently

Have students choose an expository text for sustained silent reading. Remind students that:

→ good readers pause and ask themselves questions when they don't understand a text or become confused. Then they reread to find the answers.

→ as they read, they should look for causes and effects to understand why or how something happens.

### Read Purposefully

Have students record causes and effects on Graphic Organizer 86 as they read independently. After they finish, students can conduct a Book Talk about what they read.

→ Students should share their organizers and answer this question: *What was the most interesting fact you learned about this topic?*

→ They should also tell the group if there were any sections they reread to increase their understanding.

# On Level

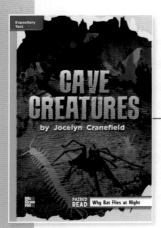

**Lexile** 900
*TextEvaluator*™ 35

---

**OBJECTIVES**

**CCSS** Explain the relationships or interactions between two or more individuals, events, ideas, or concepts in a historical, scientific, or technical text based on specific information in the text. **RI.5.3**

**CCSS** Use context to confirm or self-correct word recognition and understanding, rereading as necessary. **RF.5.4c**

---

**ACADEMIC LANGUAGE**

• *cause, effect, expository text*

• Cognates: *causa, efecto, texto expositivo*

## Leveled Reader:
## *Cave Creatures*

### Before Reading

→ Read the Essential Question with students.

→ Have students preview the title, table of contents, and first page of *Cave Creatures* and predict what they think the selection will be about. Encourage students to confirm or revise their predictions as they read.

### Review Genre: Expository Text

Tell students that this selection is an expository text. Expository text provides factual information about a topic. Main ideas within the text are supported by evidence and key details. The text may include features such as headings, captions, labels, maps, charts, or graphs. Have students identify features of expository text in *Cave Creatures*.

### During Reading

#### Close Reading

**Note Taking** Ask students to use their graphic organizer as they read.

**Pages 2–3** *Consult the map and side bar on page 3 and tell a partner where Krubera Cave is located. Ask your partner to tell you the cave's depth.* (near the Black Sea; at least 7,188 feet)

**Pages 4–5** *Some creatures, such as bats, sleep or take shelter in caves, but they hunt outside the caves. Using paragraph clues, turn to a partner and explain the term* echolocation. (determining the position of objects by making high-pitched sounds and then listening for an echo)

**Pages 6–7** *What conditions cause the creatures that live in the twilight zone to adapt?* (coolness, dampness, and lack of food and light) *With a partner, paraphrase the adaptations some creatures have as a result of these conditions.* (strong senses of hearing and touch, the ability to glow, and long antennae)

**Pages 8–9** *Although plants cannot grow in caves, there are plant-based nutrients in caves. Where do they come from?* (Rain and streams bring twigs, leaves, seeds, and insects into caves; the droppings of animals such as bats and cave crickets include recycled plant material.)

**Go Digital**

**Leveled Readers**

**Use Graphic Organizer**

*What process causes this material to become food for cave creatures?* (Mold, fungi, and bacteria break down the organic material.)

**Pages 10–12** *The dark zone lacks light, plants, and wind. How did the need to live in the dark zone affect the development of troglobites?* (They developed small bodies, long limbs, lengthy antennae, and the ability to detect small vibrations or smells in order to move in the dark.)

**Pages 13–15** *What are some extreme cave conditions that cause creatures to adapt? Paraphrase the text and identify these conditions with a partner.* (hot or sub-zero temperatures, the emission of toxic gas)

**Pages 16–17** *How do scientists learn about cave creatures and their adaptations?* (They climb, dive, or squeeze into cold dark spaces and observe and photograph them. They examine them in laboratories.)

## After Reading

**Respond to Reading** Revisit the Essential Question and ask students to complete the Respond to Reading section on page 18.

*Analytical Writing* **Write About Reading** Check that students have correctly identified and described three cave creatures and their adaptations.

### Fluency: Rate and Accuracy

**Model** Model reading page 5 with proper rate and accuracy. Next reread the page aloud and have students read along with you.

**Apply** Have students practice reading with partners.

## PAIRED READ

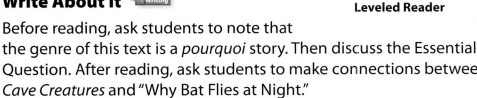

**Leveled Reader**

# "Why Bat Flies at Night"

### Make Connections: Write About It *Analytical Writing*

Before reading, ask students to note that the genre of this text is a *pourquoi* story. Then discuss the Essential Question. After reading, ask students to make connections between *Cave Creatures* and "Why Bat Flies at Night."

## 🧪 FOCUS ON SCIENCE

Students can extend their knowledge of adaptations by completing the science activity on page 24. **STEM**

## Literature Circles

Ask students to conduct a literature circle using the Thinkmark questions to guide the discussion. You may wish to have a whole-class discussion, using information from both selections in the Leveled Reader, about how living things are adapted to their environment.

# Level Up

Level-up lessons available online.

**IF** students read the **On Level** fluently and answered the questions,

**THEN** pair them with students who have proficiently read the **Beyond Level** and have students

- partner-read the **Beyond Level** main selection.
- identify multiple causes and effects.
- identify multiple effects of one cause or vice versa.

## A C T **A**ccess **C**omplex **T**ext

The **Beyond Level** challenges students through more **domain-specific words** and **complex sentence structures**.

# → On Level

# Vocabulary

## REVIEW VOCABULARY WORDS

**OBJECTIVES**

CCSS Demonstrate understanding of figurative language, word relationships, and nuances in word meanings. Use the relationships between particular words (e.g., synonyms, antonyms, homographs) to better understand each of the words. **L.5.5c**

**I Do** Display the *dormant* **Visual Vocabulary Card** and say aloud the word set *dormant, resting, active, sleeping*. Point out that the word *active* does not belong.

**We Do** Say aloud the word set *agile, quick, nimble, clumsy*. With students, identify the word that does not belong (*clumsy*) and discuss why.

**You Do** Using the word sets below, display the remaining cards one at a time, saying aloud the word set. Ask students to identify the word that does not belong.

*cache, hide, store, display*

*forage, look, ignore, search*

*frigid, hot, cold, icy*

*insulates, exposes, protects, warms*

## CONTEXT CLUES

**OBJECTIVES**

CCSS Determine or clarify the meaning of unknown and multiple-meaning words and phrases based on *grade 5 reading and content*, choosing flexibly from a range of strategies. Use context (e.g., cause/effect relationships and comparisons in text) as a clue to the meaning of a word or phrase. **L.5.4a**

**I Do** Remind students that they can use context clues to find a word's meaning. Display the Comprehension and Fluency passage on **Your Turn Practice Book** pages 273–274. Choral-read the third paragraph.

**Think Aloud** The second sentence describes what a structural adaptation is, and the rest of the paragraph gives an example of an animal whose body has adapted. I think that *structural* refers to the way a body is organized.

**We Do** Have students read aloud paragraph 4 on page 273 and find *behavioral* in the first sentence. Point out that the comparison word *act* appears in the next sentence, and the rest of the paragraph describes different actions animals take. Have students use these clues to define *behavioral*.

**You Do** Have partners use paragraph clues to determine the meanings of *nocturnal* (page 273, paragraph 4), *hibernate* (page 274, paragraph 2), *cold-blooded* (page 274, paragraph 3), *mobs* and *Predators* (page 274, paragraph 4).

# Comprehension

## REVIEW TEXT STRUCTURE: CAUSE AND EFFECT

**OBJECTIVES**

CCSS Explain the relationships or interactions between two or more individuals, events, ideas, or concepts in a historical, scientific, or technical text based on specific information in the text. **RI.5.3**

Remind students that in an informational text, an author may use a cause-and-effect text structure to explain how or why something happens. Some causes and effects are directly stated, while others are implied. Signal words such as *because of, as a result, if/then, so, since,* and *when* alert readers to a cause and effect in the text.

Have volunteers read the fourth paragraph of the Comprehension and Fluency passage on **Your Turn Practice Book** pages 273–274. Model how to use the signal word *since* to identify a cause and effect: *Since it is so hot during the day* (cause), *many animals are nocturnal* (effect).

Have partners read the rest of the passage. Tell them to stop after each paragraph and identify causes and effects that are described in the text. Remind them that causes and effects may be stated directly or students may have to infer them. Direct students to use these causes and effects to identify the text's message about animals in the desert.

## SELF-SELECTED READING

**OBJECTIVES**

CCSS Explain the relationships or interactions between two or more individuals, events, ideas, or concepts in a historical, scientific, or technical text based on specific information in the text. **RI.5.3**

Ask and answer questions to increase understanding.

### Read Independently

Have students choose an expository text for sustained silent reading.

→ Remind students to pause and ask themselves questions when they do not understand the text or become confused. They can reread to find answers.

→ Tell students to identify causes and effects in the text in order to better understand why or how something happens.

### Read Purposefully

Encourage students to read different books to learn about a variety of scientific subjects.

→ Have them record causes and effects in the text on Graphic Organizer 86.

→ They can use this organizer to help summarize the text.

→ Ask students to share their reactions to the book with classmates.

# → Beyond Level

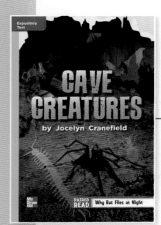

**Lexile** 1010
*TextEvaluator*™ 43

---

## OBJECTIVES

**CCSS** Explain the relationships or interactions between two or more individuals, events, ideas, or concepts in a historical, scientific, or technical text based on specific information in the text. **RI.5.3**

**CCSS** Use context to confirm or self-correct word recognition and understanding, rereading as necessary. **RF.5.4c**

---

## ACADEMIC LANGUAGE
• *cause, effect, expository text*
• Cognates: *causa, efecto, texto expositivo*

## Leveled Reader:
## *Cave Creatures*

### Before Reading

→ Have students read the Essential Question.

→ Have students preview the title, table of contents, and first page of *Cave Creatures* to make predictions about the content. Encourage students to confirm or revise their predictions as they read.

### Review Genre: Expository Text

Tell students that this selection is an expository text. Expository text provides factual information about a topic. Main ideas within the text are supported by evidence and key details. The text may include features such as headings, captions, labels, maps, charts, or graphs. Have students identify features of expository text in *Cave Creatures*.

### During Reading

#### Close Reading
**Note Taking:** Ask students to use their graphic organizer as they read.

**Pages 2–3** *Study the map and the diagram. How does the comparison between the cave and the buildings cause you to think differently about caves?* (Caves form another vast world that exists beneath the surface.)

**Pages 4–5** *Why do trogloxenes, such as bats, spend just a part of their lives in caves?* (They have to return to the outside world for food.)

**Pages 6–7** *With a partner, paraphrase the text and discuss how the glowworm and the cave weta are uniquely adapted to survive in the twilight zone.* (The glowworm illuminates its abdomen to attract prey; the cave weta uses long antennae to navigate and find food.)

**Pages 8–9** *Read the sidebar titled "Cave Lions." What causes caves to be good places for scientists to learn about the past?* (Stable conditions enable the skeletons of animals to be preserved for a long time.)

**Pages 10–12** *What is the effect of skin pigment? Why would animals without skin pigment likely not survive for long in an outdoor environment?* (protection from the sun and predators; Animals without pigment in an outside environment would likely burn or be eaten.)

**Go Digital**

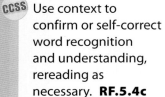

**Leveled Readers**

**Use Graphic Organizer**

**Pages 13–15** *Why are certain animals called extremophiles? What are some examples of the conditions in which they live?* (They can survive in extreme conditions, such as sub-zero temperatures and in places that emit toxic gases.) *What does* frigid *mean, based on clues in the paragraph on page 15?* (The clues *ice* and *sub-zero temperatures* indicate that it means "very cold.")

**Pages 16–17** *How do we learn about cave creatures and their adaptations?* (Scientists such as biologists, archaeologists, paleontologists, or geologists climb, dive, or squeeze into the cold, dark spaces of caves and observe and photograph these creatures.)

## After Reading

**Respond to Reading** Revisit the Essential Question and ask students to complete the Respond to Reading on page 18.

**Write About Reading** Check that students have correctly identified and described five cave creatures and their adaptations.

### Fluency: Rate and Accuracy

**Model** Model reading page 5 with proper rate and accuracy. Next, reread the page aloud and have students read along with you.

**Apply** Have students practice reading their passage with partners.

## PAIRED READ

**Leveled Reader**

### "Why Bat Flies at Night"

#### Make Connections:
**Write About It** *Analytical Writing*

Before reading, ask students to note that the genre of this text is a *pourquoi* story. Then discuss the Essential Question. After reading, ask students to write connections between what they learned about how living things adapt to their environments in *Cave Creatures* and "Why Bat Flies at Night."

 **FOCUS ON SCIENCE**

Students can extend their knowledge of adaptations by completing the science activity on page 24. **STEM**

### Literature Circles

Ask students to conduct a literature circle using the Thinkmark questions to guide the discussion. You may wish to have a whole-class discussion, using information in both selections of the Leveled Reader, about how living things are adapted to their environment.

## Gifted and Talented

**Synthesize** Based on information in the Leveled Reader selections, lead students to list different causes for animal adaptation. Record these causes on a board. Then have partners research an animal that has adapted due to one or more of these causes. Students should identify where the animal lives, what adaptations it has developed, and why its living conditions led to the adaptations. Tell students to present their research in the form of cause-and-effect charts.

→ Beyond Level

# Vocabulary

## REVIEW DOMAIN-SPECIFIC WORDS

**CCSS OBJECTIVES**
Acquire and use accurately grade-appropriate general academic and domain-specific words and phrases, including those that signal contrast, addition, and other logical relationships. **L.5.6**

**Model** Use the **Visual Vocabulary Cards** to review the meaning of the words *adaptation* and *hibernate*. Write genre-related sentences on the board using the words.

Write the words *dromedary* and *fennec* on the board and discuss the meanings with students. Then help students write sentences using these words.

**Apply** Have students work in pairs to review the meanings of the words *conditions* and *harsh*. Then have partners write sentences using these words.

## CONTEXT CLUES

**CCSS OBJECTIVES**
Determine or clarify the meaning of unknown and multiple-meaning words and phrases based on *grade 5 reading and content,* choosing flexibly from a range of strategies. Use context (e.g., cause/effect relationships and comparisons in text) as a clue to the meaning of a word or phrase. **L.5.4a**

**Model** Read aloud the fourth paragraph of the Comprehension and Fluency passage on **Beyond Reproducibles** pages 273–274.

**Think Aloud** I'm not sure what the word *nocturnal* means, so I will read ahead. The next sentence indicates that noctural animals come out at night. Now I know that *nocturnal* must mean "active at night."

Point out the word *behavioral* in the first sentence of the fourth paragraph. Have students find the comparison word *act* and read the description of actions desert animals take to survive to find the meaning of *behavioral*.

**Apply** Have pairs of students read the rest of the passage. Ask them to use paragraph clues to determine the meanings of *structural* (page 273, paragraph 3), *hibernate* (page 274, paragraph 2), *cold-blooded* (page 274, paragraph 3), *mobs* and *Predators* (page 274, paragraph 4.)

**Analyze** Challenge students to find paragraph clues for other words in the passage. Have them make a three-column chart and write the word in the first column, the paragraph clue in the second column, and the meaning in the third column. Remind them to use a thesaurus or dictionary as needed. Have students share their completed charts.

# Comprehension

## REVIEW TEXT STRUCTURE: CAUSE AND EFFECT

**OBJECTIVES**

 Explain the relationships or interactions between two or more individuals, events, ideas, or concepts in a historical, scientific, or technical text based on specific information in the text. **RI.5.3**

 **Model** Review that in a nonfiction text, an author may use cause-and-effect text structure to explain how or why something happens. Some causes and effects are directly stated, while others are implied. Signal words such as *because of, as a result, if/then,* and *when* signal cause and effect.

Have students read the third paragraph of the Comprehension and Fluency passage on **Beyond Reproducibles** pages 273–274. Work with them using the signal word *so* to identify a cause and effect related to the gundi's survival in the desert: *the animal's body has changed* (cause) *so that it can survive in the climate* (effect).

 **Apply** Have students identify the causes and effects in the rest of the passage and fill out Graphic Organizer 86 independently. Remind them to look for signal words and that they may need to identify causes and effects when they are not stated directly. Have students share their completed organizers with the class.

## SELF-SELECTED READING

**OBJECTIVES**

 Explain the relationships or interactions between two or more individuals, events, ideas, or concepts in a historical, scientific, or technical text based on specific information in the text. **RI.5.3**

Ask and answer questions to increase understanding.

### Read Independently

Have students choose an expository text for sustained silent reading.

→ As students read, have them record causes and effects on Graphic Organizer 86.

→ Remind them to ask questions as they read and to reread to find the answers in the text.

### Read Purposefully

Encourage students to keep a reading journal. Ask them to read a variety of expository texts to increase their knowledge.

→ Students can write summaries of the books in their journals.

→ Ask students to share their reactions to the books with classmates.

 **Independent Study** Challenge students to discuss how their books relate to the weekly theme of adaptations. What have they learned from all of their reading materials about the ways that living things, including human beings, adapt to their environment?

**English Language Learners**

**Reading/Writing Workshop**

---

**OBJECTIVES**

**CCSS** Explain the relationships or interactions between two or more individuals, events, ideas, or concepts in a historical, scientific, or technical text based on specific information in the text. **RI.5.3**

---

**LANGUAGE OBJECTIVE**

Identify cause-and-effect relationships within text.

---

**ACADEMIC LANGUAGE**

• *context clues, cause, effect*

• Cognates: *causa, efecto*

## Shared Read
### *Mysterious Oceans*

View "Mysterious Oceans"

**Before Reading**

### Build Background

Read the Essential Question: *How are living things adapted to their environment?*

→ Explain the meaning of the Essential Question, including the vocabulary in the question: *When something has adapted, it has changed to fit a situation. An environment is a surrounding area.*

→ **Model an answer:** *The Thorny Devil, an Australian lizard, has adapted to the dry, desert environment in which it lives. Its body has ridges that channel water into its mouth.*

→ Ask students a question that ties the Essential Question to their own background knowledge: *Turn to a partner and discuss an example of how you have adapted to your environment.* Call on several pairs to share their ideas.

**During Reading**

### Interactive Question-Response

→ Ask questions that help students understand the meaning of the text after each paragraph.

→ Reinforce the meanings of key vocabulary.

→ Ask students questions that require them to use key vocabulary.

→ Reinforce strategies and skills of the week by modeling.

## Page 411

### Deep Diving

**Paragraph 1**

Point to the photograph of the giant tube worms. *This creature lives on the dark ocean floor. How has it adapted?* Have students complete this frame: *To adapt to this environment, the tube worm has no ____, no ____, and no ____.* (mouth, eyes, stomach)

**Paragraph 2**

Hold up two fingers. *Most of the ocean is two miles deep.* Have students repeat. Hold up seven fingers. *The deepest part of the ocean is seven miles deep.* Have students echo you.

**Paragraph 3**

### Explain and Model Context Clues

*Remember that context clues in a paragraph can help us understand new words. The word* harsh *is used to describe the environment on the ocean floor. The words "frigid temperatures" and "lack of sunshine" also describe this environment. This helps me understand that* harsh *means "severe and threatening."*

**Paragraph 4**

*Do we know a lot or a little about the deep ocean?* (a little) *What is one of the things that remains a mystery?* (whether animals hibernate or cache food)

## Page 412

### Amazing Adaptations

**Paragraph 1**

*How do some people travel to the deep ocean floor?* (in submarines)

**Paragraph 2**

 **Explain and Model Cause and Effect**

*Remember that one way to understand animal adaptation is to identify causes and effects. Tell a partner one thing that has caused creatures that live in the deep ocean to adapt.* (lack of food)

**Paragraph 3**

*How have starfish adapted to the lack of food in the deep ocean?* (They grab shrimp with pincers, or claws, attached to the ends of their five arms.)

**Paragraph 4**

*Act out for your partner how the anglerfish has adapted to the lack of food in the deep ocean.*

## Page 413

### Heated Habitats

**Paragraph 1**

Begin a drawing of the ocean floor that contains a crack. Have students take turns adding and labeling the following elements: seawater rushing into the crack, magma heating the water, water bursting out to create geysers and hot springs.

**Paragraph 2**

*Do warm areas near geysers and hot springs attract or keep away life?* Draw students' attention to the photograph of the vent habitat. (The warmth attracts life.)

**Paragraph 3**

*How do these creatures survive?* (They make food out of the chemicals in the vents.)

**Paragraph 4**

*Is it likely that scientists will discover more new species on the ocean floor?* (yes)

### After Reading

**Make Connections**

→ Review the Essential Question: *How are living things adapted to their environment?*

→ Make text connections.

→ Have students complete **ELL Reproducibles** pages 273–275.

# English Language Learners

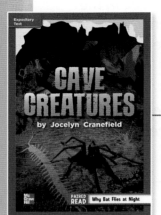

**Lexile** 750
*TextEvaluator™* 25

---

---

**ACADEMIC LANGUAGE**
- *cause, effect, expository text*
- Cognates: *causa, efecto, texto expositivo*

## Leveled Reader:
### *Cave Creatures*

**Leveled Readers**

### Before Reading

**Preview**

→ Read the Essential Question: *How are living things adapted to their environment?*

→ Refer to Creature Comforts: *How do adaptations help living things?*

→ Preview *Cave Creatures* and "Why Bat Flies at Night": *Our purpose for reading is to learn about how animals that live in caves are adapted to their environment.*

**Vocabulary**

Use the **Visual Vocabulary Cards** to pre-teach the ELL vocabulary: *features, survive, efficiently, extends*. Use the routine found on the cards.

### During Reading

**Interactive Question-Response**

**Note Taking:** Ask students to use the graphic organizer on **ELL Reproducibles** page 272. Use the questions below after each page is read with students. As you read, use the glossary definitions to define vocabulary in context and visuals to help students understand key vocabulary.

**Use Graphic Organizer**

**Pages 2–3** Show the photographs. Describe the caves with students: *deep, dark, empty, stone. Do creatures in caves adapt and change?* (yes)

**Pages 4–5** Explain that some creatures sleep in caves, but they find food outside the caves. Point to the photographs of bats. Say and have students repeat: *Bats sleep in caves. They hunt for insects outside. Name another creature that sleeps in caves and hunts outside.* (skunks)

**Pages 6–9** *One part of a cave is called the twilight zone. It is cool, wet, and dim.* Point to the photographs of the glowworm and the cave weta. *What adaptations did these creatures make in cool, wet, and dim caves?* (strong senses of hearing and touch; ability to glow; long antennae)

**Pages 10–12** Point to the dark zone on page 12. Say and have students repeat: *Another part of a cave is dark and silent.* Have students close their eyes and stay silent. Discuss what they feel or sense. *What adaptations did these creatures make in dark and silent caves?* (small bodies, long limbs, tiny or no eyes, can notice vibrations and smells)

**Pages 13–16** *What is challenging about the conditions in some caves?* (They are too cold, too hot, or too toxic.) Define *extreme* for students and point out the Spanish cognate *extremo(a). The animals that live in extreme places are called ____.* (extremophiles)

## After Reading

**Respond to Reading** Revisit the Essential Question and ask students to complete the Respond to Reading section on page 18.

**Write About Reading** Check that students have correctly identified and described three cave creatures and their adaptations.

### Fluency: Rate and Accuracy

**Model** Model reading page 5 with proper rate and accuracy. Next, reread the page aloud and have students read along with you.

**Apply** Have students practice reading with partners.

---

**PAIRED READ**

## "Why Bat Flies at Night"

### Make Connections:
### Write About It

Before reading, point out that the genre of this text is a *pourquoi* story and discuss the Essential Question. After reading, ask students to list connections between what they learned about adaptations from *Cave Creatures* and "Why Bat Flies at Night."

**Leveled Reader**

 **FOCUS ON SCIENCE**

Students can extend their knowledge of adaptations by completing the activity on page 24. **STEM**

---

## Literature Circles

Ask students to conduct a literature circle using the Thinkmark questions to guide the discussion. You may wish to have a whole-class discussion, using both Leveled Reader selections, about how animals adapt.

## Level Up

Level-up lessons available online.

**IF** students read the **ELL Level** fluently and answered the questions,

**THEN** pair them with students who have proficiently read **On Level** and have ELL students

• echo-read the **On Level** main selection with their partners.

• list words with which they have difficulty.

• discuss these words with their partners.

### A C T Access Complex Text

The **On Level** challenges students by including more **domain-specific words** and **complex sentence structures**.

**English Language Learners**

# Vocabulary

## PRETEACH VOCABULARY

**OBJECTIVES**

 Acquire and use accurately grade-appropriate general academic and domain-specific words and phrases, including those that signal contrast, addition, and other logical relationships. **L.5.6**

**LANGUAGE OBJECTIVE**
Use vocabulary words.

 **I Do**
Preteach vocabulary from "Mysterious Oceans" following the Vocabulary Routine found on the **Visual Vocabulary Cards** for the words *adaptation, agile, cache, dormant, forage, frigid, hibernate,* and *insulates.*

 **We Do**
After completing the Vocabulary Routine for each word, point to the word on the Card and read the word with students. Ask them to repeat the word.

 **You Do**
Have students work with a partner to use two or more words in sentences or questions. Then have each pair read the sentences aloud.

| Beginning | Intermediate | Advanced/High |
|---|---|---|
| Help students write the sentences correctly and read them aloud. | Ask students to write one sentence and one question. | Challenge students to write one sentence and one question for each word. |

## REVIEW VOCABULARY

**OBJECTIVES**

 Acquire and use accurately grade-appropriate general academic and domain-specific words and phrases, including those that signal contrast, addition, and other logical relationships. **L.5.6**

**LANGUAGE OBJECTIVE**
Use vocabulary words.

 **I Do**
Review the previous week's vocabulary words. The words can be reviewed over a few days. Read each word aloud pointing to the word on the **Visual Vocabulary Card**. Have students repeat after you. Then follow the Vocabulary Routine on the back of each card.

 **We Do**
Display the Visual Vocabulary Cards one at a time and have students call out the words. Give the definition if students cannot guess the word from the picture.

 **You Do**
In pairs, have students take turns showing the cards and reading the words. Then have them work together to write a sentence for each word.

| Beginning | Intermediate | Advanced/High |
|---|---|---|
| Help students read aloud the sentences. | Ask students to include a context clue in each sentence. | Have students use two or more vocabulary words in each sentence. |

## CONTEXT CLUES

CCSS

**OBJECTIVES**
Determine or clarify the meaning of unknown and multiple-meaning words and phrases based on grade 5 reading and content, choosing flexibly from a range of strategies. Use context (e.g., cause/effect relationships and comparisons in text) as a clue to the meaning of a word or phrase. **L.5.4a**

**LANGUAGE OBJECTIVE**
Identify and use context clues.

Read aloud the third paragraph of the Comprehension and Fluency passage on **ELL Reproducibles** pages 273–274. Explain that using clues in the paragraph can help students find the meaning of words. They can reread or read ahead to look for a description, example, synonym, or antonym.

**Think Aloud** I am not sure what *structural* means so I will read ahead. The word *structural* is used to describe adaptations, and the next sentence mentions changes to an animal's body. This helps me understand that, in this context, *structural* means "related to the body."

Have students point to the word *behavioral* in the fourth paragraph on page 273. Point out that the word *act* in the next sentence is a synonym for *behave*. The rest of the passage describes how desert animals act, or behave.

Have partners use paragraph clues to determine the meaning of *hibernate* (page 274, paragraph 2), *cold-blooded* (page 274, paragraph 3), *mobs,* and *predators* (page 274, paragraph 4).

| **Beginning** | **Intermediate** | **Advanced/High** |
|---|---|---|
| Identify the context clues for students and help them determine the meanings of the words. | Ask students to locate and read aloud the word on the page and identify paragraph clues. | Have students explain how they used paragraph clues to determine the meaning of the word. |

## ADDITIONAL VOCABULARY

CCSS

**OBJECTIVES**
Acquire and use accurately grade-appropriate general academic and domain-specific words and phrases, including those that signal contrast, addition, and other logical relationships. **L.5.6**

**LANGUAGE OBJECTIVE**
Use academic vocabulary and high-frequency words.

List some academic language and high-frequency words from "Mysterious Oceans": *species, survive, prey;* and *Cave Creatures*: *explore, classify, discovered.* Define each word for students: *To survive is to keep living.*

Model using the words for students in a sentence: *We all need food to survive. A fish might survive by hiding from its enemies.* Then provide sentence frames and complete them with students: *A _____ might survive by _____.*

Have pairs make up their own sentence frames for the class to complete.

| **Beginning** | **Intermediate** | **Advanced/High** |
|---|---|---|
| Provide the sentence frames and help students fill them in correctly. | Have students include a context clue in each sentence. | Have students include more than one missing word in their sentences. |

# English Language Learners
## Writing/Spelling

## WRITING TRAIT: SENTENCE FLUENCY

 **OBJECTIVES**
Write routinely over extended time frames (time for research, reflection, and revision) and shorter time frames (a single sitting or a day or two) for a range of discipline-specific tasks, purposes, and audiences. **W.5.10**

**LANGUAGE OBJECTIVE**
Use a variety of sentence structures.

 **I Do** Explain that good writers use a combination of short, simple sentences and longer, compound or complex sentences to make their writing varied and interesting. Read the Expert Model passage aloud as students follow along. Point out the simple and complex sentences.

 **We Do** Read aloud "Amazing Adaptations" from "Mysterious Oceans" as students follow along. Discuss how the varied sentence structure keeps the writing lively and clear. Record examples of each type of sentence structure. Model writing a paragraph with varied sentence structures.

 **You Do** Have pairs write a short paragraph, using a variety of sentence structures.

| Beginning | Intermediate | Advanced/High |
|---|---|---|
| Help students expand or shorten the sentences in their paragraphs to achieve variety. | Have students revise, using at least one simple, one compound, and one complex sentence. | Have students revise, vary the sentence structure, and edit for errors. |

## SPELL WORDS FROM MYTHOLOGY

 **OBJECTIVES**
Spell grade-appropriate words correctly, consulting references as needed. **L.5.2e**

**LANGUAGE OBJECTIVE**
Spell words from mythology.

 **I Do** Read aloud the Spelling Words on page T164, segmenting them into syllables. Have students repeat the words. Discuss how each word is related to mythology.

 **We Do** Read the Dictation Sentences on page T165 aloud for students. With each sentence, read the underlined word slowly, segmenting it into syllables. Have students repeat after you and write the word.

 **You Do** Display the words. Have students exchange their list with a partner to check the spelling and write the words correctly.

| Beginning | Intermediate | Advanced/High |
|---|---|---|
| Have students copy the words with correct spelling and say the words aloud. | After students have corrected their words, have pairs quiz each other. | After students have corrected their words, have them explain which words were difficult and why. |

# Grammar

## NEGATIVES

 CCSS

**OBJECTIVES**
Demonstrate command of the conventions of standard English grammar and usage when writing or speaking. **L.5.1**

**LANGUAGE OBJECTIVE**
Identify and use negatives.

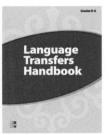

**Language Transfers Handbook**

Speakers of Cantonese, Korean, and Spanish may omit the helping verbs in negative statements. Work with these students to identify and use helping verbs in negative sentences.

 **I Do**

Remind students that a negative is a word or phrase that means *no*. Contrast negative and positive words to show how they are different. For example, write: *nobody/somebody, never/always, nowhere/everywhere.* Then write: *We are not ready for the party.* Point out the negative word *not*. Explain that negative contractions are made up of a verb with the word *not*. Give examples: *are not/aren't, do not/don't.* Write: *We aren't ready for the party.* Have students identify the negative contraction.

 **We Do**

Write the sentences below on the board. Have students use a negative word or phrase to complete each sentence. Then have them say: *The negative (word/phrase) is _____.*

> The dogs _____ playing well together.

> We _____ need to practice for the game any more.

> My bag is so full that there is _____ to put this book.

 **You Do**

Write a list of negative words and phrases, including contractions, on the board. Have students work in pairs to choose one word, one phrase, and one contraction and use them in sentences. Have them read their sentences aloud.

| **Beginning** | **Intermediate** | **Advanced/High** |
|---|---|---|
| Help students copy their sentences and underline the negative in each one. Read the sentence aloud for students to repeat. | Ask students to underline the negative in each sentence. | Have students write positive sentences to go along with the negative sentences. Have them explain how the sentences are different. |

For extra support, have students complete the activities in the **Grammar Practice Reproducibles** during the week, using the routine below.

→ Explain the grammar skill.

→ Model the first activity in the Grammar Practice Reproducibles.

→ Have the whole group complete the next couple of activities, then do the rest with a partner.

→ Review the activities with correct answers.

# Weekly Assessment

 **TESTED SKILLS**

| ✓COMPREHENSION: | ✓VOCABULARY: | ✓WRITING: |
|---|---|---|
| Text Structure: Cause and Effect **RI.5.3** | Context Clues: Paragraph Clues **L.5.4a** | Writing About Text **RI.5.3, W.5.9b** |

## Assessment Includes

→ Performance Tasks

→ Approaching-Level Assessment online PDFs

**Fluency Goal** 129 to 149 words correct per minute (WCPM)

**Accuracy Rate Goal** 95% or higher

Administer oral reading fluency assessments using the following schedule:

→ **Weeks 1, 3, 5** Provide Approaching-Level students at least three oral reading fluency assessments during the unit.

→ **Weeks 2 and 4** Provide On-Level students at least two oral reading fluency assessments during the unit.

→ **Week 6** If necessary, provide Beyond-Level students an oral reading fluency assessment at this time.

**Also Available: Selection Tests online PDFs**

**Go Digital!** www.connected.mcgraw-hill.com

# Using Assessment Results

| TESTED SKILLS | If ... | Then ... |
|---|---|---|
| **COMPREHENSION** | Students answer 0–6 multiple-choice items correctly ... | ... assign Lessons 76–78 on Cause and Effect from the *Tier 2 Comprehension Intervention online PDFs.* |
| **VOCABULARY** | Students answer 0–6 multiple-choice items correctly ... | ... assign Lesson 142 on Using Paragraph Context Clues from the *Tier 2 Vocabulary Intervention online PDFs.* |
| **WRITING** | Students score less than "3" on the constructed responses ... | ... assign Lessons 76–78 on Cause and Effect and/or Write About Reading Lesson 200 from the *Tier 2 Comprehension Intervention online PDFs.* |
|  | Students have a WCPM score of 120–128 ... | ... assign a lesson from Section 1, 7, 8, 9, or 10 of the *Tier 2 Fluency Intervention online PDFs.* |
| | Students have a WCPM score of 0–119 ... | ... assign a lesson from Section 2, 3, 4, 5, or 6 of the *Tier 2 Fluency Intervention online PDFs.* |

# Response to Intervention

Use the appropriate sections of the *Placement and Dignostic Assessment* as well as students' assessment results to designate students requiring:

 **Intervention Online PDFs**

**WonderWorks Intervention Program**

**Text Complexity Range for Grades 4–5**

| Lexile | |
|---|---|
| 740 | 1010 |
| *TextEvaluator™* | |
| 23 | 51 |

Reading/Writing Workshop

# TEACH AND MODEL

CCSS **Shared Read** Genre • Biography

## Words to Save the World

*The Work of Rachel Carson*

**Essential Question**
**What impact do our actions have on our world?**

Read about how the biologist Rachel Carson used the power of writing to change the world.

424

Sometimes, the quietest voice can spark the most clamorous outrage. Combining her love of nature with a belief in scientific accuracy, the soft-spoken writer Rachel Carson raised awareness about environmental issues. As a result, the U.S. government strengthened the rules and regulations regarding the use of chemical pesticides. Many people consider Rachel's book *Silent Spring* the foundation of today's environmental movement.

### Early Influences

Rachel was born in Springdale, Pennsylvania, in 1907. Throughout her childhood, her mother encouraged her to explore the **landscape** surrounding the family's farm. Often equipped with binoculars, Rachel developed a love of nature that affected many of her decisions. For example, she first chose to study English literature and writing when she went to college. However, she later decided to study biology. While studying at a marine laboratory, she became fascinated by the **glistening** and shimmering seascape.

From an early age, Rachel had loved to write. These writing skills proved useful to her career. She began by creating radio programs for the U.S. Bureau of Fisheries. She then became an editor and librarian for the agency. While she was working, she submitted her own articles to newspapers and magazines. Rachel eventually published three books about the ocean and its **native** plants and animals. This trilogy included *Under the Sea-Wind*, *The Sea Around Us*, and *The Edge of the Sea*.

**Rachel supported her ideas with well-researched facts.**

◀ **Rachel preferred working alone as she gathered information.**

425

## ✔ Vocabulary

export

glistening

influence

landscape

native

plantations

restore

urged

## 🔍 Close Reading of Complex Text

**Shared Read** "Words to Save the World," 424–431

**Genre** Biography

**Lexile** 980L

ETS *TextEvaluator™* 62

## Minilessons

| | |
|---|---|
| ✔ **Comprehension Strategy** | Ask and Answer Questions, T210–T211 |
| ✔ **Comprehension Skill** | Text Structure: Problem and Solution, T212–T213 |
| ✔ **Genre** | Biography, T214–T215 |
| ✔ **Vocabulary Strategy** | Synonyms and Antonyms, T216–T217 |
| ✔ **Writing Traits** | Ideas, T222–T223 |
| **Grammar Handbook** | Sentence Combining, T226–T227 |

## ✔ Tested Skills CCSS

👉 **Go** Digital

www.connected.mcgraw-hill.com

**Essential Question**
What impact do our actions have
on the world?

WEEK 4

# APPLY *WITH* CLOSE READING

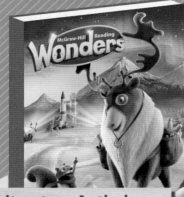

**Literature Anthology**

Literature Anthology

## Complex Text

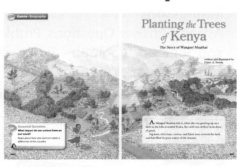

**PAIRED READ**

*Planting the Trees of Kenya,* 490–501
**Genre** Biography
**Lexile** 1030L
ETS. *TextEvaluator™* 45

"The Park Project," 504–505
**Genre** Expository Text
**Lexile** 950L
ETS. *TextEvaluator™* 42

## Differentiated Text

**Leveled Readers** *Include Paired Reads*

APPROACHING
**Lexile** 760L
ETS. *TextEvaluator™* 37

ON LEVEL
**Lexile** 890L
ETS. *TextEvaluator™* 48

BEYOND
**Lexile** 970L
ETS. *TextEvaluator™* 52

ELL
**Lexile** 790L
ETS. *TextEvaluator™* 42

## Extended Complex Text

*Spiders: Biggest! Littlest!*
**Genre** Expository Text
**Lexile** 820L
ETS. *TextEvaluator™* 13

*Earth Heroes:
Champions of the Wilderness*
**Genre** Collection of
Biographies
**Lexile** 920L
ETS. *TextEvaluator™* 53

**Classroom
Library
lessons available
online.**

**Classroom Library**

# TEACH AND MANAGE

## How You Teach

### INTRODUCE

**Weekly Concept**
Making a Difference

**Reading/Writing Workshop**
**420–421**

### TEACH

**Close Reading**
"Words to Save the World"

**Minilessons**
Ask and Answer Questions, Problem and Solution, Biography, Synonyms and Antonyms, Writing Traits

**Reading/Writing Workshop**
**424–433**

### APPLY

**Close Reading**
*Planting the Trees of Kenya*
"The Park Project"

**Literature Anthology**
**490–505**

☞ **Go Digital**

 Interactive Whiteboard

 Interactive Whiteboard

Mobile

## How Students Practice

### WEEKLY CONTRACT

**PDF Online**

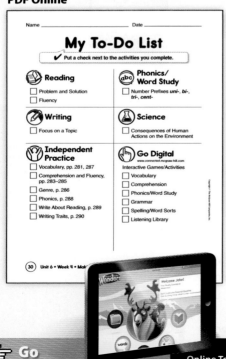

### LEVELED PRACTICE AND ONLINE ACTIVITIES

**Your Turn Practice Book**
**281–290**

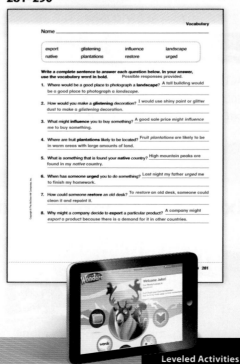

**Leveled Readers**

☞ **Go Digital**

Online To-Do List

Leveled Activities

Writer's Workspace

*Go Digital!* www.connected.mcgraw-hill.com

## DIFFERENTIATE

**SMALL GROUP INSTRUCTION**

**Leveled Readers**

## INTEGRATE

**Research and Inquiry**
Research Display, T220

**Text Connections**
Compare Impact of Human Actions, T221

**Write About Reading**
*Analytical Writing* Write an Analysis, T221

## ASSESS

**Weekly Assessment**
**337–348**

**Mobile**

**Online Research and Writing**

**Online Assessment**

---

# LEVELED WORKSTATION CARDS

More Activities on back

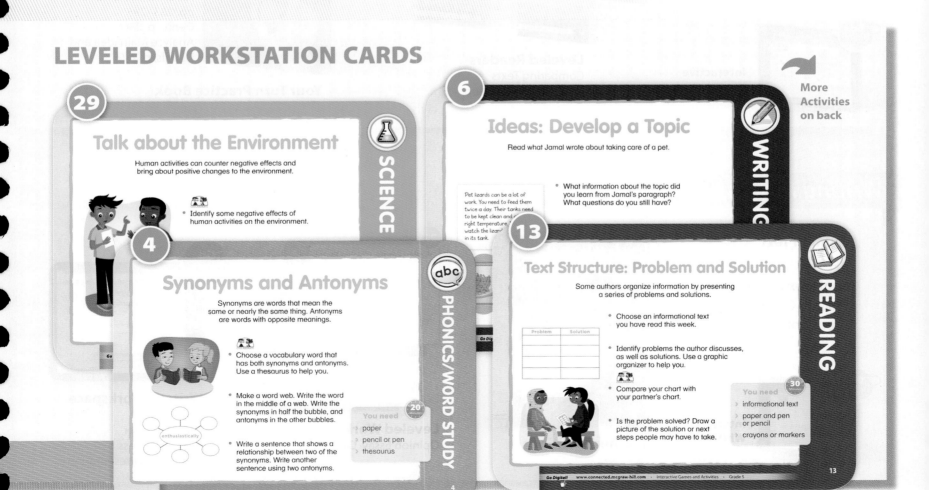

**29**

### Talk about the Environment

Human activities can counter negative effects and bring about positive changes to the environment.

• Identify some negative effects of human activities on the environment.

*SCIENCE*

**4**

### Synonyms and Antonyms

Synonyms are words that mean the same or nearly the same thing. Antonyms are words with opposite meanings.

• Choose a vocabulary word that has both synonyms and antonyms. Use a thesaurus to help you.

• Make a word web. Write the word in the middle of a web. Write the synonyms in half the bubble, and antonyms in the other bubbles.

enthusiastically

• Write a sentence that shows a relationship between two of the synonyms. Write another sentence using two antonyms.

You need
> paper
> pencil or pen
> thesaurus

**20** Minutes

*PHONICS/WORD STUDY*

**6**

### Ideas: Develop a Topic

Read what Jamal wrote about taking care of a pet.

Pet lizards can be a lot of work. You need to feed them twice a day. Their tanks need to be kept clean and c right temperature. watch the lizard in its tank.

• What information about the topic did you learn from Jamal's paragraph? What questions do you still have?

*WRITING*

**13**

### Text Structure: Problem and Solution

Some authors organize information by presenting a series of problems and solutions.

• Choose an informational text you have read this week.

| Problem | Solution |
|---------|----------|
|         |          |
|         |          |
|         |          |

• Identify problems the author discusses, as well as solutions. Use a graphic organizer to help you.

• Compare your chart with your partner's chart.

• Is the problem solved? Draw a picture of the solution or next steps people may have to take.

You need
> informational text
> paper and pen or pencil
> crayons or markers

**30**

*READING*

*Go Digital!* www.connected.mcgraw-hill.com • Interactive Games and Activities • Grade 5

# DEVELOPING READERS AND WRITERS

## *Write About Reading* • Analytical Writing

### Write to Sources and Research

Text Structure: Problem and Solution, T212–T213

Note Taking, T217B, T217O

Summarize, T217N

Problem and Solution, T217N

Make Connections: Essential Question, T217N, T217P, T221

Key Details, T217P

Research and Inquiry, T220

Analyze Main Idea and Details, T221

Comparing Texts, T233, T241, T245, T251

Predictive Writing, T217B

**Teacher's Edition**

Summarize, p. 503
Problem and Solution, p. 503

**Literature Anthology**

**Leveled Readers**
Comparing Texts
Problem and Solution

**Interactive Whiteboard**

Problem and Solution, pp. 283–285
Genre, p. 286
Analyze Main Idea and Details, p. 289

**Your Turn Practice Book**

## *Writing Process* • Genre Writing

### Opinion Text
Opinion Letter, T350–T355

### Conferencing Routines
Teacher Conferences, T352
Peer Conferences, T353

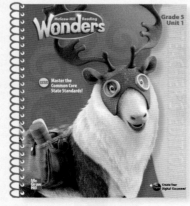

**Interactive Whiteboard**

**Teacher's Edition**

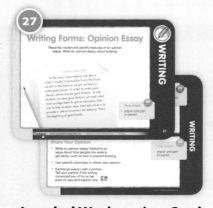

**Leveled Workstation Card**
Opinion Essay, Card 27

**Writer's Workspace**
Opinion Text:
Opinion Letter
Writing Process
Multimedia Presentations

## Writing Traits • Write Every Day

**Writing Trait: Ideas**
Focus on a Topic, T222–T223

**Conferencing Routines**
Teacher Conferences, T224
Peer Conferences, T225

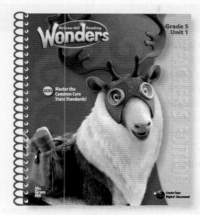

**Teacher's Edition**

Ideas: Focus on a
Topic, pp. 432–433

**Reading/Writing Workshop**

**Interactive Whiteboard**

Ideas:
Develop a
Topic, 6

**Leveled Workstation Card**

Ideas: Focus on a Topic,
p. 290

**Your Turn Practice Book**

## Grammar and Spelling

**Grammar**
Sentence Combining,
T226–T227

**Spelling**
Number Prefixes *uni-, bi-,
tri-, cent-,* T228–T229

**Interactive Whiteboard**

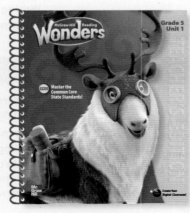

**Teacher's Edition**

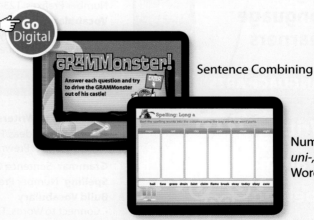

Sentence Combining

Number Prefixes
*uni-, bi-, tri-, cent-*
Word Sorts

**Online Spelling and Grammar Games**

# SUGGESTED LESSON PLAN

✔ **TESTED SKILLS** CCSS

| | DAY 1 | DAY 2 |
|---|---|---|

## READING

### Whole Group

**Teach, Model and Apply**

Reading/Writing Workshop

**DAY 1**

**Build Background** Making a Difference, T202–T203

**Listening Comprehension** Interactive Read Aloud: "Science Makes a Difference!," T204–T205

**Comprehension**
- Preview Genre: Biography, T214–T215
- Preview Strategy: Ask and Answer Questions, T210–T211

✔ **Vocabulary** Words in Context, T206–T207

**Practice** *Your Turn* 281

**Close Reading of Complex Text** "Words to Save the World," 424–427

**DAY 2**

✔ **Comprehension**
- Strategy: Ask and Answer Questions, T210–T211
- Skill: Text Structure: Problem and Solution, T212–T213
- Write About Reading *Analytical Writing*
- Genre: Informational Text, T214–T215

✔ **Vocabulary** Strategy: Synonyms and Antonyms, T216–T217

**Practice** *Your Turn* 282–287

## DIFFERENTIATED INSTRUCTION   Choose across the week to meet your students' needs.

### Small Group

**Approaching Level**

**DAY 1**

**Leveled Reader** *Marjory Stoneman Douglas: Guardian of the Everglades,* T232–T233

**Word Study/Decoding** Review Words with Number Prefixes, T234 ②

**Vocabulary**
- Review High-Frequency Words, T236 ②
- Identify Related Words, T237

**DAY 2**

**Leveled Reader** *Marjory Stoneman Douglas: Guardian of the Everglades,* T232–T233

**Vocabulary** Review Vocabulary Words, T236 ②

**Comprehension**
- Identify Important Events, T238 ②
- Review Text Structure: Problem and Solution, T239

**On Level**

**DAY 1**

**Leveled Reader** *Marjory Stoneman Douglas: Guardian of the Everglades,* T240–T241

**Vocabulary** Review Vocabulary Words, T242

**DAY 2**

**Leveled Reader** *Marjory Stoneman Douglas: Guardian of the Everglades,* T240–T241

**Comprehension** Review Text Structure: Problem and Solution, T243

**Beyond Level**

**DAY 1**

**Leveled Reader** *Marjory Stoneman Douglas: Guardian of the Everglades,* T244–T245

**Vocabulary** Review Domain-Specific Words, T246

**DAY 2**

**Leveled Reader** *Marjory Stoneman Douglas: Guardian of the Everglades,* T244–T245

**Comprehension** Review Text Structure: Problem and Solution, T247

**English Language Learners**

**DAY 1**

**Shared Read** "Words to Save the World," T248–T249

**Word Study/Decoding** Review Words with Number Prefixes, T234

**Vocabulary**
- Preteach Vocabulary, T252
- Review High-Frequency Words, T236

**DAY 2**

**Leveled Reader** *Marjory Stoneman Douglas: Guardian of the Everglades,* T250–T251

**Vocabulary** Review Vocabulary, T252

**Writing** Writing Trait: Ideas, T254

**Grammar** Sentence Combining, T255

## LANGUAGE ARTS   Writing Process: Opinion Letter T350–T355                Use with Weeks 4–6

### Whole Group

**Writing**

**Grammar**

**Spelling**

**Build Vocabulary**

**DAY 1**

✔ **Readers to Writers**
- Writing Trait: Ideas/Focus on a Topic, T222–T223
- Writing Entry: Prewrite and Draft, T224

**Grammar** Sentence Combining, T226

**Spelling** Number Prefixes *uni-, bi-, tri-, cent-,* T228

**Build Vocabulary**
- Connect to Words, T230
- Academic Vocabulary, T230

**DAY 2**

**Readers to Writers**
- Writing Entry: Revise, T224

**Grammar** Sentence Combining, T226

**Spelling** Number Prefixes *uni-, bi-, tri-, cent-,* T228

**Build Vocabulary**
- Expand Vocabulary, T230
- Review Homophones, T230

| DAY 3 | DAY 4 | DAY 5 Review and Assess |
|---|---|---|

### READING

**Word Study/Decoding** Number Prefixes *uni-*, *bi-*, *tri-*, *cent-*, T218–T219
**Practice** *Your Turn* 288

**Close Reading** *Planting the Trees of Kenya*, 490–503  *Analytical Writing*

Literature Anthology

**Fluency** Expression and Phrasing, T219
**Integrate Ideas** *Analytical Writing*
• Research and Inquiry, T220

**Practice** *Your Turn* 283–285

**Close Reading** "The Park Project," 504–505
*Analytical Writing*

**Integrate Ideas** *Analytical Writing*
• Research and Inquiry, T220
• Text Connections, T221
• Write About Reading, T221

**Practice** *Your Turn* 289

### DIFFERENTIATED INSTRUCTION

**Leveled Reader** *Marjory Stoneman Douglas: Guardian of the Everglades*, T232–T233
**Word Study/Decoding** Build Words with Number Prefixes, T234 (TIER 2)
**Fluency** Expression and Phrasing, T238 (TIER 2)
**Vocabulary** Synonyms and Antonyms, T237

**Leveled Reader** Paired Read: "The Story of the Tree Musketeers," T233 *Analytical Writing*
**Word Study/Decoding** Practice Words with Number Prefixes, T235

**Leveled Reader** Literature Circle, T233
**Comprehension** Self-Selected Reading, T239

---

**Leveled Reader** *Marjory Stoneman Douglas: Guardian of the Everglades*, T240–T241
**Vocabulary** Synonyms and Antonyms, T242

**Leveled Reader** Paired Read: "The Story of the Tree Musketeers," T241 *Analytical Writing*

**Leveled Reader** Literature Circle, T241
**Comprehension** Self-Selected Reading, T243

---

**Leveled Reader** *Marjory Stoneman Douglas: Guardian of the Everglades*, T244–T245
**Vocabulary**
• Synonyms and Antonyms, T246
• Analyze, T246
*Gifted and Talented*

**Leveled Reader** Paired Read: "The Story of the Tree Musketeers," T245 *Analytical Writing*

**Leveled Reader** Literature Circle, T245
**Comprehension**
• Self-Selected Reading, T247
• Independent Study: Make a Difference, T247
*Gifted and Talented*

---

**Leveled Reader** *Marjory Stoneman Douglas: Guardian of the Everglades*, T250–T251
**Word Study/Decoding** Build Words with Number Prefixes, T234
**Vocabulary** Synonyms and Antonyms, T253
**Spelling** Words with Number Prefixes, T254

**Leveled Reader** Paired Read: "The Story of the Tree Musketeers," T251 *Analytical Writing*
**Vocabulary** Additional Vocabulary, T253
**Word Study/Decoding** Practice Words with Number Prefixes, T235

**Leveled Reader** Literature Circle, T251

### LANGUAGE ARTS

**Readers to Writers**
• Writing Entry: Prewrite and Draft, T225
**Grammar** Mechanics and Usage, T227
**Spelling** Number Prefixes *uni-*, *bi-*, *tri-*, *cent-*, T229
**Build Vocabulary**
• Reinforce the Words, T231
• Synonyms and Antonyms, T231

**Readers to Writers**
• Writing Entry: Revise, T225
**Grammar** Sentence Combining, T227
**Spelling** Number Prefixes *uni-*, *bi-*, *tri-*, *cent-*, T229
**Build Vocabulary**
• Connect to Writing, T231
• Shades of Meaning, T231

**Readers to Writers**
• Writing Entry: Share and Reflect, T225
**Grammar** Sentence Combining, T227
**Spelling** Number Prefixes *uni-*, *bi-*, *tri-*, *cent-*, T229
**Build Vocabulary**
• Word Squares, T231
• Morphology, T231

# DIFFERENTIATE TO ACCELERATE

## A C T Scaffold to Access Complex Text

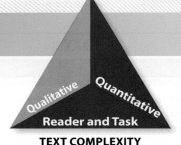

**IF** the text complexity of a particular selection is too difficult for students

**THEN** see the references noted in the chart below for scaffolded instruction to help students Access Complex Text.

Qualitative / Quantitative
**Reader and Task**
**TEXT COMPLEXITY**

| | Reading/Writing Workshop | Literature Anthology | Leveled Readers | Classroom Library |
|---|---|---|---|---|
| |  |  |  Approaching / On Level / Beyond / ELL |  |
| **Quantitative** | "Words to Save World: The Work of Rachel Carson"<br>**Lexile** 980<br>*TextEvaluator* 62 | *Planting the Trees of Kenya*<br>**Lexile** 1030<br>*TextEvaluator* 45<br><br>"The Park Project"<br>**Lexile** 950<br>*TextEvaluator* 42 | **Approaching Level**<br>**Lexile** 760<br>*TextEvaluator* 37<br><br>**Beyond Level**<br>**Lexile** 970<br>*TextEvaluator* 52 | **On Level**<br>**Lexile** 890<br>*TextEvaluator* 48<br><br>**ELL**<br>**Lexile** 790<br>*TextEvaluator* 42 | *Spiders: Biggest! Littlest!*<br>**Lexile** 820<br>*TextEvaluator* 13<br><br>*Earth Heroes: Champions of the Wilderness*<br>**Lexile** 920<br>*TextEvaluator* 53 |
| **Qualitative** | **What Makes the Text Complex?**<br>• **Organization** Cause and Effect T209<br>• **Specific Vocabulary** Word Parts T217<br><br><br>**A C T** *See Scaffolded Instruction in Teacher's Edition T209 and T217.* | **What Makes the Text Complex?**<br>• **Genre** Biography T217A, T217K<br>• **Sentence Structure** T217C<br>• **Prior Knowledge** Farming T217E; Kenyan History T217I; Oklahoma City T217O<br>• **Connection of Ideas** Impact T217G<br><br>**A C T** *See Scaffolded Instruction in Teacher's Edition T217A–T217P.* | **What Makes the Text Complex?**<br>• **Specific Vocabulary**<br>• **Prior Knowledge**<br>• **Sentence Structure**<br>• **Connection of Ideas**<br>• **Genre**<br><br>**A C T** *See Level Up lessons online for Leveled Readers.* | | **What Makes the Text Complex?**<br>• Genre<br>• Specific Vocabulary<br>• Prior Knowledge<br>• Sentence Structure<br>• Organization<br>• Purpose<br>• Connection of Ideas<br><br>**A C T** *See Scaffolded Instruction in Teacher's Edition T360-T361.* |
| **Reader and Task** | The Introduce the Concept lesson on pages T202–T203 will help determine the reader's knowledge and engagement in the weekly concept. See pages T208–T217 and T220–T221 for questions and tasks for this text. | The Introduce the Concept lesson on pages T202–T203 will help determine the reader's knowledge and engagement in the weekly concept. See pages T217A–T217P and T220–T221 for questions and tasks for this text. | The Introduce the Concept lesson on pages T202–T203 will help determine the reader's knowledge and engagement in the weekly concept. See pages T232–T233, T240–T241, T244–T245, T250–T251, and T220–T221 for questions and tasks for this text. | | The Introduce the Concept lesson on pages T202–T203 will help determine the reader's knowledge and engagement in the weekly concept. See pages T360-T361 for questions and tasks for this text. |

## Monitor and *Differentiate*

**IF** you need to differentiate instruction

**THEN** use the Quick Checks to assess students' needs and select the appropriate small group instruction focus.

### ✔ Quick Check

**Comprehension Strategy** Ask and Answer Questions T211

**Comprehension Skill** Text Structure: Problem and Solution T213

**Genre** Biography T215

**Vocabulary Strategy** Synonyms and Antonyms T217

**Word Study/Fluency** Number Prefixes *uni-, bi-, tri-, cent-,* Expression and Phrasing T219

**If No →**

| | |
|---|---|
| Approaching Level | Reteach T232–T239 |
| ELL | Develop T248–T255 |

**If Yes →**

| | |
|---|---|
| On Level | Review T240–T243 |
| Beyond Level | Extend T244–T247 |

## Level Up with Leveled Readers

**IF** students can read their leveled text fluently and answer comprehension questions

**THEN** work with the next level up to accelerate students' reading with more complex text.

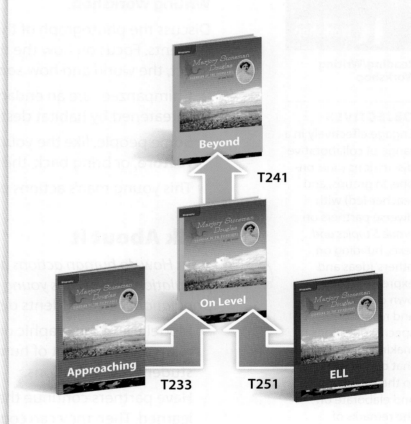

Beyond T241

On Level T233 T251 ELL

Approaching

## ENGLISH LANGUAGE LEARNERS
### SCAFFOLD

**IF** ELL students need additional support **THEN** scaffold instruction using the small group suggestions.

| Reading/Writing Workshop "Words to Save the World: The Work of Rachel Carson" T248–T249 | Leveled Reader *Mary Stoneman Douglas: Guardian of the Everglades* T250–T251 "The Story of the Tree Musketeers" T251 | Additional Vocabulary T253 environment  research nature  valuable refugees  voice | Synonyms and Antonyms T253 | Writing Trait: Ideas T254 | Spelling Words with Number Prefixes T254 | Grammar Sentence Combining T255 |
|---|---|---|---|---|---|---|

**Note: Include ELL Students in all small groups based on their needs.**

#  Introduce the Concept

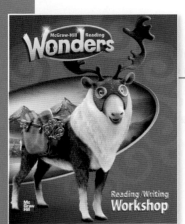

**Reading/Writing Workshop**

---

**OBJECTIVES**

**CCSS** Engage effectively in a range of collaborative discussions (one-on-one, in groups, and teacher-led) with diverse partners on *grade 5 topics and texts,* building on others' ideas and expressing their own clearly. Pose and respond to specific questions by making comments that contribute to the discussion and elaborate on the remarks of others. **SL.5.1c**

---

Build background knowledge on how people can make a difference.

---

**ACADEMIC LANGUAGE**
• *influence, restore*
• Cognates: *influir, restaurar*

---

## Build Background

**MINILESSON 10 Mins**

### ESSENTIAL QUESTION
***What impact do our actions have on our world?***

Have students read the Essential Question on page 420 of the **Reading/Writing Workshop**.

Discuss the photograph of the young man and the chimpanzees with students. Focus on how the the young man's actions **influence,** or affect, the world and how some human actions have a negative impact.

→ Chimpanzees are an endangered species. Their population is threatened by habitat destruction and hunting.

→ Some people, like the young man in the photograph, are working to **restore**, or bring back, the chimpanzee population.

→ This young man's actions positively **influence** the world.

## Talk About It

**Ask:** *How do human actions negatively **influence** the chimpanzee population? How is this young man helping to **restore** the chimpanzee population?* Have students discuss in pairs or groups.

→ Model using the graphic organizer to generate words and phrases related to the effect of human action on the environment. Add students' contributions.

→ Have partners continue the discussion by sharing what they have learned. Then they can complete the organizer.

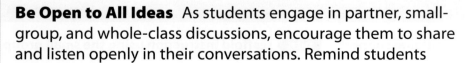

### Collaborative Conversations

**Be Open to All Ideas** As students engage in partner, small-group, and whole-class discussions, encourage them to share and listen openly in their conversations. Remind students

→ that all ideas, questions, or comments are important and should be heard; they should respect the opinions of others.

→ not to be afraid to ask a question if something is unclear.

→ to offer opinions, even if they differ from others' viewpoints.

**Go Digital**

**Discuss the Concept**

**Watch Video**

**View Photos**

**Use Graphic Organizer**

**Weekly Concept** Making a Difference

**Essential Question**
What impact do our actions have on our world?

*Go Digital!*

# Show How You Care

Human beings influence events all over the world. When human actions have a negative impact on the environment, many people must work to help restore it. Their actions can make a big difference.

▶ I always wanted to take care of animals, so I studied to be a veterinarian. My studies led me to a special interest in chimpanzees.

▶ Working to protect this species is one way I can have a positive impact on the world.

## Talk About It

Write words you have learned about making a difference. Then talk about actions you have taken that have had an impact on the world.

Making a Difference

420

421

**READING/WRITING WORKSHOP, pp. 420–421**

---

ELL ENGLISH LANGUAGE LEARNERS
SCAFFOLD

| Beginning | Intermediate | Advanced/High |
|---|---|---|
| **Use Visuals** Say: *We can make a difference in our world.* Point to the photograph. Say: *This young man is taking care of the chimpanzees. He is helping to restore, or repair, the chimpanzees' health.* Have students repeat after you. Ask: *Is he making a difference in a good way or a bad way?* Elaborate on responses. | **Describe** Have students describe how the young man in the photograph helps the chimpanzees. Ask: *How is this young man making a difference in our world?* Encourage students to use a concept word in their responses. Correct students' responses as needed. | **Discuss** Ask students to discuss how the young man in the photograph can influence, or affect, the chimpanzee population in positive ways. Ask: *What are some ways you would like to positively influence the world?* Clarify responses and elicit details as needed. |

**GRAPHIC ORGANIZER 140**

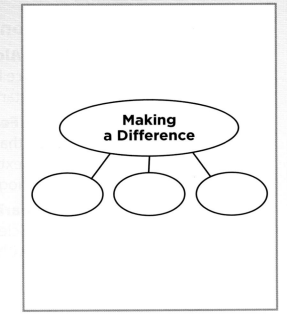

Making a Difference

# Listening Comprehension

MINILESSON
**10**
Mins

## Interactive Read Aloud

**Go Digital**

**View Images**

### OBJECTIVES

CCSS Summarize a written text read aloud or information presented in diverse media and formats, including visually, quantitatively, and orally. **SL.5.2**

- Listen for a purpose.
- Identify characteristics of a biography.

### ACADEMIC LANGUAGE

- *biography, ask and answer questions*
- Cognate: *biografía*

### Connect to Concept: Making a Difference

Tell students that the actions we take can have an impact on the world around us. Let students know that you will be reading aloud a passage about the life of a scientist whose work made a difference in protecting our planet from pollution.

### Preview Genre: Biography

Explain that the text you will read aloud is a biography. Discuss features of biographies:

→ tells the true story of a person's life

→ is about someone from the past or present

→ often includes photos and illustrations

### Preview Comprehension Strategy: Ask and Answer Questions

Point out that readers can form questions before beginning to read a biography, such as: *Why is this person's life important? How did this individual make a difference in the world?* They can then read on to find the answers to their questions. Readers can continue to ask and answer questions during and after their reading to better understand the text.

Use the Think Alouds on page T205 model the strategy.

### Respond to Reading

**Think Aloud Clouds** Display Think Aloud Master 1: *I wonder...* to reinforce how you used the ask and answer questions strategy to understand content.

**Genre Features** With students, discuss the elements of the Read Aloud that let them know it is a biography. Ask them to think about other texts that you have read or they have read independently that were biographies.

**Summarize** Have students restate the most important information from "Science Makes a Difference!" in their own words. Have them take turns with a partner to summarize key details.

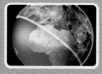

**Model Think Alouds**

**Genre Chart**

# Science Makes a Difference!

In 1995, Mario Molina and two other scientists were awarded one of the most prestigious prizes in the world, the Nobel Prize in Chemistry. They received it for their work showing that certain chemicals pose a terrible threat to the ozone layer. The ozone layer, a layer of gas in the atmosphere above Earth, protects the planet from the sun's harmful radiation.

Molina and his colleague conducted research that helped change attitudes about pollution. Their work also inspired actions to protect the atmosphere. **1**

## Mario Molina's Education

Molina was born in Mexico in 1943. Even as a boy, he was fascinated by science. He attended school briefly in Europe, but was educated mostly in Mexico.

After graduating from college, Molina spent several years traveling, studying, and teaching. Then he attended graduate school in the United States and received his Ph.D. in physical chemistry in 1973.

## Groundbreaking Research

Molina joined a group of scientists working at the University of California in Irvine. There, Molina studied how chemicals affect the atmosphere. He and another scientist found that certain chemicals seriously damage the ozone layer. These chemicals are called chlorofluorocarbons, or CFCs. Molina and the other scientist published their findings in 1974. At the time, CFCs were widely used in everything from spray cans to air conditioners. No one wanted to hear that CFCs created problems. **2**

Molina continued to do experiments on the dangers of CFCs. Scientists and policy makers began to pay attention. Then, in the mid-1980s, another group of scientists discovered a hole in the ozone layer over Antarctica. The damage could be traced to the effects of CFCs. Now the world was ready to listen!

By 2010, most nations in the world had banned the use of specific chemicals that harm the ozone layer. Molina and other scientists had taken action to help create a safer world for all living things. **3**

**1** **Think Aloud** To check my understanding, I can **ask and answer a question**: "What is this section mostly about?" It is about Mario Molina, a scientist who showed how chemicals harm the ozone layer.

**2** **Think Aloud** To be sure I understand the scientific information, I **ask and answer a question**: "What are CFCs?" I read on to find the answer: CFCs are chemicals that were once widely used, but harmful to the ozone layer.

**3** **Think Aloud** When I finish reading, I **ask and answer questions** to understand the selection: "What is the main idea?" I think it is that Molina made a difference in the world through his research, which showed that CFCs harm the ozone layer.

Andersen Ross/Blend Images/Getty Images

# → Vocabulary

**Reading/Writing Workshop**

OBJECTIVES

CCSS Acquire and use accurately grade-appropriate general academic and domain-specific words and phrases, including those that signal contrast, addition, and other logical relationships (e.g., *however, although, nevertheless, similarly, moreover, in addition*). **L.5.6**

ACADEMIC LANGUAGE
• *influence, restore*
• Cognates: *influir, restaurar*

**MINILESSON 10 Mins**

## Words in Context

### Model the Routine

Introduce each vocabulary word using the Vocabulary Routine found on the **Visual Vocabulary Cards**.

**Visual Vocabulary Cards**

Vocabu

Define:

Example:

Ask:

> **Vocabulary Routine**
>
> <u>Define:</u> When something is **glistening**, it is shining.
>
> <u>Example:</u> The glistening wrapping paper made the gift look really special.
>
> <u>Ask:</u> What other materials create a glistening effect?

**Go Digital**

glistening

**Use Visual Glossary**

### Definitions

→ **export**   To **export** an item is to sell or trade it to another country. **Cognate:** *exportar*

→ **influence**   When you **influence** people, you try to change or affect their thoughts or behavior. **Cognate:** *influir*

→ **landscape**   A **landscape** is a region's landforms or a stretch of land that can be seen from a place.

→ **native**   When someone is **native** to a place, they were born there. **Cognate:** *nativo*

→ **plantations**   **Plantations** are large farms. **Cognate:** *plantaciones*

→ **restore**   To **restore** is to bring something back to its original form or condition. **Cognate:** *restaurar*

→ **urged**   If you are **urged** to do your chores, you are strongly encouraged or persuaded to do them.

### Talk About It

COLLABORATE

Have partners look at each photograph and discuss the definition of each word. Ask students to choose three words and write questions for their partners to answer.

## CCSS Words to Know

# Vocabulary

Use the picture and the sentences to talk with a partner about each word.

**export**

Ships transport many goods made for **export** overseas.

*What goods might be produced for export to other countries?*

**glistening**

The **glistening** wrapping paper made the gift look really special.

*What other materials create a glistening effect?*

**influence**

Mrs. Garcia pointed out information that could **influence** Anna's voting decision.

*Who might influence your decisions each day?*

**landscape**

From our cabin, we see a **landscape** of mountains, trees, and a clear blue lake.

*What landscape would you like to visit?*

**native**

Penguins are **native** to Antarctica.

*What animals are native to your state or area?*

**plantations**

Flying over the land, we had a view of farms and **plantations** below.

*What kinds of things are grown on plantations?*

**restore**

The upholsterer worked to **restore** the antique chair to its original condition.

*What else might you restore by repairing?*

**urged**

My mom **urged** my baby brother to eat his food.

*What kinds of foods are growing children urged to eat?*

### Your Turn COLLABORATE

Pick three words. Write three questions for your partner to answer.

*Go Digital!* Use the online visual glossary

422

423

**READING/WRITING WORKSHOP, pp. 422–423**

## ELL ENGLISH LANGUAGE LEARNERS SCAFFOLD

### Beginning

**Use Visuals** Point to the photograph for *glistening*. Say: *The glistening gift is wrapped in shiny red paper.* Have students repeat after you. Ask: *Could you see a glistening lake on a sunny day?* Elaborate on students' responses.

### Intermediate

**Describe** Have students describe the gift in the photograph. Review the meaning of *glistening*. Have students repeat. Ask students to talk with partners about other things that might glisten, or shine. Assist with pronunciation as needed.

### Advanced/High

**Discuss** Ask pairs to discuss the photograph of the gift. Have them talk about a time when they've seen something glistening. Provide this sentence frame: *I saw a glistening _____ when I was _____.* Clarify responses as needed.

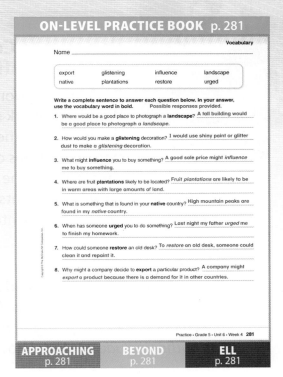

**ON-LEVEL PRACTICE BOOK p. 281**

Name _____

| export | glistening | influence | landscape |
| native | plantations | restore | urged |

Write a complete sentence to answer each question below. In your answer, use the vocabulary word in bold. Possible responses provided.

1. Where would be a good place to photograph a **landscape**? A tall building would be a good place to photograph a *landscape*.

2. How would you make a **glistening** decoration? I would use shiny paint or glitter dust to make a *glistening* decoration.

3. What might **influence** you to buy something? A good sale price might *influence* me to buy something.

4. Where are fruit **plantations** likely to be located? Fruit *plantations* are likely to be in warm areas with large amounts of land.

5. What is something that is found in your **native** country? High mountain peaks are found in my *native* country.

6. When has someone **urged** you to do something? Last night my father *urged* me to finish my homework.

7. How could someone **restore** an old desk? To *restore* an old desk, someone could clean it and repaint it.

8. Why might a company decide to **export** a particular product? A company might *export* a product because there is a demand for it in other countries.

Practice • Grade 5 • Unit 6 • Week 4 **281**

| APPROACHING p. 281 | BEYOND p. 281 | ELL p. 281 |

VOCABULARY **T207**

CCSS **Shared Read** > Genre • Biography

# Words to Save the World

## The Work of Rachel Carson

**Essential Question**

**What impact do our actions have on our world?**

Read about how the biologist Rachel Carson used the power of writing to change the world.

424

Sometimes, the quietest voice can spark the most clamorous outrage. Combining her love of nature with a belief in scientific accuracy, the soft-spoken writer Rachel Carson raised awareness about environmental issues. As a result, the U.S. government strengthened the rules and regulations regarding the use of chemical pesticides. Many people consider Rachel's book *Silent Spring* the foundation of today's environmental movement.

### Early Influences

Rachel was born in Springdale, Pennsylvania, in 1907. Throughout her childhood, her mother encouraged her to explore the **landscape** surrounding the family's farm. Often equipped with binoculars, Rachel developed a love of nature that affected many of her decisions. For example, she first chose to study English literature and writing when she went to college. However, she later decided to study biology. While studying at

◄ **Rachel preferred working alone as she gathered information.**

a marine laboratory, she became fascinated by the **glistening** and shimmering seascape.

From an early age, Rachel had loved to write. These writing skills proved useful to her career. She began by creating radio programs for the U.S. Bureau of Fisheries. She then became an editor and librarian for the agency. While she was working, she submitted her own articles to newspapers and magazines. Rachel eventually published three books about the ocean and its **native** plants and animals. This trilogy included *Under the Sea-Wind*, *The Sea Around Us*, and *The Edge of the Sea*.

**Rachel supported her ideas with well-researched facts.**

425

---

**READING/WRITING WORKSHOP, pp. 424–425**

# Shared Read

**Reading/Writing Workshop**

**Lexile** 980   *TextEvaluator™* 62

## Connect to Concept: Making a Difference

Explain that "Words to Save the World: The Work of Rachel Carson" demonstrates the impact one person's actions can have on our world. Read "Words to Save the World: The Work of Rachel Carson" with students. Note that the vocabulary words are highlighted.

## Close Reading

**Reread Paragraph 1:** Reread the first paragraph of the selection with students. Ask: *What kind of information does this paragraph contain? Why does the author include it?* Model how to cite evidence.

I learn that Rachel Carson raised awareness about environmental issues and that, as a result, regulations on pesticide use were strengthened. This paragraph summarizes the impact of Rachel's work. Perhaps the author included it to capture readers' attention and encourage them to read on.

**Reread Paragraph 2:** Model how to use information in the paragraph to identify the genre.

In the first sentence, I read that Rachel was born in Springdale, Pennsylvania, in 1907. *In 1907* is a time-order signal phrase, as is the phrase *Throughout her childhood* in the next sentence. These details help me understand that the selection is a biography that will relate events in Rachel's life in the order in which they happened.

**Rachel Carson's research revealed that DDT caused damage to birds and eggs.**

### A Call to Action

The success of Rachel's books allowed her to devote more time to her own projects. She built a cottage close to the sea on the coast of Maine. Soon, however, a letter arrived from some old friends, Olga and Stuart Huckins. They described problems resulting from the spraying of DDT on their private wildlife sanctuary. Chemical companies had developed DDT as an effective solution to crop-eating insects on farms and **plantations**. At the Huckins's sanctuary, however, the chemical also seemed to be harming birds.

In response, Rachel hired assistants to help research the Huckins's claim. Worried by the slow pace of their work, she decided to continue alone. By publishing her findings, she hoped

to warn about the dangers of these new chemicals. In order to dramatize the situation, she **urged** readers to imagine a world without songbirds. The book's title, *Silent Spring,* describes this possible result of pesticide abuse.

*Silent Spring* prompted readers to raise their voices in unison against the chemical corporations. They demanded an investigation into pesticides and implored the government to restrict their use. In response, President John Kennedy created a Congressional committee to study the matter. Rachel testified before this group and provided facts and information to **influence** its decisions.

**Though a pesticide may target insects, animals can also feel its effects.**

#### Sample Food Chains

| TROPHIC LEVEL | GRASSLAND BIOME | OCEAN BIOME |
|---|---|---|
| Primary Producer | grass | phytoplankton |
| Primary Consumer | grasshopper | zooplankton |
| Secondary Consumer | rat | fish |
| Tertiary Consumer | snake | seal |

426

### A Strong Reaction

Meanwhile, the chemical companies struggled to counter Rachel's claims. Despite her reasonable approach to the problem, they tried to depict her accusations as irrational. They published articles and reports that mocked her writing style and belittled her ideas. Advertisements on television proclaimed the safety of their products. When these ads did not change public opinion, they pulled financial support from programs that featured Rachel.

Rachel worried that once pesticides poisoned an area, it might be impossible to **restore** the

**Carson understood the power her words had to educate others, especially children.**

environment to its original state. "Man's attitude toward nature is today critically important simply because we have now acquired a fateful power to alter and destroy nature," she said in an interview. Her testimony led to restrictions on certain pesticides in the United States. Even so, chemical companies continued to produce them for **export** to other countries.

Rachel Carson died shortly after *Silent Spring* was published, but her voice survives within her books. Her love of nature endures, along with her quiet desire to preserve and protect the natural world.

##### Make Connections

What impact did the publication of *Silent Spring* have on the makers of pesticides such as DDT? **ESSENTIAL QUESTION**

Think about a time when you wrote or spoke about something that needed to change. What impact did your words have? **TEXT TO SELF**

427

**READING/WRITING WORKSHOP, pp. 426–427**

## Make Connections

### ESSENTIAL QUESTION

Encourage students to go back into the text for evidence as they discuss the impact the publication of *Silent Spring* had on the makers of pesticides. Ask students to explain, using the text, what impact our actions can have on our world.

## Continue Close Reading

Use the following lessons for focused rereadings.

→ Ask and Answer Questions, pp. T210–T211

→ Text Structure: Problem and Solution, pp. T212–T213

→ Biography, pp. T214–T215

→ Synonyms and Antonyms, pp. T216–T217

## A C T Access Complex Text

### ▶ Organization

Lead students through the chain of cause-and-effect relationships on pages 426–427.

→ *What effect did the message of* Silent Spring *have on the public?* (Readers asked the government to restrict pesticide use.)

→ *What did public reaction cause President Kennedy to do?* (create a Congressional committee to study the matter)

→ *What did the chemical companies do as a result of the outcry?* (mock Rachel's ideas; pull financial support from her programs)

# → Comprehension Strategy

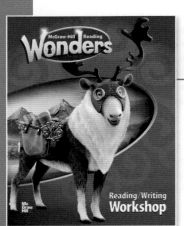

 **MINILESSON**
**10** **Mins**

## Ask and Answer Questions

**Go**
**Digital**

**Present the Lesson**

**Reading/Writing Workshop**

 **OBJECTIVES**

**CCSS** Quote accurately from a text when explaining what the text says explicitly and when drawing inferences from the text. **RI.5.1**

Ask and answer questions about text to increase understanding.

**ACADEMIC LANGUAGE**
• ask and answer questions, biography
• Cognate: *biografía*

### 1 Explain

Explain to students that they can **ask and answer questions** before, during, and after reading to increase their understanding of biographies.

→ Point out that students can ask themselves questions about a text before they even begin to read. Before reading "Words to Save the World: The Work of Rachel Carson," for example, they might ask, "What is this biography going to tell me about Rachel Carson?" or "How did Rachel Carson have an impact on the world?"

→ Students can also ask themselves questions while they read. If they are confused by the information they read, then they should ask questions about specific details in the text and then reread a paragraph or section to find answers.

→ Finally, students can ask questions about a text after they read. Answering these questions helps ensure that they understand the selection as a whole and can identify its main idea.

### 2 Model Close Reading: Text Evidence

Model how to use information in the first paragraph of "Words to Save the World: The Work of Rachel Carson" to ask questions that you will answer as you continue reading. The answer to the question "What did Rachel Carson write about?" can be found in the last paragraph on page 425 and the second paragraph on page 426. The answer to the question "Why did her books have influence?" can be found in the last paragraph on page 426.

### 3 Guided Practice of Close Reading

**COLLABORATE**

Have pairs reread the section "A Call to Action" on page 426 and ask questions about possible responses to *Silent Spring*. Have partners find the answers to their questions by rereading the rest of the biography. Partners should also ask each other questions about other sections of the text and then reread for the answers.

## CCSS Comprehension Strategy

# Ask and Answer Questions

Readers ask themselves questions about the text before, during, and after their reading. Asking and answering questions helps you focus, as well as check your understanding of a text.

 **Find Text Evidence**

As you read "Words to Save the World" on page 425, you can ask yourself questions about Rachel Carson and the effects she had on the world around her.

**page 425**

Sometimes, the quietest voice can spark the most clamorous outrage. Combining her love of nature with a belief in scientific accuracy, the soft-spoken writer Rachel Carson raised awareness about environmental issues. As a result, the U.S. government strengthened the rules and regulations regarding the use of chemical pesticides. Many people consider Rachel's book *Silent Spring* the foundation of today's environmental movement.

**Early Influences**

Rachel was born in Springdale, Pennsylvania, in 1907. Throughout a marine laboratory, she became fascinated by the **glistening** and shimmering seascape.

From an early age, Rachel had loved to write. These writing skills proved useful to her career. She began by creating radio programs for the U.S. Bureau of Fisheries. She then became an editor and librarian for the agency. While she was working, she submitted her own articles to newspapers and magazines. Rachel eventually published three books about the ocean and its **native** plants and animals. This trilogy included *Under the Sea-Wind, The Sea Around Us,* and *The Edge of the Sea.*

*I read that Rachel Carson was a writer whose work had major effects on our country. I ask myself, "What did she write about? Why did her books have influence?" I will read on to find answers.*

### Your Turn

COLLABORATE

Reread the section "A Call to Action" on page 426. Form questions about possible responses to Rachel's book. Then look for answers. Use the strategy Ask and Answer Questions as you read.

428

**READING/WRITING WORKSHOP, p. 428**

## Monitor and *Differentiate*

 **Quick Check**

Are students able to form questions about possible responses to Rachel Carson's book? Do they reread to find the answers?

### Small Group Instruction

If No → | **Approaching Level** | Reteach p. T232
| **ELL** | Develop p. T249

If Yes → | **On Level** | Review p. T240
| **Beyond Level** | Extend p. T244

| Beginning | Intermediate | Advanced/High |
|---|---|---|
| **Understand** Reread the first paragraph. Point out difficult words and phrases such as *clamorous, outrage, accuracy, environmental,* and *chemical pesticides.* Define them. Help students replace them with words or phrases they know. Ask: *Did Rachel increase people's knowledge about problems in the environment?* (yes) | **Identify** Have students reread the first paragraph on page 425. Ask: *What effect did Rachel Carson's writing have on the use of chemical pesticides?* (Rules and regulations about their use were strengthened.) Point out that this section may be confusing because it summarizes information that will be explained in detail later in the text. | **Demonstrate Comprehension** Have students reread the first paragraph on page 425. Elicit from students why this section may be confusing. Ask: *What questions about Rachel Carson's work and its effects are unanswered in this brief summary? Where can you find answers to these questions? Turn to a partner and explain.* |

### ON-LEVEL PRACTICE BOOK pp. 283–284

Comprehension and Fluency

Name _____

**Read the passage. Use the ask and answer questions strategy to guide your reading.**

**The Father of Earth Day**

12    Imagine a world where black clouds of pollution blanketed the sky and
26    rivers ran orange from toxic waste. What would the world be like if the
40    soil was too poisoned to grow food and bald eagles had been hunted to
53    extinction? That world might exist today, if not for the actions of Senator
   Gaylord Nelson.

55 **A Commitment to Conservation**

59    Gaylord Nelson developed an affection for nature growing up in the
70    woods of northern Wisconsin. As an adult, he brought his love of the
83    land to his political career. When he became governor of Wisconsin in
95    1959, he worked hard to protect and care for his state's natural resources.
108    His Outdoor Recreation Acquisition Program preserved thousands of
116    acres of unspoiled land. The program bought private lands and turned
127    them into wildlife habitats and public parks. Nelson also created a
138    Youth Conservation Corps. The Corps taught young people about the
148    environment while giving them jobs cleaning and caring for the state's
159    natural areas.
161    In 1962 Nelson was elected to the U.S. Senate. He hoped to do
174    for the country what he had done for the state of Wisconsin: protect
187    the environment. He found that few of his fellow senators shared his
199    concerns. Nelson hoped President John F. Kennedy could generate support
209    for environmental issues. In 1963 the senator helped plan a national
220    conservation tour for the president, but the tour did not create the support
233    for environmental issues that Nelson hoped it would.

Practice · Grade 5 · Unit 6 · Week 4 **283**

| **APPROACHING** pp. 283–284 | **BEYOND** pp. 283–284 | **ELL** pp. 283–284 |
|---|---|---|

# → Comprehension Skill

**Reading/Writing Workshop**

**MINILESSON 10 Mins**

## Text Structure: Problem and Solution

**Go Digital**

Present the Lesson

### 1 Explain

Explain to students that a text's structure is the way ideas within it are organized. Remind students that they learned about cause-and-effect text structure earlier in the unit. Tell them that an author can also organize a text by presenting a series of **problems and solutions**.

→ While texts organized by causes and effects focus on *why* things happen, problem and solution texts focus on *how* the subject overcomes challenges and solves problems.

→ As they read a biography, students can monitor their understanding by asking themselves, "What problem was the subject facing?" They should then continue reading to find out what actions he or she took to solve it.

→ Point out that understanding the problems and challenges a person faced can help readers better identify with and appreciate that person and can make reading about him or her more interesting.

### 2 Model Close Reading: Text Evidence

Identify two problems and their solutions that are described in the section "A Call to Action" on page 426. Then model how to include this information in the graphic organizer.

*Analytical Writing* **Write About Reading: Summary** Model how to use the notes from the organizer to write a brief summary of the problems Rachel Carson faced and the solutions she found.

### 3 Guided Practice of Close Reading

COLLABORATE
Have students work in pairs to continue reading the section "A Call to Action." Point out that sometimes solutions create new problems. Students should use the graphic organizer to record other problems and solutions described in the section.

*Analytical Writing* **Write About Reading: Compare and Contrast** Ask pairs to work together to write a summary that compares and contrasts the text structures of "Words to Save the World: The Work of Rachel Carson" and "Mysterious Oceans." Select volunteers to share their summaries.

---

**OBJECTIVES**

**CCSS** Compare and contrast the overall structure (e.g., chronology, comparison, cause/effect, problem/solution) of events, ideas, concepts, or information in two or more texts. **RI.5.5**

---

**ACADEMIC LANGUAGE**

• *text structure, problem, solution*

• Cognates: *problema, solución*

---

**SKILLS TRACE**

**TEXT STRUCTURE**

**Introduce** U1W3

**Review** U1W4, U1W6, U2W1, U2W3, U4W6, U5W3, U5W4, U5W6, U6W3, U6W4

**Assess** U1, U2, U3, U5, U6

## Comprehension Skill CCSS

# Problem and Solution

Presenting **problems and solutions** is one way of organizing information in a biography. The author may describe problems encountered by subject of the text and then explain any solutions that resulted. As you read, try to identify problems and the actions taken to solve them.

 **Find Text Evidence**

*In the section "A Call to Action" on page 426, Rachel receives information about a problem with dying birds. As she attempts solutions, she finds other problems she needs to address. I can record her problem and solution process in my graphic organizer.*

| Problem | Solution |
|---|---|
| Rachel gets a letter about bird deaths due to pesticides. | She hires assistants to help research the claim. |
| The research goes too slowly. | Rachel decides to work alone. |

### Your Turn COLLABORATE

Continue to reread the section "A Call to Action" on page 426. Record the other problems and solutions in your graphic organizer.

*Go Digital!*
*Use the interactive graphic organizer*

**429**

**READING/WRITING WORKSHOP, p. 429**

## ENGLISH LANGUAGE LEARNERS
## ELL SCAFFOLD

### Beginning

**Understand** Reread the first two paragraphs of "A Call to Action." Ask: *Did Rachel Carson's friends have a problem?* (yes) *Were people spraying chemicals that hurt animals?* (yes) *Did Rachel help solve the problem by hiring people to do research?* (yes) Help students identify the problem and solution: *The problem was _____. The solution was _____.*

### Intermediate

**Describe** Help students reread the first two paragraphs of "A Call to Action." Ask: *What problem did Rachel Carson's friends face? What did Carson do in response?* Then have partners describe another problem and solution in the text. *The problem was _____. The solution was _____.*

### Advanced/High

**Explain** Have students reread the first two paragraphs of "A Call to Action." Students should discuss the problems Carson faced and how she solved them. Then have them explain to partners how they identified the problems and solutions.

---

## Monitor and *Differentiate*

### ✓ Quick Check

Are students able to identify problems and solutions in the text and record them in the graphic organizer?

### Small Group Instruction

| | | |
|---|---|---|
| If No → | **Approaching Level** | **Reteach p. T239** |
| | **ELL** | **Develop p. T249** |
| If Yes → | **On Level** | **Review p. T243** |
| | **Beyond Level** | **Extend p. T247** |

---

 **ON-LEVEL PRACTICE BOOK** pp. 283–285

Comprehension: Problem and Solution and Fluency

Name _____

A. Reread the passage and answer the questions. Possible responses provided.

1. What problem did Gaylord Nelson encounter in the U.S. Senate when he tried to get support for environmental issues?
   Few of his fellow senators thought that environmental issues were important.

2. What gave Senator Nelson an idea for a solution?
   He read about college students protesting the Vietnam War and thought that he could hold a demonstration for the environment.

3. In what way did Senator Nelson's call for demonstrations on Earth Day help the environment?
   Millions of people took part, which convinced Congress to pass environmental legislation. Earth Day is still observed every year and it raises awareness about protecting the environment.

B. Work with a partner. Read the passage aloud. Pay attention to expression and phrasing. Stop after one minute. Fill out the chart.

| | Words Read | – | Number of Errors | = | Words Correct Score |
|---|---|---|---|---|---|
| First Read | | – | | = | |
| Second Read | | – | | = | |

Practice · Grade 5 · Unit 6 · Week 4 **285**

| **APPROACHING** pp. 283–285 | **BEYOND** pp. 283–285 | **ELL** pp. 283–285 |
|---|---|---|

# Genre: Informational Text

**Reading/Writing Workshop**

**OBJECTIVES**

CCSS Interpret information presented visually, orally, or quantitatively (e.g., in charts, graphs, diagrams, time lines, animations, or interactive elements on Web pages) and explain how the information contributes to an understanding of the text in which it appears. **RI.4.7**

CCSS By the end of the year, read and comprehend informational texts, including history/ social studies, science, and technical texts, at the high end of the grade 4–5 text complexity band independently and proficiently. **RI.5.10**

**ACADEMIC LANGUAGE**
• *biography, illustration*
• Cognates: *biografía, ilustración*

## Biography

**Go Digital**

**Present the Lesson**

### 1 Explain

Share with students the following key characteristics of a **biography:**

→ A biography tells the true story of someone's life and is written in the third person. The subject of a biography may be someone who lived in the past or someone who is living today.

→ A biography often includes text features such as photographs and illustrations, which usually have captions that provide additional information about them.

→ Photographs, illustrations, and captions help clarify information in the text. They may also help readers understand key concepts or events related to the subject's life.

### 2 Model Close Reading: Text Evidence

Model using details on page 425 of "Words to Save the World: The Work of Rachel Carson" to help you understand that the selection is a biography that tells about Rachel Carson's life and work and their impact. Then point to the illustration on page 426.

**Use Illustrations** Remind students that an illustration is a picture or diagram that clarifies information. Explain that this illustration depicts sample food chains.

Read the caption aloud and tell students that it draws a conclusion from information in one of the food chains—that is, because other animals eat insects targeted by pesticides, those animals are also impacted by the harsh chemicals. Ask: *How does the illustration help you better understand ideas described in the text?*

### 3 Guided Practice of Close Reading

Have students work in pairs to identify and list three details in "Words to Save the World: The Work of Rachel Carson" that help them understand the subject of the biography. Have students share and compare their findings with the class.

**Genre** Informational Text

# Biography

"Words to Save the World: The Work of Rachel Carson" is a biography.

A **biography:**
- Tells the true story of someone else's life
- May be about someone who lived in the past or is living today, written in the third-person
- May include text features such as illustrations

 **Find Text Evidence**

*I can tell that "Words to Save the World: The Work of Rachel Carson" is a biography. It tells about her childhood, life, and work. The illustration helps me understand why her work was important.*

**page 426**

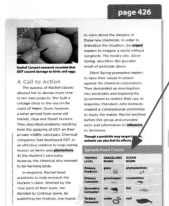

**Use Illustrations** An illustration is a picture or diagram that clarifies information. The illustrations in a biography may help the reader understand key concepts related to the life or work of the subject.

**Your Turn** COLLABORATE

List three details in "Words to Save the World: The Work of Rachel Carson" that help you understand the subject of this biography.

430

**READING/WRITING WORKSHOP, p. 430**

## ELL ENGLISH LANGUAGE LEARNERS SCAFFOLD

### Beginning

**Recognize** Have students point to the illustration on page 426. Ask: *Is this illustration about people or animals?* (animals) Explain that the illustration shows food chains. It shows what different animals eat. Then have students point to the caption. Read it aloud. Explain that it tells why the information in the web was important to Rachel.

### Intermediate

**Understand** Have students locate the illustration and caption on page 426. Ask: *What does this illustration show?* (food chains) *What conclusion can you draw about pesticides from this information?* (Pesticides could hurt many animals.) Have partners discuss how the illustration and caption support the text. Restate responses.

### Advanced/High

**Describe** Have students locate text features characteristic of a biography. Ask: *What information do the illustration and caption on page 426 present? How do they support the text?* Ask partners to discuss: *Would the illustration be clear without the caption? How do these text features work together?* Elicit details to support responses.

## Monitor and *Differentiate*

 **Quick Check**

Are students able to list three details from the text that help them understand the subject of the biography?

### Small Group Instruction

| | | |
|---|---|---|
| If No → | Approaching Level | Reteach p. T233 |
| | ELL | Develop p. T251 |
| If Yes → | On Level | Review p. T241 |
| | Beyond Level | Extend p. T245 |

**ON-LEVEL PRACTICE BOOK** p. 286

*Genre/Text Feature*

Name _____

**Conserving the Wild**

Dr. Edgar Wayburn spent most of his days saving lives as a physician. However, he spent his spare time saving wilderness areas and creating national parks. As president of the Sierra Club for many years, he urged politicians to protect wild landscapes. His greatest achievement was the Alaska National Interests Land Conservation Act, or ANILCA. In 1999, Dr. Wayburn received the Presidential Medal of Freedom. The award honored his remarkable influence on environmentalism. Dr. Wayburn died in 2010 at the age of 103.

Wayburn helped to protect millions of acres in Alaska.

Answer the questions about the text.

1. **What genre of text is this? How do you know?**
   It is a biography, because it gives readers facts about the life and achievements of Dr. Edgar Wayburn, a real person.

2. **What aspect or part of Dr. Wayburn's life is featured in this text?**
   Dr. Wayburn's work as a conservationist is featured.

3. **How does the text feature relate to the text?**
   The map illustrates the large areas of land protected by ANILCA, which Dr. Wayburn worked to pass.

4. **How does the heading relate to both the text and the text feature?**
   The word "conserving" in the heading relates to the main idea of the text. Dr. Wayburn helped to conserve wild areas, which are illustrated on the map.

286 Practice • Grade 5 • Unit 6 • Week 4

| APPROACHING | BEYOND | ELL |
|---|---|---|
| p. 286 | p. 286 | p. 286 |

# Vocabulary Strategy

**Reading/Writing Workshop**

**OBJECTIVES**

**CCSS** Demonstrate understanding of figurative language, word relationships, and nuances in word meanings. Use the relationship between particular words (e.g., synonyms, antonyms, homographs) to better understand each of the words.
**L.5.5c**

---

**ACADEMIC LANGUAGE**
- *synonym, antonym*
- Cognates: *sinónimo, antónimo*

**MINILESSON**
**10 Mins**

## Synonyms and Antonyms

### 1 Explain

Remind students that **synonyms** are words that have the same, or almost the same, meaning. **Antonyms** are words that have the opposite, or nearly the opposite, meaning.

→ Tell students to be on the lookout for words that may be synonyms or antonyms within a section of text.

→ Explain that recognizing a pair of synonyms or a pair of antonyms can help them better understand the meaning of each word or identify the meaning of an unfamiliar word in the pair.

### 2 Model Close Reading: Text Evidence

Model using context clues to identify an antonym of the word *clamorous* on page 425 of "Words to Save the World: The Work of Rachel Carson." Point out that the text sets up a contrast between the words *quietest* and *clamorous*. Although Rachel's voice was quiet, it provoked a loud response from others.

### 3 Guided Practice of Close Reading

**COLLABORATE**

Have students work in pairs identify a synonym or antonym for *regulations* (synonym: *rules*), *reasonable* (antonym: *irrational*), and *mocked* (synonym: *belittled*). Encourage partners to reread the text for context clues that help them identify synonyms or antonyms. Then ask them to explain how the meanings of the words are similar or different.

**Go Digital**

**Present the Lesson**

---

**SKILLS TRACE**

**SYNONYMS AND ANTONYMS**

**Introduce** U4W1

**Review** U4W1, U4W2, U5W1, U6W4

**Assess** U4, U6

## Vocabulary Strategy  CCSS

# Synonyms and Antonyms

**Synonyms** are words that have the same, or almost the same, meaning. **Antonyms** are words that have the opposite, or nearly the opposite, meaning. The relationship between synonyms or antonyms in the same sentence or paragraph can help you better understand the meaning of each word.

### Find Text Evidence

*In the first sentence of "Words to Save the World: The Work of Rachel Carson" on page 425 most* clamorous *must be an antonym of* quietest. *The word* clamorous *helps show that her quiet voice provoked a noisy, loud response from others.*

> Sometimes, the quietest voice can spark the most clamorous outrage.

### Your Turn

COLLABORATE

Find a synonym or antonym in the same sentence or paragraph as each of the following words in "Words to Save the World." Explain how the meanings are the same or different.

**regulations,** *page 425*
**reasonable,** *page 427*
**mocked,** *page 427*

431

**READING/WRITING WORKSHOP, p. 431**

## A C T Access Complex Text

### ▶ Specific Vocabulary

Remind students that word parts are another tool they can use to unlock word meaning.

→ Introduce the following number prefixes: *uni-* (one), *bi-* (two), *tri-* (three).

→ *Rachel Carson produced a trilogy of books about the ocean. How many did she write?* (*tri-* means "three," so three books)

→ *Carson's readers raised their voices "in unison" against pesticides. What does this mean?* (Carson's readers spoke out together, as though they had one voice.)

---

## Monitor and *Differentiate*

### ✓ Quick Check

Can students use context clues to help them identify synonyms or antonyms of words in the text?

⬇

### Small Group Instruction

If No → | Approaching Level | Reteach p. T237
| ELL | Develop p. T253
If Yes → | On Level | Review p. T242
| Beyond Level | Extend p. T246

---

**ON-LEVEL PRACTICE BOOK** p. 287

Vocabulary Strategy: **Synonyms and Antonyms**

Name _____

Read each passage and underline the word that is either a synonym or an antonym for the word in bold. Use the synonym or antonym to write a definition of the word in bold. Possible responses provided.

1. Gaylord Nelson developed an **affection** for nature growing up in the woods of northern Wisconsin. As an adult, he brought his love of the land to his political career.

   love or caring feeling

2. When he became governor of Wisconsin in 1959, he worked hard to **protect** and care for his state's natural resources. His Outdoor Recreation Acquisition Program **preserved** thousands of acres of unspoiled land.

   protected; kept safe

3. The program purchased **private** lands and converted them into wildlife habitats and public parks.

   owned by an individual; not owned by the public

4. Nelson hoped President John F. Kennedy could **generate** support for environmental issues. In 1963 the senator helped plan a national conservation tour for the president, but the tour did not produce the amount of support for environmental issues that Nelson hoped it would.

   to create or bring about; to produce

5. Nelson wanted Congress to pass such laws, but he needed to show that people supported the **legislation**.

   laws passed by a governing body

6. Nelson called for pro-environment **demonstrations** around the country. The protests were held on April 22, 1970, the day Nelson called Earth Day.

   protests or rallies for a particular cause

Practice • Grade 5 • Unit 6 • Week 4 **287**

| APPROACHING p.287 | BEYOND p. 287 | ELL p.287 |

# Develop Comprehension

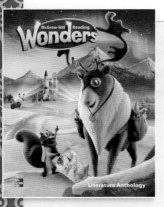

**Literature Anthology**
*Complex sentence structure and the connection of ideas place this selection above Lexile range. Content is grade-level appropriate.*

## *Planting the Trees of Kenya*

**Text Complexity Range**

**Lexile**

740        1010   *1030

**TextEvaluator™**

23       45       51

## Options for Close Reading

→ Whole Class

→ Small Group

→ Independent

**CCSS Genre · Biography**

**? Essential Question**
**What impact do our actions have on our world?**
Read about how one woman made a difference in her country.

**Go Digital!**

490

# A C T  **A**ccess **C**omplex **T**ext

## What makes this text complex?

▷ **Genre**

▷ **Sentence Structure**

▷ **Prior Knowledge**

▷ **Connection of Ideas**

## ▶ Genre

Remind students that biographers write about their subjects in different ways.

→ *How does this biography of Wangari Maathai sound like a story?* (The author begins, "As Wangari Maathai tells it," which sounds like a tale. Figurative language, such as "the earth was clothed in its dress of green," also makes this sound like a story.)

# Planting *the* Trees *of* Kenya ①

The Story of Wangari Maathai

written and illustrated by
Claire A. Nivola

As Wangari Maathai tells it, when she was growing up on a farm in the hills of central Kenya, the earth was clothed in its dress of green.
Fig trees, olive trees, crotons, and flame trees covered the land, and fish filled the pure waters of the streams.

491

**LITERATURE ANTHOLOGY,** pp. 490–491

## Predictive Writing

Have students read the title and study the illustrations. Have them write their predictions about what the story will be about. Tell them that Kenya is located in Africa.

## ESSENTIAL QUESTION

Ask a student to read aloud the Essential Question. Have students discuss how this biography might help them answer the question.

## Note Taking:
## Use the Graphic Organizer *Analytical Writing*

As students read the selection, ask them to take notes by filling in the graphic organizer on **Your Turn Practice Book page 282** to identify the problem-and-solution text structure.

## ① Text Feature: Illustrations

Look at the illustration on pages 490–491. Who do you think is pictured? (Wangari) How does the title connect to the illustration? (Both the title and the illustration show that this selection is about trees.)

---

**ELL** ELLs may need support in understanding figurative language. Review the difference between literal and figurative meanings. For example, the metaphor "dress of green" is figurative. The dress is not real, or literal; rather, it's a comparison used to convey meaning.

→ *What is "clothed in its dress of green"?* (the earth)
→ Read aloud the last sentence on page 491. *What things mentioned in this sentence are literally green?* (trees and the land)
→ *To what is the author comparing the dress of green?* (to the trees and land on the earth)

# Develop Comprehension

**2 Author's Craft: Figurative Language**

Authors make comparisons to cause readers to think about objects in new ways. Look at the comparison between frogs' eggs and necklace beads. Reread the last sentence on page 492. What is this type of comparison called? (simile) Paraphrase the comparison to show your understanding. How does this comparison cause you to think differently about frogs' eggs? (Even frogs' eggs can have beauty.) How does the author's language show how Wangari feels about nature? (It shows that she thinks nature is beautiful.)

The fig tree was sacred then, and Wangari knew not to disturb it, not even to carry its fallen branches home for firewood. In the stream near her homestead where she went to collect water for her mother, **2** she played with **glistening** frogs' eggs, trying to gather them like beads into necklaces, though they slipped through her fingers back into the clear water.

492

## A C T  Access Complex Text

### ▶ Sentence Structure

Point out that in using long sentences, such as the last one on page 492, the author can include many details that are part of a single moment. Phrases and clauses are often set off by commas so the sentence is easier to read.

→ *What part of the sentence tells what Wangari was doing?* ("…she played with glistening frogs' eggs")

→ *Look at the other details in the sentence. Where did Wangari play?* (She played in the stream.)

→ *When did Wangari play?* (She played while collecting water.)

→ *What happened to the eggs?* (They slipped back into the water.)

Her heart was filled with the beauty of her **native** Kenya when she left to attend a college run by Benedictine nuns in America, far, far from her home. There she studied biology, the science of living things. It was an inspiring time for Wangari. The students in America in those years dreamed of making the world better. The nuns, too, taught Wangari to think not just of herself but of the world beyond herself.

493

 **3 Text Feature: Illustrations**

Study the illustration on pages 492–493. How does the artist show that nature is sacred to Wangari? Turn to a partner and discuss the answer. (Possible response: The tree is much larger than the human figure, and the figure's face is upturned toward the tree with a look of appreciation. The illustration has a lot of green, which is a color found all over nature.)

 **4 Genre: Biography**

It is very common for a biography to mention some influences that shaped the main subject's life. Turn to a partner and paraphrase the influences listed on page 493 that helped shape Wangari's life. (Wangari left Kenya to study biology at an American college run by Benedictine nuns. Her fellow students and the nuns influenced her to make the world a better place.)

**ELL** Help ELLs understand the lengthy sentences in the paragraph on page 492. Break the second sentence into phrases, or units of meaning. Read the sentence aloud, pausing at each comma and using gestures to help support meaning.

Assign each phrase to partners or small groups. Lead students in a sequential choral reading.

→ Have students practice reading the sentence on their own. Remind them to pause as they encounter each comma, as commas are used to separate units of meaning.

# Develop Comprehension

## ⑤ Author's Craft: Exaggeration

Sometimes authors use exaggeration to bring attention to a point. How does the author use exaggeration on page 494? Why does she say this? (The author says Wangari had been away for five years, "but they might have been twenty" to demonstrate how much the land in Kenya had changed.)

## ⑥ Skill: Cause and Effect

Cause and effect is often included in the problem-and-solution text structure. Sometimes the effect of a certain action is also the problem presented in a text. On page 495, what is the cause-and-effect structure? (Because the people had forgotten to care for the land, the land became weak and the people's lives became harder.) What is the problem? (The land became weak and the people's lives became harder.) What clue words typically help a reader identify cause-and-effect structure? (*since, because, as a result, so, when, if/then*)

How eagerly she returned to Kenya! How full of hope and of all that she had learned!

⑤ She had been away for five years, only five years, but they might have been twenty—so changed was the **landscape** of Kenya.

Wangari found the fig tree cut down, the little stream dried up, and no trace of frogs, tadpoles, or the silvery beads of eggs. Where once there had been little farms growing what each family needed to live on and large **plantations** growing tea for **export**, now almost all the farms were growing crops to sell. Wangari noticed that the people no longer grew what they ate but bought food from stores. The store food was expensive, and the little they could afford was not as good for them as what they had grown themselves, so ⑥ that children, even grownups, were weaker and often sickly.

494

# A C T  Access Complex Text

## ▶ Prior Knowledge

Clarify why some Kenyans became weak and sickly when they started growing food to sell rather than to eat. Explain that food, especially fruits and vegetables, grown in your own garden is fresher and often more nutritious than processed food bought in stores.

Draw a T-chart with the headings *Benefits* and *Drawbacks*. Ask: *What might be some benefits and drawbacks of growing crops to sell?* (Possible responses: Benefits: provides an income for farmers; growing fresh food helps others. Drawbacks: time-consuming; hard work; can require a lot of water and soil ; foods to eat are bought at the store)

She saw that where once there had been richly wooded hills with grazing cows and goats, now the land was almost treeless, the woods gone. So many trees had been cut down to clear the way for more farms that women and children had to walk farther and farther in search of firewood to heat a pot or warm the house. Sometimes they walked for hours before they found a tree or bush to cut down. There were fewer and fewer trees with each one they cut, and much of the land was as bare as a desert. **7**

Without trees there were no roots to hold the soil in place. Without trees there was no shade. The rich topsoil dried to dust, and the wind blew it away. Rain washed the loose earth into the once-clear streams and rivers, dirtying them with silt.

> **STOP AND CHECK**
>
> **Ask and Answer Questions**
> How has Kenya changed since Wangari left? Find details to support your answer.

495

**LITERATURE ANTHOLOGY, pp. 494–495**

---

**7 Strategy: Ask and Answer Questions**

**Teacher Think Aloud** I know that I can improve my understanding of a text if I **ask and answer questions** about it. For example, I might ask: *What has happened to the trees in Kenya?* I can reread the text to find the answer. I learn that many trees were cut down to clear land for big farms. Then I can ask: *What effect did this have on the people of Kenya?* I reread to find the answer: People had to walk for hours just to get firewood to heat their food or warm their homes.

**STOP AND CHECK**

**Ask and Answer Questions** How has Kenya changed since Wangari left? (Kenya has become dry and lifeless. The fig tree and farms are gone. The stream where Wangari once collected frogs' eggs is now dry, and the land is treeless. Wind has blown away top soil and has dirtied the streams and rivers.)

---

**ELL** To help ELLs understand how the change in food affected people, point out the last sentence on page 494. Draw students' attention to the word *weaker*.

→ Explain that *weak*, meaning "without strength," describes the people after they ate store-bought food instead of food they grew themselves.

→ Point out other comparative adjectives in the selection, such as *farther* and *fewer* on page 495. Ask: *What is the root word of the word* fewer? (few)

→ Use if/then sentence frames to clarify students' understanding of *weaker* and *fewer: If people eat too much store-bought food, then they may get _____.* (weaker) *If there are _____ trees, then people must walk farther for fire wood.* (fewer)

# Develop Comprehension

## 8 Vocabulary: Synonyms and Antonyms

The first paragraph on page 496 states that "the women of the countryside complained." What word in the next paragraph is a synonym for *countryside*? (land) On page 496, the author uses the words *weak* and *suffering* to describe the land. Use a thesaurus to find antonyms for these words. (strong, healthy, sufficient)

## 9 Skill: Problem and Solution

On page 496, what clue words do you see that indicate there is a problem to be solved? (*problem, solution*) What additional problems do the Kenyans face? On page 497, what does Wangari suggest for solving these problems? Add this information to your organizer.

| Problem | Solution |
|---------|----------|
| There was a lack of natural resources, such as trees, grass, and water. | Gather seeds, prepare the soil, plant and tend the seeds, and dig holes to find water. |

"We have no clean drinking water," the women of the countryside complained, "no firewood to cook with. Our goats and cows have nothing to graze on, so they make little milk. Our children are hungry, and we are poorer than before."

Wangari saw that the people who had once honored fig trees and **8** now cut them down had forgotten to care for the land that fed them. Now the land, weak and suffering, could no longer take care of the people, and their lives became harder than ever.

The women blamed others, they blamed the government, but Wangari was not one to complain. She wanted to do something. "Think of what we ourselves are doing," she **urged** the women. "We are cutting down the trees of Kenya.

"When we see that we are part of the problem," she said, "we can become part of the solution." She had a simple and big idea.

"Why not plant trees?" she asked the women.

496

## A C T  Access Complex Text

### ▶ Connection of Ideas

A biography often shows the impact that its main subject has on people. Help students connect what Wangari learned at her American school to the way she interacts with the women of Kenya. Read aloud the dialogue at the end of page 496, beginning with "Think of what we ourselves are doing."

→ *Who cut down the trees?* (the people of Kenya)

→ *Who can solve the problem?* (the people of Kenya)

→ *How does this relate to what the nuns taught Wangari at college?* (The people of Kenya should think of not just themselves, but the world beyond themselves.)

She showed them how to collect tree seeds from the trees that remained. She taught them to prepare the soil, mixing it with manure. She showed them how to wet that soil, press a hole in it with a stick, and carefully insert a seed. Most of all she taught them to tend the growing seedlings, as if they were babies, watering them twice a day to make sure they grew strong.

It wasn't easy. Water was always hard to come by. Often the women had to dig a deep hole by hand and climb into it to haul heavy bucketfuls of water up over their heads and back out of the hole. An early nursery in Wangari's backyard failed; almost all the seedlings died. But Wangari was not one to give up, and she showed others how not to give up.

Many of the women could not read or write. They were mothers and farmers, and no one took them seriously.

**STOP AND CHECK**

**Ask and Answer Questions** Why was it difficult to plant trees? Find details in the text to help you.

497

**LITERATURE ANTHOLOGY,** pp. 496–497

---

## ⑩ Strategy: Ask and Answer Questions

**Teacher Think Aloud** This selection tells about the difficulty in planting trees successfully. What evidence can I find that proves planting trees was difficult?

Prompt students to apply the strategy in a Think Aloud by rereading page 497. Tell students to note details about women in Kenyan society.

**Student Think Aloud** I can reread the section about growing trees to find proof of the women's difficulties. I know that finding water was not easy and that caused the biggest problem in growing the trees. The text also states that "An early nursery in Wangari's backyard failed; almost all of the seedlings died." That is proof that planting trees was difficult for the women in Kenya.

**STOP AND CHECK**

**Ask and Answer Questions** Why was it difficult to plant trees? (It was difficult to find water to tend the seedlings.)

---

**ELL** Help ELLs understand the response of the Kenyan people to Wangari's words. Point out the illustration on page 497.

→ *Were the people complaining or working?* (They were working.)

→ *What were they doing?* (They were getting water for the trees.)

→ *Who helped to solve the problem in Kenya?* (The women of Kenya.)

→ *Complete this sentence: Your actions can _____ a problem.* (help fix)

# Develop Comprehension

**11 Vocabulary: Synonyms and Antonyms**

The land in Kenya is a main focus of this selection. The author uses many terms as synonyms for *land*. What other synonyms for *land* are on page 498? (*woods, plots,* and *hills*) What other synonyms for *land* have you read in this selection so far? (*countryside, landscape,* and *plantations*)

**12 Strategy: Ask and Answer Questions**

Reread the last paragraph on page 498. Think of a question such as, "Why did people change their attitudes about the women's work?" Paraphrase your answer with a partner. Include examples from the text.

**Student Think Aloud** Previously, no one took women seriously because they were not educated. When I reread I find out that the men changed their attitudes because they saw evidence of the women's success: growing trees and gardens.

But they did not need schooling to plant trees. They did not have to wait for the government to help them. They could begin to change their own lives.

All this was heavy work, but the women felt proud. Slowly, all around them, they could begin to see the fruit of the work of their hands. The woods were growing up again. Now when they cut down a tree, they planted two in its place. Their families were healthier, eating from the fruit trees they had planted and from the vegetable plots filled again with the yams, cassava, pigeon peas, and sorghum that grew so well. They had work to do, and the work brought them together as one, like the trees growing together on the newly wooded hills.

The men saw what their wives, mothers, and daughters were doing and admired them and even joined in.

498

## A C T Access Complex Text

▶ **Prior Knowledge**

Point out the reference to the soldiers on page 499. Students may not be familiar with Kenyan history, which includes some periods of turmoil. For example, during the 1950s there was a rebellion against the British, who had colonized Kenya. In the early 1980s, there was a coup, or rebellion, against the government. In 2007, a presidential election caused conflicts among supporters of the two candidates.

→ *What was Wangari's attitude toward the soldiers?* (She thought the soldiers would do a better job of protecting the country if they worked to preserve the land. To Wangari, preserving the land is another way of protecting the people.)

Wangari gave seedlings to the schools and taught the children how to make their own nurseries.

She gave seedlings to inmates of prisons and even to soldiers.  "You hold your gun," she told the soldiers, "but what are you protecting? The whole country is disappearing with the wind and water. You should hold the gun in your right hand and a tree seedling in your left. That's when you become a good soldier."

499

**LITERATURE ANTHOLOGY, pp. 498–499**

## 13 Skill: Problem and Solution

On page 499, what additional solution did Wangari suggest to help the land? Add this information to your organizer.

| Problem | Solution |
|---------|----------|
| There was a lack of natural resources such as trees, grass, and water. | Gather seeds, prepare the soil, plant and tend the seeds, and dig holes for water.<br><br>Give seedlings to school children and teach them how to make their own nurseries. Also give seedlings to prisoners and soldiers. |

## 14 Skill: Make Inferences

Wangari says to the soldiers, "You hold your gun, but what are you protecting?" What is she suggesting by saying this? Use text evidence to support your answer. (Wangari is suggesting that if the people of Kenya don't take care of their land, there might not be any usable land left, and the people will have to leave. If there is no usable land and people leave, there will be nothing to protect. Earlier on page 496, the text states, "Now the land, weak and suffering, could no longer take care of the people.")

**ELL** Help students understand and pronounce the words *soldier* and *inmates* on page 499.

→ *Say the word* soldier *with me:* soldier.

→ Point out the cognates: soldier/*soldado,* prison/*prisión*.

→ Read the second sentence on page 499 with students. Explain that inmates are people in prison.

→ *To whom does Wangari give seedlings?* (She gives them to inmates and soldiers.)

# Develop Comprehension

**15** **Skill: Problem and Solution**

Pages 500–501 summarize the main problem and solution in this selection. Paraphrase the main problem. (The land was suffering and lacked vegetation.) **What did Wangari do to solve the problem?** (Wangari led a movement that resulted in the planting of thirty million trees.) **Add this information to your organizer.**

| Problem | Solution |
|---|---|
| Kenya's land was suffering and lacked trees and other vegetation. | Wangari started a movement to make Kenya green once again. Thirty million trees have been planted in thirty years. |

**15**   And so in the thirty years since Wangari began her movement, tree by tree, person by person, thirty million trees have been planted in Kenya—and the planting has not stopped.

500

## A C T  Access Complex Text

▶ **Genre**

Remind students that a biography often tells about a major contribution the subject makes, and how the contribution impacts others' lives.

→ *What effect do you think Wangari's contribution will have on Kenya? How do you know?* (It will have a lasting effect and improve people's lives. The text says the planting "has not stopped.")

**ELL** Remind students that in a biography, the author often includes quotations from the main subject. Help students who may have difficulty with the figurative language in Wangari's final quotation.

→ Help students recall that in the opening of the story, the writer refers to green trees as a "dress" that the earth wears.

"When the soil is exposed," Wangari tells us, "it is crying out for help, it is naked and needs to be clothed in its dress. That is the nature of the land. It needs color, it needs its cloth of green."

**STOP AND CHECK**

Reread How did Wangari get people to join her movement? Use the strategy Reread to help you.

501

**LITERATURE ANTHOLOGY,** pp. 500–501

→ Point out the personification of the soil "crying out for help," "clothed in its dress," and needing "its cloth of green" on page 501.

→ *Why is the soil "crying"?* (It is naked, or bare, because it has no vegetation growing on it.)

→ *What will the soil's "dress" be made of?* (green plants and trees)

**STOP AND CHECK**

**Reread** How did Wangari get people to join her movement? (Wangari modeled how to plant trees, demonstrated success, and taught others how to follow her example.)

**Return to Predictions**

Review students' predictions and purposes for reading. Ask them to answer the Essential Question. (Each action a person performs can have an effect on the environment. In this selection, the people of Kenya hurt their own land by cutting down trees. This led to a shortage of natural resources. Wangari then reversed this impact on the land by motivating people to replant trees and make the land green once again.)

**CONNECT TO CONTENT**

**DEFORESTATION AND REFORESTATION**

Deforestation occurs when people cut down large numbers of trees for housing, farming, and manufacturing purposes. Negative effects of deforestation include dry soil, water shortages, high temperatures, more greenhouse gases in the atmosphere, and loss of animal habitats. Students read about some of these consequences of human activity on the environment on page 495. In this story, Wangari's reforestation movement restores lost trees of Kenya.

**STEM**

# About the Author

## Meet the Author and the Illustrator

### Claire A. Nivola

Have students read the biography of the author and illustrator. Provide discussion prompts:

→ What inspired Claire A. Nivola to write about Wangari and the environment?

→ Wangari passed away in September 2011, after becoming the first African woman to receive the Nobel Peace Prize. How does Nivola's writing help bring attention to Wangari's work?

## Author's Purpose

### To Inform

Remind students that authors may use illustrations to show problems and solutions. Students may say that the illustrations show the changes in Kenya's landscape over time: from green, to treeless, then green again.

## Author's Craft

### Figurative Language

Explain that figurative language helps readers think about familiar objects in new ways.

→ Authors create figurative language with comparisons. For example, on page 498 the author states, "They had work to do, and the work brought them together as one, like the trees growing together on the newly wooded hills."

→ Have students find other examples of figurative language such as the one on page 497: "…she taught them to tend the growing seedlings, as if they were babies."

## About the Author and Illustrator

**Claire A. Nivola** grew up in New York City. The daughter of two artists, she drew pictures and created sculptures starting from early childhood. She also loved to read. After studying literature and history in college, she began to illustrate children's books, including one titled *Messy Rabbit* written by her mother. Other children's books she has written and illustrated include *Elisabeth* and *The Forest*.

Claire was inspired to write about Wangari Maathai after hearing her speak on the radio about her tree-growing project in Kenya, called the Green Belt Movement. Claire wanted children to understand how people's actions can harm the environment, which provides for everyone. However, she wanted her message to be hopeful. "A child is just beginning in life and needs to have hope," she said. She hopes her biography of Wangari inspires readers to make positive changes in the world.

### Author's Purpose

Claire A. Nivola wrote and illustrated *Planting the Trees of Kenya*. How did the author's illustrations help you understand the changes that took place in Kenya?

502

**LITERATURE ANTHOLOGY, pp. 502–503**

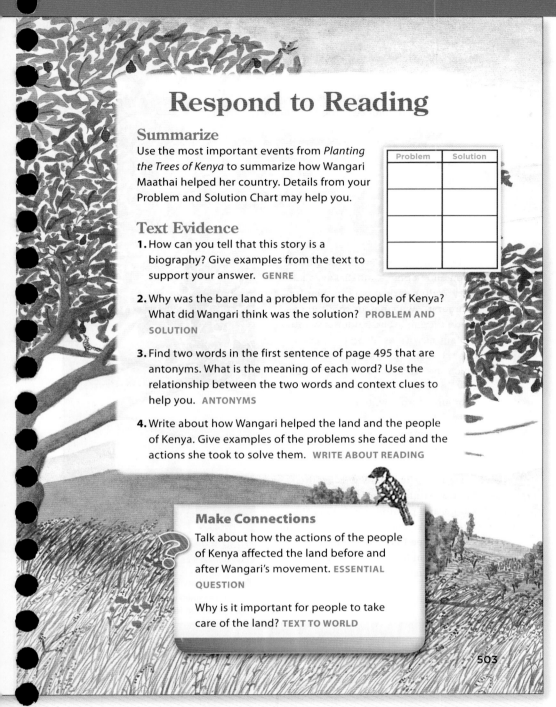

## Respond to Reading

### Summarize

Use the most important events from *Planting the Trees of Kenya* to summarize how Wangari Maathai helped her country. Details from your Problem and Solution Chart may help you.

| Problem | Solution |
|---------|----------|
|         |          |
|         |          |
|         |          |

### Text Evidence

1. How can you tell that this story is a biography? Give examples from the text to support your answer. **GENRE**

2. Why was the bare land a problem for the people of Kenya? What did Wangari think was the solution? **PROBLEM AND SOLUTION**

3. Find two words in the first sentence of page 495 that are antonyms. What is the meaning of each word? Use the relationship between the two words and context clues to help you. **ANTONYMS**

4. Write about how Wangari helped the land and the people of Kenya. Give examples of the problems she faced and the actions she took to solve them. **WRITE ABOUT READING**

> #### Make Connections
> Talk about how the actions of the people of Kenya affected the land before and after Wangari's movement. **ESSENTIAL QUESTION**
>
> Why is it important for people to take care of the land? **TEXT TO WORLD**

503

## Make Connections · *Analytical Writing*

**Essential Question** Have partners work together to cite evidence from the text to list one cause of the problem and four environmental effects. Ask students to identify solutions that reversed these effects.

**Text to World** Discuss the possible effects of replanting trees, such as keeping the soil in place, maintaining water supplies, providing food, and keeping people, animals, and the environment healthy.

# Respond to Reading

## Summarize

Review the problem and solution using students' organizers. Model how to use the information to summarize *Planting the Trees of Kenya*.

*Analytical Writing* **Write About Reading: Summarize** Remind students that a summary is a restatement of main ideas and important details.

Ask students to write a summary of the story using the problem and the solution. Remind them to begin with a sentence that names the title, genre, and subject.

## Text Evidence

1. **Genre** <u>Answer</u> The story has traits of a biography: real subject, setting, and events; facts; quotations. <u>Evidence</u> The author states that Wangari's movement led to thirty million trees being planted.

2. **Problem and Solution** <u>Answer</u> The people lacked clean drinking water, firewood, and food for livestock. Wangari wanted to teach people to plant trees to restore the land. <u>Evidence</u> She asked the women, "Why not plant trees?"

3. **Synonyms and Antonyms** <u>Answer</u> *Wooded* and *treeless* are antonyms. *Wooded* means "covered with growing trees." Treeless means "without trees." <u>Evidence</u> "The woods gone" helps define treeless. "Once there had been" and "now" show a change from woods to bare land.

4. *Analytical Writing* **Write About Reading: Problem and Solution** Wangari urged people to plant trees to restore the land. The trees grew, the land became green again, and people grew and ate fruits and vegetables, which improved their health.

# Develop Comprehension

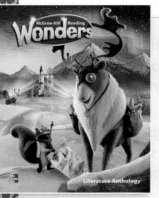

Literature Anthology

## "The Park Project"

### Text Complexity Range

**Lexile**

740 ▲ 1010
950

*TextEvaluator*™

23 ▲ 51
42

## Compare Texts  *Analytical Writing*

Students will read an expository text. Have students do a close reading of the text, **ask and answer questions** as they read, and then reread it and take notes. Then students will use their text evidence to compare and contrast this text with *Planting the Trees of Kenya*.

---

**CCSS** **Genre • Expository Text**

**Compare Texts**
Read about how students at one elementary school made a difference in their community.

# THE PARK PROJECT

Two third-grade students Adeline Dixon and Sophia Kimbell, saw that Letty Walter Park, a park in their Indiana community, was in poor condition and needed repairs. The students wanted to plant new trees along the park's creek, but that project required money, which the students did not have. So they decided to write a letter asking a community organization for money to **restore** the park.

"We wrote it by ourselves," Sophia said. "Our parents spell-checked, but that was it."

Happily, the money was granted. The two students and their classmates bought and planted trees along the park's creek. One tree was named The Survivor Tree because it had grown from a seed taken from a tree that survived the Oklahoma City bombing in 1995.

**Sophia Kimbell worked to improve Letty Walter Park in New Albany, Indiana.**

504

---

# A C T  Access Complex Text

## *What makes this text complex?*
### ▶ Prior Knowledge

### ▶ Prior Knowledge

Provide the following information about "The Survivor Tree" and the Oklahoma City bombing:

The Alfred P. Murrah Federal Building located in Oklahoma City, Oklahoma, housed many government offices. On April 19, 1995, the building was destroyed by an American in a bomb attack. Many people lost their lives.

Unfortunately, the park improvements did not last long. Later that year, powerful storms caused by a nearby hurricane destroyed most of the trees the students had planted. Only two trees remained standing, including The Survivor Tree. The third graders were saddened by the destruction, but they held on to their dream of improving the park.

Two years later, Adeline and Sophia, now fifth graders, wrote another letter to the same community organization. Again they **urged** the group to donate money so students could fix up Letty Walter Park. Again money was granted for planting trees and for further improvements, such as adding two park benches and spreading mulch—a mix of leaves and straw—on the playground.

Once they had supplies, there was plenty of work to do. More than 60 students from the local school pitched in to help. They performed a variety of tasks for their park project. Some planted trees or repainted wooden stalls. Others trimmed bushes, dug up weeds in the playground area, and removed garbage from the creek. The students even managed to **influence** their parents and others in their community to help around the park as well.

Teacher Scott Burch and students take a break beside the park's creek.

By the time all the work was completed, the park looked much greener and cleaner. Scott Burch, a teacher who helped organize the project, praised the students for what they had done. He believed that the children had learned an important lesson. "It shows the students that they can accomplish anything," he declared.

**Make Connections**
How did the students' actions have an impact on their community?
**ESSENTIAL QUESTION**

Think of another person or group you've read about who has restored a place. In what ways are the girls' actions different? Explain how each achieved results. **TEXT TO TEXT**

505

**LITERATURE ANTHOLOGY, pp. 504–505**

**1 Ask and Answer Questions**

What problem do the two girls want to solve? What is their solution?

*Analytical Writing* **Write About Reading** Write about the problem and the solution. Paraphrase your notes with a partner. (The park needs repairs. The girls write a letter, ask for money, buy trees, get volunteers to plant trees, and restore the park.)

## Make Connections *Analytical Writing*

**Essential Question** Have students paraphrase how the students' actions have impacted their community, identifying the problems and the solutions.

**Text to Text** Have student groups compare Dixon and Kimbell with Maathai. Provide focus questions: *What problems do they address? What steps are followed? What solutions do they achieve? How are the problems, steps, and solutions similar and different?* Ask a spokesperson from each group to share. (Possible responses: The park needs repairs; Kenya is bare due to tree loss. The girls write a letter to get money to buy trees; Wangari collects seeds. In both cases, volunteers plant trees to restore the area.)

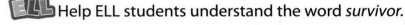

A more than 80-year-old American elm tree, located in a nearby parking lot, survived the bombing. The tree, an important symbol of survival and hope, is featured in the present-day memorial.

→ *What do the original tree and the park tree have in common?* (They have survived disasters and continue to inspire hope.)

**ELL** Help ELL students understand the word *survivor*.

→ The verb *survive* means "to continue to live after a dangerous event."

→ The suffix *-or* means "one who."

→ *What does* survivor *mean?* (one who continues to live after a dangerous event)

# → Word Study/Fluency

**MINILESSON 20 Mins**

## Number Prefixes *uni-, bi-, tri-, cent-*

**Go Digital**

**Number Prefixes** *uni-, bi-, tri-, cent-*

**Present the Lesson**

### OBJECTIVES

**CCSS** Know and apply grade-level phonics and word analysis skills in decoding words. Use combined knowledge of all letter-sound correspondences, syllabication patterns, and morphology (e.g., roots and affixes) to read accurately unfamiliar multisyllabic words in context and out of context. **RF.5.3a**

**CCSS** Read on-level prose and poetry orally with accuracy, appropriate rate, and expression on successive readings. **RF.5.4b**

Rate: 129–149 WCPM

### ACADEMIC LANGUAGE

• *expression, phrasing*

• Cognates: *expresión, fraseo*

## 1 Explain

Tell students that some common prefixes, such as *uni-, bi-, tri-,* and *cent-,* stand for numbers. Write the following on the board.

→ **uni-** means "one": A *unicycle* has one wheel.

→ **bi-** means "two": A *bicycle* has two wheels.

→ **tri-** means "three": A *tricycle* has three wheels.

→ **cent-** means "hundred": A *century* is one hundred years.

Point out that recognizing these prefixes and knowing their meanings can help students read words and determine their meanings.

## 2 Model

Write the following sentence on the board.

Everyone in the marching band wears a <u>uni</u>form during the show.

Underline the prefix *uni-,* and remind students that it means "one." Model using the meaning of the prefix to define *uniform* as "one form," or "one style of clothing."

## 3 Guided Practice

Write the following words on the board. Help students use the meanings of the number prefixes to define the words. Then have them use a dictionary to check their definitions.

| | | | |
|---|---|---|---|
| biped | bisect | triangle | binoculars |
| bilingual | centipede | tripod | unison |
| cents | unique | centimeter | triplet |

**View "Words to Save the World"**

**ELL**

Refer to the sound transfers chart to identify sounds that do not transfer in Spanish, Cantonese, Vietnamese, Hmong, and Korean.

## Read Multisyllabic Words

**Transition to Longer Words** Help students transition to reading multisyllabic words with number prefixes. Write the following prefixes and words on the board. Have students read the number prefix and the word in the second column. Then model how to read the longer words. Help students use the meaning of the number prefixes, as well as the meaning of common prefixes and suffixes, to determine the meanings of the longer words.

| | | |
|---|---|---|
| bi- | bicycle | bicyclist |
| cent- | centennial | bicentennial |
| uni- | uniform | uniformity |
| tri- | triangle | triangulation |

After the activity, have students use a dictionary to check their word meanings.

 FLUENCY ←

## Expression and Phrasing

**Explain/Model** Remind students that the use of proper expression helps make a writer's ideas clear in the text. Paying attention to phrasing, which is indicated by punctuation, helps create interest and makes the meaning of the text clear.

Model reading the first page of "Words to Save the World," **Reading/Writing Workshop** pages 424–427 Emphasize the use of proper expression and phrasing.

Remind students that you will be listening for their use of expression and phrasing as you monitor their reading during the week.

**Practice/Apply** Have partners alternate reading paragraphs in the passage, modeling the expression and phrasing you used.

## Daily Fluency Practice FLUENCY

Students can practice fluency using **Your Turn Practice Book** passages.

## Monitor and *Differentiate*

 **Quick Check**

Can students decode multisyllabic words with number prefixes? Can students read with appropriate expression and phrasing?

⬇

### Small Group Instruction

| | | |
|---|---|---|
| **If No** → | Approaching Level | Reteach pp. T234, T238 |
| | ELL | Develop pp. T251, T254 |
| **If Yes** → | On Level | Apply pp. T240–T241 |
| | Beyond Level | Apply pp. T244–T245 |

### ON-LEVEL PRACTICE BOOK p. 288

Word Study: Number Prefixes *uni-, bi-, tri-, cent-*

Name _____

| | | | |
|---|---|---|---|
| unison | triplet | unicorn | tripod |
| biweekly | bicycle | tricycle | unicycle |
| triangle | bisect | trio | uniform |
| centimeter | century | binoculars | universe |

**Read each definition below. Use clues in the definition, such as numbers and root words, to write the word from the box that matches the definition.**

1. a shape with three angles — triangle
2. one hundredth of a meter — centimeter
3. to separate into two sections — bisect
4. a cycle with three wheels — tricycle
5. a mythical animal with one horn — unicorn
6. a piece of clothing for one purpose — uniform
7. happening every two weeks — biweekly
8. a stand with three legs — tripod
9. a period of one hundred years — century
10. an optical device with two sets of lenses — binoculars
11. a cycle with only one wheel — unicycle
12. a group of three people — trio

288 Practice • Grade 5 • Unit 6 • Week 4

| APPROACHING p.288 | BEYOND p.288 | ELL p. 288 |
|---|---|---|

**Go** Digital

**www.connected.mcgraw-hill.com**
**RESOURCES**
**Research and Inquiry**

→ **Wrap Up the Week**
# Integrate Ideas

## RESEARCH AND INQUIRY

**Making a Difference**

### OBJECTIVES

**CCSS** Conduct short research projects that use several sources to build knowledge through investigation of different aspects of a topic. **W.5.7**

**CCSS** Include multimedia components (e.g., graphics, sound) and visual displays in presentations when appropriate to enhance the development of main ideas or themes. **SL.5.5**

• Take notes.
• Use skimming and scanning techniques.

### ACADEMIC LANGUAGE
*resources, display, skimming, scanning*

### Create a Research Display

Explain that students will work with partners to research the items most commonly thrown away as litter in the U.S. They will create displays of their findings, along with actual examples of items, to place on the Shared Research Board. Discuss the following steps:

**❶ Find Resources**  Have partners look for reliable print and online resources to help them identify the most commonly thrown-away items in the United States.

**❷ Research Littered Items**  Ask students to use skimming and scanning techniques to find relevant information in the resources they locate. Have them take notes about specific items that litter roadways, beaches, and waterways and the impact these items have on the environment. Use Research Process Checklist 1.

**❸ Guided Practice**  Help partners plan how to organize their information, along with images and examples of thrown-away items, on poster board.

**❹ Create the Project: Research Display**  Have partners create displays of facts, photographs, illustrations, and examples of items that are most commonly thrown away as litter. Each pair should give their display a title that reflects the content.

### Present the Research Display

Have partners add their display to the Shared Research Board. They should then discuss the displays with the class. Encourage students to suggest ways to reduce the types of litter identified in the displays.

**STEM**

# TEXT CONNECTIONS  *Analytical Writing*

## OBJECTIVES

**CCSS** Integrate information from several texts on the same topic in order to write or speak about the subject knowledgeably. **RI.5.9**

**CCSS** Engage effectively in a range of collaborative discussions with diverse partners, building on others' ideas and expressing their own clearly. Review the key ideas expressed and draw conclusions in light of information and knowledge gained from the discussions. **SL.5.1d**

### Text to Text

**Cite Evidence** Tell students they will work in groups to compare the information they have learned during the week about how human actions impact the world. Model how to make comparisons using the week's **Leveled Readers,** "Science Makes a Difference!," page T205, and "Words to Save the World," **Reading/ Writing Workshop** pages 424–427. Reread "Science Makes a Difference!" and have students review the week's selections and their notes and graphic organizers. Help them set up a Four-Door Foldable® to organize their findings. Students should record a brief summary of each problem and at least two steps the subject takes to solve the problem, and the solution.

**Present Information** Have groups meet to present their summaries and conclusions. Prompt discussion regarding the nature of problems and solutions. For example, one problem may have different solutions, or different steps may produce similar solutions. Regardless, all problems and solutions produce impacts—large or small—on the world.

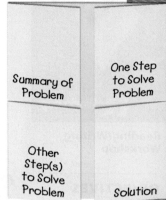

# WRITE ABOUT READING  *Analytical Writing*

## OBJECTIVES

**CCSS** Draw evidence from literary or informational texts to support analysis, reflection, and research. **W.5.9**

**CCSS** Compare and contrast the overall structure (e.g., chronology, comparison, cause/ effect, problem/ solution) of events, ideas, concepts, or information in two or more texts. **RI.5.5**

### Write an Analysis

Cite Evidence Using text evidence, students will analyze biographies to compare how two authors present events in a subject's life. Discuss how to analyze two texts by asking *how* and *why* questions.

→ How did the authors present information in each biography differently?

→ Why is the overall structure of the events important to understanding the subject's life?

Use **Your Turn Practice Book** page 289 to read and discuss the student model. Then have students select two biographies and review details they recorded about each text. Have them write to compare how each author presents information in a subject's life. Remind students that strong explanatory writing clearly states a topic and uses correct grammar and punctuation.

**Present Your Ideas** Have students share their paragraphs and discuss how the evidence they cited from the texts supports their ideas.

# → Readers to Writers

**Reading/Writing Workshop**

## Writing Traits: Ideas

### Focus on a Topic

**Expert Model** Explain that writers choose one topic to write about and formulate a main idea about that topic. They stay focused on their topic as they write, including only related information that supports or explains the main idea. They leave out information that does not relate to the main idea about the topic. When writing to share an opinion about a topic, writers include only reasons that clearly support and explain the opinion.

 **Read aloud** the expert model from "Words to Save the World: The Work of Rachel Carson." Ask students to listen for the writer's topic. Have students talk with a partner about the information the writer included that relates to the topic.

**Student Model** Remind students that writers choose one topic and organize their ideas around that topic. Read aloud the student model "A Deserving Citizen." As students follow along, have them identify the topic of the passage.

 **Invite** partners to talk about the model and the changes the writer made to keep the passage focused on the topic. Ask them to suggest other changes Olivia could make to focus ideas on her topic.

**Go Digital**

**Expert Model**

**Student Model**

### OBJECTIVES

**CCSS** Write opinion pieces on topics or texts, supporting a point of view with reasons and information. **W.5.1**

**CCSS** Write routinely over extended time frames (time for research, reflection, and revision) and shorter time frames (a single sitting or a day or two) for a range of discipline-specific tasks, purposes, and audiences. **W.5.10**

- Analyze models to identify focused writing.
- Write about a good citizen.
- Revise writing to focus on one topic.

### ACADEMIC LANGUAGE

- *focus, topic, related*
- Cognate: *relacionado*

 **Genre Writing**

**Opinion Writing**

For full writing process lessons and rubrics see:

→ Book Review, pp. T344–T349

→ Opinion Letter, pp. T350–T355

## CCSS Writing Traits — Ideas

# Readers to...

Writers usually **focus on a topic**, organizing their work around a main idea that is stated in a topic sentence early on in the text. In the paragraphs and sections that follow, they develop ideas related to the topic. Pay attention to the topic as you reread this passage from "Words to Save the World: The Work of Rachel Carson."

### Focus on a Topic

Which sentence establishes the topic of this paragraph?

Choose another sentence from the paragraph. How does it continue to focus on this topic?

**Expert Model**

From an early age, Rachel had loved to write. These writing skills proved useful to her career. She began by creating radio programs for the U.S. Bureau of Fisheries. She then became an editor and librarian for the agency. While she was working, she submitted her own articles to newspapers and magazines. Rachel eventually published three books about the ocean and its native plants and animals. This trilogy included *Under the Sea-Wind, The Sea Around Us,* and *The Edge of the Sea.*

432

# Writers

Olivia wrote a narrative to nominate a classmate for an award. Read Olivia's revision of this section.

**Student Model**

## A Deserving Citizen

Ty Kuhli deserves a good citizenship
award. His work in the library. Last
for    His efforts made the library better.
year he helped put the old card
catalog on the computer. He created
In addition,
a section for Braille books. It's in
the front corner. As if that were not
enough, he started a weekly program.
Volunteers read aloud to people with
vision inparments. Ty gladly shares
sp
his ideas. He still works to make our
and         tirelessly
library a fun place to visit.

433

**Editing Marks**

∧ Add
⌃ Add a comma.
◞ Take out.
SP Check spelling.
≡ Make a capital letter.

**Grammar Handbook**
Prepositional Phrases
See page 472.

### Your Turn

✔ What was Olivia's topic sentence?
✔ Find prepositions and the prepositional phrases Olivia used.
✔ Tell how Olivia's revisions improved her narrative.

*Go Digital!*
Write online in Writer's Workspace

---

**READING/WRITING WORKSHOP, pp. 432–433**

---

## ELL ENGLISH LANGUAGE LEARNERS SCAFFOLD

Provide support to help English Language Learners understand the writing trait.

| Beginning | Intermediate | Advanced/High |
|---|---|---|
| **Respond Orally** Help students complete the sentence frames. *The first sentence tells the topic: Ty deserves ____ for his work in the ____. Other sentences tell about the topic. He helped put the card catalog on ____. He also created a section for ____.* | **Practice** Ask students to complete the sentence frames. *The topic is ____. The other sentences support the topic by giving details about ____. For example, Ty helped ____. He created ____. He also ____.* | **Understand** Check for understanding. Ask: *What is the topic of the passage? How do you know? What do the other sentences in the passage tell?* |

# Writing Every Day: Ideas

**DAY**
 **1**

**DAY**
 **2**

## Writing Entry: Focus on a Topic

**Prewrite** Provide students with the prompt below.

*Choose a person you think deserves a good citizen award. Give reasons to support your opinion.*

Have partners list people that deserve an award. Ask them to jot down the reasons each person deserves an award.

**Draft** Have each student select a person to write about. Remind students to focus on their topic in their drafts.

## Focus on a Topic

Use **Your Turn Practice Book** page 290 to model focusing on a topic.

*Sonia Cruz deserves a good citizen award. She volunteers as a crossing guard for our school. She enjoys hiking and fishing. She also volunteers in the library every Friday. Her favorite book is* The Giver.

Model deleting the third sentence, which does not relate to the topic of why Sonia deserves the award.

Guide students to delete another sentence that does not relate to the topic.

## Writing Entry: Focus on a Topic

**Revise** Have students revise their writing from Day 1 by deleting details that do not support the topic.

Use the **Conferencing Routines**. Circulate among students and stop briefly to talk with individuals. Provide time for peer review.

**Edit** Have students use Grammar Handbook page 472 in the **Reading/Writing Workshop** to edit for errors in prepositional phrases.

# Conferencing Routines

## Teacher Conferences

**STEP 1**

Talk about the strengths of the writing.

*You provide a strong argument as to why _____ should win the award.*

**STEP 2**

Focus on how the writer uses the target trait for the week.

*You clearly stated your topic, but this detail does not relate to your main idea. Replace or delete it.*

**STEP 3**

Make concrete suggestions for revisions. Have students work on a specific assignment, such as those to the right, and then meet with you to review progress.

**DAY**

**3**

## Writing Entry: Focus on a Topic

**Prewrite** Ask students to search their Writer's Notebook for topics for a new draft. Or provide a prompt, such as the following:

*Is it more rewarding to help others or help yourself? Give reasons for your opinion.*

**Draft** Once students have chosen their topics, ask them to create a word web with the topic in the center. Then have them add related details they might include in their writing. Students can use their webs to begin their drafts.

**DAY**

**4**

## Writing Entry: Focus on a Topic

**Revise** Have students revise the draft writing from Day 3 by making sure they have focused on their topic. As students revise, hold teacher conferences with individual students. You may also wish to have students work with partners to peer conference.

**Edit** Invite students to review the rules for prepositional phrases on Grammar Handbook page 472 in the **Reading/Writing Workshop** and then check their drafts for errors.

**DAY**

**5**

## Share and Reflect

Discuss with the class what they learned about focusing on a topic. Invite volunteers to read and compare draft text with text that has been revised. Have students discuss the writing by explaining the importance of focusing on a topic. Allow time for individuals to reflect on their own writing progress and record observations in their Writer's Notebooks.

McGraw-Hill Companies Inc./Ken Karp, photographer

### Suggested Revisions

Provide specific direction to help focus young writers.

**Focus on a Sentence**
Read the draft and target one sentence for revision. *Your topic is _____. Revise this sentence to focus on the topic.*

**Focus on a Section**
Underline a section that needs to be revised. Provide specific suggestions. *Your topic is _____. This section is mostly about the topic. Remove any sentences that do not relate to the topic.*

**Focus on a Revision Strategy**
Underline a section. Have students use a specific revision strategy, such as deleting sentences. *Delete sentences that do not focus on the topic.*

# Peer Conferences

Focus peer response groups on maintaining a focus in writing.

- ☑ What is the topic?
- ☑ Which sentences relate to the topic?
- ☑ Which sentences should be removed because they do not relate to the topic?

**Grammar: Sentence Combining**

**Reading/Writing Workshop**

### OBJECTIVES

**CCSS** Use correlative conjunctions (e.g., *either/or, neither/nor*). **L.5.1e**

**CCSS** Use punctuation to separate items in a series. **L.5.2a**

**CCSS** Use knowledge of language and its conventions when writing, speaking, reading, or listening. Expand, combine, and reduce sentences for meaning, reader/listener interest, and style. **L.5.3a**

Proofread sentences.

**Go Digital**

**Sentence Combining**

**Grammar Activities**

---

## DAY 1

**DAILY LANGUAGE ACTIVITY**

**When she first arrived she didn't know nobody in our class. She is the most shyest girl in school.** (1: arrived,; 2: anyone; 3: the shyest)

### Introduce Sentence Combining

→ **Sentence combining** is reducing two or more simple sentences into one sentence.

→ Two simple sentences about the same subject can be combined into one compound sentence. They can also be combined with a compound predicate.

→ The **correlative conjunctions** *either/or* and *neither/nor* can be used to combine sentences.

Have partners discuss combining sentences using page 453 of the Grammar Handbook in **Reading/Writing Workshop**.

---

## DAY 2

**DAILY LANGUAGE ACTIVITY**

**Dear mrs Roberts,**
**You're cake tasted so well!**
**sincerely, Megan** (1: Mrs.; 2: Your; 3: good; 4: Sincerely)

### Review Sentence Combining

Remind students that sentences can be combined by using conjunctions.

### Combining Sentences with Adjectives, Adverbs, and Prepositional Phrases

→ Adding an adjective can combine two sentences that tell about the same noun.

→ If two sentences tell about the same action, adding an adverb can combine them.

→ If two sentences tell about the same location, adding a prepositional phrase can combine them.

---

 **TALK ABOUT IT**

**COLLABORATE**

### COMBINE SENTENCES

Have pairs write two simple sentences about how their actions can affect the world. The sentences should have the same subject. Students then combine their partner's sentences into one sentence.

### COMBINE TWO INTO ONE

Have groups choose a noun and an action. Ask students to write simple sentences on index cards and to use a noun and an action in each sentence. Then put the cards in a pile. Have students choose two cards at a time and then combine the sentences.

**DAY**  **3**

**DAY 5**

## DAILY LANGUAGE ACTIVITY

**When I am sick my mom makes me soop. She also brings me my green old blanket.** (1: sick,; 2: soup; 3: old green)

## DAILY LANGUAGE ACTIVITY

**Jordan pitched good on May 13 2012. She is the better pitcher in the league.** (1: well; 2: May 13,; 3: best)

## DAILY LANGUAGE ACTIVITY

**We ate italian food on sunday. It has a red, yummy sauce.** (1: Italian; 2: Sunday; 3: yummy red)

## Mechanics and Usage: Commas and Colons

→ Use commas in the greeting and closing of a friendly letter (e.g., *Dear Brandy, Your friend,*).

→ Use commas in addresses and dates (e.g., *Round Rock, TX; March 18, 2012*).

→ Use commas to separate items in a series (e.g., *Monday, Tuesday, Wednesday, and Thursday*).

→ Use a colon after a salutation or greeting in a business letter (e.g., *Dear Senator Rogers:*)

→ A colon is used to separate hours, minutes, and seconds: *6:45*.

→ Use a colon to introduce lists.

Refer students to Grammar Handbook pages 478–479.

**See Grammar Practice Reproducibles pp. 141–145.**

## Proofread

Have students correct errors in this letter:

> Dear melanie:
>
> I need these things from the store apples grapes, bread, and eggs. Could you pick it up by 3;00!
>
> Thanks
> Jill

(1: Melanie,; 2: store:; 3: apples, 4: them; 5: 3:00?; 6: Thanks, )

Have students check their work using Grammar Handbook pages 478–479 on colons and commas.

## Assess

Use the Daily Language Activity and Grammar Practice Reproducibles page 145 for assessment.

## Reteach

Use Grammar Practice Reproducibles pages 141–144 and selected pages from the Grammar Handbook for additional reteaching. Remind students that it is important to combine sentences to add variety to writing and speaking.

Check students' writing for use of the skill and listen for it in their speaking. Assign Grammar Revision Assignments in their Writer's Notebooks as needed.

## REVISE WITH FEEDBACK

Have students choose a topic and write a paragraph. Students share with a partner who then suggests ways to combine the sentences in the paragraph. Students then revise their paragraphs.

## REDUCE FOUR SENTENCES

Display these sentences: *Lyn wore a cap. It had a duck on the bill. The duck was red. The cap was inexpensive.* Have partners work together to combine the sentences. Have students share and compare their work.

## NAME THAT SENTENCE

Display a few paragraphs from this week's readings that allow for sentence combining. Have students combine sentences and share them with the class.

# Spelling: Number Prefixes *uni-, bi-, tri-, cent-*

**OBJECTIVES**

**CCSS** Spell grade-appropriate words correctly, consulting references as needed.
**L.5.2e**

## Spelling Words

| | | |
|---|---|---|
| tripod | bicycle | centipede |
| triplet | tricycle | centimeter |
| unicorn | unicycle | century |
| uniform | triangle | binoculars |
| unison | bisect | universe |
| biweekly | trio | university |
| triple | unify | |

**Review** cereal, terrace, atlas
**Challenge** bilingual, trilogy

## Differentiated Spelling

**Approaching Level**

| | | |
|---|---|---|
| tripod | bicycle | centipede |
| triplet | tricycle | centimeter |
| unicorn | unicycle | century |
| uniform | tricolor | bimonthly |
| unit | bilevel | unity |
| biweekly | trio | university |
| triple | unify | |

**Beyond Level**

| | | |
|---|---|---|
| triumvirate | bilingual | centipede |
| triplet | tricycle | centimeter |
| unicorn | unicycle | century |
| unilateral | triangle | binoculars |
| unison | bisect | universe |
| binary | trio | university |
| triathlon | trilogy | |

## DAY 1

### Assess Prior Knowledge

Read the spelling words aloud, emphasizing the prefix in each word.

Explain that some common prefixes stand for numbers. Underline the prefixes in these words as you pronounce them: <u>uni</u>cycle, <u>bi</u>cycle, <u>tri</u>pod, and <u>cent</u>ury. Explain the meanings of the prefixes: *uni-* means "one"; *bi-* means "two"; *tri-* means "three"; *centi- (cent-)* means "hundred."

Demonstrate sorting spelling words by number prefixes under the key words *uniform, bicycle, tripod,* and *century.* Sort a few spelling words. Ask students to name other everyday words with the same prefixes.

Use the Dictation Sentences from Day 5 to give the pretest. Say the underlined word, read the sentence, and repeat the word. Have students write the words. Then have students check their papers.

## DAY 2

### Spiral Review

Review these words from mythology: *cereal, terrace, atlas.* Read each sentence below, repeat the review word, and have students write the word.

1. I prefer oatmeal to cold <u>cereal</u>.
2. The couple had breakfast on the hotel's lovely <u>terrace</u>.
3. Lynn searched for the capital of Romania in an <u>atlas</u>.

Have students trade papers and check their spellings.

**Challenge Words** Review this week's spellings of number prefixes. Read each sentence below, repeat the challenge word, and have students write the word.

1. The <u>bilingual</u> woman speaks Spanish and English.
2. Nikki bought a popular <u>trilogy</u> of books to read during winter break.

Have students check and correct their spellings and write the words in their word study notebooks.

## WORD SORTS

**COLLABORATE**

### OPEN SORT

Have students cut apart the **Spelling Word Cards** in the Online Resource Book and initial the back of each card. Have them read the words aloud with partners. Then have partners do an **open sort**. Have them record their sorts in their word study notebooks.

### PATTERN SORT

Complete the **pattern sort** from Day 1 by using the boldfaced key words on the Spelling Word Cards. Point out the different number prefixes. Partners should compare and check their sorts. Have them record their sorts in their word study notebooks.

## DAY 3

### Word Meanings

Have students copy the cloze sentences below into their word study notebooks. Say the sentences aloud. Then ask students to fill in the blanks with a spelling word.

1. My _____ got dirty when I fell in some mud. (uniform)
2. The photographer set up her camera on a _____. (tripod)
3. Paul hopes to earn a scholarship to the state's best _____. (university)

Challenge students to create cloze sentences for their other spelling, review, or challenge words. Have students post their sentences on the board.

## DAY 4

### Proofread and Write

Write these sentences on the board. Have students circle and correct each misspelled word.

1. Julian got a bycycle to replace the trycycle he'd outgrown. (bicycle, tricycle)
2. I spotted a treeo of bluejays with my binnoculars. (trio, binoculars)
3. The byweekly paper has been published for a centtury. (biweekly, century)
4. The unniform for the univversity team is red and gold. (uniform, university)

**Error Correction** Remind students that the spelling of each number prefix remains the same from word to word.

**See Phonics/Spelling Reproducibles pp. 169–174.**

### SPEED SORT

Have partners do a **speed sort** to see who is fastest and then compare and discuss their sorts. Then have them do a word hunt in this week's readings to find words with number prefixes. Have them record the words in their word study notebooks.

### BLIND SORT

Have partners do a **blind sort**: one reads a Spelling Word Card; the other tells under which key word it belongs. Have students explain how they sorted the words. Then have them play Go Fish with the cards, using words with *uni-*, *bi-*, *tri-*, and *cent-* prefixes as the "fish."

## DAY 5

### Assess

Use the Dictation Sentences for the posttest. Have students list the misspelled words in their word study notebooks. Look for students' use of these words in their writings.

**Dictation Sentences**

1. A <u>tripod</u> supports the camera.
2. The <u>triplet</u> looks like her sisters.
3. The <u>unicorn</u> is a graceful creature.
4. I wore my school <u>uniform</u>.
5. The group spoke in <u>unison</u>.
6. The magazine comes <u>biweekly</u>.
7. Our city is <u>triple</u> the size of yours.
8. Jackie likes to ride her <u>bicycle</u>.
9. Ted prefers the <u>tricycle</u>.
10. The clown rode a <u>unicycle</u>.
11. A <u>triangle</u> has three sides.
12. To <u>bisect</u> is to divide into two.
13. A <u>trio</u> of singers performed.
14. Pep rallies can <u>unify</u> the school.
15. The <u>centipede</u> crawled slowly.
16. Tanya measured a <u>centimeter</u>.
17. A <u>century</u> is one hundred years.
18. I looked through the <u>binoculars</u>.
19. The <u>universe</u> is a big place.
20. He attends a state <u>university</u>.

Have students self-correct their tests.

# Build Vocabulary

## OBJECTIVES

**CCSS** Determine or clarify the meaning of unknown and multiple-meaning words and phrases based on grade 5 reading and content, choosing flexibly from a range of strategies. **L.5.4**

**CCSS** Demonstrate understanding of figurative language, word relationships, and nuances in word meanings. Use the relationship between particular words (e.g., synonyms, antonyms, homographs) to better understand each of the words. **L.5.5c**

Expand vocabulary by adding inflectional endings and suffixes.

### Vocabulary Words

| | |
|---|---|
| export | native |
| glistening | plantations |
| influence | restore |
| landscape | urged |

## Go Digital

**Vocabulary**

**Vocabulary Activities**

---

## DAY 1

### Connect to Words

Practice this week's vocabulary.

1. Where might the United States **export** a product?
2. Would you describe a diamond or a rock as **glistening**?
3. How do advertisements **influence** people?
4. Describe the **landscape** we see from the window.
5. Which country is your **native** country?
6. Are you likely to find a **plantation** in a city or in the country?
7. What do people **restore**?
8. Have you ever **urged** a friend to do something?

---

## DAY 2

### Expand Vocabulary

Help students generate different forms of this week's words by adding, changing, or removing inflectional endings.

→ Draw a T-chart on the board. Write *plantations* in the second column. Then write *plantation* in the first column. Read aloud the words with students.

→ Have students share sentences using each form of *plantations*.

→ Students can fill in the chart for *export* and *landscape*, and then share sentences using the different forms of the words.

→ Have students copy the chart in their word study notebooks.

---

# BUILD MORE VOCABULARY

**COLLABORATE**

## ACADEMIC VOCABULARY

→ Display *accuracy, awareness,* and *regulations.*

→ Define the words and discuss their meanings with students.

→ Write *unaware* under *awareness.* Have partners look up and define words with the same root. Write the words under *awareness.* Have partners ask and answer questions using the words.

→ Repeat with *accuracy* and *regulations.*

## HOMOPHONES

Remind students that homophones sound alike but have different meanings and spellings.

→ Write *hall* and *haul.* Ask students to tell what each word means.

→ Ask partners to brainstorm and discuss other homophone pairs.

→ Have students write sentences for two of the word pairs in their list.

→ Have students write the word pairs and sentences in their word study notebooks.

**DAY**
**3**

## Reinforce the Words

Review this week's and last week's vocabulary words. Have students orally complete each sentence stem.

1. My <u>native</u> language is _____.
2. Sam <u>urged</u> us to care for the <u>landscape</u> by _____.
3. This food is an <u>export</u> from _____.
4. I saw a <u>glistening</u> _____.
5. We visited two <u>plantations</u>, where we saw _____.
6. Squirrels <u>forage</u> for and <u>cache</u> _____.
7. <u>Dormant</u> plants can survive <u>frigid</u> weather by _____.
8. The <u>agile</u> dancers can _____.
9. One thing that <u>insulates</u> people from cold is _____.

**DAY**
**4**

## Connect to Writing

→ Have students write sentences in their word study notebooks using this week's vocabulary.

→ Tell them to write sentences that provide word information they learned from this week's readings.

→ **ELL** Provide the Day 3 sentence stems 1–5 for students needing extra support.

**Write About Vocabulary** Have students write something they learned from this week's words in their word study notebooks. For example, they might write about things they've seen *glistening* or about people who have had an *influence* on their lives.

**DAY**
**5**

## Word Squares

Ask students to create Word Squares for each vocabulary word.

→ In the first square, students write the word. (e.g., *glistening*)

→ In the second square, students write their own definition of the word and any related words, such as synonyms. (e.g., *gleaming, shining*)

→ In the third square, students draw a simple illustration that will help them remember the word. (e.g., drawing of star shining brightly in the sky)

→ In the fourth square, students write nonexamples, including antonyms for the word. (e.g., *dull, lackluster*)

Have partners discuss their squares.

### SYNONYMS AND ANTONYMS

Elicit from students the definition of synonyms and antonyms.

→ Display **Your Turn Practice Book pages 283–284.** Model using the synonym *love* to figure out the meaning of *affection* in the second paragraph.

→ Have students complete page 287.

→ Partners can confirm meanings in a print or online dictionary.

### SHADES OF MEANING

Point out that some of the meanings of *restore* have positive connotations. Draw a word web and write *restore* in the center.

→ Have small groups use a thesaurus to find words with similar meanings and add them to the web (e.g., *reinstate, refurbish, rebuild, renew, replenish*).

→ Ask groups to underline the words with positive connotations (*renew, replenish*). Have groups share their webs with the class.

### MORPHOLOGY

Use *urged* as a springboard for students to learn more words. Draw a T-chart. Write the base word *urge* in the left column.

→ In the right column of the T-chart, write *-ent* and *-ency*. Discuss how the suffixes change the meaning and part of speech.

→ Have students add the suffixes to *urge*. Review the meanings of the new words.

→ Ask partners to do a search for other words with these suffixes.

# → Approaching Level

## Leveled Reader:
## *Marjory Stoneman Douglas: Guardian of the Everglades*

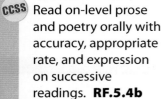

**Lexile** 760
*TextEvaluator*™ 37

---

### OBJECTIVES

**CCSS** Explain the relationships or interactions between two or more individuals, events, ideas, or concepts in a historical, scientific, or technical text based on specific information in the text. **RI.5.3**

**CCSS** Read on-level prose and poetry orally with accuracy, appropriate rate, and expression on successive readings. **RF.5.4b**

---

### ACADEMIC LANGUAGE
• biography, problem, solution, ask and answer questions
• Cognates: *biografía, problema, solución*

---

## Go Digital

**Leveled Readers**

---

### Before Reading

#### Preview and Predict

→ Read the Essential Question with students.

→ Have students preview the title, table of contents, and first page of *Marjory Stoneman Douglas: Guardian of the Everglades*. Students should predict what they think the selection will be about. Encourage them to confirm or revise their predictions as they read.

#### Review Genre: Biography

Tell students that this text is a biography. A biography tells the true story of someone's life. The author of a biography uses third person and presents factual information about the subject's life, influences, contributions, and obstacles. Have students identify features of a biography in *Marjory Stoneman Douglas: Guardian of the Everglades*.

### During Reading

#### Close Reading

**Note Taking:** Ask students to use their graphic organizer as they read.

**Page 2** *Contrast the way that Douglas viewed the Everglades with the way many other people viewed it.* (Many people saw a useless swamp; Douglas saw the Everglades' rich variety of life and beauty.)

**Pages 3–6** *Douglas used her skills as a writer to solve problems. What problems did she work to solve with her writing?* (suffering caused by World War I, lack of women's rights, lack of decent living conditions, threats to the Everglades from developers) *What synonym on page 5 helps you better understand the meaning of* plight? (*suffering*)

**Pages 7–9** *The author includes excerpts from Douglas's writing, including this metaphor: the Everglades are a glistening "river of grass." To what does Douglas compare the Everglades?* (a river) *Discuss how this comparison might cause people to view the Everglades differently.* (A river is something free, wild, and beautiful. This comparison may have helped people view the Everglades in the same way and want to protect them.)

**Use Graphic Organizer**

**Pages 10–12** *What antonym in the text helps you better understand the meaning of* inhospitable? *(welcoming) Despite the acres set aside as a national park, threats to the Everglades continued. How did Douglas solve the problem of loss of water in the Everglades, which would affect the ecosystem of Southern Florida?* (She asked polluters to clean up the water and pushed to get rid of canals.)

**Pages 13–14** *Ask a partner a question about how Marjory Douglas's actions impacted the environment and the larger world. Your partner should answer the question by paraphrasing information from the text.*

### After Reading

**Respond to Reading** Revisit the Essential Question and ask students to complete the Respond to Reading section on page 15.

**Analytical Writing** **Write About Reading** Check that students have correctly used text details to explain how Douglas helped the Everglades and the people of Florida.

### Fluency: Expression and Phrasing

**Model** Model reading page 9 with proper expression and phrasing. Next reread the page aloud and have students read along with you.

**Apply** Have students practice reading the passage with partners.

## PAIRED READ

**Leveled Reader**

# "The Story of the Tree Musketeers"

### Make Connections: Write About It ✎ *Analytical Writing*

Before reading, ask students to note that the genre of this text is expository text. Then discuss the Essential Question. After reading, ask students to write connections between what they learned from *Marjory Stoneman Douglas: Guardian of the Everglades* and "The Story of the Tree Musketeers."

## FOCUS ON SCIENCE

Students can extend their knowledge of environmental issues by completing the activity on page 20. **STEM**

### Literature Circles

Ask students to conduct a literature circle using the Thinkmark questions to guide the discussion. You may wish to have a whole-class discussion, using information in both selections of the Leveled Reader, about the impact our actions have on the world.

## Level Up

**Level-up lessons available online.**

**IF** students read the **Approaching Level** fluently and answered the questions

**THEN** pair them with students who have proficiently read the **On Level** and have students

• echo-read the **On Level** main selection.

• mark with self-stick notes a problem and solution described in the biography.

### A C T Access Complex Text

The **On Level** challenges students by including more **domain-specific words** and **complex sentence structures**.

# → Approaching Level

## Word Study/Decoding

### REVIEW WORDS WITH NUMBER PREFIXES

**TIER 2**

**OBJECTIVES**
**CCSS** Know and apply grade-level phonics and word analysis skills in decoding words. Use combined knowledge of all letter-sound correspondences, syllabication patterns, and morphology (e.g., roots and affixes) to read accurately unfamiliar multisyllabic words in context and out of context. **RF.5.3a**

Decode words with number prefixes *uni-* and *bi-*.

**I Do** Review with students that many common prefixes stand for numbers. Remind students that *uni-* means "one," and *bi-* means "two." Write these prefixes and their meanings on the board.

**We Do** Write the word *unicycle* on the board and read the word aloud. Underline the number prefix *uni-*. Model how to use the meaning of the prefix *uni-* to determine that *unicycle* is a cycle with one wheel.

**You Do** Add the words *bicycle* and *uniform* to the board. Read the words aloud. Have students identify each number prefix and tell its meaning. Then have them use the meanings of the number prefixes to determine the meanings of *bicycle* and *uniform*.

### BUILD WORDS WITH NUMBER PREFIXES

**TIER 2**

**OBJECTIVES**
**CCSS** Use combined knowledge of all letter-sound correspondences, syllabication patterns, and morphology (e.g., roots and affixes) to read accurately unfamiliar multisyllabic words in context and out of context. **RF.5.3a**

Build words with number prefixes *bi-*, *tri-*, and *cent-*.

**I Do** Display the **Word-Building Cards** *bi* and *tri* and remind students that *tri-* means "three." Write the words *monthly* and *annual* on the board. Read them aloud.

**We Do** Work with students to combine the Word-Building Cards and words to create new words. Have them chorally read the words *bimonthly* and *triannual*. Have students use the meanings of the number prefixes to determine the meanings of the words.

**You Do** Write on the board other words and word parts such as *focal, angle,* and *igrade*. Display the Word-Building Cards *bi, tri,* and *cent* ("hundred") and ask students to add them to the words or word parts to build new words (*bifocal, triangle, centigrade*). Have them determine the meaning of each word, using the number prefixes and a dictionary as necessary.

## PRACTICE WORDS WITH NUMBER PREFIXES

**OBJECTIVES**

(CCSS) Know and apply grade-level phonics and word analysis skills in decoding words. Use combined knowledge of all letter-sound correspondences, syllabication patterns, and morphology (e.g., roots and affixes) to read accurately unfamiliar multisyllabic words in context and out of context. **RF.5.3a**

Practice words with number prefixes *uni-*, *bi-*, *tri-*, and *cent-*.

 **I Do** Write these words on the board: *unify, triplet*. Read each word aloud, identify the number prefix and its meaning, and give the meaning of the word.

 **We Do** Write the words *unicellular* and *bivalve* on the board. Model how to decode and figure out the meaning of the first word. Then have students decode and give the meaning of the remaining word. As necessary, help them identify and define the number prefix in each word.

 **You Do** To provide additional practice, write these words on the board. Read aloud the first word, identify the number prefix, and give the word's meaning.

| | | | |
|---|---|---|---|
| unique | centimeter | bilingual | triathlete |
| biweekly | universe | centipede | bilevel |
| triangle | centennial | tricolor | union |

Then have students read aloud the remaining words. Ask them to identify each number prefix and give the meaning of each word. Have them use a dictionary, as necessary.

Afterward, point to the words in the list in random order for students to read chorally.

### ELL ENGLISH LANGUAGE LEARNERS

For the **ELLs** who need **phonics, decoding,** and **fluency** practice, use scaffolding methods as necessary to ensure students understand the meaning of the words. Refer to the **Language Transfers Handbook** for phonics elements that may not transfer in students' native languages.

# Approaching Level

## Vocabulary

### REVIEW HIGH-FREQUENCY WORDS

**TIER 2**

 **OBJECTIVES**
Acquire and use accurately grade-appropriate general academic and domain-specific words and phrases, including those that signal contrast, addition, and other logical relationships (e.g., *however, although, nevertheless, similarly, moreover, in addition*).
**L.5.6**

 **I Do** Use **High-Frequency Word Cards** 231–240. Display one word at a time, following the routine:

Display the word. Read the word. Then spell the word.

 **We Do** Ask students to state the word and spell the word with you. Model using the word in a sentence and have students repeat after you.

 **You Do** Display the word. Ask students to say the word then spell it. When completed, quickly flip through the word card set as students chorally read the words. Provide opportunities for students to use the words in speaking and writing. For example, provide sentence starters such as *I wish I could* _____. Ask students to write each word in their Writer's Notebook.

### REVIEW VOCABULARY WORDS

**TIER 2**

**OBJECTIVES**
Acquire and use accurately grade-appropriate general academic and domain-specific words and phrases, including those that signal contrast, addition, and other logical relationships (e.g., *however, although, nevertheless, similarly, moreover, in addition*).
**L.5.6**

 **I Do** Display each **Visual Vocabulary Card** and state the word. Explain how the photograph illustrates the word. State the example sentence and repeat the word.

 **We Do** Point to the word on the card and read the word with students. Ask them to repeat the word. Engage students in structured partner talk about the image as prompted on the back of the vocabulary card.

 **You Do** Display each visual in random order, hiding the word. Have students match the definitions and context sentences of the words to the visuals displayed.

## IDENTIFY RELATED WORDS

**OBJECTIVES**

 Demonstrate understanding of figurative language, word relationships, and nuances in word meanings. Use the relationship between particular words (e.g., synonyms, antonyms, homographs) to better understand each of the words. **L.5.5c**

 **I Do** Display the *glistening* **Visual Vocabulary Card** and say aloud the word set *glistening, gleaming, dull, shiny*. Point out that the word *dull* does not belong.

 **We Do** Display the vocabulary card for the word *export*. Say aloud the word set *export, distribute, sell, keep*. With students, identify the word that does not belong and discuss why.

 **You Do** Using the word sets below, display the remaining cards one at a time, saying aloud the word set. Ask students to identify the word that does not belong.

landscape, scenery, interior, outdoors

native, inborn, foreign, natural

plantations, homesteads, farms, cities

urged, begged, discouraged, insisted

influence, guide, persuade, obstruct

restore, return, undo, reinstate

## SYNONYMS AND ANTONYMS

**OBJECTIVES**

 Demonstrate understanding of figurative language, word relationships, and nuances in word meanings. Use the relationship between particular words (e.g., synonyms, antonyms, homographs) to better understand each of the words. **L.5.5c**

Use synonyms and antonyms to determine the meaning of unfamiliar words.

**I Do** Remind students that synonyms have the same, or almost the same, meaning. Antonyms have the opposite, or nearly the opposite, meaning. Students can use a pair of synonyms or antonyms in a text to better understand the meaning of an unfamiliar word in the pair. Display the Comprehension and Fluency passage on **Approaching Reproducibles** pages 283–284. Choral-read the second paragraph. Point to the word *affection* in the phrase *affection for nature*.

**Think Aloud** I see the phrase *love of the land* in the second sentence, which helps me recognize that *affection* is a synonym for *love*. So affection for nature is a love of or fondness for nature.

 **We Do** Have students point to the word *private* in paragraph 2. Point out the antonym *public* in the same sentence. Guide students to use the meaning of *public* ("can be used by everyone") to understand that *private* has the opposite meaning ("can be used only by a certain individual or group").

 **You Do** Have partners use the relationship between synonyms and antonyms to better understand the meanings of *generate* (page 283, paragraph 3) and *demonstrations* (page 284, paragraph 3).

# → Approaching Level

## Comprehension

### FLUENCY

 **OBJECTIVES**
Read on-level prose and poetry orally with accuracy, appropriate rate, and expression on successive readings. **RF.5.4b**

Read fluently with good expression and phrasing.

 **I Do** Explain that phrasing means grouping words that go together. Reading with expression means changing the sound of one's voice to show meaning or place emphasis. Read the first paragraph of the Comprehension and Fluency passage on **Approaching Reproducibles** pages 283–284. Tell students to listen for the way you group words into phrases, pausing slightly after the phrase, and how you raise your voice slightly at the end of a question.

 **We Do** Read the next two paragraphs aloud, and have students repeat each sentence after you while imitating your phrasing and expression. Point out that you grouped several words into phrases that made sense and that you emphasized the most important words in each sentence.

 **You Do** Have partners take turns reading sentences from the Comprehension and Fluency passage. Remind them to focus on reading with correct phrasing and good expression. Listen in and provide corrective feedback as needed by modeling proper fluency.

### IDENTIFY IMPORTANT EVENTS

**TIER 2**

 **OBJECTIVES**
Explain the relationships or interactions between two or more individuals, events, ideas, or concepts in a historical, scientific, or technical text based on specific information in the text. **RI.5.3**

Identify important events.

 **I Do** Remind students that in a biography, the author relates many events in a subject's life. Identifying those that are most important, including challenges the person faced and actions he or she took to solve those problems, can help readers better understand the impact the person had on the world.

 **We Do** Read the first two paragraphs of the Comprehension and Fluency passage on **Approaching Reproducibles** pages 283–284. Guide students to identify important events in Gaylord Nelson's life and record them in a list.

 **You Do** Have students read the rest of the passage. After each paragraph, have them write down other important events in Gaylord Nelson's life. Review their lists with them and help them explain why the events they chose are important.

## REVIEW TEXT STRUCTURE: PROBLEM AND SOLUTION

**OBJECTIVES**

Explain the relationships or interactions between two or more individuals, events, ideas, or concepts in a historical, scientific, or technical text based on specific information in the text. **RI.5.3**

 Remind students that an author can organize a text by presenting a series of problems and solutions. In a biography, the author may describe a problem the subject faced and then describe the action the subject took to solve or overcome the problem.

 Choral-read the first two paragraphs of the Comprehension and Fluency passage on **Approaching Reproducibles** pages 283–284. Refer to the list of important events the students have already compiled. Model how to use these events to identify the problems Gaylord Nelson faced (how to protect natural resources) and ways he solved them (starting a program that turned private land into wildlife areas and public parks).

 Have partners read the rest of the passage and identify problems that Gaylord Nelson faced and the actions he took to solve them.

## SELF-SELECTED READING

**OBJECTIVES**

Explain the relationships or interactions between two or more individuals, events, ideas, or concepts in a historical, scientific, or technical text based on specific information in the text. **RI.5.3**

Ask and answer questions to increase understanding.

### Read Independently

Have students choose a biography for sustained silent reading. Remind students that:

→ good readers ask themselves questions about a text before, while, and after they read. They look for answers in the text to make sure they understand it.

→ as they read, they should look for problems the subject has faced and how he or she solved them.

### Read Purposefully

Have students record problems and solutions on Graphic Organizer 142 as they read independently. After students finish, they can conduct a Book Talk about what they read.

→ Students should share their organizers and answer this question: *How did the person solve problems in his or her own life and the world at large?*

→ They should also tell the group if there were any sections they reread to increase their understanding.

**On Level**

## Leveled Reader:
# *Marjory Stoneman Douglas: Guardian of the Everglades*

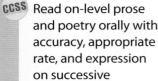

**Lexile** 890
*TextEvaluator*™ 48

---

### OBJECTIVES

**CCSS** Explain the relationships or interactions between two or more individuals, events, ideas, or concepts in a historical, scientific, or technical text based on specific information in the text. **RI.5.3**

**CCSS** Read on-level prose and poetry orally with accuracy, appropriate rate, and expression on successive readings. **RF.5.4b**

---

### ACADEMIC LANGUAGE

• biography, problem, solution, ask and answer questions

• Cognates: *biografía, problema, solución*

---

**Go Digital**

**Leveled Readers**

**Use Graphic Organizer**

### Before Reading

→ Read the Essential Question with students.

→ Have students preview the title, table of contents, and first page of *Marjory Stoneman Douglas: Guardian of the Everglades*. Students should predict what they think the selection will be about. Encourage them to confirm or revise their predictions as they read.

### Review Genre: Biography

Tell students that this text is a biography. A biography tells the true story of someone's life. The author of a biography uses third person and presents factual information about the subject's life, influences, contributions, and obstacles. Have students identify features of a biography in *Marjory Stoneman Douglas: Guardian of the Everglades*.

### During Reading

#### Close Reading

**Note Taking:** Ask students to use their graphic organizer as they read.

**Pages 2–3** *Contrast the way that many people viewed the Everglades with the way Douglas viewed it.* (Many viewed it as a useless swamp, but Douglas recognized its rich variety of life, uniqueness, and beauty.)

**Pages 4–5** *What environmental issues did Douglas's father attempt to address in his newspaper?* (the preservation of Miami's older neighborhoods and the Everglades) *What synonym on page 5 helps you better understand the meaning of* plight? (*suffering*)

**Pages 6–9** *Douglas also used her skills as a writer to address important social and environmental issues of the day. What issues did she address?* (decent living conditions, women's rights, protection of the Everglades, assistance for the poor) *With a partner, discuss why writing might be a good way to impact the world.* (Writers are able to reach and possibly influence many people when they publish.) *Douglas described the Everglades as a "river of grass." To what does Douglas compare the Everglades in this metaphor?* (a river) *How might the comparison influence readers?* (They might learn to view the Everglades more positively.)

**Pages 10–12** *How would draining water in the Everglades create potential problems for the ecosystem of Southern Florida?* (It would become a semitropical desert, and plants, animals, and people would not have enough water.) *What antonym on page 11 helps you understand the meaning of* inhospitable? (*welcoming*)

**Pages 13–14** *What additional threats to the Everglades did Douglas work to solve?* (Developers planned to build an airport near the Everglades, which Douglas helped prevent. She also pushed to make polluters clean up the water and to get rid of canals.)

## After Reading

**Respond to Reading** Revisit the Essential Question and ask students to complete the Respond to Reading section on page 15.

**Write About Reading** Check that students have correctly used text details to explain how Douglas helped the Everglades and the people of Florida.

### Fluency: Expression and Phrasing

**Model** Model reading page 9 with proper expression and phrasing. Next reread the page aloud and have students read along with you.

**Apply** Have students practice reading with partners.

## PAIRED READ

# "The Story of the Tree Musketeers"

**Make Connections:**
**Write About It**

**Leveled Reader**

Before reading, ask students to note that the genre of this text is expository text. Then discuss the Essential Question. After reading, ask students to write connections between what they learned from *Marjory Stoneman Douglas: Guardian of the Everglades* and "The Story of the Tree Musketeers" about the impact our actions can have on our environment.

## FOCUS ON SCIENCE

Students can extend their knowledge of environmental issues by completing the activity on page 20. **STEM**

# Literature Circles

Ask students to conduct a literature circle using the Thinkmark questions to guide the discussion. You may wish to have a whole-class discussion, using information in both selections in the Leveled Reader, about the impact our actions have on our world.

# Level Up

Level-up lessons available online.

**IF** students read the On Level fluently and answered the questions

**THEN** pair them with students who have proficiently read the Beyond Level and have students

- partner-read the Beyond Level main selection.
- list several problems and solutions described in the biography.

## A C T Access Complex Text

The Beyond Level challenges students through more complex **organizational structures** and **connection of ideas**.

 **On Level**

# Vocabulary

## REVIEW VOCABULARY WORDS

**OBJECTIVES**
CCSS Acquire and use accurately grade-appropriate general academic and domain-specific words and phrases, including those that signal contrast, addition, and other logical relationships (e.g., *however, although, nevertheless, similarly, moreover, in addition*). **L.5.6**

**I Do** Use the **Visual Vocabulary Cards** to review the key selection words *export, glistening, landscape, native, plantations,* and *urged*. Point to each word, read it aloud, and have students chorally repeat it.

**We Do** Ask these questions and help students respond.
→ When you *export* goods, do you bring them into or take them out of the country?
→ Would a ring or a piece of paper likely be *glistening*?
→ Would a picture of a *landscape* show the outdoors or indoors?

**You Do** Have students work in pairs to respond to these questions.
→ Is a person who is a *native* of a city born there or in a different place?
→ Are *plantations* most like towns or farms?
→ Are people frequently *urged* to vote or to eat junk food?

## SYNONYMS AND ANTONYMS

**OBJECTIVES**
CCSS Demonstrate understanding of figurative language, word relationships, and nuances in word meanings. Use the relationship between particular words (e.g., synonyms, antonyms, homographs) to better understand each of the words. **L.5.5c**

**I Do** Students can use a pair of synonyms or antonyms in a text to better understand the meaning of an unfamiliar word in the pair. Display the Comprehension and Fluency passage on **Your Turn Practice Book** pages 283–284. Read aloud the second paragraph and point to *affection*.

**Think Aloud** The phrase *love of the land* in the next sentence helps me recognize that *affection* and *love* are synonyms.

**We Do** Point to the word *preserved* in the same paragraph. Ask students to identify the synonym in the previous sentence.

**You Do** Have partners identify the synonyms or antonyms they use to determine the meanings of *generate* (page 283, paragraph 3), *legislation* (page 284, paragraph 2), *demonstrations* (page 284, paragraph 3), and *individuals* (page 284, paragraph 6).

# Comprehension

## REVIEW TEXT STRUCTURE: PROBLEM AND SOLUTION

**OBJECTIVES**

**CCSS** Explain the relationships or interactions between two or more individuals, events, ideas, or concepts in a historical, scientific, or technical text based on specific information in the text. **RI.5.3**

 Remind students that authors can organize a text by presenting a series of problems and solutions. In a biography, the author may describe a problem the subject faced and the action the subject took to solve or overcome it.

 Have volunteers read the first two paragraphs of the Comprehension and Fluency passage on **Your Turn Practice Book** pages 283–284. Guide students to identify a problem that Gaylord Nelson faced (preserving natural resources) and the action he took to solve it (turned private land into wildlife habitats and public parks).

 Have partners read the rest of the passage and identify the problems Gaylord Nelson faced and the actions he took to solve them. Remind them that a problem may be presented in one paragraph, and the solution may appear in a later paragraph or paragraphs.

## SELF-SELECTED READING

**OBJECTIVES**

**CCSS** Explain the relationships or interactions between two or more individuals, events, ideas, or concepts in a historical, scientific, or technical text based on specific information in the text. **RI.5.3**

Ask and answer questions to increase understanding.

### Read Independently

Have students choose a biography for sustained silent reading.

→ Remind them to ask questions as they read and to look for answers in the text.

→ Tell students to identify the problems the subject faced as well as his or her attempts to solve these problems.

### Read Purposefully

Encourage students to read different books to learn about a variety of important people.

→ Have them fill in the problems and solutions on Graphic Organizer 142.

→ They can use this organizer to help them summarize important information about the subject's life and work.

→ Ask students to share their reactions to the book with classmates.

# → Beyond Level

## Leveled Reader:
### *Marjory Stoneman Douglas: Guardian of the Everglades*

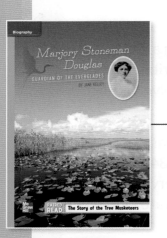

**Lexile** 970
*TextEvaluator*™ 52

Go
Digital

**Leveled Readers**

**Use Graphic Organizer**

---

### OBJECTIVES

**CCSS** Explain the relationships or interactions between two or more individuals, events, ideas, or concepts in a historical, scientific, or technical text based on specific information in the text. **RI.5.3**

**CCSS** Read on-level prose and poetry orally with accuracy, appropriate rate, and expression on successive readings. **RF.5.4b**

---

### ACADEMIC LANGUAGE

• *biography, problem, solution, ask and answer questions*

• Cognates: *biografía, problema, solución*

---

## Before Reading

→ Have students read the Essential Question.

→ Have students preview the title, table of contents, and first page of *Marjory Stoneman Douglas: Guardian of the Everglades* to make predictions about the content. Encourage students to confirm or revise their predictions as they read.

### Review Genre: Biography

Tell students that this text is a biography. A biography tells the true story of someone's life. The author of a biography uses third person and presents factual information about the subject's life, influences, contributions, and obstacles. Have students identify features of a biography in *Marjory Stoneman Douglas: Guardian of the Everglades*.

## During Reading

### Close Reading

**Note Taking:** Ask students to use their graphic organizer as they read.

**Pages 2–3** *Why does the author of the biography include quotations from Douglas and details about her childhood?* (Quotations and biographical details help readers better understand the subject of a biography.) *How does Douglas's writing show that her view of the Everglades was different from many other people's?* (She described the Everglades' uniqueness, simplicity, diversity, and harmony. Others saw only a useless swamp.)

**Pages 4–6** *How did Douglas's family help her become a writer who worked to solve social problems?* (Her grandmother and aunt sent her to college. Her father gave her a writing job at his newspaper, shared his passion for social issues, and eventually helped her become assistant editor of the newspaper.) *What synonym on page 5 helps you better understand the meaning of* plight? (*suffering*)

**Pages 7–9** *Read excerpts from Douglas's writing about the Everglades. What traits make them effective? Discuss your ideas with a partner.* (She uses a metaphor, "river of grass," and sensory language to encourage readers to recognize the Everglades' beauty and want to protect it.)

**Pages 10–11** *What antonym in the text helps you better understand the meaning of* inhospitable? (*welcoming*)

**Pages 12–13** *How did Douglas's efforts help protect the Everglades?* (She established an organization called Friends of the Everglades to protest and prevent the construction of an airport near the Everglades. She also pushed to make polluters clean up the water and to get rid of canals that diverted water from the area.)

**Page 14** *Why was the Everglades Forever Act passed?* (to preserve the quality and quantity of the water in order to maintain the balance of plant and animal life in the Everglades)

## After Reading

**Respond to Reading** Revisit the Essential Question and ask students to complete the Respond to Reading section on page 15.

**Analytical Writing** **Write About Reading** Check that students have explained how Douglas helped the Everglades and the people of Florida.

### Fluency: Expression and Phrasing

**Model** Model reading page 9 with proper expression and phrasing. Next reread the page aloud and have students read along with you.

**Apply** Have students practice reading with partners.

## PAIRED READ

**Leveled Reader**

# "The Story of the Tree Musketeers"

### Make Connections: Write About It **Analytical Writing**

Before reading, ask students to note that the genre of this text is expository text. Then discuss the Essential Question. After reading, ask students to write connections between what they learned from *Marjory Stoneman Douglas: Guardian of the Everglades* and "The Story of the Tree Musketeers."

 **FOCUS ON SCIENCE**

Students can extend their knowledge of environmental issues by completing the activity on page 20. **STEM**

## Literature Circles

Ask students to conduct a literature circle using the Thinkmark questions to guide the discussion. You may wish to have a whole-class discussion, using information in both selections in the Leveled Reader, about the impact our actions have on our world.

## Gifted and Talented

**Synthesize** Based on the Leveled Reader selections, lead students to identify different types of current environmental problems. Record these problems on the board. Then have partners choose and research an individual or group that is working to solve one of these problems. Have them identify obstacles the group faces, potential solutions it has proposed, and results to date. Tell students to present their research to the class in problem-and-solution charts.

## Beyond Level

# Vocabulary

## REVIEW DOMAIN-SPECIFIC WORDS

 **OBJECTIVES**
**CCSS** Acquire and use accurately grade-appropriate general academic and domain-specific words and phrases, including those that signal contrast, addition, and other logical relationships. **L.5.6**

 **Model**

Use the **Visual Vocabulary Cards** to review the meaning of the words *influence* and *restore*. Write genre-related sentences on the board using the words.

Write the words *pollution* and *toxic* on the board and discuss the meanings with students. Then help students write sentences using these words.

 **Apply**

Have students work in pairs to review the meanings of the words *conservation* and *habitats*. Then have partners write sentences using these words.

## SYNONYMS AND ANTONYMS

 **OBJECTIVES**
**CCSS** Demonstrate understanding of figurative language, word relationships, and nuances in word meanings. Use the relationship between particular words (e.g., synonyms, antonyms, homographs) to better understand each of the words. **L.5.5c**

 **Model**

Read aloud the second paragraph of the Comprehension and Fluency passage on **Beyond Reproducibles** pages 283–284.

**Think Aloud** I'm not sure what the word *preserved* means, but I see the words *protect* and *care for* in the previous sentence. The words are used in similar ways, so I believe they are synonyms. I think that the word *preserved* means "protected and cared for."

Reread aloud the second paragraph on page 283 and point out the word *private*. Point out that the word *public* in the same sentence is an antonym.

 **Apply**

Have pairs of students read the rest of the passage. Ask them to use synonyms and antonyms to determine the meanings of *generate* (page 283, paragraph 3), *protesting* (page 284, paragraph 1), *legislation* (page 284, paragraph 2), *demonstrations* (page 284, paragraph 3), and *individuals* (page 284, paragraph 6.)

 **Analyze** Challenge students to use a thesaurus to identify a synonym and an antonym for three other words in the passage. Have them make a three-column chart and write the word in the first column, a synonym in the second column, and an antonym in the third column.

# Comprehension

## REVIEW TEXT STRUCTURE: PROBLEM AND SOLUTION

**OBJECTIVES**
Explain the relationships or interactions between two or more individuals, events, ideas, or concepts in a historical, scientific, or technical text based on specific information in the text. **RI.5.3**

 **Model** Review that problem and solution is one kind of text structure. In a biography, the author often describes a problem the subject faced and describes the action the subject took to solve or overcome the problem.

Have students read the first two paragraphs of the Comprehension and Fluency passage on **Beyond Reproducibles** pages 283–284. Work with them to identify the problems that Gaylord Nelson faced with preserving natural resources and the actions he took to solve them by creating wildlife habitats and public parks.

 **Apply** Have students record problems and solutions in the rest of the passage on Graphic Organizer 142. Remind them that a problem may be presented early in the text while the solution may be described in later paragraphs. Then have students share their completed organizers with the class.

## SELF-SELECTED READING

**OBJECTIVES**
Explain the relationships or interactions between two or more individuals, events, ideas, or concepts in a historical, scientific, or technical text based on specific information in the text. **RI.5.3**

Ask and answer questions to increase understanding.

### Read Independently

Have students choose a biography for sustained silent reading.

→ As students read, have them record problems and solutions on Graphic Organizer 142.

→ Remind them to ask questions before, while, and after they read and to look for answers in the text.

### Read Purposefully

Encourage students to keep a reading journal. Ask them to read biographies about other famous people to increase their understanding of the genre.

→ Students can write summaries of the books in their journals.

→ Ask students to share their reactions to the books with classmates.

 **Independent Study** Challenge students to discuss how their books relate to the weekly theme of making a difference. What have they learned about the impact our actions have on our world?

# → English Language Learners

## Shared Read

## *Words to Save the World: The Work of Rachel Carson*

**Reading/Writing Workshop**

---

**OBJECTIVES**

**CCSS** Explain the relationships or interactions between two or more individuals, events, ideas, or concepts in a historical, scientific, or technical text based on specific information in the text. **RI.5.3**

---

**LANGUAGE OBJECTIVE**

Identify problems and solutions within a text.

---

**ACADEMIC LANGUAGE**

• *problem, solution, synonym, antonym*

• Cognates: *problema, solución, sinónimo, antónimo*

---

### Before Reading

#### Build Background

Read the Essential Question: *What impact do our actions have on the world?*

→ Explain the meaning of the Essential Question, including the vocabulary in the question: *To have an impact on something is to have an effect.*

→ **Model an answer:** *Every action produces one or more effects. For example, if you drink water from a water bottle, you create trash. This trash must be thrown away. This trash then has an effect on the environment.*

→ Ask students a question that ties the Essential Question to their own background knowledge: *Turn to a partner and discuss how some of your actions may impact the world.* Call on several pairs to share their ideas.

### During Reading

#### Interactive Question-Response

→ Ask questions that help students understand the meaning of the text after each paragraph.

→ Reinforce the meanings of key vocabulary.

→ Ask students questions that require them to use key vocabulary.

→ Reinforce strategies and skills of the week by modeling.

**Go Digital**

**View "Words to Save the World: The Work of Rachel Carson"**

## Page 425

### Paragraph 1

Explain that Rachel Carson was a person who loved nature and wrote about it. When she saw problems, she wanted to find solutions. Lead students in a choral reading of the opening paragraph.

Point to the phrase *raised awareness. When people are aware, they are paying attention. Rachel Carson wanted people to think about the environment.*

**Model Problem and Solution** Remind students that some texts introduce a problem and then present a solution. Ask students to think about these questions as they read: *What was the problem? How did Rachel Carson solve it?*

### Early Influences

#### Paragraph 1

**Explain and Model Synonyms and Antonyms** *Remember that writers sometimes provide readers with synonyms for new words. Which word in the paragraph has a meaning similar to* glistening? (shimmering) *Which word has a meaning related to the word* landscape? (seascape)

#### Paragraph 2

*What skills did Rachel Carson have that might help her solve environmental problems?* (She was a writer, an editor, and a librarian. She loved nature and shared this love by writing about it.)

## Page 426

### A Call to Action

#### Paragraph 1

Discuss the diagram and read the caption. *The pesticide DDT was used to kill insects. Why was it harming birds?* (Birds eat insects.)

#### Paragraph 2

*Rachel Carson wrote the book* Silent Spring *to _____.* (teach people about the dangers of pesticide use)

### Paragraph 3

*Remember that one way to understand how people impact the world is to identify problems and solutions. How did people solve the problem created by DDT?* (protest, investigation, study, and testimony)

## Page 427

### A Strong Reaction

#### Paragraph 1

*Were the chemical companies happy about Rachel Carson's claims?* (no)

#### Paragraph 2

Read Rachel Carson's quotation aloud. Have students demonstrate understanding by completing this restatement: *Science has given some people the power to _____ nature, so it is the responsibility of other people to _____ nature.* (destroy; save/protect)

#### Paragraph 3

*How did Carson use her words to preserve and protect the natural world?* (She wrote books and spoke publicly about environmental issues.)

Return to the questions you asked while modeling problem and solution and have partners answer. *What was the problem?* (chemical pesticides) *How did Rachel Carson solve it?* (She wrote *Silent Spring.*) *How did Rachel Carson impact the world?* (The government strengthened rules and regulations.)

### After Reading

#### Make Connections

→ Review the Essential Question: *What impact do our actions have on the world?*

→ Make text connections.

→ Have students complete **ELL Reproducibles** pages 283–285.

# → English Language Learners

## Leveled Reader:
## *Marjory Stoneman Douglas: Guardian of the Everglades*

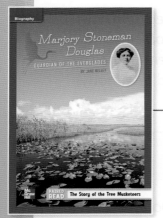

**Lexile** 790
*TextEvaluator* 42

---

**OBJECTIVES**

**CCSS** Explain the relationships or interactions between two or more individuals, events, ideas, or concepts in a historical, scientific, or technical text based on specific information in the text. **RI.5.3**

**CCSS** Read on-level prose and poetry orally with accuracy, appropriate rate, and expression on successive readings. **RF.5.4b**

---

**ACADEMIC LANGUAGE**

• *biography, problem, solution, ask and answer questions*

• Cognates: *biografía, problema, solución*

**Go Digital**

**Leveled Readers**

### Before Reading

#### Preview

→ Read the Essential Question: *What impact do our actions have on our world?*

→ Refer to Show How You Care: *What are some specific actions you take every day that impact the world?*

→ Preview *Marjory Stoneman Douglas: Guardian of the Everglades* and "The Story of the Tree Musketeers": *Our purpose for reading is to describe the effect of human activities on the environment.*

#### Vocabulary

Use the **Visual Vocabulary Cards** to pre-teach the ELL vocabulary: *encouraged, expand, preserve.* Use the routine found on the cards. Point out the cognate: *preservar.*

### During Reading

#### Interactive Question-Response

**Note Taking:** Ask students to use the graphic organizer on **ELL Reproducibles** page 282. Use the questions below after each page is read with students. As you read, use the glossary definitions to define vocabulary in context and visuals to help students understand key vocabulary.

**Page 2** Point to the photograph and describe the Everglades. Have students repeat after you: *grassy, wet, green, brown,* and so on. *Some people thought the Everglades were useless. Did Marjory Stoneman Douglas think they were useless? (no)*

**Pages 3–6** Explain that Marjory Stoneman Douglas wrote about the Everglades. *What skills helped Douglas become a writer?* (reading, researching, editing, speaking, reporting) Pantomime these skills.

**Pages 7–9** Use these frames: *Some people viewed the Everglades as a useless _____. Douglas viewed the Everglades as _____. She used _____ to change people's minds.* (swamp; valuable; her words)

**Use Graphic Organizer**

**Pages 10–13** *What was a problem the Everglades faced?* (People wanted to drain the water and use the land for crops and construction.) *How did Douglas help solve the problem the Everglades faced?* (She wrote, spoke, and formed support groups.)

**Page 14** Point out that Douglas believed two things would save the Everglades. *What are the two things?* (laws and education) *Did Douglas have a good or bad impact on the world?* (good)

## After Reading

**Respond to Reading** Revisit the Essential Question and ask students to complete the Respond to Reading section on page 15.

*Analytical Writing* **Write About Reading** Check that students have correctly used text details to explain how Douglas helped the Everglades and the people of Florida.

### Fluency: Expression and Phrasing

**Model** Model reading page 9 with proper expression and phrasing. Next, reread the page aloud and have students read along with you.

**Apply** Have students practice reading with partners.

**PAIRED READ**

## "The Story of the Tree Musketeers"

**Leveled Reader**

### Make Connections: Write About It *Analytical Writing*

Before reading, ask students to note that the genre of this text is expository text. Then discuss the Essential Question. After reading, ask students to list connections between what they learned from *Marjory Stoneman Douglas: Guardian of the Everglades* and "The Story of the Tree Musketeers."

 **FOCUS ON SCIENCE**

Students can extend their knowledge of life science by completing the activity on page 20. **STEM**

 **Literature Circles**

Ask students to conduct a literature circle using the Thinkmark questions to guide the discussion. You may wish to use both Leveled Reader selections to conduct a whole-class discussion about how people can take action to impact the world.

## Level Up

Level-up lessons available online.

**IF** students read the **ELL Level** fluently and answered the questions

**THEN** pair them with students who have proficiently read **On Level** and have ELL students

• echo-read the **On Level** main selection with their partners.

• list words with which they have difficulty.

• discuss these words with their partners.

 **A C T Access Complex Text**

The **On Level** challenges students by including more **domain-specific words** and **complex sentence structures**.

# → English Language Learners

# Vocabulary

## PRETEACH VOCABULARY

**OBJECTIVES**
Acquire and use accurately grade-appropriate general academic and domain-specific words and phrases, including those that signal contrast, addition, and other logical relationships. **L.5.6**

**LANGUAGE OBJECTIVE**
Use vocabulary words.

 Preteach vocabulary from "Words to Save the World: The Work of Rachel Carson" following the Vocabulary Routine found on the **Visual Vocabulary Cards** for the words *export, glistening, influence, landscape, native, plantations, restore,* and *urged.*

 After completing the Vocabulary Routine for each word, point to the word on the card and read the word with students. Ask them to repeat the word.

 Have students work with a partner to use two or more words in sentences or questions. Then have each pair read the sentences aloud.

| Beginning | Intermediate | Advanced/High |
|---|---|---|
| Help students write the sentences correctly and read them aloud. | Ask students to write one sentence and one question. | Challenge students to write one sentence and one question for each word. |

## REVIEW VOCABULARY

**OBJECTIVES**
Acquire and use accurately grade-appropriate general academic and domain-specific words and phrases, including those that signal contrast, addition, and other logical relationships. **L.5.6**

**LANGUAGE OBJECTIVE**
Use vocabulary words.

 Review the previous week's vocabulary words. The words can be reviewed over a few days. Read each word aloud, pointing to the word on the **Visual Vocabulary Card**. Have students repeat after you. Then follow the Vocabulary Routine on the back of each card.

 Display each Visual Vocabulary Card one at a time and have students call out the words.

 In pairs, have students take turns showing the cards and reading the words. Then have them work together to write a sentence for each word.

| Beginning | Intermediate | Advanced/High |
|---|---|---|
| Help students write the sentences and read them aloud. | Ask students to include a context clue in each sentence. | Have students use two or more vocabulary words in each sentence. |

# SYNONYMS AND ANTONYMS

## OBJECTIVES

Demonstrate understanding of figurative language, word relationships, and nuances in word meanings. Use the relationships between particular words (e.g., synonyms, antonyms, homographs) to better understand each of the words. **L.5.5c**

## LANGUAGE OBJECTIVE

Identify and use synonyms and antonyms.

 **I Do**

Read aloud the second paragraph of the Comprehension and Fluency passage on **ELL Reproducibles** pages 283–284. Review synonyms and antonyms with students. Explain that looking for a synonym or antonym will help them figure out the meaning of *affection*.

**Think Aloud** I'm not sure what *affection* means. Following the word, I see the words "or liking." This tells me that *affection* and *liking* have similar meanings. They are synonyms.

**We Do**

Have students point to the word *private* in the second paragraph on page 283. Point out that the word *public* in the same sentence is an antonym. Ask what *public* means and guide students to form the opposite meaning for *private*.

**You Do**

Have partners use synonyms and antonyms to determine the meaning of *legislation* (page 284, paragraph 2), *demonstrations* (page 284, paragraph 3), and *individuals* (page 284, paragraph 6).

| Beginning | Intermediate | Advanced/High |
|---|---|---|
| Identify the synonym and antonym clues for students and guide them to determine meanings. | Ask students to locate and read aloud the word on the page and identify synonym or antonym clues. | Have students explain how they used synonym or antonym clues to determine the meaning of the word. |

# ADDITIONAL VOCABULARY

## OBJECTIVES

Acquire and use accurately grade-appropriate general academic and domain-specific words and phrases, including those that signal contrast, addition, and other logical relationships. **L.5.6**

## LANGUAGE OBJECTIVE

Use academic vocabulary and high-frequency words.

**I Do**

List some academic vocabulary and high-frequency words from "Words to Save the World": *environment, nature, voice*; and *Marjory Stoneman Douglas*: *research, refugees, valuable*. Define each word for students: *Nature is the physical world and things in it that are not made by people.*

**We Do**

Model using the words in a sentence: *Sunflowers and birds are things found in nature. Rachel Carson studied nature even as a young girl.* Then provide sentence frames and complete them with students: _____ *are found in nature.*

 **You Do**

Have students choose one or two words to illustrate. Have partners exchange drawings and guess the word that they depict.

| Beginning | Intermediate | Advanced/High |
|---|---|---|
| Help students determine an appropriate picture to illustrate each word. | Have students write a definition of the word below their drawing. | Have students write a definition and sentence to accompany their drawing. |

# English Language Learners
## Writing/Spelling

---

### WRITING TRAIT: IDEAS

**OBJECTIVES**

 Write routinely over extended time frames (time for research, reflection, and revision) and shorter time frames (a single sitting or a day or two) for a range of discipline-specific tasks, purposes, and audiences. **W.5.10**

**LANGUAGE OBJECTIVE**
Focus on one topic in writing.

 Explain that good writers choose one central idea, or topic, to write about. Read the Expert Model passage aloud as students follow along and identify the topic and the related information.

 Read aloud one passage from "Words to Save the World" as students follow along. Identify the topic. Discuss how the information in the passage connects to the topic. Then use a word web to record the topic and related information. Model writing a paragraph that includes a topic and related information.

 Have students write their own short paragraph, using the word web and focusing on one topic.

| Beginning | Intermediate | Advanced/High |
|---|---|---|
| Help students add details to their paragraph that support the main idea. | Have students revise, making sure the sentences all relate to the topic, and editing for errors. | Have students revise, adding information related to the topic, deleting unrelated details, and editing for errors. |

---

### SPELL WORDS WITH NUMBER PREFIXES

**OBJECTIVES**

 Spell grade-appropriate words correctly, consulting references as needed. **L.5.2e**

**LANGUAGE OBJECTIVE**
Spell words with number prefixes *uni-*, *bi-*, *tri-*, and *cent-*.

 Read aloud the Spelling Words on page T228, segmenting them into syllables and stressing the prefix in each word. Point out the words where the prefix is the accented syllable.

 Read the Dictation Sentences on page T229 aloud, reading the underlined word slowly and stressing the prefix. Have students repeat the word and write it.

 Display the words. Have students exchange their list with a partner to check the spelling and write the words correctly.

| Beginning | Intermediate | Advanced/High |
|---|---|---|
| Have students copy the words with correct spelling and say the word aloud. | After students have corrected their words, have pairs quiz each other. | After students have corrected their words, have students explain which words were difficult and why. |

# Grammar

## SENTENCE COMBINING

**CCSS**

**OBJECTIVES**
Use knowledge of language and its conventions when writing, speaking, reading, or listening. Expand, combine, and reduce sentences for meaning, reader/listener interest, and style. **L.5.3a**

**LANGUAGE OBJECTIVE**
Combine simple sentences.

**Language Transfers Handbook**

Speakers of Hmong may use two main verbs consecutively without conjunctions or connectors. Reinforce the use of conjunctions in compound sentences and compound subjects or predicates.

**I Do**
Remind students that sentence combining is reducing two or more simple sentences into one sentence. Explain that a simple sentence expresses one complete thought. Write on the board: *I ate my salad. I drank my milk.* Point out that the simple sentences are about a similar subject, so they can be combined into a compound sentence. Write on the board: *I ate my salad and drank my milk.* Then write on the board: *The peach is sweet. It is juicy. The peach is sweet and juicy.* Explain that you can combine two sentences by joining similar ideas.

**We Do**
Write the sentences below on the board. Have students combine the sentences using the conjunction provided.

> *We can hike. We can swim.* (or)
>
> *I went to New York City. I did not go to Long Island.* (but)
>
> *The dragon is green. It is scaly.* (and)

**You Do**
Write a list of simple sentences on the board. Have partners choose two simple sentences and combine them into a compound sentence. Have them read their sentences aloud.

| Beginning | Intermediate | Advanced/High |
|---|---|---|
| Help students copy their sentences and help them underline the two similar ideas. Read the combined sentence aloud for students to repeat. | Ask students to underline the two similar ideas in their compound sentence and tell how the ideas are related. | Have students combine two simple sentences into a compound sentence and then make two simple sentences out of one compound sentence with related ideas. |

For extra support, have students complete the activities in the **Grammar Practice Reproducibles** during the week, using the routine below.

→ Explain the grammar skill.

→ Model the first activity in the Grammar Practice Reproducibles.

→ Have the whole group complete the next couple of activities, then do the rest with a partner.

→ Review the activities with correct answers.

# PROGRESS MONITORING

## Weekly Assessment

| ✔ **COMPREHENSION:** | ✔ **VOCABULARY:** | ✔ **WRITING:** |
|---|---|---|
| Text Structure: Problem and Solution **RI.5.5** | Synonyms and Antonyms **L.5.5c** | Writing About Text **RI.5.5, W.5.9b** |

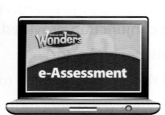

### Assessment Includes

→ Performance Tasks

→ Approaching-Level Assessment online PDFs

**Fluency Goal** 129 to 149 words correct per minute (WCPM)

**Accuracy Rate Goal** 95% or higher

Administer oral reading fluency assessments using the following schedule:

→ **Weeks 1, 3, 5** Provide Approaching-Level students at least three oral reading fluency assessments during the unit.

→ **Weeks 2 and 4** Provide On-Level students at least two oral reading fluency assessments during the unit.

→ **Week 6** If necessary, provide Beyond-Level students an oral reading fluency assessment at this time.

**Also Available: Selection Tests online PDFs**

*Go Digital!* www.connected.mcgraw-hill.com

# Using Assessment Results

| TESTED SKILLS | If ... | Then ... |
|---|---|---|
| **COMPREHENSION** | Students answer 0–6 multiple-choice items correctly ... | ... assign Lessons 82–84 on Problem and Solution from the ***Tier 2 Comprehension Intervention online PDFs.*** |
| **VOCABULARY** | Students answer 0–6 multiple-choice items correctly ... | ... assign Lesson 169 on Synonyms and Antonyms from the ***Tier 2 Vocabulary Intervention online PDFs.*** |
| **WRITING** | Students score less than "3" on the constructed responses ... | ... assign Lessons 82–84 on Problem and Solution and/or Write About Reading Lesson 200 from the ***Tier 2 Comprehension Intervention online PDFs.*** |
| **FLUENCY** | Students have a WCPM score of 120–128 ... | ... assign a lesson from Section 1, 7, 8, 9, or 10 of the ***Tier 2 Fluency Intervention online PDFs.*** |
| | Students have a WCPM score of 0–119 ... | ... assign a lesson from Section 2, 3, 4, 5, or 6 of the ***Tier 2 Fluency Intervention online PDFs.*** |

# Response to Intervention

Use the appropriate sections of the ***Placement and Dignostic Assessment*** as well as students' assessment results to designate students requiring:

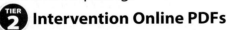 **Intervention Online PDFs**

 **WonderWorks Intervention Program**

**Text Complexity Range for Grades 4–5**

| Lexile | |
|---|---|
| 740 | 1010 |
| *TextEvaluator™* | |
| 23 | 51 |

McGraw-Hill Reading

**Wonders**

**Reading/Writing Workshop**

McGraw Hill

# TEACH AND MODEL

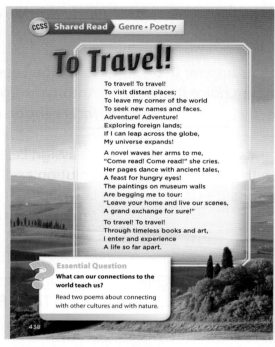
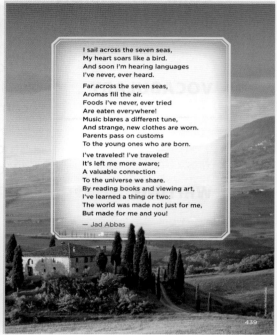

**CCSS** Shared Read ▶ Genre · Poetry

## To Travel!

To travel! To travel!
To visit distant places;
To leave my corner of the world
To seek new names and faces.
Adventure! Adventure!
Exploring foreign lands;
If I can leap across the globe,
My universe expands!

A novel waves her arms to me,
"Come read! Come read!" she cries.
Her pages dance with ancient tales,
A feast for hungry eyes!
The paintings on museum walls
Are begging me to tour:
"Leave your home and live our scenes,
A grand exchange for sure!"

To travel! To travel!
Through timeless books and art,
I enter and experience
A life so far apart.

I sail across the seven seas,
My heart soars like a bird.
And soon I'm hearing languages
I've never, ever heard.

Far across the seven seas,
Aromas fill the air.
Foods I've never, ever tried
Are eaten everywhere!
Music blares a different tune,
And strange, new clothes are worn.
Parents pass on customs
To the young ones who are born.

I've traveled! I've traveled!
It's left me more aware;
A valuable connection
To the universe we share.
By reading books and viewing art,
I've learned a thing or two:
The world was made not just for me,
But made for me and you!

— Jad Abbas

**? Essential Question**
**What can our connections to the world teach us?**
Read two poems about connecting with other cultures and with nature.

438 · 439

## ✔ Vocabulary

blares
connection
errand
exchange

## 🔍 Close Reading of Complex Text

**Shared Read** "To Travel" and "Wild Blossoms," 438–445
**Genre** Poetry
**Lexile** N/A
**ETS** *TextEvaluator™* N/A

## Poetry Terms

assonance
consonance
imagery
personification

## Minilessons

✔ **Genre** ............................... Lyric and Narrative, T274–T275
✔ **Comprehension Skill** ............... Point of View, T276–T277
✔ **Literary Elements** ................. Assonance and Consonance, T278–T279
✔ **Vocabulary Strategy** .............. Personification, T280–T281
✔ **Writing Traits** .................... Word Choice, T286–T287
**Grammar Handbook** .................. Prepositional Phrases, T290–T291

## ✔ Tested Skills **CCSS**

☞ **Go** Digital

www.connected.mcgraw-hill.com

OUT IN THE WORLD

**Essential Question**
What can our connections to the world teach us?

WEEK 5 →

# APPLY WITH CLOSE READING

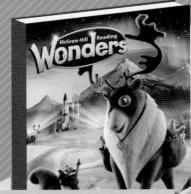

**Literature Anthology**

## Complex Text

**PAIRED READ**

*"You Are My Music"* and *"You and I,"* 506–509
**Genre** Poetry
**Lexile** N/A
ⓔⓣⓢ *TextEvaluator*™ N/A

*"A Time to Talk,"* 510–511
**Genre** Poetry
**Lexile** N/A
ⓔⓣⓢ *TextEvaluator*™ N/A

## Differentiated Text

**Leveled Readers** *Include Paired Reads*

APPROACHING
**Lexile** 730L
ⓔⓣⓢ *TextEvaluator*™ 42

ON LEVEL
**Lexile** 790L
ⓔⓣⓢ *TextEvaluator*™ 51

BEYOND
**Lexile** 940L
ⓔⓣⓢ *TextEvaluator*™ 61

ELL
**Lexile** 610L
ⓔⓣⓢ *TextEvaluator*™ 24

## Extended Complex Text

*No Talking*
**Genre** Realistic Fiction
**Lexile** 820L
ⓔⓣⓢ *TextEvaluator*™ 45

*The Midnight Fox*
**Genre** Realistic Fiction
**Lexile** 990L
ⓔⓣⓢ *TextEvaluator*™ 45

**Classroom Library**

Classroom Library lessons available online.

No Talking: Illustration © Mark Elliott

# TEACH AND MANAGE

## How You Teach

### INTRODUCE

**Weekly Concept**
Out in the World

**Reading/Writing Workshop**
434–435

### TEACH

**Close Reading**
"To Travel!" and "Wild Blossoms"

**Minilessons**
Lyric and Narrative Poem, Point of View, Assonance and Consonance, Personification, Writing Traits

**Reading/Writing Workshop**
438–447

### APPLY

**Close Reading**
"You Are My Music" and "You and I"

"A Time to Talk"

**Literature Anthology**
506–511

👉 **Go Digital**

**Interactive Whiteboard**

**Interactive Whiteboard**

**Mobile**

## How Students Practice

### WEEKLY CONTRACT

**PDF Online**

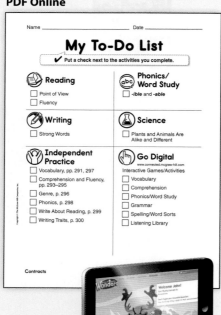

Name _____    Date _____

## My To-Do List
✔ Put a check next to the activities you complete.

📖 **Reading**
☐ Point of View
☐ Fluency

🔤 **Phonics/ Word Study**
☐ *-ible* and *-able*

✍ **Writing**
☐ Strong Words

🧪 **Science**
☐ Plants and Animals Are Alike and Different

**Independent Practice**
☐ Vocabulary, pp. 291, 297
☐ Comprehension and Fluency, pp. 293–295
☐ Genre, p. 296
☐ Phonics, p. 298
☐ Write About Reading, p. 299
☐ Writing Traits, p. 300

**Go Digital**
www.connected.mcgraw-hill.com
Interactive Games/Activities
☐ Vocabulary
☐ Comprehension
☐ Phonics/Word Study
☐ Grammar
☐ Spelling/Word Sorts
☐ Listening Library

Contracts

### LEVELED PRACTICE AND ONLINE ACTIVITIES

**Your Turn Practice Book**
**291–300**

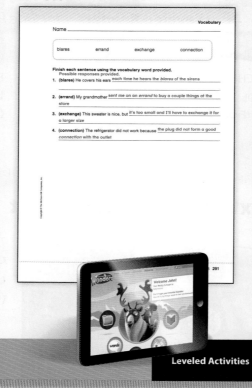

Name _____

**Vocabulary**

| blares | errand | exchange | connection |

Finish each sentence using the vocabulary word provided.
Possible responses provided.

1. (blares) He covers his ears each time he hears the *blares* of the sirens

2. (errand) My grandmother sent me on an *errand* to buy a couple things of the store

3. (exchange) This sweater is nice, but it's too small and I'll have to exchange it for a larger size

4. (connection) The refrigerator did not work because the plug did not form a good *connection* with the outlet

291

**Leveled Readers**

👉 **Go Digital**

**Online To-Do List**

**Leveled Activities**

**Writer's Workspace**

## DIFFERENTIATE

**SMALL GROUP INSTRUCTION**

**Leveled Readers**

Mobile

## INTEGRATE

**Research and Inquiry**
Summary of an Interview, T284

**Text Connections**
Compare Speakers, T285

**Write About Reading**
*Analytical Writing* Write an Analysis, T285

Online Research
and Writing

## ASSESS

**Weekly Assessment**
**349–360**

Online
Assessment

---

# LEVELED WORKSTATION CARDS

**More Activities on back**

### 30 — Connections Among Us — SCIENCE

All plants and animals, including humans, are alike in some ways and different in others. Children inherit certain traits from their parents. Children also acquire, or gain, certain traits as they grow and change.

| Inherited Traits | Acquired Traits |
|---|---|
| | |

- Research traits you inherit, or are born with. Then research traits you acquire over time.

**You need** — 20 Minutes
> paper or poster board
> pencils, crayons

### 14 — Word Choice: Strong Words — WRITING

Read this part of Tanya's narrative about her ice hockey game.

I saw the clock ticking down as I skated onto the ice. At the last second, my teammate passed me the puck. I quickly flicked puck with my stick. S... crowd's cheers fille... had scored my...

- Identify strong words Tanya uses to help create a picture for the reader.

- Find places where Tanya could add

### 14 — Personification — PHONICS/WORD STUDY

Personification is figurative language that gives human characteristics to non-human things.

The wind is knocking at my window.

The wind raced up and grabbed my hat.

- Think of two non-human things that move or seem to behave in human ways. List them.

- Write a description of how it moves, acts, or seems to be like a person.

- Show your personifications to another pair for feedback. Can they visualize what you mean?

- Make a "Personification Poster." Write and illustrate your personifications.

**You need** — 25 Minutes
> paper and pen or pencil
> poster paper
> colored pencils, crayons, or markers

Go Digital! www.connected.mcgraw-hill.com • Interactive Games and Activities • Grade 5    14

### 7 — Point of View — READING

In literature, point of view refers to the way a story or poem is told, either in the first- or third-person. Details tell you how the narrator or speaker feels about events.

**Activity 1: Fiction**
- Choose a story you have read and take turns rereading the first few paragraphs aloud.

- Write down who is telling the story. How does the narrator feel about events? List details that show this.

**First Person**
A character in the story is the narrator.

**Third Person**
The story is told by someone who is not in the story.

**Activity 2: Poetry**
- Choose a poem you like.

- Who is speaking in the poem? Write details showing the speaker's point of view.

**You need** — 20 Minutes
> story or poem
> paper and pen or pencil

Go Digital! www.connected.mcgraw-hill.com • Interactive Games and Activities • Grade 5    7

# DEVELOPING READERS AND WRITERS

## Write to Sources and Research

Point of View, T276–T277

Note Taking, T281B, T281E

Summarize, T281D

Point of View, T281D

Make Connections: Essential Question, T281D, T281F, T285

Key Details, T281F

Research and Inquiry, T284

Analyze to Share an Opinion, T285

Comparing Texts, T297, T305, T309, T315

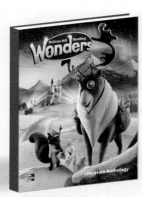

**Teacher's Edition**

**Literature Anthology**

Summarize, p. 509
Point of View, p. 509

**Interactive Whiteboard**

**Leveled Readers**
Comparing Texts
Point of View

**Your Turn Practice Book**

Point of View, pp. 293–295
Genre, p. 296
Analyze to Share an Opinion, p. 299

**Opinion Text**
Opinion Letter, T350–T355

**Conferencing Routines**
Teacher Conferences, T352
Peer Conferences, T353

**Interactive Whiteboard**

**Teacher's Edition**

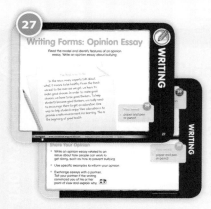

**Leveled Workstation Card**
Opinion Essay, Card 27

**Writer's Workspace**
Opinion Text: Opinion Letter
Writing Process
Multimedia Presentations

## Writing Traits • Write Every Day

**Writing Trait: Word Choice**
Strong Words, T286–T287

**Conferencing Routines**
Teacher Conferences, T288
Peer Conferences, T289

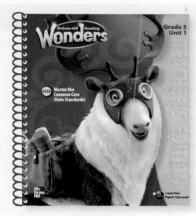

**Teacher's Edition**

Word Choice: Strong
Words, pp. 446–447

**Reading/Writing Workshop**

**Interactive
Whiteboard**

**Leveled Workstation Card**

Word Choice:
Strong Words,
14

Word Choice: Strong
Words, p. 300

**Your Turn Practice Book**

## Grammar and Spelling

**Grammar**
Prepositional Phrases,
T290–T291

**Spelling**
Suffixes -ible and -able,
T292–T293

**Interactive
Whiteboard**

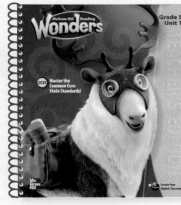

**Teacher's Edition**

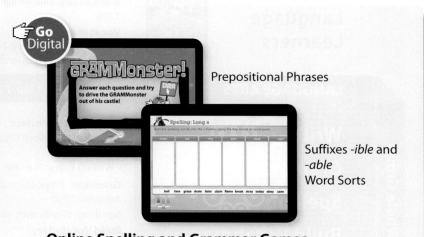

Prepositional Phrases

Suffixes -ible and
-able
Word Sorts

**Online Spelling and Grammar Games**

# SUGGESTED LESSON PLAN

✓ TESTED SKILLS CCSS

|  | DAY 1 | DAY 2 |
|---|---|---|

## READING

### Whole Group

**Teach, Model and Apply**

Reading/Writing Workshop
Workshop

**DAY 1**

**Build Background** Out in the World, T266–T267
**Listening Comprehension** Interactive Read Aloud: "The Beat," T268–T269
**Comprehension**
• Preview Genre: Lyric Poem and Narrative Poem, T274–T275
• Preview Literary Elements: Assonance and Consonance, T278–T279
✓ **Vocabulary** Words in Context, T270–T271
**Practice** Your Turn 291

**Close Reading of Complex Text** "To Travel!" and "Wild Blossoms," 438–441

**DAY 2**

✓ **Comprehension**
• Genre: Lyric Poem and Narrative Poem, T274–T275
• Skill: Point of View, T276–T277
• Write About Reading Analytical Writing
• Literary Elements: Assonance and Consonance, T278–T279
✓ **Vocabulary** Strategy: Personification, T280–T281
**Practice** Your Turn 292–297

## DIFFERENTIATED INSTRUCTION   Choose across the week to meet your students' needs.

### Small Group

**Approaching Level**

**DAY 1**
**Leveled Reader** Your World, My World, T296–T297
**Word Study/Decoding** Review Words with -able, T298 TIER 2
**Vocabulary**
• Review High-Frequency Words, T300 TIER 2
• Identify Related Words, T301

**DAY 2**
**Leveled Reader** Your World, My World, T296–T297
**Vocabulary** Review Vocabulary Words, T300 TIER 2
**Comprehension**
• Identify Key Details, T302 TIER 2
• Review Point of View, T303

**On Level**

**DAY 1**
**Leveled Reader** Flying Home, T304–T305
**Vocabulary** Review Vocabulary, T306

**DAY 2**
**Leveled Reader** Flying Home, T304–T305
**Comprehension** Review Point of View, T307

**Beyond Level**

**DAY 1**
**Leveled Reader** Helping Out, T308–T309
**Vocabulary** Review Domain-Specific Words, T310

**DAY 2**
**Leveled Reader** Helping Out, T308–T309
**Comprehension** Review Point of View, T311

**English Language Learners**

**DAY 1**
**Shared Read** "To Travel!" and "Wild Blossoms," T312–T313
**Word Study/Decoding** Review Words with -able, T298
**Vocabulary**
• Preteach Vocabulary, T316
• Review High-Frequency Words, T300

**DAY 2**
**Leveled Reader** Flying Home, T314–T315
**Vocabulary** Review Vocabulary, T316
**Writing** Writing Trait: Word Choice, T318
**Grammar** Prepositional Phrases as Adjectives and Adverbs, T319

## LANGUAGE ARTS   Writing Process: Opinion Letter T350–T355                Use with Weeks 4–6

### Whole Group

**Writing**
**Grammar**
**Spelling**
**Build Vocabulary**

**DAY 1**
✓ **Readers to Writers**
• Writing Trait: Word Choice/Strong Words, T286–T287
• Writing Entry: Prewrite and Draft, T288
**Grammar** Prepositional Phrases as Adjectives and Adverbs, T290
**Spelling** Words with -ible or -able, T292
**Build Vocabulary**
• Connect to Words, T294
• Academic Vocabulary, T294

**DAY 2**
**Readers to Writers**
• Writing Entry: Revise, T288
**Grammar** Prepositional Phrases as Adjectives and Adverbs, T290
**Spelling** Words with -ible or -able, T292
**Build Vocabulary**
• Expand Vocabulary, T294
• Review Connotation and Denotation, T294

☞ **Go** Digital

CUSTOMIZE YOUR OWN
LESSON PLANS
www.connected.mcgraw-hill.com

# WEEK 5 →

| **DAY 3** | **DAY 4** | **DAY 5** Review and Assess |
|---|---|---|

## READING

**Word Study/Decoding** Words with *-ible* or *-able*, T282–T283
**Practice** *Your Turn* 298

**Close Reading** "You Are My Music" and "You and I," 506–509

 Literature Anthology

**Fluency** Expression and Phrasing, T283
**Integrate Ideas** *Analytical Writing*
• Research and Inquiry, T284
**Practice** *Your Turn* 293–294

**Close Reading** "A Time to Talk," 510–511 *Analytical Writing*

**Integrate Ideas** *Analytical Writing*
• Research and Inquiry, T284
• Text Connections, T285
• Write About Reading, T285
**Practice** *Your Turn* 299

## DIFFERENTIATED INSTRUCTION

**Leveled Reader** *Your World, My World,* T296–T297
**Word Study/Decoding** Build Words with *-ible*, *-able*, T298 **TIER 2**
**Fluency** Expression and Phrasing, T302 **TIER 2**
**Vocabulary** Personification, T301

**Leveled Reader** Paired Read: "Do I Know You?," T297 *Analytical Writing*
**Word Study/Decoding** Practice Words with *-ible*, *-able*, T299

**Leveled Reader** Literature Circle, T297
**Comprehension** Self-Selected Reading, T303

---

**Leveled Reader** *Flying Home,* T304–T305
**Vocabulary** Personification, T306

**Leveled Reader** Paired Read: "Tell Me, Show Me," T305 *Analytical Writing*

**Leveled Reader** Literature Circle, T305
**Comprehension** Self-Selected Reading, T307

---

**Leveled Reader** *Helping Out,* T308–T309
**Vocabulary**
• Personification, T310
• Independent Study, T310

*Gifted and Talented*

**Leveled Reader** Paired Read: "A Journalistic Journey," T309 *Analytical Writing*

**Leveled Reader** Literature Circle, T309
**Comprehension**
• Self-Selected Reading, T311
• Independent Study: World Connections, T311

*Gifted and Talented*

---

**Leveled Reader** *Flying Home,* T314–T315
**Word Study/Decoding** Build Words with *-ible*, *-able*, T298
**Vocabulary** Personification, T317
**Spelling** Words with *-ible* or *-able*, T318

**Leveled Reader** Paired Read: "Fun and Play," T315 *Analytical Writing*
**Vocabulary** Additional Vocabulary, T317
**Word Study/Decoding** Practice Words with *-ible*, *-able*, T299

**Leveled Reader** Literature Circle, T315

## LANGUAGE ARTS

**Readers to Writers**
• Writing Entry: Prewrite and Draft, T289
**Grammar** Mechanics and Usage, T291
**Spelling** Words with *-ible* or *-able*, T293
**Build Vocabulary**
• Reinforce the Words, T295
• Personification, T295

**Readers to Writers**
• Writing Entry: Revise, T289
**Grammar** Prepositional Phrases as Adjectives and Adverbs, T291
**Spelling** Words with *-ible* or *-able*, T293
**Build Vocabulary**
• Connect to Writing, T295
• Shades of Meaning, T295

**Readers to Writers**
• Writing Entry: Share and Reflect, T289
**Grammar** Prepositional Phrases as Adjectives and Adverbs, T291
**Spelling** Words with *-ible* or *-able*, T293
**Build Vocabulary**
• Word Squares, T295
• Morphology, T295

# DIFFERENTIATE TO ACCELERATE

  **Scaffold to Access Complex Text**

**IF** the text complexity of a particular selection is too difficult for students

**THEN** see the references noted in the chart below for scaffolded instruction to help students Access Complex Text.

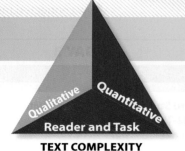

Qualitative / Quantitative
**Reader and Task**
**TEXT COMPLEXITY**

|  | Reading/Writing Workshop | Literature Anthology | Leveled Readers | Classroom Library |
|---|---|---|---|---|
|  |  |  |  |  |
| **Quantitative** | *"To Travel"*<br>**Lexile** N/A<br>*TextEvaluator* N/A | *"You and My Music"*<br>**Lexile** N/A<br>*TextEvaluator* N/A<br><br>*"A Time to Talk"*<br>**Lexile** N/A<br>*TextEvaluator* N/A | **Approaching Level**<br>**Lexile** 730<br>*TextEvaluator* 42<br><br>**Beyond Level**<br>**Lexile** 940<br>*TextEvaluator* 61 | **On Level**<br>**Lexile** 790<br>*TextEvaluator* 51<br><br>**ELL**<br>**Lexile** 610<br>*TextEvaluator* 24 | *No Talking*<br>**Lexile** 820<br>*TextEvaluator* 45<br><br>*The Midnight Fox*<br>**Lexile** 990<br>*TextEvaluator* 45 |
| **Qualitative** | **What Makes the Text Complex?**<br>• **Sentence Structure** T273<br>• **Connection of Ideas** Travel T277 | **What Makes the Text Complex?**<br>• **Genre Poem** T281A<br>• **Sentence Structure** T281C<br>• **Purpose** Meaning T281E | **What Makes the Text Complex?**<br>• **Specific Vocabulary**<br>• **Sentence Structure**<br>• **Connection of Ideas**<br>• **Genre** | **What Makes the Text Complex?**<br>• **Genre**<br>• **Specific Vocabulary**<br>• **Prior Knowledge**<br>• **Sentence Structure**<br>• **Organization**<br>• **Purpose**<br>• **Connection of Ideas** |
|  | **ACT** *See Scaffolded Instruction in Teacher's Edition T273 and T277.* | **ACT** *See Scaffolded Instruction in Teacher's Edition T281A–T281F.* | **ACT** *See Level Up lessons online for Leveled Readers.* | **ACT** *See Scaffolded Instruction in Teacher's Edition T360-T361.* |
| **Reader and Task** | The Introduce the Concept lesson on pages T266–T267 will help determine the reader's knowledge and engagement in the weekly concept. See pages T272–T281 and T284–T285 for questions and tasks for this text. | The Introduce the Concept lesson on pages T266–T267 will help determine the reader's knowledge and engagement in the weekly concept. See pages T281A–T281F and T284–T285 for questions and tasks for this text. | The Introduce the Concept lesson on pages T266–T267 will help determine the reader's knowledge and engagement in the weekly concept. See pages T296–T297, T304–T305, T308–T309, T314–T315, and T284–T285 for questions and tasks for this text. | The Introduce the Concept lesson on pages T266–T267 will help determine the reader's knowledge and engagement in the weekly concept. See pages T360-T361 for questions and tasks for this text. |

## Monitor and *Differentiate*

**IF** you need to differentiate instruction

**THEN** use the Quick Checks to assess students' needs and select the appropriate small group instruction focus.

### ✓ Quick Check

**Genre** Lyric and Narrative T275
**Comprehension Skill** Point of View T277
**Literary Elements** Assonance and Consonance T279
**Vocabulary Strategy** Personification T281
**Word Study/Fluency** Words with *-ible, -able*, Expression and Phrasing T283

**If No →**

| Approaching Level | Reteach T296–T303 |
| ELL | Develop T312–T319 |

**If Yes →**

| On Level | Review T304–T307 |
| Beyond Level | Extend T308–T311 |

## Level Up with Leveled Readers

**IF** students can read their leveled text fluently and answer comprehension questions

**THEN** work with the next level up to accelerate students' reading with more complex text.

Beyond
T305

On Level
T297

ELL
T315

Approaching

## ENGLISH LANGUAGE LEARNERS
### ELL SCAFFOLD

**IF** ELL students need additional support **THEN** scaffold instruction using the small group suggestions.

| Reading/Writing Workshop "To Travel" and "Wild Blossoms" T312–T313 | Leveled Reader *Flying Home* T314–T315 "Fun and Play" T315 | Additional Vocabulary T317 customs emotion island  languages precious variety | Personification T317 | Writing Trait: Word Choice T318 | Spelling Words with *-ible* or *-able* T318 | Grammar Prepositional Phrases as Adjectives and Adverbs T319 |

**Note: Include ELL Students in all small groups based on their needs.**

**Introduce the Concept**

**Reading/Writing Workshop**

---

**OBJECTIVES**

**CCSS** Engage effectively in a range of collaborative discussions (one-on-one, in groups, and teacher-led) with diverse partners on *grade 5 topics and texts,* building on others' ideas and expressing their own clearly. Follow agreed-upon rules for discussions and carry out assigned roles. **SL.5.1b**

**CCSS** Review the key ideas expressed and draw conclusions in light of information and knowledge gained from the discussions. **SL.5.1d**

Build background knowledge on connections to the world.

---

**ACADEMIC LANGUAGE**
*connection, exchange*

---

 **MINILESSON**
**10 Mins**

## Build Background

**ESSENTIAL QUESTION**
*What can our connections to the world teach us?*

Have students read the Essential Question on page 434 of the **Reading/Writing Workshop**. Tell them that we have a **connection**, or link, to the world through our relationships with others.

Discuss the photograph of the student sitting near the Taj Mahal in India. Remind students that an **exchange** is the act of giving one thing for another. Discuss how the ability to have an **exchange** with others strengthens our relationships.

→ Even when we are far from home, technology helps us communicate and keep our **connection** with friends and family.

→ This student is using his cell phone and laptop to stay connected with others. He has an **exchange** with others while sitting near the Taj Mahal.

→ Sharing stories and information helps us feel connected to our world.

## Talk About It

**COLLABORATE**

**Ask:** *What is something you have learned from keeping a **connection** to a person or place? How can an **exchange** with others help to expand your world?* Have students discuss in pairs or groups.

→ Model adding words to the graphic organizer about our connections to the world. Then generate words and phrases with students and add their ideas.

→ Have partners discuss what they have learned about connecting with others. Tell them to add related ideas to the organizer.

### Collaborative Conversations

**Listen Carefully** As students engage in partner, small-group, and whole-class discussions, encourage them to follow discussion rules by listening carefully to speakers. Remind students to

→ always look at the person who is speaking.

→ respect others by not interrupting them.

→ repeat peers' ideas to check understanding.

---

**Go Digital**

**Discuss the Concept**

**Watch Video**

**Use Graphic Organizer**

Weekly Concept  Out in the World

*Poetry*

**Essential Question**
What can our connections to the world teach us?

*Go Digital!*

# Keeping in Touch

As we go out into the world, we find ways to stay connected to our friends, families, and countries.

▶ Sitting within sight of the famous Taj Mahal in India, I can keep a connection with others using my cell phone and laptop.

▶ As we exchange the stories of our adventures, I feel I am a part of the larger world.

## Talk About It

Write words you have learned about connections to the world. Then talk about one thing you have learned from a connection to a person or place.

World Connections

434    435

**READING/WRITING WORKSHOP, pp. 434–435**

## ENGLISH LANGUAGE LEARNERS SCAFFOLD

**GRAPHIC ORGANIZER 61**

| Beginning | Intermediate | Advanced/High |
|---|---|---|
| **Use Visuals** Point to the photo. Say: *This student is in India, a country far away. Even so, he stays connected to his family and friends every day.* Review the meaning of the word *connection*. Elicit that related words are *link*, *bond*, and *relationship*. Ask: *What is he using to keep connections with others far away?* Repeat correct responses. | **Describe** Have students describe how the young man in the photo stays connected. Ask: *What do the cell phone and laptop help the young man do?* Guide students to use the word *connection* in their responses. Repeat students' answers, correcting for grammar. | **Discuss** Have students discuss what is happening in the photo. Ask questions to prompt them. *How does the student make connections with other people? Why is it important to stay connected to others?* Ask students to elaborate on their responses. |

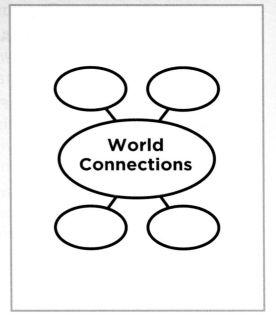

World Connections

# → Listening Comprehension

## Interactive Read Aloud

MINILESSON
**10** Mins

**Go Digital**

### OBJECTIVES

CCSS Summarize a written text read aloud or information presented in diverse media and formats, including visually, quantitatively, and orally. **SL.5.2**

- Listen for a purpose.
- Identify characteristics of lyric poems.

### ACADEMIC LANGUAGE

- *lyric poem, visualize*
- Cognates: *poema lírico, visualizar*

### Connect to Concept: Out in the World

Tell students that being out in the world often involves connecting with people who share a common experience. Explain that you will be reading aloud a poem about a girl who shares the rhythm of the crowd while experiencing a salsa concert.

### Preview Genre: Lyric Poem

Explain that the text you will read aloud is a lyric poem. Discuss features of a lyric poem:

→ expresses personal thoughts and feelings

→ has a musical quality

→ may contain rhyme and rhythm

### Preview Comprehension Strategy: Visualize

Point out to students that poems often include descriptive language that allows readers to visualize how something looks, smells, sounds, or feels. When you visualize, you picture what is happening in your mind. Visualizing can help readers understand the experience or message a poem conveys.

Use the Think Alouds on page T269 to model the strategy.

### Respond to Reading

**Think Aloud Clouds** Display Think Aloud Master 2: *I was able to picture in my mind*... to reinforce how you used the visualize strategy to understand content.

**Genre Features** With students, discuss the elements of the Read Aloud that let them know it is a lyric poem. Ask students to think about other lyric poems that you have read aloud or that they have read independently.

**Summarize** Have students restate the important events and actions in "The Beat" in their own words. Have them take turns with a partner to summarize key details.

**View Illustrations**

I was able to picture in my mind...

**Model Think Alouds**

**Use Graphic Organizer**

| Genre | Features |
|-------|----------|
|       |          |
|       |          |
|       |          |

# The Beat

Salsa dance!
Sold-out show!
Pulsing light
Trumpets and congas split the night **1**
and the beat goes seeking,
heating,
bongos leaping!
reaching through the crowd
where a girl is standing,
watching,
listening,
hanging back from the tide **2**

But the beat keeps reaching,
stirring the crowd,
shaking their shoulders,
moving their feet,
and deep inside
where the drumbeats ride
the congas and the bongos
the congas and the bongos!

And she sees
everybody moving to the driving beat
everybody shaking to the salsa beat
everybody dancing
everybody bouncing
everybody energized
connecting to each other
connecting to the beat
connecting her
to the congas and the bongos
the trumpets and timbales

And she can't hang back now
She has to dance
It's moving her arms
It's moving her feet
It's everyone together
keeping the beat! **3**

moodboard/Corbis

**1 Think Aloud** I can **visualize** the concert from the lines "Pulsing light/ Trumpets and congas split the night." This helps me imagine how the scene looks and sounds.

**2 Think Aloud** The words "hanging back from the tide" help me **visualize** the girl standing alone as all the people move in unison to the beat that sweeps through them like a tide.

**3 Think Aloud** When I read "It's everyone together/ keeping the beat!" I **visualize** the girl joining in the movement of the crowd.

# → **Vocabulary**

**Reading/Writing
Workshop**

___

**OBJECTIVES**

**CCSS** Acquire and use accurately grade-appropriate general academic and domain-specific words and phrases, including those that signal contrast, addition, and other logical relationships (e.g., *however, although, nevertheless, similarly, moreover, in addition*). **L.5.6**

___

**ACADEMIC
LANGUAGE**
*connection, exchange*

## MINILESSON 10 Mins

## Words in Context

### Model the Routine

Introduce each vocabulary word using the Vocabulary Routine found on the **Visual Vocabulary Cards**.

**Visual Vocabulary Cards**

Vocabu...
Define:
Example:
Ask:

**Vocabulary Routine**

**Define:** If something **blares**, it makes a loud, harsh sound.

**Example:** When a trumpet blares, Frankie covers his ears.

**Ask:** What might be the reason why a car horn blares?

**Go Digital**

blares

**Use Visual
Glossary**

### Definitions

→ **connection**    A **connection** is a relationship or bond with someone or something.

→ **errand**    An **errand** is a short trip to do or get something.

→ **exchange**    An **exchange** is the giving of one thing for another.

### Poetry Terms

Introduce each poetry term on **Reading/Writing Workshop** page 437.

→ **assonance**    **Assonance** is repeating words with the same vowel sound. **Cognate:** *asonancia*

→ **consonance**    A poem with **consonance** has words that contain the same middle or final consonant sound. **Cognate:** *consonancia*

→ **imagery**    When writers use **imagery**, they use words to create a picture.

→ **personification**    **Personification** is giving human qualities to things that aren't human, such as objects or animals. **Cognate:** *personificación*

### Talk About It

COLLABORATE

Have partners read the sentence and discuss the photograph for each vocabulary word and define it in their own words. Then have them choose three words and write questions for their partner to answer.

## Vocabulary

**Words to Know**

Use the picture and the sentences to talk with a partner about each word.

**blares**

When a trumpet or other loud instrument **blares**, Frankie covers his ears.

*What might be the reason why a car horn blares?*

**connection**

Ron feels a strong **connection** to the players on his soccer team.

*How would you establish a connection with a new friend?*

**errand**

My mom sent me on an **errand** to the cereal aisle of the grocery store.

*What errand would you do for a relative?*

**exchange**

Milo and his brothers were paid ten dollars in **exchange** for shoveling snow.

*What favor might you do in exchange for free movie tickets?*

436

## Poetry Terms

**personification**

Poets use **personification** to make objects, animals, or ideas resemble people.

*How might personification help describe a thunderstorm?*

**assonance**

A poem using **assonance** includes words with the same vowel sound.

*List three words that have assonance with the word moon.*

**consonance**

A poem using **consonance** includes words with the same middle or final consonant sound.

*Name three words that have consonance with the word buzz.*

**imagery**

With **imagery**, poets use words to create a vivid picture that the reader can imagine.

*What imagery might you use to describe a specific rainy day?*

**Your Turn** COLLABORATE

Pick three words. Write three questions for your partner to answer.

*Go Digital!* *Use the online visual glossary*

437

**READING/WRITING WORKSHOP, pp. 436–437**

(t to b) A. Chederos/Onoky/Corbis; Corbis Super RF/Alamy; Howard Kingsnorth/Ikon/Getty Images; Design Pics Inc./Alamy; McGraw-Hill Companies Inc./Ken Karp, photographer

 **ENGLISH LANGUAGE LEARNERS**
## SCAFFOLD

| **Beginning** | **Intermediate** | **Advanced/High** |
|---|---|---|
| **Use Visuals** Demonstrate turning up the sound on a radio, television, or other device and covering your ears. Say: *It's too loud. It blares!* Elicit that another way to say *It blares* is *It's very loud.* Point to the photograph. Ask: *Is a trumpet that blares noisy or quiet?* Elaborate on students' responses. | **Describe** Help students describe the photograph for *blares.* Review the definition and assist students with the pronunciation. Ask: *What is another thing that blares? Show me or tell me what you might do when something blares.* Clarify responses as needed. | **Discuss** Ask students to discuss the photograph for *blares* with a partner. Then have students complete a concept web using *blares* as the center concept word. Circulate and elaborate as needed. |

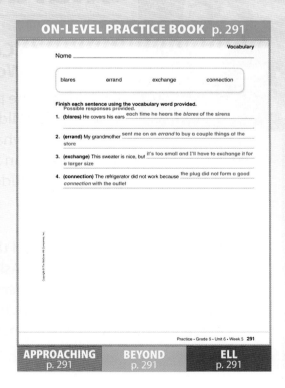

**ON-LEVEL PRACTICE BOOK** p. 291

Name _____

Vocabulary

| blares | errand | exchange | connection |

**Finish each sentence using the vocabulary word provided.**
Possible responses provided.

1. (blares) He covers his ears each time he hears the *blares* of the sirens

2. (errand) My grandmother sent me on an *errand* to buy a couple things at the store

3. (exchange) This sweater is nice, but it's too small and I'll have to exchange it for a larger size

4. (connection) The refrigerator did not work because the plug did not form a good *connection* with the outlet

Practice • Grade 5 • Unit 6 • Week 5 **291**

| **APPROACHING** p. 291 | **BEYOND** p. 291 | **ELL** p. 291 |

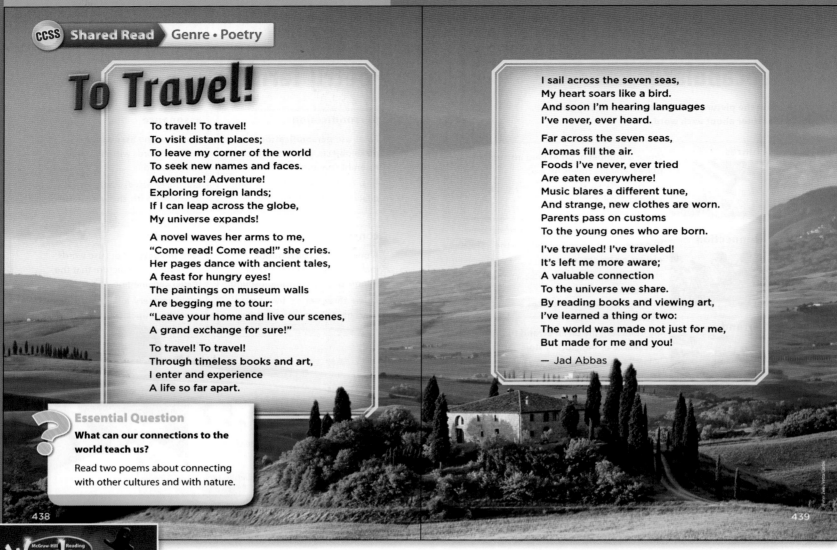

CCSS **Shared Read** Genre • Poetry

# To Travel!

To travel! To travel!
To visit distant places;
To leave my corner of the world
To seek new names and faces.
Adventure! Adventure!
Exploring foreign lands;
If I can leap across the globe,
My universe expands!

A novel waves her arms to me,
"Come read! Come read!" she cries.
Her pages dance with ancient tales,
A feast for hungry eyes!
The paintings on museum walls
Are begging me to tour:
"Leave your home and live our scenes,
A grand exchange for sure!"

To travel! To travel!
Through timeless books and art,
I enter and experience
A life so far apart.

I sail across the seven seas,
My heart soars like a bird.
And soon I'm hearing languages
I've never, ever heard.

Far across the seven seas,
Aromas fill the air.
Foods I've never, ever tried
Are eaten everywhere!
Music blares a different tune,
And strange, new clothes are worn.
Parents pass on customs
To the young ones who are born.

I've traveled! I've traveled!
It's left me more aware;
A valuable connection
To the universe we share.
By reading books and viewing art,
I've learned a thing or two:
The world was made not just for me,
But made for me and you!

— Jad Abbas

**? Essential Question**

**What can our connections to the world teach us?**

Read two poems about connecting with other cultures and with nature.

438

439

---

**Reading/Writing Workshop**

**READING/WRITING WORKSHOP, pp. 438–439**

# Shared Read

**Lexile** 000    *TextEvaluator.* 00

## Connect to Concept: Out in the World

Explain that the poems "To Travel!" and "Wild Blossoms" will demonstrate what our connections to the world can teach us. Read the poems with students.

## Close Reading

**Reread "To Travel!":**  Reread the first three stanzas of "To Travel!" with students. Ask: *Which details in these stanzas help readers understand what kind of travel the speaker is talking about?* Model how to use evidence from the poem to answer the question.

In the first stanza, the speaker talks about traveling to foreign lands and having adventures. In the second stanza, a novel and paintings invite the speaker to have adventures through reading and looking at art. I realize that "traveling" in this poem occurs in the speaker's imagination. Through books and art, we can experience new things.

**Reread "Wild Blossoms":**  Model how to identify key details that help you understand the theme.

The speaker is surprised that her grandmother is not planting neat rows. Her grandmother says she prefers a wild meadow "with plenty of variety." So the speaker and her grandmother let the seeds fly. These details suggest that sometimes life can be more joyful when it is natural and less structured.

# Wild Blossoms

One bright summer morning, my grandmother asked me to help her plant some flowers. I pedaled my bike downtown, wheels weaving between sunbeams. In the sky, clouds exchanged greetings, their language inaudible, while I, on my errand, brought a long list of seeds to the store. Back on my bike, I followed the same sensible route I always took to Grandmother's house. I watched with surprise as she tore off the tops of the seed packets and shook them willy-nilly around the backyard, then told me to do the same.

"I thought we were planting a garden," I told her, "with row after row of flowers." She said, "Oh, no! I prefer a mountain meadow, one with plenty of variety." As she talked, bees buzzed about in excitable flight, impatient for blossoms. Quick swifts and happy sparrows dipped, dove, and darted after the falling seeds. My grandmother and I danced about the backyard, arms outstretched, letting seeds loose on the wind, joyfully dreaming of the wild beauty that would fill the yard, and us, all summer.

— Amelia Campos

**Make Connections**

Describe how the speakers in the poems connect to their worlds. **ESSENTIAL QUESTION**

How do the connections described in the poems compare with your own experiences? **TEXT TO SELF**

440

441

**READING/WRITING WORKSHOP, pp. 440–441**

## Make Connections

### ESSENTIAL QUESTION
Encourage students to reread the poems for details as they discuss how the speakers in the poems connect to their worlds. Ask students to explain, using the poems, what our connections to the world can teach us.

## Continue Close Reading
Use the following lessons for focused rereadings.
→ Lyric and Narrative, pp. T274–T275
→ Point of View, pp. T276–T277
→ Assonance and Consonance, pp. T278–T279
→ Personification, pp. T280–T281

## A C T Access Complex Text

### ▶ Sentence Structure

Point out that poets often break the rules of grammar and usage to express their ideas in a more exciting or interesting way.

→ Read the first stanza of "To Travel!" Help students understand that only the last two lines form a complete sentence.

→ Point out that instead of sentences, the poet uses short phrases that begin with *to*. Ask: *What do the words* travel, visit, leave, *and* seek *have in common?* (They are all about leaving one place to go to another.)

→ *Why do you think the poet used this pattern?* (to emphasize the idea of travel in the poem)

**Genre: Poetry**

**Reading/Writing Workshop**

## OBJECTIVES

**CCSS** Explain major differences between poems, drama, and prose, and refer to the structural elements of poems (e.g., verse, rhythm, meter) and drama (e.g., casts of characters, settings, descriptions, dialogue, stage directions) when writing or speaking about a text. **RL.4.5**

**CCSS** By the end of the year, read and comprehend literature, including stories, dramas, and poetry, at the high end of the grades 4–5 text complexity band independently and proficiently. **RL.5.10**

## ACADEMIC LANGUAGE

- *lyric poem, narrative poem, dialogue, meter, rhyme, rhythm*
- Cognates: *poema lírico, poema narrativo, diálogo, métrico, rima, ritmo*

 MINILESSON **10** Mins

## Lyric and Narrative

### 1 Explain

Share with students the following key characteristics of lyric and narrative poetry:

→ **Lyric poetry** expresses thoughts and feelings. A lyric poem has a musical quality, often contains imagery, and may include rhyme and rhythm.

→ **Narrative poetry** tells a story and has characters who may communicate their thoughts, feelings, and ideas to each other and to the reader through dialogue. A narrative poem often contains imagery and may or may not have a regular meter, or a repeated pattern of sounds that gives a poem a predictable rhythm.

Explain to students that recognizing the characteristics of lyric and narrative poems can make reading poetry more interesting and enjoyable.

### 2 Model Close Reading: Text Evidence

Model how to identify "To Travel!" as a lyric poem. Explain that the line *My heart soars like a bird* expresses the speaker's feelings about traveling the world through reading books and looking at paintings. Point out the rhyme in the second and fourth lines of the first stanza and explain that the use of rhyme helps create the poem's musical quality. Also describe how the poem uses imagery in such lines as *I sail across the seven seas*.

### 3 Guided Practice of Close Reading

 Have students work in pairs to reread the poems "To Travel!" and "Wild Blossoms." Partners should compare the ways the speakers express themselves and explain how the poems are similar and different in terms of poetic elements such as rhyme, meter, and dialogue.

**Go Digital**

**Present the Lesson**

**Genre** Poetry

# Lyric and Narrative

**Lyric** poetry: • Expresses personal thoughts and feelings. • Has a musical quality and may include rhyme and rhythm. • Often contains imagery.

**Narrative** poetry: • Tells a story. • Has characters and dialogue. • May have meter. • Often contains imagery.

 **Find Text Evidence**

*I can tell that "To Travel!" is a lyric poem expressing the speaker's personal feelings. "Wild Blossoms" is a narrative poem that tells a story. Both poems contain imagery, or words that create a picture.*

page 439

I sail across the seven seas,
My heart soars like a bird.
And soon I'm hearing languages
I've never, ever heard.

Far across the seven seas,
Aromas fill the air.
Foods I've never, ever tried
Are eaten everywhere!
Music blares a different tune,
And strange, new clothes are worn.
Parents pass on customs
To the young ones who are born.

I've traveled! I've traveled!
It's left me more aware,
A valuable connection
To the universe we share.
By reading books and viewing art,
I've learned a thing or two:
The world was made not just for me,
But made for me and you!

— Jad Abbas

"To Travel!" is a lyric poem. The line *My heart soars like a bird* expresses the speaker's feelings about traveling the world. The line *I sail across the seven seas* shows imagery of traveling.

 **Your Turn**
COLLABORATE

Compare the way the speakers of "To Travel!" and "Wild Blossoms" express themselves. How are the poems similar and different?

442

**READING/WRITING WORKSHOP, p. 442**

 **Monitor and _Differentiate_**

✓ **Quick Check**

Can students compare the way the speakers in the two poems express themselves? Can they tell other ways the poems are similar and different?

⬇

**Small Group Instruction**

If No → | Approaching Level | Reteach p. T297
| ELL | Develop p. T315
If Yes → | On Level | Review p. T305
| Beyond Level | Extend p. T309

**Beginning**

**Respond Orally** Reread aloud the first four lines of "To Travel!" on page 438. Point to the words *places* and *faces* and ask: *Do these two words rhyme?* (yes) *Does the speaker in the poem sound bored or excited about travel?* (excited) Help students understand that lyric poems express feelings and often use rhyme.

**Intermediate**

**Explain** Help students reread the first stanza of "To Travel!" on page 438. Ask: *Which words in these lines rhyme? How does the speaker feel about travel? How can you tell? Turn to a partner and discuss.* Have partners complete this sentence: *This poem is an example of _____ poetry.* (lyric)

**Advanced/High**

**Demonstrate Comprehension** Have students reread the poem "To Travel!" Then have partners point out text evidence that helps them identify the poem as a lyric poem. Encourage students to use the words *rhyme, imagery,* and *feelings* in their discussions.

**ON-LEVEL PRACTICE BOOK** p. 295

Name _____

Genre/Literary Element

**Big Sky**

Standing on a small rise in the road
I saw the big sky.
I had not thought about the name
Big Sky Country
Until that moment,
And I was overwhelmed.
I thought I might explode
At the splendor.
The sun rising from the east
Bounced off soaring clouds
In the west
And shot the sky with coral.
I could turn in circles
And see the sky everywhere I looked.
Nothing blocked my view.
No trees. No mountains. No skyscrapers.
Just sky. Big sky.

**Answer the questions about the text.**

1. **What is the topic of this poem?**
The topic is Big Sky Country.

2. **How does the speaker in the poem feel? How do you know?**
Possible response: The speaker loves Big Sky Country. I know this because the speaker says, "I was overwhelmed. / I thought I might explode / At the splendor."

3. **Is this lyric poetry or narrative poetry? How do you know?**
This is lyric poetry because it expresses the speaker's personal thoughts and feelings. It is not narrative poetry because it does not tell a story.

Practice • Grade 5 • Unit 6 • Week 5 **295**

| APPROACHING p. 295 | BEYOND p. 295 | ELL p. 295 |

→ # Comprehension Skill

**Reading/Writing Workshop**

**OBJECTIVES**

CCSS Describe how a narrator's or speaker's point of view influences how events are described. **RL.5.6**

---

**ACADEMIC LANGUAGE**

• *point of view, speaker, poem, details*

• Cognates: *poema, detalles*

---

 MINILESSON **10** Mins

## Point of View

### 1 Explain

Explain that a poem's **point of view** refers to the individual way the speaker of a poem thinks and expresses ideas.

→ The speakers in many poems use the first or the third person to describe events or ideas. If the speaker describes events and ideas from the first person, the speaker refers to himself or herself using the words *I* and *me*.

→ Thinking about the words the speaker uses and the thoughts he or she expresses can help students understand the speaker's point of view.

### 2 Model Close Reading: Text Evidence

Point out that both "To Travel!" and "Wild Blossoms" describe events and ideas from the first person, using *I* and *me*. Then model identifying key details in the lyric poem "To Travel!" that help you identify the speaker's point of view, which is excited, curious, and open-minded about the world.

 *Analytical Writing* **Write About Reading: Summary** Model using the notes from the graphic organizer to write a brief summary of the speaker's thoughts about traveling through books and art.

### 3 Guided Practice of Close Reading

 COLLABORATE Have students work in pairs to reread the narrative poem "Wild Blossoms," identify key details about events and ideas in the poem, and record those details in the graphic organizer. Partners should then use those details to determine the speaker's point of view.

 *Analytical Writing* **Write About Reading: Summary** Have pairs work together to write a brief summary of how the speaker's ideas about gardens change during the poem and how this change influences how events are described.

**Go Digital**

**Present the Lesson**

---

**SKILLS TRACE**

**POINT OF VIEW**

**Introduce** U4W1

**Review** U4W2, U4W6, U5W6, U6W1, U6W5, U6W6

**Assess** U4, U6

## Comprehension Skill CCSS

# Point of View

The **point of view** is the individual way the speaker of the poem thinks. Details such as word choice and the thoughts expressed are clues to the speaker's point of view.

### Find Text Evidence

*"To Travel!" and "Wild Blossoms" are written in the first person, and they express individual points of view. I'll reread "To Travel!" to look for key details that help me figure out the speaker's point of view.*

| Details | Point of View |
|---|---|
| If I can leap across the globe, My universe expands! | The speaker is excited, curious, and open-minded about the world. |
| Her pages dance with ancient tales, A feast for hungry eyes! | |
| I've traveled! I've traveled! It's left me more aware; | |

### Your Turn

Reread the poem "Wild Blossoms." List key details in the graphic organizer. Use the details to figure out the speaker's point of view.

*Go Digital!* **Use the interactive graphic organizer**

443

**READING/WRITING WORKSHOP, p. 443**

## A C T Access Complex Text

### ▶ Connection of Ideas

Students might have difficulty understanding the kind of travel described in "To Travel!"

→ Reread the first stanza with students. Ask: *What does the speaker want to do?* (travel, explore foreign lands, go on adventures)

→ Reread the third stanza. Ask: *Is the speaker physically traveling to foreign lands? How is the speaker traveling?* (no; by reading books and looking at paintings )

→ *How are reading and viewing art like traveling, according to the speaker?* (They enable us to experience the world.)

## Monitor and *Differentiate*

### ✓ Quick Check

Can students identify key details from "Wild Blossoms" and complete the graphic organizer? Do they use these details to determine the speaker's point of view?

### Small Group Instruction

If No → | Approaching Level | Reteach p. T303
| ELL | Develop p. T313
If Yes → | On Level | Review p. T307
| Beyond Level | Extend p. T311

**ON-LEVEL PRACTICE BOOK** pp. 293–294

Comprehension: Point of View and Fluency

Name _____

A. Reread the poem and answer the questions.
Possible responses provided.

1. Is this poem a lyric or a narrative poem and how do you know?
This is a lyric poem because it tells how the speaker feels about a daily run.
It does not tell a story.

2. Write two examples of personification from the poem.
"Sun's up and smiling"; "Trees all wave to me"; "Wind kicks up its heels."

3. What point of view is used in the poem? Write a line that shows the point of view.
The poem is written from the first-person point of view. "I round the corner";
"What is it we share?"; "Well, I think I know."

B. Work with a partner. Read the passage aloud. Pay attention to expression and phrasing. Stop after one minute. Fill out the chart.

| | Words Read | – | Number of Errors | = | Words Correct Score |
|---|---|---|---|---|---|
| First Read | | – | | = | |
| Second Read | | – | | = | |

294 Practice • Grade 5 • Unit 6 • Week 5

| APPROACHING pp. 293–294 | BEYOND pp. 293–294 | ELL pp. 293–294 |
|---|---|---|

# → Literary Elements

**Reading/Writing
Workshop**

**OBJECTIVES**

**CCSS** Explain major differences between poems, drama, and prose, and refer to the structural elements of poems (e.g., verse, rhythm, meter) and drama (e.g., casts of characters, settings, descriptions, dialogue, stage directions) when writing or speaking about a text. **RL.4.5**

**ACADEMIC
LANGUAGE**
- *repetition, assonance, consonance*
- Cognate: *repetición*

 **MINILESSON 10 Mins**

## Assonance and Consonance

### 1 Explain

Explain to students that poets often repeat sounds in words to emphasize something or to create a certain effect.

→ The repetition of the same vowel sound in two or more words is called **assonance**. Assonance differs from rhyme in that words with assonance have different ending consonant sounds—as in *moon, troops, fruit.*

→ The repetition of a consonant sound in the middle or at the end of words is called **consonance**.

Point out that the use of assonance and consonance can help a poet draw the reader's attention to important words and key details in a poem.

### 2 Model Close Reading: Text Evidence

Identify examples of assonance and consonance in the lines from the second stanza of "To Travel!" on page 438. Point out how the /ā/ sound is repeated in the third line with *pages, ancient,* and *tales* and helps emphasize the contents of the novel. Then point out how the /z/ sound is repeated in *pages, tales, eyes, paintings, museum, walls,* and *scenes* and helps create a feeling of how much there is to see and do.

### 3 Guided Practice of Close Reading

Have students work in pairs to find examples of assonance and consonance in "Wild Blossoms" and explain what feelings the sounds contribute to the poem.

**Go
Digital**

**Present the
Lesson**

**CCSS** Literary Elements

# Assonance and Consonance

Poets may repeat sounds in words for emphasis or effect. **Assonance** is the repetition of the same vowel sound in two or more words. **Consonance** is the repetition of a final or middle consonant sound. The sounds contribute to a poem's feeling.

 **Find Text Evidence**

Reread the poem "To Travel!" on pages 438 and 439. Look for examples of assonance and consonance.

> | page 438 |
>
> A novel waves her arms to me,
> "Come read! Come read!" she cries.
> Her pages dance with ancient tales,
> A feast for hungry eyes!
> The paintings on museum walls
> Are begging me to tour:
> "Leave your home and live our scenes,
> A grand exchange for sure!"

*The long a sound in* pages, ancient, *and* tales *is repeated to emphasize the contents of the novel. The repetition of the /z/ sound in the words* pages, tales, eyes, paintings, museum, walls, *and* scenes *creates a feeling of how much there is to see and do.*

## Your Turn
COLLABORATE

Find examples of assonance and consonance in "Wild Blossoms." Say the words in those lines aloud. What feelings do the sounds contribute to the poem?

444

**READING/WRITING WORKSHOP, p. 444**

---

## ELL ENGLISH LANGUAGE LEARNERS SCAFFOLD

### Beginning

**Listen** Reread the second stanza of "To Travel!" Point out difficult phrases, such as *pages dance with ancient tales, A feast for hungry eyes,* and *grand exchange.* Explain their meanings. Help students replace them with more familiar phrases, such as *pages are full of old stories that I can't wait to read* and *good trade.*

### Intermediate

**Recognize** Help students reread the second stanza of "To Travel!" Guide them to identify examples of assonance. Ask: *What kind of stories do the pages of the novel contain?* (ancient tales) Then guide students to identify examples of consonance. Ask: *Where does the /z/ sound appear in most of these words?* (at the end) *Are most plural?* (yes)

### Advanced/High

**Explain** Have students reread the second stanza of "To Travel!" Have them identify and read aloud examples of assonance and consonance. Ask: *What do the words that contain each type of sound have in common? How do these sound patterns enrich the poem? Turn to a partner and discuss.*

---

## Monitor and *Differentiate*

 **Quick Check**

Are students able to find examples of assonance and consonance in "Wild Blossoms"? Can they explain what feelings the sounds contribute to the poem?

⬇

### Small Group Instruction

| | | |
|---|---|---|
| **If No** → | Approaching Level | Reteach p. T297 |
| | **ELL** | Develop p. T315 |
| **If Yes** → | On Level | Review p. T305 |
| | Beyond Level | Extend p. T309 |

---

**ON-LEVEL PRACTICE BOOK** p. 296

Literary Elements: Assonance and Consonance

Name _____

**Assonance** is the repetition of the same vowel sound in two or more words.
**Consonance** is the repetition of a consonant sound in the *middle* or at the *end* of words.

**Read the lines of the lyric poem below. Then answer the questions.**

**Running**

Feet pound the pavement,
Arms pump up and down,
Sun's up and smiling,
As I jog through the town.

Neighbors out raking,
Look up, holler, "Hi!"
Trees all wave to me,
As I dash on by.

Wind kicks up its heels,
And gives playful chase.
Whooshing and whirling,
"Come, let's have a race."

1. Find two examples of assonance in the poem. Write them below.
Answers might include: pump/up, sun's/up, wind/kicks, playful/chase.

2. Find two examples of consonance in the poem. Write them below.
Answers might include: pump/up, kicks/its.

3. How do the assonance and consonance affect the poem?
Possible response: Assonance and consonance add excitement and rhythm to the poem.

296 Practice • Grade 5 • Unit 6 • Week 5

| APPROACHING p. 296 | BEYOND p. 296 | ELL p. 296 |
|---|---|---|

# → Vocabulary Strategy

**Reading/Writing Workshop**

### OBJECTIVES

**CCSS** Determine the meaning of words and phrases as they are used in a text, including figurative language such as metaphors and similes. **RL.5.4**

**CCSS** Demonstrate understanding of figurative language, word relationships, and nuances in word meanings. Interpret figurative language, including similes and metaphors, in context. **L.5.5a**

### ACADEMIC LANGUAGE
• *personification*
• Cognate: *personificación*

### SKILLS TRACE

**PERSONIFICATION**

**Introduce** U2W4

**Review** U2W4, U3W2, U6W5

**Assess** U2, U6

 **MINILESSON 10 Mins**

## Personification

### 1 Explain

Explain to students that personification is the use of human characteristics to describe non-human things, such as animals, objects, or ideas.

→ Poets use personification to create vivid images that help the reader picture a detail or understand an idea.

→ Both "To Travel!" and "Wild Blossoms" contain examples of personification that make the poems more vivid and entertaining to readers.

### 2 Model Close Reading: Text Evidence

Identify examples of personification in "To Travel!" and discuss the effects that personification has on the poem. For example, a novel is described as waving her arms and crying, "Come read!" while paintings beg the speaker to take a tour. These descriptions make books and art seem like travel companions, exciting and alive.

### 3 Guided Practice of Close Reading

 Have students work in pairs to discuss how personification is used to describe clouds in "Wild Blossoms." Then have partners explain the effect that this use of personification has on the poem. Encourage students to share their work with the class.

**Go Digital**

**Present the Lesson**

## Vocabulary Strategy CCSS

# Personification

**Personification** is the use of human characteristics to describe non-human things, such as animals, objects, or ideas. Poets use personification to create vivid images and to help the reader picture a detail or understand an idea.

 **Find Text Evidence**

In "To Travel!" a novel is described as a person waving her arms and crying, "Come read!" The pages "dance" and eyes are described as "hungry." These human descriptions make books and their contents seem exciting and alive for the reader.

> page 438
>
> A novel waves her arms to me,
> "Come read! Come read!" she cries.
> Her pages dance with ancient tales,
> A feast for hungry eyes!

### Your Turn
COLLABORATE

How is personification used to describe clouds in "Wild Blossoms"? What is the effect of this personification on the poem?

445

**READING/WRITING WORKSHOP, p. 445**

---

## Monitor and *Differentiate*

### ✔ Quick Check

Can students explain how personification is used to describe clouds in "Wild Blossoms"? Can they describe the effect personification has on the poem?

⬇

### Small Group Instruction

If No → | **Approaching Level** | Reteach p. T301
| **ELL** | Develop p. T317

If Yes → | **On Level** | Review p. T306
| **Beyond Level** | Extend p. T310

---

## ENGLISH LANGUAGE LEARNERS SCAFFOLD

### Beginning

**Understand** Point out the words *clouds exchanged greetings* and *inaudible* in line four of "Wild Blossoms." Ask: *If something is inaudible can you hear it?* (no) Pantomime saying "hello" without actually talking. *Can clouds say or wave hello?* (no) Help students understand that the speaker is imagining the clouds' greetings.

### Intermediate

**Explain** Point out the words *clouds exchanged greetings, their language inaudible* in line four of "Wild Blossoms." *What is a way to exchange greetings without speaking?* (wave, shake hands) Ask: *How can you tell that this is an example of personification?* (because clouds cannot exchange greetings)

### Advanced/High

**Demonstrate Comprehension** Point out the words *clouds exchanged greetings, their language inaudible* in line four of "Wild Blossoms." Have students explain why this is an example of personification. Ask partners to describe what effect this example of personification has on the poem.

---

### ON-LEVEL PRACTICE BOOK p. 297

Vocabulary Strategy: **Personification**

Name _____

Read each sentence. Circle the examples of personification. Then explain the author's meaning in your own words. Use context clues to help you understand the figurative language.
Possible responses provided.

1. "Sun's up and smiling / As I jog through the town."
   The writer is using personification to show that the day is bright and beautiful.

2. "Trees all wave to me / As I dash on by."
   The writer is using personification to describe the movement of wind through the trees.

3. "Wind kicks up its heels / And gives playful chase"
   The writer is using personification to show that the wind is rushing along beside the runner.

Practice • Grade 5 • Unit 6 • Week

| APPROACHING | BEYOND | ELL |
| p. 297 | p. 297 | p. |

# Develop Comprehension

**Literature Anthology**
*Lexile and TextEvaluator scores are not provided for non-prose selections, such as poetry and drama.*

## "You Are My Music" and "You and I"

### Text Complexity Range

**Lexile**

740         1010

**TextEvaluator™**

23      **NP** NonProse*      51

## Options for Close Reading

→ Whole Class

→ Small Group

→ Independent

Grade 5
Mon 12/12

## What makes this text complex?

▶ **Genre**

▶ **Sentence Structure**

STRATEGY **T281**

WEEK 5

---

# You Are My Music
## *(Tú eres mi música)*

My older sister Ana's hands dance as she asks,
"Are you ready to go?" Down five flights and out
onto our cheerful street, a summer Saturday chorus
of honks and shouts. Hand in hand we walk four blocks

to the Pappas Family Music Store. "*Kalimera*, Mr. Pappas.
I am here to buy the guitar I have admired for so long."
How proud I feel with my savings from a year of walking
Mrs. Birnbaum's dog. Mr. Pappas's face becomes a frown.

"I am sorry, Aida, I sold it yesterday. In a week
I will have another, please come back then, *mikro pouli*,
little bird." "Be patient," Ana tells me with her hands,
"just a few more days. Let's go to Mr. Kim's for flowers."

The florist's shop smells cool and fresh, like one big rose.
"*Annyeonghaseyo*, Mr. Kim. I'd like sunflowers, please."
His smile also disappears. "Someone bought them all
this morning. I'll have more on Monday, *chamsae*, little bird."

Back outside we go into the August heat, where a siren shrieks,
every radio blares a different tune. My feet feel heavy,
my shoulders droop. Ana and I have one sweet errand more,
across the street at Castelli's Bakery. But even here,

**Essential Question**
**What can our connections to the world teach us?**
Read about how poets reflect on the connections people make with others.

**Go Digital!**

506

---

### ▶ Genre

Explain that poets choose their words carefully to convey a certain mood. Help students recognize how the assonance and rhythm in the poem convey a cheerful mood. Read aloud the first line, emphasizing the lightness of the rhythm: "Ana's hands dance as she asks …"

→ *What vowel sound is repeated?* (short *a*)

something isn't right. A note taped to the door reads,
"Closed today, cannoli tomorrow." Too many horns,
too many trucks, too hot, the worst Saturday ever.
As we walk home, Ana signs, "You will be happy soon,"

but I can't think about a time called "soon." I unlock
the door to our apartment and suddenly—what is this?
Mamá, papá, Mrs. Birnbaum, the Castellis too,
my friends Jenny Kim and Voula Pappas, cousins Raul and Rai,

a cake with icing roses, four vases full of sunflowers!
"*Feliz cumpleaños*," my family exclaims.
Voula hugs me, whispers "Happy Birthday."
Then Jenny, "*Saengil chukha hae*." "Yes, Happy Birthday!"

Mr. and Mrs. Castelli add. And everyone says, "Ooooooh"
as Ana brings in my dream guitar tied with a pink ribbon
and a card: "For Aida's eleventh birthday. *Tú eres mi música*."
Ana's hands say "Happy, happy," circles in the air.

We all make the sign for "happy," and the room ①
is filled with dancing hands, a world of music,
my cousins eating too much cake, my beautiful sister
smiling, her hands quiet now, held over her beautiful heart.

— Jean LeBlanc

507

**LITERATURE ANTHOLOGY, pp. 506–507**

## ESSENTIAL QUESTION

Ask a student to read aloud the Essential Question. Have them discuss how the poems help them answer the question.

### *Analytical Writing* Note Taking: Use Graphic Organizer

As students read the selection, have them fill in the graphic organizer on **Your Turn Practice Book page 292** for point of view.

### ① Skill: Point of View

From what point of view is this poem told? (first person) What is the speaker's point of view about the day's events in "You Are My Music"? What details support this point of view? (The speaker feels cheerful about the day's events at first, then discouraged, and then happy again. Details: "How proud I feel with my savings"; "My feet feel heavy, my shoulders droop"; "the worst Saturday ever "; "We all make the sign for 'happy'") **Add this information to your organizer.**

| Details | Point of View |
|---|---|
| "How proud I feel with my savings" | The speaker is cheerful, then discouraged, then happy again. |
| "my shoulders droop" | |
| "the worst Saturday ever " | |
| "We all make the sign for 'happy'" | |

→ *Which words are emphasized by the use of assonance?* (*Ana, hands, dance, as, asks*)

→ *How would you describe the rhythm of this line?* (The rhythm is light and musical.)

→ *What kind of mood do the assonance and rhythm create at the beginning of the poem?* (They create a cheerful, light mood.)

**ELL** Read aloud the first line of the poem, emphasizing the musical rhythm and the repeated short *a* sound. Have students read the line chorally with you.

→ *What vowel sound is repeated?* (short *a*) Point out the cognate: assonance/*asonancia*.

→ *Is the rhythm light or heavy?* (light) *What mood does a light rhythm create?* (happy)

# Develop Comprehension

## 2 Literary Element: Imagery

What image is the speaker trying to create by saying, "Only one I in the whole wide world/And millions and millions of you?" Discuss with a partner. (The speaker creates the image of being one in a million, unique in a big world.)

## 3 Literary Element: Assonance

In the poem "You and I," what vowel sounds do you hear repeated in the line "And I am a you to you, too!"? (The /o͞o/ sound repeats.) What literary element is this an example of? (assonance)

## 4 Genre: Lyric Poem

What clues tell you this is a lyric poem? (It is short, has a rhyming pattern, and expresses the speaker's feelings about a topic.) **How many stanzas are in this poem?** (three) **How do the stanzas add structure to the poem?** (The stanzas show the progression of the speaker's thoughts.)

## You and I

2   Only one I in the whole wide world
And millions and millions of you,
But every you is an I to itself
3   And I am a you to you, too!

But if I am a you and you are an I
And the opposite also is true,
It makes us both the same somehow
Yet splits us each in two.

It's more and more mysterious,
The more I think it through:
Every you everywhere in the world is an I;
4   Every I in the world is a you!

— Mary Ann Hoberman

508

YOU AND I from The Tree That Time Built. Text copyright © 2009 by Mary Ann Hoberman. Used by Permission of SourceBooks, Inc. (l) Anderson Ross/Blend Images/Getty Images; (r) JLP/Jose L. Pelaez/Corbis

**LITERATURE ANTHOLOGY, pp. 508–509**

## A C T Access Complex Text

### ▸ Sentence Structure

Explain that the pronouns *I* and *you* are sometimes treated as common nouns in the poem.

→ *In line four, which* you *is treated as a noun?* (first)
*In line five, which* I *is treated as a noun?* (second)

Point out that when the poet uses these pronouns as nouns, she is introducing *you* and *I* as larger concepts, which helps her convey her message.

**ELL** Clarify the difference between the pronouns *I* and *you*. Gesture to yourself and say *I*. Have students repeat. Gesture to a student and say *you*. Have students repeat. Then read the poem chorally, using similar gestures to help students track the references to *I* and *you*.

## Respond to Reading

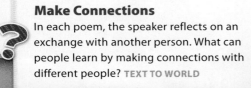

### Summarize

Use important details from "You Are My Music" to summarize the poem. Think about the connection the speaker makes with others. Details from your Point of View Chart may help you.

| Details | Point of View |
|---------|---------------|
|         |               |
|         |               |
|         |               |
|         |               |

### Text Evidence

1. Is "You and I" a narrative poem or a lyric poem? Give examples from the poem to support your answer. GENRE

2. Identify examples of assonance in the first stanza of "You Are My Music". How do the vowel sounds contribute a feeling to the poem? Say the words aloud and think about the feelings the sounds create. LITERARY ELEMENTS

3. Identify three examples of personification in "You Are My Music". How does each example add to the picture that the poet creates? PERSONIFICATION

4. Reread "You and I." Write about how the speaker's view of "you" changes throughout the poem. Use details from the poem to explain your answer. WRITE ABOUT READING

> **? Make Connections**
> In each poem, the speaker reflects on an exchange with another person. What can people learn by making connections with different people? TEXT TO WORLD

509

## Make Connections *Analytical Writing*

**Text to World** After students share what people can learn by making connections, have them discuss the cultures and traditions in their community.

**Your Turn** Have students write a narrative or lyric poem that expresses what they learned about themselves through a connection they made. Then invite students to memorize their poems to recite to the class. Have them practice fluency and using appropriate gestures.

# Respond to Reading

## Summarize

Review with students the information from their graphic organizers. Model how to use the information to summarize "You Are My Music."

*Analytical Writing* **Write About Reading: Summarize** Remind students that a summary includes the important details and may end with a statement that sums up the speaker's feelings. Ask students to write a summary, using the information in their organizers to guide them. Have students share their summaries with a partner.

## Text Evidence

1. **Genre** <u>Answer</u> It is a lyric poem. <u>Evidence</u> It does not tell a story; it states the poet's thoughts about similarities and differences of the self to others; it has a regular pattern of rhyme and rhythm.

2. **Literary Elements** <u>Answer</u> The first line has assonance. They start the poem with a lighthearted feel. <u>Evidence</u> "My older sister Ana's hands dance as she asks…"

3. **Figurative Language** <u>Answer</u> "cheerful street," "siren shrieks," "dancing hands" <u>Evidence</u> The first two examples convey a busy, noisy street. The last example adds a sense of liveliness to the image of the family.

*Analytical Writing* 4. **Write About Reading: Point of View** The speaker's view of *I* changes from thinking of *I* as *one* to *millions*: "Every you everywhere in the world is an I"; "Every I in the world is a you!" All people are an *I*, which connects them, making them the *same*.

# Develop Comprehension

## "A Time to Talk"

**Literature Anthology**

| Lexile | |
|---|---|
| 740 | 1010 |

| TextEvaluator™ | |
|---|---|
| 23 | 51 |

**NP Non-Prose***

*Lexile and TextEvaluator scores are not provided for non-prose selections, such as poetry and drama.

## Compare Texts ✎ Analytical Writing

Students will read a poem in which the poet reflects on friendship. Ask students to do a close reading of the poem and **visualize** or use other strategies they know. They will also reread, take notes, and use evidence to compare this poem with another poem they have read.

**CCSS Genre · Poetry**

**Compare Texts**

Read about how a poet reflects on a friendly exchange.

# A TIME TO TALK

1  When a friend calls to me from the road
And slows his horse to a meaning walk,
I don't stand still and look around
On all the hills I haven't hoed,
And shout from where I am, "What is it?"
No, not as there is a time to talk.
I thrust my hoes in the mellow ground,
Blade-end up and five feet tall,
And plod: I go up to the stone wall
For a friendly visit.

— Robert Frost

510

## A C T Access Complex Text

### *What makes this text complex?*
▷ **Purpose**

▷ **Purpose**

Help students recognize that poems often have a much deeper meaning than it might seem at first.

→ *Based on the words in the poem, what two main actions could the speaker have taken when his friend called from the road?* (The speaker could continue his work and shout "What is it?" or he could stop his work and greet his friend.)

**Make Connections**

Why does the speaker stop to visit with his friend? What lesson does this teach? Use details from the poem to support your ideas. **ESSENTIAL QUESTION**

Think of another poem in which a speaker makes a connection with another person. How is each speaker's experience different? **TEXT TO TEXT**

511

**LITERATURE ANTHOLOGY, pp. 510–511**

**1** **Ask and Answer Questions**

What is the speaker doing at the beginning of the poem?

**Write About Reading** With a partner, paraphrase what the speaker is doing. (The speaker is hoeing hills.)

## Make Connections

**Essential Question** Have students paraphrase and share information about the connection the speaker in "A Time to Talk" feels for his friend. Suggest they visualize the speaker's actions to help them.

**Text to Text** Have pairs of students compare the speaker in "A Time to Talk" with the speaker of another poem such as "You Are My Music." One partner can share how the speaker in "A Time to Talk" connects. (He stops work and makes time to talk with a visiting friend.) **The other partner can share how the speaker in "You Are My Music" connects.** (The speaker of "You Are My Music" connects with her sister by using sign language and holding hands as they walk down the street. The speaker also connects with her neighbors and friends by speaking in their languages.)

→ *What action does the speaker choose?* (The speaker sets down the hoes and walks over to visit with the friend.)

→ *What meaning is the author trying to get across in this poem?* (The author wants readers to recognize the importance of friendship.)

**ELL** Use a photograph to clarify the term *hoed.* Tell students *plod* is another word for walking heavily.

→ *What is the speaker doing when the friend comes by?* (hoeing the fields) *Show me how you would hoe a field.*

→ *To where does the speaker plod?* (to the stone wall) *Why?* (to talk to a friend)

# → Word Study/Fluency

**MINILESSON**
**20 Mins**

## Suffixes *-ible* and *-able*

**OBJECTIVES**

CCSS Know and apply grade-level phonics and word analysis skills in decoding words. Use combined knowledge of all letter-sound correspondences, syllabication patterns, and morphology (e.g., roots and affixes) to read accurately unfamiliar multisyllabic words in context and out of context. **RF.5.3a**

CCSS Read on-level prose and poetry orally with accuracy, appropriate rate, and expression on successive readings. **RF.5.4b**

Rate: 129–149 WCPM

**ACADEMIC LANGUAGE**
• *expression, phrasing*
• Cognates: *expresión, fraseo*

**ELL**

Refer to the sound transfers chart to identify sounds that do not transfer in Spanish, Cantonese, Vietnamese, Hmong, and Korean.

### 1 Explain

Remind students that a suffix is a group of letters added to the end of a word to make a new word. Recognizing common suffixes can help students decode words and understand their meanings. Introduce the suffixes *-ible* and *-able*. Tell students that both suffixes mean "can be done." Write the following on the board:

*wash* + *able* = *washable*: can be washed

*produce* + *ible* = *producible*: can be produced

Point to the spelling of *producible*. Explain that when *-ible* or *-able* is added to a word that ends in *e*, the *e* is usually dropped before the suffix is added.

### 2 Model

Write the following words ending in *-ible* and *-able* on the board:

digestible        learnable

Read aloud each word, underlining the *-ible* and *-able* suffixes with your finger. Model how to use the meaning of the suffix to determine the meaning of each word.

### 3 Guided Practice

Write the following words on the board. Help students identify each suffix. Then lead them to use the meaning of the suffix to determine the meaning of the whole word.

| | | |
|---|---|---|
| enjoyable | sensible | believable |
| eruptible | breakable | punishable |
| reducible | forgivable | flexible |
| bendable | likable | convertible |

**Go Digital**

**Suffixes -ible, -able**

**Present the Lesson**

**View Poems**

## Read Multisyllabic Words

**Transition to Longer Words** Help students transition to multisyllabic words with the suffixes *-ible* and *-able*. Write the following words on the board. Model how to read each word. Then have students read the words chorally as you point to them. Help students use the meaning of the suffixes, as well as the meaning of common prefixes, to determine each word's meaning.

| | |
|---|---|
| inconceivable | nonrefundable |
| unsustainable | indestructible |
| irresponsible | unreasonable |
| unbelievable | unattainable |

After students complete the activity, ask them to use two multisyllabic words from the list in sentences. Then have them share their sentences with partners.

## Expression and Phrasing

**Explain/Model** Review with students that using appropriate expression helps create interest and bring a poem to life. Rather than pausing at the end of each line of poetry, attention to punctuation can help students group words into meaningful phrases. Emphasize the use of expression and phrasing as you model reading the poem "Wild Blossoms," **Reading/Writing Workshop** pages 440–441.

Remind students that you will also be listening for their use of accuracy and appropriate rate as you monitor their reading during the week.

**Practice/Apply** Have partners take turns reading the poem, modeling the expression and phrasing you used.

## Daily Fluency Practice

Students can practice fluency using **Your Turn Practice Book** passages.

### Monitor and *Differentiate*

#### ✓ Quick Check

Can students identify the suffixes *-ible* and *-able* in words? Can they use the meaning of the suffixes to determine the meaning of each word?

#### Small Group Instruction

If No → **Approaching Level** Reteach
pp. T298, T302

**ELL** Develop
pp. T315, T318

If Yes → **On Level** Apply
pp. T304–T305

**Beyond Level** Apply
pp. T308–T309

---

**ON-LEVEL PRACTICE BOOK** p. 298

Word Study: Suffixes *-ible* and *-able*

Name _____

A. Add the suffix in parentheses to the word in bold.

|   |   | New Word |
|---|---|---|
| 1. | (able) **enjoy** | enjoyable |
| 2. | (able) **use** | usable |
| 3. | (ible) **convert** | convertible |
| 4. | (able) **comfort** | comfortable |
| 5. | (ible) **force** | forcible |
| 6. | (ible) **sense** | sensible |

B. Add the suffix *-ible* or *-able* to create a new word. Write the new word on the first line. Then write the meaning of the word on the second line.

|   |   | New Word | Meaning |
|---|---|---|---|
| 7. | afford | affordable | can be afforded |
| 8. | respect | respectable | can be respected |
| 9. | collapse | collapsible | can be collapsed |
| 10. | honor | honorable | can be honored |

298 Practice • Grade 5 • Unit 6 • Week 5

| APPROACHING | BEYOND | ELL |
|---|---|---|
| p. 298 | p. 298 | p. 298 |

☞ **Go** Digital

www.connected.mcgraw-hill.com
**RESOURCES**
**Research and Inquiry**

→ # Wrap Up the Week
# Integrate Ideas

## RESEARCH AND INQUIRY

**Out in the World**

### OBJECTIVES

CCSS Engage effectively in a range of collaborative discussions (one-on-one, in groups, and teacher-led) with diverse partners on grade 5 topics and texts, building on others' ideas and expressing their own clearly. Pose and respond to specific questions by making comments that contribute to the discussion and elaborate on the remarks of others. **SL.5.1c**

CCSS Summarize the points a speaker makes and explain how each claim is supported by reasons and evidence. **SL.5.3**

Conduct an interview.

### ACADEMIC LANGUAGE
• *interview, summary*
• Cognate: *entrevista, resumen*

## Summary of an Interview

Explain that students will choose a friend, family member, or other adult they know to interview. They will interview their subjects about their lives and then summarize the results. Discuss the following steps:

❶ **Choose a Person to Interview** Have students think about people they know and the many interesting stories they may have to tell about their lives. They should then select one of these people to interview and decide on a focus for the interview.

❷ **Plan the Interview** Have students think of questions they want to ask their subjects, keeping in mind what they already know about them. Students may use the online Interview Form to help them plan their interview.

❸ **Guided Practice** Tell students to write each interview question on an index card. Have them leave enough room on each card to take notes about the answer. Remind students to maintain eye contact with their subjects as they ask questions. Facial expressions might provide clues about areas of discussion to pursue or cut short.

❹ **Create the Project: Summary of an Interview** Have students conduct their interviews and take notes about the responses. Then have each student use his or her notes to write about what they have learned from the interview. Students may use the online Listening Checklist to evaluate their listening skills.

## Present the Summary of an Interview

Encourage students to add drawings or photographs of their subjects or important points to their summaries. Them have them post their summaries on the Shared Research Board.

# TEXT CONNECTIONS  Analytical Writing

## OBJECTIVES

**CCSS** Engage effectively in a range of collaborative discussions (one-on-one, in groups, and teacher-led) with diverse partners on grade 5 topics and texts, building on others' ideas and expressing their own clearly. Review the key ideas expressed and draw conclusions in light of information and knowledge gained from the discussions. **SL.5.1d**

### Text to Text

**Cite Evidence** Tell students they will work in groups to compare the poems they read this week. They will look at how the people in the poems learn something through their connections to the world. They will then draw some conclusions about the Essential Question: *What can our connections to the world teach us?* Model how to make comparisons using examples from "To Travel!" and "Wild Blossoms," **Reading/ Writing Workshop** pages 438–441. Review the week's poems, notes, and graphic organizers. Help students set up a Accordion Foldable® to organize their findings. Students should record a brief summary of what each speaker learned about himself or herself and then draw some conclusions related to the week's Essential Question.

Dinah Zike's
**FOLDABLES**

**Present Information** Have groups meet to present their summaries and conclusions. Prompt discussion of differences in students' interpretations of how people connect to the world and learn about themselves and in their overall conclusions.

# WRITE ABOUT READING  Analytical Writing

**Analyze to Share an Opinion**

## OBJECTIVES

**CCSS** Draw evidence from literary or informational texts to support analysis, reflection, and research. **W.5.9**

**CCSS** Determine the meaning of words and phrases as they are used in a text, including figurative language such as metaphors and similes. **RL.5.4**

### Write an Analysis

**Cite Evidence** Using evidence from a poem they have read, students will analyze a poem's imagery and give their opinion as to whether the poet created strong imagery. Discuss how to analyze a poem by asking the following questions.

→ How do some words help create a clear picture in your mind?

→ Why is a person, place, or thing in the poem easy to visualize?

Read and discuss the student model on **Your Turn Practice Book** page 299. Then have students choose a poem and review what they recorded about the details and imagery. Have them write to analyze how the author created imagery and give their opinion as to whether the poet created strong imagery. Remind students that good opinion writers have strong concluding statements and correctly use prepositional phrases as adjectives and adverbs.

**Present Your Ideas** Ask partners to share their paragraphs and discuss how the evidence they cited from the poem supports their opinions.

**Readers to Writers**

 **MINILESSON** **10** Mins

## Writing Traits: Word Choice

### Strong Words

**Expert Model** Explain that writers carefully choose strong words to make their writing interesting and clear. Writers choose strong nouns and adjectives to describe people, places, things, and ideas clearly. They choose strong verbs and adverbs describe actions clearly. Strong adverbs describe how, when, or where an action takes place. Adverbs can also appear as prepositional phrases.

 **Read aloud** the expert model from "To Travel." Ask students to listen for strong words that make the speaker's desire to travel clear and interesting. Encourage them to notice adverbs and prepositional phrases that act as adverbs, such as *across the seven seas* (where), *like a bird* (how), and *never, ever* (when). Have students work with partners to identify these examples.

**Student Model** Remind students that writers use strong words to clearly describe their topics. Read aloud the student draft "Thunderstorm." As students follow along, have them identify strong words that help them understand how the speaker feels about storms.

 **Invite** partners to talk about the draft and how Alec revises the draft to improve his word choice. Ask them to suggest other strong words that Alec might use to describe the action in the situation.

**Go Digital**

**Expert Model**

**Student Model**

---

**Reading/Writing Workshop**

### OBJECTIVES

**CCSS** Use concrete words and phrases and sensory details to convey experiences and events precisely. **W.5.3d**

**CCSS** With guidance and support from peers and adults, develop and strengthen writing as needed by planning, revising, editing, rewriting, or trying a new approach. **W.5.5**

**CCSS** Write routinely over extended time frames (time for research, reflection, and revision) and shorter time frames (a single sitting or a day or two) for a range of discipline-specific tasks, purposes, and audiences. **W.5.10**

### ACADEMIC LANGUAGE

• *nouns, adjectives, verbs, adverbs*

• Cognates: *adjectivos, verbos, adverbios*

---

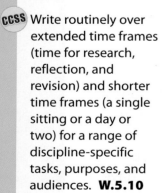 **Genre Writing**

### Opinion Writing

For full writing process lessons and rubrics, see:

→ Book Review, pp. T344–T349

→ Opinion Letter, pp. T350–T355

## CCSS Writing Traits › Word Choice

# Readers to...

Writers use **strong words** to make clear what events are taking place. These words include adverbs that tell *when*, *where*, and *how* something happens or how someone feels. Adverbs can also appear in the form of prepositional phrases. Reread this section of the poem "To Travel!"

### Strong Words

Identify **adverbs** that the poet uses to show when, where, or how something happens. How do adverbs give energy to events in this stanza?

**Expert Model**

I sail across the seven seas,
My heart soars like a bird.
And soon I'm hearing languages
I've never, ever heard.

Far across the seven seas,
Aromas fill the air.
Foods I've never, ever tried
Are eaten everywhere!

446

# Writers

Alec wrote a lyric poem showing his feelings about storms. Read Alec's revision.

**Student Model**

## Thunderstorm

Outside,
~~The~~ sky is a (thret) *sp*

Inside,        *fearfully*
I ~~worry and~~ fret!

Whenever a storm builds,

it builds in me, too!

*nervously*                              *from blue.*
I watch as the sky turns black͜

     *by my window*
I sit ͜and wait for a flash

                              *CRASH*
of lightning and a thundering ~~sound~~.

I hide with my dog, and he gives me

     a start—

his tail thumps as hard as my heart!

447

### Editing Marks

∧ Add
⩞ Add a comma.
⌐ Take out.
(SP) Check spelling.
≡ Make a capital letter.

### Grammar Handbook

**Prepositional Phrases**
See page 472.

### Your Turn

✔ Identify the strong words that Alec used.
✔ Identify the prepositional phrases as adverbs and adjectives that Alec used.
✔ Tell how revisions improved Alec's writing.

*Go Digital!*
*Write online in Writer's Workspace*

**READING/WRITING WORKSHOP, pp. 446–447**

## ELL ENGLISH LANGUAGE LEARNERS SCAFFOLD

Provide support to help English Language Learners understand the writing trait.

| Beginning | Intermediate | Advanced/High |
|---|---|---|
| **Respond Orally** Have students complete the sentence frames to understand strong words in the expert model. *The speaker sails ____.* (across the seven seas) *The speaker's heart ____ like a bird.* (soars) *____ fill the air.* (Aromas) | **Practice** Have students answer the questions. *How does the speaker describe where she sails?* (across the seven seas) *What strong word does the speaker use instead of "smells"?* (aromas) *What strong word does the speaker use to describe food?* (she's never, ever tried them) | **Understand** Ask: *How does the speaker feel about traveling?* (excited) *What are some examples of strong words that make the speaker's message clear?* (soars like a bird, never, ever, aromas) Have students talk about what they picture as they read the poem. |

# Writing Every Day: Word Choice

**DAY**

1

**DAY**

2

### Writing Entry: Strong Words

**Prewrite** Provide students with the prompt below.

*Write a lyric poem about an activity that connects you to others, such as friends or family members.*

Have students work with partners to list people and activities. Ask them to jot down strong verbs, adverbs, nouns, and adjectives about each that they might use in their drafts.

**Draft** Have students select an activity to write about. Remind students to use strong words.

### Focus on Strong Words

Use **Your Turn Practice Book** page 300 to model adding strong adverbs.

*One arm stroke following another, I keep pace.*

*Then buoyed by my team, I move forward and win.*

Model adding strong words by revising the first line:

*One arm stroke swiftly following another, I steadily keep pace.*

Discuss how the strong adverbs improve the poem. Guide students to suggest other strong words to add to the rest of the model.

### Writing Entry: Strong Words

**Revise** Have students revise their writing from Day 1 by adding two or three strong words.

Use the **Conferencing Routines**. Circulate among students and stop briefly to talk with individuals. Provide time for peer review.

**Edit** Have students use Grammar Handbook page 472 in the **Reading/Writing Workshop** to edit for errors in prepositional phrases.

# Conferencing Routines

## Teacher Conferences

**STEP 1**

Talk about the strengths of the writing.

*I can tell you feel strongly about your topic. Your personal voice really comes through!*

**STEP 2**

Focus on how the writer uses the target trait for the week.

*Add strong adverbs to help me visualize the action in your poem. For example, how (where, when) does _____ take place?*

**STEP 3**

Make concrete suggestions for other revisions. Have students work on specific assignments, such as those to the right. Then have students meet with you to review progress.

**DAY**

## Writing Entry: Strong Words

**Prewrite** Ask students to search their Writer's Notebooks for topics for a new draft. Or provide a prompt, such as the following:

*Write a lyric poem that tells your feelings about a community event, such as a parade or a fair. Make sure to use strong words.*

**Draft** Once students have chosen their topics, ask them to create a word web with the topic in the center. Have them think about strong verbs, adverbs, nouns, and adjectives that relate. Students can then use their word webs to begin their drafts.

**DAY**

## Writing Entry: Strong Words

**Revise** Have students revise their drafts from Day 3 by checking to make sure they have used strong words. As students revise, hold teacher conferences with individual students. You may also wish to have students work with partners to conduct peer conferences.

**Edit** Invite students to review the rules for prepositional phrases on Grammar Handbook page 472 in the **Reading/Writing Workshop** and then check their drafts for errors.

**DAY**

## Share and Reflect

Discuss with the class what they learned about using strong words when they write. Invite volunteers to read and compare draft text with text that has been revised. Have students discuss the writing by focusing on how strong adverbs help readers visualize action. Allow time for individuals to reflect on their own writing progress and record observations in their Writer's Notebooks.

## Suggested Revisions

Provide specific direction to help focus young writers.

**Focus on a Sentence**
Read the draft and target one sentence for revision. *Here, you might use an adverb to tell when the action takes place.*

**Focus on a Section**
Underline a section that needs to be revised. Provide specific suggestions. *This stanza sets the scene. Add some strong words so readers can create a clear picture in their minds.*

**Focus on a Revision Strategy**
Underline a section of the writing and ask the student to use a specific revision strategy, such as substituting. *Try replacing some general or overused words with more interesting, stronger words.*

# Peer Conferences

Focus peer response groups on strong words.

☑ Does the writer use strong verbs and adverbs to describe action?

☑ Does the writer use concrete nouns and interesting adjectives?

☑ Do the writer's words help you understand the speaker's feelings?

# Grammar: Prepositional Phrases

**Reading/Writing Workshop**

## OBJECTIVES

**Demonstrate command of the conventions of standard English grammar and usage when writing or speaking. Explain the function of conjunctions, prepositions, and interjections in general and their function in particular sentences. L.5.1a**

- Use objective pronouns in prepositional phrases correctly.
- Proofread sentences.

## Go Digital

**Prepositional Phrases**

**Grammar Activities**

### DAY 1

**DAILY LANGUAGE ACTIVITY**

**Because Sue believes in recycling she collects cans. She exchanges them four money.** (1: recycling,; 2: for)

### Introduce Prepositional Phrases as Adjectives

→ A **prepositional phrase** is a group of words that contains a preposition, an object, and any modifier.

→ Some common prepositions are *by, from, through, to, above, at, behind,* and *with*.

→ When a prepositional phrase acts as an adjective, it tells what kind, how many, or which one. *The first speaker <u>on the program</u> is Liz. She edited the article <u>for the magazine</u>.*

Have partners discuss prepositional phrases using page 472 of the Grammar Handbook in **Reading/Writing Workshop**.

### DAY 2

**DAILY LANGUAGE ACTIVITY**

**"Martha will you save your cans for me," asked Sue. "I will recycle them."** (1: Martha,; 2: me?)

### Review Prepositional Phrases as Adjectives

Review prepositional phrases as adjectives. Have students add prepositional phrases as adjectives to sentences. For example: *The dog ran away. Which dog? The dog <u>with the white fur</u> ran away.*

### Introduce Prepositional Phrases as Adverbs

→ When a prepositional phrase acts as an adverb, it tells how, when, or where. *Her cousin will teach <u>in San Diego</u>. The students will learn <u>from their mistakes</u>.*

## TALK ABOUT IT

**COLLABORATE**

### PLAY PREPOSITION BINGO

Have students make bingo cards writing *adjective* or *adverb* in random squares. Say sentences with a prepositional phrase used as an adjective or an adverb. Discuss with students which kind of phrase was used. Players then "X" the appropriate square on their cards.

### ROLE-PLAY A SCENE

Have students give directions that use prepositional phrases on how to get from school to an interesting place in their city. Ask other students to raise their hands when they hear a prepositional phrase.

## DAY 3

**Sue rinsed each can with water last night. Then, to save space she crushes each can.** (1: space,; 2: crushed)

### Mechanics and Usage: Pronouns in Prepositional Phrases

Present the following:

→ A prepositional phrase begins with a preposition and ends with a noun or a pronoun. *I walk with Anna.*

→ When the object of a preposition is a pronoun, use the objective case. *I walk with her.*

As students write, refer them to Grammar Handbook pages 463 and 472.

## DAY 4

**DAILY LANGUAGE ACTIVITY**

**Sues friend Olivia helps collect cans. Sue is happy to have help from them.** (1: Sue's; 2: her)

### Proofread

Have students correct errors in these sentences:

1. Joan loaned her grammar book to Wu and I. (me/us)
2. I borrowed some toys from Alex and he. (him/them)
3. My aunt asked me to go with she. (her)
4. Working together was good for he and I. (us)

Have students check their work using Grammar Handbook pages 463 and 472 on prepositional phrases.

## DAY 5

**DAILY LANGUAGE ACTIVITY**

**Sue plans to collect newspapers, to. Do you have any newspapers for she?** (1: too; 2: her)

### Assess

Use the Daily Language Activity and Grammar Practice Reproducibles page 150 for assessment.

### Reteach

Use Grammar Practice Reproducibles pages 146–149 and selected pages from the Grammar Handbook for additional reteaching. Remind students to use pronouns correctly in prepositional phrases.

Check students' writing for use of the skill and listen for it in their speaking. Assign Grammar Revision Assignments in their Writer's Notebooks as needed.

**See Grammar Practice Reproducibles pp. 146–150.**

### SIX DEGREES

Write a student's name on the board. Call on students to describe how they are connected to the student whose name is on the board, using sentences with prepositional phrases that have pronouns. For example: *I sit across from her.*

### GUESS WHO IT IS

Have students each write down three prepositions on index cards and place them in a pile. Students will take turns taking a card and using the preposition in a sentence to describe a famous person.

### PLAY SIMON SAYS

Have students play "Simon Says" and take turns being Simon, giving instructions that use prepositional phrases such as "Jump to the chalkboard," or "Simon says put a book on your desk."

# Spelling: Suffixes *-ible* and *-able*

CCSS **OBJECTIVES**
Spell grade-appropriate words correctly, consulting references as needed.
**L.5.2e**

## Spelling Words

| | | |
|---|---|---|
| enjoyable | possible | capable |
| unreasonable | breakable | sensible |
| unbelievable | favorable | laughable |
| comfortable | likable | bearable |
| convertible | usable | collapsible |
| respectable | invisible | suitable |
| affordable | honorable | |

**Review** uniform, bicycle, triangle
**Challenge** manageable, tangible

## Differentiated Spelling

**Approaching Level**

| | | |
|---|---|---|
| enjoyable | possible | capable |
| reasonable | breakable | sensible |
| favorable | laughable | erasable |
| comfortable | likable | bearable |
| convertible | usable | forcible |
| respectable | invisible | suitable |
| readable | fixable | |

**Beyond Level**

| | | |
|---|---|---|
| redeemable | inexcusable | capable |
| unreasonable | affordable | sensible |
| inseparable | favorable | laughable |
| knowledgeable | gullible | likable |
| observable | convertible | collapsible |
| respectable | reversible | suitable |
| transferable | honorable | |

## DAY 1

### Assess Prior Knowledge

Read the spelling words aloud, distinctly segmenting the syllables.

Point out the suffix *-able* at the end of *enjoyable* and draw a line under it. Explain that the suffixes *-able* and *-ible* both mean "can be," so *enjoyable* means "can be enjoyed." Point out the rule for dropping the *e* at the end of a base word when adding the suffix *-able* or *-ible*. Mention that *manageable* is an exception.

Demonstrate sorting the spelling words with the suffix pattern *-able* or *-ible* as seen in the words *capable* and *sensible*. Sort a few words. Ask students to name some other words they know with these suffixes.

Use the Dictation Sentences from Day 5 to give the pretest. Say the underlined word, read the sentence, and repeat the word. Have students write the words. Then have students check their papers.

## DAY 2

### Spiral Review

Review words with number prefixes, as in <u>uniform</u>, <u>bicycle</u>, and <u>triangle</u>. Read each sentence below, repeat the review word, and have students write the word.

1. Each rider wears a <u>uniform</u>.
2. His <u>bicycle</u> moved quickly through the mountain range.
3. The sign in the shape of a <u>triangle</u> warns riders about the wet road.

Have students trade papers and check their spellings.

**Challenge Words** Review this week's suffixes *-ible* and *-able*. Read each sentence below, repeat the challenge word, and have students write the word.

1. The project was <u>manageable</u> after we broke it into parts.
2. The high grade was a <u>tangible</u> reward for our hard work.

Have students check and correct their spellings and write the words in their word study notebooks.

 **WORD SORTS**

**COLLABORATE**

### OPEN SORT

Have students cut apart the **Spelling Word Cards** in the Online Resource Book and initial the back of each card. Have them read the words aloud with partners. Then have partners do an **open sort**. Have them record their sorts in their word study notebooks.

### PATTERN SORT

Complete the **pattern sort** from Day 1 by using the Spelling Word Cards. Point out the different suffixes. Partners should compare and check their sorts. Have them record their sorts in their word study notebooks.

**DAY**

## Word Meanings

Point out the prefix *un-* meaning "not or opposite of" in the words *unreasonable* and *unbelievable*.

Have students work with partners to add the prefix *un-* to other spelling words.

Tell students to record their lists in a chart. For each entry, have students circle the prefix, underline the base word, and place a box around the suffix. (unbreakable, unfavorable, unlikable, unusable, unaffordable, uncomfortable, unbearable, unsuitable)

Have each pair present one word from the chart.

**See Phonics/Spelling Reproducibles pp. 175–180.**

### SPEED SORT

Have partners do a **speed sort** to see who is fastest. Then have them do a word hunt in this week's readings to find words with the suffixes *-ible* and *-able*. Have them record the words in their word study notebooks.

**DAY**

## Proofread and Write

Write these sentences on the board. Have students circle and correct each misspelled word. Have students use a print or a digital dictionary to make corrections.

1. The new principal is capible and sensable. (capable, sensible)

2. Weather conditions are favorible for an enjoyible picnic. (favorable, enjoyable)

3. The convertable car is comfortible. (convertible, comfortable)

4. The affordible dress is suitible for the dance. (affordable, suitable)

**Error Correction** Point out the spelling change that occurs in some words when adding the suffixes *-ible* and *-able*.

### BLIND SORT

Have partners do a **blind sort:** one reads a Spelling Word Card; the other tells under which spelling pattern it belongs. Have students explain how they sorted the words. Then have partners take turns drawing two cards from a stack and using both words in one sentence.

**DAY** **5**

## Assess

Use the Dictation Sentences for the posttest. Have students list the misspelled words in their word study notebooks. Look for students' use of these words in their writings.

### Dictation Sentences

1. It was an <u>enjoyable</u> dinner.
2. The <u>unreasonable</u> child had a tantrum.
3. The tall tale was <u>unbelievable</u>.
4. Relax on the <u>comfortable</u> sofa.
5. We put the top down on the <u>convertible</u> car.
6. Scientists have <u>respectable</u> jobs.
7. The sale items were <u>affordable</u>.
8. Time travel is not <u>possible</u>.
9. Glass goblets are <u>breakable</u>.
10. Justin earned <u>favorable</u> grades.
11. Easy-going Leah is a <u>likable</u> girl.
12. The cracked cup was no longer <u>usable</u>.
13. The sleuth wrote with <u>invisible</u> ink.
14. The king was an <u>honorable</u> man.
15. He is <u>capable</u> of doing the job.
16. That was a <u>sensible</u> decision.
17. The silly mistakes were <u>laughable</u>.
18. Winters are hardly <u>bearable</u>.
19. We folded the <u>collapsible</u> tent.
20. These are <u>suitable</u> boots for snow.

Have students self-correct their tests.

# Build Vocabulary

**DAY**

**1**

**DAY**

**2**

## OBJECTIVES

**CCSS** Demonstrate understanding of figurative language, word relationships, and nuances in word meanings. Use the relationship between particular words (e.g., synonyms, antonyms, homographs) to better understand each of the words. **L.5.5c**

Expand vocabulary by adding inflectional endings and suffixes.

### Vocabulary Words

blares

connection

errand

exchange

## Connect to Words

Practice this week's vocabulary words.

1. What **blares**—a siren or a violin?

2. With which authors do you feel a strong **connection**?

3. What is an **errand** that you run with your parents?

4. What is an **exchange** you have made with a friend or sibling?

## Expand Vocabulary

Help students generate different forms of this week's words by adding, changing, or removing inflectional endings.

→ Draw a T-chart on the board. Write *connection* in the first column. Then write *connections* in the second column. Read aloud the words with students.

→ Have students share sentences using each form of *connection*.

→ Students can fill in the chart for *errand* and *exchange* and then share sentences using the different forms of the words.

→ Have students copy the chart in their word study notebooks.

## Go Digital

[Vocabulary]

**Vocabulary Activities**

# BUILD MORE VOCABULARY

**COLLABORATE**

## ACADEMIC VOCABULARY

Discuss important academic words. Display *assonance* and *consonance*.

→ Define each word and discuss the meanings with students.

→ Write *consonance* and *consonant* on the board. Have partners discuss how the words are related.

→ Have partners use a T-chart to generate word pairs that have either *consonance* or *assonance*.

## CONNOTATION AND DENOTATION *Review*

→ Ask: *What is the denotation, or dictionary meaning, of* blares?

→ Have partners use a thesaurus to find words with similar denotations, such as *trumpets*.

→ Have partners distinguish between the connotations of these words. Ask: *How is* blares *different from* trumpets?

→ Have students write each word's denotation and connotation in their word study notebooks.

## DAY  3

### Reinforce the Words

Review last week's and this week's vocabulary words. Have students orally complete each sentence stem.

1. The alarm <u>blares</u> when ____.

2. I ran an <u>errand</u> to ____.

3. I'd like to hear the <u>exchange</u> of ideas between ____.

4. I feel a <u>connection</u> to ____.

5. Large <u>plantations</u> produce ____.

6. The <u>glistening</u> lake ____.

7. He <u>urged</u> his dad to ____.

8. That country's biggest <u>export</u> is ____.

9. The <u>landscape</u> in my <u>native</u> country is ____.

## DAY  4

### Connect to Writing

→ Have students write sentences in their word study notebooks using this week's vocabulary.

→ Tell them to write sentences that provide word information they learned from this week's readings.

→ **ELL** Provide the Day 3 sentence stems 1–4 for students needing extra support.

**Write About Vocabulary** Have students write something they learned from this week's words in their word study notebooks. For example, they might write about *connections* they have to places and people in their city.

## DAY  5

### Word Squares

Ask students to create Word Squares for each vocabulary word.

→ In the first square, students write the word. (e.g., *errand*)

→ In the second square, students write their own definition of the word and any related words, such as synonyms. (e.g., *task, duty, chore,* or *job*)

→ In the third square, students draw a simple illustration that will help them remember the word. (e.g., drawing of a person with a shopping cart)

→ In the fourth square, students write nonexamples of the word. (e.g., *game* or *hobby*)

→ Have partners share and discuss their squares.

---

### PERSONIFICATION

Remind students that writers sometimes use personification, meaning they give human qualities to animals or objects.

→ Display **Your Turn Practice Book** page 293. Read the passage and model with the phrase *Sun's up and smiling* (line 3).

→ Have students complete page 297.

### SHADES OF MEANING

Help students generate words related to *connection*. Draw a T-chart. Head one column "Close Tie" and the other "Separation."

→ Have partners generate words to add to the T-chart.

→ Add words not included such as (close tie) *alliance, bond*; (separation) *gap, rift*.

→ Ask students to copy the words in their word study notebooks.

### MORPHOLOGY

Use *connection* as a springboard for students to review the suffix *-ion* (meaning "act or process"). Explain that writers can add this suffix to many verbs to create nouns.

→ Tell students to write the following verbs in the left column of a T-chart: *act, complete,* and *devote*.

→ In the right column, have them add *-ion* to create nouns.

→ Tell students to record the charts in their word study notebooks.

# → Approaching Level

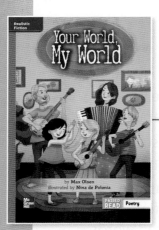

**Lexile** 730
*TextEvaluator*™ 42

---

## OBJECTIVES

**CCSS** Describe how a narrator's or speaker's point of view influences how events are described. **RL.5.6**

**CCSS** Read on-level prose and poetry orally with accuracy, appropriate rate, and expression on successive readings. **RF.5.4b**

---

## ACADEMIC LANGUAGE

• point of view, speaker, visualize, realistic fiction, poetry, personification

• Cognates: punto de vista, visualizar, ficción realista, poesía, personificación

## Leveled Reader:
## *Your World, My World*

### Before Reading

#### Preview and Predict

→ Read the Essential Question with students.

→ Have students preview the title, table of contents, and first page of *Your World, My World*. Students should use the text and illustrations to predict what they think the selection will be about.

#### Review Genre: Realistic Fiction

Tell students that this selection is realistic fiction. The characters and settings are like real people and places, and the events could actually happen in real life. As they preview the book, have students identify features of realistic fiction in *Your World, My World*.

### During Reading

#### Close Reading

**Note Taking:** Ask students to use their graphic organizer as they read.

**Pages 2–3** Reread this sentence: "At last, the bus engines chugged to life." *This is an example of personification. What nonhuman thing is given human characteristics?* (the bus engines) *Who is telling the story—Crystal, Emilia, or an outside narrator?* (an outside narrator)

**Pages 4–6** *Turn to a partner and summarize details about how Emilia and Crystal become good friends.* (They do camp activities together, they teach each other songs on the mandolin, and they e-mail after camp is over.) *In what way are Emilia and Crystal different?* (Emilia was not afraid to fly by herself. Crystal would feel nervous about such a trip.)

**Pages 7–9** Reread the first two paragraphs on page 7. *What picture forms in your mind?* (a steep trail in the mountains surrounded by trees with colorful fall leaves) *Find an example of personification in the second paragraph on page 7.* ("The trail climbed steadily.")

**Pages 10–11** *Turn to a partner and explain what Crystal does at the Roanoke Wildlife Rescue Center?* (She helps take care of orphaned or injured wild mammals.)

**Go Digital**

**Leveled Readers**

**Use Graphic Organizer**

*How do Emilia's feelings about the world around her change after her visit?* (She thinks that just because she lives in a city, it doesn't mean that she can't care for the natural environment and wildlife.)

**Pages 12–13** *What does Emilia do to care for her environment?* (She volunteers to help reduce waste at her school.) *How does Crystal react when she gets Emilia's invitation to visit in New York?* (Crystal is terrified of going to a big city. She tells her mom she doesn't want to go.)

**Pages 14–15** *What impact has Emilia had on Crystal?* (Crystal realizes that getting to know Emilia has made her want to learn more about music, the environment, and the world.) *How does Crystal's mom help convince her to go?* (Her mom says it's important for her to stand on her own two feet away from home.)

## After Reading

**Respond to Reading** Revisit the Essential Question and ask students to complete the Text Evidence questions on page 16.

**Write About Reading** Check that students have identified Crystal's point of view about leaving home and compared it to Emilia's.

### Fluency: Expression and Phrasing

**Model** Model reading page 4 with proper expression and phrasing. Next reread the page aloud and have students read along with you.

**Apply** Have students practice reading with a partner.

## PAIRED READ

### "Do I Know You?"

**Make Connections: Write About It** *Analytical Writing*

Before reading, ask students to note that the genre of this text is poetry. After reading, have students identify the speaker's point of view in the poem and tell how it influences the description of events. Have them make connections between *Your World, My World* and "Do I Know You?"

**Leveled Reader**

## FOCUS ON LITERARY ELEMENTS

Students can extend their knowledge of imagery by completing the literary elements activity on page 20.

# Literature Circles

Ask students to conduct a literature circle using the Thinkmark questions to guide the discussion. You may wish to have a whole-class discussion, using both selections in the Leveled Reader, about what our connections to the world can teach us.

# Level Up

Level-up lessons available online.

**IF** students read the **Approaching Level** fluently and answered the questions,

**THEN** pair them with students who have proficiently read the **On Level** and have students

• echo-read the **On Level** main selection.

• identify three traits of realistic fiction.

## A C T Access Complex Text

The **On Level** challenges students by including more **figurative language** and **complex sentence structures**.

# → Approaching Level

# Word Study/Decoding

## REVIEW SUFFIX *-able*

**TIER 2**

### OBJECTIVES

 Know and apply grade-level phonics and word analysis skills in decoding words. Use combined knowledge of all letter-sound correspondences, syllabication patterns, and morphology (e.g., roots and affixes) to read accurately unfamiliar multisyllabic words in context and out of context. **RF.5.3a**

Decode words with the suffix *-able*.

 Remind students that a suffix is a group of letters added to the end of a word to make a new word. Review that the suffix *-able* means "can be done." Write the word pair *enjoy, enjoyable* on the board and read it aloud. Explain that *enjoyable* means "can be enjoyed." Remind students that when the *-able* suffix is added to a word ending with an *e*, the *e* is usually dropped before the suffix is added.

 Write the word pairs *fix, fixable* and *believe, believable* on the board and read them aloud with students. Point out that when the suffix was added to the word *believe*, the final *e* was dropped. Help students define *fixable* and *believable* using the meanings of *fix* and *believe* and the suffix *-able*.

 Write the words *allowable, likable,* and *washable* on the board. Have students read them aloud and identify the suffix in each. Ask students to use the meanings of *allow, like,* and *wash* and the suffix *-able* to determine the meaning of each word.

## BUILD WORDS WITH SUFFIXES *-ible* AND *-able*

**TIER 2**

### OBJECTIVES

 Use combined knowledge of all letter-sound correspondences, syllabication patterns, and morphology (e.g., roots and affixes) to read accurately unfamiliar multisyllabic words in context and out of context. **RF.5.3a**

Build words with suffixes *-ible* and *-able*.

 Tell students that they will build words using the suffixes *-ible* and *-able*. Write each suffix as well as the words *bend* and *sense* on the board. Read each suffix and word aloud and have students repeat after you.

Work with students to combine the suffixes and words to build new words. Have them chorally read the words *bendable* and *sensible*. Lead them to define each of the words by using the meanings of the words *bend* and *sense* and the suffixes *-able* and *-ible*.

 Add the words *coach, depend,* and *convert* to the board. Have students combine these words with the suffixes *-able* and *-ible* to build new words. Then have them share their words with the class. Ask students to use the meanings of *coach, depend,* and *convert* and the suffixes *-able* and *-ible* to determine the meaning of each new word.

# PRACTICE WORDS WITH SUFFIXES *-ible* AND *-able*

## OBJECTIVES

**CCSS** Know and apply grade-level phonics and word analysis skills in decoding words. Use combined knowledge of all letter-sound correspondences, syllabication patterns, and morphology (e.g., roots and affixes) to read accurately unfamiliar multisyllabic words in context and out of context. **RF.5.3a**

Practice words with suffixes *-ible* and *-able*.

 **I Do** Write these word pairs on the board: *close, closable* and *digest, digestible*. Read the words aloud and underline the *-able* and *-ible* suffixes. Point out that when the suffix *-able* was added to *close*, the e was dropped. Define *closable* as "can be closed" and *digestible* as "can be digested."

 **We Do** Write the word pairs *break, breakable* and *flex, flexible* on the board. Underline the suffixes. Model how to determine the meaning of *breakable* using the meaning of *break* and the suffix *-able*. Then have students use the same process to determine the meaning of *flexible*.

 **You Do** To provide additional practice, write these words on the board. Read aloud the first word, and underline *-able*.

| | | |
|---|---|---|
| deliverable | reversible | learnable |
| insurable | foreseeable | mixable |
| producible | audible | passable |
| divisible | unsinkable | forgivable |

Have students read aloud the remaining words. Ask them to point out the suffix in each word. Then have students use the meanings of the suffixes and a dictionary to determine the meaning of each word.

Afterward, point to the words in the list in random order for students to read chorally.

 **ELL** **ENGLISH LANGUAGE LEARNERS**

For the **ELLs** who need **phonics, decoding,** and **fluency** practice, use scaffolding methods as necessary to ensure students understand the meaning of the words. Refer to the **Language Transfers Handbook** for phonics elements that may not transfer in students' native languages.

# → Approaching Level

# Vocabulary

## REVIEW HIGH-FREQUENCY WORDS

**TIER 2**

**OBJECTIVES**
Acquire and use accurately grade-appropriate general academic and domain-specific words and phrases, including those that signal contrast, addition, and other logical relationships (e.g., *however, although, nevertheless, similarly, moreover, in addition*). **L.5.6**

Review high-frequency words.

 **I Do** Choose review words from **High-Frequency Word Cards** 201–240. Display one word at a time, following the routine:

Display the word. Read the word. Then spell the word.

 **We Do** Ask students to state the word and spell the word with you. Model using the word in a sentence and have students repeat after you.

 **You Do** Display the word. Ask students to say the word then spell it. When completed, quickly flip through the word card set as students chorally read the words. Provide opportunities for students to use the words in speaking and writing. For example, provide sentence starters such as *I went to _____.* Ask students to write each word in their Writer's Notebook.

## REVIEW VOCABULARY WORDS

**TIER 2**

**OBJECTIVES**
Acquire and use accurately grade-appropriate general academic and domain-specific words and phrases, including those that signal contrast, addition, and other logical relationships (e.g., *however, although, nevertheless, similarly, moreover, in addition*). **L.5.6**

 **I Do** Display each **Visual Vocabulary Card** and state the word. Explain how the photograph illustrates the word. State the example sentence and repeat the word.

 **We Do** Point to the word on the card and read the word with students. Ask them to repeat the word. Engage students in structured partner talk about the image as prompted on the back of the vocabulary card.

 **You Do** Display each visual in random order, hiding the word. Have students match the definitions and context sentences of the words to the visuals displayed.

## IDENTIFY RELATED WORDS

**OBJECTIVES**

CCSS Demonstrate understanding of figurative language, word relationships, and nuances in word meanings. Use the relationship between particular words (e.g., synonyms, antonyms, homographs) to better understand each of the words. **L.5.5c**

**I Do** Display the *blares* **Visual Vocabulary Card** and say aloud the word set *blares, blasts, muffles*. Point out that the word *blasts* has almost the same meaning as *blares*.

**We Do** Display the vocabulary card for *connection*. Say aloud the word set *connection, distance, relationship*. With students, identify that *relationship* is similar in meaning to *connection*.

**You Do** Using the word sets below, display the remaining cards one at a time, saying aloud the word set. Ask students to identify the word that has almost the same meaning as the first word in each group.

> errand, trip, mistake
>
> exchange, coin, trade

## PERSONIFICATION

**OBJECTIVES**

CCSS Determine the meaning of words and phrases as they are used in a text, including figurative language such as metaphors and similes. **RL.5.4**

CCSS Demonstrate understanding of figurative language, word relationships, and nuances in word meanings. Interpret figurative language, including similes and metaphors, in context. **L.5.5a**

**I Do** Display the Comprehension and Fluency passage on **Approaching Reproducibles** page 293. Read aloud the first stanza. Point out the line *Sun's up and smiling*. Tell students that personification is the use of human characteristics to describe non-human things such as animals, objects, or ideas.

**Think Aloud** *Sun's up and smiling* is an example of personification. The sun cannot really smile like a person, but the poet describes it in human terms to create for readers the image of a bright and cheerful sunny day.

**We Do** Read the next two stanzas with students. Ask them to point to the line *Trees all wave to me* in the second stanza. With students, discuss why the line is an example of personification and what image it conveys to readers: trees blowing cheerfully in the breeze.

**You Do** Have partners find an example of personification in the third stanza. Ask them to tell what is being personified and the image created by the personification.

**Approaching Level**

# Comprehension

## FLUENCY

 **TIER 2**

### OBJECTIVES
**CCSS** Read on-level prose and poetry orally with accuracy, appropriate rate, and expression on successive readings. **RF.5.4b**

Read fluently with good expression and phrasing.

 **I Do** Explain that good readers group words into phrases and change their volume, tone, and emphasis to convey the meaning of what they read. Read the first two stanzas of the Comprehension and Fluency passage on **Approaching Reproducibles** page 293. Tell students to listen for your phrasing and the way you change your voice according to punctuation cues and the meanings of specific words.

 **We Do** Read the rest of the page aloud and have students repeat each stanza after you, matching your phrasing and expression. Point out that the rhythm and meter of the poem guide your phrasing when you read poetry aloud.

 **You Do** Have partners take turns reading stanzas from the Comprehension and Fluency passage. Remind them to focus on their phrasing and expression. Provide corrective feedback as needed by modeling proper fluency.

## IDENTIFY KEY DETAILS

 **TIER 2**

### OBJECTIVES
**CCSS** Describe how a narrator's or speaker's point of view influences how events are described. **RL.5.6**

**I Do** Review that specific words and details in a poem can be used to determine how the speaker of the poem thinks. For example, if a speaker describes slushy puddles on dreary winter day, the reader may determine that the speaker has a negative point of view about the subject of winter.

 **We Do** Read the first stanza of the Comprehension and Fluency passage on **Approaching Reproducibles** page 293. Point out the words and details that the poet includes about jogging. Explain that the lines *Feet pound the pavement* and *Sun's up and smiling* convey to the reader that the speaker is energetic and cheerful and has a positive attitude about jogging.

 **You Do** Have students read the rest of the poem. After each stanza, they should identify and write down important details about things the speaker observes while jogging, words he or she uses to describe these things, and what he or she is thinking. Review their lists with them and help them explain why the details they chose are important.

## REVIEW POINT OF VIEW

**OBJECTIVES**

CCSS Describe how a narrator's or speaker's point of view influences how events are described. **RL.5.6**

 **I Do** Remind students that point of view in a poem refers to what the speaker of a poem thinks. Being aware of the words the speaker uses and the ideas he or she expresses can help students understand the speaker's point of view.

 **We Do** Read the first stanza of the Comprehension and Fluency passage on **Approaching Reproducibles** page 293. Refer to the list of thoughts, words, and details that students have already compiled. Work with students to offer some ideas about the speaker's point of view in the poem thus far.

 **You Do** Have partners read the rest of the poem, review and add to their lists, and use the word choices, details, and thoughts they have compiled to determine the speaker's overall point of view. Ask students to discuss how the speaker's point of view influences how he or she describes events.

## SELF-SELECTED READING

**OBJECTIVES**

CCSS Describe how a narrator's or speaker's point of view influences how events are described. **RL.5.6**

Visualize sections in a text to increase understanding.

### Read Independently

Have students choose a narrative or lyric poem or selection of poems for sustained silent reading. Remind students that:

→ point of view is the individual way the speaker of a poem thinks.

→ visualizing the characters, settings, and events can help them better understand what they read.

### Read Purposefully

As they read independently, students should use Graphic Organizer 144 to record key details that help them determine the speaker's point of view. After they finish, they can conduct a Book Talk about what they read.

→ Students should share their organizers and answer this question: *What did you enjoy most about the poem or poems you read?*

→ They should also tell the group how visualizing a setting or event helped them understand the poem.

# On Level

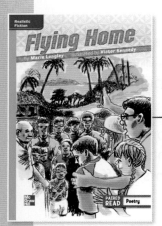

**Lexile** 790
*TextEvaluator* 51

---

### OBJECTIVES

**CCSS** Describe how a narrator's or speaker's point of view influences how events are described. **RL.5.6**

**CCSS** Read on-level prose and poetry orally with accuracy, appropriate rate, and expression on successive readings. **RF.5.4b**

---

### ACADEMIC LANGUAGE

• *point of view, speaker, visualize, realistic fiction, poetry, personification*

• Cognates: *punto de vista, visualizar, ficción realista, poesía, personificación*

## Leveled Reader:
## *Flying Home*

### Before Reading

#### Preview and Predict

→ Read the Essential Question with students.

→ Have students preview the title, table of contents, and first page of *Flying Home*. Students should use the text and illustrations to predict what they think the selection will be about.

#### Review Genre: Realistic Fiction

Tell students that this selection is realistic fiction. The characters and settings are like real people and places, and the events could actually happen in real life. As they preview the book, have students identify features of realistic fiction in *Flying Home*.

### During Reading

#### Close Reading

**Note Taking:** Ask students to use their graphic organizer as they read.

**Pages 2–5** *Why does Tane feel strange at the beginning of the story?* (It is his first visit to Tutuila, the island in American Samoa where his dad was born.) *Who is telling the story?* (an outside narrator) *What picture forms in your mind when you read page 4?* (a happy family reunion with loud voices, smiles, and hugs) *How does Sione feel about how Pago Pago has changed?* (He is disappointed because it is so modern.)

**Pages 6–10** *What can you visualize as you read the description of the reception on page 6?* (a huge, loud, overwhelming crowd) *What simile does the narrator use to describe it?* ("It was like being in the middle of a fireworks display") *Which words help you visualize what the fale looks like?* (oval shaped, see right inside and even right through it, roof made from palm fronds) *How do Tane, Marama, and Ruth feel about sleeping in a village fale?* (They are nervous and unsure. There is no bedroom, kitchen, or electricity and very little privacy.)

**Pages 11–13** *Who helps Tane connect to his father's family and village? How?* (his grandmother; She tells him that his father's family is his family and that the island is his home too.)

**Go Digital**

**Leveled Readers**

**Use Graphic Organizer**

*Find two examples of personification on page 13.* ("The sunlight danced on the glittering water"; "Tane felt the warm water embrace him") *What is one thing you visualized as you read page 13?* (sleeping on a mat with a soft breeze and listening to the waves)

**Pages 14–16** *How has Tane's behavior changed since the beginning of the story?* (He is no longer shy, and he has made good friends.) *How do Tane's grandparents feel about a western-style house?* (They prefer to live in the fale.) *How does Sione show his appreciation to the village?* (His business will build a desalination plant to provide fresh water.) *What is Tane's point of view about Tutuila at the end of the story?* (He knows that his family's connection with it is stronger than ever, and he looks forward to visiting again.)

## After Reading

**Respond to Reading** Revisit the Essential Question and ask students to complete the Text Evidence questions on page 16.

*Analytical Writing* **Write About Reading** Check that students have correctly identified Marama's point of view and compared it to Tane's, using text evidence.

### Fluency: Expression and Phrasing

**Model** Model reading page 6 with proper expression and phrasing. Next reread the page aloud and have students read along with you.

**Apply** Have students practice reading with a partner.

## PAIRED READ

### "Tell Me, Show Me"

#### Make Connections: Write About It *Analytical Writing*

Before reading, ask students to note that the genre of this text is poetry. After reading, have students identify the speaker's point of view in the poem and tell how it influences the description of events. Have them write connections between *Flying Home* and "Tell Me, Show Me."

**Leveled Reader**

### FOCUS ON LITERARY ELEMENTS

Students can extend their knowledge of imagery by completing the literary elements activity on page 20.

## Literature Circles

Ask students to conduct a literature circle using the Thinkmark questions to guide the discussion. You may wish to have a whole-class discussion, using both selections in the Leveled Reader, about what our connections to the world can teach us.

## Level Up

Level-up lessons available online.

**IF** students read the On Level fluently and answered the questions,

**THEN** pair them with students who have proficiently read the Beyond Level and have students

- partner-read the Beyond Level main selection.
- use self-stick notes to mark details that identify the characters' points of view.
- make a list of examples of personification.

### A C T  Access Complex Text

The Beyond Level challenges students by including more **figurative language** and **complex sentence structures**.

→ **On Level**

# Vocabulary

## REVIEW VOCABULARY WORDS

**OBJECTIVES**

CCSS Acquire and use accurately grade-appropriate general academic and domain-specific words and phrases, including those that signal contrast, addition, and other logical relationships (e.g., *however, although, nevertheless, similarly, moreover, in addition*). **L.5.6**

**I Do** Use the **Visual Vocabulary Cards** to review the key selection words *blares, connection, errand, exchange.* Point to each, read it aloud, and have students repeat.

**We Do** Ask these questions. Help students explain their answers.
→ What is something that *blares*?
→ Who is someone with whom you have a strong *connection*?

**You Do** Have students work in pairs to respond to these questions and explain their answers.
→ What is an *errand* you might do on the weekend?
→ What might you consider to be a fair *exchange* with a friend?

## PERSONIFICATION

**OBJECTIVES**

CCSS Determine the meaning of words and phrases as they are used in a text, including figurative language such as metaphors and similes. **RL.5.4**

CCSS Demonstrate understanding of figurative language, word relationships, and nuances in word meanings. Interpret figurative language, including similes and metaphors, in context. **L.5.5a**

**I Do** Remind students that personification is the use of human characteristics to describe non-human things. Use the Comprehension and Fluency passage on **Your Turn Practice Book** page 293 to model interpreting personification.

**Think Aloud** Line 3 of the first stanza is an example of personification. The sun cannot really smile, but describing the sun in human terms creates for readers the image of a bright and cheerful sunny day.

**We Do** Have students read the second stanza on page 293 where they encounter the line *Trees all wave to me.* Help students explain why this is an example of personification and what image it creates for readers: trees blowing cheerfully in the breeze. The speaker feels a friendly bond with nature.

**You Do** Have students work in pairs to find two examples of personification in the third stanza. Ask them to identify what is being personified and the images created by the personification.

# Comprehension

## REVIEW POINT OF VIEW

### OBJECTIVES

 **CCSS** Describe how a narrator's or speaker's point of view influences how events are described. **RL.5.6**

 **I Do** Remind students that point of view in a poem refers to what the speaker of a poem thinks. Being aware of the words the speaker uses and the ideas he or she expresses can help students understand the speaker's point of view.

 **We Do** Have a volunteer read the first stanza of the Comprehension and Fluency passage on **Your Turn Practice Book** page 293. Have students write down details shared by the speaker. Model using the speaker's word choices and use of details to determine his or her point of view about jogging.

**You Do** Have partners read the rest of the poem. Tell them to stop after each stanza and identify key words, thoughts, and details and use these to determine the speaker's overall point of view in the poem. Ask students to explain how the speaker's point of view influences how he or she describes events.

## SELF-SELECTED READING

### OBJECTIVES

 **CCSS** Describe how a narrator's or speaker's point of view influences how events are described. **RL.5.6**

Visualize sections in a text to increase understanding.

### Read Independently

Have students choose a narrative or lyric poem or selection of poems for sustained silent reading.

→ Before they read, have students preview the poem or poems, reading the title and viewing any images that appear.

→ As students read, remind them to visualize the characters, settings, and events described in the poem.

### Read Purposefully

Encourage students to read both narrative and lyric poems to learn about different subjects and kinds of speakers.

→ As students read, have them fill in Graphic Organizer 144, recording details, thoughts, and descriptions.

→ They can use the organizer to help them state the speaker's point of view and summarize the poem.

→ Ask students to share how the speaker's point of view influences how he or she describes events.

**Beyond Level**

**Lexile** 940
*TextEvaluator™* 61

---

**OBJECTIVES**

**CCSS** Describe how a narrator's or speaker's point of view influences how events are described. **RL.5.6**

**CCSS** Read on-level prose and poetry orally with accuracy, appropriate rate, and expression on successive readings. **RF.5.4b**

---

**ACADEMIC LANGUAGE**

• *point of view, speaker, visualize, realistic fiction, poetry, personification*

• Cognates: *punto de vista, visualizar, ficción realista, poesía, personificación*

---

## Leveled Reader:
## *Helping Out*

### Before Reading

**Preview and Predict**

→ Students should read the Essential Question.

→ Have students preview the title, table of contents, and first page of *Helping Out*. Students should use the text and illustrations to predict what they think the selection will be about.

**Review Genre: Realistic Fiction**

Tell students that this selection is realistic fiction. The characters and settings are like real people and places, and the events could actually happen in real life. As they preview the book, have students identify features of realistic fiction in *Helping Out*.

### During Reading

**Close Reading**

**Note Taking:** Ask students to use their graphic organizer as they read.

**Pages 2–3** *Who is telling the story?* (an outside narrator) *What words help you visualize the effects of the earthquake in Costa Rica?* (fallen buildings, people being carried out of the rubble on stretchers) *Why do the students rule out a music concert fund raiser?* (Only Chen and Jorge can play instruments; It will take too much time to organize.)

**Pages 4–5** *Identify an example of personification on page 4.* ("the room was humming with excitement") *Explain how the students plan to help the earthquake victims.* (They will ask businesses to donate food and water.) *How does Curtis feel about helping the victims?* (He thinks it is exciting to have a connection to another country.)

**Pages 6–10** *Find an example of personification on page 6.* ("his stomach began turning cartwheels") *What does this show?* (Curtis is nervous.) *Are Chen and Curtis successful at collecting donations? Explain.* (Yes. Even though they get off to a slow start and do not collect as much as other students, they still fill the trunk.) *What example of figurative language helps readers understand how disappointed Curtis is when he gets the e-mail from the Red Cross?* ("the message hit him like a slap in the face")

**Go Digital**

**Leveled Readers**

**Use Graphic Organizer**

*Why can't the Red Cross accept the students' donations?* (The cost of sending food would be more than its value, and they have no way to transport it where it is needed.) *What kind of donations does the Red Cross need instead?* (donations of money)

**Pages 11–15** *Summarize details about what the students have to do before they can sell the donated food at the market.* (ask permission from the stores who donated, revisit stores who could not donate before because they had only fresh produce, rent a stall at the market, make a sign for the stall) *How do the students end up raising so much money?* (People pay more than the asking price or donate without taking anything.) *What, according to Curtis, is the real lesson learned from the experience?* (Everyone can help. They just need to find the right way.)

## After Reading

**Respond to Reading** Revisit the Essential Question and ask students to complete the Text Evidence questions on page 16.

**Analytical Writing Write About Reading** Check that students have correctly identified Miss Johnston's point of view and cited appropriate supporting details.

### Fluency: Expression and Phrasing

**Model** Model reading page 10 with proper expression and phrasing. Next reread the page aloud and have students read along with you.

**Apply** Have students practice reading with a partner.

## PAIRED READ

**Leveled Reader**

# "A Journalistic Journey"

## Make Connections: Write About It ✏ *Analytical Writing*

Before reading, ask students to note that the genre of this text is poetry. After reading, have students identify the speaker's point of view in the poem and tell how it influences the description of events. Have them make connections between *Helping Out* and "A Journalistic Journey."

---

### FOCUS ON LITERARY ELEMENTS

Students can extend their knowledge of imagery by completing the literary elements activity on page 20.

---

## Literature Circles

Ask students to conduct a literature circle using the Thinkmark questions to guide the discussion. You may wish to have a whole-class discussion, using both selections in the Leveled Reader, about what our connections to the world can teach us.

## Gifted and Talented

**Synthesize** Have students research different areas in the world in which the Red Cross is currently giving aid. Have partners choose one of these areas and contact the Red Cross in order to find out how they can best contribute. Then have pairs write a detailed report in which they identify the area, explain why and how the Red Cross is giving aid there, and inform the class about what volunteers can do in order to best support the efforts of the Red Cross.

## Beyond Level

# Vocabulary

## REVIEW DOMAIN-SPECIFIC WORDS

**OBJECTIVES**

 Acquire and use accurately grade-appropriate general academic and domain-specific words and phrases, including those that signal contrast, addition, and other logical relationships (e.g., *however, although, nevertheless, similarly, moreover, in addition*). **L.5.6**

 **Model**  Use the **Visual Vocabulary Cards** to review the meaning of the words *connection* and *exchange*. Use each word in a context sentence.

Write the words *acknowledge* and *commitment* on the board and discuss the meanings with students. Then help students write sentences using these words.

**Apply**  Have students work in pairs to review the meanings of the words *appeal* and *contributions*. Then have partners write sentences using the words.

## PERSONIFICATION

**OBJECTIVES**

 Determine the meaning of words and phrases as they are used in a text, including figurative language such as metaphors and similes. **RL.5.4**

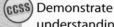 Demonstrate understanding of figurative language, word relationships, and nuances in word meanings. Interpret figurative language, including similes and metaphors, in context. **L.5.5a**

**Model**  Read aloud the first stanza of the Comprehension and Fluency passage on **Beyond Reproducibles** page 293.

**Think Aloud**  I recognize that the line *Sun's up and smiling* is an example of personification. The sun cannot really smile, but describing it in human terms creates an image for readers of a bright and cheerful sunny day.

With students, read the third stanza. Help them interpret *Wind kicks up its heels* and discuss the image it creates.

 **Apply**  Have pairs of students read the rest of the poem. Challenge them to identify as many examples of personification as they can in the poem and discuss the images they create.

 **Independent Study**  Challenge students to create an advertisement for a household product, using two or more examples of personification. Have students illustrate and present their ads.

# Comprehension

## REVIEW POINT OF VIEW

**OBJECTIVES**

 Describe how a narrator's or speaker's point of view influences how events are described. **RL.5.6**

 **Model** Remind students that point of view in a poem refers to what the speaker of a poem thinks. Being aware of the words the speaker uses and the ideas he or she expresses can help students understand the speaker's point of view.

Have students read the first stanza of the Comprehension and Fluency passage on **Beyond Reproducibles** page 293. Ask open-ended questions to facilitate discussion, such as *What does the speaker think about running? What words or phrases give you clues?* Students should support their responses with details from the poem.

 **Apply** Have students identify key words, details, and thoughts in the rest of the poem as they independently fill in Graphic Organizer 144. Then have students share their organizers and use them to state the speaker's point of view. Ask students to explain how the speaker's point of view influences how he or she describes events.

## SELF-SELECTED READING

**OBJECTIVES**

 Describe how a narrator's or speaker's point of view influences how events are described. **RL.5.6**

Visualize sections in a text to increase understanding.

### Read Independently

Have students choose a narrative or lyric poem or selection of poems for sustained silent reading.

→ As students read, have them complete Graphic Organizer 144.

→ Remind them to visualize characters, settings, and events as they read.

### Read Purposefully

Encourage students to keep a reading journal. Suggest that they select poems about topics that interest them.

→ Students can write summaries of the poem or poems in their journals.

→ Ask students to explain to the class how the point of view of the speaker of their poem is revealed in how he or she describes events.

 **Independent Study** Challenge students to consider how the poem or poems they read relate to the weekly theme of being out in the world. What do their class and independent poems suggest that our connections to the world can teach us?

# English Language Learners

**Reading/Writing Workshop**

## Shared Read
### *Poetry*

**Go Digital**

**View Poems**

### Before Reading

#### Build Background

Read the Essential Question: *What can our connections to the world teach us?*

→ Explain the meaning of the Essential Question, including the vocabulary in the question: *Connections are relationships or links with something. People have different connections to the world around us.*

→ **Model an answer:** *Appreciating art is one way to connect to the world. When I go to a museum, I see art from many places. Art can teach me about different time periods and different cultures.*

→ Ask students a question that ties the Essential Question to their own background knowledge: *Turn to a partner and discuss something you have learned about yourself from an activity, a trip, or a relationship.* Call on several pairs to share with the class.

### During Reading

#### Interactive Question-Response

→ Ask questions that help students understand the meaning of the text after each stanza.

→ Reinforce the meanings of key vocabulary.

→ Ask students questions that require them to use key vocabulary.

→ Reinforce strategies and skills of the week by modeling.

---

### OBJECTIVES

**CCSS** Determine the meaning of words and phrases as they are used in a text, including figurative language such as metaphors and similes. **RL.5.4**

**CCSS** Determine how a narrator's or speaker's point of view influences how events are described. **RL.5.6**

### LANGUAGE OBJECTIVE

Identify a speaker's point of view.

### ACADEMIC LANGUAGE

• *personification, visualize, speaker, point of view*

• Cognates: *personificación, visualizar, punto de vista*

**Page 438**

## To Travel!

**Stanza 1**
Choral-read the first stanza. Point to the exclamation points and encourage students to read with expression. *The speaker says that his universe expands when he travels. What do you think this means?* (he learns about new things)

**Stanza 2**
**Explain and Model Personification** Have students wave their arms. *Can a novel wave its arms, speak, or dance?* (no) *This is personification. The novel does things that humans do. What other example of personification do you see in this stanza?* (The pages of the novel dance. The paintings are speaking.)

**Stanza 3**
*How does the speaker travel and learn about life far away?* (He reads books and looks at art.)

**Page 439**

**Stanzas 4–5**
**Explain and Model the Strategy** *Authors use words that appeal to our senses to help us visualize, or create pictures in our mind, as we read. What senses do these words make you think about?* (hearing, smelling, tasting) *What do you picture in your mind when you read these stanzas?* (a heart flying through the air, hearing, smelling, and tasting different things)

*Customs are the traditions or different ways of doing things among a group of people.* Have students repeat the word. *An example of a custom is dancing at celebrations. What are some customs you practice?*

**Stanza 6**
**Explain and Model Speaker's Point of View** *A speaker's point of view is how he or she thinks about something. The speaker says he has learned that the world is made for everyone. He thinks that everyone can enjoy every part of the world by traveling through books and art.*

**Page 440**

## Wild Blossoms

**Lines 1–4**
*What words help you picture riding a bicycle on a sunny day?* (wheels weaving between sunbeams)

*Work with a partner to find an example of personification.* (clouds exchanged greetings)

**Lines 5–10**
*Let's pretend to be the grandmother planting seeds willy-nilly.* Demonstrate shaking out seeds on the ground without a plan.

**Page 441**

**Lines 11–20**
*Which words help you picture what the scene looks like?* (bees buzzed; swifts and sparrows dipped, dove, and darted; letting seeds loose on the wind)

*What is the speaker's reaction to how her grandmother is planting the seeds?* (She was surprised, but then she has fun planting the seeds like her grandmother does.)

### After Reading

**Make Connections**
→ Review the Essential Question: *What can our connections to the world teach us?*
→ Make text connections.
→ Have students complete **ELL Reproducibles** pages 293–294.

# English Language Learners

**Lexile** 610
*TextEvaluator* 24

---

## OBJECTIVES

**CCSS** Describe how a narrator's or speaker's point of view influences how events are described. **RL.5.6**

**CCSS** Read on-level prose and poetry orally with accuracy, appropriate rate, and expression on successive readings. **RF.5.4b**

---

## ACADEMIC LANGUAGE

• *point of view, speaker, visualize, realistic fiction, poetry*

• Cognates: *punto de vista, visualizar, ficción realista, poesía*

## Leveled Reader:
## *Flying Home*

### Before Reading

#### Preview

→ Read the Essential Question: *What can our connections to the world teach us?*

→ Refer to Keeping in Touch: *How do you stay connected to your friends and family?*

→ Preview *Flying Home* and "Fun and Play": Our purpose for reading is to learn how we are all connected to the world around us.

#### Vocabulary

Use the **Visual Vocabulary Cards** to pre-teach the ELL vocabulary: *appreciation, homeland, precious*. Use the routine found on the cards. Point out the cognate: *apreciación*.

### During Reading

#### Interactive Question-Response

**Note Taking:** Ask students to use the graphic organizer on **ELL Reproducibles** page 292. Use the questions below after each page is read with students. As you read, define vocabulary in context and use visuals to help students understand key vocabulary.

**Pages 2–3** *Where are Tane and his family going?* (American Samoa) Choral read the last paragraph. Then have students complete the sentence: *Tane feels _____ and _____.* (nervous, excited)

**Pages 4–5** Reread the last paragraph on page 5. *Sione is upset to see so many stores, restaurants, cars, and trucks. What is he worried about?* (He is worried the village has changed.)

**Pages 6–8** Read page 6. Explain that a reception is like a large party. Pantomime the feeling of being overwhelmed. *How does Tane feel?* (overwhelmed) Read page 8. *Tane feels shy with his cousins at first. When does he begin to relax?* (when they ask about his home)

**Pages 9–10** Point out the words *oval-shaped, palm fronds, tall wooden poles,* and *raised floor. How do these words help you visualize the house?* (I picture a round house on poles.)

## Go Digital

**Leveled Readers**

**Use Graphic Organizer**

**Pages 11–12** *Marama jumps out to see her cousins. Tane sits in the car. How are their feelings different?* (Marama is excited. Tane is nervous.) Read page 12. Explain the simile "you'll cook like a fish on the fire."

**Pages 13–15** Point out the words "The sunlight danced on the water…." *Can sunlight really dance?* (no) *How do Tane's feelings about the fale change?* (He is not nervous. He sleeps.) *How has Tane changed?* (He enjoys his family. He has made friends.) *What does Sione do to show how thankful he is to the village?* (His business will build a plant.)

## After Reading

**Respond to Reading** Revisit the Essential Question and ask students to complete the Text Evidence questions on page 16.

**Analytical Writing Write About Reading** Check that students have correctly identified Maramar's point of view and compared it to Tane's, using text evidence.

### Fluency: Expression and Phrasing

**Model** Model reading page 10 with proper expression and phrasing. Then reread the page aloud and have students read along with you.

**Apply** Have students practice reading with partners.

## PAIRED READ

**Leveled Reader**

### "Fun and Play"

#### Make Connections:
#### Write About It ● *Analytical Writing*

Before reading, ask students to note that the genre of this text is poetry. Then discuss the Essential Question. After reading, have students identify the speaker's point of view in the poem and tell how it influences the description of events. Have them list connections between *Flying Home* and "Fun and Play."

---

### FOCUS ON LITERARY ELEMENTS

Students can extend their knowledge of imagery by completing the activity on page 20.

---

## Literature Circles

Ask students to conduct a literature circle using the Thinkmark questions to guide the discussion. You may wish to have a whole-class discussion about connecting to the world using information from both selections in the Leveled Reader.

## Level Up

Level-up lessons available online.

**IF** students read the **ELL Level** fluently and answered the questions,

**THEN** pair them with students who have proficiently read **On Level** and have ELL students

• echo-read the **On Level** main selection.

• list words with which they have difficulty and discuss them with a partner.

### A C T ccess omplex ext

The **On Level** challenges students by including more **domain-specific words** and **complex sentence structures**.

#  English Language Learners
## Vocabulary

## PRETEACH VOCABULARY

**OBJECTIVES**
 Acquire and use accurately grade-appropriate general academic and domain-specific words and phrases, including those that signal contrast, addition, and other logical relationships. **L.5.6**

**LANGUAGE OBJECTIVE**
Use vocabulary words.

 **I Do** Preteach vocabulary from "To Travel!" and "Wild Blossoms," following the Vocabulary Routine found on the **Visual Vocabulary Cards** for the words *blares, connection, errand,* and *exchange.*

 **We Do** After completing the Vocabulary Routine for each word, point to the word on the Visual Vocabulary Card and read the word with students. Ask students to repeat the word.

 **You Do** Have students write a definition for a word of their choosing. Ask them to read the definition to a partner, and have the partner name the word that matches the definition.

| Beginning | Intermediate | Advanced/High |
|---|---|---|
| Help students write the definition correctly and read it aloud. | Ask students to write the definition as a complete sentence. | Challenge students to write a definition for each word. |

## REVIEW VOCABULARY

**OBJECTIVES**
 Acquire and use accurately grade-appropriate general academic and domain-specific words and phrases, including those that signal contrast, addition, and other logical relationships. **L.5.6**

**LANGUAGE OBJECTIVE**
Use vocabulary words.

 **I Do** Review the previous week's vocabulary words over a few days. Read each word aloud, pointing to the word on the **Visual Vocabulary Card**. Have students repeat. Then follow the Vocabulary Routine on the back of each card.

 **We Do** Review the words. Ask students to guess the word you describe. Provide clues, such as synonyms or antonyms. Have students name the word and define it or use it in a sentence.

 **You Do** In pairs, have students make a list of clues for two or more words. Ask them to read them aloud for the class to guess the word and define it or use it in a sentence.

| Beginning | Intermediate | Advanced/High |
|---|---|---|
| Help students list clue words and read them aloud. | Have students write clues as sentences. | Ask students to use synonyms or antonyms in their clues. |

# PERSONIFICATION

## OBJECTIVES

 Determine the meaning of words and phrases as they are used in a text, including figurative language such as metaphors and similes. **RL.5.4**

 Demonstrate understanding of figurative language, word relationships, and nuances in word meanings. Interpret figurative language, including similes and metaphors, in context. **L.5.5a**

### LANGUAGE OBJECTIVE
Interpret personification.

 **I Do** Read aloud the first stanza of the Comprehension and Fluency passage on **ELL Reproducibles** pages 293–294. Summarize the stanza. Point to the line "Sun's up and smiling." Explain that personification is giving human characteristics to non-human things, such as the sun.

**Think Aloud** "Sun's up and smiling" is an example of personification. The sun cannot really smile, but the poet creates a happy mood using personification, telling the reader that it is a bright, sunny day.

 **We Do** Have students read the line "Trees all wave to me" in the third stanza on page 293. Help students identify what is being personified and interpret the meaning.

 **You Do** In pairs, have students identify an example of personification in the fourth stanza and discuss what is being personified and the effect it creates.

| Beginning | Intermediate | Advanced/High |
|---|---|---|
| Help students locate and interpret the personification. | Ask students to identify and explain the personification. | Have students explain what personification adds to the poem. |

# ADDITIONAL VOCABULARY

## OBJECTIVES

 Acquire and use accurately grade-appropriate general academic and domain-specific words and phrases, including those that signal contrast, addition, and other logical relationships. **L.5.6**

### LANGUAGE OBJECTIVE
Use academic vocabulary and high-frequency words.

 **I Do** List academic language and high-frequency words from "To Travel!" and "Wild Blossoms": *customs, languages, variety;* and from *Flying Home: island, emotion, precious.* Define each word for students: *People in different countries speak different languages.*

 **We Do** Model using the words for students in a sentence: *I can speak two languages. When you travel, you might hear people speaking other languages.* Then provide sentence frames and complete them with students: *The languages I speak are _____.*

 **You Do** Have pairs make up their own sentence frames for the class to complete.

| Beginning | Intermediate | Advanced/High |
|---|---|---|
| Provide sentence frames and help students copy them. | Provide sentence starters, if necessary. | Have students define the words they used. |

# → English Language Learners
## Writing/Spelling

---

## WRITING TRAIT: WORD CHOICE

**OBJECTIVES**

 Write narratives to develop real or imagined experiences or events using effective technique, descriptive details, and clear event sequences. Use concrete words and phrases and sensory details to convey experiences and events precisely. **W.5.3d**

**LANGUAGE OBJECTIVE**
Use strong words in writing.

 **I Do** Explain that writers use strong, precise words to make story events clear. They may use adverbs that tell *where, when,* and *how* something happens. They may also use prepositional phrases. Read the Expert Model passage and identify adverbs or prepositional phrases the poet uses.

 **We Do** Read aloud the first stanza of "Wild Blossoms." Identify strong words and prepositional phrases, such as "weaving between sunbeams." Then use a word web to generate strong adverbs and prepositional phrases. Model sentences with strong words using the diagram.

 **You Do** Have pairs write a short paragraph, using the word web. They should include adverbs and prepositional phrases used as adverbs.

| Beginning | Intermediate | Advanced/High |
|---|---|---|
| Have students underline the prepositional phrases. | Have students revise, replacing weak words with stronger ones. | Have students revise to add strong adverbs and prepositional phrases. |

---

## SPELL WORDS WITH SUFFIXES *-ible* AND *-able*

**OBJECTIVES**

 Spell grade-appropriate words correctly, consulting references as needed. **L.5.2e**

**LANGUAGE OBJECTIVE**
Spell words with suffixes *-ible* and *-able*.

 **I Do** Read aloud the Spelling Words on page T292, segmenting them into syllables, and attaching a spelling to each sound. Point out the *-ible* or *-able* ending. Have students repeat the words.

 **We Do** Read the Dictation Sentences on page T293 aloud. Emphasize the underlined word, segmenting it into syllables. Have students repeat after you and write the word.

 **You Do** Display the words. Have students exchange their list with a partner to check the spelling and write the words correctly.

| Beginning | Intermediate | Advanced/High |
|---|---|---|
| Help students copy the words with correct spelling and say the words aloud. | After students correct their words, have pairs quiz each other. | Ask students to correct their words and practice writing words that were hard. |

# Grammar

## PREPOSITIONAL PHRASES AS ADJECTIVES AND ADVERBS

### OBJECTIVES

 Demonstrate command of the conventions of standard English grammar and usage when writing or speaking. **L.5.1**

### LANGUAGE OBJECTIVE

Use prepositional phrases as adjectives and adverbs.

**Language Transfers Handbook**

In Cantonese, prepositions are not used the way that they are in English. Speakers of this language may omit the preposition and may need additional support in the correct use and placement of prepositions.

 Review prepositions and prepositional phrases. Explain that a prepositional phrase that acts as an adjective tells *what kind, how many,* or *which one.* Write the following sentence, underlining the prepositional phrase: *The girl <u>with the blue backpack</u> is my friend.* Then tell students that a prepositional phrase that acts as an adverb tells *where, when,* or *how.* Write the following sentence, underlining the prepositional phrase: *My Aunt Lois lives <u>in Arizona</u>.*

 Write the sentence frames below on the board. Have students complete each prepositional phrase with a preposition. Guide them to tell whether the phrase is acting as an adjective or an adverb. Have them read the sentences aloud.

> *Lupe lives _____ Washington Street.* (on, adverb)
>
> *George works _____ the city government.* (for, adjective)
>
> *I like the horse _____ the golden mane.* (with, adjective)

 Brainstorm a list of prepositions with students. Have partners write two sentences, one with a prepositional phrase used as an adjective and one with a prepositional phrase used as an adverb. Have students read their sentences aloud.

| Beginning | Intermediate | Advanced/High |
|---|---|---|
| Help students write their sentences and tell whether the prepositional phrase is an adjective or an adverb. Read the sentences aloud. Have students repeat. | Ask students to underline the prepositional phrase they used in each sentence and tell what kind it is. | Challenge students to write sentences with more than one prepositional phrase. |

For extra support, have students complete the **Grammar Practice Reproducibles** during the week, using this routine:

→ Explain the grammar skill.

→ Model the first activity in the Grammar Practice Reproducibles.

→ Have the whole group complete the next couple of activities, then review the rest with a partner.

→ Review the activities with correct answers.

# PROGRESS MONITORING

## Weekly Assessment

**CCSS** **TESTED SKILLS**

| ✔**COMPREHENSION:** | ✔**VOCABULARY:** | ✔**WRITING:** |
|---|---|---|
| Point of View **RL.5.6** | Personification **RL.5.4** | Writing About Text **RL.5.4, W.5.9** |

**Assessment Includes**

→ Performance Tasks

→ Approaching-Level Assessment online PDFs

**Fluency Goal**  129 to 149 words correct per minute (WCPM)

**Accuracy Rate Goal**  95% or higher

Administer oral reading fluency assessments using the following schedule:

→ **Weeks 1, 3, 5**  Provide Approaching-Level students at least three oral reading fluency assessments during the unit.

→ **Weeks 2 and 4**  Provide On-Level students at least two oral reading fluency assessments during the unit.

→ **Week 6**  If necessary, provide Beyond-Level students an oral reading fluency assessment at this time.

**Also Available: Selection Tests online PDFs**

*Go Digital!*  www.connected.mcgraw-hill.com

# Using Assessment Results

| TESTED SKILLS | If ... | Then ... |
|---|---|---|
| **COMPREHENSION** | Students answer 0–6 multiple-choice items correctly ... | ... assign Lessons 37–39 on Point of View from the *Tier 2 Comprehension Intervention online PDFs.* |
| **VOCABULARY** | Students answer 0–6 multiple-choice items correctly ... | ... assign Lesson 167 on Personification from the *Tier 2 Vocabulary Intervention online PDFs.* |
| **WRITING** | Students score less than "3" on the construction responses ... | ... assign Lessons 37–39 on Point of View and/or Write About Reading Lesson 194 from the *Tier 2 Comprehension Intervention online PDFs.* |
| **FLUENCY** | Students have a WCPM score of 120–128 ... | ... assign a lesson from Section 1, 7, 8, 9, or 10 of the *Tier 2 Fluency Intervention online PDFs.* |
| | Students have a WCPM score of 0–119 ... | ... assign a lesson from Section 2, 3, 4, 5, or 6 of the *Tier 2 Fluency Intervention online PDFs.* |

# Response to Intervention

Use the appropriate sections of the *Placement and Dignostic Assessment* as well as students' assessment results to designate students requiring:

**TIER 2** **Intervention Online PDFs**

**TIER 3** **WonderWorks Intervention Program**

# REVIEW AND EXTEND

## Reader's Theater

*'Round the World with Nellie Bly*

**Genre** Play

**Fluency** Accuracy, Rate, and Prosody

## Reading Digitally

TIME FOR KIDS "The Tortoise and the Solar Plant"

**Comprehension** Close Reading

**Study Skills** Using Online Sources

**Research** Navigate Links to Information

*Go Digital!*

## Level Up Accelerating Progress

| From **APPROACHING** To **ON LEVEL** | From **ON LEVEL** To **BEYOND LEVEL** | From **ENGLISH LANGUAGE LEARNERS** To **ON LEVEL** | From **BEYOND LEVEL** To **SELF-SELECTED TRADE BOOK** |

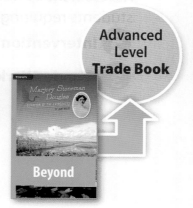

Advanced Level **Trade Book**

# *ASSESS*

## Presentations

### Research and Inquiry
Project Presentations
Project Rubric

### Writing
Opinion Writing Presentations
Writing Rubric

Juice Images/age fotostock

## Unit Assessments

**UNIT 6 TEST**

**FLUENCY**

## Evaluate Student Progress

Use the McGraw-Hill Reading Wonders eAssessment reports to evaluate student progress and help you make decisions about small group instruction and assignments.

→ Student and Class Assessment Report

→ Student and Class Standards Proficiency Report

→ Student Profile Summary Report

Juice Images/age fotostock

# SUGGESTED LESSON PLAN

|  | DAY 1 | DAY 2 |
|---|---|---|

## READING

### Whole Group

Reader's Theater
"'Round the World with Nellie Bly"

"The Tortoise and the Solar Plant"

| DAY 1 | DAY 2 |
|---|---|
| **Reader's Theater,** T326<br>"'Round the World with Nellie Bly"<br>Assign Roles<br>Model Fluency: Accuracy, Rate, and Prosody | **Reader's Theater,** T326<br>"'Round the World with Nellie Bly"<br>Model Fluency: Accuracy, Rate, and Prosody<br>**Reading Digitally,** T328<br>TIME "The Tortoise and the Solar Plant"<br>**Research and Inquiry,** T330–T331<br>Giving a Presentation |

**Research and Inquiry Projects**

## DIFFERENTIATED INSTRUCTION  Level Up to Accelerate

### Small Group

**Approaching Level**

| DAY 1 | DAY 2 |
|---|---|
| **Level Up to On Level**<br>*Marjory Stoneman Douglas: Guardian of the Everglades,* T336<br>**Spiral Review** Comprehension Skills Unit 6 Revised PDFs Online • *Analytical Writing* | **Level Up to On Level**<br>*Marjory Stoneman Douglas: Guardian of the Everglades,* T336<br>**Spiral Review** Comprehension Skills Unit 6 Revised PDFs Online • *Analytical Writing* |

**On Level**

| DAY 1 | DAY 2 |
|---|---|
| **Level Up to Beyond Level**<br>*Marjory Stoneman Douglas: Guardian of the Everglades,* T337 | **Level Up to Beyond Level**<br>*Marjory Stoneman Douglas: Guardian of the Everglades,* T337 |

**Beyond Level**

| DAY 1 | DAY 2 |
|---|---|
| **Level Up to Self-Selected Trade Book,** T339 | **Level Up to Self-Selected Trade Book,** T339 |

**English Language Learners**

| DAY 1 | DAY 2 |
|---|---|
| **Level Up to On Level**<br>*Marjory Stoneman Douglas: Guardian of the Everglades,* T338 | **Level Up to On Level**<br>*Marjory Stoneman Douglas: Guardian of the Everglades,* T338 |

## Writing Process  LANGUAGE ARTS

### Whole Group

**Writing**

| DAY 1 | DAY 2 |
|---|---|
| **Share Your Writing,** T334<br>Opinion Writing<br>Prepare to Present Your Writing | **Share Your Writing,** T334<br>Opinion Writing<br>Discuss Peer Feedback |

| DAY 3 | DAY 4 | DAY 5 |
|---|---|---|
| **Reading Digitally,** T328 <br> TIME "The Tortoise and the Solar Plant" <br> *Analytical Writing* | **Reader's Theater,** T326 <br> Performance | **Research and Inquiry,** T332–T333 <br> Presentations <br> ✔ **Unit Assessment,** T340–T341 |
| **Research and Inquiry Projects** | **Research and Inquiry Projects** *Analytical Writing* | |
| **Level Up to On Level** <br> *Marjory Stoneman Douglas: Guardian of the Everglades,* T336 <br> **Spiral Review** Comprehension Skills <br> Unit 6 Revised PDFs Online *Analytical Writing* | **Level Up to On Level** <br> "The Story of the Tree Musketeers," T336 | **Level Up to On Level** <br> Literature Circle, T336 |
| **Level Up to Beyond Level** <br> *Marjory Stoneman Douglas: Guardian of the Everglades,* T337 | **Level Up to Beyond Level** <br> "The Story of the Tree Musketeers," T337 | **Level Up to Beyond Level** <br> Literature Circle, T337 |
| **Level Up to Self-Selected Trade Book,** T339 | **Level Up to Self-Selected Trade Book,** T339 | **Level Up to Self-Selected Trade Book,** T339 |
| **Level Up to On Level** <br> *Marjory Stoneman Douglas: Guardian of the Everglades,* T338 | **Level Up to On Level** <br> "The Story of the Tree Musketeers," T338 | **Level Up to On Level** <br> Literature Circle, T338 |
| **Share Your Writing,** T334 <br> Opinion Writing <br> Rehearse Your Presentation | **Share Your Writing,** T334 <br> Present Your Opinion Writing <br> Evaluate Your Presentation | **Share Your Writing,** T335 <br> Opinion Writing <br> Portfolio Choice |

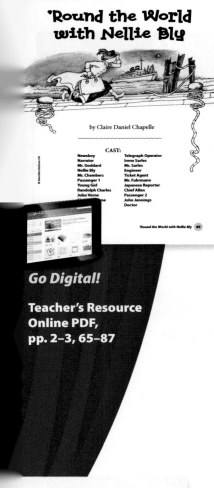

'Round the World
with Nellie Bly

by Claire Daniel Chapelle

CAST:
| | |
|---|---|
| Newsboy | Telegraph Operator |
| Narrator | Irene Sarles |
| Mr. Goddard | Mr. Sarles |
| Nellie Bly | Engineer |
| Mr. Chambers | Ticket Agent |
| Passenger 1 | Mr. Fuhrmann |
| Young Girl | Japanese Reporter |
| Randolph Charles | Chief Allen |
| Jules Verne | Passenger 2 |
| | John Jennings |
| | Doctor |

'Round the World with Nellie Bly

**Go Digital!**

**Teacher's Resource
Online PDF,
pp. 2–3, 65–87**

# 'Round the World with Nellie Bly

## Introduce the Play

Explain that *'Round the World with Nellie Bly* is a play set in 1888, when Nellie Bly, a newspaper reporter, set out to travel around the world in 75 days and share her adventures with readers. Distribute the Elements of Drama handout and scripts from the **Teacher's Resource Online PDF,** pages 2–3, 65–87.

→ Review the features of a play.

→ Review the cast of characters.

→ Review information provided by the narrator about the setting, explaining that sensational journalism was popular at the time Nellie Bly was writing for the *World*. Few women worked outside the home, and even fewer had jobs like Nellie Bly's.

## Shared Reading

Model reading the play as students follow along in their scripts.

**Focus on Vocabulary** Stop and discuss any vocabulary words that students may not know. You may wish to teach:

→ gimmick

→ sensational

→ itinerary

→ avid

→ palatial

→ enchants

**Model Fluency** As you read each part, state the name of the character and read the part, emphasizing the appropriate phrasing and expression.

## Discuss Each Role

→ After reading the part of the narrator, ask students to identify what information the narrator gives about the play.

→ After reading each character part, ask partners to note the character's traits. Model how to find text evidence that tells them about the characters.

## Assign Roles

If you need additional roles, you can assign the parts of the narrator and Nellie Bly to more than one student.

## Practice the Play

Each day, allow students time to practice their parts in the play. Pair fluent readers with less fluent readers. Pairs can echo read or chorally read their parts. As needed, work with less fluent readers to mark pauses in their scripts using one slash for a short pause and two slashes for longer pauses.

Throughout the week, have students work on the **Reader's Theater Workstation Activity Card 29.**

Once students have practiced reading their parts several times, allow students time to practice performing the script.

## Perform the Reader's Theater

→ Remind students to focus on their scripts as the play is being performed and read along, even when they are not in the scene.

→ As a class, discuss how performing a play aloud is different from reading it silently. Have students discuss with a partner what they liked about performing and what they found difficult.

# ACTIVITIES

## ALL ABOUT THE NARRATOR

Some plays use a narrator to move the plot along and announce a new setting. The narrator does not interact with the other characters in the play. Instead, the narrator gives the audience information.

Reread 'Round the World with Nellie Bly, paying close attention to the narrator's lines. Then discuss these questions with a small group:

**1.** How does the narrator describe the first setting?

**2.** What are two things the narrator says that go beyond the characters' dialogue?

**3.** How does the narrator move the plot along?

**4.** What does the narrator say about Nellie's challenge at the end of the play?

## DIRECT THE SHOW

Unlike some plays, 'Round the World with Nellie Bly has no stage directions. The narrator only briefly describes what characters are doing. Have partners pick three pages and write more detailed stage directions. Then ask:

**1.** Why might a playwright choose not to include stage directions?

**2.** How might stage directions affect the actors' performances?

## ENGLISH LANGUAGE LEARNERS

**ELL**

→ Review the definitions of difficult words and phrases, including *bleary-eyed, gripsack, racking my brains, bureau, positively, dreadful,* and *astonished.*

→ Team an ELL student with a fluent reader who is also reading the part of the narrator. Have each reader take turns reading the lines. Determine which reader will read which lines at the performance.

→ Work with students on pronunciation and comprehension of difficult words, as well as on intonation.

# Reading Digitally

## The Tortoise and the Solar Plant

### Before Reading

**Preview**  Scroll through the online article "The Tortoise and the Solar Plant" at www.connected.mcgraw-hill.com and have students identify text features. Clarify how to navigate through the article. Point out the interactive features, such as **hyperlinks**, **pop-ups, maps,** and **diagrams**. Explain that you will read the article together first and then access these features.

### Close Reading Online

**Take Notes**  Scroll back to the top and read the article aloud. As you read, ask questions to focus students on the problem of building a solar-powered plant and how people have worked to solve it. Have students take notes on the problem and solutions using Graphic Organizer 142. After each section, have partners paraphrase the main ideas, giving text evidence. Make sure students understand homophones, such as *site/sight, hole/whole,* and *it's/its*.

**Access Interactive Features**  Help students access the interactive elements by clicking each feature. Discuss what information these elements add to the text.

Tell students they will reread parts of the article to help them answer a question: *How does the government help preserve endangered animals?*

Have students skim to find text detailing actions the government has taken to protect endangered animals. Have partners share what they find.

**Navigate Links to Information**  Remind students that online texts may include **hyperlinks**, colored or underlined text on a Web page that connects to another Web page with related information.

Do an online search about endangered animals. Model using a hyperlink to jump to another Web page. Discuss any information on the new Web page related to the question *How does the government help preserve endangered animals?* Examine the Web page with students and make a list of relevant facts and supporting details. Remind students to evaluate the information for accuracy, currency, and signs of bias.

 **OBJECTIVES**
**CCSS** Draw on information from multiple print or digital sources, demonstrating the ability to locate an answer to a question quickly or to solve a problem efficiently. **RI.5.7**

 **CCSS** Conduct short research projects that use several sources to build knowledge through investigation of different aspects of a topic. **W.5.7**

**ACADEMIC LANGUAGE**
• *homophones, preserve, endangered, protect*
• Cognates: *homófonos, proteger*

## WRITE ABOUT READING *Analytical Writing*

**Summarize** Review students' graphic organizers. Model using the information to summarize "The Tortoise and the Solar Plant."

Ask students to write a summary of the article, stating the problem and the actions people have taken to solve it. Partners should discuss their summaries.

**Make Connections** Have students compare what they learned about how we are all connected with what they have learned about other connections in texts they have read in this unit.

## TAKE A STAND

**Preserving Habitats**

Have students research and write about the following question: *Why is it important to protect animal habitats?* Encourage students to take notes and make an outline of the ideas and evidence they find. For example:

→ Building solar-powered plants in the Mojave Desert could have killed off the desert tortoises there.

As students write, remind them to state their opinion clearly, organize their ideas logically, cite any sources they use, and end with a strong concluding statement.

## RESEARCH ONLINE

**Spelling** Remind students that spelling key words correctly will lead them to better search results. Point out that the word *Mojave* is also spelled *Mohave*, but that *Mojave* is the current spelling. Students should choose search results that use the current spelling in hopes of finding the most recent information.

Similarly, point out that misspelled information often makes it clear that a Web site is not reliable. Explain that watching for proper spelling and using it to search will help students locate useful research material.

## INDEPENDENT STUDY

**Investigate**

**Choose a Topic** Students should brainstorm questions related to the article. They might ask: *What other habitats have been threatened by human activity?* Then have students choose a question to research. Help them narrow it.

**Conduct Internet Research** Review the importance of spelling key words correctly and looking for misspelled words on Web sites. Use a few sites as examples of good or unreliable information.

**Present** Have groups present a round-table discussion on the topic of threatened habitats.

# RESEARCH AND INQUIRY

**The Big Idea:** *How are we all connected?*

**Assign the Projects** Break students into five groups. Assign each group one of the five projects that follow or let groups self-select their project. Before students begin researching, present these minilessons.

## Research Skill: Giving a Presentation

### OBJECTIVES

**CCSS** With some guidance and support from adults, use technology, including the Internet, to produce and publish writing as well as to interact and collaborate with others; demonstrate sufficient command of keyboarding skills to type a minimum of two pages in a single sitting. **W.5.6**

**CCSS** Conduct short research projects that build knowledge through investigation of different aspects of a topic. **W.5.7**

**CCSS** Recall relevant information from past experiences or gather relevant information from print and digital sources. **W.5.8**

**CCSS** Include multimedia components (e.g., graphics, sound) and visual displays in presentations when appropriate to enhance the development of main ideas or themes. **SL.5.5**

### Communicating Clearly

→ Effective speakers make eye contact with the audience, use an appropriate rate and volume of speech, and use gestures and nonverbal cues that complement the information. Finally, they choose language that is appropriate for their topic and audience.

→ Explain that formal language is used in informational presentations and persuasive speeches when the audience includes an adult, such as a teacher or principal. Formal presentations use more advanced vocabulary, avoid contractions, and follow grammar rules exactly.

→ Informal language may be used in dialogue, humorous speeches, or when addressing an audience of one's peers. It is more acceptable to use contractions and slang in an informal presentation.

### Organizing and Enhancing Presentations

Effective, engaging speakers deliver organized and interesting presentations. Their presentations are clear and easy to follow and often enhanced by multimedia or visual components.

→ Presentations are usually organized into an introduction, a body, and a conclusion. A strong introduction captures the audience's interest. It clearly states the topic, theme, or purpose of the presentation.

→ The body of the presentation contains the main content and ideas. It must be organized and easy to follow. For example, when giving oral instructions, it makes sense to organize the steps in sequence.

→ The conclusion ends the presentation by restating the main points. It may also leave the audience with something to think about.

→ Students may choose to include technology or visuals to enhance a presentation. Diagrams, charts, graphic organizers, slide shows and visual presentations that include music or video clips can engage the audience and illustrate important ideas.

Go Digital

**COLLABORATE**
Post student questions and monitor student online discussions. Create a Shared Research Board.

# Choose a Project!

## 1 An Oral Presentation

**ESSENTIAL QUESTION**
*How do different groups contribute to a cause?*

**Goal**
Research teams will research groups that specialize in emergency response or disaster relief, then summarize what they have learned in a formal oral presentation.

## 2 A List of Guidelines

**ESSENTIAL QUESTION**
*What actions can we take to get along with others?*

**Goal**
Research teams will create a list of guidelines for using social media in a safe and respectful way and present those guidelines to the class.

## 3 A Slide Show

**ESSENTIAL QUESTION**
*How are living things adapted to their environment?*

**Goal**
Research teams will create a slide show about an animal found on the island of Madagascar and its adaptations to its environment.

**STEM**

## 4 A Rap or Jingle

**ESSENTIAL QUESTION**
*What impact do our actions have on our world?*

**Goal**
Research teams will do research and write a rap or jingle that explains how a disposable item can be reused in a creative new way.

**STEM**

## 5 A Mock Interview

**ESSENTIAL QUESTION**
*What can our connections to the world teach us?*

**Goal**
Research teams will research a foreign person who is admired by the group and dramatize a mock interview with that person.

# RESEARCH AND INQUIRY

**Distribute the Research Roadmap Online PDF. Have students use the roadmap to complete the project.**

## Conducting the Research

**STEP 1** **Set Research Goals**

Discuss with students the Essential Question and the research project. As appropriate, have them look at the Shared Research Board for information they have already gathered. Each group should

→ make sure they are clear on their research focus and end product.

→ review the class Web site to help them generate search terms and questions.

**STEP 2** **Identify Sources**

Have the group brainstorm where they can find the information they need. Sources might include

→ reliable Web sites, such as those of governments or reputable organizations.

→ wildlife magazines or nonfiction books.

→ periodicals about the environment.

Review examples of primary sources and suggest that students examine photographs, interviews, or blog posts related to their topics.

**STEP 3** **Find and Record Information**

Have students review the strategies presented on page T330. Then have them do research. Suggest that students write a question they have on one side of a note card and the information they find to answer the question on the other side.

**STEP 4** **Organize**

After team members have completed their research, they can review and analyze the information they collected. Students should classify and categorize their notes into an outline to determine the main ideas and important details. Remind students they may not need all of the information they gathered.

**STEP 5** **Synthesize and Present**

Have teams synthesize their research and decide on a final message.

→ Encourage students to create props, visual aids, or graphic displays for their presentation or performance.

→ Students should check that their key ideas are included and their findings relate to the Big Idea.

### Audience Participation

→ Encourage the audience to share the most interesting thing they learned.

→ Have students discuss how the presentation relates to the Essential Question.

# Review and Evaluate

Distribute the Student Checklist and Project Rubric Online PDFs. Use the Project Rubric and the Teacher Checklist below to evaluate students' research and presentations.

## Student Checklist

### Research Process

- ☑ Did you narrow your focus for your research?
- ☑ Did you create a research plan for your project?
- ☑ Did you give credit to all your sources?
- ☑ Did you evaluate the information you collected?

### Presenting

- ☑ Did you practice your presentation?
- ☑ Did you sequence your ideas logically?
- ☑ Did you support your topic with appropriate facts and details?
- ☑ Did you make eye contact with your audience?
- ☑ Did you answer the Essential Question and Big Idea?
- ☑ Did you use multimedia components or visual displays to enhance your presentation?

## Teacher Checklist

### Assess the Research Process

- ☑ Selected a focus.
- ☑ Used multiple sources to gather information.
- ☑ Cited sources for information.
- ☑ Used time effectively and collaborated well.

### Assess the Presentation

- ☑ Spoke clearly and at an appropriate pace and volume.
- ☑ Used appropriate gestures.
- ☑ Maintained eye contact.
- ☑ Established a main message that answered the Essential Question and Big Idea.
- ☑ Used appropriate visuals and technology.
- ☑ Shared responsibility and tasks among all group members.

### Assess the Listener

- ☑ Listened quietly and politely.
- ☑ Made appropriate comments and asked clarifying question.
- ☑ Responded with an open mind to different ideas.

# Research and Inquiry Rubric

| 4 Excellent | 3 Good | 2 Fair | 1 Unsatisfactory |
|---|---|---|---|
| **The student** | **The student** | **The student** | **The student** |
| → presents information clearly. | → presents information adequately. | → attempts to present information. | → may show little grasp of the task. |
| → includes many details. | → provides adequate details. | → may offer few or vague details. | → may present irrelevant information. |
| → may include sophisticated observations. | → includes relevant observations. | → may include few or irrelevant personal observations. | → may reflect extreme difficulty with research or presentation. |

# Celebrate Share Your Writing

## Presentations

### Giving Presentations

Now is the time for students to share one of the pieces of opinion writing that they have worked on through the unit.

You may wish to invite parents or students from other classes to the Publishing Celebrations.

### Preparing for Presentations

Tell students that they will need to prepare in order to best present their writing.

Allow students time to rehearse their presentations. Encourage them to reread their writing a few times. This will help them become more familiar with their pieces so that they won't have to read word by word as they present.

Students should consider any visuals or digital elements that they may want to use to present their book reviews and opinion letters. Discuss a few possible options with students.

→ Can they share a copy of the book they have reviewed?

→ Is there a video about the topic of their opinion letter that might provide background information or support their point of view?

→ Is there a Web site or multimedia presentation that offers additional information about the issue?

Students can practice presenting to a partner in the classroom. They can also practice with family members at home, or in front of a mirror. Share the following checklist with students to help them focus on important parts of their presentation as they rehearse. Discuss each point on the checklist.

### Speaking Checklist

Review the Speaking Checklist with students as they practice.

☑ Have all of your notes and visuals ready.

☑ Take a few deep breaths.

☑ Stand up straight.

☑ Look at the audience.

☑ Speak clearly and slowly, particularly when communicating complex information.

☑ Speak loud enough so everyone can hear.

☑ Emphasize important points in your argument.

☑ Use appropriate gestures.

☑ Hold your visual aids so everyone can see them.

☑ Use facial expressions to convey appropriate emotions to your audience.

## Listening to Presentations

Remind students that they will be part of the audience for other students' presentations. A listener serves an important role. Review with students the following Listening Checklist.

---

### Listening Checklist

**During the presentation**

☑ Pay attention to how the speaker uses facts and details to support opinions.

☑ Notice how the speaker includes visual elements to enhance main ideas.

☑ Take notes on one or two things with which you agree or disagree.

☑ Write one question or comment you have about the information.

☑ Do not talk during the presentation.

**After the presentation**

☑ Tell why you liked the presentation.

☑ Ask a question or make a comment based on the information presented.

☑ Only comment on the presentation when it is your turn.

☑ If someone else makes the same comment first, elaborate on that person's response.

---

## Portfolio Choice

Ask students to select one finished piece of writing, as well as two revisions, to include in their writing portfolio. As students consider their choices, have them use the questions below.

### Published Writing

Does your writing

→ share an opinion and logically organize reasons to support the opinion?

→ have a strong conclusion?

→ have few or no spelling and grammatical errors?

→ demonstrate neatness when published?

### Writing Entry Revisions

Do your revisions show

→ strong opinions with supporting details?

→ information that is clearly connected to the topic?

→ varied sentence structure?

→ time-order signal words to indicate the sequence of events described?

---

**Go Digital**

**PORTFOLIO**
Students can submit their writing to be considered for inclusion in their digital Portfolio. Students' portfolios can be shared with parents.

Juice Images/age fotostock

# Level Up Accelerating Progress

**Leveled Reader**

## Approaching Level to On Level

### *Marjory Stoneman Douglas: Guardian of the Everglades*

Level Up Lessons also available online

### Before Reading

**Preview** Discuss what students remember about Marjory Stoneman Douglas and her work to protect the Everglades. Tell them they will be reading a more challenging version of *Marjory Stoneman Douglas: Guardian of the Everglades*.

**Vocabulary** Use the Visual Vocabulary Cards and routine to review.

### A C T During Reading

▶ **Specific Vocabulary** Review new content-area words. Model how to use word parts or context clues to determine the meaning of *hydrologist, Seminoles, diminutive,* and *quadrupled*.

▶ **Connection of Ideas** Students may need help connecting and synthesizing information from paragraph to paragraph. Model paraphrasing Marjory's words in paragraph 2 on page 2. Have students state the main idea based on key details. Then have them turn to a partner and paraphrase paragraph 3 on page 2. Discuss how paragraphs 2 and 3 are related—they show Marjory's feelings about the Everglades.

▶ **Sentence Structure** Students may need help understanding the different kinds of questions the author asks. See pages 2, 3, and 9. Chorally read the first two questions in paragraph 1 on page 2. Then ask: *Are these the narrator's questions to readers?* (yes) *Why do you think the narrator poses these questions?* (to make readers take a closer look at the Everglades)

### After Reading

Ask students to complete the Respond to Reading on page 15. Have students complete the Paired Read and hold Literature Circles.

**Leveled Reader**

**OBJECTIVES**
By the end of the year, read and comprehend informational texts, including history/ social studies, science, and technical texts, at the high end of the grades 4–5 complexity band independently and proficiently.
**RI.5.10**

# On Level
## to Beyond Level

## Marjory Stoneman Douglas: Guardian of the Everglades

**Level Up Lessons also available online**

### Before Reading

**Preview** Discuss what students remember about Marjory Stoneman Douglas and her work to protect the Everglades. Tell them they will be reading a more challenging version of *Marjory Stoneman Douglas*.

**Vocabulary** Use the Visual Vocabulary Cards and routine to review.

### A C T  During Reading

▶ **Specific Vocabulary** Review new content-area words. Model using context clues or word parts to determine the meaning of *saturated*, *idyllic*, *inhabited*, and *conserving*.

▶ **Connection of Ideas** Students may need help connecting and synthesizing ideas from section to section. Model for students how to connect the information in the section they just read to information in the previous section. Students may find it helpful to identify the main idea of each section after reading it in order to connect it to the next section.

▶ **Sentence Structure** Students may need help understanding more complex sentences. Read aloud the following sentence on page 13: *Although she was best known for her work to save and restore the Everglades, she was concerned about all aspects of protecting and conserving the natural world.* Simplify the sentence: *Marjory was best known for her work to save the Everglades. However, she was also concerned about all aspects of protecting the natural world.* Have students read the complex sentence aloud.

### After Reading

Ask students to complete the Respond to Reading on page 15. Have students complete the Paired Read and hold Literature Circles.

# Level Up Accelerating Progress

**Leveled Reader**

**OBJECTIVES**

**CCSS** By the end of the year, read and comprehend informational texts, including history/social studies, science, and technical texts, at the high end of the grades 4–5 complexity band independently and proficiently.
**RI.5.10**

## English Language Learners to On Level

### *Marjory Stoneman Douglas: Guardian of the Everglades*

**Level Up Lessons also available online**

### Before Reading

**Preview** A biography gives facts and details about a real person's life. Discuss what students remember about Marjory Stoneman Douglas.

**Vocabulary** Use the Visual Vocabulary Cards and routine to review. Point out cognates: *influenciar, plantaciones*.

### A C T During Reading

▶ **Specific Vocabulary** Show students how to identify context clues that will help them figure out the meaning of more difficult words, such as *unique* in paragraph 2 on page 2. Point out that the words "different from anywhere else" define *unique*. Provide a simple definition. (one of a kind) Repeat for other words.

▶ **Connection of Ideas** Students may need help connecting the quotations from Marjory Stoneman Douglas with the main text. See pages 2, 8, 11, and 14. Paraphrase the quotes in simpler language. Discuss how the quote relates to the surrounding text.

▶ **Sentence Structure** Students may need help understanding the different kinds of questions the author asks. Explain that sometimes the narrator may ask questions of the readers. (page 2) The narrator may also pose questions that he or she thinks the reader might have. (pages 3 and 9) Chorally read the first two questions in paragraph 1 on page 2. Ask: *Are these the narrator's questions to readers?* (yes) *Why do you think the narrator asks these questions?* (to make readers take a closer look at the Everglades)

### After Reading

Ask students to complete the Respond to Reading on page 15. Have students complete the Paired Read and hold Literature Circles.

**Leveled Reader**

**OBJECTIVES**

**CCSS** By the end of the year, read and comprehend literature, including stories, dramas, and poetry, at the high end of the grades 4–5 text complexity band independently and proficiently.
**RL.5.10**

**CCSS** By the end of the year, read and comprehend informational texts, including history/social studies, science, and technical texts, at the high end of the grades 4–5 text complexity band independently and proficiently.
**RI.5.10**

**Advanced Level Trade Book**

# Beyond Level
# to Self-Selected Trade Book

## Independent Reading

**Level Up Lessons** also available online

### Before Reading

Together with students identify the particular focus of their reading based on the text they choose. Students who have chosen the same title will work in groups to closely read the selection.

### Close Reading

**Taking Notes** Assign a graphic organizer for students to use to take notes as they read. Reinforce specific comprehension focus from the unit by choosing one of the graphic organizers that best fits the book.

**Examples:**

| **Fiction** | **Informational Text** |
| --- | --- |
| Theme | Text Structure: Cause and Effect |
| Graphic Organizer 102 | Graphic Organizer 86 |

**Ask and Answer Questions** Remind students to ask questions as they read. Suggest that they fold a sheet of paper in half vertically and record questions and page numbers on one side. As students meet, have them discuss the section that they have read. They can discuss the questions they noted and work together to find text evidence to support their answers. Have them write their answers on the other half of the paper.

### After Reading

**Write About Reading**

Have students work together to respond to the text using text evidence to support their writing.

**Examples:**

| **Fiction** | **Informational Text** |
| --- | --- |
| How do the characters' words and actions reveal the theme? What is the theme? | How is the text organized? Why is this organization effective? |

# SUMMATIVE ASSESSMENT

# Unit Assessment

 **TESTED SKILLS**

| ✔ **COMPREHENSION:** | ✔ **VOCABULARY:** | ✔ **ENGLISH LANGUAGE CONVENTIONS:** | ✔ **WRITING:** |
|---|---|---|---|
| • Theme **RL.5.2**<br>• Text Structure: Cause and Effect **RI.5.3**<br>• Text Structure: Problem and Solution **RI.5.5**<br>• Point of View **RL.5.6** | • Homophones **L.5.4a**<br>• Connotation and Denotation **L.5.4c**<br>• Context Clues: Paragraph Clues **L.5.4a**<br>• Synonyms and Antonyms **L.5.5c**<br>• Personification **RL.5.4** | • Adverbs **L.3.1a, L.4.1a**<br>• Adverbs That Compare **L.3.1g**<br>• Negatives **L.5.1, L.5.2**<br>• Sentence Combining **L.5.1e, L.5.3a**<br>• Prepositional Phrases **L.5.1a** | • Writing About Text **W.5.9a–b**<br>• Writing Prompt-Opinion **W.5.1a–d** |

## Assessment Includes
→ Performance Tasks
→ Writing Prompt

## Additional Assessment Options

Conduct assessments individually using the differentiated passages in *Fluency Assessment.* Students' expected fluency goal for this Unit is **129–149 WCPM** with an accuracy rate of 95% or higher.

### Running Records

Use the instructional reading level determined by the Running Record calculations for regrouping decisions. Students at Level 50 or below should be provided reteaching on specific Comprehension skills.

# Using Assessment Results

| TESTED SKILLS | If ... | Then ... |
|---|---|---|
| **COMPREHENSION** | Students answer 0–9 multiple-choice items correctly ... | ... reteach the necessary skills using Lessons 34–39, 76–78, and 82–84 from the ***Tier 2 Comprehension Intervention online PDFs.*** |
| **VOCABULARY** | Students answer 0–7 multiple-choice items correctly ... | ... reteach the necessary skills using Lessons 142, 167, 169, 170, and 172 from the ***Tier 2 Vocabulary Intervention online PDFs.*** |
| **ENGLISH LANGUAGE CONVENTIONS** | Students answer 0–7 multiple-choice items correctly ... | ... reteach the necessary skills using Lessons 36–40 from the ***Tier 2 Writing and Grammar Intervention online PDFs.*** |
| **WRITING** | Students score less than "2" on short-response items and "3" on extended constructed response items ... | ... reteach tested skills using appropriate lessons from the Strategies and Skills and/or Write About Reading sections in the ***Tier 2 Comprehension Intervention online PDFs.*** |
| | Students score less than "3" on the writing prompt ... | ... reteach the necessary skills using the ***Tier 2 Writing and Grammar Intervention online PDFs.*** |
| **FLUENCY** | Students have a WCPM score of 0–128 ... | ... reteach tested skills using the ***Tier 2 Fluency Intervention online PDFs.*** |

# Response to Intervention

Use the appropriate sections of the ***Placement and Dignostic Assessment*** as well as students' assessment results to designate students requiring:

**2** **Intervention Online PDFs**

**3** **WonderWorks Intervention Program**

**Reevaluate Student Grouping**

View the ***McGraw-Hill Reading Wonders eAssessment Class Unit Assessment*** reports available for this Unit Assessment. Note students who are below the overall proficiency level for the assessment, and use the reports to assign small group instruction for students with similar needs.

**Genre Writing**

 **Reading Extended Complex Text**

**Literature Anthology**

**Your Own Text**

**Program Information**

**Scope and Sequence**

**Index**

 **Correlations**

## Genre Writing: Opinion

*Writing Process*

## Reading Extended Complex Text

*Model Lesson*

Literature Anthology

## Program Information

## For Additional Resources

*Go Digital*

Review Comprehension Lessons

Unit Bibliography

Word Lists

Literature and Informational Text Charts

Web Sites

Resources

www.connected.mcgraw-hill.com

# OPINION TEXT Book Review

## EXPERT MODEL

**EXPERT MODEL**

### OBJECTIVES

CCSS Write opinion pieces on topics or texts, supporting a point of view with reasons and information. Provide logically ordered reasons that are supported by facts and details. **W.5.1b**

### ACADEMIC LANGUAGE

• *book review, prewrite, purpose, audience, logical order*

• Cognate: *orden lógico*

### Read Like a Writer

When writing a book review, the writer includes a summary of the book, followed by an opinion of the work. A writer gives reasons for his or her opinion, and explains those reasons using evidence from the book.

Readers may seek out book reviews *before* they read a book to see if the topic or genre might interest them. Sometimes readers like to read book reviews *after* they have read the work to see if the reviewer agrees with their own opinions.

Provide copies of the Expert Model Online PDF 101 and the Features of a Book Review Online PDF 102 in Writer's Workspace.

**Go Digital**

Writer's Workspace

### Features of a Book Review

→ It clearly states the writer's opinion about the book.

→ It introduces the book and provides a short summary.

→ It gives clear reasons for the writer's opinion.

→ It supports the opinion with reasons, facts, and details.

→ It often ends with a recommendation to readers.

### Discuss the Expert Model

Use the questions below to prompt discussion of the features of a book review.

→ What is the writer's opinion of this book? (He thinks it is an important book and he learned a lot by reading it. He found the book's story about the restoration of a polluted river inspiring.)

→ How does the writer introduce the book? (He names the book and the author and tells the reader what *A River Ran Wild* is about.)

→ How does the writer support his opinion of the book? (He uses facts about the pollution of the Nashua River, which went from being a healthy body of water to a polluted one, and details about Marion Stoddart's work in restoring the river.)

→ What recommendation does the writer make to readers? (He recommends the book to anyone who has an interest in the environment and in being a responsible citizen.)

# PREWRITE

## Discuss and Plan

**Purpose** Discuss with students the purpose for writing a book review. They will share an opinion about a book and explain why they have that opinion. Book reviews are intended to convince readers to agree with the writer's opinion.

**Audience** Encourage students to think about who will read their book review, such as classmates, school newspaper readers, or family members. Ask: *What do you want your readers to do after they have read your book review?*

## Teach the Minilesson

**Logical Order** Explain that in book reviews, writers give reasons for their opinion and support it with evidence, such as facts, details, quotations, or examples. Writers put their reasons in an order that makes sense to readers. Since the purpose is to convince the reader to agree with your point of view, writers consider which reason will have the biggest impact on readers. They may choose to put their strongest reason either first or last, where it will stand out most to readers.

Distribute copies of the Model Graphic Organizer Online PDF 103 in Writer's Workspace. Point out that Malcolm planned out his summary and the reasons and evidence that support his opinion. He decided on a logical way to order his reasons.

### Your Turn

**Choose Your Topic** Have students work with partners or in small groups to brainstorm books they have read and about which they would like to share an opinion. Ask questions to prompt thinking.

→ What book have you read that you would like to review?

→ What is your opinion of the book?

→ What facts and details support your opinion?

→ How will you order this evidence logically?

Have students record their topics in their Writer's Notebooks.

**Plan** Provide students with copies of the blank Graphic Organizer Online PDF 104 in Writer's Workspace. Ask students to use the graphic organizer to plan their summary and organize their reasons and evidence logically.

## ENGLISH LANGUAGE LEARNERS

### Beginning

**Demonstrate Comprehension** List opinion phrases *I thought, I liked, I did not like*. Have students draw a picture based on one of the phrases.

### Intermediate

**Explain** Provide the stem: *I like this book because it is _____.* Ask for adjectives that describe the book and write them on the board.

### Advanced/High

**Expand** Have partners summarize their chosen books in a few sentences; then ask each other questions to elaborate.

## MODEL GRAPHIC ORGANIZER

**Model Graphic Organizer • 103**

*A River Ran Wild*

| Summary | Opinion |
|---|---|
| Native Americans lived along the Nashua River banks. But soon industry began to grow. Trees were cut down and the factories polluted the water, and animals lost their homes. But Marion Stoddart started a group to restore the river, and today, the river has improved. | This book is important for people to read. |

| Reasons | Evidence |
|---|---|
| 1. It shows what can happen to rivers if they aren't treated with care.<br>2. It gives an example of how to stand up and fight for a cause. | 1. The author's clear descriptions showed the river before and after industry arrived.<br>2. The water became so polluted that fish, birds, and animals disappeared.<br>1. Marion Stoddart founded the Nashua River Watershed Association.<br>2. She helped get laws passed to protect the river. |

Unit 6 • Book Review

# OPINION TEXT Book Review

## DRAFT

### OBJECTIVES

**CCSS** Introduce a topic or text clearly, state an opinion, and create an organizational structure in which ideas are logically grouped to support the writer's purpose. **W.5.1a**

**CCSS** Provide a concluding statement or section related to opinion presented. **W.5.1d**

### ACADEMIC LANGUAGE

• *draft, organization, revise, strong conclusions*

• Cognates: *organización, revisar, conclusiones*

### Discuss the Student Draft Model

Provide copies of the Student Draft Model Online PDF 105 in Writer's Workspace. Review the features of a book review.

### Teach the Minilesson

**Organization** Explain that a book review begins with an introduction that names the book and states the writer's opinion. The introduction is followed by a brief summary of the book. In a fiction book review, the summary describes the characters, setting, plot, and theme. In a nonfiction book review, the writer tells the topic of the book and sums up the author's main points. After summarizing the text, the writer uses paragraphs to organize reasons and evidence that explain his or her opinion about the book. A book review ends with a conclusion that may sum up the main points, make a recommendation to readers, or leave readers with a final thought. Look at the Student Model. Ask students to identify the introduction, summary, reasons and evidence, and conclusion.

### Your Turn

**Write a Draft** Have students review the graphic organizer they prepared in Prewrite. Remind them to organize their book reviews logically.

**Go Digital**

Writer's Workspace

# Conferencing Routines

## Teacher Conferences

**STEP 1**

Talk about the strengths of the writing.

*The conclusion does a good job of summing up your reasons for recommending the book.*

**STEP 2**

Focus on how the writer uses a writing trait.

*You varied the sentence structure in your book review, making it interesting to read. Try adding transitions to connect one sentence to the next.*

**STEP 3**

Make concrete suggestions for revision.

*Your summary would be stronger if you took out some of the more specific details you found interesting and focused instead on the author's main ideas.*

# REVISE

## Discuss the Revised Student Model

Distribute copies of the Revised Student Model Online PDF 106 in Writer's Workspace. Read the model aloud and have students note the revisions that Keysha made. Use the specific revisions to show how the writer rearranged ideas to make the order more logical, refined word choice, and combined sentences to make the writing flow better.

## Teach the Minilesson

**Strong Conclusions** In a book review, the conclusion restates the writer's opinion. It may sum up the key points, and it often describes the type of reader who may or may not enjoy the book. This is the writer's last chance to convince readers, so it should leave a strong impression.

Have students identify an example of a revision in the Revised Student Model that made the conclusion stronger.

## Your Turn

**Revise** Have students use the peer review routine and questions to review their partner's draft. Then have students select suggestions from the peer review to incorporate into their revisions. Provide the Revise and Edit Checklist Online PDF 108 in Writer's Workspace to guide them as they revise. Suggest that they consider whether their conclusion is strong and convincing. Circulate as students work, and conference as needed.

### REVISED STUDENT MODEL

Revised Student Model • Book Review • 106

### The Story of Ruby Bridges
by Keysha R.

I enjoyed reading *The Story of Ruby Bridges*, by Robert Coles, the true story of a 6-year-old girl who helped change history. Ruby became the first African American student to attend William Frantz elementary school, an all-white school. It tells about Ruby's move from Mississippi to New Orleans at a young age. It tells about her hard working family, and her determined spirit. This story takes place during the civil rights movement in New Orleans in 1960.

I enjoyed reading this book because it helped me understand the hardships African American students faced in the 1960s. At the time of the story African American and white children went to separate schools in many areas of the United States. A judge decided that this was against the law, and ordered schools to be desegregated—that means opened to members of all races. I think this was a well idea. The judge wanted to show people that both African American and white children should recieve an equal good education. Ruby was one of the first students chosen to go to a desegregated school.

I was also interested in learning what Ruby's school days were like. On Ruby's first day at her new school, angry crowds gathered outside. Ruby went into the building by federal marshals, who made sure she was not harmed. Ruby went through the same thing every day for weeks and months.

Unit 6 • Book Review

## Peer Conferences

Review with students the routine for peer review of writing. They should listen carefully as the writer reads his or her work aloud. Begin by telling what they liked about the writing. Then ask a question that will help the writer think more about the writing. Finally, make a suggestion that will make the writing stronger.

Use these questions for peer review:

- ✔ Does the writing have a clear introduction and strong conclusion?
- ✔ Does the writer summarize the book being discussed?
- ✔ Does the writer state an opinion and give reasons for it?
- ✔ Are there supporting facts and details?

# OPINION TEXT Book Review

## PROOFREAD/EDIT AND PUBLISH

**OBJECTIVES**

**CCSS** Produce clear and coherent writing in which the development and organization are appropriate to task, purpose, and audience. **W.5.4**

**CCSS** With guidance and support from peers and adults, develop and strengthen writing as needed by planning, revising, editing, rewriting, or trying a new approach. **W.5.5**

**ACADEMIC LANGUAGE**

• proofread, edit, publish, present, rubric
• Cognates: publicar, presentar

### Discuss the Edited Student Model

Provide copies of the Edited Student Model Online PDF 107 in Writer's Workspace. Read the model aloud and have students note the editing changes that Keysha made. Use the specific edits to show how editing for capitalization, spelling, grammar, and punctuation improves the book review.

### Your Turn

**Edit**  Have students use the edit questions from the Revise and Edit Checklist online PDF 108 in Writer's Workspace to guide them as they review and edit their drafts independently. Remind them to read for one type of error at a time.

### Publish

For the final presentation of their book reviews, have students choose a format for publishing. Students may want to consider:

| Print Publishing | Digital Publishing |
|---|---|
| Class Book Review Collection | Writer's Workspace |
| Newspaper Book Review | Class Blog |
| Book Jacket | Online Review |

Remind students to format their final drafts using standard margins and formatting. Encourage students to work on their keyboarding skills by typing their book reviews in a single sitting. If time allows, encourage students to incorporate multimedia elements, such as photos, illustrations, or audio clips featuring an excerpt of the book they reviewed.

**Go Digital**

Writer's Workspace

**EDITED STUDENT MODEL**

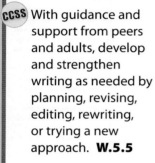

Edited Student Model • Book Review • 107

**The Story of Ruby Bridges**
by Keysha R.

I enjoyed reading *The Story of Ruby Bridges*, by Robert Coles, the true story of a 6-year-old girl who helped change history. Ruby became the first African American student to attend William Frantz elementary school, an all-white school. It tells about Ruby's move from Mississippi to New Orleans at a young age. It tells about her hard working family, and her determined spirit. This story takes place during the civil rights movement in New Orleans in 1960.

I enjoyed reading this book because it helped me understand the hardships African American students faced in the 1960s. At the time of the story African American and white children went to separate schools in many areas of the United States. A judge decided that this was against the law, and ordered schools to be desegregated—that means opened to members of all races. I think this was a good idea. The judge wanted to show people that both African American and white children should receive an equal good education. Ruby was one of the first students chosen to go to a desegregated school.

I was also interested in learning what Ruby's school days were like. On Ruby's first day at her new school, angry crowds gathered outside. Ruby went into the building by federal marshals, who made sure she was not harmed. Ruby went through the same thing every day for weeks and months.

Unit 6 • Book Review

# EVALUATE

## Discuss Rubrics

Guide students as they use the Book Review Rubric Online PDF 109 in Writer's Workspace. Explain that students can improve their writing by using rubrics to identify areas that might need further work. Review the bulleted points on the rubric with the class.

→ **Focus and Coherence** Does the book review present a clear opinion with supporting details?

→ **Organization** Does it present reasons and evidence in logical order?

→ **Ideas and Support** Does it include relevant evidence that explains the writer's reasons?

→ **Word Choice** Does the writing include transitions that connect the writer's opinion and reasons?

→ **Voice/Sentence Fluency** Does the writing show strong interest in the book and connect to readers? Does the writer use a variety of sentences that flow smoothly?

→ **Conventions** Is the book review free of errors?

### BOOK REVIEW RUBRIC

Writing Rubric • 109

**Book Review Rubric**

| | |
|---|---|
| **4 Excellent** | • presents a clear opinion with relevant supporting details<br>• presents reasons and evidence in a logical order and uses transitions to connect ideas<br>• shows strong interest in the issue and connects to readers<br>• the conclusion relates to the topic and leaves readers with an interesting final thought<br>• uses a variety of sentences that flow smoothly<br>• is free or almost free of errors |
| **3 Good** | • presents a clear opinion with supporting details<br>• reasons and evidence are orderly logically but lacks some transitions<br>• shows interest in the issue and connects to readers<br>• the conclusion relates to the topic<br>• uses a variety of complete sentences<br>• has minor errors that do not confuse the reader |
| **2 Fair** | • presents an opinion, but supporting details are weak<br>• presents reasons, but not in logical order and lacks transitions<br>• shows little connection with readers<br>• has a conclusion is present but does not relate well to the body of the review<br>• sentence structure is choppy and awkward<br>• makes frequent errors that confuse the reader |
| **1 Unsatisfactory** | • does not present an opinion<br>• is poorly organized with disconnected ideas<br>• is dull and unconvincing<br>• does not include a conclusion<br>• uses run-on sentences and sentence fragments<br>• makes serious and repeated errors in spelling and grammar |

Unit 6 • Book Review

## Your Turn

**Reflect and Set Goals** After students have evaluated their book reviews, tell them to reflect on their progress as writers. Encourage them to consider areas where they feel they have shown improvement, and to identify what areas need further improvement. Have them set writing goals to prepare for their conference with the teacher.

### Conference with Students

Use the Book Review Rubric online PDF 109 and the Anchor Papers online PDF 110 in Writer's Workspace as you evaluate student writing. The anchor papers provide samples of papers that score from 1 to 4. These papers reflect the criteria described in the rubric. Anchor papers offer a standard against which to judge writing.

Review with individual students the writing goals they have set. Discuss ways to achieve these goals and suggest any further areas of improvement students may need to target.

# OPINION TEXT Opinion Letter

## EXPERT MODEL

**EXPERT MODEL**

### OBJECTIVES

**CCSS** Write opinion pieces on topics or texts, supporting a point of view with reasons and information. Introduce a topic or text clearly, state an opinion, and create an organizational structure in which ideas are logically grouped to support the writer's purpose. **W.5.1a**

### ACADEMIC LANGUAGE

• *prewrite, purpose, audience, develop support*

### Read Like a Writer

Explain that writing a letter is a common way to express an opinion about a topic and convince readers to share that opinion. Opinion letters often ask readers to take action.

Public officials often give speeches to present opinions to an audience for a given purpose, such as in support of a cause or as a call for action. Both written and spoken opinions rely on the use of rhetoric—the art of effective speaking or writing.

Provide copies of the Expert Model Online PDFs 111–112 in Writer's Workspace. Read Vice President Gore's speech about the preservation of Yellowstone National Park and the opinion letter to the school board. Discuss the similarities between the speech and the opinion letter. Then provide copies of the Features of an Opinion Letter Online PDF 113.

**Go Digital**

**Writer's Workspace**

### Features of an Opinion Letter

→ It includes the parts of a formal letter.

→ It clearly states the writer's opinion about a topic.

→ It supports the writer's opinion with clear reasons and relevant evidence, including facts and details.

→ It organizes reasons and evidence in a logical order, often saving the strongest reason for last.

→ It uses linking words to connect ideas.

→ It provides a conclusion that asks readers to take action.

### Discuss the Expert Model

Use the questions below to discuss the features of an opinion letter.

→ To whom is the opinion letter addressed? Who is the writer of the letter? (the Desert Creek School District Board of Education; Manuel S. Ruiz, president of the Desert Creek Parent Teacher Association)

→ What is the writer's opinion about the topic? (The annual fifth grade trip to the Desert Creek Nature Center should not be cancelled.)

→ What facts or details does he provide to support his opinion? (Children enjoy it; it offers hands-on programs; it is the only facility of its kind.)

→ How does the letter conclude? (The writer suggests alternate funding so the trip can go on as scheduled.)

# PREWRITE

## Discuss and Plan

**Purpose** Explain that the purpose in writing an opinion letter is to convince readers to share their opinion about the topic they have chosen. An important part of the purpose is to ask the reader to take action.

**Audience** Encourage students to think about who will read their letters, such as a teacher, principal, or town official. Remind students to use a voice that is appropriate for the audience of a formal letter. Ask: *What action do you want your readers to take as a result of your opinion letter?*

## Teach the Minilesson

**Develop Support** Explain that an effective opinion letter introduces the topic clearly. The writer states a controlling idea—or opinion—in the opening paragraph. Reasons and evidence are logically grouped into supporting paragraphs. The main idea of each paragraph gives a reason for the writer's opinion. That reason is supported by relevant facts and details. Remind students that all of the information they include must relate to their opinion.

Distribute copies of the Model Graphic Organizer Online PDF 114 in Writer's Workspace. Point out that Manuel Ruiz organized his letter by listing reasons that support his opinion, or controlling idea, and by grouping together facts and details that support each reason.

## Your Turn

**Choose Your Topic** Have students work with partners or in small groups to brainstorm situations or problems in their neighborhoods or school about which they have an opinion. Remind them to establish a controlling idea that can be supported with facts and details.

→ Think about something that is or is not happening in your school or neighborhood that you would like to change.

→ How would you like to change it? Why would these changes be an improvement?

→ What facts or details can you use to support your opinion?

Have students record their topics in their Writer's Notebooks.

**Plan** Provide students with copies of the blank Graphic Organizer Online PDF 115 in Writer's Workspace. Ask students to use the graphic organizer to organize their opinion letters.

## ENGLISH LANGUAGE LEARNERS

### Beginning

**Demonstrate Comprehension** Identify parts of a letter and point to them on the Expert Model. Have students repeat. Have them share to whom they will write their letters.

### Intermediate

**Explain** Point out signal words in the Expert Model: *As a result, consequently.* Provide sentence frames to practice signal words.

### Advanced/High

**Expand** Have partners discuss which reason in the Expert Model is most convincing and why.

## MODEL GRAPHIC ORGANIZER

**Model Graphic Organizer • 114**

**Opinion:** The annual fifth-grade trip to the Desert Creek Nature Center should continue.

| Reasons | Evidence |
|---|---|
| A state of the art environmental center fosters an interest in nature. | The center has programs, exhibits, and special events, exhibit gallery, a small theater, a library, and program rooms. |
| | Visitors get to spend time outdoors, exploring the trails. |
| The programs for students in grades K–5 create understanding and appreciation of the environment. | Students get hands-on experiences with naturalists. |
| | Students can study marshes, woods, rivers, and lakes in our community. |
| | In fifth grade, students learn about watersheds and hydrology. They also learn how to identify trees. |
| The fifth-grade trip to the nature center is an important learning experience for students. | It is the only facility of its kind in our county. |
| | 60,000 people participate each year, including 12,000 school children. |

Unit 6 • Opinion Letter

# OPINION TEXT Opinion Letter

## DRAFT

### OBJECTIVES

**CCSS** Write opinion pieces on topics or texts, supporting a point of view with reasons and information. Link opinion and reasons using words, phrases, and clauses (e.g., *consequently*, *specifically*). **W.5.1c**

**CCSS** Provide a concluding statement or section related to the opinion presented. **W.5.1d**

### ACADEMIC LANGUAGE
- draft, transitions, revise, strong conclusions
- Cognates: *transiciones, revisar, conclusiones*

### Discuss the Student Draft Model

Review the features of an opinion letter. Provide copies of the Student Draft Model Online PDF 116 in Writer's Workspace. Read the draft and have students identify the features. Point out the date, salutation, body, closing, and signature.

### Teach the Minilesson

**Transitions** Tell students that a successful opinion letter uses transitional words, phrases, and clauses to connect the writer's opinion and reasons. Transitions allow the reader to understand how supporting facts and details relate to the writer's opinion. Some transitions signal a cause-and-effect relationship, such as *consequently* or *as a result*. Other transitions signal an example that illustrates a point, such as *for example* or *specifically*. Transitions may also signal order, such as *first*, *second*, and *finally*.

Read paragraph three of the Student Model. Ask students to identify the transition word *therefore* and discuss how it connects the last sentence of the paragraph with the previous sentence.

### Your Turn

**Write a Draft** Have students review the graphic organizer they prepared in Prewrite. Remind them to use transitions as they draft.

**Go Digital**

Writer's Workspace

# Conferencing Routines

## Teacher Conferences

**STEP 1**

Talk about the strengths of the writing.

*You used transitions effectively. I could clearly understand how your reasons and evidence connect to your opinion.*

**STEP 2**

Focus on how the writer uses a writing trait.

*You focused on one controlling idea and all of your facts and details related to that idea.*

**STEP 3**

Make concrete suggestions for revision.

*Be sure to include all the parts of a formal letter.*

# REVISE

## Discuss the Revised Student Model

Distribute copies of the Revised Student Model Online PDF 117 in Writer's Workspace. Read the model aloud. Have students note the revisions that Gabe made. Use the revisions to show how adding transitions, changing the order of ideas, and adding details made the letter clearer.

## Teach the Minilesson

**Strong Conclusions** The conclusion of an opinion letter sums up the writer's argument and asks readers to take action. Should readers do something? Should they think or feel a certain way about the writer's topic? The conclusion is the place to drive home this call to action. It is the last chance to convince readers, so writers often craft a strong final thought that readers will remember.

Have students look at the Revised Student Model. Discuss how the writer made the conclusion stronger by adding the last five words.

## Your Turn

**Revise** Have students use the peer review routine and questions to review their partner's draft. Then have students select suggestions from the peer review to incorporate into their revisions. Provide the Revise and Edit Checklist Online PDF 119 in Writer's Workspace to guide them. Suggest they check that their letters have a strong conclusion. Circulate as students work, and conference as needed.

### REVISED STUDENT MODEL

Revised Student Model • Opinion Letter • 117

Editor in Chief
*The waterside times*
4523 Main Street
Waterside, Florida 34301

To the Editor:

   I went for a walk last Sunday morning along Vanderbilt Beach and picked up six bags of garbage cans and bottles that people had discarded along the shoreline. I was amazed and disappointed by the large amount of litter there. The beach is no longer an enjoyable place to visit. In fact, every time I visit the beach, it is mostly empty. The citizens of Waterside need to work together to clean up our beaches to make it safe not only for visitors, but also for the fish and animals that call it home.

   Waste and litter at our beaches threaten some of our favorite marine wildlife. Hundreds of species of fish and animals accidentally eat litter. Or they become tangled up in litter. Plastic, paper, fishing line, netting, and rope have harmed turtles, fish, birds, dolphins, seals, and other aquatic animals. Litter is often mistaken for food and is eaten by marine life, causing choking, starvation, or poisoning.

   Litter is harmful to the Gulf of Mexico. There are many ways that litter can reach the Gulf. It can be blown in directly by wind, it can go down a storm drain and be emptied into the Gulf, or it can enter a river or stream and drift down to the

Unit 6 • Opinion Letter

## Peer Conferences

Review with students the routine for peer review of writing. They should listen carefully as the writer reads his or her work aloud. Begin by telling what they liked about the writing. Then ask a question that will help the writer think more about the writing. Finally, make a suggestion that will make the writing stronger.

Use these questions for peer review:

- ☑ Does the opinion letter open with a clear opinion, or controlling idea?
- ☑ Is the opinion supported by details?
- ☑ Do transitions connect the opinion and supporting reasons?
- ☑ Does the opinion letter end with a strong conclusion and call to action?

# OPINION TEXT Opinion Letter

Writing Process Lesson 2

## PROOFREAD/EDIT AND PUBLISH

### Discuss the Edited Student Model

Provide copies of the Edited Student Model online PDF 118 in Writer's Workspace. Read the model aloud and have students note the editing changes that Gabe made. Use the specific edits to show how editing for complete sentences, spelling, verb tenses, punctuation, and subject-verb agreement improves the opinion letter.

### Your Turn

**Edit** Have students use the questions from the Revise and Edit Checklist online PDF 119 to guide them as they review and edit their drafts independently. Remind them to read for one type of error at a time.

### Publish

For the final presentation of their opinion letters, have students choose a format for publishing. Students may want to consider:

| Print Publishing | Digital Publishing |
|---|---|
| School-wide Letter Writing Campaign | Writer's Workspace |
| Letter to the School Newspaper | Class Website |
| Letter to the Local Newspaper | E-mail |

Remind students to use proper formatting for their final drafts and include the five parts of a formal letter: date, salutation, body, closing, and signature.

**Go Digital**

Writer's Workspace

### EDITED STUDENT MODEL

Edited Student Model • Opinion Letter • 118

Editor in Chief
*The waterside times*
4523 Main Street
Waterside, Florida 34301

To the Editor:

I went for a walk last Sunday morning along Vanderbilt Beach and picked up six bags of garbage,cans,and bottles that people had discarded along the shoreline. I was amazed and disappointed by the large amount of litter there. The beach is no longer an enjoyable place to visit. In fact, every time I visit the beach, it is mostly empty. The citizens of Waterside need to work together to clean up our beaches to make it safe not only for visitors, but also for the fish and animals that call it home.

Waste and litter at our beaches threaten some of our favorite marine wildlife. Hundreds of species of fish and animals accidentally eat litter,Or they become tangled up in litter. Plastic, paper, fishing line, netting, and rope have harmed turtles, fish, birds, dolphins, seals, and other aquatic animals. Litter is often mistaken for food and is eaten by marine life, causing choking, starvation, or poisoning.

Litter is harmful to the Gulf of Mexico. There are many ways that litter can reach the Gulf. It can be blown in directly by wind, it can go down a storm drain and be emptied into the Gulf, or it can enter a river or stream and drift down to the

Unit 6 • Opinion Letter

# EVALUATE

## Discuss Rubrics

Guide students as they use the Opinion Letter Rubric Online PDF 120 in Writer's Workspace. Explain that students can improve their writing by using rubrics to identify areas that might need further work. Review the bulleted points on the rubric with the class.

→ **Focus and Coherence** Does the opinion letter present a clear opinion with relevant evidence, including facts and details?

→ **Organization** Does it organize reasons and evidence in a logical order? Does it include all parts of a formal letter?

→ **Ideas and Support** Does it have a strong conclusion that asks readers to take action?

→ **Word Choice** Does it link opinions and reasons using words, phrases and clauses?

→ **Voice/Sentence Fluency** Does the opinion letter show strong interest in the issue and connect to readers?

→ **Conventions** Is the letter free of errors?

**OPINION LETTER RUBRIC**

Writing Rubric • 120

| Opinion Letter Rubric | |
|---|---|
| **4 Excellent** | • presents a clear opinion with relevant evidence, including facts and details<br>• organizes reasons and evidence in a logical order<br>• links opinions and reasons using words, phrases, and clauses<br>• shows strong interest in the issue and uses a formal voice<br>• has a strong conclusion that asks readers to take action<br>• includes all parts of a formal letter<br>• is free or almost free of errors |
| **3 Good** | • presents a clear opinion supported by mostly relevant evidence, including facts and details<br>• presents reasons and evidence in a logical order<br>• links ideas using some transitional words, phrases, or clauses<br>• shows interest in the issue and uses a formal voice<br>• has a conclusion that asks readers to take action<br>• includes most parts of a formal letter<br>• has minor errors that do not confuse the reader |
| **2 Fair** | • attempts to present an opinion, but reasons are weakly supported<br>• reasons and evidence are not in a logical order<br>• transitional words, phrases, or clauses occasionally connect ideas<br>• shows little connection with readers and voice is inconsistent<br>• includes a confusing or unconvincing conclusion<br>• includes some parts of a formal letter<br>• makes frequent errors that confuse the reader |

Unit 6 • Opinion Letter

## Your Turn

**Reflect and Set Goals** After students have evaluated their opinion letters, tell them to reflect on their progress as writers. Encourage them to consider areas where they feel they have shown improvement, and to identify what areas need further improvement. Have them set writing goals to prepare for their conference with the teacher.

### Conference with Students

Use the Opinion Letter Rubric and the Anchor Papers Online PDFs 120–121 in Writer's Workspace as you evaluate student writing. The anchor papers provide samples of papers that score from 1 to 4. These papers reflect the criteria described in the rubric. Anchor papers offer a standard against which to judge writing.

Review with individual students the writing goals they have set. Discuss ways to achieve these goals and suggest any further areas of improvement students may need to target.

## Close Reading Routine

### Read the Text · *What does the author tell us?*

#### Assign the Reading

Depending upon the needs of your students, you can

→ ask students to read the text silently.

→ read the text together with students.

→ read the text aloud.

#### Take Notes

Students generate questions and take notes about aspects of the text that might be confusing for them. Encourage students to note

→ difficult vocabulary words or phrases.

→ details that are not clear.

→ information that they do not understand.

Students complete a graphic organizer to take notes on important information from the text.

### Reread the Text · *What does the text mean?*

#### Ask Text Dependent Questions/Generate Questions

Students reread and discuss and take notes on important shorter passages from the text. Students should

→ generate questions about the text.

→ work with partners or small groups to answer questions using text evidence.

### Write About the Text · *Think about what the author wrote.*

Students write a response to the text, using evidence from the text to support their ideas or arguments.

# Use the Literature Anthology

## Getting Ready

**Close Reading of *The Friend Who Changed My Life,***
pages 450–461

Use the suggestions in the chart to assign reading of the text and to chunk the text into shorter passages for rereading.

**ESSENTIAL QUESTION** *What actions can we take to get along with others?*

Ask students to discuss the different ways they have learned to get along with others.

| **Suggested Pacing** | |
| --- | --- |
| **Days 1–3** | **Read** |
| | pp. 450–454 |
| | pp. 455–457 |
| | pp. 458–461 |
| **Days 4–8** | **Reread** |
| | pp. 450–451 |
| | pp. 452–454 |
| | pp. 455–457 |
| | pp. 458–459 |
| | pp. 460–461 |
| **Days 9–10** | **Write** |
| | **About Text** |

## Read the Text  *What does the author tell us?*

### Assign the Reading

Ask students to read the text independently. You may want to read together pages 451–454 due to difficult vocabulary and expressions used in the text.

### Take Notes

As students read, ask them to generate questions and other notes on features they find difficult to understand. For this selection, students may note:

→ words and idioms they do not know.

→ the order of events and pacing of the story.

→ how past and present events are connected.

Model for students how to take notes.

**Think Aloud**  In the second paragraph on page 452, the narrator tells her mother that her bruises are from playing on the jungle gym. I wonder why she says this instead of telling the truth. I will keep reading to find the answer.

> p. 452
> Why doesn't the narrator tell her mother the truth about her bruises?

Assign **Graphic Organizer 102** to help students take notes on how the author reveals the theme.

As students share their questions and notes, use the Access Complex Text suggestions on pages T89A–T89L to help address features about the text that students found difficult.

### Reread the Text   *What does the text mean?*

**Ask Text Dependent Questions/Generate Questions**

Ask students to reread the shorter passages from the text, focusing on how the author presents a story about a valuable friendship. Ask questions about

→ **Theme, pages 450–454, 458–461**

→ What do the characters say and do?

→ What happens to the characters?

→ **Character Development, pages 452–454, 458-461**

→ How does the author develop the characters?

→ **Word Choice, pages 455–457**

→ How does the author's word choice affect the meaning of the text?

→ **Literary Elements, pages 455–457**

→ How does the author vary the pacing? Why might she do this?

→ What descriptive details does the author include? How do they help readers?

Use the prompts on Teacher Edition pages T89A–T89L for suggested text dependent questions. Remind students that they are to look back into the text to cite evidence to support their answers.

Model citing text evidence as needed.

Why is it surprising when Mary Lou says that she might hit the narrator? Do you think Mary Lou will follow through on her threat? Why, or why not?

**Think Aloud**   On page 453, the text says that Mary Lou has "a gentle giant appearance." Then Mary Lou rescues the narrator and causes Theresa to back away. This evidence shows that it is surprising when Mary Lou says she might hit the narrator because she has been described as gentle and protective. Mary Lou says "if you don't stick up for yourself, things will get worse." This evidence suggests that Mary Lou will not really hit the narrator. She just wants her to stick up for herself.

As they reread each section, students should continue to generate their own questions about the text. As each student shares a question, ask all students to go back into the text to find text evidence to answer the question. Encourage students to

→ point out the exact place within the text they found the evidence.

→ reread and paraphrase the section of the text that they think supports their answer.

→ discuss how strong the evidence cited is in answering the question.

→ identify when an answer to a question cannot be found in the text.

## Write About the Text   *Think about what the author wrote.*

### Essential Question

Have students respond in writing to the Essential Question using evidence from the text.

What actions can we take to get along with others?

Students should use their notes and graphic organizers to cite evidence from the text to support their answer.

Model how to use notes to respond to the Essential Question:

**Think Aloud**  I review all the notes I took while reading to find text evidence that can help me answer the question. My notes on page 459 say that the narrator and Theresa join Mary Lou in leaving the slumber party, even though it is embarrassing. The shared experience of leaving the party together provided the narrator and Theresa with an opportunity to get to know each other better and discover things they have in common. I can use that information to support my answer. Then I will read through the rest of my notes to find additional text evidence that I can use.

Students can work with a partner and use their notes and graphic organizer to locate evidence that can be used to answer the question. Encourage students to discuss the strength of the evidence cited and give arguments about what may be strong or weak about a particular citation.

# READING Extended Complex Text

Model Lesson

## Use Your Own Text

### Classroom Library

Classroom Library lessons available online.

*No Talking*
**Genre** Realistic Fiction

**Lexile** 820
*TextEvaluator*™ 45

*Spiders: Biggest! Littlest!*
**Genre** Expository Text

**Lexile** 820
*TextEvaluator*™ 13

*The Midnight Fox*
**Genre** Realistic Fiction

**Lexile** 990
*TextEvaluator*™ 45

*Earth Heroes: Champions of the Wilderness*
**Genre** Biography

**Lexile** 920
*TextEvaluator*™ 53

or Choose from your own **Trade Books**

→ Use this model with a text of your choice. Go online for title specific classroom library book lessons.

→ Assign reading of the text. You may wish to do this by section or chapters.

→ Chunk the text into shorter important passages for rereading.

→ Present an Essential Question. You may want to use the Unit Big Idea.

### Read the Text  *What does the author tell us?*

#### Assign the Reading

Ask students to read the assigned sections of the text independently. For sections that are more difficult for students, you may wish to read the text aloud or ask students to read with a partner.

#### Take Notes

As students read, ask them to take notes on difficult parts of the text. Model how to take notes on

→ identifying details or parts that are unclear.

→ words they do not know.

→ ways in which information or events are connected.

→ the genre of the text.

You may wish to have students complete a graphic organizer, chosen from within the unit, to take notes on important information as they read. The graphic organizer can help them summarize the text.

No Talking: Illustration © Mark Elliott

Help students access the complex text features of the text. Scaffold instruction on the following features as necessary:

- → Purpose
- → Genre
- → Specific Vocabulary
- → Sentence Structure
- → Connection of Ideas
- → Organization
- → Prior Knowledge

## Reread the Text    *What does the text mean?*

### Ask Text Dependent Questions/Generate Questions

 Ask students to reread the shorter passages from the text, focusing on how the author provides information or develops the characters, setting, and plot. Focus questions on the following:

| Literature Selections | Informational Text |
|---|---|
| Character, Setting, and Plot Development | Main Idea and Supporting Key Details |
| Word Choice | Word Choice |
| Genre | Text Structure |
| Point of View | Text Features |
|  | Genre |
|  | Author's Point of View |

Have students discuss questions they generated. As each student shares a question, ask all students to go back into the text to find text evidence to answer the question. Encourage students to

- → point out the exact place within the text they found the evidence.
- → reread and paraphrase the section of the text that they think supports their answer.
- → discuss how strong the evidence cited is in answering the question.
- → identify when an answer to a question cannot be found in the text.

## Write About the Text    *Think about what the author wrote.*

### Essential Question

Have students respond in writing to the Essential Question, considering the complete text. Students can work with a partner and use their notes and graphic organizer to locate evidence that can be used to answer the question.

# SCOPE & SEQUENCE

| | K | 1 | 2 | 3 | 4 | 5 | 6 |
|---|---|---|---|---|---|---|---|
| **READING PROCESS** | | | | | | | |
| **Concepts About Print/Print Awareness** | | | | | | | |
| Recognize own name | | | | | | | |
| Understand directionality (top to bottom; tracking print from left to right; return sweep, page by page) | ✔ | | | | | | |
| Locate printed word on page | ✔ | | | | | | |
| Develop print awareness (concept of letter, word, sentence) | ✔ | | | | | | |
| Identify separate sounds in a spoken sentence | ✔ | | | | | | |
| Understand that written words are represented in written language by a specific sequence of letters | ✔ | | | | | | |
| Distinguish between letters, words, and sentences | ✔ | | | | | | |
| Identify and distinguish paragraphs | | | | | | | |
| Match print to speech (one-to-one correspondence) | ✔ | | | | | | |
| Name uppercase and lowercase letters | ✔ | | | | | | |
| Understand book handling (holding a book right-side-up, turning its pages) | ✔ | | | | | | |
| Identify parts of a book (front cover, back cover, title page, table of contents); recognize that parts of a book contain information | ✔ | | | | | | |
| **Phonological Awareness** | | | | | | | |
| Recognize and understand alliteration | | | | | | | |
| Segment sentences into correct number of words | | | | | | | |
| Identify, blend, segment syllables in words | | ✔ | | | | | |
| Recognize and generate rhyming words | ✔ | ✔ | | | | | |
| Identify, blend, segment onset and rime | ✔ | ✔ | | | | | |
| **Phonemic Awareness** | | | | | | | |
| Count phonemes | ✔ | ✔ | | | | | |
| Isolate initial, medial, and final sounds | ✔ | ✔ | | | | | |
| Blend spoken phonemes to form words | ✔ | ✔ | | | | | |
| Segment spoken words into phonemes | ✔ | ✔ | | | | | |
| Distinguish between long- and short-vowel sounds | ✔ | ✔ | | | | | |
| Manipulate phonemes (addition, deletion, substitution) | ✔ | ✔ | | | | | |
| **Phonics and Decoding /Word Recognition** | | | | | | | |
| Understand the alphabetic principle | ✔ | ✔ | | | | | |
| Sound/letter correspondence | ✔ | ✔ | ✔ | ✔ | | | |
| Blend sounds into words, including VC, CVC, CVCe, CVVC words | ✔ | ✔ | ✔ | ✔ | | | |
| Blend common word families | ✔ | ✔ | ✔ | ✔ | | | |

| KEY | ✔ = Assessed Skill |
|---|---|
| | Tinted panels show skills, strategies, and other teaching opportunities. |

| | K | 1 | 2 | 3 | 4 | 5 | 6 |
|---|---|---|---|---|---|---|---|
| Initial consonant blends | | ✔ | ✔ | ✔ | | | |
| Final consonant blends | | ✔ | ✔ | ✔ | | | |
| Initial and medial short vowels | ✔ | ✔ | ✔ | ✔ | ✔ | ✔ | ✔ |
| Decode one-syllable words in isolation and in context | ✔ | ✔ | ✔ | ✔ | | | |
| Decode multisyllabic words in isolation and in context using common syllabication patterns | | ✔ | ✔ | ✔ | ✔ | ✔ | ✔ |
| Distinguish between similarly spelled words | ✔ | ✔ | ✔ | ✔ | ✔ | ✔ | ✔ |
| Monitor accuracy of decoding | | | | | | | |
| Identify and read common high-frequency words, irregularly spelled words | ✔ | ✔ | ✔ | ✔ | | | |
| Identify and read compound words, contractions | | ✔ | ✔ | ✔ | ✔ | ✔ | ✔ |
| Use knowledge of spelling patterns to identify syllables | | ✔ | ✔ | ✔ | ✔ | ✔ | ✔ |
| Regular and irregular plurals | ✔ | ✔ | ✔ | ✔ | ✔ | ✔ | ✔ |
| Long vowels  (silent e, vowel teams) | ✔ | ✔ | ✔ | ✔ | ✔ | ✔ | ✔ |
| Vowel digraphs (variant vowels) | | ✔ | ✔ | ✔ | ✔ | ✔ | ✔ |
| r-Controlled vowels | | ✔ | ✔ | ✔ | ✔ | ✔ | ✔ |
| Hard/soft consonants | | ✔ | ✔ | ✔ | ✔ | ✔ | ✔ |
| Initial consonant digraphs | | ✔ | ✔ | ✔ | ✔ | ✔ | |
| Medial and final consonant digraphs | | ✔ | ✔ | ✔ | ✔ | ✔ | |
| Vowel diphthongs | | ✔ | ✔ | ✔ | ✔ | ✔ | ✔ |
| Identify and distinguish letter-sounds (initial, medial, final) | ✔ | ✔ | ✔ | | | | |
| Silent letters | | ✔ | ✔ | ✔ | ✔ | ✔ | ✔ |
| Schwa words | | | | ✔ | ✔ | ✔ | ✔ |
| Inflectional endings | | ✔ | ✔ | ✔ | ✔ | ✔ | ✔ |
| Triple-consonant clusters | | ✔ | ✔ | ✔ | ✔ | ✔ | |
| Unfamiliar and complex word families | | | | ✔ | ✔ | ✔ | ✔ |
| **Structural Analysis/Word Analysis** | | | | | | | |
| Common spelling patterns (word families) | | ✔ | ✔ | ✔ | ✔ | ✔ | ✔ |
| Common syllable patterns | | ✔ | ✔ | ✔ | ✔ | ✔ | ✔ |
| Inflectional endings | | ✔ | ✔ | ✔ | ✔ | ✔ | ✔ |
| Contractions | | ✔ | ✔ | ✔ | ✔ | ✔ | ✔ |
| Compound words | | ✔ | ✔ | ✔ | ✔ | ✔ | ✔ |
| Prefixes and suffixes | | ✔ | ✔ | ✔ | ✔ | ✔ | ✔ |
| Root or base words | | | ✔ | ✔ | ✔ | ✔ | ✔ |
| Comparatives and superlatives | | | ✔ | ✔ | ✔ | ✔ | ✔ |
| Greek and Latin roots | | | ✔ | ✔ | ✔ | ✔ | ✔ |
| **Fluency** | | | | | | | |
| Apply letter/sound knowledge to decode phonetically regular words accurately | ✔ | ✔ | ✔ | ✔ | ✔ | ✔ | ✔ |
| Recognize high-frequency and familiar words | ✔ | ✔ | ✔ | ✔ | ✔ | ✔ | ✔ |
| Read regularly on independent and instructional levels | | | | | | | |
| Read orally with fluency from familiar texts (choral, echo, partner, Reader's Theater) | | | | | | | |
| Use appropriate rate, expression, intonation, and phrasing | | ✔ | ✔ | ✔ | ✔ | ✔ | ✔ |
| Read with automaticity (accurately and effortlessly) | | ✔ | ✔ | ✔ | ✔ | ✔ | ✔ |

| | K | 1 | 2 | 3 | 4 | 5 | 6 |
|---|---|---|---|---|---|---|---|
| Use punctuation cues in reading | | ✔ | ✔ | ✔ | ✔ | ✔ | ✔ |
| Adjust reading rate to purpose, text difficulty, form, and style | | | | | | | |
| Repeated readings | | | | | | | |
| Timed readings | | ✔ | ✔ | ✔ | ✔ | ✔ | ✔ |
| Read with purpose and understanding | | ✔ | ✔ | ✔ | ✔ | ✔ | ✔ |
| Read orally with accuracy | | ✔ | ✔ | ✔ | ✔ | ✔ | ✔ |
| Use context to confirm or self-correct word recognition | | ✔ | ✔ | ✔ | ✔ | ✔ | ✔ |

## READING LITERATURE

### Comprehension Strategies and Skills

| | K | 1 | 2 | 3 | 4 | 5 | 6 |
|---|---|---|---|---|---|---|---|
| Read literature from a broad range of genres, cultures, and periods | | ✔ | ✔ | ✔ | ✔ | ✔ | ✔ |
| Access complex text | | ✔ | ✔ | ✔ | ✔ | ✔ | ✔ |
| Build background | | | | | | | |
| Preview and predict | | | | | | | |
| Establish and adjust purpose for reading | | | | | | | |
| Evaluate citing evidence from the text | | | | | | | |
| Ask and answer questions | ✔ | ✔ | ✔ | ✔ | ✔ | ✔ | ✔ |
| Inferences and conclusions, citing evidence from the text | ✔ | ✔ | ✔ | ✔ | ✔ | ✔ | ✔ |
| Monitor/adjust comprehension including reread, reading rate, paraphrase | | | | | | | |
| Recount/Retell | ✔ | ✔ | | | | | |
| Summarize | | | ✔ | ✔ | ✔ | ✔ | ✔ |
| Story structure (beginning, middle, end) | ✔ | ✔ | ✔ | ✔ | ✔ | ✔ | ✔ |
| Visualize | | | | | | | |
| Make connections between and across texts | | ✔ | ✔ | ✔ | ✔ | ✔ | ✔ |
| Point of view | | ✔ | ✔ | ✔ | ✔ | ✔ | ✔ |
| Author's purpose | | | | | | | |
| Cause and effect | ✔ | ✔ | ✔ | ✔ | ✔ | ✔ | ✔ |
| Compare and contrast (including character, setting, plot, topics) | ✔ | ✔ | ✔ | ✔ | ✔ | ✔ | ✔ |
| Classify and categorize | | ✔ | ✔ | | | | |
| Literature vs informational text | ✔ | ✔ | ✔ | | | | |
| Illustrations, using | ✔ | ✔ | ✔ | ✔ | | | |
| Theme, central message, moral, lesson | | ✔ | ✔ | ✔ | ✔ | ✔ | ✔ |
| Predictions, making/confirming | ✔ | ✔ | ✔ | | | | |
| Problem and solution (problem/resolution) | | ✔ | ✔ | ✔ | ✔ | ✔ | ✔ |
| Sequence of events | ✔ | ✔ | ✔ | ✔ | ✔ | ✔ | ✔ |

### Literary Elements

| | K | 1 | 2 | 3 | 4 | 5 | 6 |
|---|---|---|---|---|---|---|---|
| Character | ✔ | ✔ | ✔ | ✔ | ✔ | ✔ | ✔ |
| Plot development/Events | ✔ | ✔ | ✔ | ✔ | ✔ | ✔ | ✔ |
| Setting | ✔ | ✔ | ✔ | ✔ | ✔ | ✔ | ✔ |
| Stanza | | | | | ✔ | ✔ | ✔ | ✔ |
| Alliteration | | | | | | | ✔ | ✔ |
| Assonance | | | | | | | ✔ | ✔ |
| Dialogue | | | | | | | | |

**KEY**  ✔ = Assessed Skill
Tinted panels show skills, strategies, and other teaching opportunities.

| | K | 1 | 2 | 3 | 4 | 5 | 6 |
|---|---|---|---|---|---|---|---|
| Foreshadowing | | | | | | ✔ | ✔ |
| Flashback | | | | | | ✔ | ✔ |
| Descriptive and figurative language | | ✔ | ✔ | ✔ | ✔ | ✔ | ✔ |
| Imagery | | | | | ✔ | ✔ | ✔ |
| Meter | | | | | ✔ | ✔ | ✔ |
| Onomatopoeia | | | | | | | |
| Repetition | | ✔ | ✔ | ✔ | ✔ | ✔ | ✔ |
| Rhyme/rhyme schemes | | ✔ | ✔ | ✔ | ✔ | ✔ | ✔ |
| Rhythm | | ✔ | ✔ | | | | |
| Sensory language | | | | | | | |
| Symbolism | | | | | | | |
| **Write About Reading/Literary Response Discussions** | | | | | | | |
| Reflect and respond to text citing text evidence | | ✔ | ✔ | ✔ | ✔ | ✔ | ✔ |
| Connect and compare text characters, events, ideas to self, to other texts, to world | | | | | | | |
| Connect literary texts to other curriculum areas | | | | | | | |
| Identify cultural and historical elements of text | | | | | | | |
| Evaluate author's techniques, craft | | | | | | | |
| Analytical writing | | | | | | | |
| Interpret text ideas through writing, discussion, media, research | | | | | | | |
| Book report or review | | | | | | | |
| Locate, use, explain information from text features | | ✔ | ✔ | ✔ | ✔ | ✔ | ✔ |
| Organize information to show understanding of main idea through charts, mapping | | | | | | | |
| Cite text evidence | ✔ | ✔ | ✔ | ✔ | ✔ | ✔ | ✔ |
| Author's purpose/ Illustrator's purpose | | | | | | | |
| **READING INFORMATIONAL TEXT** | | | | | | | |
| **Comprehension Strategies and Skills** | | | | | | | |
| Read informational text from a broad range of topics and cultures | ✔ | ✔ | ✔ | ✔ | ✔ | ✔ | ✔ |
| Access complex text | | ✔ | ✔ | ✔ | ✔ | ✔ | ✔ |
| Build background | | | | | | | |
| Preview and predict | ✔ | ✔ | ✔ | | | | |
| Establish and adjust purpose for reading | | | | | | | |
| Evaluate citing evidence from the text | | | | | | | |
| Ask and answer questions | ✔ | ✔ | ✔ | ✔ | ✔ | ✔ | ✔ |
| Inferences and conclusions, citing evidence from the text | ✔ | ✔ | ✔ | ✔ | ✔ | ✔ | ✔ |
| Monitor and adjust comprehension including reread, adjust reading rate, paraphrase | | | | | | | |
| Recount/Retell | ✔ | ✔ | | | | | |
| Summarize | | | ✔ | ✔ | ✔ | ✔ | ✔ |
| Text structure | ✔ | ✔ | ✔ | ✔ | ✔ | ✔ | ✔ |
| Identify text features | | ✔ | ✔ | ✔ | ✔ | ✔ | ✔ |
| Make connections between and across texts | ✔ | ✔ | ✔ | ✔ | ✔ | ✔ | ✔ |

| | K | 1 | 2 | 3 | 4 | 5 | 6 |
|---|---|---|---|---|---|---|---|
| Author's point of view | | | | ✔ | ✔ | ✔ | ✔ |
| Author's purpose | | ✔ | ✔ | | | | |
| Cause and effect | ✔ | ✔ | ✔ | ✔ | ✔ | ✔ | ✔ |
| Compare and contrast | ✔ | ✔ | ✔ | ✔ | ✔ | ✔ | ✔ |
| Classify and categorize | | ✔ | ✔ | | | | |
| Illustrations and photographs, using | ✔ | ✔ | ✔ | ✔ | | | |
| Instructions/directions (written and oral) | | ✔ | ✔ | ✔ | ✔ | ✔ | ✔ |
| Main idea and key details | ✔ | ✔ | ✔ | ✔ | ✔ | ✔ | ✔ |
| Persuasion, reasons and evidence to support points/persuasive techniques | | | | | | ✔ | ✔ |
| Predictions, making/confirming | ✔ | ✔ | | | | | |
| Problem and solution | | ✔ | ✔ | ✔ | ✔ | ✔ | ✔ |
| Sequence, chronological order of events, time order, steps in a process | ✔ | ✔ | ✔ | ✔ | ✔ | ✔ | ✔ |

## Writing About Reading/Expository Critique Discussions

| | K | 1 | 2 | 3 | 4 | 5 | 6 |
|---|---|---|---|---|---|---|---|
| Reflect and respond to text citing text evidence | | ✔ | ✔ | ✔ | ✔ | ✔ | ✔ |
| Connect and compare text characters, events, ideas to self, to other texts, to world | | | | | | | |
| Connect texts to other curriculum areas | | | | | | | |
| Identify cultural and historical elements of text | | | | | | | |
| Evaluate author's techniques, craft | | | | | | | |
| Analytical writing | | | | | | | |
| Read to understand and perform tasks and activities | | | | | | | |
| Interpret text ideas through writing, discussion, media, research | | | | | | | |
| Locate, use, explain information from text features | | ✔ | ✔ | ✔ | ✔ | ✔ | ✔ |
| Organize information to show understanding of main idea through charts, mapping | | | | | | | |
| Cite text evidence | | ✔ | ✔ | ✔ | ✔ | ✔ | ✔ |
| Author's purpose/Illustrator's purpose | | | | | | | |

## Text Features

| | K | 1 | 2 | 3 | 4 | 5 | 6 |
|---|---|---|---|---|---|---|---|
| Recognize and identify text and organizational features of nonfiction texts | | ✔ | ✔ | ✔ | ✔ | ✔ | ✔ |
| Captions and labels, headings, subheadings, endnotes, key words, bold print | ✔ | ✔ | ✔ | ✔ | ✔ | ✔ | ✔ |
| Graphics, including photographs, illustrations, maps, charts, diagrams, graphs, time lines | ✔ | ✔ | ✔ | ✔ | ✔ | ✔ | ✔ |

## Self-Selected Reading/Independent Reading

| | K | 1 | 2 | 3 | 4 | 5 | 6 |
|---|---|---|---|---|---|---|---|
| Use personal criteria to choose own reading including favorite authors, genres, recommendations from others; set up a reading log | | | | | | | |
| Read a range of literature and informational text for tasks as well as for enjoyment; participate in literature circles | | | | | | | |
| Produce evidence of reading by retelling, summarizing, or paraphrasing | | | | | | | |

## Media Literacy

| | K | 1 | 2 | 3 | 4 | 5 | 6 |
|---|---|---|---|---|---|---|---|
| Summarize the message or content from media message, citing text evidence | | | | | | | |
| Use graphics, illustrations to analyze and interpret information | ✔ | ✔ | ✔ | ✔ | ✔ | ✔ | ✔ |
| Identify structural features of popular media and use the features to obtain information, including digital sources | | | | ✔ | ✔ | ✔ | ✔ |
| Identify reasons and evidence in visuals and media message | | | | | | | |
| Analyze media source: recognize effects of media in one's mood and emotion | | | | | | | |

**KEY**   ✔ = Assessed Skill
Tinted panels show skills, strategies, and other teaching opportunities.

| | K | 1 | 2 | 3 | 4 | 5 | 6 |
|---|---|---|---|---|---|---|---|
| Make informed judgments about print and digital media | | | | | | | |
| Critique persuasive techniques | | | | | | | |

## WRITING

### Writing Process

| | K | 1 | 2 | 3 | 4 | 5 | 6 |
|---|---|---|---|---|---|---|---|
| Plan/prewrite | | | | | | | |
| Draft | | | | | | | |
| Revise | | | | | | | |
| Edit/proofread | | | | | | | |
| Publish and present including using technology | | | | | | | |
| Teacher and peer feedback | | | | | | | |

### Writing Traits

| | K | 1 | 2 | 3 | 4 | 5 | 6 |
|---|---|---|---|---|---|---|---|
| Conventions | | ✔ | ✔ | ✔ | ✔ | ✔ | ✔ |
| Ideas | | ✔ | ✔ | ✔ | ✔ | ✔ | ✔ |
| Organization | | ✔ | ✔ | ✔ | ✔ | ✔ | ✔ |
| Sentence fluency | | ✔ | ✔ | ✔ | ✔ | ✔ | ✔ |
| Voice | | ✔ | ✔ | ✔ | ✔ | ✔ | ✔ |
| Word choice | | ✔ | ✔ | ✔ | ✔ | ✔ | ✔ |

### Writer's Craft

| | K | 1 | 2 | 3 | 4 | 5 | 6 |
|---|---|---|---|---|---|---|---|
| Good topic, focus on and develop topic, topic sentence | | | ✔ | ✔ | ✔ | ✔ | ✔ |
| Paragraph(s); sentence structure | | | ✔ | ✔ | ✔ | ✔ | ✔ |
| Main idea and supporting key details | | | ✔ | ✔ | ✔ | ✔ | ✔ |
| Unimportant details | | | | | | | |
| Relevant supporting evidence | | | ✔ | ✔ | ✔ | ✔ | ✔ |
| Strong opening, strong conclusion | | | ✔ | ✔ | ✔ | ✔ | ✔ |
| Beginning, middle, end; sequence | | ✔ | ✔ | ✔ | ✔ | ✔ | ✔ |
| Precise words, strong words, vary words | | | ✔ | ✔ | ✔ | ✔ | ✔ |
| Figurative and sensory language, descriptive details | | | | | | | |
| Informal/formal language | | | | | | | |
| Mood/style/tone | | | | | | | |
| Dialogue | | | | ✔ | ✔ | ✔ | ✔ |
| Transition words, transitions to multiple paragraphs | | | | ✔ | ✔ | ✔ | ✔ |
| Select focus and organization | | | ✔ | ✔ | ✔ | ✔ | ✔ |
| Points and counterpoints/Opposing claims and counterarguments | | | | | | | |
| Use reference materials (online and print dictionary, thesaurus, encyclopedia) | | | | | | | |

### Writing Applications

| | K | 1 | 2 | 3 | 4 | 5 | 6 |
|---|---|---|---|---|---|---|---|
| Writing about text | ✔ | ✔ | ✔ | ✔ | ✔ | ✔ | ✔ |
| Personal and fictional narrative (also biographical and autobiographical) | ✔ | ✔ | ✔ | ✔ | ✔ | ✔ | ✔ |
| Variety of expressive forms including poetry | ✔ | ✔ | ✔ | ✔ | ✔ | ✔ | ✔ |
| Informative/explanatory texts | ✔ | ✔ | ✔ | ✔ | ✔ | ✔ | ✔ |
| Description | ✔ | ✔ | ✔ | ✔ | | | |
| Procedural texts | | | ✔ | ✔ | ✔ | ✔ | ✔ |
| Opinion pieces or arguments | ✔ | ✔ | ✔ | ✔ | ✔ | ✔ | ✔ |
| Communications including technical documents | | | ✔ | ✔ | ✔ | ✔ | ✔ |

| | K | 1 | 2 | 3 | 4 | 5 | 6 |
|---|---|---|---|---|---|---|---|
| Research report | ✔ | ✔ | ✔ | ✔ | ✔ | ✔ | ✔ |
| Responses to literature/reflection | | | | ✔ | ✔ | ✔ | ✔ |
| Analytical writing | | | | | | | |
| Letters | | ✔ | ✔ | ✔ | ✔ | ✔ | ✔ |
| Write daily and over short and extended time frames; set up writer's notebooks | | | | | | | |

## Penmanship/Handwriting

| | K | 1 | 2 | 3 | 4 | 5 | 6 |
|---|---|---|---|---|---|---|---|
| Write legibly in manuscript using correct formation, directionality, and spacing | | | | | | | |
| Write legibly in cursive using correct formation, directionality, and spacing | | | | | | | |

# SPEAKING AND LISTENING

## Speaking

| | K | 1 | 2 | 3 | 4 | 5 | 6 |
|---|---|---|---|---|---|---|---|
| Use repetition, rhyme, and rhythm in oral texts | | | | | | | |
| Participate in classroom activities and discussions | | | | | | | |
| Collaborative conversation with peers and adults in small and large groups using formal English when appropriate | | | | | | | |
| Differentiate between formal and informal English | | | | | | | |
| Follow agreed upon rules for discussion | | | | | | | |
| Build on others' talk in conversation, adding new ideas | | | | | | | |
| Come to discussion prepared | | | | | | | |
| Describe familiar people, places, and things and add drawings as desired | | | | | | | |
| Paraphrase portions of text read alone or information presented | | | | | | | |
| Apply comprehension strategies and skills in speaking activities | | | | | | | |
| Use literal and nonliteral meanings | | | | | | | |
| Ask and answer questions about text read aloud and about media | | | | | | | |
| Stay on topic when speaking | | | | | | | |
| Use language appropriate to situation, purpose, and audience | | | | | | | |
| Use nonverbal communications such as eye contact, gestures, and props | | | | | | | |
| Use verbal communication in effective ways and improve expression in conventional language | | | | | | | |
| Retell a story, presentation, or spoken message by summarizing | | | | | | | |
| Oral presentations: focus, organizational structure, audience, purpose | | | | | | | |
| Give and follow directions | | | | | | | |
| Consider audience when speaking or preparing a presentation | | | | | | | |
| Recite poems, rhymes, songs | | | | | | | |
| Use complete, coherent sentences | | | | | | | |
| Organize presentations | | | | | | | |
| Deliver presentations (narrative, summaries, research, persuasive); add visuals | | | | | | | |
| Speak audibly (accuracy, expression, volume, pitch, rate, phrasing, modulation, enunciation) | | | | | | | |
| Create audio recordings of poems, stories, presentations | | | | | | | |

## Listening

| | K | 1 | 2 | 3 | 4 | 5 | 6 |
|---|---|---|---|---|---|---|---|
| Identify musical elements in language | | | | | | | |
| Determine the purpose for listening | | | | | | | |
| Understand, follow, restate, and give oral directions | | | | | | | |
| Develop oral language and concepts | | | | | | | |

| KEY | ✔ = Assessed Skill |
|---|---|
| | Tinted panels show skills, strategies, and other teaching opportunities. |

| | K | 1 | 2 | 3 | 4 | 5 | 6 |
|---|---|---|---|---|---|---|---|
| Listen openly, responsively, attentively, and critically | | | | | | | |
| Listen to identify the points a speaker makes | | | | | | | |
| Listen responsively to oral presentations (determine main idea and key details) | | | | | | | |
| Ask and answer relevant questions (for clarification to follow-up on ideas) | | | | | | | |
| Identify reasons and evidence presented by speaker | | | | | | | |
| Recall and interpret speakers' verbal/nonverbal messages, purposes, perspectives | | | | | | | |

## LANGUAGE

### Vocabulary Acquisition and Use

| | K | 1 | 2 | 3 | 4 | 5 | 6 |
|---|---|---|---|---|---|---|---|
| Develop oral vocabulary and choose words for effect | | | | | | | |
| Use academic language | | ✔ | ✔ | ✔ | ✔ | ✔ | ✔ |
| Identify persons, places, things, actions | | ✔ | ✔ | ✔ | | | |
| Classify, sort, and categorize words | ✔ | ✔ | ✔ | ✔ | ✔ | ✔ | ✔ |
| Determine or clarify the meaning of unknown words; use word walls | | ✔ | ✔ | ✔ | ✔ | ✔ | ✔ |
| Synonyms, antonyms, and opposites | | ✔ | ✔ | ✔ | ✔ | ✔ | ✔ |
| Use context clues such as word, sentence, paragraph, definition, example, restatement, description, comparison, cause and effect | | ✔ | ✔ | ✔ | ✔ | ✔ | ✔ |
| Use word identification strategies | | ✔ | ✔ | ✔ | ✔ | ✔ | ✔ |
| Unfamiliar words | | ✔ | ✔ | ✔ | ✔ | ✔ | ✔ |
| Multiple-meaning words | | ✔ | ✔ | ✔ | ✔ | ✔ | ✔ |
| Use print and online dictionary to locate meanings, pronunciation, derivatives, parts of speech | | ✔ | ✔ | ✔ | ✔ | ✔ | ✔ |
| Compound words | | ✔ | ✔ | ✔ | ✔ | ✔ | ✔ |
| Words ending in -er and -est | | ✔ | ✔ | ✔ | ✔ | ✔ | |
| Root words (base words) | | ✔ | ✔ | ✔ | ✔ | ✔ | ✔ |
| Prefixes and suffixes | | ✔ | ✔ | ✔ | ✔ | ✔ | ✔ |
| Greek and Latin affixes and roots | | | ✔ | ✔ | ✔ | ✔ | ✔ |
| Denotation and connotation | | | | | ✔ | ✔ | ✔ |
| Word families | | ✔ | ✔ | ✔ | ✔ | ✔ | ✔ |
| Inflectional endings | | ✔ | ✔ | ✔ | ✔ | ✔ | ✔ |
| Use a print and online thesaurus | | | ✔ | ✔ | ✔ | ✔ | ✔ |
| Use print and online reference sources for word meaning (dictionary, glossaries) | ✔ | ✔ | ✔ | ✔ | ✔ | ✔ | ✔ |
| Homographs | | | | ✔ | ✔ | ✔ | ✔ |
| Homophones | | | ✔ | ✔ | ✔ | ✔ | ✔ |
| Contractions | | ✔ | ✔ | ✔ | | | |
| Figurative language such as metaphors, similes, personification | | | ✔ | ✔ | ✔ | ✔ | ✔ |
| Idioms, adages, proverbs, literal and nonliteral language | | | ✔ | ✔ | ✔ | ✔ | ✔ |
| Analogies | | | | | | | |
| Listen to, read, discuss familiar and unfamiliar challenging text | | | | | | | |
| Identify real-life connections between words and their use | | | | | | | |
| Use acquired words and phrases to convey precise ideas | | | | | | | |
| Use vocabulary to express spatial and temporal relationships | | | | | | | |
| Identify shades of meaning in related words | ✔ | ✔ | ✔ | ✔ | ✔ | ✔ | ✔ |
| Word origins | | | | ✔ | ✔ | ✔ | ✔ |

| | K | 1 | 2 | 3 | 4 | 5 | 6 |
|---|---|---|---|---|---|---|---|
| Morphology | | | | ✔ | ✔ | ✔ | ✔ |
| **Knowledge of Language** | | | | | | | |
| Choose words, phrases, and sentences for effect | | | | | | | |
| Choose punctuation effectively | | | | | | | |
| Formal and informal language for style and tone including dialects | | | | | | | |
| **Conventions of Standard English/Grammar, Mechanics, and Usage** | | | | | | | |
| Sentence concepts: statements, questions, exclamations, commands | | ✔ | ✔ | ✔ | ✔ | ✔ | ✔ |
| Complete and incomplete sentences; sentence fragments; word order | | ✔ | ✔ | ✔ | ✔ | ✔ | ✔ |
| Compound sentences, complex sentences | | | | ✔ | ✔ | ✔ | ✔ |
| Combining sentences | | ✔ | ✔ | ✔ | ✔ | ✔ | ✔ |
| Nouns including common, proper, singular, plural, irregular plurals, possessives, abstract, concrete, collective | | ✔ | ✔ | ✔ | ✔ | ✔ | ✔ |
| Verbs including action, helping, linking, irregular | | ✔ | ✔ | ✔ | ✔ | ✔ | ✔ |
| Verb tenses including past, present, future, perfect, and progressive | | ✔ | ✔ | ✔ | ✔ | ✔ | ✔ |
| Pronouns including possessive, subject and object, pronoun-verb agreement, indefinite, intensive, reciprocal; correct unclear pronouns | | ✔ | ✔ | ✔ | ✔ | ✔ | ✔ |
| Adjectives including articles, demonstrative, proper, adjectives that compare | | ✔ | ✔ | ✔ | ✔ | ✔ | ✔ |
| Adverbs including telling how, when, where, comparative, superlative, irregular | | ✔ | ✔ | ✔ | ✔ | ✔ | ✔ |
| Subject, predicate; subject-verb agreement | | ✔ | ✔ | ✔ | ✔ | ✔ | ✔ |
| Contractions | | ✔ | ✔ | ✔ | ✔ | ✔ | ✔ |
| Conjunctions | | | | ✔ | ✔ | ✔ | ✔ |
| Commas | | | ✔ | ✔ | ✔ | ✔ | ✔ |
| Colons, semicolons, dashes, hyphens | | | | | | ✔ | ✔ |
| Question words | | | | | | | |
| Quotation marks | | | ✔ | ✔ | ✔ | ✔ | ✔ |
| Prepositions and prepositional phrases, appositives | | ✔ | ✔ | ✔ | ✔ | ✔ | ✔ |
| Independent and dependent clauses | | | | | | ✔ | ✔ |
| Italics/underlining for emphasis and titles | | | | | | | |
| Negatives, correcting double negatives | | | | | ✔ | ✔ | ✔ |
| Abbreviations | | | ✔ | ✔ | ✔ | ✔ | ✔ |
| Use correct capitalization in sentences, proper nouns, titles, abbreviations | | ✔ | ✔ | ✔ | ✔ | ✔ | ✔ |
| Use correct punctuation | | ✔ | ✔ | ✔ | ✔ | ✔ | ✔ |
| Antecedents | | | | ✔ | ✔ | ✔ | ✔ |
| Homophones and words often confused | | | ✔ | ✔ | ✔ | ✔ | ✔ |
| Apostrophes | | | | ✔ | ✔ | ✔ | ✔ |
| **Spelling** | | | | | | | |
| Write irregular, high-frequency words | ✔ | ✔ | ✔ | | | | |
| ABC order | ✔ | ✔ | | | | | |
| Write letters | ✔ | ✔ | | | | | |
| Words with short vowels | ✔ | ✔ | ✔ | ✔ | ✔ | ✔ | ✔ |
| Words with long vowels | ✔ | ✔ | ✔ | ✔ | ✔ | ✔ | ✔ |
| Words with digraphs, blends, consonant clusters, double consonants | | ✔ | ✔ | ✔ | ✔ | ✔ | ✔ |
| Words with vowel digraphs and ambiguous vowels | | ✔ | ✔ | ✔ | ✔ | ✔ | ✔ |

**KEY** ✔ = Assessed Skill
Tinted panels show skills, strategies, and other teaching opportunities.

| | K | 1 | 2 | 3 | 4 | 5 | 6 |
|---|---|---|---|---|---|---|---|
| Words with diphthongs | | ✔ | ✔ | ✔ | ✔ | ✔ | ✔ |
| Words with r-controlled vowels | | ✔ | ✔ | ✔ | ✔ | ✔ | ✔ |
| Use conventional spelling | | ✔ | ✔ | ✔ | ✔ | ✔ | ✔ |
| Schwa words | | | | ✔ | ✔ | ✔ | ✔ |
| Words with silent letters | | | ✔ | ✔ | ✔ | ✔ | ✔ |
| Words with hard and soft letters | | | ✔ | ✔ | ✔ | ✔ | ✔ |
| Inflectional endings including plural, past tense, drop final e and double consonant when adding -ed and -ing, changing y to i | | ✔ | ✔ | ✔ | ✔ | ✔ | ✔ |
| Compound words | | ✔ | ✔ | ✔ | ✔ | ✔ | ✔ |
| Homonyms/homophones | | | ✔ | ✔ | ✔ | ✔ | ✔ |
| Prefixes and suffixes | | ✔ | ✔ | ✔ | ✔ | ✔ | ✔ |
| Root and base words (also spell derivatives) | | | | ✔ | ✔ | ✔ | ✔ |
| Syllables: patterns, rules, accented, stressed, closed, open | | | | ✔ | ✔ | ✔ | ✔ |
| Words with Greek and Latin roots | | | | | | ✔ | ✔ |
| Words from mythology | | | | | | ✔ | ✔ |
| Words with spelling patterns, word families | | ✔ | ✔ | ✔ | ✔ | ✔ | ✔ |

## RESEARCH AND INQUIRY

### Study Skills

| | K | 1 | 2 | 3 | 4 | 5 | 6 |
|---|---|---|---|---|---|---|---|
| Directions: read, write, give, follow (includes technical directions) | | | ✔ | ✔ | ✔ | ✔ | ✔ |
| Evaluate directions for sequence and completeness | | | | ✔ | ✔ | ✔ | ✔ |
| Use library/media center | | | | | | | |
| Use parts of a book to locate information | | | | | | | |
| Interpret information from graphic aids | | ✔ | ✔ | ✔ | ✔ | ✔ | ✔ |
| Use graphic organizers to organize information and comprehend text | | ✔ | ✔ | ✔ | ✔ | ✔ | ✔ |
| Use functional, everyday documents | | | | ✔ | ✔ | ✔ | ✔ |
| Apply study strategies: skimming and scanning, note-taking, outlining | | | | | | | |

### Research Process

| | K | 1 | 2 | 3 | 4 | 5 | 6 |
|---|---|---|---|---|---|---|---|
| Generate and revise topics and questions for research | | | | ✔ | ✔ | ✔ | ✔ |
| Narrow focus of research, set research goals | | | | ✔ | ✔ | ✔ | ✔ |
| Find and locate information using print and digital resources | | ✔ | ✔ | ✔ | ✔ | ✔ | ✔ |
| Record information systematically (note-taking, outlining, using technology) | | | | ✔ | ✔ | ✔ | ✔ |
| Develop a systematic research plan | | | | ✔ | ✔ | ✔ | ✔ |
| Evaluate reliability, credibility, usefulness of sources and information | | | | | | ✔ | ✔ |
| Use primary sources to obtain information | | | | | ✔ | ✔ | ✔ |
| Organize, synthesize, evaluate, and draw conclusions from information | | | | | | | |
| Cite and list sources of information (record basic bibliographic data) | | | | | ✔ | ✔ | ✔ |
| Demonstrate basic keyboarding skills | | | | | | | |
| Participate in and present shared research | | | | | | | |

### Technology

| | K | 1 | 2 | 3 | 4 | 5 | 6 |
|---|---|---|---|---|---|---|---|
| Use computer, Internet, and other technology resources to access information | | | | | | | |
| Use text and organizational features of electronic resources such as search engines, keywords, e-mail, hyperlinks, URLs, Web pages, databases, graphics | | | | | | | |
| Use digital tools to present and publish in a variety of media formats | | | | | | | |

# INDEX

## A

KEY   3 = Unit 3

# H

# I

# M

KEY  3 = Unit 3

# Q

# R

# S

**Scaffolding.** *See* Access complex text; English Language Learners: scaffold.

**Science, 1:** T92, T197, T217J, T220, T233, T241, T245, T251, T261, T281B, T284, T297, T305, T309, T315, T329, T331, **2:** T69, T133, T153L, T156, T169, T177, T181, T187, T197, T217T, T233, T241, T245, T251, T261, T331, **3:** T69, T89R, T92, T133, T153H, T156, T169, T177, T181, T187, T197, T217L, T233, T241, T245, T249, T251, T331, **4:** T92, T197, T217F, T220, T233, T241, T245, T249, T251, T261, T329, T331, **5:** T5, T133, T153L, T156, T169, T177, T181, T187, T197, T217F, T217H, T220, T233, T241, T245, T251, T261, T281B, T281D, T284, T297, T305, T309, T315, T329, T331, **6:** T133, T153J, T156, T169, T177, T181, T187, T197, T217L, T220, T233, T241, T245, T251, T261, T329, T331

*See also* Literacy workstation activity cards.

**Science fiction.** *See under* Genre: fiction.

**Scoring rubrics**
research and inquiry projects, **Units 1–6:** T333
writing, **Units 1–6:** T30, T94, T158, T222, T286, T349, T355

**Self-correction strategies.** *See* Monitor and Clarify.

**Self-monitoring strategies.** *See* Monitor and Clarify.

**Self-selected reading, Units 1–6:** T47, T51, T55, T111, T115, T119, T175, T179, T183, T239, T243, T247, T303, T307, T311

**Sentences.** *See* Grammar: sentences; Writer's Craft: strong sentences; Writing traits: sentence fluency.

**Sequence of events.** *See* Comprehension skills: sequence; Writing traits: organization.

**Setting.** *See* Comprehension skills: setting.

**Setting purposes for reading, 1:** T58, T186, T250, T314, **2:** T58, T186, T250, T314, **3:** T58, T186, T250, T314, **4:** T58, T186, T250, T314, **5:** T58, T186, T250, T314, **6:** T58, T186, T250, T314

**Shared Read, Units 1–6:** T16–T17, T56–T57, T80–T81, T120–T121, T144–T145, T184–T185, T208–T209, T248–T249, T272–T273, T312–T313, T326

**Sharing circles.** *See* Literature Circle.

**Signal words, 1:** T148–T149, T153L, T212–T213, T222, T224–T225, **2:** T20, T148–T149, T174–T175, **3:** T89J, T153G, T217G, **4:** T158, T190, **5:** T148, T153P, T175, T179, T183, T212, **6:** T23, T149, T150, T153F, T153T, T175, T179, T183, T335

**Similes, 1:** T41, T49, T53, T59, **2:** T88–T89, T89H, T89K, T89P, T103, T109, T114, T118, T121, T125, T230, T294, **4:** T217N, T280–T281, T281C, T295, T301, T306, T310, T317, T352, **5:** T22, T25E–T254, T89H, T89J, T102, **6:** T25B, T25O, T217C

**Small Group Options.** *See* Approaching Level Options; Beyond Level Options; English Language Learners; On Level Options.

**Social studies, 1:** T5, T28, T69, T133, T153T, T156, T169, T177, T181, T187, T197, **2:** T5, T25P, T28, T41, T49, T53, T59, T331, **3:** T5, T261, T281B, T284, T297, T309, T315, T331, **4:** T5, T41, T49, T53, T59, T69, T133, T153N, T156, T169, T177, T181, T187, T329, T331, **5:** T53, T69, T92, T331, **6:** T5, T69, T331

*See also* Literacy workstation activity cards.

**Speaking skills and strategies**
*See also* Fluency: speaking checklist; Listening; Literature Circle.
act it out, **1:** T121, **2:** T185, **3:** T57, T252, **4:** T99, T123, **5:** T252, **6:** T185, T314
add new ideas, **1:** S6, T202, **5:** T202, **6:** T10
ask and answer questions, **1:** S20, T74, **2:** T74, **3:** T202, **4:** T10, T202, **5:** T10
audio presentation, **1:** T354, **2:** T331
be open to all ideas, **1:** S20, **2:** T138, **3:** T10, **6:** T74, T202
checklist, **Units 1–6:** T333, T334
debate, **1:** T331, **3:** T331, **5:** T227
dramatic presentation, **2:** T331
English Language Learner,
demonstrate, **1:** T275, **2:** T277, T281, **3:** T351, **4:** T275, T277, T279, **6:** T87, T275
explain, **1:** T19, T21, T25, T83, T89, T149, T151, T213, T215, T279, T281, **2:** T19, T21, T83, T87, T89, T149, T223, T277, T279, **3:** T25, T85, T87, T149, T153, T211, T215, T277, T279, T281, **4:** T21, T23, T87, T89, T149, T153, T211, T215, T277, **5:** T275, T281, **6:** T21, T83, T149, T151, T213, T275, T279
express, **2:** T217, **3:** T23, T25, **4:** T153
respond orally, **1:** T31, T95, T159, T223, T287, **2:** T153, T213, T223, T277, T287, **3:** T147, T211, T277, T287, **4:** T87, T95, T159, T223, T275, T277, T287, **5:** T31, T95, T159, T213, T223, T277, T287, **6:** T31, T95, T159, T223, T275, T287
formal presentation, **4:** T331, **5:** T331
mock interview, **5:** T331, **6:** T331
multimedia presentation, **5:** T331
oral presentations, **1:** S35, T28, T29, T92, T93, T156, T157, T220, T221, T284, T285, T331, T334, **2:** T28, T29, T92, T93, T156, T157, T220, T221, T284, T285, T331, **3:** T29, T92, T93, T156, T157, T220, T221, T284, T285, **4:** T28, T29, T92, T93, T157, T220, T221, T285, **5:** T28, T29, T92, T93, T156, T157, T221, T285, **6:** T29, T92, T93, T156, T157, T220, T221, T285, T331
perform commercial, **5:** T227
persuasive presentation, **1:** T331, **2:** T284, **5:** T331
poster, **3:** T331
present advertisement, **6:** T310
present ideas, **4:** T285

retell, **1:** T119, T148, T187, **3:** T217P, **4:** T28, T168, T187
role-play, **2:** T11, **6:** T89D, T89P
Reader's Theater, **1:** T326–T327, **2:** T326–T327, **3:** T326–T327, **4:** T326–T327, **5:** T326–T327, **6:** T326–T327
speak slowly and clearly, **1:** S35, **2:** T156, T220, **4:** T220
speech, **1:** T284, **5:** T331
summarize/summaries, **1:** T12, T76, T140, T204, T268, **2:** T12, T76, T140, T204, T268, **3:** T76, T140, T204, T268, **4:** T12, T76, T92, T140, T204, T220, T268, **5:** T12, T29, T76, T140, T204, T268, **6:** T12, T29, T76, T140, T204, T221, T268
take on discussion roles, **1:** S20, T10, **2:** T202, **3:** T138, **4:** T138, **5:** T74, T138
take turns talking, **1:** S6, T266, **2:** T10, **3:** T266, **4:** T74, **6:** T138
visual and digital elements, **1:** T92, 334, **2:** T334, **3:** T334, **4:** T334, **5:** T92, T334, **6:** T334
web site/podcast, **5:** T156

**Speech, 1:** T284, **4:** T84–T85, T185, T284, **5:** T331, **6:** T92, T334

**Speed Sort, Units 1–6:** T37, T101, T165, T229, T293

**Spelling, Units 1–6:** T36–T37, T100–T101, T164–T165, T228–T229, T292–T293
*See also* English Language Learners: writing/spelling; Phonics/Word Study.
analogies, **1:** T37, **2:** T37, T293, **4:** T101, **5:** T165, **6:** T165
antonyms, **1:** T37, **2:** T37, **3:** T37, **5:** T165
assess, **Units 1–6:** T37, T101, T165, T229, T293
assess prior knowledge, **Units 1–6:** T36, T100, T164, T228, T292
challenge words, **Units 1–6:** T36, T100, T164, T228, T292
closed syllables, **1:** S29, **2:** T292–T293, T318, **3:** T36
cloze sentences, **1:** T293, **3:** T101, **5:** T229, **6:** T101, T229
consonant + *le* syllables, **1:** S29, **3:** T228–T229, T254, T292
contractions, **2:** T228–T229, T254, T292
definitions, **3:** T165, **4:** T165, **5:** T37, T293
dictation sentences, **Units 1–6:** T37, T101, T165, T229, T293
differentiated spelling, **Units 1–6:** T36, T100, T164, T228, T292
diphthongs, **2:** T62
error correction, **Units 1–6:** T37, T101, T165, T229, T293
homographs, **4:** T154–T155, T164–T165, T170–T171, T190, T228
homophones, **5:** T90–T91, T100–T101, T106–T107, T126, T164
inflectional endings, **2:** T154–T155, T164–T165, T170–T171, T190, T228
link to spelling, **1:** S30
long vowels, **1:** T126, T164
number prefixes *uni-, bi-, tri-, cent-,* **6:** T218–T219, T228–T229, T234–T235, T254, T292

# T

# W

**Common Core State Standards Correlations**

**English Language Arts**

# College and Career Readiness Anchor Standards for READING

The K-5 standards on the following pages define what students should understand and be able to do by the end of each grade. They correspond to the College and Career Readiness (CCR) anchor standards below by number. The CCR and grade-specific standards are necessary complements—the former providing broad standards, the latter providing additional specificity—that together define the skills and understandings that all students must demonstrate.

## Key Ideas and Details

1. Read closely to determine what the text says explicitly and to make logical inferences from it; cite specific textual evidence when writing or speaking to support conclusions drawn from the text.

2. Determine central ideas or themes of a text and analyze their development; summarize the key supporting details and ideas.

3. Analyze how and why individuals, events, and ideas develop and interact over the course of a text.

## Craft and Structure

4. Interpret words and phrases as they are used in a text, including determining technical, connotative, and figurative meanings, and analyze how specific word choices shape meaning or tone.

5. Analyze the structure of texts, including how specific sentences, paragraphs, and larger portions of the text (e.g., a section, chapter, scene, or stanza) relate to each other and the whole.

6. Assess how point of view or purpose shapes the content and style of a text.

## Integration of Knowledge and Ideas

7. Integrate and evaluate content presented in diverse media and formats, including visually and quantitatively, as well as in words.

8. Delineate and evaluate the argument and specific claims in a text, including the validity of the reasoning as well as the relevance and sufficiency of the evidence.

9. Analyze how two or more texts address similar themes or topics in order to build knowledge or to compare the approaches the authors take.

## Range of Reading and Level of Text Complexity

10. Read and comprehend complex literary and informational texts independently and proficiently.

# **CCSS** Common Core State Standards
# English Language Arts

## Grade 5

Each standard is coded in the following manner:

| Strand | Grade Level | Standard |
|--------|-------------|----------|
| RL | 5 | 1 |

## Reading Standards for Literature

| Key Ideas and Details | *McGraw-Hill Reading Wonders* |
|---|---|
| **RL.5.1** | Quote accurately from a text when explaining what the text says explicitly and when drawing inferences from the text. | **READING/WRITING WORKSHOP:** Unit 1: 26, 40, 41 Unit 2: 113, 142 Unit 3: 170, 171, 212 Unit 4: 242, 243, 256, 257 Unit 5: 315, 329 Unit 6: 386, 387, 401, 402<br>**LITERATURE ANTHOLOGY:** Unit 1: 14, 18, 20, 25, 33, 35, 39, 41, 89 Unit 2: 129, 133, 137, 155, 169, 171, 179, 181 Unit 3: 185, 190, 192, 195, 202, 207, 213 Unit 4: 275, 277, 291, 293, 297, 343 Unit 5: 359, 377, 379 Unit 6: 434, 437, 443, 445, 454, 457, 461, 463, 509, 511<br>**LEVELED READERS:** Unit 1, Week 1: *Parker's Plan* (A), *Can-do Canines* (O), *Cleaning Up the Competition* (B) Unit 1, Week 2: *Dog Gone* (A), *Shhh! It's a Surprise!* (O), *Lost and Found* (B) Unit 2, Week 4: *The Lion's Whiskers* (A), *The Riddle of the Drum: A Tale from Mexico* (O), *Clever Manka* (B) Unit 3, Week 2: *Over the Top* (A), *In Drama Valley* (O), *Welcome to the Wilds* (B) Unit 4, Week 2: *The Mysterious Teacher* (A), *The Unusually Clever Dog* (O), *The Surprise Party* (B) Unit 5, Week 2: *The Picture Palace* (A), *Hard Times* (O), *Woodpecker Warriors* (B) Unit 6, Week 2: *Winning Friends* (A), *Enemy or Ally?* (O), *Jamayla to the Rescue* (B)<br>**YOUR TURN PRACTICE BOOK:** 3–5, 13–15, 63–65, 83–85, 103–105, 113–115, 163–165, 203–205, 213–215, 223–225, 263–265<br>**READING WORKSTATION ACTIVITY CARDS:** 22<br>**TEACHER'S EDITION:** Unit 1: T25P, T29, T89I, T89L, T93 Unit 2: T89P, T93, T217G, T217P, T221 Unit 3: T25N, T89E, T89G, T89P, T93 Unit 4: T25P, T29, T89E, T89L, T93 Unit 5: T25G, T25N, T89H, T89J, T89P, T93 Unit 6: T25H, T25M, T25P, T89H, T89K |
| **RL.5.2** | Determine a theme of a story, drama, or poem from details in the text, including how characters in a story or drama respond to challenges or how the speaker in a poem reflects upon a topic; summarize the text. | **READING/WRITING WORKSHOP:** Unit 2: 141, 155 Unit 3: 170, 171, 184, 185 Unit 4: 299 Unit 6: 387, 400, 401<br>**LITERATURE ANTHOLOGY:** Unit 1: 25, 41 Unit 2: 133, 171, 179 Unit 3: 185, 190, 195, 207, 213 Unit 4: 275, 277, 293, 343 Unit 5: 359, 377, 379 Unit 6: 434, 437, 445, 454, 457, 463, 509, 511<br>**LEVELED READERS:** Unit 2, Week 4: *The Lion's Whiskers* (A), *The Riddle of the Drum: A Tale from Mexico* (O, ELL), *Clever Manka* (B) Unit 2, Week 5: *Clearing the Jungle* (A), *I Want to Ride!* (O, ELL), *Changing Goals* (B) Unit 3, Week 1: *All the Way from Europe* (A), *Dancing the Flamenco* (O, ELL), *A Vacation in Minnesota* (B) Unit 3, Week 2: *Over the Top* (A), *In Drama Valley* (O, ELL), *Welcome to the Wilds* (B) Unit 4, Week 5: *Tell Me the Old, Old Stories* (A), *From Me to You* (O, ELL), *Every Picture Tells a Story* (B) Unit 6, Week 1: *Mrs. Gleeson's Records* (A), *Norberto's Hat* (O, ELL), *The Victory Garden* (B) Unit 6, Week 2: *Winning Friends* (A), *Enemy or Ally?* (O, ELL), *Jamayla to the Rescue* (B)<br>**YOUR TURN PRACTICE BOOK:** 83–85, 93–94, 103–105, 113–115, 193–194, 199, 253–255, 259, 263–265<br>**READING WORKSTATION STUDY CARDS:** 6<br>**TEACHER'S EDITION:** Unit 2: T212, T217P, T239, T243, T247, T249, T276, T281D, T303, T307, T311, T313 Unit 3: T20, T25N, T47, T51, T55, T57, T84, T89C, T89F, T89P Unit 4: T276, T281B, T285, T303, T307, T311, T313 Unit 6: T20, T25L, T25P, T29, T84, T111, T115, T119, T121 |

# Reading Standards for Literature

| Key Ideas and Details | McGraw-Hill Reading Wonders |
|---|---|
| **RL.5.3** Compare and contrast two or more characters, settings, or events in a story or drama, drawing on specific details in the text (e.g., how characters interact). | **READING/WRITING WORKSHOP:** Unit 2: 113 Unit 5: 315, 329 <br> **LITERATURE ANTHOLOGY:** Unit 2: 133 Unit 4: 293 Unit 5: 359, 379 Unit 6: 463 <br> **LEVELED READERS:** Unit 2, Week 2: *The Bird of Truth* (A), *The Talking Eggs* (O, ELL), *Three Golden Oranges* (B) Unit 5, Week 1: *King of the Board* (A), *Snap Happy* (O, ELL), *No Place Like Home* (B) Unit 5, Week 2: *The Picture Palace* (A), *Hard Times* (O, ELL), *Woodpecker Warriors* (B) <br> **YOUR TURN PRACTICE BOOK:** 62–65, 202–205, 212–215 <br> **READING WORKSTATION ACTIVITY CARDS:** 3, 4, 5 <br> **TEACHER'S EDITION:** Unit 2: T84, T89C, T89G, T89J, T89K, T89N, T89P Unit 5: T20, T25B, T25F, T25I, T25K, T25N, T84, T89E, T89I, T89K, T89M, T89P |

| Craft and Structure | McGraw-Hill Reading Wonders |
|---|---|
| **RL.5.4** Determine the meaning of words and phrases as they are used in a text, including figurative language such as metaphors and similes. | **READING/WRITING WORKSHOP:** Unit 1: 43 Unit 2: 115 Unit 3: 173 Unit 4: 301 Unit 5: 331 Unit 6: 389 <br> **LITERATURE ANTHOLOGY:** Unit 1: 41 Unit 2: 133 Unit 3: 195 Unit 4: 343 Unit 5: 379 Unit 6: 445 <br> **YOUR TURN PRACTICE BOOK:** 17, 67, 107, 197, 217 <br> **TEACHER'S EDITION:** Unit 1: T88, T89B, T89L, T89M, T109, T114, T118, T125 Unit 2: T88, T109, T114, T118, T125 Unit 3: T24, T25C, T25I, T25K, T25N Unit 4: T280, T281, T281A, T281C, T281D, T281F, T301, T306, T310, T317 Unit 5: T88, T89E, T89G, T109, T114, T118, T125 Unit 6: T24, T25C, T25E, T25H, T25I, T25P |
| **RL.5.5** Explain how a series of chapters, scenes, or stanzas fits together to provide the overall structure of a particular story, drama, or poem. | **READING/WRITING WORKSHOP:** Unit 4: 300 <br> **LITERATURE ANTHOLOGY:** Unit 2: 132 Unit 4: 343 <br> **LEVELED READERS:** Unit 4, Week 2: *The Mysterious Teacher* (A), *The Unusually Clever Dog* (O, ELL), *The Surprise Party* (B) <br> **YOUR TURN PRACTICE BOOK:** 99, 166, 196 <br> **READING WORKSTATION ACTIVITY CARDS:** 26, 27 <br> **TEACHER'S EDITION:** Unit 2: T81, T89G, T285 Unit 4: T86, T89E, T89F, T89G, T89K, T104, T105, T112, T113, T116, T117, T121–T123, T278, T350 Unit 5: T25I |
| **RL.5.6** Describe how a narrator's or speaker's point of view influences how events are described. | **READING/WRITING WORKSHOP:** Unit 4: 243, 257 Unit 5: 316 Unit 6: 443 <br> **LITERATURE ANTHOLOGY:** Unit 4: 277, 293 Unit 5: 358 Unit 6: 462 <br> **LEVELED READERS:** Unit 4, Week 1: *Paul Bunyan* (A), *Pecos Bill* (O, ELL), *An Extraordinary Girl* (B) Unit 4, Week 2: *The Mysterious Teacher* (A), *The Unusually Clever Dog* (O, ELL), *The Surprise Party* (B) Unit 6, Week 5: *Your World, My World* (A), *Flying Home* (O, ELL), *Helping Out* (B) <br> **YOUR TURN PRACTICE BOOK:** 153–155, 159, 163–165 <br> **READING WORKSTATION ACTIVITY CARDS:** 7 <br> **TEACHER'S EDITION:** Unit 4: T20, T25C, T25E, T25J, T25M, T25P, T29, T47, T51, T55, T57, T84, T89C, T89E, T89I, T89L, T111, T115, T119, T121, T274 Unit 5: T22, T25E Unit 6: T276, T281B, T281D, T303, T307, T311, T313 |

| Integration of Knowledge and Ideas | McGraw-Hill Reading Wonders |
|---|---|
| **RL.5.7** Analyze how visual and multimedia elements contribute to the meaning, tone, or beauty of a text (e.g., graphic novel, multimedia presentation of fiction, folktale, myth, poem). | **READING/WRITING WORKSHOP:** Unit 2: 114 <br> **YOUR TURN PRACTICE BOOK:** 6, 9, 66 <br> **READING WORKSTATION ACTIVITY CARDS:** 8 <br> **TEACHER'S EDITION:** Unit 1: T22, T23, T25F, T25J, T29, T89K Unit 2: T86, T89E, T89O, T217I, T217N, T284 Unit 3: T25B, T89B, T93 Unit 4: T25E, T28 <br> www.connected.mcgraw-hill.com: **RESOURCES:** <br> READING/WRITING WORKSHOP: Unit 2: 108–115, 136–143 Unit 6: 438–445 <br> LITERATURE ANTHOLOGY: Unit 2: 118–133, 156–171 Unit 3: 198–213 <br> STUDENT PRACTICE: Approaching Reproducibles: 6, 9, 66 Beyond Reproducibles: 6, 9, 66 <br> ELL Reproducibles: 6, 9, 66 <br> MEDIA: Video, Images |
| **RL.5.8** (Not applicable to Literature) | |

## Reading Standards for Literature

| Integration of Knowledge and Ideas | McGraw-Hill Reading Wonders |
|---|---|
| **RL.5.9** Compare and contrast stories in the same genre (e.g., mysteries and adventure stories) on their approaches to similar themes and topics. | **LITERATURE ANTHOLOGY:** Unit 1: 45 Unit 2: 137, 155 Unit 4: 281, 297 Unit 5: 363 Unit 6: 489<br>**LEVELED READERS:** Unit 1, Week 2: *Dog Gone* (A), *Shhh! It's a Surprise!* (O, ELL), *Lost and Found* (B)<br>**READING WORKSTATION ACTIVITY CARDS:** 9<br>**TEACHER'S EDITION:** Unit 1: T29, T93, T105, T113, T117, T123 Unit 2: T89R, T89T, T93, T105, T113, T117, T123, T221 Unit 3: T29, T93 Unit 4: T25R, T25T, T89N, T89P, T93 Unit 5: T25P, T25R |

| Range of Reading and Level of Text Complexity | McGraw-Hill Reading Wonders |
|---|---|
| **RL.5.10** By the end of the year, read and comprehend literature, including stories, dramas, and poetry, at the high end of the grades 4–5 text complexity band independently and proficiently. | **READING/WRITING WORKSHOP:** These Units reflect the range of text complexity found throughout the book.<br>Unit 1, Week 1: "A Fresh Idea," 22; **Unit 2, Week 2:** "A Modern Cinderella," 108; **Unit 2, Week 4:** "The Magical Lost Brocade," 136; **Unit 3, Week 1:** "A Reluctant Traveler," 166; **Unit 3, Week 2:** "Survivaland," 180; **Unit 4, Week 1:** "How Mighty Kate Stopped the Train," 238; **Unit 4, Week 2:** "Where's Brownie?," 252; **Unit 5, Week 1:** "Miguel in the Middle," 310; **Unit 5, Week 2:** "The Day the Rollets Got Their Moxie Back," 324; **Unit 6, Week 2:** "The Bully," 396; **Unit 6, Week 5:** "To Travel!," 438<br>**LITERATURE ANTHOLOGY:** These Units reflect the range of text complexity found throughout the book.<br>**Unit 1, Week 1:** *One Hen*, 10; **Unit 2, Week 2:** *Where the Mountain Meets the Moon*, 118; **Unit 2, Week 4:** *Blancaflor*, 156; **Unit 2, Week 5:** *Stage Fright*, 176; **Unit 3, Week 2:** *Weslandia*, 198; **Unit 4, Week 1:** *Davy Crockett Saves the World*, 262; **Unit 4, Week 2:** *A Window Into History*, 282; **Unit 5, Week 2:** *Bud, Not Buddy*, 364; **Unit 6, Week 1:** *The Unbreakable Code*, 430; **Unit 6, Week 2:** *The Friend Who Changed My Life*, 450; **Unit 6, Week 5:** *You Are My Music*, 506<br>**LEVELED READERS: Unit 1, Week 1:** *Parker's Plan* (A), *Can-do Canines* (O, ELL), *Cleaning Up the Competition* (B) **Unit 2, Week 2:** *The Bird of Truth* (A), *The Talking Eggs* (O, ELL), *Three Golden Oranges* (B) **Unit 2, Week 4:** *The Lion's Whiskers* (A), *The Riddle of the Drum: A Tale from Mexico* (O, ELL), *Clever Manka* (B) **Unit 3, Week 1:** *All the Way from Europe* (A), *Dancing the Flamenco* (O, ELL), *A Vacation in Minnesota* (B) **Unit 3, Week 2:** *Over the Top* (A), *In Drama Valley* (O, ELL), *Welcome to the Wilds* (B) **Unit 4, Week 1:** *Paul Bunyan* (A), *Pecos Bill* (O, ELL), *An Extraordinary Girl* (B) **Unit 4, Week 2:** *The Mysterious Teacher* (A), *The Unusually Clever Dog* (O, ELL), *The Surprise Party* (B) **Unit 4, Week 5:** *Tell Me the Old, Old Stories* (A), *From Me to You* (O, ELL), *Every Picture Tells a Story* (B) **Unit 5, Week 2:** *The Picture Palace* (A), *Hard Times* (O, ELL), *Woodpecker Warriors* (B) **Unit 6, Week 1:** *Mrs. Gleeson's Records* (A), *Norberto's Hat* (O, ELL), *The Victory Garden* (B) **Unit 6, Week 5:** *Your World, My World* (A), *Flying Home* (O, ELL), *Helping Out* (B)<br>**YOUR TURN PRACTICE BOOK:** 16, 86, 106, 116, 266<br>**READING WORKSTATION ACTIVITY CARDS:** 24, 26, 27, 30<br>**TEACHER'S EDITION: Unit 1:** T22, T25A–T25P **Unit 2:** T86, T89A–T89T, T214, 217A–T217P, T274, T281A–T281F **Unit 3:** T22, T25A–T25N, T86, T89A–T89P **Unit 4:** T22, T25A–T25T, T86, T89A–T89L, T104–T105, T112–T113, T116–T117, T274, T281A–T281F **Unit 5:** T22, T25A–T25R, T86, T89A–T89P **Unit 6:** T86, T89A–T89R, T274, T281A–T281F |

# Reading Standards for Informational Text

| Key Ideas and Details | | McGraw-Hill Reading Wonders |
|---|---|---|
| **RI.5.1** | Quote accurately from a text when explaining what the text says explicitly and when drawing inferences from the text. | **READING/WRITING WORKSHOP:** Unit 1: 54, 55, 68 Unit 2: 98, 99, 126, 128 Unit 3: 198, 199, 212, 213 Unit 4: 271 Unit 5: 342, 356 Unit 6: 414, 428<br>**LITERATURE ANTHOLOGY:** Unit 1: 49, 54, 61, 63, 72, 78, 81, 85 Unit 2: 100, 103, 109, 113, 141, 145, 147, 151 Unit 3: 220, 223, 227, 231, 241, 246, 249, 251 Unit 4: 303, 307, 311, 315, 319, 324, 328, 332, 337 Unit 5: 388, 393, 397, 399, 409, 417, 419, 421 Unit 6: 473, 478, 485, 495, 497, 501, 503, 505<br>**LEVELED READERS:** Unit 1, Week 3: *Save This Space!* (A, O, B) Unit 2, Week 1: *The Bill of Rights* (A, O, B) Unit 3, Week 4: *The Power of a Team* (A, O, B) Unit 4, Week 3: *Jane Addams: A Woman of Action* (A, O, B) Unit 5, Week 4: *Mars* (A, O, B) Unit 6, Week 3: *Cave Creatures* (A, O, B)<br>**YOUR TURN PRACTICE BOOK:** 23–25, 33–35, 53–55, 73–75, 123–125, 133–135, 173–175, 183–185, 223–225, 233–235, 273–275, 283–285<br>**READING WORKSTATION ACTIVITY CARDS:** 22<br>**TEACHER'S EDITION:** Unit 1: T153R, T217K, T217R, T221, T281D Unit 2: T25H, T25R, T153F, T153N, T157 Unit 3: T153N, T153P, T217L, T217P, T221 Unit 4: T153C, T153I, T153R, T157, T217R Unit 5: T153H, T153P, T217R, T221, T285 Unit 6: T153K, T153R, T217J, T217N, T221 |
| **RI.5.2** | Determine two or more main ideas of a text and explain how they are supported by key details; summarize the text. | **READING/WRITING WORKSHOP:** Unit 3: 199, 213, 226 Unit 4: 270, 284<br>**LITERATURE ANTHOLOGY:** Unit 3: 231, 251 Unit 4: 315, 337<br>**LEVELED READERS:** Unit 3, Week 3: *Weather Patterns* (A, O, B, ELL) Unit 3, Week 4: *The Power of a Team* (A, O, B, ELL) Unit 4, Week 3: *Jane Addams: A Woman of Action* (A, O, B, ELL) Unit 4, Week 4: *The Delta* (A, O, B, ELL)<br>**YOUR TURN PRACTICE BOOK:** 123–125, 133–135<br>**READING WORKSTATION ACTIVITY CARDS:** 10<br>**TEACHER'S EDITION:** Unit 3: T148, T153C, T153F, T153H, T153J, T153K, T153M, T153P, T175, T179, T183, T185, T212, T217C, T217H, T217M, T217P, T239, T243, T247, T249, T274 Unit 4: T146, T153G, T153L, T153R, T210, T217K, T217M, T217R Unit 5: T274 |
| **RI.5.3** | Explain the relationships or interactions between two or more individuals, events, ideas, or concepts in a historical, scientific, or technical text based on specific information in the text. | **READING/WRITING WORKSHOP:** Unit 1: 55 Unit 5: 357 Unit 6: 415<br>**LITERATURE ANTHOLOGY:** Unit 1: 63 Unit 5: 388, 399, 403, 409, 417, 421, 427 Unit 6: 473, 483, 485<br>**LEVELED READERS:** Unit 1, Week 3: *Save This Space!* (A, O, B, ELL) Unit 5, Week 4: *Mars* (A, O, B, ELL) Unit 6, Week 3: *Cave Creatures* (A, O, B, ELL)<br>**YOUR TURN PRACTICE BOOK:** 23–25, 233–235, 273–275<br>**READING WORKSTATION ACTIVITY CARDS:** 11<br>**TEACHER'S EDITION:** Unit 1: T153D, T153F, T153H, T153I, T153K, T153M, T1530 Unit 5: T217D, T217E, T217H, T217L, T217P Unit 6: T153C, T153E, T153G, T153I, T153L, T212 |

# Reading Standards for Informational Text

| Craft and Structure | | McGraw-Hill Reading Wonders |
|---|---|---|
| **RI.5.4** | Determine the meaning of general academic and domain-specific words and phrases in a text relevant to a *grade 5 topic or subject area.* | **LITERATURE ANTHOLOGY:** Unit 1: 63, 85, 93 Unit 2: 113, 151 Unit 3: 231, 251, 259 Unit 4: 315, 337 Unit 5: 399, 427 Unit 6: 485, 503<br>**YOUR TURN PRACTICE BOOK:** 37, 57, 77, 127, 137, 147, 187, 227, 237, 247, 277<br>**TEACHER'S EDITION:** Unit 1: T153J, T153R, T216, T217C, T217R Unit 2: T24, T25I, T25R, T153G, T153N Unit 3: T153D, T153P, T216, T217J, T217P Unit 4: T153K, T153R, T216, T217E, T217R Unit 5: T152, T153B, T153P, T217B, T217R Unit 6: T153D, T153R, T173, T178, T182, T185 |
| **RI.5.5** | Compare and contrast the overall structure (e.g., chronology, comparison, cause/effect, problem/solution) of events, ideas, concepts, or information in two or more texts. | **LITERATURE ANTHOLOGY:** Unit 1: 95<br>**YOUR TURN PRACTICE BOOK:** 289<br>**READING WORKSTATION ACTIVITY CARDS:** 15<br>**TEACHER'S EDITION:** Unit 1: T212 Unit 2: T148 Unit 5: T212 Unit 6: T212, T221 |
| **RI.5.6** | Analyze multiple accounts of the same event or topic, noting important similarities and differences in the point of view they represent. | **READING/WRITING WORKSHOP:** Unit 1: 56, 82 Unit 3: 226 Unit 5: 372<br>**LITERATURE ANTHOLOGY:** Unit 1: 93 Unit 3: 259 Unit 5: 427<br>**LEVELED READERS:** Unit 1, Week 5: *What About Robots?* (A, O, B, ELL)<br>**YOUR TURN PRACTICE BOOK:** 43–45, 143–145, 243–245, 249<br>**READING WORKSTATION ACTIVITY CARDS:** 16<br>**TEACHER'S EDITION:** Unit 1: T150, T274, T276, T281C, T281D, T296–T297, T304–T305, T308–T309, T314–T315 Unit 3: T274, T276, T281C, T281D, T281F Unit 5: T278, T279, T281D, T285 |

| Integration of Knowledge and Ideas | | McGraw-Hill Reading Wonders |
|---|---|---|
| **RI.5.7** | Draw on information from multiple print or digital sources, demonstrating the ability to locate an answer to a question quickly or to solve a problem efficiently. | **READING WORKSTATION ACTIVITY CARDS:** 19<br>**TEACHER'S EDITION:** Unit 1: T157, T285, T328, T329 Unit 2: T29, T157, T328, T329 Unit 3: T157, T285, T328, T329 Unit 4: T92, T156, T157, T221, T328, T329 Unit 5: T156, T221, T285, T328, T329 Unit 6: T29, T93, T328, T329<br>www.connected.mcgraw-hill.com: **RESOURCES:**<br>**READING/WRITING WORKSHOP:** Unit 4: 272<br>**RESEARCH & INQUIRY:** Weekly Lessons: Units 1–6 **Research Roadmaps:** Units 1–6<br>**CARDS:** Reading Workstation Activity Cards: 19 |
| **RI.5.8** | Explain how an author uses reasons and evidence to support particular points in a text, identifying which reasons and evidence support which point(s). | **READING/WRITING WORKSHOP:** Unit 1: 83, 84 Unit 3: 227, 228 Unit 4: 271, 285 Unit 5: 371<br>**LITERATURE ANTHOLOGY:** Unit 1: 62, 93 Unit 3: 259 Unit 4: 337 Unit 5: 427<br>**LEVELED READERS:** Unit 3, Week 5: *The Anasazi* (A, O, B, ELL), Unit 5, Week 5: *The Great Plains* (A, O, B, ELL)<br>**YOUR TURN PRACTICE BOOK:** 43–45, 46, 143–145, 146, 149, 173–175, 183–185, 189, 243–245<br>**READING WORKSTATION ACTIVITY CARDS:** 20<br>**TEACHER'S EDITION:** Unit 1: T274, T276, T281C, T281D Unit 3: T276, T278, T281C, T281D, T303, T307, T311, T313 Unit 4: T148, T153F, T153R, T212, T217H, T221 Unit 5: T276, T281D, T303, T307, T311, T313 |
| **RI.5.9** | Integrate information from several texts on the same topic in order to write or speak about the subject knowledgeably. | **LITERATURE ANTHOLOGY:** Unit 1: 95<br>**READING WORKSTATION ACTIVITY CARDS:** 21<br>**TEACHER'S EDITION:** Unit 1: T157, T220, T221 Unit 2: T28, T29, T156, T157, T329 Unit 3: T156, T157, T220, T221, T329 Unit 4: T92, T157, T220, T221, T329 Unit 5: T156, T157, T220, T329 Unit 6: T29, T156, T157, T221, T329 |

# Reading Standards for Informational Text

| Range of Reading and Level of Text Complexity | McGraw-Hill Reading Wonders |
|---|---|
| **RI.5.10** By the end of the year, read and comprehend informational texts, including history/social studies, science, and technical texts, at the high end of the grades 4–5 text complexity band independently and proficiently. | **READING/WRITING WORKSHOP:** These Units reflect the range of text complexity found throughout the book. <br> **Unit 1, Week 3:** "A Life in the Woods," 50; **Unit 1, Week 4:** "Fantasy Becomes Fact," 64 <br> **Unit 2, Week 1:** "Creating a Nation," 94; **Unit 2, Week 3:** "Growing in Place: The Story of E. Lucy Braun," 122; **Unit 3, Week 3:** "Patterns of Change," 194; **Unit 4, Week 3:** "Frederick Douglass: Freedom's Voice," 266; **Unit 4, Week 4:** "Power from Nature," 280; **Unit 5, Week 4:** "Changing Views of Earth," 352; **Unit 5, Week 5:** "Should Plants and Animals from Other Places Live Here?," 366; **Unit 6, Week 3:** "Mysterious Oceans," 410; **Unit 6, Week 4:** "Words to Save the World: The Work of Rachel Carson," 424 <br> **LITERATURE ANTHOLOGY:** These Units reflect the range of text complexity found throughout the book. <br> **Unit 1, Week 3:** *Camping with the President*, 46; **Unit 1, Week 4:** *The Boy Who Invented TV*, 68; **Unit 2, Week 1:** *Who Wrote the U.S. Constitution?*, 96; **Unit 2, Week 3:** *The Boy Who Drew Birds*, 138; **Unit 3, Week 3:** *The Story of Snow*, 216; **Unit 3, Week 5:** *Machu Picchu: Ancient City*, 256; **Unit 4, Week 3:** *Rosa*, 298; **Unit 4, Week 4:** *One Well*, 320; **Unit 5, Week 4:** *When Is a Planet Not a Planet?*, 404; **Unit 6, Week 3:** *Survival at 40 Below*, 468; **Unit 6, Week 4:** *Planting the Trees of Kenya*, 490 <br> **LEVELED READERS: Unit 1, Week 4:** *Snapshot! The Story of George Eastman* (A, O, B, ELL) **Unit 2, Week 1:** *The Bill of Rights* (A, O, B, ELL) **Unit 2, Week 3:** *Norman Borlaug and the Green Revolution* (A, O, B, ELL) **Unit 3, Week 3:** *Weather Patterns* (A, O, B, ELL) **Unit 3, Week 4:** *The Power of a Team* (A, O, B, ELL) **Unit 4, Week 3:** *Jane Addams: A Woman of Action* (A, O, B, ELL) **Unit 4, Week 4:** *The Delta* (A, O, B, ELL) **Unit 5, Week 3:** *Ocean Threats* (A, O, B, ELL) **Unit 5, Week 4:** *Mars* (A, O, B, ELL) **Unit 6, Week 3:** *Cave Creatures* (A, O, B, ELL) <br> **YOUR TURN PRACTICE BOOK:** 26, 36, 76, 125, 136, 176, 226, 276, 286 <br> **READING WORKSTATION ACTIVITY CARDS:** 25, 30 <br> **TEACHER'S EDITION: Unit 1:** T150, T153A–T153V, T214, T217A–T217R, T281E–T281F <br> **Unit 2:** T22, T25A–T25V, T150, T153A–T153N **Unit 3:** T150, T153A–T153T, T278, T281A–T281F <br> **Unit 4:** T150, T153A–T153V, T214, T217A–T217T **Unit 5:** T214, T217A–T217R, T278, T281A–T281F <br> **Unit 6:** T150, T153A–T153R, T214, T217A–T217P |

# Reading Standards: Foundational Skills

| Phonics and Word Recognition | *McGraw-Hill Reading Wonders* |
|---|---|
| **RF.5.3** | Know and apply grade-level phonics and word analysis skills in decoding words. |
| **RF.5.3a** Use combined knowledge of all letter-sound correspondences, syllabication patterns, and morphology (e.g., roots and affixes) to read accurately unfamiliar multisyllabic words in context and out of context. | **LITERATURE ANTHOLOGY:** Unit 1: 85, 93 Unit 2: 151 Unit 3: 231, 251 Unit 4: 315 Unit 5: 421, 427 <br> **WORD STUDY WORKSTATION ACTIVITY CARDS:** 16–30 <br> **YOUR TURN PRACTICE BOOK:** 8, 18, 28, 38, 48, 58, 68, 78, 88, 98, 108, 118, 128, 138, 148, 158, 168, 178, 188, 198, 208, 218, 228, 238, 248, 258, 268, 278, 288, 298 <br> **TEACHER'S EDITION:** Unit 1: T26–T27, T40–T41, T48–T49, T52–T53, T90–T91, T154–T155, T218–T219, T282–T283 Unit 2: T26–T27, T90–T91, T104–T105, T112–T113, T116–T117, T154–T155, T218–T219, T282–T283 Unit 3: T26–T27, T90–T91, T154–T155, T168–T169, T176–T177, T180–T181, T218–T219, T282–T283 Unit 4: T26–T27, T90–T91, T154–T155, T218–T219, T232–T233, T240–T241, T244–T245, T282–T283 Unit 5: T26–T27, T154–T155, T218–T219, T282–T283, T296–T297, T304–T305, T308–T309 Unit 6: T26–T27, T40–T41, T48–49, T52–T53, T90–T91, T154–T155, T218–T219, T282–T283 |

| Fluency | *McGraw-Hill Reading Wonders* |
|---|---|
| **RF.5.4** | Read with sufficient accuracy and fluency to support comprehension. |
| **RF.5.4a** Read on-level text with purpose and understanding. | **LEVELED READERS:** Unit 1, Week 2: *Dog Gone* (A), *Shhh! It's a Surprise!* (O, ELL), *Lost and Found* (B); Unit 2, Week 3: *Norman Borlaug and the Green Revolution* (A, O, B, ELL); Unit 3, Week 1: *All the Way from Europe* (A), *Dancing the Flamenco* (O, ELL), *A Vacation in Minnesota* (B); Unit 4, Week 5: *Tell Me the Old, Old Stories* (A), *From Me to You* (O, ELL), *Every Picture Tells a Story* (B); Unit 5, Week 3: *Ocean Threats* (A, O, B, ELL); Unit 6, Week 2: *Winning Friends* (A), *Enemy or Ally?* (O, ELL), *Jamayla to the Rescue* (B) <br> **READING WORKSTATION ACTIVITY CARDS:** 29 <br> **WORD STUDY WORKSTATION ACTIVITY CARDS:** 25, 26 <br> **TEACHER'S EDITION:** Unit 1: T27, T91, T155, T219, T283 Unit 2: T27, T91, T155, T219, T283 Unit 3: T27, T91, T155, T219, T283 Unit 4: T27, T91, T155, T219, T283 Unit 5: T27, T91, T155, T219, T283 Unit 6: T27, T91, T155, T219, T283 |
| **RF.5.4b** Read on-level prose and poetry orally with accuracy, appropriate rate, and expression on successive readings. | **LEVELED READERS:** Unit 1, Week 2: *Dog Gone* (A), *Shhh! It's a Surprise!* (O, ELL), *Lost and Found* (B); Unit 2, Week 3: *Norman Borlaug and the Green Revolution* (A, O, B, ELL); Unit 3, Week 1: *All the Way from Europe* (A), *Dancing the Flamenco* (O, ELL), *A Vacation in Minnesota* (B); Unit 4, Week 5: *Tell Me the Old, Old Stories* (A), *From Me to You* (O, ELL), *Every Picture Tells a Story* (B); Unit 5, Week 3: *Ocean Threats* (A, O, B, ELL); Unit 6, Week 2: *Winning Friends* (A), *Enemy or Ally?* (O, ELL), *Jamayla to the Rescue* (B) <br> **READING WORKSTATION ACTIVITY CARDS:** 28 <br> **YOUR TURN PRACTICE BOOK:** 5, 15, 25, 35, 45, 55, 65, 75, 85, 95, 105, 115, 125, 135, 145, 155, 165, 175, 185, 195, 205, 215, 225, 235, 245, 255, 265, 275, 285, 294 <br> **TEACHER'S EDITION:** Unit 1: T27, T155, T219 Unit 2: T27, T91, T155, T169, T177, T181, T219, T283 Unit 3: T91, T155, T219, T233, T241, T245, T283 Unit 4: T27, T91, T219, T283, T297, T305, T309 Unit 5: T27, T91, T155, T219, T283 Unit 6: T27, T155, T219, T283 |
| **RF.5.4c** Use context to confirm or self-correct word recognition and understanding, rereading as necessary. | **LEVELED READERS:** Unit 1, Week 2: *Dog Gone* (A), *Shhh! It's a Surprise!* (O, ELL), *Lost and Found* (B); Unit 2, Week 3: *Norman Borlaug and the Green Revolution* (A, O, B, ELL); Unit 3, Week 1: *All the Way from Europe* (A), *Dancing the Flamenco* (O, ELL), *A Vacation in Minnesota* (B); Unit 4, Week 5: *Tell Me the Old, Old Stories* (A), *From Me to You* (O, ELL), *Every Picture Tells a Story* (B); Unit 5, Week 3: *Ocean Threats* (A, O, B, ELL); Unit 6, Week 2: *Winning Friends* (A), *Enemy or Ally?* (O, ELL), *Jamayla to the Rescue* (B) <br> **TEACHER'S EDITION:** Unit 1: T27, T41, T49, T53, T59 Unit 2: T27, T41, T49, T53, T91 Unit 3: T155, T169, T177, T181, T187 Unit 4: T91, T105, T219, T241, T245 Unit 5: T219, T233, T241, T245, T251 Unit 6: T155, T169, T177, T181, T187 |

# College and Career Readiness Anchor Standards for WRITING

The K-5 standards on the following pages define what students should understand and be able to do by the end of each grade. They correspond to the College and Career Readiness (CCR) anchor standards below by number. The CCR and grade-specific standards are necessary complements—the former providing broad standards, the latter providing additional specificity—that together define the skills and understandings that all students must demonstrate.

### Text Types and Purposes

1. Write arguments to support claims in an analysis of substantive topics or texts, using valid reasoning and relevant and sufficient evidence.

2. Write informative/explanatory texts to examine and convey complex ideas and information clearly and accurately through the effective selection, organization, and analysis of content.

3. Write narratives to develop real or imagined experiences or events using effective technique, well-chosen details, and well-structured event sequences.

### Production and Distribution of Writing

4. Produce clear and coherent writing in which the development, organization, and style are appropriate to task, purpose, and audience.

5. Develop and strengthen writing as needed by planning, revising, editing, rewriting, or trying a new approach.

6. Use technology, including the Internet, to produce and publish writing and to interact and collaborate with others.

### Research to Build and Present Knowledge

7. Conduct short as well as more sustained research projects based on focused questions, demonstrating understanding of the subject under investigation.

8. Gather relevant information from multiple print and digital sources, assess the credibility and accuracy of each source, and integrate the information while avoiding plagiarism.

9. Draw evidence from literary or informational texts to support analysis, reflection, and research.

### Range of Writing

10. Write routinely over extended time frames (time for research, reflection, and revision) and shorter time frames (a single sitting or a day or two) for a range of tasks, purposes, and audiences.

# CCSS Common Core State Standards
# English Language Arts
## Grade 5

Each standard is coded in the following manner:

| Strand | Grade Level | Standard |
|--------|-------------|----------|
| W | 5 | 1 |

## Writing Standards

| Text Types and Purposes | McGraw-Hill Reading Wonders |
|-------------------------|------------------------------|
| **W.5.1** | Write opinion pieces on topics or texts, supporting a point of view with reasons and information. |
| **W.5.1a** | Introduce a topic or text clearly, state an opinion, and create an organizational structure in which ideas are logically grouped to support the writer's purpose. | **WRITING WORKSTATION ACTIVITY CARDS:** 26, 27 <br> **TEACHER'S EDITION: Unit 1:** T93 **Unit 3:** T345, T347, T351 **Unit 4:** T160, T161 **Unit 5:** T224, T225 **Unit 6:** T224, T225, T329, T345, T346, T347, T351 |
| **W.5.1b** | Provide logically ordered reasons that are supported by facts and details. | **TEACHER'S EDITION: Unit 3:** T288, T289, T345, T346, T351, T353 **Unit 4:** T160, T161 **Unit 5:** T224, T225 **Unit 6:** T329, T345, T351 |
| **W.5.1c** | Link opinion and reasons using words, phrases, and clauses (e.g., *consequently*, *specifically*). | **YOUR TURN PRACTICE BOOK:** 150 <br> **TEACHER'S EDITION: Unit 3:** T29, T288, T289, T349, T352 **Unit 4:** T224, T225 **Unit 5:** T221 **Unit 6:** T352, T353, T355 |
| **W.5.1d** | Provide a concluding statement or section related to the opinion presented. | **YOUR TURN PRACTICE BOOK:** 250 <br> **WRITING WORKSTATION ACTIVITY CARDS:** 9 <br> **TEACHER'S EDITION: Unit 3:** T347, T353 **Unit 5:** T288, T289, T318 **Unit 6:** T285, T329, T346, T347, T353 |
| **W.5.2** | Write informative/explanatory texts to examine a topic and convey ideas and information clearly. |
| **W.5.2a** | Introduce a topic clearly, provide a general observation and focus, and group related information logically; include formatting (e.g., headings), illustrations, and multimedia when useful to aiding comprehension. | **WRITING WORKSTATION ACTIVITY CARDS:** 2, 8, 10, 11 <br> **TEACHER'S EDITION: Unit 2:** T224, T225, T345, T346, T348, T351, T352, T354 **Unit 3:** T92, T329 **Unit 4:** T285 **Unit 5:** T32, T33, T254, T345, T346, T348, T351, T352, T354, T355 **Unit 6:** T28, T32, T33 <br> www.connected.mcgraw-hill.com: **RESOURCES:** <br> **RESEARCH & INQUIRY: Research Roadmaps:** Units 1–6 **Note-taking Tools:** Units 1–6 <br> **WRITER'S WORKSPACE:** Unit 2, Unit 5 <br> **CARDS:** Writing Workstation Activity Cards: 2, 8, 10, 11 |
| **W.5.2b** | Develop the topic with facts, definitions, concrete details, quotations, or other information and examples related to the topic. | **LITERATURE ANTHOLOGY: Unit 4:** 337 <br> **YOUR TURN PRACTICE BOOK:** 60, 80, 130 <br> **WRITING WORKSTATION ACTIVITY CARDS:** 3, 6, 30 <br> **TEACHER'S EDITION: Unit 2:** T32, T33, T62, T160, T161, T190, T329, T346, T351–T353, T355 **Unit 3:** T92, T160, T161, T329 **Unit 4:** T220 **Unit 5:** T190, T254, T285, T346, T349, T351, T353 |

# Writing Standards

| Text Types and Purposes | | McGraw-Hill Reading Wonders |
|---|---|---|
| **W.5.2c** | Link ideas within and across categories of information using words, phrases, and clauses (e.g., *in contrast, especially*). | **YOUR TURN PRACTICE BOOK:** 220<br>**WRITING WORKSTATION ACTIVITY CARDS:** 13, 17, 19<br>**TEACHER'S EDITION:** Unit 4: T157 Unit 5: T96, T97, T347 Unit 6: T29 |
| **W.5.2d** | Use precise language and domain-specific vocabulary to inform about or explain the topic. | **WRITING WORKSTATION ACTIVITY CARDS:** 15<br>**TEACHER'S EDITION:** Unit 1: T190 Unit 2: T347, T355 Unit 5: T346, T349 |
| **W.5.2e** | Provide a concluding statement or section related to the information or explanation presented. | **YOUR TURN PRACTICE BOOK:** 140<br>**TEACHER'S EDITION:** Unit 2: T346, T353 Unit 3: T92, T224, T225, T254, T329 Unit 5: T347, T352 Unit 6: T29, T221 |
| **W.5.3** | Write narratives to develop real or imagined experiences or events using effective technique, descriptive details, and clear event sequences. | |
| **W.5.3a** | Orient the reader by establishing a situation and introducing a narrator and/or characters; organize an event sequence that unfolds naturally. | **YOUR TURN PRACTICE BOOK:** 70<br>**WRITING WORKSTATION ACTIVITY CARDS:** 5, 7, 22<br>**TEACHER'S EDITION:** Unit 1: T224, T225, T254, T345, T351 Unit 2: T96, T97, T126, T254 Unit 4: T96, T97, T345, T347 Unit 6: T96, T97 |
| **W.5.3b** | Use narrative techniques, such as dialogue, description, and pacing, to develop experiences and events or show the responses of characters to situations. | **YOUR TURN PRACTICE BOOK:** 20, 109, 170<br>**WRITING WORKSTATION ACTIVITY CARDS:** 1, 5, 22, 28<br>**TEACHER'S EDITION:** Unit 1: T32, T33, T96, T97, T345, T347, T351 Unit 4: T96, T97, T126, T346 |
| **W.5.3c** | Use a variety of transitional words, phrases, and clauses to manage the sequence of events. | **YOUR TURN PRACTICE BOOK:** 40, 270<br>**WRITING WORKSTATION ACTIVITY CARDS:** 7, 17, 19<br>**TEACHER'S EDITION:** Unit 1: T224, T225, T347, T351 Unit 4: T345 Unit 5: T126 Unit 6: T96, T97, T126 |
| **W.5.3d** | Use concrete words and phrases and sensory details to convey experiences and events precisely. | **YOUR TURN PRACTICE BOOK:** 10, 30<br>**WRITING WORKSTATION ACTIVITY CARDS:** 1, 14, 18<br>**TEACHER'S EDITION:** Unit 1: T32, T33, T62, T160, T161, T346, T352 Unit 2: T288, T289, T318 Unit 4: T288, T289, T318, T351, T353 Unit 6: T288, T289, T318 |
| **W.5.3e** | Provide a conclusion that follows from the narrated experiences or events. | **WRITING WORKSTATION ACTIVITY CARDS:** 23<br>**TEACHER'S EDITION:** Unit 1: T225, T351, T353 Unit 4: T345, T347 |
| **Production and Distribution of Writing** | | **McGraw-Hill Reading Wonders** |
| **W.5.4** | Produce clear and coherent writing in which the development and organization are appropriate to task, purpose, and audience. (Grade-specific expectations for writing types are defined in standards 1–3 above.) | **WRITING WORKSTATION ACTIVITY CARDS:** 12, 24<br>**TEACHER'S EDITION:** Unit 1: T33, T97, T161, T225, T345, T347, T348 Unit 2: T32, T126, T160, T225, T348 Unit 3: T33, T97, T161, T225, T345, T347, T348 Unit 4: T33, T97, T161, T225, T345, T347, T348 Unit 5: T33, T97, T161, T225, T345, T347, T348 Unit 6: T33, T97, T161, T225, T345, T347, T348 |
| **W.5.5** | With guidance and support from peers and adults, develop and strengthen writing as needed by planning, revising, editing, rewriting, or trying a new approach. (Editing for conventions should demonstrate command of Language standards 1–3 up to and including grade 5.) | **TEACHER'S EDITION:** Unit 1: T32, T96, T160, T224, T345, T346, T347, T348 Unit 2: T96, T160, T224, T351, T352, T353, T354 Unit 3: T32, T96, T160, T225, T351, T352, T353, T354 Unit 4: T32, T96, T126, T345, T346, T347, T348 Unit 5: T32, T96, T160, T224, T345, T346, T347, T348 Unit 6: T32, T96, T160, T224, T345, T346, T347, T348 |

## Writing Standards

| Production and Distribution of Writing | | *McGraw-Hill Reading Wonders* |
|---|---|---|
| **W.5.6** | With some guidance and support from adults, use technology, including the Internet, to produce and publish writing as well as to interact and collaborate with others; demonstrate sufficient command of keyboarding skills to type a minimum of two pages in a single sitting. | **TEACHER'S EDITION:** Unit 1: T330–T332, T348, T354 **Unit 2:** T156, T330–T332, T348, T354 **Unit 3:** T330–T332, T348, T354 **Unit 4:** T330–T332, T333, T348, T354 **Unit 5:** T156, T330–T332, T348, T354 **Unit 6:** T330–T332, T348, T354<br>www.connected.mcgraw-hill.com: **RESOURCES:**<br>RESEARCH & INQUIRY: Weekly Lessons: Units 1–6<br>WRITER'S WORKSPACE: Units 1–6<br>TEACHER RESOURCES: Writer's Checklists/Proofreading Marks |

| Research to Build and Present Knowledge | | *McGraw-Hill Reading Wonders* |
|---|---|---|
| **W.5.7** | Conduct short research projects that use several sources to build knowledge through investigation of different aspects of a topic. | **WRITING WORKSTATION ACTIVITY CARDS:** 30<br>**TEACHER'S EDITION:** Unit 1: T28, T92, T156, T220, T330, T331, T332 **Unit 2:** T28, T92, T156, T330, T331, T332 **Unit 3:** T28, T92, T156, T220, T330, T331, T332 **Unit 4:** T28, T92, T156, T220, T330, T331, T332 **Unit 5:** T92, T156, T220, T284, T351, T352, T353, T354 **Unit 6:** T28, T156, T220, T330, T331, T332 |
| **W.5.8** | Recall relevant information from experiences or gather relevant information from print and digital sources; summarize or paraphrase information in notes and finished work, and provide a list of sources. | **WRITING WORKSTATION ACTIVITY CARDS:** 30<br>**TEACHER'S EDITION:** Unit 1: S35, S36, T220, T329, T330, T331, T332 **Unit 2:** T92, T156, T284 **Unit 3:** T28, T92, T156, T220, T284 **Unit 4:** T28, T92, T156, T220, T284, T330, T331, T332 **Unit 5:** T28, T92, T156, T220, T351, T354 **Unit 6:** T28, T92, T156, T330, T331, T332<br>www.connected.mcgraw-hill.com: **RESOURCES:**<br>RESEARCH & INQUIRY: Note-taking Tools: Units 1–6<br>WRITER'S WORKSPACE: Units 1–6<br>TIME FOR KIDS ONLINE ARTICLES: Units 1–6<br>CARDS: Writing Workstation Activity Cards: 29, 30 |
| **W.5.9** | Draw evidence from literary or informational texts to support analysis, reflection, and research. | |
| **W.5.9a** | Apply *grade 5 Reading standards* to literature (e.g., "Compare and contrast two or more characters, settings, or events in a story or a drama, drawing on specific details in the text [e.g., how characters interact]"). | **LITERATURE ANTHOLOGY:** Unit 1: 25, 41 **Unit 2** 133, 171 **Unit 3:** 213, 277 **Unit 4:** 293 **Unit 5:** 359, 379 **Unit 6:** 445, 463<br>**YOUR TURN PRACTICE BOOK:** 9, 19, 69, 79, 109, 119, 159, 169, 209, 219, 259, 269<br>**TEACHER'S EDITION:** Unit 1: T25P, T29, T89L, T93 **Unit 2:** T89P, T93, T217P, T221 **Unit 3:** T25N, T29, T89P, T93 **Unit 4:** T25P, T29, T89L, T93 **Unit 5:** T25N, T29, T89P, T93 **Unit 6:** T25P, T29, T89N, T93 |
| **W.5.9b** | Apply *grade 5 Reading standards* to informational texts (e.g., "Explain how an author uses reasons and evidence to support particular points in a text, identifying which reasons and evidence support which point[s]"). | **LITERATURE ANTHOLOGY:** Unit 1: 63, 85 **Unit 2:** 113, 151 **Unit 3:** 231, 251 **Unit 4:** 315, 337 **Unit 5:** 399, 421 **Unit 6:** 485, 503<br>**YOUR TURN PRACTICE BOOK:** 29, 39, 59, 89, 129, 139, 149, 279, 289<br>**TEACHER'S EDITION:** Unit 1: T153R, T157, T217R, T221, T285 **Unit 2:** T25R, T29, T153N, T157 **Unit 3:** T153P, T157, T221, T285 **Unit 4:** T153R, T157, T217R, T221 **Unit 5:** T153P, T157, T217R, T221, T285 **Unit 6:** T153R, T157, T217N, T221 |

| Range of Writing | | *McGraw-Hill Reading Wonders* |
|---|---|---|
| **W.5.10** | Write routinely over extended time frames (time for research, reflection, and revision) and shorter time frames (a single sitting or a day or two) for a range of discipline-specific tasks, purposes, and audiences. | **LITERATURE ANTHOLOGY:** Unit 1: 25, 41, 63, 85 **Unit 2:** 113, 133, 151, 171, 179 **Unit 3:** 195, 213, 231, 251, 277 **Unit 4:** 293, 315, 337, 343 **Unit 5:** 353, 379, 399, 429 **Unit 6:** 445, 463, 485, 503, 509<br>**YOUR TURN PRACTICE BOOK:** 9, 19, 29, 39, 49, 59, 69, 79, 89, 99, 109, 119, 129, 139, 149, 159, 169, 179, 189, 199, 209, 219, 229, 239, 249, 259, 269, 279, 289, 299<br>**TEACHER'S EDITION:** Unit 1: T32, T33, T96, T103, T160 **Unit 2:** T29, T32, T33, T96, T97 **Unit 3:** T93, T97, T160, T161, T345, T346, T347, T348 **Unit 4:** T221, T224, T351, T352, T353, T354 **Unit 5:** T285, T288, T289, T344, T347, T349 **Unit 6:** T345, T346, T347, T351, T352 |

# College and Career Readiness Anchor Standards for
# SPEAKING AND LISTENING

The K-5 standards on the following pages define what students should understand and be able to do by the end of each grade. They correspond to the College and Career Readiness (CCR) anchor standards below by number. The CCR and grade-specific standards are necessary complements—the former providing broad standards, the latter providing additional specificity—that together define the skills and understandings that all students must demonstrate.

| Comprehension and Collaboration |
|---|
| **1.** Prepare for and participate effectively in a range of conversations and collaborations with diverse partners, building on others' ideas and expressing their own clearly and persuasively. |
| **2.** Integrate and evaluate information presented in diverse media and formats, including visually, quantitatively, and orally. |
| **3.** Evaluate a speaker's point of view, reasoning, and use of evidence and rhetoric. |
| **Presentation of Knowledge and Ideas** |
| **4.** Present information, findings, and supporting evidence such that listeners can follow the line of reasoning and the organization, development, and style are appropriate to task, purpose, and audience. |
| **5.** Make strategic use of digital media and visual displays of data to express information and enhance understanding of presentations. |
| **6.** Adapt speech to a variety of contexts and communicative tasks, demonstrating command of formal English when indicated or appropriate. |

## CCSS Common Core State Standards
# English Language Arts

## Grade 5

**Each standard is coded in the following manner:**

| Strand | Grade Level | Standard |
|--------|-------------|----------|
| SL | 5 | 1 |

## Speaking and Listening Standards

| Comprehension and Collaboration | | McGraw-Hill Reading Wonders |
|---|---|---|
| **SL.5.1** | Engage effectively in a range of collaborative discussions (one-on-one, in groups, and teacher-led) with diverse partners on *grade 5 topics and texts*, building on others' ideas and expressing their own clearly. | |
| **SL.5.1a** | Come to discussions prepared, having read or studied required material; explicitly draw on that preparation and other information known about the topic to explore ideas under discussion. | **LITERATURE ANTHOLOGY:** Unit 1: 25, 29, 41, 63, 67, 85, 89 Unit 2: 113, 117, 133, 137, 151, 171 Unit 3: 195, 213, 231, 251 Unit 4: 277, 293, 315, 337 Unit 5: 359, 379, 403 Unit 6: 445, 463, 485, 503 **TEACHER'S EDITION:** Unit 1: S5, S19, T25P, T25T, T89L Unit 2: T29, T93, T157, T221, T285 Unit 3: T25N, T29, T89P, T93, T153P Unit 4: T25P, T29, T89L, T93, T157 Unit 5: T89P, T89T, T93, T157, T221 Unit 6: T25P, T89N, T93, T157, T221 |
| **SL.5.1b** | Follow agreed-upon rules for discussions and carry out assigned roles. | **TEACHER'S EDITION:** Unit 1: S6, T10, T92, T138, T202, T266 Unit 2: T10, T138, T202, T266 Unit 3: T74, T138, T220, T266 Unit 4: T74, T138, T266 Unit 5: T74, T138, T266 Unit 6: T156, T266 |
| **SL.5.1c** | Pose and respond to specific questions by making comments that contribute to the discussion and elaborate on the remarks of others. | **READING/WRITING WORKSHOP:** Unit 1: 19, 33, 47, 61, 75 Unit 2: 91, 105, 119, 133, 147 Unit 3: 163, 177, 191, 205, 219 Unit 4: 235, 249, 263, 277, 291 Unit 5: 307, 321, 335, 349, 363 Unit 6: 379, 393, 407, 421, 435 **LITERATURE ANTHOLOGY:** Unit 1: 25, 29, 41, 63, 67, 85, 89 Unit 2: 113, 117, 133, 137, 151, 171 Unit 3: 195, 213, 231, 251 Unit 4: 277, 293, 315, 337 Unit 5: 359, 379, 403 Unit 6: 445, 463, 485, 503 **TEACHER'S EDITION:** Unit 1: S5, T10, T25R, T74, T266 Unit 2: T10, T74, T138, T153P Unit 3: T10, T146, T202, T266 Unit 4: T10, T89G, T890, T153T, T202 Unit 5: T10, T74, T138, T202, T210 Unit 6: T10, T138, T146, T210, T266 |
| **SL.5.1d** | Review the key ideas expressed and draw conclusions in light of information and knowledge gained from the discussions. | **TEACHER'S EDITION:** Unit 1: S6, S19, S35, T138, T285 Unit 2: T29, T93, T157, T221, T285 Unit 3: T29, T93, T157, T221, T285 Unit 4: T29, T93, T157, T221, T285 Unit 5: T29, T93, T157, T221, T266, T285 Unit 6: T29, T93, T157, T221, T285 |
| **SL.5.2** | Summarize a written text read aloud or information presented in diverse media and formats, including visually, quantitatively, and orally. | **TEACHER'S EDITION:** Unit 1: T12, T76, T140, T204, T268, T281E, T296–T297, T304–T305, T308–T309, T326 Unit 2: T12, T17, T76, T89E, T140, T153D, T204, T268, T326 Unit 3: T12, T76, T140, T153C, T153I, T204, T217D, T268, T326 Unit 4: T12, T76, T140, T204, T268, T326 Unit 5: T12, T76, T140, T204, T268, T326 Unit 6: T12, T76, T140, T204, T268, T326 |
| **SL.5.3** | Summarize the points a speaker makes and explain how each claim is supported by reasons and evidence. | **TEACHER'S EDITION:** Unit 1: T268, T335 Unit 2: T335 Unit 3: T268, T335 Unit 4: T335 Unit 5: T268, T335 Unit 6: T335 |

## Speaking and Listening Standards

| Presentation of Knowledge and Ideas | | McGraw-Hill Reading Wonders |
|---|---|---|
| **SL.5.4** | Report on a topic or text or present an opinion, sequencing ideas logically and using appropriate facts and relevant, descriptive details to support main ideas or themes; speak clearly at an understandable pace. | **TEACHER'S EDITION:** Unit 1: T92, T156, T284, T333, T334 Unit 2: T220, T333, T334 Unit 3: T284, T333, T334 Unit 4: T220, T333, T334 Unit 5: T285, T333, T334 Unit 6: T92, T156, T333, T334 |
| **SL.5.5** | Include multimedia components (e.g., graphics, sound) and visual displays in presentations when appropriate to enhance the development of main ideas or themes. | **TEACHER'S EDITION:** Unit 1: T92, T156, T220, T354 Unit 2: T354 Unit 3: T220, T348, T354 Unit 4: T329, T348, T354 Unit 5: T92, T156 Unit 6: T28, T156, T220, T284, T348 |
| **SL.5.6** | Adapt speech to a variety of contexts and tasks, using formal English when appropriate to task and situation. (See grade 5 Language standards 1 and 3 for specific expectations.) | **TEACHER'S EDITION:** Unit 1: S35, T333, T334 Unit 2: T333, T334 Unit 3: T220, T333, T334 Unit 4: T333, T334 Unit 5: T333, T334 Unit 6: T333, T334 |

# College and Career Readiness Anchor Standards for
# LANGUAGE

The K-5 standards on the following pages define what students should understand and be able to do by the end of each grade. They correspond to the College and Career Readiness (CCR) anchor standards below by number. The CCR and grade-specific standards are necessary complements—the former providing broad standards, the latter providing additional specificity—that together define the skills and understandings that all students must demonstrate.

### Conventions of Standard English

1. Demonstrate command of the conventions of standard English grammar and usage when writing or speaking.

2. Demonstrate command of the conventions of standard English capitalization, punctuation, and spelling when writing.

### Knowledge of Language

3. Apply knowledge of language to understand how language functions in different contexts, to make effective choices for meaning or style, and to comprehend more fully when reading or listening.

### Vocabulary Acquisition and Use

4. Determine or clarify the meaning of unknown and multiple-meaning words and phrases by using context clues, analyzing meaningful word parts, and consulting general and specialized reference materials, as appropriate.

5. Demonstrate understanding of figurative language, word relationships, and nuances in word meanings.

6. Acquire and use accurately a range of general academic and domain-specific words and phrases sufficient for reading, writing, speaking, and listening at the college and career readiness level; demonstrate independence in gathering vocabulary knowledge when encountering an unknown term important to comprehension or expression.

# English Language Arts

## Grade 5

Each standard is coded in the following manner:

| Strand | Grade Level | Standard |
|--------|-------------|----------|
| L | 5 | 1 |

## Language Standards

| Conventions of Standard English | | McGraw-Hill Reading Wonders |
|---|---|---|
| **L.5.1** | Demonstrate command of the conventions of standard English grammar and usage when writing or speaking. | |
| **L.5.1a** | Explain the function of conjunctions, prepositions, and interjections in general and their function in particular sentences. | **READING/WRITING WORKSHOP:** Unit 6: 433, 446, 447 **Grammar Handbook:** 452, 453, 457, 471, 472 <br> **TEACHER'S EDITION:** Unit 1: T35, T98, T99, T162, T163, T191, T221, T226, T227, T255, T286, T319 **Unit 2:** T290, T291, T319 **Unit 3:** T286 **Unit 4:** T336 **Unit 5:** T34, T35, T98, T127 **Unit 6:** T224–T226, T255, T285, T286, T288–T291, T318, T319 |
| **L.5.1b** | Form and use the perfect (e.g., *I had walked*; *I have walked*; *I will have walked*) verb tenses. | **READING/WRITING WORKSHOP:** Grammar Handbook: 461 <br> **TEACHER'S EDITION:** Unit 3: T162, T290, T291 |
| **L.5.1c** | Use verb tense to convey various times, sequences, states, and conditions. | **READING/WRITING WORKSHOP:** Grammar Handbook: 458, 461 <br> **TEACHER'S EDITION:** Unit 1: T348, T354 **Unit 2:** T153J, T154, T155, T170, T171, T348, T354 **Unit 3:** T34, T35, T63, T93, T98, T99, T127, T157, T162, T163, T191, T290, T291, T319, T348, T354 **Unit 4:** T348 **Unit 5:** T354 **Unit 6:** 354 |
| **L.5.1d** | Recognize and correct inappropriate shifts in verb tense. | **READING/WRITING WORKSHOP:** Unit 3: 189 Grammar Handbook: 459 <br> **TEACHER'S EDITION:** Unit 1: T348, T354 **Unit 2:** T348, T354 **Unit 3:** T93, T96–T99, T127, T290, T291, T319, T348, T354 **Unit 4:** T348 **Unit 5:** T354 **Unit 6:** 354 |
| **L.5.1e** | Use correlative conjunctions (e.g., *either/or*, *neither/nor*). | **TEACHER'S EDITION:** Unit 1: T98 **Unit 3:** T286 **Unit 6:** T226 |
| **L.5.2** | Demonstrate command of the conventions of standard English capitalization, punctuation, and spelling when writing. | |
| **L.5.2a** | Use punctuation to separate items in a series. | **TEACHER'S EDITION:** Unit 1: T99 **Unit 4:** T291 **Unit 6:** T227 |
| **L.5.2b** | Use a comma to separate an introductory element from the rest of the sentence. | **TEACHER'S EDITION:** Unit 1: T99, T226, T227, T286 **Unit 5:** T34, T98, T99, T127 |
| **L.5.2c** | Use a comma to set off the words *yes* and *no* (e.g., *Yes, thank you*), to set off a tag question from the rest of the sentence (e.g., *It's true, isn't it?*), and to indicate direct address (e.g., *Is that you, Steve?*). | **READING/WRITING WORKSHOP:** Grammar Handbook: 479 <br> **TEACHER'S EDITION:** Unit 1: T35, T99, T286 |

# Language Standards

| Conventions of Standard English | | McGraw-Hill Reading Wonders |
|---|---|---|
| **L.5.2d** | Use underlining, quotation marks, or italics to indicate titles of works. | **READING/WRITING WORKSHOP:** Grammar Handbook: 480<br>**TEACHER'S EDITION:** Unit 2: T291 Unit 3: T227 Unit 5: T163 |
| **L.5.2e** | Spell grade-appropriate words correctly, consulting references as needed. | **TEACHER'S EDITION:** Unit 1: T36–37, T100–101, T164–T165, T228–T229, T292–T293<br>**Unit 2:** T36–T37, T100–101, T164–T165, T228–T229, T292–T293 **Unit 3:** T36–37, T100–101, T164–T165, T228–T229, T292–T293 **Unit 4:** T36–37, T100–101, T164–T165, T228–T229, T292–T293 **Unit 5:** T36–37, T100–101, T164–T165, T228–T229, T292–T293 **Unit 6:** T36–37, T100–101, T164–T165, T228–T229, T292–T293 |

| Knowledge of Language | | McGraw-Hill Reading Wonders |
|---|---|---|
| **L.5.3** | Use knowledge of language and its conventions when writing, speaking, reading, or listening. | |
| **L.5.3a** | Expand, combine, and reduce sentences for meaning, reading/listener interest, and style. | **READING/WRITING WORKSHOP:** Unit 6: 418 Grammar Handbook: 452, 453, 468<br>**TEACHER'S EDITION:** Unit 1: T33, T290, T291, T319, T347, T353 **Unit 2:** T347, T353 **Unit 3:** T347, T353 **Unit 4:** T347, T353 **Unit 5:** T35, T99, T347, T353 **Unit 6:** T158, T160, T161, T226, T227, T347, T353 |
| **L.5.3b** | Compare and contrast the varieties of English (e.g., dialects, registers) used in stories, dramas, or poems. | **READING/WRITING WORKSHOP:** Unit 5: 330<br>**TEACHER'S EDITION:** Unit 5: T86, T89C, T89I, T89M |

| Vocabulary Acquisition and Use | | McGraw-Hill Reading Wonders |
|---|---|---|
| **L.5.4** | Determine or clarify the meaning of unknown and multiple-meaning words and phrases based on *grade 5 reading and content,* choosing flexibly from a range of strategies. | |
| **L.5.4a** | Use context (e.g., cause/effect relationships and comparisons in text) as a clue to the meaning of a word or phrase. | **READING/WRITING WORKSHOP:** Unit 1: 29 Unit 2: 101 Unit 3: 173, 187, 229 Unit 4: 287 Unit 5: 317, 345 Unit 6: 389, 417<br>**LITERATURE ANTHOLOGY:** Unit 1: 25, 63 Unit 2: 113, 179 Unit 3: 195, 213, 259 Unit 5: 359, 399 Unit 6: 445, 485<br>**YOUR TURN PRACTICE BOOK:** 7, 57, 107, 147, 187, 207, 227, 277<br>**WORD STUDY WORKSTATION ACTIVITY CARDS:** 1–3<br>**TEACHER'S EDITION:** Unit 1: T25C, T25D, T25H, T25L, T25P, T153C, T153J, T153K, T153R, T217E, T217H, T217K, T217R **Unit 2:** T24, T25E, T25G, T25I, T39, T153E, T166 **Unit 3:** T24, T25K, T25N, T39, T88, T89D, T89E, T89H, T89I, T89P, T153B, T153I, T166, T217I, T230, T280, **Unit 4:** T25, T88, T152, T153A, T153I, T153O, T166, T216, T217C, T217E, T217M, T217R, T231 **Unit 5:** T24, T25D, T25N, T39, T152, T153B, T167, T217E, T217K **Unit 6:** T24, T25H, T89A, T89C, T89K, T152, T153C, T153D, T153G, T153K, T153R |
| **L.5.4b** | Use common, grade-appropriate Greek and Latin affixes and roots as clues to the meaning of a word (e.g., *photograph, photosynthesis*). | **READING/WRITING WORKSHOP:** Unit 1: 71, 85 Unit 2: 129 Unit 3: 201, 215 Unit 5: 359, 373<br>**LITERATURE ANTHOLOGY:** Unit 1: 85, 93 Unit 2: 151 Unit 3: 231, 251 Unit 5: 421<br>**YOUR TURN PRACTICE BOOK:** 37, 47, 77, 127, 137, 237, 247<br>**WORD STUDY WORKSTATION ACTIVITY CARDS:** 7–11<br>**TEACHER'S EDITION:** Unit 1: T216, T217C, T217R, T231, T280, T281B, T295 **Unit 2:** T38, T152, T153F, T153G, T153N, T167 **Unit 3:** T152, T153D, T153P, T167, T216, T217J, T217P, T231 **Unit 4:** T38, T230 **Unit 5:** T216, T217B, T217H, T217R, T231, T280, T281C, T295 **Unit 6:** T25I, T38, T89K |
| **L.5.4c** | Consult reference materials (e.g., dictionaries, glossaries, thesauruses), both print and digital, to find the pronunciation and determine or clarify the precise meaning of key words and phrases. | **WORK STUDY WORKSTATION ACTIVITY CARDS:** 5<br>**TEACHER'S EDITION:** Unit 1: T24, T39, 133 (Reading Workstation Activity Cards), T167, T216, T217E, T217K, T231, T280, T284, T295; **Unit 2:** T24, T39, T25E, T152, T167, T261 (Reading Workstation Activity Cards), T295; **Unit 3:** T25C, T89E, T152; **Unit 4:** T24, T170, T171; **Unit 5:** T152, T153I; Unit 6: T88, T89Q, T153C |

# Language Standards

| Vocabulary Acquisition and Use | | McGraw-Hill Reading Wonders |
|---|---|---|
| **L.5.5** | Demonstrate understanding of figurative language, word relationships, and nuances in word meanings. | |
| **L.5.5a** | Interpret figurative language, including similes and metaphors, in context. | **READING/WRITING WORKSHOP:** Unit 2: 115, 143 Unit 4: 301, 303 Unit 5: 316 Unit 6: 445 **LITERATURE ANTHOLOGY:** Unit 2: 133, 171 Unit 4: 343, 345 Unit 6: 509 **YOUR TURN PRACTICE BOOK:** 67, 87, 197, 297 **WORD STUDY WORKSTATION ACTIVITY CARDS:** 13, 14 **TEACHER'S EDITION:** Unit 1: T89A, T89B, T89L, 153K, T217F, T217M Unit 2: T88, T89H, T89K, T89P, T103, T216, T217B, T217P, T230, T231, T294 Unit 4: T280, T281C, T281D, T281F, T352 Unit 5: T102 Unit 6: T280, T281D, T295 |
| **L.5.5b** | Recognize and explain the meaning of common idioms, adages, and proverbs. | **READING/WRITING WORKSHOP:** Unit 1: 43 Unit 4: 259 Unit 5: 331 **LITERATURE ANTHOLOGY:** Unit 1: 41 Unit 4: 293 Unit 5: 379 **YOUR TURN PRACTICE BOOK:** 17, 167, 217 **WORD STUDY WORKSTATION ACTIVITY CARDS:** 12 **TEACHER'S EDITION:** Unit 1: T89A, T89B, T89L, T230 Unit 3: T38 Unit 4: T88, T89D, T89L, T103 Unit 5: T88, T89C, T89E, T89G, T89P, T103 Unit 6: T102 |
| **L.5.5c** | Use the relationship between particular words (e.g., synonyms, antonyms, homographs) to better understand each of the words. | **READING/WRITING WORKSHOP:** Unit 1: 57 Unit 2: 157 Unit 4: 245 Unit 6: 389, 431 **LITERATURE ANTHOLOGY:** Unit 1: 63 Unit 2: 179 Unit 4: 277 Unit 6: 503 **YOUR TURN PRACTICE BOOK:** 27, 97, 157, 287 **WORD STUDY WORKSTATION ACTIVITY CARDS:** 4–6 **TEACHER'S EDITION:** Unit 1: T153J, T153R, T294, T295 Unit 2: T103, T195, T231, T280, T281C, T281D, T295 Unit 4: T24, T25L, T25P, T39, T102, T167, T295 Unit 5: T38, T167, T231 Unit 6: T216, T217G, T217I, T217N |
| **L.5.6** | Acquire and use accurately grade-appropriate general academic and domain-specific words and phrases, including those that signal contrast, addition, and other logical relationships (e.g., *however, although, nevertheless, similarly, moreover, in addition*). | **READING/WRITING WORKSHOP:** Unit 1: 55, 69, 72 Unit 2: 99 Unit 3: 230, 231 Unit 4: 288, 289 **YOUR TURN PRACTICE BOOK:** 1, 11, 21, 31, 41, 51, 81, 91, 101, 111, 121, 131, 141, 171, 191, 241, 251, 261, 271, 281, 291 **TEACHER'S EDITION:** Unit 1: T14, T38, T78, T102, T142, T148, T153L, T166, T206, T212, T222–T225, T230, T270, T273, T294, T344, T346–T348, T350–T352, T354 Unit 2: T14, T20, T38, T78, T102, T142, T166, T206, T230, T270, T294, T344, T346, T348, T350, T352, T354 Unit 3: T14, T38, T78, T89J, T102, T142, T153J, T166, T206, T230, T270, T286–T289, T294, T344, T346, T348, T350, T352, T354 Unit 4: T14, T38, T78, T102, T142, T166, T206, T222–T225, T230, T270, T294, T344, T346, T348, T350, T352, T354 Unit 5: T14, T38, T78, T94–97, T102, T142, T166, T206, T230, T270, T294, T332, T344, T346–T348, T350, T352, T354 Unit 6: T14, T34, T38, T78, T94, T102, T142, T166, T206, T230, T270, T294, T344, T346, T348, T350, T352, T354 |

# CCSS Language Progressive Skills

Below are the grades 3 and 4 Language standards indicated by CCSS to be particularly likely to require continued attention in grade 5 as they are applied to increasingly sophisticated writing and speaking.

## Language Standards

| Standard | | McGraw-Hill Reading Wonders |
|---|---|---|
| **L.3.1f** | Ensure subject-verb and pronoun-antecedent agreement. | **TEACHER'S EDITION:** Unit 1: T348 Unit 2: T348 Unit 3: T34, T35, T63, T255, T348 Unit 4: T34, T35, T63, T98, T99, T157, T162, T163, T227, T348 Unit 5: T98, T99, T348 Unit 6: T348 |
| **L.3.3a** | Choose words and phrases for effect. | **READING/WRITING WORKSHOP:** Unit 1: 44 Unit 2: 143 Unit 3: 174, 188 Unit 4: 302 Unit 5: 403, 445<br>**YOUR TURN PRACTICE BOOK:** 10, 20, 30, 100, 120, 200<br>**WRITING WORKSTATION ACTIVITY CARDS:** 14, 16, 18, 21<br>**TEACHER'S EDITION:** Unit 1: T30, T32, T33, T94, T96, T158, T160, T161, T345, T346, T350, T352 Unit 2: T286, T288, T289 Unit 3: T94, T96, T97, T126 Unit 4: T286, T288, T289, T318, T350, T351, T352 Unit 6: T286, T288, T289, T318, T350, T352 |
| **L.4.1f** | Produce complete sentences, recognizing and correcting inappropriate fragments and run-ons. | **TEACHER'S EDITION:** Unit 1: T34, T35, T63, T162, T163, T290, T291, T319, T348, T354 Unit 2: T63, T252, T348, T354 Unit 3: T348, T354 Unit 4: T348, T354 Unit 5: T348, T354 Unit 6: T348, T354 |
| **L.4.1g** | Correctly use frequently confused words (e.g., *to, too, two*; *there, their*). | **READING/WRITING WORKSHOP:** Unit 6: 389<br>**WORD STUDY WORKSTATION ACTIVITY CARDS:** 6<br>**TEACHER'S EDITION:** Unit 1: T25L Unit 2: T228 Unit 4: T285, T290, T291, T319 Unit 5: T90, T91, T100, T101, T106, T107, T126 Unit 6: T24, T25, T39, T45, T50, T54, T61, T230 |
| **L.4.3a** | Choose words and phrases to convey ideas precisely. | **READING/WRITING WORKSHOP:** Unit 1: 58 Unit 2: 158 Unit 6: 446<br>**YOUR TURN PRACTICE BOOK:** 30, 80, 100, 300<br>**WORKSTATION ACTIVITY CARDS:** 15<br>**TEACHER'S EDITION:** Unit 1: T158, T160, T161, T190, T349, T353 Unit 2: T97, T157, T158, T160, T161, T286, T288, T289, T318, T344, T347, T350, T352 Unit 3: T285 Unit 4: T286, T353 Unit 5: T158, T161, T285, T346 Unit 6: T318 |
| **L.4.3b** | Choose punctuation for effect. | **TEACHER'S EDITION:** Unit 1: T25G, T34, T35, T153G, T217G Unit 2: T25G, T89I, T217C Unit 4: T291 Unit 5: T217E Unit 6: T217C, T227 |